THRIVING ON CHAOS

Prescriptions for a World Turned Upside Down

Creating Total Customer Responsiveness

The Guiding Premise	**C-1:**	Specialize/Create Niches/Differentiate
The Five Basic Value-Adding Strategies	**C-2:**	Provide Top Quality, as Perceived by the Customer
	C-3:	Provide Superior Service/Emphasize the Intangibles
	C-4:	Achieve Extraordinary Responsiveness
	C-5:	Be an Internationalist
	C-6:	Create Uniqueness
The Four Capability Building Blocks	**C-7:**	Become Obsessed with Listening
	C-8:	Turn Manufacturing into a Marketing Weapon
	C-9:	Make Sales and Service Forces into Heroes
	I-1–I-10:	Pursue Fast-Paced Innovation (see below)
The Evolving Firm	**C-10:**	Launch a Customer Revolution

Pursuing Fast-Paced Innovation

The Guiding Premise	**I-1:**	Invest in Applications-Oriented Small Starts
The Four Key Strategies	**I-2:**	Pursue Team Product/Service Development
	I-3:	Encourage Pilots of Everything
	I-4:	Practice "Creative Swiping"
	I-5:	Make Word-of-Mouth Marketing Systematic
Management Tactics to Encourage Innovation	**I-6:**	Support Committed Champions
	I-7:	"Model" Innovation/Practice Purposeful Impatience
	I-8:	Support Fast Failures
	I-9:	Set Quantitative Innovation Goals
The New Look Firm	**I-10:**	Create a Corporate Capacity for Innovation

Achieving Flexibility by Empowering People

The Guiding Premises	**P-1:**	Involve Everyone in Everything
	P-2:	Use Self-Managing Teams
The Five Supports (Add Them)	**P-3:**	Listen/Celebrate/Recognize
	P-4:	Spend Time Lavishly on Recruiting
	P-5:	Train and Retrain
	P-6:	Provide Incentive Pay for Everyone
	P-7:	Provide an Employment Guarantee
The Three Inhibitors (Take Them Away)	**P-8:**	Simplify/Reduce Structure
	P-9:	Reconceive the Middle Manager's Role
	P-10:	Eliminate Bureaucratic Rules and Humiliating Conditions

340-460

Learning to Love Change: A New View of Leadership at All Levels

The Guiding Premise	**L-1:**	Master Paradox
The Three Leadership Tools for Establishing Direction	**L-2:**	Develop an Inspiring Vision
	L-3:	Manage by Example
	L-4:	Practice Visible Management
Leading by Empowering People	**L-5:**	Pay Attention! (More Listening)
	L-6:	Defer to the Front Line
	L-7:	Delegate
	L-8:	Pursue "Horizontal" Management by Bashing Bureaucracy
The Bottom Line: Leading as Love of Change	**L-9:**	Evaluate Everyone on His or Her Love of Change
	L-10:	Create a Sense of Urgency

Building Systems for a World Turned Upside Down

The Guiding Premise	**S-1:**	Measure What's Important
Reconceiving the System Tools of Control and Empowerment	**S-2:**	Revamp the Chief Control Tools
	S-3:	Decentralize Information, Authority, and Strategic Planning
Establishing Trust Via Systems	**S-4:**	Set Conservative Goals
	S-5:	Demand Total Integrity

ALSO BY TOM PETERS

In Search of Excellence
(with Robert H. Waterman, Jr.)

A Passion for Excellence
(with Nancy Austin)

THRIVING ON CHAOS

Handbook for a Management Revolution

TOM PETERS

Harper Perennial
A Division of HarperCollins*Publishers*

To
ROGER MILLIKEN
and
WILLIAM DONALD SCHAEFER

two whose flexibility of mind and raging
impatience with inaction have inspired
the most dramatic and fruitful
organizational revolutions
I've witnessed

Thriving on Chaos with Tom Peters is
now available on videocassette. Contact
Video Publishing House, Inc., Schaumburg, IL,
by calling 1-800-824-8889.

The Excellence Audit, a set of organizational assessment tools (including software) based
on the "prescriptions" in *Thriving on Chaos*, is available from The Tom Peters Group;
1-800-333-8878.

A hardcover edition of this book was originally published in 1987 by Alfred A. Knopf, Inc.
It is here reprinted by arrangement with Alfred A. Knopf, Inc.

Portions of this book appeared in the *Los Angeles Times* and the *Washington Post*.

Acknowledgments of permission to reprint previously published material will be found following the index.

First Perennial Library edition published 1988. First HarperPerennial edition published 1991.

LIBRARY OF CONGRESS CATALOG CARD NUMBER: 88-45121

ISBN: 0-06-097184-3

92 93 94 95 MPC 20 19 18 17 16 15 14 13

Three outstanding attitudes—obliviousness to the growing disaffection of constituents, primacy of self-aggrandizement, [and the] illusion of invulnerable status—are persistent aspects of folly.

Barbara Tuchman
The March of Folly

Contents

Preface   Rx: Revolution!   xiii

I Prescriptions for a World Turned Upside Down   1

    1: Facing Up to the Need for Revolution   3
    2: Using the Prescriptions: The Essentials of
         Proactive Management   43

II Creating Total Customer Responsiveness   57

    C-1: Specialize/Create Niches/Differentiate   61
    C-2: Provide Top Quality, as Perceived by the
           Customer   79
    C-3: Provide Superior Service/Emphasize the
           Intangibles   109
    C-4: Achieve Extraordinary Responsiveness   131
    C-5: Be an Internationalist   151
    C-6: Create Uniqueness   167
    C-7: Become Obsessed with Listening   177
    C-8: Turn Manufacturing into a Marketing Weapon   195
    C-9: Make Sales and Service Forces into Heroes   213
  C-10: Launch a Customer Revolution   227

III Pursuing Fast-Paced Innovation   235

    I-1: Invest in Applications-Oriented Small Starts   239
    I-2: Pursue Team Product/Service Development   257

/ CONTENTS

I-3: Encourage Pilots of Everything 269
I-4: Practice "Creative Swiping" 279
I-5: Make Word-of-Mouth Marketing Systematic 291
I-6: Support Committed Champions 297
I-7: "Model" Innovation/Practice Purposeful
  Impatience 307
I-8: Support Fast Failures 315
I-9: Set Quantitative Innovation Goals 327
I-10: Create a Corporate Capacity for Innovation 333

IV Achieving Flexibility by Empowering People 339

P-1: Involve Everyone in Everything 343
P-2: Use Self-Managing Teams 357
P-3: Listen/Celebrate/Recognize 367
P-4: Spend Time Lavishly on Recruiting 379
P-5: Train and Retrain 387
P-6: Provide Incentive Pay for Everyone 399
P-7: Provide an Employment Guarantee 413
P-8: Simplify/Reduce Structure 425
P-9: Reconceive the Middle Manager's Role 441
P-10: Eliminate Bureaucratic Rules and Humiliating
  Conditions 453

V Learning to Love Change: A New View of
Leadership at All Levels 467

L-1: Master Paradox 473
L-2: Develop an Inspiring Vision 483
L-3: Manage by Example 497
L-4: Practice Visible Management 511
L-5: Pay Attention! (More Listening) 525
L-6: Defer to the Front Line 535
L-7: Delegate 545
L-8: Pursue "Horizontal" Management by Bashing
  Bureaucracy 555
L-9: Evaluate Everyone on His or Her Love of
  Change 561
L-10: Create a Sense of Urgency 569

VI Building Systems for a World Turned Upside Down 579

  S-1: Measure What's Important   583
  S-2: Revamp the Chief Control Tools   597
  S-3: Decentralize Information, Authority, and
      Strategic Planning   609
  S-4: Set Conservative Goals   619
  S-5: Demand Total Integrity   627

Second Thoughts   635

Appendix   655

Acknowledgments   667

Notes   671

Index   685

Contents

X. Building Systems for a World Turned Upside Down

Preface

RX: REVOLUTION!

Few would take exception to the conclusion that our sales forces are not sufficiently cherished. But how many are ready to consider doubling the sales force—in the next 36 months? And all would nod when urged to get marketers out with customers more. But would you sign up for putting marketers in the field 50 percent of the time? Improving quality—we all salute that, too. But will you accept a challenge to cut defects by 90 percent in 36 months? I'd guess that most would agree when the idea of tying pay to performance (for everyone) comes up. But are you ready to institute a bonus that amounts to 50 percent of base pay (a third of total pay)?

Revolution: It's a word business people have trouble with, and justifiably so. But our competitive situation is dire. The time for 10 percent staff cuts and 20 percent quality improvements is past. Such changes are not good enough.

Many of the ideas in this book will be new to readers of *In Search of Excellence* and *A Passion for Excellence;* others will be familiar. But *the rate of change demanded by the prescriptions in this book and the boldness of the goals suggested will be unfailingly new—and frightening.*

So this book *is* about a revolution—a necessary revolution. It challenges everything we thought we knew about managing, and often challenges over a hundred years of American tradition. Most fundamentally, the times demand that flexibility and love of change replace our long-standing penchant for mass production and mass markets, based as it is upon a relatively predictable environment now vanished.

Titling a book is never easy—the "selling proposition" must be presented in no more than a half-dozen words. Finding the right title here was especially tough. After much discussion I decided to be adamant about "revolution," palatable or not. But the most vigorous debate involved the choice of a preposition: "amidst" versus "on." The competitive situation was (and will be) chaotic—so "chaos" was easy. And it's not hard to sign up for "thriving." But was it to be "Thriving *amidst* Chaos" or "Thriving *on* Chaos"?

To thrive "amidst" chaos means to cope or come to grips with it, to succeed in spite of it. But that is too reactive an approach, and misses the point. The true objective is to take the chaos as given and learn to thrive *on* it. The winners of tomorrow will deal *proactively* with chaos, will look at the chaos per se as the source of market advantage, not as a problem to be got around. Chaos and uncertainty are (will be) market opportunities for the wise; capitalizing on fleeting market anomalies will be the successful business's greatest accomplishment. It is with that in mind that we must proceed.

West Tinmouth, Vermont   TOM PETERS
June 1987

I

PRESCRIPTIONS FOR A WORLD TURNED UPSIDE DOWN

1

Facing Up to the Need for Revolution

Can America make it? A huge trade imbalance, a sliding currency, falling real wages and a dismal productivity record. A decade ago, these were the hallmarks of a struggling British economy. Today they characterize an American economy which is struggling . . . against fierce competition from the Far East.

Financial Times (of London)
May 9, 1987

EXCELLENCE ISN'T

There are no excellent companies. The old saw "If it ain't broke, don't fix it" needs revision. I propose: "If it ain't broke, you just haven't looked hard enough." Fix it anyway.

No company is safe. IBM is declared dead in 1979, the best of the best in 1982, and dead again in 1986. People Express is the model "new look" firm, then flops twenty-four months later.

In 1987, and for the foreseeable future, there is no such thing as a "solid," or even substantial, lead over one's competitors. Too much is changing for anyone to be complacent. Moreover, the "champ to chump" cycles are growing ever shorter—a "commanding" advantage, such as Digital Equipment's current edge in networks that allow vast numbers of computers to interact with one another, is probably good for about eighteen months, at best.

3

There are two ways to respond to the end of the era of sustainable excellence. One is frenzy: buy and sell businesses in the brave hope of staying out in front of the growth industry curve. This is the General Electric idea: in the last six years, it has acquired over 325 businesses at a cost of over $12 billion, and dumped more than 225, getting $8 billion in return.

The second strategy is paradoxical—meeting uncertainty by emphasizing a set of new basics: world-class quality and service, enhanced responsiveness through greatly increased flexibility, and continuous, short-cycle innovation and improvement aimed at creating new markets for both new and apparently mature products and services.

The latter is Ford's approach to transformation. Quality really has become Job One at Ford. The once all-powerful finance function has assumed a less dominant role, and manufacturing, the prime source of quality, is no longer low in the organizational pecking order. And product development techniques have been set on their ear with the unconventional, but wildly successful, Team Taurus approach; it combined supplier, worker, dealer, and customer input from the start.

If the word "excellence" is to be applicable in the future, it requires wholesale redefinition. Perhaps: "Excellent firms don't believe in excellence—only in constant improvement and constant change." That is, excellent firms of tomorrow will cherish impermanence—and thrive on chaos.

THE ACCELERATING AMERICAN DECLINE

You need not look far to find cause for alarm:

1. Our average business productivity grew at 3 percent a year from 1950 to 1965. From 1965 to 1973, the rate was 2 percent; and since 1973, it's barely crept along at 1 percent. Manufacturing productivity looks worse. It grew at 2.5 percent a year from 1950 to 1985; that contrasts with Japan at 8.4 percent, Germany and Italy at 5.5 percent, France at 5.3 percent, Canada at 3.5 percent—and much-maligned Britain at 3.1 percent.

2. U.S. per capita GNP, called by some the truest measure of a nation's international economic standing, slipped below Japan's in 1986;

it also trails the per capita GNP of such European nations as West Germany, Switzerland, Sweden, and Denmark.

3. The average wage for a 25–34-year-old white male declined 26 percent from 1973 to 1983 in constant dollars; the comparable figure for 35–44-year-olds was little better, a decline of 14 percent. This figure is more useful to look at than others. Given the increase in work force participation by women, overall family income has slowly risen. But the economic fate of the individual white male remains the bellwether indicator of progress (or lack of it).

4. The national savings rate, long the lowest in the industrial world, continues to decline. Despite supply-side economic stimulants such as the 1981 tax cut, savings as a share of disposable personal income plummeted from 7.5 percent to 3.9 percent from 1981 to 1986. At year's end 1986, it stood at 2.8 percent. Only our dramatic shift as a nation from premier net lender to premier net borrower has kept investment afloat.

5. In 1986, 138 banks failed, the largest number in one year since the Great Depression; the pace in 1987 is ahead of 1986's. By contrast, 10 banks toppled in 1981.

6. Economists estimate that as many as 30 million people have been dislocated by the "restructuring" in manufacturing during the last decade. Since 1980, the Fortune 500 have shed a staggering 2.8 million jobs.

7. The plain truth is that every major manufacturing or service firm—from the Bank of America and Citicorp, to Du Pont and General Motors, to IBM and Intel and the Hospital Corporation of America—is undergoing trauma.

Alarming as these indicators are—and a host of similar ones—it is the chaos in trade that is most revealing of our poor performance. It alone provides the harsh, industry-by-industry evidence of our decline.

The fact that the trade deficit is currently (April 1987) running at $152 billion, despite the dollar's plunge against the yen and mark since September 1985, is a powerful indication that, while the problem may have been exacerbated by the dollar's strength of a few years back, we are getting clobbered primarily because of the generally poor quality of what we produce and a failure, as a result of questionable service and slow responsiveness, to make use of our onshore, close-to-the-world's-biggest-market advantage.

Textile-makers all but gave up decades ago, and begged for protective relief; while foreign wages were and are often still low, the industry's repeated failure to modernize and adapt to new market needs was the root cause. Then, one by one, steel, autos, and machine tools also begged for—and got—access to the protectionist trough. Finally, 1986 brought the spectacle of Silicon Valley's once proud barons spending more time in Washington than at the factory; their pleas for protection against Japan's alleged "dumping" (selling below cost to gain market share) culminated in the imposition of tariffs of 100 percent on certain Japanese electronics products. But though Japanese hands are not entirely clean, it was long-term disinterest in the factory (the nuts and bolts of producing top-quality products) and arrogance toward even large customers that most severely damaged our semiconductor industry—not Japanese "dumping" or protectionist barriers within Japan.

In 1986, despite continuing bright spots such as computers and aircraft, even the trade balance in high-technology goods went into the red. That was also a first-time losing year for construction equipment and agriculture. In the latter case, despite billions in subsidies, we have simply not awakened to the fact that most of the rest of the world, including India and China, is now self-sufficient in grain. Commodity prices in general remain in a trough, and any upticks are likely to be temporary. That is, the United States can no longer depend on its natural resources to be a source of enduring trade surplus.

A Decline in Service Too

The various service industries are faring little better than manufacturing and agriculture. A formidable $41 billion positive trade balance in services in 1981 has all but disappeared. In a recent *Harvard Business Review* article, "Will Service Follow Manufacturing into Decline?," James Brian Quinn and Christopher Gagnon were glum:

> It will take hard and dedicated work not to dissipate our broad-based lead in services, as we did in manufacturing. Many of the same causes of lost position are beginning to appear. Daily we encounter the same inattention to quality, [over]emphasis on scale economies rather than customers' concerns and short-term financial orientation that earlier injured manufacturing. Too many service companies have . . . concentrated on cost-cutting efficiencies they can quantify, rather than on adding to their product's value by

listening carefully and . . . providing the services their customers genuinely want. Haven't we heard this once before? The cost of losing this battle is unacceptably high. . . . If [services] are disdained or mismanaged, the same forces that led to the decline of U.S. manufacturing stand ready to cut them to pieces.

That's bad news indeed, since the service sector now employs 75 percent of us.

Some Rays of Light, but on Net, Trouble

To be sure, the picture isn't entirely grim. And many of these indicators have their flip sides. For instance, although Japanese productivity growth has been several times ours in recent years, we still hold an absolute productivity advantage over the Japanese. In absolute terms they are far ahead of us in targeted industries (steel, autos, semiconductors), but far behind in others (agriculture, the service sector as a whole).

And while the Fortune 500 continue their job-shedding binge, our vital capital markets, among other things, have spurred a small-business-led surge in job creation, in high-tech as well as hamburgers.

Yet, while the bag is mixed, almost all leading indicators—e.g., productivity growth, competitive assessments of leading industries such as financial services and semiconductors, the trade balances with almost any other industrialized nation—clearly show that our postwar economic hegemony is at an end. Though we still harbor fond memories of days when the rules of the game governed everyone but us, we are now, at best, "one of the big players"; decisions of the Japanese and German ministries of finance are at least as important as those of the U.S. Federal Reserve Board or Department of the Treasury.

All of this is, of course, exacerbated by our failure to come to grips with our awesome budget deficit. One simply can't (1) run a constant deficit of $100 to $200 billion a year, (2) blithely devalue the dollar by over 50 percent vis-à-vis Japan, and (3) shift from chief creditor to chief debtor nation overnight—while expecting the economic waters to remain calm. The U.S. standard of living has declined, by definition, as the dollar has plummeted. More inflation surely looms if the dollar is not stabilized. And a recession may well lie ahead.

Thus, it is essential to address the macroeconomic folly of continued deficits, among other matters. But it is equally important not to be lulled by the glib talk of macroeconomic wizards. Sound macroeconomic policy will help, but the underlying source of our problematic economic performance is a cataclysmic change in competitive conditions, which has in surprisingly short order turned almost every traditional U.S. strength, at the level of the individual firm, into weakness.

AN ERA OF UNPRECEDENTED UNCERTAINTY

Merging and Demerging: Shuffle for Shuffle's Sake

Madness *is* afoot. On the same day in early March 1987, Chrysler buys AMC and USAir swallows Piedmont.

The Chrysler move comes amidst predictions of overcapacity in U.S. auto production—and not long after a decision at General Motors to shut down eleven plants. In the airline industry, prior to late 1986, only USAir, Piedmont, Delta, and American had eschewed major mergers; they also happened to be the four most profitable airlines, with number one American making twenty-four times as much as United, which was the largest airline in 1986 and fraught with problems after trying to swallow much of Pan Am. In 1987, Texas Air will be biggest, after swallowing Continental, Eastern, and People Express. Its digestion problems are all too well documented. So why have the four best so quickly succumbed to major mergers?

Don't look to GE for an answer. On the one hand, its former top strategic planner (now a line executive vice-president) is quoted by *Business Week* in early 1987 as saying that nine out of ten acquisitions "are a waste of time and a destruction of shareholders' value." Then the same article goes on to report that GE is thinking of acquiring United Technologies—a conglomerate with revenues of $16 billion.

Certainly most studies suggest that, in general, mergers don't pan out. For instance, business strategist Michael Porter, of the Harvard Business School, recently concluded a study of merger behavior among thirty-three big U.S. firms from 1950 through 1980. As a group, they subsequently unloaded 53 percent of all their acquisitions during this period and sold off a whopping 74 percent of their acquisitions in unrelated new fields (those purchases that were to have made them safe by positioning them in "guaranteed" growth sectors, according to the press releases). Likewise, when consultants McKinsey & Co. made an extensive study in 1986 of mergers between 1972 and 1983 that involved the two hundred largest public corporations, they determined that a mere 23 percent were successful (as measured by an increase in value to shareholders). The highest success rate (33 percent) was found with small acquisitions made in related fields, the lowest (8 percent) resulted from the merger of large firms whose operations were in unrelated areas.

Structural economist Frederic Scherer has observed, after years of meticulous study: "On average, mergers decrease efficiency." An economist at the Securities and Exchange Commission was more blunt: Asked to comment on a proposal to further relax antitrust restrictions, he replied, "Most industries in which we have competitive difficulties are not exactly filled with pigmy companies. . . . You don't put two turkeys together and make an eagle."

The mergers do grab headlines. But Ray Miles, dean of the business school of the University of California at Berkeley, is not alone when he points out, "Current 'merger mania' notwithstanding, it seems likely that the 1980s and 1990s will be known as decades of large-scale disaggregation." New terms such as "breakup value" and "de-integration" are heard daily in the halls of the Fortune 500. A 1987 *Forbes* analysis of Litton Industries, caustically titled "But the Grass Looked Greener Over There," speaks eloquently to the overall issue of frenzied buying and selling:

> Restructuring. The magic word of the mid-1980s. Just say the syllables: re-struc-tur-ing. They cure all ills, excuse all past mistakes and justify huge writedowns in assets. But does restructuring always accomplish what it originally sets out to accomplish? The trouble with much of what goes on in the name of restructuring is that it is a policy for tomorrow based on today's known circumstances. Take the case of Litton Industries, Inc. That $4.5 billion (revenues) conglomerate has been repeatedly restructured in its 33-year history. The latest restructuring, completed in 1985, refocused the company into three main lines of business, each of which looked extremely promising when the restructuring began four years earlier. Alas. Soon after the reorganization was essentially complete, each of the three chosen businesses ran into problems. . . . The

Litton of the future is essentially in place, says [its chief executive officer]. "Now our job for the next several years is to make what we have perform." But one wonders: Will Litton have to restructure again in a few years? Or will management finally settle down to making what it has work?

Mergers and de-mergers are just one part of the madness. Strategies change daily, and the names of firms, a clear indicator of strategic intent, change with them. In rapid succession, U.S. Steel became USX, American Can became Primerica, and United Airlines became Allegis for a while. General Electric has been a bit more coy than the rest; it has not made the official change to GE, but "encourages" the use of the initials rather than the words. The new names share a common trait—they're all more vague than their predecessors.

So U.S. Steel is almost out of steel, as the change in its name suggests. And why not? The year of the change, 1986, brought LTV, the second-largest U.S. steelmaker after swallowing Republic Steel in 1984, to bankruptcy. The company, with $8.2 billion in revenues, became the biggest industrial firm ever to go belly up. (Texaco, at $32 billion, eclipsed the record in early 1987. Most record-breaking feats these days seem to be bad-news stories.)

Internationalism: Yes and No

Despite protectionist movements in the United States and other nations, transactions that cross international borders are sharply on the rise. Seldom does a week pass without major joint ventures among partners from more than one country. Nomura buys into Salomon Brothers. Boeing and the Japanese make a deal. McDonnell-Douglas then attempts to join up with Airbus Industries in an effort to match Boeing's newest partnership.

Global financing is also changing the landscape. On the one hand, financial markets are opening up rapidly, and everyone is increasingly connected to everyone else. High-speed computers and communications technology make possible the arrangement of the most exotic financing in a dozen currencies in a matter of days—which facilitates such developments in manufacturing as "global sourcing," wherein firms shop freely among several nations, usually for the lowest-cost source of numerous components. This in turn brings increasing de-integration or "hollow-ing" of firms; tasks routinely done inside most firms, from watering the plants in the lobby to manufacturing subcomponents, are now subcontracted to outsiders small and large, domestic and foreign.

But strong as the trend toward transcending national boundaries is, the countertrend is also strong. Protection is one element. Debt is another. The United States has lent a trillion dollars to developing countries, and about two-thirds of that debt is held by private banks. Huge debt restructurings are common, and more major defaults, such as Brazil's in early 1987, are anticipated. The quandary is inescapable. The only way the debt-strapped nations can pay back their loans is by exporting what they produce, whether manufactured goods or commodities. This drives them to aggressive selling tactics, which trigger a further protectionist response. Talk about Catch-22.

Predictability Is a Thing of the Past

Nothing is predictable. Currency-exchange transactions now total $80 trillion a year, only $4 trillion of which is required to finance trade in goods and services. The rest is essentially currency speculation, one reason that the overall financial situation has been labeled the "Casino Society." The prices of the major currencies, once stable within 1 percent over decades, now swing 5 percent a week, and 50 percent a year. The prices of energy, agricultural products, and metals are also volatile.

So we don't know from day to day the price of energy or money. We don't know whether protection and default will close borders, making a mess of global sourcing and trade alike, or whether global financing will open things up further.

We don't know whether merging or de-merging makes more sense, and we have no idea who will be partners with whom tomorrow or next week, let alone next month.

We don't know who our competitors will be, or where they will come from. New foreign competition appears each day—not only in new services and end products (1986 was the year of the Hyundai and the Yugo, and 1987 brings Daihatsu, the ninth Japanese auto company to export to the United States), but also in the form of the invisible subcomponents of purportedly American products (at one point most of the innards of the IBM personal computer were made abroad).

New competitors financed by venture capital and a sustained market for Initial Public Offerings (IPOs) spring up like mushrooms in banking and health care and pizza delivery and temporary business services, and in semiconductors, supercomputers, and biotechnology, too. Other "new" competitors are units spun off from big firms (often following a hostile takeover or a leveraged buy-out, two of a vast number of new financing schemes speeding the pace of corporate overhaul) or down-sized, newly autonomous units within big firms.

Technology's Unsettling Impact—On Everything

Technology is yet another wild card affecting every aspect of doing business. As mentioned, it has revolutionized financing. It has also forever changed:

1. Manufacturing: The technology of miniaturization is (a) reducing optimal factory size dramatically and (b) allowing factories of all sizes to turn out a huge variety of products, with greatly reduced setup times.

2. Design: Such innovations as computer-aided engineering are slashing the length of design-to-manufacture cycles.

3. Distribution: Electronics, computer, and telecommunications technologies are making it possible to (a) shorten substantially the time required between order and delivery, (b) poll customers instantly, (c) engage in almost numberless permutations and combinations of globe-spanning partnerships. They are also (d) breathing new life into the independent user, such as the corner grocer, whose optical scanner and computer give him newfound power in dealing with big producers. Likewise, (e) distribution companies, such as Ingram in books and McKesson in drugs, make it possible for smaller user firms to achieve almost all the purchase-price economies that big buyers can achieve.

4. Product definition: There is a blurring of service/product distinctions, given the enhancement of almost every product, from tractors to bank cards, by "software" services and the "intelligence-added" features provided courtesy of the microprocessor.

Consumers Are on the Move Too

On the consuming end of things, more uncertainty is added. Tastes are changing: (1) Thanks to the Japanese, Germans, and others, there is a vastly increased awareness of quality. (2) The rapid rise in the number of women in the work force and of two-wage-earner families leads to new needs (e.g., convenience goods and services). (3) Changes in the kinds of jobs available and, hence, in the distribution of incomes may create something like a two-class society—with an increased number of "haves" demanding greater variety and quality, and an increased number of "have-nots" demanding more durable basic goods, in the face of increasingly poor prospects. And (4) with a TV or two in every home, and a car or two in most driveways, the demand for these products is shifting from a desire for the product per se, almost regardless of quality, to a demand for customized alternatives with special features tailored for ever narrower market segments.

The Interaction of Forces: All Bets Are Off

Of course, more important than any one of these sets of uncertainties—financial, international, technological, or markets/tastes—is the interaction among them. For instance, the drive for more product variety is abetted by the technology which can meet such needs, the explosion of international competitors (producers of both end products and subcomponents) with a piece of the action, and the similar, finance-driven explosion of start-up domestic firms vying for a piece of the more specialized action too.

Sum up all these forces and trends, or, more accurately, multiply them, then add in the fact that most are in their infancy, and you end up with a forecaster's nightmare. But the point is much larger, of course, than forecasting. The fact is that *no firm can take anything in its market for granted*.

Suppose you are considering next year's strategy for a maturing product. Here's what you might well find:

▶ a new Korean competitor
▶ an old Japanese competitor continuing to reduce costs and improve quality
▶ a dozen domestic start-ups, each headed by talented people claiming a technology breakthrough
▶ one old-line domestic competitor that has slashed overhead costs by 60 percent and is de-integrating via global sourcing as fast as it can
▶ another old-line domestic competitor that has just fended off a hostile takeover; in doing so, it may have (odds 50 percent) sold off the division that competes with you to another strong competitor with a great distribution system

► a competitor that has just introduced an electronics-based distribution system that wires it to each of its 2,500 principal distributors, slashing the time required to fill orders by 75 percent

► yet another competitor that is tailor-making its products to suit the requirements or tastes of tiny groups of customers, thanks to a new, flexible Computer Integrated Manufacturing (CIM) system

► consumers demanding consistently high quality in every component of the product, from inner workings to fits and finishes

► a wildly gyrating currency market that confounds your own global sourcing decisions

► the probable interruption of supply from two offshore manufacturing plants where governments have defaulted on loan interest and principle payments

It is because this scenario is now *average*—for every banker, health care administrator, public utility executive, and soup maker, let alone computer maker—that our organizations *all* require major surgery. Violent and accelerating change, now commonplace, will become the grist of the opportunistic winner's mill. The losers will view such confusion as a "problem" to be "dealt" with.

OLD ASSUMPTIONS ASKEW

Today, only a small motivated firm with . . . highly qualified labor and good vertical mobility instead of oppressive hierarchy can hold up in a world whose principal characteristic is instability.

> Andrea Saba
> *Submerged Industry,*
> on the dominant role of
> the gray economy in spearheading
> Italy's economic revival

Henry Ford made great contributions, but his Model T was not a quality car.

> W. Edwards Deming
> father of statistical
> process control and the
> Japanese quality revolution

U.S. industry, run as it was by our forefathers in the tradition of our ancestors, grew big and powerful and restless. We built the biggest steel mills, the biggest oil refineries, the biggest chemical plants, the largest automobile assembly lines, the largest smelters in the world. Boy, could we make product! We didn't always make the best, but we made the most at the lowest price and U.S. industry became a model for the rest of the world. We were the model for size, productivity, for efficiency—but not necessarily for quality. You've heard the expressions, "It ran like a Swiss watch," or "It had the precision of a German machine." We in the U.S. really didn't care. We left the specialized, high quality niche in the marketplace to others, while we concentrated on huge scale, high volume, mass production economics. . . . But then in the '60s and '70s we began to get some hint . . . that some of our assumptions were askew. For one thing, we started to experience some competition from foreign producers—not just because they could make their products cheaper and faster, but because they were, for God's sake, better. The car didn't fall apart at 30,000 miles, and when you bought their television set, it didn't mean taking the repairman into the family.

> Dr. Irving G. Snyder, Jr.
> Vice President and Director
> of Research & Development
> Dow Chemical USA
> from a speech: "The
> Quality Revolution—It
> Just Ain't in Our Genes"

Two assumptions at the very core of our economic system are now causing untold harm: (1) bigger is better, and biggest is best; (2) labor (human beings at work) is to be ever more narrowly specialized, or eliminated if possible.

THE AMERICAN PENCHANT FOR GIANTISM

Big, not best, has always been the American calling card. In fact, I bet you can't drive more than seventy-five miles in any direction, from anywhere in the United States, without running into a "biggest in the world" of some sort. Wide-open spaces and an apparently limitless frontier set it all in motion. U.S. farmers, starting with the Pilgrims, would cultivate land, wear it out, and blithely move west five miles. Today almost every farm you see is a history lesson told by hulks of rusted cars and agricultural equipment, and homes and yards are filled with broken Christmas toys and power lawn mowers.

Have you ever seen a rusted auto or tractor body in Germany, Switzerland, or Japan? The Europeans and the Japanese have lived within limits for centuries, and have had to be more careful with resources—that is, quality-conscious.

When we began to manufacture, we adopted agriculture's early habits—mass, not quality. Big railroads spurred us on by making vast markets for cheap goods accessible to industry. Railroad tycoons then used naked power to create and control huge business combinations; independents who wouldn't go along faced outrageous rail rates and were often forced out of business. The rise of big combines coincided with the War Department's perfection of mass-production techniques starting in the Civil War and culminating little more than a half-century later, during World War I. Britain may have invented most tools of mass production, but Americans copied and perfected them, and applied them to commercial use. (It's ironic that we are now the premier inventors, and Japan the "copycat" perfecters.)

This all-American system—long production runs, mass operations—paid off with victory in World Wars I and II, and cemented subsequent U.S. economic dominance. But we won World War II with *more* tanks and planes, not, in general, *better* ones. And then overseas economies revived and started looking to our enticing markets. Their only entryways were through niche markets and by offering superb quality to overcome our skepticism, such as that engendered by the inferior image of Japanese products in 1955.

The emphasis on quality fit nicely with European and Japanese skills, in particular their bent for craft (non-specialized) labor and their use of the worker as the primary means of adding value to a product. As well, their historic lack of excessive vertical integration (as in the Ford Motor Company, which once owned the iron mines from which came the iron for the steel forged in the River Rouge mills that in turn went into the cars) provided unique flexibility and was the basis for the short production runs needed to conquer small niche markets. We stuck to our penchant for big, becoming enamored of large-scale automation after

16

World War II. The Japanese took our unused designs for smaller, more flexible machine tools, cornered that market, and also raised rapid product changeover to a high art.

And so today, we are in trouble. Quality and flexibility will be the hallmarks of the successful economy for the foreseeable future. A recent poll of Korean businessmen, *Fortune* reports, revealed that "they preferred Japanese suppliers to American by a margin of two to one. The Koreans complained about mediocre product quality, slow delivery times, and poor service, and added that U.S. companies were reluctant to accept small orders." (This is all the more dramatic, given the long-standing enmity between the Japanese and the Koreans.)

The Koreans are right, but it is gut-wrenching to turn our backs on bigness. GE chairman Jack Welch tells security analysts he wants his company to be number one in "market value"—to be worth the most on the stock market. Does he want to be remembered for superb products? for creating jobs? Who knows? He seldom talks about products; and as for jobs, GE has slashed over 100,000 jobs from its payroll, not counting acquisitions, since he came aboard. And as one *Forbes* writer puts it, GE's Fairfield headquarters "has the look and feel of a colossal investment banking house on the prowl for takeover targets"—with nary a product in sight.

Size drives even entrepreneurs, who all too quickly drift from a desire to be special to a desire to be big, and, they anticipate, safe. People Express founder Don Burr's ill-fated acquisition of Frontier Airlines is all too typical.

Listen to the chatter when the Fortune 500 comes out. Few chiefs comment on their profit or return on assets. The question is: "What's your rank?" "Making the Fortune 500"—an attribute based on size alone—is the Holy Grail for most nonmembers; moving up is the Holy Grail for most members.

The Japanese Passion Whose Time Has Come

There are two principal schools of thought about the Japanese miracle. Economists would have us believe their success is due to consistent, conservative macro-economic policy—the confluence of interest between companies and their bankers, and between the bankers and the government. For instance, the conservative alliance represented by the all-powerful Ministry of Finance and the more visible Ministry of International Trade and Industry (MITI) directs low-cost loans to targeted industries and protects youthful (or recovering) industries. The sociologists and management theorists sing a different tune, explaining the same phenomenon in terms of group cohesion, lifetime employment, and other management and family (e.g., child-rearing) practices.

The plain fact is, of course, that both have a point. Both factors have contributed to Japan's success.

But there are other, more novel explanations that make sense too. One such focuses on the unique, age-old Japanese passion for smallness, in a world where the advantages of smallness seem to be fast eclipsing the once generally perceived value of giantism. For instance, in *Smaller Is Better: Japan's Mastery of the Miniature,* Korean writer O-Young Lee suggests that "Japan, with its tradition of smaller is better . . . its sensitivity to information, is perfectly positioned to take the lead in the coming age of reductionism."

Lee does a thorough job of tracing the roots of Japan's attachment to smallness. Japanese fairy tales, for example, feature "little giants" who turn needles into swords, bowls into boats, in contrast to such characters of Western folk legend as Paul Bunyan. But the language may provide the most important clue. For instance, the Japanese word for "craftsmanship" is literally "delicate workmanship," and that for feminine beauty is "detailed woman." On the other hand, "large" is literally "not delicately crafted" and "worthless" is "not packed in." There are many more prefixes, more frequently used, that mean "small" than "big." And so on.

The folding fan, miniature gardening, the tea ceremony, and other ritual staples of Japanese life all stem, according to Lee, from a passion for reductionism. For meditation, the Japanese naturally gravitate to small spaces—small inner courts, say, within already small houses—while Americans (and Koreans and Chinese, for that matter) head for the wide-open spaces when they need to reflect. In fact, the Japanese are contemptuous of almost everything large, says Lee, adding that "Nothing comes harder to the Japanese than living with objects of no use. They cannot bear the unnecessary, the excess."

This deep-seated Japanese trait has major economic consequences in these, the early days of the electronic (miniaturization) age. Sony, for instance, has pioneered in miniaturization—of tape recorders and radios (the Walkman), of VCRs (see also page 197), and of the disk audio, and now video, player.

Though it was a U.S. firm that invented the transistor, and initially supplied transistors to Sony, it was Sony which first mastered the consumer application of the technology. Many other examples, of course, could be added, such as the development of the first electronic calculator by Sharp in 1963. Lee concludes: "That reduction is a hallmark of Japanese electronics should come with little surprise if we recall our discussion of the [Japanese] rock garden. . . . the essence of rock gardening aesthetic was summed up in the words of the garden designer Tessen Soki: 'A thousand miles is shrunk down to one foot.' " (Japan's total dominance of the market in miniaturized consumer goods is illustrated by its astonishing $9 billion positive trade balance in consumer electronics alone,* which is nearly half the size of its more ballyhooed automotive surplus.)

In summary, says Lee, "It has been a thousand years since Sei Shonagon wrote, 'All things small, no matter what they are, all things small are beautiful.' How ironic that we should now be hearing the same refrain from the other side of the Pacific!"

One need look no further than a 1987 Mazda ad in a Lufthansa in-flight magazine for evidence supporting Lee's thesis. The ad simply could not have been conceived in America. Its beautiful artwork features a photograph of eleven ancient, delicately crafted Japanese wooden combs. The ad's lead was "Combing Through the Details." The copy proceeds:

A comb looks like a very simple item. But it is deceptively simple. We tend to forget that in the past combs were all hand made. That every tooth, and the space between each tooth, was filed to the same width. This uniformity is all the more astonishing when we remember it was achieved by eye. One mistake and the comb would be ruined. This made combs valuable possessions. And the fact that they were personal items engendered the belief in ancient Japan that one's comb was the repository of one's soul. No wonder the making of it was approached with an almost religious devotion. The comb, an example of how devotion to the basics can lead to simply stun-

*The overall annual U.S. electronic trade deficit with Japan runs over $20 billion.

ning results. Mazda. Where a devotion to the basics of automotive engineering leads to simply stunning results.

The ad, then, (1) uses the small and delicate as exemplar (a comb in this instance), (2) underscores the tie to ancient Japan and craftsmanship, and (3) "sells" the emphasis on details as Mazda's principal competitive strength.

Now GM has tried a similar tack, using the lead line "No one sweats the details like GM." The similarity is superficial, to say the least. "Sweat" and the image of delicate and ancient combs are, figuratively and literally, worlds apart!

Re-interpreting History I: Has Big Ever Been More Efficient?

The new market realities demand flexibility and speed. The new technologies permit their achievement—but only if we turn our backs decisively on our love affair with size and its handmaidens, stability and predictability. And a useful step in weaning ourselves from the obsession with size might be to recognize that it has never yielded the promised results.

"Bigness has not delivered the goods, and this fact is no longer a secret." With these words, economists Walter Adams (a former president of Michigan State University) and James Brock launch their 1986 book *The Bigness Complex.* After a review of hundreds of studies, they conclude: "Scientific evidence has not been kind to the apostles of bigness and to their mythology."

Adams and Brock don't even require us to deal with the many forces—the instability, the technology of miniaturization, the explosion in products, services, and competitors, and the changing markets just described—that are all currently pushing toward the predominance of smaller enterprises or business units. They argue, and my own observations coincide with theirs, that the highly touted economies of scale have never been all they were cracked up to be.

In fact, astute observers of the industrial landscape have been questioning the efficiency of bigness for decades. A report on U.S. Steel done by a management consultant in the 1930s concluded even then that the firm was "a big, sprawling, inert giant, whose production operations were improperly coordinated; with an inadequate knowledge of the costs or the relative profitability of the many thousands of items it sold; with production and cost standards generally below those considered everyday practice in other industries; with inadequate knowledge of its domestic markets and no clear appreciation of its opportunity in foreign markets; with less efficient production facilities than its rivals had."

Also in the 1930s, the legendary General Motors chairman Alfred Sloan turned self-critical, observing that "in practically all our activities we seem to suffer from the inertia resulting from our great size. . . . There are so many people involved and it requires such a tremendous effort to put something new into effect that a new idea is likely to be considered insignificant in comparison with the effort that it takes to put it across. . . . Sometimes I am almost forced to the conclusion that General Motors is so large and its inertia so great that it is impossible for us to be leaders."

In a classic 1956 study, economist Joe Bain examined the cost advantages flowing to multi-plant, as opposed to single-plant, firms in twenty industries. In no case was owning more than one plant a major advantage! More recently, Frederic Scherer studied the fate of fifteen former subsidiaries of conglomerates that had been sold to their former managers. All but one showed substantial improvements in profit—despite the heavy burden of debt incurred in the buyouts. Among the reasons for the dramatic improvement, Scherer notes these: "Cost-cutting opportunities that had previously gone unexploited were seized. Austere offices were substituted for lavish ones. Staffs were cut back sharply. . . . Inexpensive computer services were found to substitute for expensive in-house operations. Make vs. buy decisions were reevaluated and lower-cost alternatives were embraced. Efforts were made to improve labor-management relations by removing bureaucratic constraints that had been imposed by the previous conglomerate's headquarters. Tight inventory controls were implemented, cutting holding costs by as much as one-half."

The movement toward efficiency through smallness is accelerating in virtually every industry today. Language itself provides the first clue:

▶ In steel, there is an unsung U.S. success story—the one-third of the market now held by profitable, fast-growing firms such as Nucor Corporation and Chaparral Steel. These two have excelled in "mini-mills." Now, the *mini-mill* is about to be eclipsed by the *micro-mill:* further miniaturization, thanks to new technologies, will make it economical to dot little mills every 25 miles or so along the road, in support of local markets.

► A recent *Industry Week* analysis of Allen-Bradley observes that "the Milwaukee-based firm found that its motor starters were losing market share to imports. . . . The design was obsolescent. . . . the company designed and built a . . . *minifactory* [my emphasis] to make them in Milwaukee. Allen-Bradley has cashed in on the flexibility of its *'factory within a factory'* [my emphasis]. It has boosted the variety of starters from 125 originally to 600—without adding floorspace or hardware. . . . Its flexibility gives the company a quick-response capability that translates into a marketplace edge. . . . Now it exports motor starters again and is recouping its domestic share as well."

► In photo-finishing, the *mini-lab* is allowing corner shops with a $250,-000 line of credit to do what only Kodak could do ten years ago. The same is true in optometry, where the same word is in vogue.

► The evidence even cascades from the shelves of the corner grocery store, where, for example, the products of a host of *micro-brewers* are pushing the venerable Budweiser to the rear.

More sweeping evidence comes from *U.S. News & World Report*'s year-end analysis for 1986. It attributes much of the productive vitality of the Los Angeles basin—population about 13 million—to the astonishing fact that "some 90 percent of those employed in the . . . area work in small firms with fewer than 50 people that can change course fast to stay competitive."

Once upon a not-so-ancient time, as noted above, Ford owned the mines that provided the iron that went into the steel from which its cars were made. Today, too much of such vertical integration is hurting many of the old industrial giants. For instance, most of Chrysler's $500-per-car cost advantage over GM accrues from the fact that it purchases 70 percent of its components outside the firm; the comparable GM proportion is 30 percent. Not surprisingly, de-integration is now a strategic priority at GM. As Gordon Forward, founder of Chaparral, puts it, "The big is coming out of manufacturing in this country." The *Economist* confirms the trend:

Disbursement of production towards ever-smaller manufacturing units is progressing remorselessly. . . . Industrial boutiques [those new terms again], run by small, independent operators with all the latest computer-aided . . . techniques are emerging as contractors to mainstream corporations, many of which might eventually be forced to offload their own manufacturing units and buy in tailor-made products. . . . [That is], Henry Ford's soul-destroying, wealth-creating assembly lines are out of date. Most of the things factories make now—be they cars, cameras or candlesticks—come in small batches designed to gratify fleeting market whims. The successful manufacturing countries in the 21st century will be those whose factories change their products fastest.

Reinterpreting History II: Has Big Ever Been More Innovative?

After efficiency, the second advantage of bigness touted by its advocates has been innovativeness. On this point, the authors of *The Bigness Complex* begin by presenting the advocates' conventional wisdom—

Ostensibly, giant firms might be presumed for a variety of reasons to be superior inventors and innovators: They can afford to hire armies of the best brains and to outfit them in elaborate, extensive and sophisticated laboratories. Their massive size should permit them to bear the potential losses of risky research into fundamentally new products and production processes. They can further reduce risks by operating a large portfolio of individual projects, so that the success of any one project can compensate for the failures and losses of other projects. They have established channels of distribution and that should enable them to quickly bring new products to market.

—and then proceed to slash away:

Reality and the available evidence show that despite all these theoretical advantages, small firms . . . are far more efficient innovators than industrial giants . . . small firms are more prolific inventors than giant companies; small firms exert significantly greater research and development effort than large ones; small firms devise and develop inventions at substantially lower costs than large firms; and the giant organizations seem to suffer a number of debilitating and apparently endemic disadvantages as regards invention and innovation.

Adams and Brock review numerous studies, such as one by the National Science Board (part of the National Science Foundation) which reveals that only 34 percent of major technical innovations come from

23

giant firms (over 10,000 employees)—far less than those firms' share of industrial output. Moreover, "the smallest firms produced about four times as many innovations per R&D dollar as the middle-size firms and 24 times as many as the largest firms."

They continue with this *coup de grâce:* "Nor do giant firms display any appetite for undertaking more fundamental and risky research projects. That is, contrary to the image that bigness is conducive to risk-taking, there is no statistically significant tendency for corporate behemoths to conduct a disproportionately large share of the relatively risky R&D or of the R&D aimed at entirely new products and processes. On the contrary, they generally seem to carry out a disproportionately small share of the R&D aimed at entirely new products and processes." Yet another study reveals that large firms spend three to ten times more than small ones to develop similar new products. Even firms venerated for research, such as Du Pont, are challenged by these authors: "A study . . . found the bulk of the firm's commercially important products to have been invented *outside* the firm."

Brock and Adams do a much-needed job in conveying the macroeconomists' view of the shortcomings of size. Eli Ginzberg of Columbia University and George Vojta, formerly Citicorp's top strategic planner, examine the phenomenon from the managerial perspective in *Beyond Human Scale: The Large Corporation at Risk:*

> The large corporation at risk moves along a familiar path. Growth in earnings and return on capital tend to moderate. Often the deceleration of the rate of profits conceals an accumulation of potential corporate deficits, which are permitted to remain hidden, at least for a time, by accounting conventions and/or regulatory procedures. . . . [A] slow secular decline in a major arena is often misread as a cyclical phenomenon that time will cure. This misreading allows top management to procrastinate before taking corrective action. . . .
>
> Burdened by the high costs of internal coordination and ineffective utilization of its human resources, the large enterprise is increasingly vulnerable to the entry of small and medium firms into its markets. Its vulnerability is usually in the specialized segments of these markets, where the small firm can be more attentive and responsive to selected customer groups. These new competitors,

unburdened by massive prior investments and free of the heavy costs of internal coordination, are frequently able to offer superior products and thereby capture the small end of the market. The large-scale competitor must therefore focus increasingly on the upper end, where transaction size and gross profitability are still large enough to cover its costs. Over time, many large corporations must yield large segments of what had earlier been highly profitable markets to the new competition. . . . At this stage the firm is on the brink of major trauma. It confronts large write-offs, is vulnerable to takeover bids, and may even have to file for bankruptcy.

While these two studies contain damning evidence, neither emphasizes the degree to which current trends are underscoring the inadequacies of bigness. The best contemporary analysis has been done by Michael Piore and Charles Sabel of MIT in *The Second Industrial Divide*. They catalogue "the break-up of mass markets," "the decomposition of large markets," "the disintegration of mass markets," "particularized demand," and, the ultimate, "fragmented markets becoming pulverized." Surprisingly, they are not talking about new arenas such as biotechnology and semiconductors, but about chemicals, steel, textiles, autos, and computers. And they propose a survivor's strategy, "flexible specialization," by which they mean smaller economic units or firms providing a wider variety of products for narrower markets. I will discuss such a strategy below. The point here is simply this: What has been the most venerated tradition in American economics, or, indeed, the American psyche—that big is good; bigger is better; biggest is best—isn't so. It wasn't so. And it surely won't be so in the future.

THE OTHER AMERICAN TRADITION: MINIMIZATION OF LABOR'S ROLE

If bigness is now problematic (and never really was very good), what about that other sacred cow of the American economic belief system, the minimization of the role of labor? It began with a unique American device—the specializing of jobs into narrow skills. The Japanese and Europeans have a centuries-old craft-guild tradition (based on broad-based skills). Extreme specialization never took root in either setting. But neither the craft tradition nor the craftsmen came to America with the great waves of immigrants; instead, there were masses of illiterate peasants to labor in our giant factories. And when labor finally did organize, the result was to lock in place the narrow job jurisdictions that the moguls of mass production had so painstakingly invented.

The central idea behind narrow job classifications is the conception of labor as a mechanical tool; cost minimization (low wages) and the widespread application of labor-replacing automation are natural concomitants. So is the fact that old American firms and, more frighteningly, new ones thoughtlessly ship work offshore to find cheaper labor. No one speaks more eloquently of the stark choices we face than Robert Reich in *Tales of a New America:*

> . . . high wage economies can no longer depend on standardized mass production. Big Ideas . . . can be shipped in blueprints or electronic symbols anywhere on the globe. Workers in South Korea, Taiwan, or Mexico can churn out turbo-charged automatic vacuums just as well as American workers can, and for far lower wages. Indeed, today [an inventor] is as likely to license a South Korean or Taiwanese company to manufacture the [Big Idea] as he is to sell out to Westinghouse. If Westinghouse does get hold of [the] Big Idea, it is apt to build its own factory overseas.
>
> In a world where routine production is footloose and billions of potential workers are ready to underbid American labor, competitive advantage lies not in one-time breakthroughs but in continual improvements. Stable technologies get away. Keeping a technology requires elaborating upon it continuously, developing variations and small improvements in it that better meet particular needs. . . .
>
> Where innovation is continuous, and products are ever more tailored to customers' particular needs, the distinction between goods and services begins to blur. Thus when robots and computerized machine tools are linked through software that allows them to perform unique tasks, customer service becomes a part of production. When a new alloy is molded to be a specified weight and tolerance, service accounts for a significant part of the value added. . . . Reports that American workers can no longer compete in manufacturing and must shift to services are only half-right. More precisely, they can keep high wages only by producing goods with

a large component of specialized services, or to state the same thing differently, providing services integral to the production and use of specific goods.

The point is this: In the new global economy, nearly everyone has access to Big Ideas and the machines and money to turn them into standardized products, at about the same time, and on roughly the same terms. *The older industrial economies have two options: They can try to match the wages for which workers elsewhere are willing to labor. Or they can compete on the basis of how quickly and well they can transform ideas into incrementally better products* [my emphasis].

The first path—toward stable mass production—relies on cutting labor costs and leaping into wholly new product lines as old ones are played out. For managers this path has meant undertaking (or threatening) massive layoffs, moving (or threatening to move) to lower-wage states and countries, parceling out work to lower-cost suppliers, automating to cut total employment, and diversifying into radically different goods and services. For workers this path has meant defending existing jobs and pay scales, grudgingly conceding lower wages and benefits, shifting burdens by accepting lower pay scales for newly-hired workers, seeking protection from foreign competition, and occasionally striking.

The second path . . . involves increasing labor value. For managers this path means continuously retraining employees for more complex tasks, automating in ways that cut routine tasks and enhance worker flexibility and creativity, diffusing responsibility for innovation, taking seriously labor's concern for job security and giving workers a stake in improved productivity via profit-linked bonuses and stock plans. For workers this second path means accepting flexible job classifications and work rules, agreeing to wage rates linked to profits and productivity improvements, and generally taking greater responsibility for the soundness and efficiency of the enterprise. The second path also involves a closer and more permanent relationship with other parties that have a stake in the firm— suppliers, dealers, creditors, even the towns and cities in which the firm resides.

On this second path, all those associated with the firm become partners in its future. . . . Each member of the enterprise participates in its evolution. All have a commitment to the firm's continued success. Both paths can boost profits and improve competitiveness in the short run. But only the second can maintain and improve America's standard of living over time.

A Grim Prognosis

Today's and tomorrow's winning hand is becoming increasingly clear—quality and flexibility. Essential to them both are (1) smaller units and (2) highly skilled workers serving as the chief source of incremental improvements in products and services.

Is it a simple case of what "goes around, comes around"? Long-standing Japanese and European traditions—less dependence on big scale, more dependence on broadly skilled labor—are now conducive to economic success. Our denigration of these two factors may prove disastrous.

Worse yet, we have no tradition to fall back on as we seek new models. This is not, as some have labeled it, a "back to basics" movement. Quality and flexibility through skilled labor have never been an American custom.

THE SHAPE OF THE NEW
AMERICAN COMPETITOR

Uniformity has given way to broader choices. . . . Mass markets have splintered. Size has lost its significance as it becomes increasingly clear that a company's rank in the *Fortune 500* is of limited importance.

> Martin Davis
> Chairman, Gulf + Western
> *Fortune,* December 1985

In the face of the uncertainties catalogued above, there are those who *are* thriving, in every economic sector. Interestingly, the winners increasingly share common traits. Most pronounced is the emergence of the specialist producer of high value-added goods or services,* or niche creator, which is either a stand-alone firm or a downsized, more entrepreneurial unit of a big firm.

Specialists in Steel, Autos, and Chemicals . . .

A quick *tour d'horizon* admits no exception to this trend. Begin with the toughest of industries, steel. While USX, LTV, Bethlehem, and the rest of the integrated firms totter, mini-mill/micro-mill leaders such as Nucor Corporation and Chaparral, and specialists like Worthington Industries, thrive. Productivity in each of these large firms is several times the industry average. Worker involvement is uniformly high, and quality and responsiveness to customers are phenomenal. In many markets, business is being won back from overseas.

The auto market is flying apart. Hyundais dot the highway. Chrysler's president says we will soon have "the Big Thirty, not the Big Three," and industry analyst Maryann Keller comments that "The U.S. market [has become] a collection of niche markets." Chrysler was following a niche strategy when it acquired AMC primarily for its Jeep Division. And Ford has won by adding value to its product through design distinction and high quality. GM, on the other hand, has been losing out: aiming for the "mass market" that no longer exists, it produced lookalike models, and did not deign to enter small niches, such as that for four-wheel drive and turbos, until very late in the game. The huge firm, says Keller, was "nibbled to death rather than chewed" by smaller, more highly focused competitors.

In chemicals, big firms are writing off billions of dollars in assets in basic commodity chemicals aimed at undifferentiated markets; they are racing, instead, into what the industry calls "downstream" (closer to the river's mouth, or customers) products—numerous specialty, high value-added chemicals to address the narrow needs of smaller markets. Monsanto had a rosy profit picture in 1986; in just five years it has reduced

---

*The term "high value-added" will be routinely used throughout the book. By it I simply mean products or services which emphasize innovative design tailored for narrow markets and resulting from more intense listening to customers; superior quality; exceptional service and responsiveness to customers. This is in contrast to the Model T strategy—"any color as long as it's black"—followed by so many firms to this day.

its dependence on bulk chemicals from 26 percent to 3 percent of assets. Du Pont is creating numerous swift-moving business units, closer to the market.

. . . and Computers and Semiconductors

In September 1986, *Financial World* reviewed the computer industry, observing: "Despite analysts' predictions of an industry shakeout, that only a handful of huge companies would survive, the computer industry is actually *more* fragmented than ever." The *Economist*, in January 1987, concurred: "The way in which market forces have humbled IBM is a lesson to trustbusters everywhere. Only a few years ago the American Justice Department and the EEC Commission threatened to break it up or maim it, so as to end its near-monopoly of the computer market. Today it is struggling to remain a blue-chip. In 1986 it suffered a 27 percent fall in net profits . . . while increasing its sales by a tiny 2.5 percent to $51 billion. Can IBM now mount as successful a counter-attack against its competitors as it did against too-hasty trustbusters?"

In fact, IBM is under attack from the world of the future (Hypres is succeeding, where a quarter-billion-dollar IBM development project failed, in introducing the first products using exotic Josephson Junction technology)—and in supercomputers (Cray et al.), superminicomputers (Convex et al.), engineering work stations (Apollo et al.), minicomputers and networks (Digital Equipment et al.), and personal computers (Apple et al.). A February 1987 issue of *High Technology* assesses the state of the vital "parallel/multiprocessor computers" market. It lists nineteen products, from Elxisi's 6400 to Sequent's Balance 2100 to BBN's Butterfly to NCube. Elxisi? BBN? Who?

In semiconductors, the commodity, or so-called merchant chip, market, once dominated by Fairchild, National Semiconductor, et al., has all but been lost to Japan. We were victimized even in this new arena by our century-old addiction to mass production and our aversion to labor. With a few exceptions such as IBM, which produces chips only for internal consumption, the big U.S. producers emphasized invention over polishing manufacturing skills. Mass production facilities were built willy-nilly as product demand soared. The best engineers did not go into production. Silicon Valley's labor practices, except for engineers, often make Detroit's look humanistic. Since demand exceeded supply in the days in which these firms' philosophies were taking shape, rudeness, not responsiveness, was the approach to customer affairs.

Now the worm has turned, as it did on Detroit. Computer companies and other purchasers not only found the Japanese chip to be of higher quality, they found the Japanese firm to be more responsive to their needs—from 6,000 miles away—than their next-door neighbors.

The way out of the box, if there is one, appears to be customer-centered specialization. Thus Intel is betting much of its future on an entrepreneurial Application Specific Integrated Circuit (ASIC) unit—a group whose operations are entirely separated from those of the rest of the firm. The greater good-news story in U.S. semiconductors, however, may be the 113 specialist start-ups between 1977 and 1986 that constitute the so-called Third Wave; only six have failed, and the new bunch will do over $2 billion in sales in 1987. Some, such as LSI Logic, which was just founded in 1981 but is projecting sales of $300 million in 1987, have become powerhouses. They give us a wide lead in what may well turn out to be the most important part of the industry.

Forget Bigness in Packaged Goods Too

The story is repeated in packaged goods and foods. Take Kitchen Privileges of Alexandria, Virginia, a specialist firm that serves specialists. It is a commercial kitchen (seventeen ovens, walk-in freezer, etc.) specifically designed to be rented. And it is, by giants such as Campbell Soup, to help test-market new products, and by start-ups like Ultimate Brownies. Consumers, especially in the burgeoning two-worker-family sector, are demanding more and more fresh specialized products. Big producers such as Campbell and entrepreneurs by the thousand are satisfying them by deluging a market increasingly fragmented into niches with goods designed to fit.

Campbell has in fact had two sweeping reorganizations in the last five years. The first created over fifty fleet-of-foot business units, the second decentralized marketing into regional offices in an effort to get closer to the distribution channel. Flexible manufacturing systems the firm is introducing add yet another dimension of responsiveness.

Procter & Gamble is following a similar path, attempting to streamline its very hierarchical, functionally centered organization. The firm's past successes cannot be denied, but its old approach is far too cumbersome for today's fast-changing markets.

Ditto the Service Sector

The situation in the service sector is no different. The business section of the January 3, 1987, issue of the Kansas City *Times* proclaims: "Niche stores again outdo retail giants in holiday sales." The new household names and profit stars in retailing are firms such as The Limited, The Gap, and Nordstrom. Even the specialists are specializing—The Limited's Victoria's Secret, Limited Express, and Henri Bendel; The Gap's Banana Republic. Meanwhile, the giants, from Safeway to Carter Hawley-Hale, sputter, fight takeover threats, and attempt to transform their cavernous retail spaces into collections of Limited-like boutiques. (Counter-trends can be found, to be sure, such as warehouse stores in retailing. However, these stores will likely end up with a very limited share of the market. In fact, sales per store in warehouse operations have been declining since 1983.)

In financial services, the "financial supermarket," with its one-stop shopping for all financial services, died stillborn: for example, Merrill Lynch, formulator of the idea, sold off its commercial real estate unit in 1986. And the giant banks, with rare exceptions, look much less "solid" than only a few years ago; the Bank of America is the premier acute-care case—while superregionals such as Banc One of Columbus, Ohio, are surging ahead and smaller specialists such as the University National Bank & Trust of Palo Alto, California, are growing fast and yielding eye-popping returns to assets. Indeed, a look at *Business Week*'s 1986 list of the top 200 banks reveals that the further down the list you go, the better the returns get. Only one of the twenty-three biggest banks (The Morgan) returned more than 1 percent on assets, while fully twenty of the smallest fifty topped that magic mark.

In health care, too, the mega-firms like American Medical International and Hospital Corporation of America were seen as the wave of the future just a few years ago. They roamed the countryside gobbling up small hospitals, and some experts were predicting that most health care in the United States would be delivered by a half-dozen firms by the mid-nineties. Now the giants are struggling. On May 31, 1987, for instance, HCA announced that it was selling off 104 hospitals, for $1.8

billion; it is left with 75, some 50 psychiatric centers, and a number of management contracts. On the other hand, regional hospitals that have specialized are doing well. So are ambulatory-care centers and superspecialists such as ServiceMaster, a Chicago-area firm whose principal business is contracting to clean hospitals. It's over a billion dollars in size, with a five-year return to equity that was tops among the *Business Week 1000* in 1986. (Incidentally, ServiceMaster is going great guns with its mundane but specialized service in Japan, too.)

More evidence of the specialist advance in services is the burgeoning of temporary services and franchising. Only a few years ago the word "temp" brought to mind stenographers and receptionists. The industry, which grew at a compound annual rate of almost 20 percent from 1970 to 1984, now provides temporary semiconductor workers, trial lawyers, and even executives. Call Kelly today for that secretary substitute, and they'll ask you if you want a WordStar or a MacWrite person.

Typical of the specialist winner in franchising is Minit-Lube, or "McOil Change," as *Forbes* dubbed the several-hundred-unit chain:

> Stand in the spotless driveway of Minit-Lube, a fast-growing auto lubrication franchise, where cars are streaming into Minit-Lube's bays, three abreast. Why is this chain so successful? Perhaps it is because, aside from the drive-through car bays, Minit-Lube looks nothing like a greasy automotive business. It's clean, painted white and surrounded by neatly trimmed, lush landscaping. . . . The place should have been named McOil Change. The customer pulls up, is greeted by a smiling employee trained to make eye contact. The customer then places the standard order—a check or fill of brake and power-steering fluids, motor oil, battery water and filters for air and oil. Thereafter, a uniformed service team springs into action. One pops the hood to check and fill fluids. Another vacuums the interior and cleans windows. A third, from a pit below, works his way along the drive shaft, grease gun and wrench in hand, lubricating joints, draining the oil and replacing the filter. Within ten minutes the driver is on his way. The bill: $20. Sears charges the same just for an oil change and lubrication, and it can take up to an hour.

The Winning Look Is Clear

This tour is hardly complete, but it does give the flavor of the sorts of firms that are turning up winners. And even were most of the recent mergers to reverse history's trend and work, the movement toward specialization and more moderately sized business units would in no way be blocked. A GE swallows an RCA, but its first move is to put each acquired business unit, such as NBC, through a starvation diet, similar to the one GE's homegrown corporate and business unit staffs have been subjected to. The truly close-to-the-market units within GE and its acquisitions, and within Du Pont, IBM, and P&G, are being reshaped to look and act more like The Limited, Minit-Lube, or Worthington Industries.

Take all the evidence together, and a clear picture of the successful firm in the 1990s and beyond emerges. It will be:

► flatter (have fewer layers of organization structure)
► populated by more autonomous units (have fewer central-staff second-guessers, more local authority to introduce and price products)
► oriented toward differentiation, producing high value-added goods and services, creating niche markets
► quality-conscious
► service-conscious
► more responsive
► much faster at innovation
► a user of highly trained, flexible people as the principal means of adding value

Figure 1 summarizes the case I've made so far. A series of forces, arrayed on the left side of the chart, are interacting with one another to create a completely new context for doing business, labeled "outcome." The outcome can only be dealt with, I believe, by firms which share a common set of traits, labeled "shape of a winner."

It is that shape, and the attainment of it in short order, which this book addresses.

THE GOOD NEWS: THERE IS GOOD NEWS

You want evidence of transformation not led by major mergers? How about Ford at $60 billion, Chrysler at $23 billion, Dana at $4 billion, Brunswick at $3 billion, Milliken at $2 billion, Campbell Soup at $4 billion, McKesson at $6 billion? You want examples of those squarely in the middle of it? Try Du Pont or Procter & Gamble. How about winners who have hiccuped but so far not made a major misstep in tumultuous markets? Consider Cray, Apple, Digital Equipment, Nucor, Worthington, Chaparral, ServiceMaster, American Airlines, Banc One, Federal Express, The Limited, Nordstrom.

But is there anyone big who seems to have known the formula all along? I began this discussion by declaring that there were no excellent companies. Were I to admit an exception, it would be 3M. If ever there was a perpetual-motion machine, it is this $9 billion firm. Its trick has been to understand value-added differentiation and perpetual market creation long before such tactics became necessary. Every unit of the corporation, whether it serves "mature" markets or exotic new ones, is charged with continual reinvention. And the firm's minimum acceptable profit margins per unit are astronomical—only attainable with truly superior products and service.

So in every industry there are places to visit, people to learn from. Johnsonville Sausage of Sheboygan Falls, Wisconsin, installed a remarkable organization structure, with little hierarchy, lots of employee involvement, and substantial profit-sharing; its market share in the Milwaukee area soared from 7 to 50 percent in ten years. I wrote about the firm in *U.S. News & World Report*—and was delighted to learn that the column spurred visits by plant managers from 3M and General Mills. Another column, about the stellar customer service and economic performance of Sewell Village Cadillac of Dallas, led to a visit by a team from a Procter & Gamble plant.

So the role models are there—in steel, textiles, and autos, as well as computers, retailing, health care, and banking.

Generic Uncertainty

- Oil @ $5 or $35 a barrel
- 1 trillion Eurodollars
- $80 trillion in annual currency = trading/gyrating exchange rates
- Casino society (junk bonds, availability of venture capital, strong market for initial public offerings, leveraged buyouts)
- $1 trillion in developing-country debt
- Mergers, divestitures, de-integration, joint ventures
- Record business and bank failures (and record start-ups)

Technology Revolution

- Design (fast collection of customer data, reduced design-to-manufacture time)
- Manufacturing (smaller, more flexible factories)
- Distribution (electronic linkages, power to customers)

New Competitors

FOREIGN
- Developed (e.g. Japan, Germany)
- Newly industrialized (e.g. Korea)
- Rapidly industrializing (e.g. Brazil)

DOMESTIC
- Smaller firms resulting from the entrepreneurial explosion
- Downsized and de-integrated units within big firms, spun-off elements from big firms

Changing Tastes

- More options
- Two-wage-earner families
- More affluence (top third)
- Less affluence (bottom third)
- Saturation of markets for the "commodities" of yesteryear
- Demand for superior quality

Figure 1: **Forces at Work and Their Apparent Resolution**

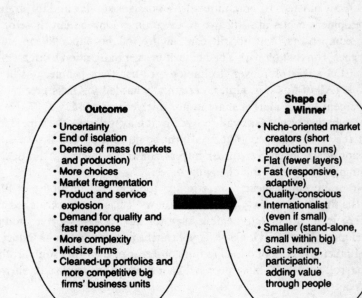

Outcome

- Uncertainty
- End of isolation
- Demise of mass (markets and production)
- More choices
- Market fragmentation
- Product and service explosion
- Demand for quality and fast response
- More complexity
- Midsize firms
- Cleaned-up portfolios and more competitive big firms' business units

Shape of a Winner

- Niche-oriented market creators (short production runs)
- Flat (fewer layers)
- Fast (responsive, adaptive)
- Quality-conscious
- Internationalist (even if small)
- Smaller (stand-alone, small within big)
- Gain sharing, participation, adding value through people

THE BAD NEWS: PACE

General Motors was and remains a pioneer in workplace experiments. From its joint venture with Toyota called the New United Motor Manufacturing, Inc. (NUMMI), to its assembly plant in Lakewood, Georgia, a lot has been going on.

But not enough. The firm's relative cost position has deteriorated. Its management ranks, despite radical (by past standards) surgery, remain hopelessly bloated. Its committee-driven designs still lag and its product development cycles are still two to three times longer than those of its best competitors. And it still can't figure out how to take on small markets. Top that off with a bad case of merger indigestion from Hughes and EDS alike. Moreover, technology, rather than people, is still its theme. (All of this was, almost certainly, what led to GM's precipitous 20 percent loss of market share in just one year, as of May 1987. Never mind whether or not GM will recover, as it may well do—the simple fact that the world's largest industrial firm could tumble that fast, despite extraordinary incentives to car buyers aimed at stemming the tide, is stunning evidence of the changing times.)

No one is complacent. Ford, though topping GM in profits in 1986 for the first time in sixty-two years, knows it has barely scratched the surface in its attempt to achieve superior quality and shorter product development cycles. It looks to Toyota as the premier firm in its industry. IBM is scurrying, too; one long-time observer of the firm estimates that its payroll has 50,000 more people than it needs to accomplish its current mission.

But is even Ford moving fast enough? It's not at all clear. Radical changes in organizational structure and procedures are called for. Layers of management must be reduced in most big firms by 75 percent. Product development time and order lead time must be slashed by 90 percent. Electronic/telecommunication linkups to customers and suppliers must be developed posthaste. Just listening to customers and dealers needs to become the norm—and as yet it's not.

All this adds up to a requirement, not for structural or procedural tinkering, but for a revolution in organization: more autonomous units— guided by a coherent vision rather than by memorandums and managers-as-cops, and manned by involved workers with a big stake in the action and hell-bent upon constant improvement. And this in turn means that new attitudes are also required—especially commitment on the part of managers to the idea that suppliers, workers, unions, distributors, and customers are all partners in the common endeavor.

But the wholesale changes in attitude have not yet occurred, and without them we are doing immeasurably dumb things. We are, for example, letting work drift offshore in pursuit of the lowest-cost production. But, as I'll argue below, to lose control of the plant is to lose control of the future—of quality, responsiveness, and the source of most innovation, which in manufacturing industries occurs in the palpable, on-premises interaction among plant team, designer, marketer, and customer.

We are misusing automation. Americans still see it as a tool to reduce the need for labor, not as a tool to aid labor in adding value to the product. In consequence, efforts to staff our plants with robots are not working.

We are still churning businesses, via merger and divestiture, in hopes of obtaining some ideal portfolio, fit for the future. There is none. No industry is safe. There is no such thing as a safe, fast-growth haven. The new attitudes toward people and adding value are required as much in financial services and entertainment as in autos and steel. Look at the revolution wrought by The Limited or Federal Express, linking people power and computer network power; most service firms are light-years behind.

This book is dedicated to Roger Milliken of Milliken & Co. His genius in 1980 was to see that the answer to competition in the "mature" textile market was unparalleled quality attained largely through people. He revolutionized the company then. But he's almost unique because he saw in 1984 that the first revolution was wholly inadequate to meet the worldwide competitive challenge. So he made another revolution, reordering every relationship in the firm in pursuit of unparalleled customer responsiveness. Two revolutions in six years.

It is Roger Milliken's brand of urgency—and taste for radical reform—that must become the norm. For Milliken's two revolutions (and the firm was a star to begin with) are still only barely meeting the competitive challenge.

IMPLICATIONS FOR PUBLIC POLICY

This book is meant to serve as a handbook for management. Management, I believe, holds the key to a competitive resurgence in the United States. Nonetheless, certain policy prods could help immeasurably in speeding the necessary transformation.

As a conclusion to this introductory analysis, I will offer only the barest of outlines—suggestions for several steps that policymakers can take:

1. Promote more, not less, competition. That is, turn up the heat. First, pass no protectionist legislation. Protect an industry, ancient and recent history alike suggest, and it gets sloppier, or at least fails to improve at an acceptable rate. Playing fields are not, and never have been, level. We should utilize existing trade management legislation, which is fully adequate, and not add more. The objective is to get better and different, not to try to hide from a newly energized world economy. (In this regard, the trade bill which will likely pass in 1987—the most restrictive since Smoot-Hawley in 1930—is a giant step backwards.)

Second, don't tie the corporate raiders' hands. Raiders are no altruists, and their acts cause much unnecessary pain. And, to be sure, some of the moves corporations make to forestall raiders are dysfunctional—for example, making inappropriate mergers so as to create a balance sheet that scares a raider off, or shuttling jobs offshore in a crash, but ultimately misguided, effort to slash costs. But on balance, the raiders are, along with the Japanese, the most effective force now terrorizing inert corporate managements into making at least some of the moves, such as downsizing, that should have been made years ago.

Third, get rid of the entire capital-gains tax after a certain holding period passes. The start-up firms are the breath of fresh air in the economy—we encouraged them with the 1981 capital-gains tax break, and have now discouraged them with the omnibus tax act of 1986. In general, support financial incentives that favor start-ups and spin-offs/divestitures such as leveraged buyouts.

2. Retool and involve the work force. The work force must become the prime source of value added. We need to give employers the incentive to hire people and constantly upgrade skills. First, provide a special tax incentive for all funds, including employee wage costs, spent on training and pay-for-knowledge programs. Provide a further tax incentive for wage increases that result directly from skill upgrading. Provide general tax deductibility for employee off-the-job skill upgrading, whether or not it's related to the current job. I also support, to aid displaced workers, some form of Individual Training Account, as proponents have labeled it. Sizable tax-deductible contributions by employees, similar to IRAs, might be made over an extended period. The money would revert to the employee at retirement or some such time, but upon displacement would be issued, in voucher form, for use in certified training programs.

A second, sweeping plank is aimed at giving employers an even higher incentive to hire and involve employees. Inspired, in particular, by the ideas discussed by Martin Weitzman in *The Share Economy,* I propose, for employers, that a major, old-fashioned investment tax credit plan be allowed on wages distributed as bonuses via profit-distributing bonus plans and quality- and productivity-based gain-sharing plans. For employees, I suggest a big tax exemption, possibly with limits, for all income from profit-distribution and productivity-based gain-sharing plans. (Such a bold incentive would be required to compensate for greater uncertainty—the real possibility of lower pay in bad times.)

Third, greater employee assurance is required as foreign competition heats up even further, and smaller firms become increasingly dominant. Extended and increased trade adjustment assistance is desirable to combat the former (though it should be highly skewed to force rapid enrollment in retraining programs, for instance). Portable pensions and other dislocation-ameliorating housing and health-care programs will be required as well.

3. Stop the mindless offshore job drift. The loss of jobs per se may be less significant than the loss of control of our destiny, as certain manufacturing activities migrate offshore. I propose a new form of domestic content legislation. The term is usually applied to the percentage of domestic content in imports. My alternative is to provide some tax credit for domestic products, based upon the percentage of domestic content, up to, say, 50 percent. A particularly thorny subset of this issue is start-ups—for instance, high-tech firms—that never do establish their own manufacturing operations. The capital-gains tax formula for start-ups could be a sliding one, depending on the percent of value added by onshore manufacture.

4. Push internationalism. We need to shed our lingering isolationism.

Concepts I support include (a) a value-added tax (VAT) to pay for the programs I have proposed here, but excluding goods sold for export, (b) tax benefits favorable to Americans working abroad, (c) provision of more readily available financing sources for smaller or mid-sized firms seeking export markets, and (d) educational incentives to induce much more foreign-language education.

5. Support expanded research and development. The R&D tax credit and the basic-research credit which supports business and university linkages will both be phased out by the end of 1988, thanks to the 1986 tax act. At the least, they should be restored. Support for high levels of basic research, especially in non-defense areas, is a must. Additionally, we might provide special tax breaks to firms that bring university researchers on board, or that support cooperative education programs, especially in engineering and science.

This brief sketch is not meant to be exhaustive. It does not include any mention of major policy levers that influence the overall business climate (arenas where others are more expert than I), and it includes only some of the types of policies that would hasten the transformation of our firms.*

I find myself turning more frequently to public policy considerations because of my growing frustration. The changes are being made—by management. The changes can be made—by management. But they are not being made fast enough by management. The issue is not the unions. Nor is it "unfair" Japanese practices, unless learning our language or paying attention to details that commercial and individual consumers care about is unfair.

We must look at what's working, and move fast to adapt and emulate the best. The speed of the transition is the most pressing issue.

---

*It also flies in the face of the basic intention of tax reform—less use of the tax code to manipulate firms' outcome. While I acknowledge the adverse consequences of thousands of special interest loopholes, I think this is precisely the wrong time to turn our back on the most effective weapon to aid rapid industrial transformation—tax policy.

2

Using the Prescriptions: The Essentials of Proactive Management

"NICE TO DO" BECOMES "MUST DO"

The history of the forty-five prescriptions that are the essence of this book is the history of *In Search of Excellence*. In short, a "nice-to-do" in 1979 (when the excellence research began) has become a "must-do" in the late 1980s.

It soon became apparent that the "excellence phenomenon," and the associated explosion of concern with management's performance, was not leading to rapid enough transformation by most firms. The modest effort of my colleagues and myself to focus on application of the principles for success we had described was spearheaded by a five-day executive seminar. It is officially called Implementing In Search of Excellence.

The spirit of implementation of the new, especially in sizable organizations, is best embodied by Kelly Johnson's original Lockheed "Skunk Works" (discussed extensively in *A Passion for Excellence*). A modest-sized band toiled under Johnson's guidance for forty-four years. In the process it delivered working prototypes, and often production models, of some forty-one new aircraft or other complex systems. Included were the F-104 Starfighter, the durable C-130, the renowned U-2, and the exotic SR-71 "blackbird" spy plane.

Again and again Johnson would deliver the goods in a tenth the expected time at a tenth the expected cost—and with a product both advanced and reliable. This sort of "corpocracy" beater was the symbol we were looking for. So the seminar became Skunk Camp, and the participants, naturally enough, became Skunks. Though the words are amusing, the objective, as with Johnson's original band, was deadly serious.

The people who came surprised us. After a first session attended mostly by our heroes (chicken magnate Frank Perdue, Dana turnaround boss Ren McPherson, et al.), the regular meetings were dominated by: (1) people who headed midsized companies and (2) action takers, such as plant or division managers, from giant firms.

Plant managers from Ford and Crown Zellerbach attended, as did division general managers from 3M. But more typical was the response of Buckman Labs. The firm is a privately held, $110 million maker of specialty chemicals based in Memphis, Tennessee; already well run, it has sent some twenty-four executives, from both U.S. and foreign operations, to our seminars.

The sessions, then, were filled with activists, not theorists. They bought the message of *Search* and *Passion,* and were hell-bent and determined to get on with it. So we were increasingly pressed by our customers to move beyond the case studies and examples in the two books to hard-edged answers to the question: "What in the heck are we supposed to *do?*" Thus "the promises" were born, drafted early one morning, seven in number. They have evolved into these prescriptions. I'll address their structure presently.

A different kind of evolution was more important. The original tone of presentation was: "Here's some nifty stuff you might do first, folks. Take it or leave it." But the evidence kept pouring in: America wasn't cutting it in any industry, either service or manufacturing. Banks, hospitals, and semiconductor firms alike were shutting their doors. GM, IBM, and Du Pont were quaking.

So a nice-to-do "reduce product development cycle time" became a hard-edged "reduce product development cycle time by 75 percent," and then became "reduce product development cycle time by 75 percent in the next two to three years." An innocuous "reduce the layers" became a sharp "no more than five layers in an organization of any size"—and "get rid of all first-line supervisors." "Get people involved" became "get everyone involved in almost everything, train like the dickens, and introduce major pay-for-knowledge and profit-distribution plans—NOW."

Thus the hastily sketched, "nice to do" promises have become a manifesto for radical organizational reform, a handbook for a management revolution. And the objective is not to be excellent, because "to be" implies stasis and there is no place to stand anymore; the only excellent firms are those that are rapidly evolving.

PRESCRIPTIONS FOR A WORLD TURNED UPSIDE DOWN

Five areas of management constitute the essence of proactive performance in our chaotic world: (1) an obsession with responsiveness to customers, (2) constant innovation in all areas of the firm, (3) partnership—the wholesale participation of and gain sharing with all people connected with the organization, (4) leadership that loves change (instead of fighting it) and instills and shares an inspiring vision, and (5) control by means of simple support systems aimed at measuring the "right stuff" for today's environment.

In each area except the last I will present ten prescriptions. Each of the total of forty-five, with no exceptions, is an urgent call for radical reform. Following the logic developed in the preceding chapter, for instance, the first "customer" prescription demands a radical shift of the firm's entire portfolio toward highly differentiated products, delivered via a strategy aimed at creating niche markets. It is my advice for bankers, retailers, hospital administrators, computer makers, and city managers alike.

The next prescription uses another "hot" word, urging a quality revolution. Why revolution? Simple. I've looked at dozens of "quality programs" closely, hundreds casually, and read and talked with the gurus. Everybody has a quality program—but only the tiniest handful, such as Ford, Milliken, and the Paul Revere Life Insurance Company, are really making a difference. Thus I spell out twelve steps, each bold, which represent the minimum basis for a quality revolution.

And on the challenges go, all the way to the last of the forty-five, which stresses integrity. Of course, integrity has always been important. But even its meaning has changed. If we are to depend increasingly on people's wholesale involvement, then integrity is more of an issue than ever—integrity, as I've come to see it, means that if there are no employee bonuses, there are no executive bonuses. It means trusting first-line employees to do all the quality control, after providing them with the tools and training required to execute.

The endpapers of this book list the forty-five prescriptions in abbreviated form. Two obvious questions pop out at once: What do you do first? How do you pace the introduction of the ideas?

There is a happy and an unhappy answer. The happy answer is that many of the prescriptions support each other. Doing one aids implementation of another. For instance, the twenty-five people, leadership, and systems prescriptions all exist solely to speed the customer and innovation goals established in the customer and innovation sections.

The bad news: *You can't do it all at once, but you must.* Fail to get on with almost all of this agenda at a brisk pace and you're in for trouble. Part of the reason is that explosion of domestic and foreign competitors: Some competitor is already beating you to the punch on most of these bold ideas in some segments of your market right now. But you can't do everything at once, and I do provide some guidelines for getting started. Still, your own sense of your competitive situation must be the guide to picking a starting point. And, of course, various parts of the organization can work with different intensity on different ideas.

Hard Evidence Supports Each Bold Goal

It's essential to note that there is no speculation involved in any of these prescriptions. First, they are born of the radically altered business environment in which we find ourselves. They are need-driven, pure and simple.

Second, each idea has already been anticipated by a few leaders in virtually every industry. There's not a hint of "it would really be nice to wire ourselves up to our customers." PPG (once Pittsburgh Plate Glass), Milliken, Federal Express, McKesson, et al. have done it. More are doing it every day.

The Prescriptions and the Public Sector

Maryland governor William Donald Schaefer led the dramatic transformation of Baltimore during his fifteen years as mayor. A compulsion for action, unmatchable energy, and an astonishing ability to be in touch with the city's people marked his tenure. That is why he joins Roger Milliken in my dedication.

In a late-1986 letter to me, Schaefer stated that "the same principles of success prevail" in the public as in the private sector. Many would debate Schaefer on that point. I'm not one of them. My own career includes over four years in two managerial assignments in Washington, one as a young Navy lieutenant at the Pentagon, one as a White House coordinator of drug treatment and law enforcement programs. Both jobs were humble ones, especially the first. So I have observed failure and success as an insider, and from watching the likes of Schaefer and General Bill Creech, former commander of the giant Air Force Tactical Air Command, whose dramatic organization turnaround was chronicled at length in *A Passion for Excellence*.

It *is* the same. Even the language is the same among the best in the public sector—that is, the customer is identified and made central to all affairs in the top schools, cities, state agencies. Such is the talk even in a newly invigorated IRS. Procedures have been radically simplified by the best public sector leaders. First-line-employee involvement and improvement programs in pursuit of responsive service are the essential concern of the top public sector bosses.

To address the similarities while attempting to deal with linguistic differences, I have included a brief section called "Public Parallels" at the end of those prescriptions whose translation to the public sector, in my experience, has been most difficult.

The Prescriptions as Management Theory

The prescriptions constitute a first draft, if you will, of a theory of management. I add this point because it is increasingly clear that we need a new theory of management, or at least some new generally accepted principles. It is audacious to proclaim these prescriptions as a first draft of generally accepted principles, yet I do.

They draw from the most thoughtful theorists of both macro- and micro-economics. They join the firm to worldwide financial flows and expected international conditions (and uncertainties). They are also consistent with the more sound of the various sociological and psychological theories on the internal states of organizations. Consideration is given to information theory, especially to so-called internal transaction costs (better called communication and coordination costs) that affect scale economies, flexibility, and responsiveness so greatly. Finally, the diverse impacts of changing technology on every aspect of the internal and external dealings of the organization are considered. Thus while all of the prescriptions are grounded in empirical evidence, all have been passed through a number of purely theoretical frameworks as well.

Why is this important to the practitioner, who is, after all, the book's customer? For at least two reasons, as it turns out. First, it is an essential test of soundness that extreme empirical observations—and, by conventional standards, the prescriptions are extreme—be consistent with some larger set of theoretical ideas. Otherwise, the extreme observations could be suspect as anomalies from which it is dangerous to generalize.

Second, each manager, from newly promoted supervisor to the chief executive of a big firm, has, and indeed needs, a pocket theory of management. It is seldom formal, to be sure, but more likely an implicit list of "ten things I really believe" that can be wheedled out of anyone with some effort. So each reader-practitioner has a theory. I want to challenge it, or reinforce it, as the case may be.

That said, what is the theory, beyond the specifics of each of the forty-five prescriptions? In summary:

1. The customer responsiveness prescriptions add up to a view of a "porous" organization listening intently to its customers and adjusting rapidly. The porosity induces the flexibility and responsiveness necessary to satisfy minute differences in demand—thence, an ever-changing portfolio of highly differentiated, high-value-added products/services. If we are to sustain our relatively high-wage economy, we must learn to add value across the board.

2. The prescriptions for fast-paced innovation suggest that more starts on new things, in every function, by every person, must be made in order to adapt as fast as the ever-faster-changing environment requires. Given that premise, the need arises for tolerance of well-intended failures and persistent champions of innovation if the state of excitation necessary to deal with the exploding competitive picture is to be maintained.

3. The flexibility-through-empowered-people prescriptions, which deal with high involvement, minimal hierarchy, and increased rewards based upon new performance parameters (quality, responsiveness), are wholly consistent with the more freewheeling, fast-reacting organization pictured in the customer and innovation sections. Highly trained and thus more flexible workers, with a big stake in the action, are a must for constant adaptation to customer needs and constant innovation.

4. The leadership prescriptions essentially address only two questions: First, "how do you induce people to love change as much as they've hated it in the past?" And then, "how do you lead/guide/control what looks like anarchy by normal standards?" That is, how do you deal with very short production runs *and* higher quality *and* treating every customer as a "market segment," and also get line workers involved in everything from budgets to quality control, while paring middle management to the bone? New notions of "control," such as creating an inspiring vision and being out and about, replace traditional controls by means of written policy directives filtering down from a remote headquarters.

5. The systems prescriptions add up to revolution, too: They redefine the traditional—and ever-important—process of measurement and control. Measure the "right stuff" (quality, flexibility, innovation) is the plea. Share information, heretofore considered confidential, with everyone in order to engender fast action on the line. That is, systems must *abet* our revolutionary agenda rather than impede it, as they most often do today.

These are the general themes you can expect. I can't overstate the extreme nature of the challenge I unashamedly lay down. Some months ago, after a marketing conference, I did some scribbling on a napkin while flying home. I listed the major activities of a business. Then I listed the way it "was/is" and the way it "must become" as column headings. To my dismay, in all ten basic areas, almost a 180 degree flip-flop was required. I called my sketch "a world turned upside down." This list, summarized as Figure 2 (see pages 52–53), provided a major spur to the writing of this book.

The themes are already familiar: a flow of power to the field, the need to act fast, adapt fast, and destroy traditional functional barriers—all in the service of rapid, value-added market creation. But as you subsequently read and reflect on these prescriptions, pay special attention to the time "denominator"—for example, in the fourth customer prescription you'll find the outrageous *demand* that you link up electronically with 75 percent of your biggest customers within the next 24 months. I have become a fanatic about quantifying—but a new sort of quantifying. I insist upon quantifying the "soft stuff"—quality, service, customer linkups, innovation, organizational structure, people involvement, and even how much time you spend breaking down inappropriate inter-functional barriers. We must move from lip service to the ideas of *In Search of Excellence, A Passion for Excellence,* and 1,000 other books just as good or better, to setting challenging goals for implementation. It's an unalterable fact: others in your industry, from Korea to Kalamazoo, are meeting and exceeding my most "outrageous demands" as you read this.

USING THIS BOOK

Many strategies are available for organizing a book. I have chosen a handbook format. In the course of hundreds of seminars, numerous important ideas have surfaced. In each of the five major business areas, there were hundreds of candidates for the final list of five or ten prescriptions.

As a result, though we have forty-five specific "suggestions" (prescriptions), each one, even at this level of dis-aggregation, is complex. Each prescription includes some supporting data (case examples, summaries of others' research), but is principally organized into specific suggestions for action. Finally, based upon my experience, a short list of possible near-term "first steps" is presented.

I propose that you skim any of the five sections and pick the areas that appear most relevant to your current competitive situation. Size up yourself (and your competition) vis-à-vis the sweeping proposals that a given prescription lays out. Then (1) move to corroborate the validity of the idea in your own setting and (2) select some pragmatic steps to be taken in two weeks to sixty days that will allow you to both (a) collect data and (b) seek pilot sites for first tests of the proposals.

The Tension

I hope to induce tension. On the one hand, it is imperative—in each and every one of the forty-five areas—that you consider bold goals, really bold goals, in fact. On the other hand, it is at least as important that you pick some "next 72 hours" steps—i.e., get going!

In May 1987, I was part of a seminar with an established building products firm. The discussion quickly turned to responsiveness to customers (distributors). The group worked on some challenging goals, and developed one for an order turnaround process that amounted to a 100 percent improvement on their current performance. Some gasped and more than a few snickered at the possibility of such a "promise."

Yet I stood up and threw cold water on the idea, suggesting that, given the competitive scene, the group consider an improvement of 400 to 600 percent—and described several other groups, from similar old-line firms, that had done at least that much.

I think I was right—and so, later, did the firm's president (he acknowledged, for instance, that some small competitors were already beating my "bold goal" suggestion). Such non-incremental goals, which will require you to "zero base" the business and seek completely new ways of organizing everything—from accounting systems to organizational structure to training to equipment layout and distribution network relations—are a commonplace necessity today.

Rather than accepting or rejecting the call for boldness, we (the group and a colleague and I) decided to accept the 400 to 600 percent improvement as given for the next 36 hours of the seminar, acting as if it could be done. So we plunged headlong into the process of looking for dramatic and mundane first steps, to be taken in the next two days to sixty days, that would facilitate implementation of the goal.

I can't conclude with a hearty "They did it." I can tell you that they accepted the challenge, did come up with very practical—and bold and mundane—first steps, and mounted several pilots, which produced promising results in the thirty days immediately following the end of the seminar (at which point this book went to press).

I commend them—and such an approach.

Caveats

I have proposed a piecemeal reading of the book, in an effort to deal with real-world implementation. There are two major problems with such an approach—issues of attitude and issues of connectedness.

Attitude. The book—each part, each prescription—is about attitude:

Figure 2: **A World Turned Upside Down**

		Was/Is	Must Become
1.	Marketing	Mass markets, mass advertising, violent battles to shift a share point, functional integrity of marketing pros	Market creation, niche focus, innovation from being closer to markets, thriving on market fragmentation, ceaseless differentiation of any product (no matter how mature)
2.	International	"Global" brands which are managed from the U.S., international as an adjunct activity, for big firms only	Focus on new market creation, development done offshore from the start, essential strategy for firms of all sizes
3.	Manufacturing	Emphasis on volume, cost, hardware, functional integrity	Primary marketing tool (source of quality, responsiveness, innovation), part of product design team from the start, short runs, flexibility, people *supported by* automation
4.	Sales and Service	Second-class citizens, "move the product" predominates	Heroes, relationship managers (with every customer, even in retail), major source of value added, prime source of new product ideas

	Was/Is	Must Become
5. Innovation	Driven by central R&D, big projects the norm, science-rather than customer-driven, cleverness of design more important than fits and finishes, limited to new products	Small starts in autonomous and decentralized units the key, everyone's business, driven by desire to make small and customer-noticeable improvements
6. People	Need tight control, try to specialize and diminish role	People as prime source of value added, can never train or involve too much, big financial stake in the outcome
7. Structure	Hierarchical, functional integrity maintained	Flat, functional barriers broken, first-line supervisors give way to self-managed teams, middle managers as facilitators rather than turf guardians
8. Leadership	Detached, analytic, centralized strategy planning, driven by corporate staffs	Leader as lover of change and preacher of vision and shared values, strategy development radically bottom-up, all staff functions support the line rather than vice versa

53

	Was/Is	Must Become
9. Management Information Systems (MIS)	Centralized for the sake of consistency, internally aimed	Information use and direct customer/ supplier linkups as a strategic weapon managed by the line, decentralization of MIS a must
10. Financial Management and Control	Centralized, finance staff as cop	Decentralized, most finance people to the field as "business team members," high spending authority down the line

for instance, turning the organization inside out (making it porous to customer and distributors and suppliers) and turning it upside down (encouraging participation, information-sharing, and wholly new roles for supervisors/managers at all levels).

There is, then, a feel to the prescriptions taken as a whole—what they add up to in terms of the way we think about people, customers, relationships (adversarial versus cooperative)—that requires a more or less front-to-back reading. Unless you address the deep-seated attitude issues (see the prior discussion of scale economies and labor's historic role), you miss the point.

Connectedness. There are two issues here. First, each of the five or ten prescriptions in each section is closely interrelated with the others in that section. Each section's introduction, as well as some of the commentary in each prescription, underscores this point. For instance, most participation programs fail. The reasons are many, including failure to train, failure to simplify structure, and failure to reward (pay for) good performance. Thus, the ten prescriptions for achieving flexibility through people are close to meaningless if taken separately; they must be considered together, as a unit. (That doesn't mean that you don't "start somewhere." Rather, you must keep all ten in mind at all times—and work on all ten, albeit at different rates in different places.)

The second issue here is the relation of each set of five or ten prescriptions to the other four sets. Each of the five sets is designed to support the other four, and vice versa. You cannot achieve, say, the customer responsiveness goals unless you buy into all the rest. Furthermore, everything in the book follows from the first set of prescriptions, and especially the first six. This book is market-driven! The first six customer responsiveness strategies are essential for survival. The rest of the book, in many respects, is about implementing these strategies.

Format

Handbooks, by definition, are meant for ready—and repeated—reference. That is why we've chosen a format that breaks the book not into chapters, but into 45 parts, each containing one of the prescriptions. Moreover, each prescription begins with a summary which covers its main points and specifies the most important subsidiary goals. Additionally, most prescriptions contain detailed lists of suggested actions, based upon the best practice of firms that are most successfully preparing for the future.

I strongly urge you to use the central elements of each prescription as a basis for competitor comparison. How are you doing on *each* dimension of the prescription? How is your best (new, small, old and refurbished, international) competitor doing? Do my goals sound outrageous? If so, think again, please—that is, look again at the very best unit in your firm, or your very best small competitor. Careful reflection, I suspect, will reveal that in fact someone in your industry has already surpassed each of the apparently ever-so-bold goals prescribed herein.

This handbook is intended to push you to the limit, time and again. Get to work on a practical improvement project, assess the early results—and then look at the bold goals (and evidence for their necessity); then redouble your efforts, and your pace.

Learning to Love Change

There is no prescription which says it outright. Yet it lurks on every page. It is the true revolution to which the title refers. The world has not just "turned upside down." It is turning in every which way at an accelerating pace.

To meet the demands of the fast-changing competitive scene, we must simply learn to love change as much as we have hated it in the past. Our organizations are designed, down to the tiniest nuts and bolts and forms and procedures, for a world where tomorrow is today, plus or minus one-one-thousandth of one percent.

Our factories are not built to compete with micro-brewers (beer) and micro-mills (steel) or "boutique factories" (very specialized shops with very specialized and advanced machine tools). Our accounting systems are not designed to deal with machines that can produce hundreds of different parts an hour. And our strategic planning systems are not designed to deal with the appearance of a host of new and largely unexpected competitors in a given year.

Every variable is up for grabs, and we are meeting (not meeting, in general) the challenge with inflexible factories, inflexible systems, inflexible front-line people—and, worst of all, inflexible managers who still yearn for a bygone era where presiding over the opening of new wings of hospitals and new plants was about the most strenuous chore to be performed.

Today, loving change, tumult, even chaos is a prerequisite for survival, let alone success. It is to that end—exploring what it means to succeed by loving change—that this book is devoted.

II

CREATING TOTAL *C*USTOMER RESPONSIVENESS

SECTION SUMMARY

Only those who become attached to their customers, figuratively and literally, and who move most aggressively to create new markets—for fast-growing and mature products alike—will survive.

Figure 3 describes the relationships among the ten customer responsiveness prescriptions. C-1, the Guiding Premise, follows from the case developed in Part I. Success—in health care, food, or computers—will go to those who add value by developing customized products or services that create new market niches.

Prescriptions C-2 through C-6 are the Five Basic Value-Adding Strategies for attaining the superordinate objective specified in C-1. These are: C-2, the provision of exceptional quality, as perceived by the customer; C-3, the provision of exceptional service, emphasizing the intangible attributes of any product or service; C-4, the achievement of extraordinary responsiveness by creating electronic or other tight linkages to the customer; C-5, exploiting international market opportunities, regardless of firm size or market maturity; and C-6, positioning the business unit or organization in a way that creates a clear sense of its uniqueness in everyone's mind—customer, distributor, supplier, employee.

The Five Basic Value-Adding Strategies are in turn supported by the Four Capability Building Blocks. The first, C-7, is a pervasive obsession—including every person and every function in the organization—with listening to customers. The next two delineate revised—and heroic—roles for neglected functions: C-8 demands the transformation of manufacturing from "cost center to be optimized" to a prime marketing tool; C-9 proposes the elevation of the sales and service functions to positions of commanding importance and the lionizing of their people. The fourth basic capability building block—achieving fast-paced innovation—is the subject of the next set of prescriptions, I-1 through I-10.

The customer responsiveness prescriptions add up to a revolution in corporate life—the wholesale external orientation of everyone in the firm, the achievement of extraordinary flexibility in response to what in the past would have been called customer whims. C-10 summarizes the "feel" of that revolution.

Figure 3: **Creating Total Customer Responsiveness**

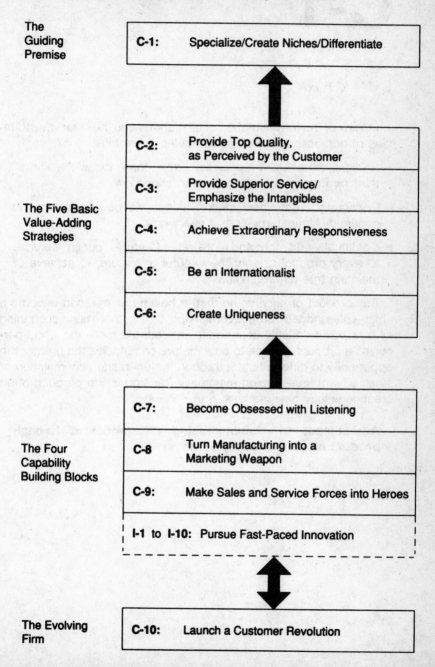

The Guiding Premise

C-1: Specialize/Create Niches/Differentiate

The Five Basic Value-Adding Strategies

C-2: Provide Top Quality, as Perceived by the Customer

C-3: Provide Superior Service/Emphasize the Intangibles

C-4: Achieve Extraordinary Responsiveness

C-5: Be an Internationalist

C-6: Create Uniqueness

The Four Capability Building Blocks

C-7: Become Obsessed with Listening

C-8 Turn Manufacturing into a Marketing Weapon

C-9: Make Sales and Service Forces into Heroes

I-1 to **I-10:** Pursue Fast-Paced Innovation

The Evolving Firm

C-10: Launch a Customer Revolution

C-1

SUMMARY

In view of the fragmentation of all markets and the clear-cut strategies of domestic and foreign competitors, we must:

▶ Radically emphasize "specialist" rather than "mass"/"volume" thinking throughout our entire portfolio—now.

▶ Constantly create new market niches via new products and continuous transformation of every product.

▶ Continually add more and more value (features, quality, service) to every product or service, youthful or mature, to achieve or maintain true differentiation.

Any product or service, no matter how mundane, can become a "high-value-added" product or service; that is, there is no such thing as a nondifferentiable commodity. Indeed, the more the world perceives a product/service to be a mature commodity, the greater the opportunity to differentiate it through the unending accumulation of small advantages—which eventually transforms the product, often creating wholly new markets in the process.

Add at least ten value-increasing "differentiators" to each product or service every 90 days.

C-1

Specialize/Create Niches/Differentiate

. . . the Japanese pulled the rug out from under U.S. manufacturing. They figured they could break America's stronghold in many markets only by offering customers a broader choice of goods. That would attack the key weakness of mass manufacturing: It depends on long, stable production runs. By totally revamping the factory and finding methods that could rapidly inject a stream of new products into the market, [they ensured that] the U.S. would be unable to keep pace. It was a stunning strategic coup that marked the end of an era. The Japanese created a manufacturing infrastructure that can respond with blazing speed to market demands and changing opportunities. . . . few U.S. companies have the manufacturing talent necessary to mount an effective response. The experts can tick off only 30 or so.

Business Week, April 1987

The fastest growing companies on the fringe of this year's *Fortune 500* hold strong positions in specialized markets.

"The Riches in Market Niches"
Fortune, April 1987

The car market has become increasingly fragmented. . . . General Motors will have to become Specific Motors, offering . . . a wider variety of cars for narrower markets . . . in the new world of low-volume production runs.

"The Economy of the 1990s"
Fortune, February 1987

More than anything else, today's [successful] hospitals specialize, specialize, specialize.

Training, April 1987

There has been an explosion in the last four or five years in specialty foods.

Louie Gonzalez, Safeway Stores
May 1987

On an Eastern Airlines flight early in 1987, I noticed something odd in the little pocket at the front of the cabin where schedules are usually placed. It turned out to be a MasterCard credit application—or, rather, an application for an Eastern Airlines MasterCard. Each time you use the card, at a restaurant or photo shop, you get bonus miles.

Two days later, in Rutland, Vermont, I saw another newly printed credit card application while purchasing some pots and pans. The Vermont National Bank, with the Contemporary Downtown Business Association as co-sponsor, was offering a Downtown Rutland Shopping Card—"no annual fee, low annual interest rate of 16.5%, 25 day grace period, free 'Downtown Dollars.'" (Free "Downtown Dollars" means a rebate of 1 percent on all purchases, issued twice a year, and usable at any participating merchant's establishment.)

These two examples are typical of the blizzard of new financial service products that are being launched daily—from both traditional and nontraditional sources, and encompassing partnerships of all sorts.* Similar blizzards mark any industry you can name. For instance, there's the Oklahoma City hospital beset with cost problems, whose cinnamon rolls happened to win a citywide bake-off; it now has a separate catering division providing bakery products for Marriott, among others.

---

*In fact, there has recently arisen a whole new segment of the credit card business, called "affinity cards." For instance, Ducks Unlimited of Reno, Nevada, offers a Visa card with a picture of a duck landing on a marsh; some of the interest paid in by cardholders goes to preserve marshland for ducks.

MARKET CREATORS

A banker friend offers this advice: "Niche or be niched." In Part I of this book I made the case which underpins this prescription. For a series of reasons, including (1) an explosion of new and relatively small competitors, as well as foreign competitors looking for toeholds in every U.S. market, (2) growing instability in the marketplace, and (3) the technology revolution, we are fast entering the era of the flexible specialist. The observation is as valid for the service sector as for manufacturing. And it is as valid for large firms, which must reshape themselves to keep up, as for small or midsized ones.

The language is a dead giveaway: "micro-brewers" (beer), "minimills" and "micro-mills" (steel), "minilabs" (photo finishing, optometry), "minifactory," "industrial boutique," "boutique farming," "designer tomatoes," "custom semiconductor," "gourmet semiconductor," "de-integrate," "de-organize," "de-massify," "collection of niche markets," "flexible manufacturing systems," "de-merge," "hollow [corporation/hospital]," "store within a store," "factory within a factory," "particularized demand," "de-layering," "subcontracting," "temporary services," "de-conglomerate," "sell off," "spin off," "breakup value," "flattened [organizational] pyramid," "[market] fractured into subsegments." None of these terms was in use in 1975. Yet I ran across each, some several times, in the space of a month in late 1986.

A recent analysis by the highly respected Strategic Planning Institute (SPI), using their extensive PIMS (Profit Impact of Market Strategy) data base,* shows that return on investment in market segments of less than $100 million averages 27 percent, while the return in large ($1 billion and over), less differentiated markets averages 11 percent—quite a difference. And in their landmark study of midsized firms, *The Winning Performance: How America's High Growth Mid-Size Companies Succeed,* Don Clifford and Dick Cavanagh observed that niche-creating,

---

*The PIMS data base contains detailed, confidential data on product lines from over 3,000 business units representing all sectors of the economy. The data base was formed within General Electric in 1972. SPI is now an independent entity in Cambridge, Massachusetts. *The PIMS Principles,* by Drs. Robert Buzzell and Bradley Gale, published in 1987, summarizes the SPI research.

high-value-adding strategies marked over 95 percent of their winners in every sector of the economy.

I made a brief tour of the landscape in Part I, suggesting the sorts of changes that are occurring. Figure 4 summarizes that tour and includes a few other examples as well: name the industry and you'll find (1) the emergence of specialist small and midsized firms and (2) large firms trying to reconfigure to better enable themselves to compete in the specialist world.

Thus, this first prescription reflects the fast-changing macro- and micro-economic environment. If you are not reconfiguring your organization to become a fast-changing, high-value-adding creator of niche markets, you are simply out of step.

The attitudes that mark the niche market creators, as opposed to traditional market sharers, are aptly described by Silicon Valley marketing expert Regis McKenna:

> *Marketing should focus on market creation, not market sharing* [my emphasis]. Most people in marketing have what I call a "market-share mentality." They identify established markets, then try to figure a way to get a piece of the market. . . . All these strategies are aimed at winning market share from other companies in the industry.
>
> In fast-changing industries, however, marketers need a new approach. Rather than thinking about *sharing* markets, they need to think about *creating* markets. Rather than taking a bigger slice of the pie, they must try to create a bigger pie. Or better yet, they should bake a new pie.
>
> Market-sharing and market-creating strategies require very different sorts of thinking. Market-share strategies [emphasize] advertising, promotion, pricing, and distribution. Customers are interested primarily in price and availability. The supplier with the best financial resources is likely to win.
>
> Market-creating strategies are much different. In these strategies, managers think like entrepreneurs. They are challenged to create new ideas. The emphasis is on applying technology, educating the market, developing the industry infrastructure, and creating new standards. The company with the greatest innovation and creativity is likely to win.
>
> . . . If companies think only about sharing the markets, they will

never get involved in emerging businesses. They'll take a look at the business, decide that the "pie" is too small, and move on to other possibilities.

That is exactly what happened in the personal-computer business. Dozens of major companies investigated the market for inexpensive computers in the mid-1970s. At the time, these computers were used primarily by hobbyists—that is, enthusiasts who enjoyed tinkering with the machines. . . .

But a few companies, companies such as Apple and Tandy, looked at the business with a market-creation mentality. They looked beyond the hobbyists and saw that small businessmen and professionals might eventually use the machines—if only the machines were designed and marketed a bit differently. Rather than focusing on what *was* they focused on what *might be.*

Figure 4: **The Trend Toward Niche Market Creation in America**

Sector	Typical Thriving Niche Creators	Major Firms Reorganizing/ Becoming Niche Creators
Manufacturing/ Agriculture		
Steel and Metals	Worthington, Nucor, Chaparral, Alleghany Ludlum, Fansteel, Stahl Specialty, Philips	Inland
Autos		Chrysler, Ford
Chemicals	Liquid Air, Sealed Air, Safety-Kleen, Hexcel Chemical Products, Buckman Labs	Du Pont, Monsanto
Textiles	Nantucket Industries, Russell Corp., Golden Needles Knitting and Glove	Milliken

Figure 4: *(continued)*

Sector	Typical Thriving Niche Creators	Major Firms Reorganizing/ Becoming Niche Creators
Forest Products	Elgin Corrugated Box, Trus Joist	
Semiconductors	LSI Logic, Siliconix, Cypress Semiconductor	Intel, Advanced MicroDevices, Texas Instruments
Computers	Cray Research, Sun Microsystems, Convex, Compaq, Apple	IBM, NCR
Packaged Goods	Salad Singles, Orval Kent, Dreyer's Grand, Anchor Steam	Campbell Soup, Procter & Gamble
Farming	Perdue Farms, Chianina Lite Beef, Inc., Denair	
Service		
Retailing	The Limited, Nordstrom, The Gap, 7-Eleven	Sears, Safeway, Kroger
Distribution	McKesson, Williams-Sonoma, Ingram	Spiegel
Financial Services	Banc One, Stillwater National, Citytrust, University National Bank & Trust, Barnett Banks	Continental Illinois
Health Care	ServiceMaster, Emergency Management Services, Nuclear Medical Associates, Health Management	

Figure 4: *(continued)*

Sector	Typical Thriving Niche Creators	Major Firms Reorganizing/ Becoming Niche Creators
	Professionals, Caremark, El Camino Hospital, the Mayo Clinic	Hospital Corporation of America
Temporary Services	Editorial Experts, The Mortgage Professionals	
Trucking/Busing	Ryder System, Peter Pan	

Midsize firms and fast-growth industries are not the only arenas in which specialization and market creation can occur. Other PIMS analyses point out that differentiation works as well in declining as in growing markets. Economist William Hall goes further, concluding after extensive research that the top differentiators in "mature" industries (e.g., tires, cigarettes) actually outperform the best differentiators in growth industries. Thus, any firm's strategy can—and should—be shifted radically toward niche creation.

DIFFERENTIATING "COMMODITIES"

Anything—a first draft said "almost anything," but I scrapped the "almost"—can be turned into a value-added product or service for a well-defined or newly created market. Consider:

The Milliken shop towels. "Shop towel" is a euphemism for "rag." Textile-maker Milliken & Co. has a vital rag/shop towel business (towels, dust mops, and the like for factories, hospitals, and similar establishments), growing like the blazes with returns on investment of more than 50 percent. How can a domestic textile producer do that?

Simple: A rag is not a rag. The shop towels are sold to industrial launderers who in turn rent them to the ultimate user. Milliken trains the salespeople of its customers (the industrial launderers), develops promotional material for them, and held a whopping thirty-three days of executive-level "user conferences" for customers in 1985. A few other services in 1986 included: Shop Towel Product Workshop I–IV; telecommunications seminars; seminars on selling skills; audiovisual sales aids for their customers; production seminars; customer tours of Milliken plants; on-line, computer based order entry and freight optimization systems to maximize responsiveness and minimize shipping costs; market research assistance; use of the Milliken Data Access System, which gives the customer, via computer link-up, access to various Milliken marketing aids; sales leads generated by participation in conventions; participatory management seminars; Customer Action Teams (see below, C-4); and Partners for Profit seminars on quality improvement. In other words, the works. And the list expands each month. Beyond even all this, though, customers most commend Milliken for its extraordinarily rapid response to special needs.

Learning to sell mops and rags is no picnic at Milliken. Classroom training for a neophyte rag salesperson amounts to twenty-two grueling weeks, followed by a year's on-the-job trial with small accounts. Most computer firms don't prepare their salespeople that well!

Milliken has turned the humble shop towel into a high-value-added, greatly differentiated product. In fact, it has created a new product and a new market through its value/service/responsiveness-added approach. Milliken essentially runs its customers' businesses for them, using the rags sold as an excuse to provide value-adding services. This "for certain" commodity is not a commodity at all. Moreover, doing business this way has become typical for Milliken. It launches hundreds of Customer Action Teams and Partners for Profit programs each year; every one is an unabashed attempt to de-commoditize a product and create a new market, by constantly improving quality, adding features, and increasing service and responsiveness—in order to improve its customers' profitability.

Elgin's boxes. During the last fifteen years, most big paper companies have been hemorrhaging badly, with frighteningly low utilization rates in their giant plants. Their main defensive tactic has been vicious price-cutting. Yet since 1970 independent producers of corrugated boxes have increased their share of the market, in that $16 billion industry, from 12 to 30 percent. Elgin Corrugated Box Company of Elgin, Illinois, provides a fine example of one of these smaller winners. Business is so good that the $13 million firm will add a new plant in 1987 to serve its low-growth market around Chicago. Why?

Elgin's logo gives away one-third of the secret: "Our job is to make QUALITY product at the best [production line] speeds we can. Not to run FAST with the best quality we can." Quality is Elgin's hallmark—in a host of big and small ways. It spends on better ink for the printing on the box. It uses a more expensive A-flute corrugation (the flute is the inner fold of paper between the two outer layers), requiring more material, rather than the more common C-flute; the former is much stronger. Jury-rigged machines (old, but adapted many times) make sharper corners—and so on, ad infinitum.

The other two components of Elgin's competitive edge are service and responsiveness to its customers' needs. Elgin has not been late in shipping an order (it fills roughly 280 per week) for over six years! Moreover, it gleefully takes on small, difficult orders that larger firms won't touch. Its relatively small, flexible plant makes such custom work both possible and profitable. And the small custom orders often lead to big ones. "If they'll do the tough stuff for us," says one customer, "then we'll give them the bread-and-butter orders too."

In sum, Elgin does not consider its boxes a "commodity"; to the contrary, it adds value to its product every step of the way—and gains a decisive advantage in a business that many have written off as "dying" in our high-wage economy.

(Elgin, Illinois, is home to another specialist in another competitive industry. Community hospitals are struggling, with hospital occupancy rates at 65 percent and declining despite the loss of thousands of beds nationwide each year since 1965. Yet the 300-bed community hospital in Elgin is thriving, having specialized by creating "radiation therapy facilities that rival those of the Mayo Clinic," according to *Healthcare Forum*.)

"Gold Seal" laser parts—and more. A Silicon Valley laser products firm got all its employees engaged in product improvement, focusing on such "mundane" areas as packaging. Packaging for even a tiny $500 laser part was upgraded: Instead of a nondescript plastic bag, there was a gold seal label, an ebony-colored mounting for the part, and a vacuum seal (increasing shelf life). The company successfully offered the "new" product—to highly sophisticated customers—at a 20 percent premium.

In another part of the business, the president and his senior colleagues gave customers—doctors who often have trouble with laser calibration—their home phone numbers. Sales increased by 30 percent. The phone didn't ring much; the president got only one call in the first 120 days. But the gesture alone doubled customer confidence in and comfort with the product.

The list could be added to endlessly. One division of American Standard, the world's premier supplier of quality toilets, bathtubs, etc., is confronted with all the problems of a mature business. The billion-dollar division has recently added a $25,000, top-of-the-line, combined bathtub and home entertainment center. It includes a device that gives you a video picture, from the tub, of whoever is knocking at the door. The division's overall objective is nothing less than re-conceiving the role of the bathroom.

Or take American Express Travelers Cheques—97 years old in 1987 and going strong. Over $20 billion worth will be sold this year, and revenues are growing at 20 percent a year, despite a declining dollar that has made foreign travel much more expensive. The key? Amex keeps developing new features. Refund approval, after losing your checks, now takes less than six minutes; replacement checks will be delivered almost anywhere in three hours or less.

And young Federal Express does much more than just meet the promise of guaranteed overnight delivery which launched the company; it is constantly expanding its service offerings. For instance, a huge distribution center in Memphis stocks such urgently needed items as medical supplies and computer parts. They are stockpiled by Federal Express customers, such as IBM; one quick call and Federal Express will have the critical item on its way to an IBM customer in dire need.

Differentiation makes a difference! Furthermore, anything, from rags to laser parts, can be differentiated—and differentiated decisively over time.

Constant Differentiation: Japan's Edge

A deeply ingrained habit of constant differentiation is the essence of Japan's economic success. It's called kaizen, which management consultant Masaaki Imai describes as "ongoing improvement involving everyone." It is, he says, "the most important difference between Japanese and Western management." Economist Masanori Moritani, in his book *Japa-*

nese Technology, elaborates: "One of the characteristics of competition in Japan is the establishment of small distinctions between one's own product and similar products made by other manufacturers. These tend to be minor improvements in convenience, function, miniaturization and the like. . . . Five, six or even as many as ten companies may be producing virtually identical products, but upon close examination, you will find a number of small innovations in each. Since each firm is rapidly making such improvements in its goods, the cumulative effect is immense. In two or three years, the product can be completely transformed."

A Word or Two of Caution

Though there is no limit to the ability to differentiate profitably, there can be misguided differentiation:

1. Don't offer wildly exaggerated differentiation that the market doesn't want. Take Regent Air, former provider of luxury cross-country flights—at $3,240 per round trip. The firm found a severely limited market at that price. It shut down in 1986.

2. Don't negate useful—and expensive—differentiation by underattending to other parts of the product-service package. The fruits of differentiation may also be denied as a result of weakness in a neglected part of an operation. For instance, how many "new look" $175-a-night hotels have sprung up, with stunning architectural opulence—but where service is more reminiscent of a $20-a-night fleabag? Customers' memories of the poor service tend to far outweigh the impressive decor. Many of these hotels have found occupancy far below expected levels, and as overbuilding in this segment continues, I'd predict some outright failures.

A similar pitfall is illustrated by the marketing classic from the pet food industry. A renowned manufacturer broke the bank on market research—for instance, testing numerous packaging variables to make the new product uniquely attractive to the purchaser. It paid off, at first. But soon low repeat purchases scuttled the product. Everyone loved it—except the dogs.

3. Don't let premature implementation of exotic technology trip you up. Some producers of highly differentiated products fail as a result of being too far ahead of their time. The first automated teller machines and the first picture phones in the United States were fiascoes. A decade or

more passed before automated tellers caught on—and the jury is *still* out on picture phones.

4. Don't forget that it's not differentiated until the customer understands the difference. Sometimes a new idea is on target, but still is not "sold"—i.e., communicated—effectively. Scandinavian Air System's chief, Jan Carlzon, tells of a fare-reduction campaign launched years ago at the Swedish domestic airline, Linjeflyg. The program was called "F50," to indicate fares at an attractive 50 percent off. But F50 flopped. When Carlzon took over the airline, he retained the idea, but renamed it the "Twenty Dollar Plan," signifying the actual fare. The switch from technical argot to plain talk caused the program to catch fire. Carlzon explains: "What people don't understand doesn't exist."

While differentiation is a winning strategy, it obviously requires thoughtfulness. That said, however, the plain fact is that nine out of ten executives underestimate their ability to differentiate. Who would have ever thought that Milliken could charge a premium price for rags, or that Federal Express, by guaranteeing overnight delivery, could charge a premium amounting to several hundred percent on mail?

Quantify Your Differentiators

I offer one last demanding piece of advice: Quantify. I am attempting to quantify almost everything. It can be done, no matter how apparently qualitative the attribute. Therefore I urge you to set a tough, quantitative target for adding "differentiators," as I call them, to every product and every service you provide. Specifically, I suggest ten every 90 days—and frankly, that's far too low.

The point is that though the differentiators are individually mundane, they can be collectively awesome in impact, redefining an entire segment of an industry, as Milliken's "shop towels" do. No one is stuck with a commodity. To the contrary, I repeatedly observe that the more the world perceives the product to be a commodity, the greater the opportunity to differentiate and create new and unexpected niches through the unending accumulation of small advantages.

A FINAL WORD ON ADDING VALUE:
THE HAPPY-SAD STORY OF PEOPLE EXPRESS
AND THE MODEL T

No person changed the industrial landscape in this century more profoundly than Henry Ford. The $360 Model T automobile provided previously unimaginable opportunities to the American public, and monuments to Ford are deservedly large. Yet Ford held on far too long to the narrow vision that his Model T represented, and almost lost the company as a result. He yielded market share to General Motors, which eventually nearly closed the price gap and then beat Ford hands down by providing a diverse product line and by offering financing for all GM customers.

Today Ford is having its greatest relative resurgence in over sixty years—which is how long it took to recover from the Model T mentality. And today—oh, irony!—GM is suffering from a strategy reminiscent of the Ford of old, emphasizing volume and cloning all its models to look alike, while it is Ford that has regained its touch through distinctive styling (e.g., the Taurus) and features (e.g., turbos), and generally superior quality (with special attention to fits and finishes).

The recent swallowing of People Express Airlines by Texas Air recalls Ford's nearly catastrophic decline earlier in this century—and despite the unhappy ending, founder Don Burr nonetheless deserves monuments almost as great as those to Ford. For, like Ford, Burr significantly expanded the horizons and possibilities for millions of Americans by making air transportation affordable. Thanks to him, it's now hard to remember that less than a decade ago flying was almost the exclusive province of businesspersons and the well-to-do.

Rushing to take advantage of the federal deregulation of airlines, Burr and People Express forced overwhelming and lasting changes on other, more established air systems—such as the across-the-board use of efficient hub-and-spoke networks. Perhaps the changes would have come without Burr or People Express (would there have been some other version of the Model T without Ford?). Still, Burr's boldness surely shortened the process by years.

So what happened? Over a four-year period, competitors, by reducing their overhead drastically, closed much of the once imposing difference between People's cost per seat per mile and their own, while at the same time continuing to provide the amenities that People did not. The result: Burr was left with a customer-perception problem similar to that which the Model T eventually acquired—available in "any color as long as it's black." Despite the belated investment of hundreds of millions of dollars in a new terminal and a new reservation system, People was burdened by ineradicable memories of the dingy and congested North Terminal at Newark, of ridiculous overbooking incidents and a primitive reservation system that turned the entire community of travel agents against the airline.

At the same time, while matching People on price, other airlines poured more and more money into reservation systems and other notable value-adding differentiation strategies. American Airlines, in particular, under aggressive chief Bob Crandall, did almost step for step to People what GM, under Alfred Sloan, did to the first Mr. Ford. And now, with People gone, fares are on the rise, though they will never again reach heights that will exclude most of the public from flying. (Frank Lorenzo of Texas Air, which acquired People, continues to play the "discounter's roulette," but the plain fact is that the days of no-frills flying—air travel as a commodity—are probably gone, and the deepest discounts have an increasing number of strings attached.)

An almost exact parallel seems to be unfolding in the telecommunications industry. MCI was the all-time giant-slayer, destroying AT&T's monopoly. Even more proactively than People, in the early 1980s MCI took advantage of the drift toward less regulation, providing a no-frills alternative long-distance service to AT&T's at a discount of up to 50 percent. In doing so it started a major and permanent revolution from which many customers have benefited immeasurably.

Again, however, the price gap is closing, and MCI's no-frills image is fast becoming an almost intractable millstone, as AT&T's genuinely high level of service and superior transmission quality are now proving to be a decisive value-added advantage.

The strategic implications of these three cases, and a host of other, less prominent ones that could have been discussed, are profound. A no-frills provider takes advantage of or creates a true discontinuity by providing a widespread, low price/low cost, undifferentiated product or service. In the marketplace, both older and newer players respond as basic economic theory proclaims they must—by narrowing the price/cost gap.

Once the gap is somewhat narrowed and a new, substantially lower-than-the-start plateau is reached, <u>the winning strategy for the long haul</u> becomes differentiation—<u>via service, quality, and variety.</u>

The first Henry Ford at Ford, People Express's Don Burr, and MCI's Bill McGowan deserve the accolades that have been heaped upon them. But the pioneer no-frills provider almost inevitably sows the seeds of its own destruction. Its position is ultimately fragile and vulnerable to the clever differentiator, which will likely win both the customers and the profits over the medium to long term. (It is important to note, in the context of this book's emphasis on the speed of market transformation, that Ford had a run of 19 years with the Model T, from 1908 to 1927; People and MCI were in trouble within a couple of years of their great triumphs.)

PUBLIC PARALLELS

Public sector manager: Send off to the governor's office in Michigan for the state's latest annual report. Michigan is back! Unemployment is surprisingly low; vitality on numerous fronts is high. The annual report details a vast array of innovative, "value-added" programs that have spurred development, despite the auto industry's continued disarray and domestic manufacturing's downsizing. A small business explosion has been encouraged; retraining has been supported. State pension funds have been tapped to provide venture capital for start-up firms. Unique partnerships have been formed by the bushel.

In *The High-Flex Society,* economist Pat Choate offers another example of a state's value-adding, differentiation strategy:

Franklin [Electric Company], an electric motor manufacturer, decided to open a plant in Wilburton, Oklahoma, in 1981. Since the company needed a hundred workers to wind, assemble, test, and package submersible electric motors, it asked the Oklahoma State Department of Vocational and Technical Education to prepare a training program for the workers who would be hired. The company and the department formed a team composed of company representatives and state training specialists and engineers. Together, they identified specific training needs and devised a pre-employment orientation for trainees, manuals for the various jobs, and a schedule for all activities. . . . The state provided equipment for worker orientation. The company provided the training equipment the workers would use once [its] facility was in operation, making the curriculum realistic and job-specific. Faculty was drawn from both state personnel and company supervisors. . . . The Franklin experience is by no means unique. By 1985, seventeen years after Oklahoma began providing such customized training assistance, the service had been used by more than 500 firms. Some have been large international companies such as General Motors and Weyerhaeuser, while many have been smaller companies such as Franklin.

Start-up training is only part of the training service Oklahoma provides. To ensure that those who require remedial assistance can also participate in these programs, Oklahoma offers individual pre-entry-level training. . . . The program is popular with Oklahoma political leaders because it produces visible results at a low cost— the average sum per trainee has been $141. Most important, graduates have a very good chance of getting a job. Nearly three-quarters of the more than fifty thousand persons who enrolled in this program between 1968 and 1985 finished the training and were employed. . . .

In 1980, the state initiated an extension program to help firms increase their productivity. Much as county agents assist farmers in applying improved agricultural techniques, these industrial specialists counsel firms on how to improve production processes, time management, work scheduling, and employee involvement. This program has been particularly popular with small and medium-sized firms, which typically have had little opportunity to consult with productivity experts.

The relentless pursuit of jobs has become a city and state obsession. Some follow the same low-cost strategy that so many "commodity" manufacturers use; they offer a vast array of tax-reducing holidays and gimmicks. The danger is that they get trapped, as do their industrial counterparts, in a downward spiral: price is their only weapon, and as the amenities (education, infrastructure) deteriorate, no price is low enough to induce employers to come. The smart boosters, therefore, while surely price-conscious, principally use a value-adding, differentiating strategy—stressing amenities and creative, growth-oriented partnership programs.

FIRST STEPS

1. Read on. Prescriptions C-2 through C-6 develop the five basic value-adding, differentiation-oriented, market-creating strategies: (a) top quality, (b) service that emphasizes the intangibles, (c) responsiveness, (d) becoming an internationalist, and (e) creating true uniqueness in the customer's mind.
2. Take one slumbering product or service, or one in each product or service family. In the next 60 days, meet intensively with (a) end-user customers, (b) members of the distribution channel, (c) suppliers, (d) people at all levels from all functions in your organization. Devise a low-investment strategy for *radical* differentiation of the product or service via value-adding steps; relaunch the product or service in the next six months.
3. Finally, add such a "differentiation assessment" to your normal strategic-planning program. But beware—grand plans are not the answer; start adding differentiators now.

C-2

SUMMARY

With high-quality products and services being provided by new, especially foreign, competitors; and with quality being increasingly demanded by industrial and individual customers, every firm must:

▶ Mount a quality improvement revolution.

▶ Ensure that quality is always defined in terms of customer perceptions.

A quality revolution means eating, sleeping, and breathing quality. Management obsession and persistence at all levels are essential. But the passion must be matched with a detailed process. And, always, the customer must be present—as the chief definer of what's important.

Cut supplier, company, and distribution system product/ service failure rates by 90 percent in the next three years. Get everyone involved, starting in the next 90 days, in a radical program of continuous quality improvement.

C-2

Provide Top Quality, as Perceived by the Customer

The best of ours are [now] about as good as the worst of theirs, and that is a tremendous achievement.

> Robert E. Cole
> University of Michigan,
> commenting on the improvement
> in U.S. auto quality vis-à-vis Japan
> *Fortune,* February 1987

Percentage of West Germans who say "Made in America" is a mark of quality: 6.

> Roper survey, reported
> in *Harper's,* March 1987

Tennant Company was known for producing top-quality floor maintenance equipment. But during my visits with our Japanese joint-venture partner in the late 1970s, I had been hearing complaints—sometimes bitter—about hydraulic leaks in our most successful machines. Back home, I began asking questions: Why were the hydraulic leaks happening only in the machines we sent to Japan, and not in those we were selling in the U.S., where, in fact, we were selling many *more* of the same machine?

As it turned out, the leaks weren't just happening in Japan. The machines we sold here at home were leaking too. The difference was that U.S. customers accepted the leaks. If a drop of oil appeared on a freshly polished floor, they simply wiped it up. In Japan, the leak was cause for complaint. Japanese customers expected better quality. . . .

At about the same time, we faced our first serious competition in Japan from the lift-truck division of Toyota when it announced its entry into the sweeper business. The news spread in our company, and suddenly everything we'd been hearing about Japanese cars, Japanese stereos, and Japanese television sets versus U.S. cars, stereos, and television sets began to take on new meaning.

Those events, all happening in 1979, motivated us to begin our journey toward quality. We have found that like all important ideas, quality is very simple. So simple, in fact, that it is difficult for people to understand.

> Roger Hale
> chief executive officer
> Tennant Company
> in *Quest for Quality*

It has always been remarkable to me the extent to which people can hold certain assumptions inviolate even in the face of compelling evidence to the contrary. Nowhere has my amazement been greater than when I've watched healthcare professionals confront the issue of quality. There is a common assertion, of course, that "quality is a given"—that the quality of care provided by physicians and hospitals is "roughly equivalent." . . . Unfortunately, it is a ridiculous contention. . . . The power of owning a "high quality" position can be overwhelming. In Baltimore and in the surrounding area extending in a 100-mile radius, for instance, consumer preference for Johns Hopkins consistently runs above 50 percent. Similar patterns can be discerned for Massachusetts General and the Cleveland Clinic. In an era when most hospitals are hard put to define how they differ from their neighbors, no point of differentiation is likely to prove more powerful than quality.

> J. Daniel Beckham
> *Healthcare Forum*
> March–April 1987

THE CRUSHING QUALITY PROBLEM

Every day's news brings new, painful evidence. A poll shows that Koreans prefer Japanese over American suppliers by a wide margin (see Part I)—chief reason: problematic American quality. An analyst reviews Japan's closed markets; a principal reason for them—Japan's low opinion, across the board, of the quality of American products. The Limited, fearful of a trade war and in response to the declining dollar, is trying to line up American suppliers to replace part of its vast overseas network. The chief roadblock—the unreliability of American suppliers on quality.

The United States is getting clobbered in steel, autos, semiconductors, construction, and financial services alike. The causes, the voices of protectionism would have us believe, are closed markets, aggressive marketing (dumping), and differences in cost, particularly of labor. But the plaintive voices of customers and the cold, hard data tell a different story: For the most part, the quality of made-in-America goods and services is questionable; perhaps "stinks" is often a more accurate word. Yet, fifteen years after the battering began, quality is still not often truly at the top of the American corporate agenda.

THE LONG IGNORED EVIDENCE:
QUALITY EQUALS PROFIT

The evidence of the value customers place on quality surrounds us—from Federal Express, The Morgan Bank, Nordstrom, American Airlines, and Disney in the service sector to Maytag, Ford, and Digital Equipment in manufacturing. And the anecdotal evidence is matched by systematic evidence. For example, every survey of auto quality shows that U.S.-made cars, except, recently, for Ford's, still bring up the rear by a long shot—and the loss of market share to foreign producers continues even in the face of the increasing prices of many foreign cars as the dollar declined.

The remarkable PIMS data base, also cited in C-1, is decisive. For a decade after establishing the data base, PIMS researchers argued that market share was the primary begetter of profits. But a re-analysis of the data led to a startling and more robust conclusion: High market share does indeed bring profit; however, sustainable market share comes primarily through leadership in what the PIMS researchers call "relative perceived product or service quality"—"relative" meaning vis-à-vis competitors, and "perceived" meaning as seen through the customer's rather than the provider's eyes. PIMS researchers now call relative quality "the most important single factor affecting a business unit's [long-term] performance," and a recent PIMS newsletter to members concluded: "When we examine the options for maintaining the lead in value, we find that changes in relative quality have a far more potent effect on market share than do changes in price."

PIMS assesses both technical and "soft" factors (judgments about a firm's responsiveness, for example) in customers' views of competing product offerings, holding price constant. On average, those firms whose products score in the top third on relative perceived product quality outearn those in the bottom third by a two-to-one margin. Moreover, this conclusion does not vary substantially by sector (service sector vs. manufacturing sector, consumer products vs. industrial-user goods), geography (North America vs. Europe), or market trajectory (low growth vs. high growth, low inflation vs. high inflation).

TRW provides a useful test, since it is a microcosm of the U.S. economy, with products ranging from one-megabit semiconductors to auto parts and financial and information services. In 1985, Dr. John Groocock, recently retired vice-president for quality at TRW, applied the PIMS ideas to his $6 billion firm; using customers' evaluations of quality as his measure, he assessed 148 product lines in forty-seven TRW business units, and compared them with 560 product lines of the company's competition.

The results? The top third of TRW's business units (with a quality score, as perceived by customers, of 4.6 out of a possible 5) out-earned the bottom third (with a score of 1.9—which amounts to "average quality" vis-à-vis competitors) by a three-to-one margin. The top third had a 26.6 percent return on assets employed, versus 8.9 percent for the bottom third. The top third's 7.7 percent return on sales more than doubled the bottom third's 2.9 percent. Groocock concluded: "The PIMS results for quality are so impressive that it is surprising that they have had so little effect on American management."

A 1985 Gallup survey for the American Society for Quality Control assessed the extent to which customers are willing to pay more for quality; the results startled even those who commissioned the survey: "It would appear that most consumers are willing to pay to get the quality in a product they desire. . . . On average consumers report that they would pay about a third more for a better quality car ($13,581 versus $10,000). Consumers would be willing to pay about 50 percent more for a better quality dishwasher ($464 rather than $300) and proportionately more for a television or sofa they thought was of better quality ($497 rather than $300 for a TV, $868 rather than $500 for a sofa). Finally, consumers claim they would, on average, pay twice as much for a better quality pair of shoes ($47.00) than for an average quality pair ($20.00)." The proportion who would pay nothing extra for the higher quality was 10 percent for automobiles, 4 percent for dishwashers, 3 percent for shoes, 6 percent for TVs, and 4 percent for sofas. Frighteningly, the survey also found that people with higher incomes and Westerners, two consumer categories considered "leading indicators," were by far the most dissatisfied with the quality of American products.

For ten years I have pored over studies and observed grocers, retailers, express mail companies, and hardware distributors; manufacturers of textiles and steel (from structural grade construction steel to precision parts for transmissions) and washing machines and autos. I have studied furniture makers and makers of two-by-fours and high-tech wood joists and producers of cardboard boxes and tents. I have examined the methods and results of theme park operators, baseball franchise owners, chicken and beef and vegetable and pig farmers, cookie makers, ice-cream makers, soup makers, computer makers, and semiconductor makers. My unequivocal findings: (1) customers—individual or industrial, high tech or low, science-trained or untrained—will pay a lot for better, and especially *best,* quality; moreover, (2) firms that provide that quality will thrive; (3) workers in all parts of the organization will become energized by the opportunity to provide a top-quality product or service; and (4) no product has a safe quality lead, since new entrants are constantly redefining, for the customer, what's possible.

So why does all this remain the best-kept secret in North America?

QUALITY IN THE U.S.A.: SOME QUANTITATIVE ASSESSMENTS

The U.S. auto industry remains central to the American economy, affecting semiconductor makers and health care providers as well as its own workers and communities. Protection from imports in the form of quotas was laid on in 1981, to provide a "breathing space"—now in its sixth year—during which the United States would "catch up.".

The results? While there has been some improvement, the yawning gap in quality between the domestic product and the foreign (especially Japanese) has not closed. The Rogers Survey, done only for industry insider use, but leaked and published in *Fortune,* measures "TGWs," or Things Gone Wrong, in the first eight months of new-car ownership per 100 cars produced. Chrysler is worst with an average score of 285 and GM is next to last at 256. Ford, which was last among domestic producers in 1980 with a score of 392, has leapt to best by far, with a score of 214. The average for Japanese models, however, is still miles ahead, with a score of 132 TGWs. Indeed, the worst Japanese performer is about equal to the best of GM and Chrysler, confirming Bob Cole's comment.

Pollster and industry consultant J. D. Power of Los Angeles is best known for its influential automobile CSI—Customer Satisfaction Index. On the quality component of the index, the Japanese are decisively in the lead, with an average score of 134 (on this index, higher is better). The Americans have passed the Europeans, but manage only a 90 (average is 100). Ford again leads comfortably with an above-average 107, and Chrysler and GM bring up the rear. In this poll, GM at 83 edged out Chrysler at 85 for most awful.

⋎ Another important Power survey assesses dealers' opinions on vehicle reliability and dependability. By this measure, 63 percent of cars manufactured in Asia were considered "very acceptable" and 9 percent were considered "unacceptable." Only 23 percent of cars made in the United States were very acceptable, while 26 percent were unacceptable.

Finally, *Consumer Reports* conducts a major "frequency of repair" survey each year. The most recent results, from 450,000 respondents, are not comforting. Just 1 percent of GM's cars were ranked "above average," while 69 percent scored "below average." Japan, by contrast, had 88 percent above average and *none* below average. Chrysler scored better than GM on this poll, with 13 percent above and "only" 70 percent below average. But hold on. That includes Chrysler's Japanese-made cars; remove them and the 13 percent drops to 4 percent, and the 70 percent jumps to 83 percent.

The purpose of printing these numbers is to underscore the chasm that exists between us and our competitors in the area of quality. The problem is not, as former UAW president Doug Fraser once said to me, that "we did take our eye off the ball a bit." We are behind by orders of magnitude—and not only in autos. We must squarely confront this fact, in order to realize the urgency with which we must attack the quality issue.

More important than the numbers is the generic impression—America doesn't make quality goods, and is worse on service/responsiveness than on quality. Such a perception gap would take a decade or more to reverse, even if we were hard at work today. I belabor this point, because I still encounter such skepticism among U.S. executives (much more than from any line worker). "Where's your evidence?" they commonly ask. I'm inclined to be smart-alecky and say, "Where's your counterevidence?" But I usually don't say that. Instead, I produce the evidence. And yet, as often as not, though I cite the source and produce the originals of the studies I still get blank stares; and not infrequently, in the face of the hard evidence, the skeptism is not only not removed, but turns to raw belligerence of the "it's just not so" variety. Then, I usually get very quiet—because I am scared.

TWELVE ATTRIBUTES OF A QUALITY REVOLUTION

If you accept the above—the bad-news evidence and the indications that quality pays—what do you do about it? The answer is a systematic program. Glib words. Tough to execute. Many have started. Most have foundered. In the last few years, I have read all I could find on the subject and observed close up uniquely successful quality improvement programs at IBM, Tennant Company, Milliken & Co.,* Ford, the Paul Revere Life Insurance Company, First Chicago (the bank), Worthington Industries, the Air Force's Tactical Air Command, Federal Express, and several other organizations. The top programs share a dozen traits:

1. Management obsessed with quality. First comes top management's attention—or obsession, as I prefer to call it. What does that mean? It's visceral—the anguish and anger of Roger Milliken at a tiny defect in a

---

*Quality expert Phil Crosby says that these first three firms have the best quality improvement programs in America.

tiny order. I've watched him call his whole great ship to general quarters over a "small" problem that others wouldn't even have seen or heard about, let alone acted upon.

One of the best descriptions of the emotional component of mounting a quality revolution appeared in *The Big Time,* a study of the Harvard Business School's class of 1949. Conrad Jones, a top executive at the consultants Booz, Allen & Hamilton, painted this picture:

. . . Let me tell you about two meetings I sat in on. Both were with companies that were having some problems with quality control. One company was professionally managed. Their approach to the problem was to analyze everything. How many doors, say, were falling off? What *percentage* of doors were falling off? How much would it cost to stick 'em back on? What were the chances of getting sued? How much advertising would it take to counteract the bad publicity? Not once did they actually talk about the doors, the hinges, or why the hell they were falling off. They weren't interested in solving the problem, they just wanted to manage the mess. The other meeting was at Coleman Stove. . . . They were having a problem with some boilers that were cracking. So picture it—the Executive Committee assembles, there's the usual small talk. . . . Then the service department comes in with the reports, the clipboards, the yellow pencils, and everybody hunkers down for a serious discussion. Well, you know how long that meeting lasted? About thirty seconds: Old Man Coleman sits bolt upright in his chair and bellows out: "You mean we've got goods out there that aren't working? Get 'em back. Replace 'em, and find out why, goddammit." And that was the end of the meeting. There was no financial analysis. There was no legal analysis. There was no customer-relations analysis. There was *no* goddam analysis. The issue was the integrity of the product—which meant there was no issue at all. We stand by it, and that's that.

I will soon turn to talk of systems and measurements, but it is essential to begin with emotion. In a recent New York *Times* article, Gulf + Western chairman Martin Davis, ruminating on today's uniquely tumultuous environment, asserts, "You can't become emotionally attached to any particular asset." An "asset" presumably means a business, its products and its people. What bunk! I can't conceive of one of the Nordstrom brothers saying that, or Leon Gorman, L. L. Bean's chairman, or Federal

Express founder Fred Smith, or Roger Milliken, or "Old Man Coleman." Quality begins precisely with emotional attachment, no ifs, ands, or buts. As Apple's former top manufacturing executive (now chief financial officer) Debi Coleman puts it: "I don't think you should ever manage anything that you don't care passionately about."

Top management commitment means lots of big and little things. For instance, is quality at the top of the agenda—every agenda? (See also prescription L-3.) At Milliken, President Tom Malone reports that the first four hours of every monthly President's Meeting (an operating review) are devoted exclusively to quality. "And it would be that way," he adds, "if the office were burning down as we met."

A Texas Instruments executive describes a variation on this theme: "In years past, we traditionally held quarterly reviews with top corporate executives. For the past three years or so, these financial reviews have been discontinued. In their place, we hold a review four times per year with top management that is devoted solely to quality and productivity."

Jim Harrington, senior IBM quality manager and 1986 chairman of the American Society for Quality Control, makes the more general point: "Now step back and take a look at your calendar. Are you spending as much time controlling the quality of your department's output as you are investing in cost and schedules? . . . If you don't have time for quality and don't value it enough to be interested in it, how can you expect your employees to? . . . Plant managers hold production status meetings in which quality, schedules, and costs are reviewed. Normally, schedules are addressed first, then costs, then quality—if there is time. . . . [But] if quality is really the most important factor, then it should be first on every agenda."

Another key to top management commitment is the potent use of symbols. (Again, see also prescription L-3.) A few years ago a new Ford Thunderbird was a sure bet for *Motor Trend*'s "car of the year," an assessment that not only strokes egos but means big dollars too. As in the world of Hollywood's Oscars, however, a car must be released for production by a certain date to qualify. In what one Ford executive described as "the shot heard round the world," the company held up the release, forgoing the almost certain prize, because the car's quality was not yet up to snuff for a production model. In the most powerful way, Ford had demonstrated its new commitment to quality—the commitment that played such a vital role in the company's extraordinary performance in 1986.

Likewise, Tennant executives brought the company to full alert with a single symbolic stroke as they launched their quality program in 1980. As a first step, before their ameliorative quality improvement program was in place, they cut the number of rework mechanics, the firm's highest-paid assemblers, in half—from twenty to ten (there are only two today). The message: There will be no more rework—we will do it right the first time.

A third element of top management commitment is perhaps the most challenging—persisting through program doldrums. A serious quality commitment is forever. Some have called Toyota the most quality-oriented big company in quality-conscious Japan. One key to its success has been the mundane suggestion system, made not so mundane at Toyota. We often act as if Japan's giants sprang to life as world-class organizations. Not so. In 1960, Toyota's suggestion system snared just 5,001 submissions (about six-tenths of one suggestion per worker), only 33 percent of which were implemented. Twenty-two persistent years later, in 1982, that number had increased 381-fold, to 1,905,682 suggestions, or 32.7 per worker. Moreover, 95 percent were implemented.

With no exception, quality program leaders report that programs stall around the 12–18-month mark, no matter how much energy and organization have gone into them. Award programs become stale. Team leaders are worn out. The first full round of training is complete. The easy-to-find problems have been solved. Moreover, there are doldrums every couple of years thereafter—forever. At these points, which appear unavoidable, most lose heart. Commitment means gritting your teeth and dreaming up as many new wrinkles as you can to pump life back into the program.

There is a final element of commitment. As my seminars, at which a mass of ideas has been presented, wind down, obviously frustrated participants frequently shout out, "So what, exactly, do I do first?" Here's the answer I give: "Starting this afternoon, don't walk past a shoddy product or service without comment and action—ever again!"

A brochure is going out to customers. You've already missed your deadline. Five thousand have been printed, inserted into envelopes, addressed and sealed, and are packed and ready to be taken to the post office. Your small unit's cash flow is pinkish to red in hue. And then you discover a single typo on page two, in the small print. Should you walk past it or act? Easy. Act—throw it out!

It doesn't matter whether the firm has 15 or 150,000 employees. Whether you are section head or chairman of the board. If you knowingly ignore a tiny act of lousy service or poor quality, you have destroyed your credibility and any possibility of moral leadership on this issue. Period.

I have dwelled on management commitment for the very reason that most experts ignore it. Yes, they put it at the top of their list, in a knee-jerk fashion; but they devote about two paragraphs in a 500-page book to it, and then move on to the nuts and bolts, the "real stuff." They never define precisely what this seemingly soft and squishy item means. Yes, it is about attitudes; but the attitude of abiding and emotional commitment must also be translated into practical actions, which show up on the calendar each day.

Pounding Away

Recall Roger Hale's comment about the floor cleaner's hydraulic leak, noticed only by his Japanese customers. He launched the Tennant quality revolution in 1979. Hale did many things right, and made a number of errors, too. But above all, he and his firm have persisted. Miracles have occurred, but they are unfailingly miracles of pounding away. Let's return to the hydraulic leak, and look at Tennant's progress, as reported in *Quest for Quality:*

First Year (1981):	Team learned about hydraulics, including the best assembly methods. Team set own goals. Average performance: 1 leak per *216* joints. Note: Average machine has about 150 joints; therefore, almost every machine leaked.
Second Year:	Developed extensive training programs. Developed and printed training manuals. Trained managers, supervisors, assemblers, and engineers. Purchasing department set supplier goals. Replumbed test machines [using] new methods; reduced number of joints and overall fitting and hose costs by 10 percent per machine. Average performance: 1 leak per *509* joints.

Third Year: Reduced number of hydraulic hose and fitting suppliers from 16 to 2. Average performance: 1 leak per *611* joints.

Fourth Year: Introduced newly plumbed products at year end.

Fifth Year: Gave training update to all assembly people. Reduced number of suppliers from 2 to 1. Note: Reduced hose and fitting costs by 10 percent by single-sourcing. Average performance: 1 leak in *1,286* joints. Not one customer reported a leak from any machine shipped this year. Received National Fluid Power Association's PRO Award for our work in this area.

Sixth Year: Average performance: 1 leak per *2,800* joints. Zero field-reported leaks.

Now, that's hanging in!

---

2. There is a guiding system, or ideology. Most quality programs fail for one of two reasons: They have system without passion, or passion without system. You must have both.

This is not the place, nor am I the expert, to make a recommendation other than "Have a system." There's a lot of controversy here: Should you follow Deming (W. Edwards Deming, father of the Japanese quality revolution via statistical process control)? Or Phil Crosby, author of *Quality Is Free,* and so prominent that GM bought a 10 percent stake in his firm? Or Armand Feigenbaum's "Total Quality Control"? Or Joseph Juran? Or invent a system of your own?

Eventually you will develop your own scheme if you are successful. But I strongly recommend that you not begin with a Chinese menu. Pick one system and implement it religiously. Frankly, it makes little difference which system you choose, among the top half-dozen or so, as long as it is thorough and followed rigorously.

3. Quality is measured. "What gets measured gets done" is a wonderful old saw. "Measurement is the heart of any improvement process. If something cannot be measured, it cannot be improved," says IBM's

Harrington. You must start by measuring the "poor-quality cost," precisely and in detail. Poor-quality cost includes such items as manufacturing (or any other function's) rework, warranty costs, cost of repair or return of poor goods from suppliers, and inspection costs. IBM, Milliken, et al., after substantial initial resistance, have decisively demonstrated that the cost of poor quality can be measured in every function —from the executive secretarial pool to engineering to the sales force to the plant.

The measurement must begin at the outset of the program. Among other things, if done right, it will inject energy into the program as the size of the problem—and the opportunity—comes into view. Though the experts agree on little else, they do concur on the poor-quality cost: it absorbs about 25 percent of all your people and all your assets in manufacturing firms to do the rework and other tasks caused by poor quality; the costs of poor quality in service firms absorb a staggering 40 percent of people and assets. IBM says the costs of poor quality run from 15 to 40 percent of gross revenues, depending on the maturity of the product.

Measurement should be visible. Electronic scoreboards glow in many Milliken plants, tracking quality progress by the hour; big charts and readable graphs are on public display in accounting, personnel, and data processing too. Huge TICs (team improvement charts) dot IBM.

It can also be straightforward, as Richard Schonberger describes it in *World Class Manufacturing:* "Data recording comes first. The tools are cheap and simple: pencils and chalk. Give those simple tools for recording data to each operator. Then make it a natural part of the operator's job to record disturbances and measurements on charts and blackboards. The person who records data is inclined to analyze, and the analyzer is inclined to think of solutions." Schonberger goes on to illustrate with, for instance, the system of Display Boards that marks Hewlett-Packard's Greeley, Colorado, operation.

Caution: Though I am a "measurement freak," as one colleague put it, I acknowledge a downside. Measurement must be done by the participants; that is, by the natural work group, team, or department itself. It must not be done "to" such groups by an accounting department or by an "audit" or "inspector" brigade. If it is, there is a high risk (1) that the process will become bureaucratic and (2) that turf fights and squabbles over interpretation of data will break out, setting true involvement back considerably. Ford is so finance- and numbers-driven that it av-

91

oided measurement for a long time, fearing that the powerful finance bureaucracy would usurp the quality program, as it had so many others.

4. Quality is rewarded. In the people prescriptions, I will discuss forms of rewards in general (see P-7). At this juncture, I simply want to urge you to reward contributions to quality improvement.

Quality targets are part of Ford's executive compensation plan. For Ford managers in general in 1986, 40 to 65 percent of their bonus was based on contributions to quality, just 20 percent on contributions to profit. Quality targets are the primary incentive variable in Perdue Farms' executive pay scheme. They are part of everyone's performance evaluation at IBM. Adding a big component of quality-based incentive compensation caused an early breakthrough in top management's attitude at Tennant.

Rewards based on quality are part of IBM's program with suppliers too. For instance, with one division's cable suppliers, the premium price is paid for 0.0 to 0.2 percent defects; for a 0.21 to 0.3 percent defect level, $2.00 per cable is knocked off the price; for 0.31 percent and over, there is a $4.00 reduction. With this system in place, a defect rate that had averaged 0.11 percent for years rapidly dropped to .04 in 60 days—and stayed there.

5. Everyone is trained in technologies for assessing quality. Instruct everyone in problem cause-and-effect analysis, rudimentary statistical process control, and group-problem-solving and interaction techniques. Some train only first-line supervisors. This is a serious mistake. The chairman of the board should take the course—Roger Milliken went to Crosby's Quality College; IBM's chairman took its basic course. More important, every person in the company should be extensively trained.

"Training is the key," says a Tennant executive; every Tennant manager had taken at least five courses in quality control by 1985. Richard Schonberger's *World Class Manufacturing* includes a chapter titled "Training: The Catalyst." He warns: "Western industry must put substantially more resources into training to match the prodigious sums the World Class Manufacturing companies in Japan and Germany invest in it." Japanese consultant Masaaki Imai concurs: "There is a Japanese axiom: 'Quality control starts with training and ends in training.'"

6. Teams involving multiple functions/systems are used. Once more, ideological firestorms await you. Paul Revere's quality program quarterback, Pat Townsend, champions *non*voluntary quality circles—and makes a vigorous and well-documented case, replete with success. The

Japanese, on the other hand, use only voluntary quality circles. Tennant sides with the Japanese. Crosby rejects quality circles as such, but embraces teams: Error Cause Removal Teams or Corrective Action Teams formed as needed, with members drawn from various sites as necessary, to take on a specific problem. The team disbands when the problem is solved, and thus doesn't deterioriate into a weekly sewing circle—that is, another bureaucratic exercise.

In any case—and many would place this point at the top of their lists—it is vital to engage in multi-function problem-solving and to target business systems that cross several functional boundaries (order entry, engineering changes, etc.). Ford and IBM both say they wasted years before realizing that <u>most quality improvement opportunities lie outside the natural work group</u> (for instance, a section of fifteen within accounts receivable). Tennant and Milliken launched multi-function teams from the start. In fact, Tennant's first team was a multi-function group working on an automatic floor scrubber; it reduced defects per machine from 1.3 to 0.4 in its year of existence. Tennant tries to be sure that every team has members who can run interference in each major function.

Masaaki Imai contends that the "natural" work group is *not* the key to Japanese success. Instead, he says, "Cross-functional management is the major organizational tool in realizing [Total Quality Control] improvement goals." IBM's quality improvement process emphasizes the systems that hold the functions (and firm) together. An "owner" has been assigned to each business system—for example, one that deals with implementing engineering changes, which may start in the field, involve a lab or two, several plants, and eventually field service. Typically, IBM and others found that such processes, which bridge functions and units, fall through the cracks and are not relentlessly updated. IBM has now raised business system quality improvement to a near-science. Every system is painstakingly and quantitatively scored as to effectiveness. Special Process Improvement Teams grind away, and a sophisticated, thirteen-step Process Analysis Technique has been developed and honed.

IBM's reasons for the move are clear, as explained by corporate quality director Edward Kane:

The billing process consists of 14 major cross-functional activities which are logically related but physically dispersed among 255 marketing branches and 25 regional offices, a similar number of field service locations, and several headquarters operations and manufac-

93

turing sites. The work is cross-functional and nonsequential within any function. It is tied together by a complex information system. Overall, 96 percent of the invoices are accurate, but because of the high cost of adjusting those that are incorrect, *54 percent of the total resource was devoted to cost of quality* [my emphasis].

A deeper issue emerges here for the first time that is addressed more fully in the people prescriptions (especially P-9). We must fundamentally shift our managerial philosophy from adversarial to cooperative. Protecting functional fiefdoms and hoarding information is the American middle management norm. The seemingly straightforward plea in this prescription for cross-functional quality teams peels off but one layer of a big onion.

7. Small is very beautiful. There is no such thing as an insignificant improvement. Paul Revere's Townsend expounds:

Many teams received credit for things as simple and as small as moving a file cabinet ten feet closer to the one person who has frequent use of it. A quality idea? Technically, perhaps not—but the inconvenient location of that cabinet had most likely been a matter of irritation fifteen times a day for the person who had to walk the extra dozen or so steps. Could it have been moved prior to the Quality Has Value process? Perhaps in theory it could have been, but the person being inconvenienced did not believe it, or did not want to go through the hassle of asking permission through however many layers of management that it would have taken.

Milliken leaders declare that the plaudits now go to those who admit to/revel in having lots of problems—that is, lots of quality improvement opportunities. It's no longer okay to give the traditional, macho "everything's on schedule" response—amidst the rubble of an obviously noncompetitive factory or distribution operation.

8. There is constant stimulation. Create endless "Hawthorne Effects."* I referred to the 12–18-month doldrums before. The antidote is new goals, new themes, new rewards, new team champions, new team

---

*After the 1930s Western Electric experiments which inadvertently demonstrated that productivity increased when a work situation was constantly attended to and stimulated, regardless of the precise type of intervention—lights up, productivity up; lights down, productivity up again.

configurations, new celebratory events. Change everything, in fact, except the structure of the basic system (see point #2 above).

No item in the improvement process is too small to use in generating and sustaining momentum—or too insignificant for concern. In a program Revere's Townsend launched in his second year, as part of an effort to keep things lively, names were randomly drawn out of a pot each week; if the person picked happened to be wearing his or her Quality Has Value pin, he or she was awarded a free lunch. Townsend discovered that women were not well represented among the winners. The reason, it turned out, was the pin. Designed by a man, it had a tie tack fastener, which made holes in women's dresses or blouses. When an optional charm design was offered, the participation of the women shot up. On such details are wars—and quality revolutions—won or lost.

9. There is a parallel organization structure devoted to quality improvement. Create a "shadow quality organization." Tennant's includes a Steering Committee, a Recognition Committee, a Zero Defect Day Celebration Committee. Unexpected stars have been born in the process; Tennant executives note: "Champions can . . . come from the ranks of the hourly workers. A welder who became involved in one of the first quality small groups in his department became its informal leader. Then he volunteered for the second company-wide Quality Team. From there he went to the Zero Defect Day planning committee. As he learned more and did more, he became an articulate spokesman for quality within the company. In 1983, he and his co-workers were asked to make a presentation at the Tennant Company-sponsored Japanese Management Association Meeting. Now, this former welder is a supervisor—and a champion for quality company-wide." At Revere, too, the parallel structure has become a new source of promotion and an unofficial alternate career advancement channel.

Caution: Many correctly warn that if such "parallel" structures are not carefully controlled, they can deteriorate into a new, inertia-inducing layer of bureaucracy.

10. Everyone plays: Suppliers especially, but distributors and customers too, must be a part of the organization's quality process. The task, once more, is a challenging one. Milliken trains its suppliers. Milliken and Tennant form joint improvement teams with suppliers (Milliken's are called Partners for Profit—see C-1). Symbols help: IBM calls all suppliers Business Associates. Ford takes out full-page ads in papers such as *The Wall Street Journal* and *USA Today* to praise suppliers with top quality records. More fundamentally, what's required is mutually dependent, lasting relationships (see also I-2, on team product development, particularly the discussion of Ford's Taurus project). Almost all agree, for instance, that the number of suppliers must be drastically reduced—recall Tennant's hydraulic leaks, which were also much reduced when the number of suppliers was reduced, in two steps, from sixteen to one.

Tennant's Doug Hoelscher, vice-president for engineering/manufacturing/purchasing, reports on an early approach to a supplier:

> ... I got the phone number of our largest supplier—not surprisingly, the one with which we were having the largest number of quality-related problems. I was apprehensive about calling the president to tell him that there "might be" some quality-related problems with his product that he "might not" know about.
>
> His response: "Why the hell are you calling me? I have people to handle these kinds of things."
>
> I took a deep breath and explained that at Tennant Company we were trying a new approach. Our CEO and I wanted to become more involved with our counterparts in key supplier companies, and we had set a goal of reducing our supplier base by 10 percent per year over the next five years. I seemed to have his attention. I told him I hoped he was interested in keeping our business and invited him to a meeting. He reluctantly agreed.
>
> At the meeting, we showed him documentation outlining the percentage of parts received from his company that we had to reject because of poor workmanship. It became obvious to him that the product he was selling was not of the quality his people had led him to believe. His shoulders drooped. "What do you want me to do?" he asked.
>
> "Ship us the product as promised," we said. We then explained that we didn't expect zero-defect products immediately, and that we could work with him to meet our expectations. We had three requirements:
> 1. Set annual improvement goals.
> 2. Meet with us annually to review progress against those goals.
> 3. Become a fully-qualified supplier by meeting those goals.
> In turn, we said, we would send him semi-annual reports showing

his company's performance. As long as he continued to show improvement and eventually became qualified, we would continue to purchase from him.

The result has been a much more satisfying relationship with a key supplier. His company did set and meet goals. We continue to purchase parts from them, and they are a part of our group of major suppliers. We now provide quarterly updates to each member of that group, and many participate in our ZD [Zero Defects] Day programs. Meeting our quality goals has become a joint effort. When a company depends as we do on outsiders for so many components of its product, cooperation for quality not only makes sense, it is absolutely essential.

Analogously, all parts of the company must be part of the program—MIS, personnel, accounting and treasury, sales, order entry, shipping. Quality programs limited to the factory or operations center will fizzle. Milliken and Revere are especially proud, and rightly so, of the intensive involvement of their field sales/service forces in quality control. These independent-minded domains are usually very skeptical about participating, but can become the source of phenomenal improvements.

11. When quality goes up, costs go down. Quality improvement is the primary source of cost reduction. I continue to hear all too much chatter about the "quality/cost trade-off." For one kind of quality—i.e., extra features—there is, of course, a trade-off. The hand-stitched leather seats in an Aston-Martin cost a bundle. But overall, perfecting quality saves money. As noted, poor quality has a huge, documentable cost.

In *Augustine's Laws,* Norman Augustine, president of Martin Marietta, has recast data from a study of the room air conditioner industry, conducted by Harvard's David Garvin. The result is depicted in Figure 5. Augustine concludes: "As greater quality is built into a product, the cost of achieving quality does not increase but rather decreases."

The elementary force at work is simplification. Almost all quality improvement comes via simplification of design, manufacturing, layout, processes and procedures. For example, the redesign of the second generation of Hewlett-Packard's HP-150 touch screen personal computer reduced the number of parts from 270 to 130 and the number of suppliers from 120 to 50. Quality soared and costs plummeted.

In fact, there is an interesting asymmetry which has profound conse-

Figure 5: **Room Air Conditioner Industry**

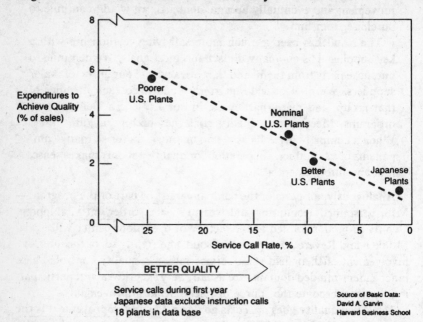

Expenditures to
Achieve Quality
(% of sales)

Poorer
U.S. Plants

Nominal
U.S. Plants

Better
U.S. Plants

Japanese
Plants

Service Call Rate, %

BETTER QUALITY

Service calls during first year
Japanese data exclude instruction calls
18 plants in data base

Source of Basic Data:
David A. Garvin
Harvard Business School

quences. Cost reduction campaigns do not often lead to improved quality; and, except for those that involve large reductions in personnel, they don't usually result in long-term lower costs either. On the other hand, effective quality programs yield not only improved quality but lasting cost reductions as well. And all this doesn't even touch upon increased revenues from more sales resulting from improved quality.

12. Quality improvement is a never-ending journey. There is no such thing as a top-quality product or service. All quality is relative. Each day, each product or service is getting relatively better or relatively worse, but it never stands still. Ford is doing well now, but Toyota, which Ford sees as its principal competition, is implementing 5,000 new suggestions a day.

These dozen factors, as imposing as they may collectively be, still don't begin to do justice to the best quality improvement programs. There is something almost mystical about them: "This program is what we're all about." "It's who we are." "This program *is* Tennant." Such is the stem-to-stern feel of the programs that deserve to be called quality revolutions. Sadly, anything less than an all-out, "This *is* us" approach will fall into disuse within 18 months, becoming one more "program of the year" skeleton that haunts management's effort to be taken seriously about anything.

The goals must—and can—be bold. I recommend a target of 90 percent reduction in defects in three years, with a 25 percent reduction in the first 12 to 18 months. Between 1978 and 1984, Tennant reduced the cost of poor quality from 17 to 8 percent of sales, cut manufacturing rework hours from 33,900 to 6,800 a year (while sales were growing), and introduced state-of-the-industry warranties to boot. To aim for less is to be less than serious.

Some Startling Results from a Quality Program in Action

A few examples, from *Excellence: The IBM Way,* by H. James (Jim) Harrington, underscore the huge potential that IBM found as its quality program got into full swing:

▶ Error-free installation of new products. When a major new system is launched, though computing power is significantly increased from the start, it usually takes years to iron out bugs that result in downtime. After starting its quality program, IBM audaciously decreed that this post-launch learning curve would, ipso facto, no longer exist. A new machine was to have better "availability" than the machine it replaced and the competition's best—from the start. Harrington reports: "For years we had believed that a defect-free installation of our large computers was impossible because of their complexity. . . . But once we focused on error-free installation, the process immediately began to improve. Today the 308X series is seven times better than its predecessor product in terms of defect-free installation . . . [and] installation time has been cut by a factor of three."

▶ Enormous improvement opportunities in mature products. IBM uses about 2,000,000 flat ribbon cables a year to connect electronic circuits. Harrington says, "This is a well-known technology moved out to vendors years ago. . . . Massive amounts of rework had been built into the product estimate and treated as normal expected yield. A young industrial engineer . . . mustered up enough interest from management so that a team was assigned to attack the high defect rates." Scrap per cable dropped from 94 cents to 28 cents, and rework dropped from 25 to 4 percent. Problems in final tests fell from 12 to 1.2 percent. "Our annual savings," Harrington notes, "are $5,000,000."

▶ Software coding yields to the improvement process. Process improvement technologies were applied to software, where quality is in part measured in terms of defects per 1,000 lines of code. An institute was even set up to abet the process. A threefold improvement ensued over a six-year period.

▶ Stunning results from improving mundane accounting practices. Accounting data entry was 98 percent accurate at the outset. But that means 20,000 to 30,000 miscodes per day! In two years, the number dropped to 0.4 percent, a fivefold improvement.

▶ Supplier partnerships hit paydirt. "In the 1970s we made the mistake of talking to our suppliers in terms of AQLs [Acceptable Quality Levels] when we should have been talking parts per million," says Harrington. "I am convinced that if in the 1970s we had been talking parts per million, today we would be talking parts per billion." Typical improvements, from 1980 to 1983, measured as defects per million: transistors, from 2,800 to 200, a 14-fold improvement; transformers, 4,200 to 100, a 42-fold rise in quality; and capacitors, from 9,300 to 80, a 116-fold rise.

Such are the opportunities, from the complex to the less complex, from the new to the old, from hardware to software to accounting.

QUALITY MUST BE JUDGED AS THE CUSTOMER PERCEIVES IT

The advice this prescription has proffered so far is vital. But it still misses the boat. After four wildly successful years of pounding away at "quality," Milliken found that a second revolution was required—to become more responsive to customers. Tennant and Ford, and even IBM, have likewise moved beyond early definitions of quality improvement and are paying more attention to the customer.

Crosby will assert that his process is oriented toward the customer. I am his fan, but he is not. Getting better, within specifications (which are at least, in theory, partially determined by the customer), is not enough. Dow's Irving Snyder is on target:

> Quality is not just an inspector. It's not just in the product. . . . But what is it? How do we define it so that we can get a handle on it and cope with it? . . . I asked about 50 methods editors to help me define quality in terms of the key element they work with—specifications. Here are some of the answers I received: "A specification is a minimum requirement to which we produce a product." "A specification tells the manufacturing plant what to produce." "A specification tells the salesperson what he'll be selling." "A specification spells out the limits within which we can produce a satisfactory product." These were all very interesting, I told them. But nobody picked up on the fundamental reason we have specs in the first place, and that is: "Specifications should define what it takes to satisfy the customer." Period. This is what quality is all about: the customer's perception of excellence. And quality is our response to that perception.
>
> Let me give you an example. One of our customers in Europe came to us several years ago with his own testing spec for carpet foam backing. We were a bit put out that someone thought they could test it better than we could. We told him not to worry. Dow measures for foam stability, molecular weight distribution, particle size conformity, percent of unreacted monomer, adhesion strength—all the vital things. We told him, "You're going to get the best there is, real quality!" Well, three times we tried to ship him the order, and three times he sent it back. Now, that gets annoying. So we asked him, "What's the deal?" And he told us, "Your product can't pass my roll-stool test!"
>
> "Roll-stool test? What's that?" Well, what he did was take the bottom half of an office chair, that is, the undercarriage and casters, put a weight on it, and spin it around on a piece of test carpet 30,000 times. He even had a little counter to keep track, day and night. If the carpet sample didn't delaminate from the foam, you passed the test and got the order. Ours didn't pass, so back we went to the laboratory. Eventually, we gave him a product that would withstand 80,000 revolutions before delaminating. The lesson was pain-

fully clear: Quality is what the customer says he needs, not what our tests indicate is satisfactory.

Caution: The Customer's Perception of Quality Can Be Perverse

I have owned a GMC truck for over a year. Nothing major has gone wrong with it—no dropped transmission or oil leaks. It's worse than that: About eight little things have gone wrong, such as the failure of a light which indicates whether or not the truck is in four-wheel drive and a loose, rattling latch on the glove box.

The problem is that even collectively these irritating problems aren't enough to warrant the inconvenience of a visit to the dealer. Therefore, and here's the rub, each time I get in the truck, it's as if a brightly lit map of GM's failure to attend to detail flashes before my eyes.

Frankly, in terms of my perceptions, GM would have been better off if the transmission had failed. I would have gotten it fixed immediately, it would have been done with, and my memory of it would have dimmed.

The Moral Dimension of Quality

In the winter of 1987, a new magazine appeared, *Quality: America's Guide to Excellence.* One of the lead articles began with this statement: "We have to grant quality its moral dimension. . . . It should be recognized as a virtue—something to be sought for its own sake—not just a profitable strategy. To the Swiss, with their passion for grace and precision in everything from pocket knives to highway bridges, quality is second nature. Can we import not just Swiss products but the attitudes behind them?"

Quality is practical, and factories and airlines and hospital labs must be practical. But it is also moral and aesthetic. And it is perceptual and subjective. It is delivering above expectation. It is a startling little touch that makes you smile at the designer's or production shop's care for you, the customer. Marketing expert Phil Kotler, of Northwestern, calls this the "delight factor"—it's at the opposite end of the perception scale from the "perverseness" phenomenon noted above.

Ford is coming to understand this. Its Taurus and Sable are filled with such features, including my favorite, a coffee cup holder. Many are following in Ford's footsteps. Some declare that a packaging and industrial design renaissance is sweeping from Europe and Japan to the United States.

On the other hand, we have a long way to go. As I was changing a tire recently, I was struck by the rough surface of the $8.95 lug wrench I was using. It could be a work of art, like the $8.00 mallet I bought in Hammerfest, Norway, in the summer of 1986—it's so attractive that when I'm not using it, I display it on a shelf in my den!

The Japanese aesthetic sense is centuries old. Within the Toyota or Sony Walkman lie the modern outcroppings of the tea ceremony. After all, the Shinto religion, according to Joseph Campbell in *The Masks of God: Oriental Mythology,* is marked by "seamstresses [who] hold requiem services for lost and broken needles." *Inc.* provides corroboration:

Although Japanese lumbermen and construction firms had long been customers for whole logs shipped from the Pacific Northwest, they had rarely bought finished lumber from the region's mills. Quality had been a big part of it: as with so many other products from consumer appliances to food, the Japanese tended to be finicky customers. And in the case of lumber, they liked it cut to exacting traditional Japanese specifications. How the wood looked—not merely how strong it was or how much it weighed—was a primary concern.

. . . [F]orester Adolph Hertrich followed the path traveled so many times by the Japanese themselves during the 1960s as they began their industrial conquest of the United States. He traveled extensively throughout Japan, meeting with potential customers and inspecting the facilities of their Japanese lumber suppliers, taking careful notes wherever he went. . . . By the mid-1970s, he had begun to redesign his mill from head saw to edger to trim saw. . . . And most important, foremen were instructed by Japanese specialists on the complex lumber-grading systems that are based on such aesthetic factors as color and graining—categories that change depending on the region of Japan in which a customer is located. It took Hertrich and his people two years before they were finally confident and able to impress prospective Japanese customers. And to press the point still further, they even built a traditional Japanese guest house from their own lumber and invited overseas guests to spend the night there. To the Japanese businessman, who has always suffered from some cultural discomfort when dealing with Westerners, this willingness to accommodate was a powerful and persuasive marketing strategy.

And it has paid off handsomely. Today, while many local mills lie idle, Vanport's 170 nonunion workers labor at double shifts. Sales last year reached $27 million, 90% of which are destined for Japan. The company has been consistently profitable.

From the Taurus gas cap to the roll-stool test, from guest houses in Oregon to ceremonies for broken needles, quality is a complex subject. The twelve-trait program to revolution is a big part of it, but not all of it by a long shot.

PATTERNS AND PRIORITIES IN QUALITY PROGRAMS

Each of the quality improvement programs I have observed most closely, at Milliken, Tennant, IBM, Ford, and the Paul Revere Life Insurance Company, has followed a tortuous path to success. The similarities are instructive.

Milliken began in 1981 with a pure quality improvement thrust, helped by Phil Crosby. It focused from the start on quality teams within the natural work area, cross-functional teams, and suppliers. About two years into the process Milliken added the reluctant sales group to its quality program. At the three-year mark, it shifted attention to customer issues, mounting a series of multi-functional teams to work on them. The final phase of the Milliken program took the customer emphasis a giant step further, aiming for order-of-magnitude improvements in overall customer responsiveness.

Tennant's program, also spurred by Crosby, has followed a similar path, beginning with the emphasis on quality and including suppliers and cross-functional teams from the outset. About seven years into their program, Tennant, too, came to the conclusion that a new emphasis on the customer was needed, that customers had not been central enough to the program during its early years.

IBM worked on quality within the natural work group at first. About three years into the program, the abiding importance of cross-functional systems to the quality of almost everything became evident. Systems improvement emerged as the all-out obsession of the quality process. Now, in 1986 and 1987, IBM has learned that it, too, was not listening adequately to its customers. Customers have become the focus of renewed concern.

The early Ford emphasis was on employee involvement, working with the unions; it focused on the natural work group. Then, as mentioned, Ford, like IBM a couple of years before it, moved radically in the direction of quality improvement via an emphasis on cross-functional systems improvement. Six or seven years into the process, Ford is now focusing attention on the customer.

Paul Revere began with an emphasis on the individual work group at headquarters, but moved quickly to include field selling and servicing operations. Step three for Revere was the inclusion of cross-functional activities.

Two points emerge. First is the not immediately obvious need to emphasize improvement in the subtle but controlling cross-functional systems; as noted, Ford and IBM believe they lost years by not realizing the importance of these systems. Second, even in the best programs the quality improvement activities, though they certainly had a dramatic impact on customers' acceptance of the product, were not sufficiently focused on the customer. Groocock of TRW and Crosby worked together at ITT for years and, technically, they define quality quite similarly. Yet Groocock's clear emphasis, developed in his work at TRW, is on the customer; Crosby, by contrast, gives lip service to the customer, but is primarily concerned with meeting technical specifications.

It is noteworthy that Crosby's favorite exemplars, Milliken, Tennant, and IBM, have reached similar conclusions, several years into the process. Their improvements in quality had not automatically taken them close enough to the customer, especially according to the customers' *perceptions* of quality.

So the natural progression goes something like this: (1) quality within the natural work group; (2) quality jointly with suppliers; (3) quality in field sales and service and marketing operations; (4) quality improvement through cross-functional teams and systems improvement; and finally (5) a shift of emphasis to the customer. Figure 6 surveys the experiences of the five firms.

105

Though these prescriptions are written to suggest that one should "do it all," it is clear that the agenda is overfull. One could argue that Milliken or Tennant or Ford or IBM or Revere could have changed its tune earlier, from the natural work group to the field to cross-functional systems to the customer, but I'm not sure of that. In all cases, there was much to learn. "Do it all at once" is tempting, but not very practical, advice.

Figure 6 : **Patterns of Progression**

STEP	MILLIKEN	IBM	TENNANT	FORD	PAUL REVERE
1. Quality within natural work group	1*	1	1	1	1
2. Quality with suppliers	1	1	1	2	
3. Quality with field sales/service	2	1	2		2
4. Cross-functional teams	1	1	1	2	3
5. Quality via systems improvement	4	2	2	3	1
6. Quality as close to the customer	3	3	3	4	
7. Quality as total customer responsiveness (see C-4)	4				

* 1 means did at the outset; 2 means next wave of emphasis, etc.

PUBLIC PARALLELS

Reread #3 and #11 in the description above of a quality revolution. Poor-quality cost is as sound a notion in the public sector as in the private. With increasing budget pressure, a quality revolution will allow you to have your cake and eat it too: improve service delivery and cut its cost simultaneously.

Incidentally, the same caution holds in the public as in the private sector. Quality is defined by the customer's perception of service delivery, not the legislative parameters of a particular program. Callousness or indifference in the delivery of an inherently helpful service destroys much of its benefit.

FIRST STEPS

1. What do you feel about quality and its role—in your gut? Is it a consuming passion, or one more competitive weapon? Think about this question for a long time.
2. Starting today, if you are serious, never again knowingly walk past poor quality—in any form—delivered by your firm without taking dramatic and decisive action, almost regardless of the cost.
3. Collect reams of data on quality—internally and from customers. Go off-site for three days of intense debate. Are you up to mounting a true quality revolution? Will anything short of such a revolution do?
4. From the start, ensure that the customer is a major part of the program, and that the customer's perceptions drive the program. Embarrassing or not, invite customers to every quality analysis/ program meeting—from the outset.

C-3

SUMMARY

Increasingly, competitive advantage in a crowded market will stem from "service added":

► Become a service fanatic, emphasizing service in the customer's terms.

► Consider every customer to be a potential lifelong customer, generating word-of-mouth referrals; therefore, emphasize the relationship with the customer over time.

► Attend especially to the intangible attributes of the product or service.

Service pays! Customers for hamburgers, aircraft engines, fashion goods, bank loans, health care, and semiconductors buy far more than an interest rate or technical specifications. Over the long haul, relationships, based upon perceptions formed over time, are more important than so-called tangible traits. Every product and service can be completely redefined on the basis of "service/intangibles added." Service, on average, is so bad that a barrage of tiny positives can overwhelm the customer and the competition. Remember, the average customer is neither a crook nor an idiot. Caution: Service is more than smiles—at the very best it's attitude and supporting systems.

Measure customer satisfaction, in customers' terms and emphasizing the intangibles. Measure it regularly for all members of the distribution channel. Tie measurement directly to compensation and performance evaluation. Design support systems, training programs, etc., based upon the "lifetime value" of the customer. Append at least three tangible and three intangible "service added" features to every product/service offering, every 90 days.

C-3

Provide Superior Service/Emphasize the Intangibles

The United States has been terrible as it applies to customer service. When the history of American business is written, I think that's going to be the most incredible part of the historian's view of what we did during the sixties and seventies. I mean, we killed the goose that laid the golden egg. . . . Somehow, management let employees believe the customers weren't important.

Fred Smith
founder, Federal Express
March 1987

WHERE SUPERLATIVE SERVICE IS THE NORM

So you want to buy a suit? Well, one of our seminar participants did. He is an executive for a large national retailer, headquartered in Portland, Oregon. His two daughters and his wife are Nordstrom fans. They constantly bubble about it and pester him to shop there. He was frankly fed up with all the talk. Moreover, despite their comments to the contrary, he secretly suspected that Nordstrom charged an arm and a leg. (Nordstrom's policy is to match anyone's price for a garment, if asked to do so.)

But he did need a suit badly. And a major sale was going on. At worst, he figured, he didn't have too much to lose, especially with the sale. Reluctantly, he went to Nordstrom.

The service in the store was good, he had to admit. And he did find a fine suit on sale, although he also picked up a second suit—at full price. Nordstrom promises same-day alterations. He noted, however, that there was a little asterisk next to the promise—next-day alteration was promised during sales. He chortled at this small chink in the armor.

He came back at 5:45 P.M. the next day to pick up his suits. It was fifteen minutes before closing. He needed the suits for a trip that night.

To his surprise, though he'd only been there once, his salesperson greeted him by name! The fellow then trotted upstairs to pick up the suits. Five minutes passed. The salesperson reappeared—without the goods. They hadn't been finished.

Though he needed the suits, our friend admits to secret glee. Without the suits, he took off for a Monday appointment in Seattle, after which he proceeded to Dallas for the big meeting of the trip.

He checked into his hotel and went up to his room. A message light informed him that a package had arrived for him. A bellhop fetched it—Federal Express, mailing fee $98. Yes, it was from Nordstrom. In it were his two suits. On top of them were three $25 silk ties (which he hadn't ordered) thrown in gratis! There was also a note of apology from the salesperson, who had called his home and learned his travel arrangements from one of his daughters. With a smile of resignation, he admits that he's now a believer.

Specialty retailer Nordstrom has grown sevenfold since 1978, from $225 million to $1.9 billion. Its ad budget is a small fraction of the industry's average, yet sales per square foot, tops among department stores, are three times higher than the industry norm. Moreover, Nordstrom has generated growth internally (no acquisitions) and made most of its gains in the viciously competitive Southern California market.

Its secret? A matchless level of service. If you live in the West, you can't talk about Nordstrom service, because practically everyone has a bizarre Nordstrom story, and you will be inundated with "But I can top that." And that's the point. Though the Portland executive's story is a bit extreme, only slightly less remarkable tales are truly commonplace. ("The store was officially closed. They kept it open for 15 minutes while I looked for a present for my friend. I was already late to the party. And they wrapped it, too, with no sense of being rushed. It was the most beautiful package at the party"—ho hum.)

The sparkling dressing rooms have fresh flowers. No dressing-room matron impedes your entry, demanding to know how many pieces you're carrying in, then giving you an appropriately coded tag to certify the number. No thief-proof wires on the coats (I call them "Macy lines") prevent you from trying them on.

Your salesperson can cash checks, take returns, and do gift wrapping on the spot, instead of shuttling you off to a long line in an out-of-the-way and dingy corner. And those returns? Nordstrom takes anything. Employees even declare that Jim Nordstrom once said, "I don't care if they roll a Goodyear tire into the store, if they say they paid $200 for it, give them the $200." And, yes, the salesperson will routinely know your name after one trip, as was the case with our Oregon friend. He or she will be collecting numerous other facts as well in precious "personal books."

Sophisticated bankers from Morgan, IBM marketing executives, and Harvard marketing professor Ted Levitt are variously given credit for developing the term "relationship management." It is usually applied to sales of mainframe computers, huge corporate loans, and similar sizable transactions. Nordstrom applies the term to retailing with unparalleled skill and zest. Even if you haven't had a problem, as a regular customer you can expect a flood of gifts (flowers on your birthday, etc.) and personal notes from your Nordstrom salesperson.

But Nordstrom won't talk to outsiders like me. Why? Fear of giving away secrets? No, sincere humility. Vice-president Betsy Sanders proclaims, "If we were as good as people say, then there wouldn't need to be shopping malls, only Nordstrom!"

SERVICE PAYS HANDSOMELY

Nordstrom, Federal Express, IBM, The Morgan Bank, Frito-Lay, American Express, McDonald's, Disney, and all too few others seem to understand that service pays. The PIMS data base once more provides decisive support. It split a sample of firms into those rated as better and those rated as worse than average on service—by their customers. The better performers on service charged about 9 percent more for their goods. They grew twice as fast as well, and picked up market share at 6 percent a year, while the also-rans lost share at 2 percent a year. The bottom line: a 12 percent return on sales for the top half in service as seen by the customer, versus a paltry 1 percent for the rest. Some difference!

Beneath such gross indicators are more finely tuned ones. A study by Technical Assistance Research Programs revealed these facts: Twenty-six of every twenty-seven customers who have a bad experience with you fail to report it. The principal reason is not surprising: They expect no satisfaction if they do bug you. The scary part comes next—some 91 percent of those who complain won't come back. Scarier yet, the statistic on dropouts holds as true for $1,000 purchases as for $1.79 ones. And perhaps worst of all, the average person who has been burned tells nine to ten colleagues; 13 percent of the malcontents will spread the bad news to twenty or more people.

There is some hope. The data show that, depending on the industry, you can get 82 to 95 percent of these customers back, if you resolve the complaint in a timely and thoughtful fashion. Other studies are even more optimistic. A well-handled problem usually breeds more loyalty than you had before the negative incident.

Finally, the study yields a clincher: It costs five times more to go out and get a new customer than it does to maintain a customer you already have. Anyone who's been a salesperson for even a day agrees that there's no lousier way to live than depending on cold calls. Developing expanded business with today's customers and thriving via the "word" on your reputation that they broadcast is a less stressful—and more profitable—way to live. Yet all too often our market development budgets, in allocations of both time and money, are skewed toward snazzy activities aimed at attracting first-time users, with today's customer taken for granted.

FOCUS ON THE "OUTER RINGS": THE TOTAL PRODUCT CONCEPT

The Total Product Concept of Harvard's Ted Levitt provides a device to aid systematic analysis of this prescription:

Figure 7

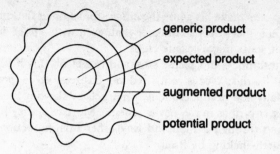

- generic product
- expected product
- augmented product
- potential product

Consider Nordstrom: At the *generic* level, the store provides four walls and the categories of goods traditional to an upscale specialty clothing retailer. At the *expected* level, hours are standard and fashions are timely. At the *augmented* level, Nordstrom spends heavily to "overstaff" the sales floor by traditional standards—with "overpaid" people by traditional standards. It likewise "overspends" to ensure the availability of more sizes and colors than usual. And it "overspends" again to maintain numerous, close-to-the-market buying offices which cater to specialized, local tastes.

It is at the *potential* level, however, that Nordstrom really lives its "No Problem at Nordstrom" logo: the flowers in the dressing rooms; a grand piano, with pianist, in each store; the losses from the few who doubtless do take advantage of the "return anything" policy; the empowerment of salespeople to deal with almost all problems on the spot; the routine performance of exceptional acts of service, such as the ones described above.

As you, the customer, traverse Levitt's rings, from generic to potential, you realize that Nordstrom is not "a specialty clothing retailer." It is, and many have so labeled it, "an experience," "a phenomenon," or, as one of my computer company friends calls it, "a provider of a lifetime, user-friendly relationship, only marginally associated with clothing per se!"

In the same vein, Federal Express has redefined "mail service." And Ray Smith of the Louisville Redbirds has transformed minor-league baseball: spotless washrooms, cleaned several times per game; seats steam-cleaned and hand-wiped before each game; freshly squeezed orange juice and the best nachos around; players available to sign balls; kids encouraged to run on the field after the game; and an endless array of special events make his game the choice for summer family entertainment in Louisville—with attendance that, even with a poor field record, tops that of some major-league clubs.

The bottom line—and please stop and reflect on this if you don't at first agree—is this: Nordstrom, Federal Express, et al. have created fundamentally new products and new markets by skewing their attention to the outer two rings in the Levitt scheme. Moreover, they have invariably done so through a thousand tiny differentiating actions, none of which is earth-shaking by itself.

This is so important because the converse attitude is all too prevalent. Spend time around engineering firms, and most of the chatter is about their products' technical performance—the generic circle. Hang out with bankers, and again the generic—the price of money—dominates conversation. While I acknowledge the importance of the generic, I am urging a flip-flop: most of the organization's attention should center on repositioning the product and creating whole new markets by emphasizing the two outer Levitt rings.

Figure 8

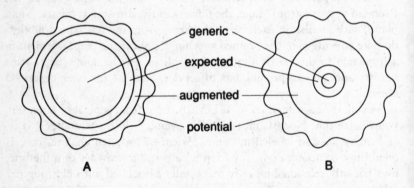

generic
expected
augmented
potential

A   B

The value of this advice is rising from "useful" to "essential"—"service added" is increasingly becoming the competitive battleground in every market. That is, traditional strategic thinking, in retailing and manufacturing, can be depicted as Figure 8A, in which the "generic" dominates. The effective organization of tomorrow—auto company, custom semiconductor maker, insurance firm—will pay attention as shown in Figure 8B, that is, will emphasize service added via the "augmented" and "potential" rings.

ATTEND TO THE INTANGIBLES

Little Things Mean a Lot

Computer retailer ValCom launched a program called CARE, for Customers Are Really Everything. The centerpiece has been working at an expanding list labeled "A Little Thing Means a Lot." Small touches, such as the following, are constantly added to the firm's selling package: "Send monthly newsletter to customers with spotlight on key customers. Spot management visits to key accounts. Send small gifts to customers. Send thank-you notes with store logos. Salespeople saying thank you with sales invoice. Call back customers 30 days after sale is delivered— see how they are doing. Provide support service index for customer's Rolodex of names and addresses. Return phone calls the same day. Put label on computer with phone number of store. Take a picture of the customers and their computer system and post it in your store; mail them a copy. Have framed customer satisfaction letters on store walls. Provide bag with store logo on it for customer to carry diskettes, ribbons, etc. 'Keep-in-touch' program: mail thank you once every three months to current customers acknowledging their continued support. Circle/high-light phone number to call for questions on invoice." It adds up.

Little things mean a lot even in what appears to be the most clear-cut commodity arena. Here's a letter addressed to the Granite Rock Company of Watsonville, California:

March 24, 1987

Dear Sirs:

I am sending you this letter to express my gratitude with your service. I was very impressed with the human manner (as opposed to a machine-like manner) that my situation was handled. . . . I had ordered 7.25 yards for a simple 10 × 40 slab, broom finish. When the driver showed up on time, to say the least, we were off to a great start. The driver was friendly, and cooperative which I would say is not a common trait. After pouring out the truck [he] noticed I

115

was having a hard time . . . as my laborer didn't show up, and he helped to speed things up. . . . As it turned out I was one wheelbarrow short and had no way to make it work without it. After using the truck's radio to communicate with the batch plant and drivers, he found a truck very near by with less than a yard on its way back to the plant. The second driver was able to find the job quickly, save my ass and do it all politely. To top it off I was only charged for the extra one-quarter yard I used, as opposed to a one-yard minimum. . . . If my service was a fluke then oh-well, but I tend to think that it was all a reflection of the attitude in which Granite Rock is run. Also there is no way to say clearly enough how nice it is to have pleasant drivers who are able to be a service instead of just another randy ass concrete truck driver. You can be sure I will call upon this company again when we have work in your area.

Sincerely,
Contractor

The Power of Call-Backs

At a recent seminar, we devoted a half-day to the perception of service. The talk among insurance company executives, hospital administrators, and auto-component manufacturers at one point gravitated to "call-backs." It seemed that each succeeding participant had a more astounding tale to tell about the potency of a call from an executive or manager following a purchase or a repair. Even, said one, a call to see if a bid had arrived was received with wonderment—no one had ever bothered to do that before, according to a crusty auto company purchasing executive.

This small, human touch in an increasingly impersonal world can go a long way toward cementing a customer relationship. Domino Pizza's top franchisee (based on repeat business), Phil Bressler, attributes much of his success to calling 100 customers per week. He insists that call-backs be given priority over the shop's nightly accounting closeout. His explanation: "Nobody's ever bought a pie from us because we had a great closeout."

High-tech Intangibles

So the transformational possibilities of Levitt's outer rings hold for pizzas and concrete. They hold as well for manufacturing firms, as Caterpillar, Boeing, and IBM demonstrate daily. They hold for health-care service: a group of hospital administrators at one of our seminars came up with about 250 service intangibles beyond the generic procedure for which the patient is admitted. Indeed, even (or especially) in the arena of the highest technology, the intangibles are paramount, as Regis McKenna points out in *The Regis Touch:*

[I]t is common for a company to boast that its product . . . is 25 percent more powerful than any competing product. Indeed, an incredible number of positioning strategies center on price and "specsmanship." (That is, promoting a product by its superior technical specifications, or "specs.") . . . Companies are much better off if they establish positions based on what I call "intangible" factors, qualities such as reliability and service. Unlike price and technical specs, intangibles don't fit neatly onto a product-comparison chart. . . . But intangibles are much more powerful as positioning levers. . . .

The power of intangible positioning became clear to me a few years ago when I was doing a market survey for Intel. As part of the survey, I talked to a number of engineers about a certain memory chip. I remember asking one engineer why he selected the Intel chip. This chip was a fairly technical product, and you might have expected the engineer to answer in technical argot: "The memory had an access time of so many nanoseconds," or "Its power dissipation is only such-and-such." That didn't happen. Instead, the engineer told me his company buys almost all its chips from Intel, so it was natural to buy the new chip from Intel too. Had he evaluated the new product? Not really. "We just tend to buy from Intel because we have a business relationship there," he explained. "We know where they are going and we trust the company. . . ." Most buying decisions are made the same way. Product managers spend days, if not weeks, drawing up charts and graphs that compare products on the basis of specifications and price. But buying decisions are rarely based on these objective standards. The important product comparisons come from the minds of those in the market-place. And in people's minds, it is intangible factors that count.

Under-promise, Over-deliver

With competition heating up in every market, firms are forced to promise the moon to get an order, especially that first order. Right?

Wrong. With an explosion of competitors, many of them new and without track records, reliability, rather than overly aggressive promises, is the most valuable strategic edge, especially for the mid- to long haul. While getting faster at responding to customers is imperative (see C-4), living up to commitments has never been worth more.

A survey of banks, summarized by Citytrust marketing vice-president Skip Morse, supports this point. Banks with lower customer ratings tend to respond, for instance, to an early-morning customer query with, "We'll be back to you by noon," or "We'll be back to you." Then they get back to the customer at, say, 3 P.M. The top-rated banks, such as The Morgan, reply, "We'll be back to you by close of business today"—and they are—at 4 P.M., for example.

The paradox: Those banks which, objectively speaking, perform bet-ter—that is, which actually get the job done first—are frequently rated lower by customers than those they have apparently outperformed. Cus-tomers turn thumbs down on banks that fail to keep promises (3 P.M. instead of noon) or that are vague ("We'll get back to you"), and unfail-ingly prefer slightly less aggressive promises if these are honored.

I experienced the same phenomenon in quick succession at a hotel and a service station. Although the hotel's menu promised that room service would start at 6:15 A.M., when I called at 6:20 A.M., I was subjected to a tinny tape-recorded message saying, "Room service will be open at six-thirty." Though I'm a morning coffee devotee, the 15 minutes is no big deal, in absolute terms. But the delay was infuriating in light of the promise made; my perception was that I was getting rotten service—a perception compounded by the hotel's high rates.

Similarly, when I ordered an unusual-sized tire from a local service station, I was surprised and delighted to be assured (twice) that I could pick it up just four hours later. I was busy then, so I said I'd return the next morning and left that station feeling much better about its unusually high gas prices, which appeared to be offset by its service responsiveness.

I rearranged the next morning's schedule, and popped in at 9 A.M. To my dismay, the tire hadn't even been ordered—and my morning was shot. One more shattered expectation. And once again the issue was the perception, not the absolute: I had originally expected getting the tire to take a couple of days, at least, and had been more than willing to wait.

I realized how important all this was when I had an ever so tiny reverse experience of "over-delivery," and from an airline no less. Airlines just don't tell the truth very often. We all know that "ten minute delay" is a code phrase for either (1) "hour delay" or (2) "I don't have the foggiest notion when, or if, the darn thing will ever take off."

But once I felt the power of the truth. A downpour swept La Guardia, and all takeoffs were halted. When we moved onto the taxiway after the storm had passed, and with the underventilated plane already approaching Black Hole of Calcutta status, the pilot said, "We're fifteenth in line, and we'll be off in forty-five minutes." There were lots of groans, but we settled in. About 30 minutes later we were off—and I felt as though I'd been given a great gift. The fact is that it's memorable over a year later. Now had that pilot followed the routine—"There are a buncha planes ahead of us. It'll be 'bout fifteen minutes"—the same 30-minute wait would have been just one more "over-promise, under-deliver" episode.

Some intriguing evidence from the health-care field bears on this issue. Surgical patients who are told, in detail, of the nature of post-operative agony recover as much as one-third faster than those left in the dark.

Suppose a patient is told that she or he will suffer severe shortness of breath for four or five days following surgery. Even if the symptoms persist a bit longer than average, the patient is prepared to deal with it. The uninformed patient panics, believing that the operation was a failure. No amount of post-operative explanation helps ("They're lying—I'm dying"). Even if the uninformed patient's shortness of breath lasts less than the norm, his or her emotional distress frequently sets back overall recovery.

We all seek predictability. In fact, the more uncertain, frightening, and complex the situation (such as today's competitive scene), the more we grasp for predictability. That's why I'm not at all surprised at the bank study or health-care findings.

And yet, as much as we may relate to such stories of frustrating, unkept promises when we are on the receiving end (patient, individual consumer, commercial purchaser), we tend to underrate this concern when we plan our own firm's strategy.

Take, for instance, groups I have worked with from two fine companies (building products, packaging materials), both renowned for top-flight product quality. Both have been meeting with customers to learn how they are perceived in the marketplace. Both have been surprised that their renowned quality has been less the focus of attention than their good, or occasionally bad, record for responsiveness. That is, despite quality that is demonstrably superior to their chief competitors', more than 80 percent of the customer feedback harps on responsiveness and reliability. Quite frequently, "second-rate firms" (as their competitors— my clients—see them, based upon relative quality) have received high overall marks from customers because they have unfailingly met their commitments.

"I can't get over it," one executive pondered. "I expected them to talk about various quality enhancements, including some problems we've had with a new product. Instead, they went on and on about a small, late order here or an especially responsive act there."

Quality is important, to be sure. So is absolute response time. And price. But at least as important as any of these is keeping your word. In fact, I've boiled it down to a simple formula:

$$CP = \frac{D}{E}.$$

Customer perception (CP) equals delivery (D) divided by expectation (E). Maximizing CP is essential in the squishy, real world, where perception of the intangibles is really everything.

Treat the Customer as an Appreciating Asset

When the Federal Express courier enters my office, she should see "$180,000" stamped on the forehead of our receptionist. My little twenty-five-person firm runs about a $1,500-a-month Fed Ex bill. Over ten years, that will add up to $180,000. I suggest that this simple device, calculating the ten-year (or, alternatively, lifetime) value of a customer can be very powerful—and has sweeping implications.

Grocer Stew Leonard got me started on this. He says, "When I see a frown on a customer's face, I see $50,000 about to walk out the door."

His good customers buy about $100 worth of groceries a week. Over ten years, that adds up to roughly $50,000. We all agree that repeat trade is the key to business success. This simple quantifying device provides a way to add potency to the idea.

Here are two other examples. Average lifetime auto purchases will total about $150,000, not including repair work. Given the remarkably low dealer loyalty of car buyers these days, might it not make a difference if dealers and their employees focused on this big number? Or suppose you frequent a good restaurant twice a month for a six-person business dinner. You're worth about $75,000 every ten years to that establishment.

Imposing as they are, these figures are just the tip of the iceberg. The repeat customer is also any firm's principal vehicle for powerful word-of-mouth advertising. Conservatively, suppose a lifelong, happy customer sells just one colleague on becoming a lifelong customer of your fine restaurant, grocery store, or Federal Express, as the case may be. Suddenly, the regular customer's value to the restaurant doubles from $75,000 to $150,000, including that likely word-of-mouth referral. And that sign on my receptionist's forehead should now be read by the Fed Ex person as $360,000 rather than $180,000.

There's a third step in the progression. If the restaurant's waiter handles five tables a night, he or she is catering to 5 × $150,000, or $750,000, worth of potential business. The numbers are stunning for Fed Ex. If our courier has forty regular stops at businesses my size (which would be normal), she is managing each day a "portfolio" of customers worth 40 × $360,000, or $14 million, to Federal Express!

So the three-step formula is: First, estimate the ten-year or lifelong value of a customer, based upon the size and frequency of a good customer's average transaction. Then multiply that number by two, to take into account the word-of-mouth factor. Finally, multiply the new total by the average number of customers served per day by the sales, service, dispatch, or other front-line person or group. The result is the lifelong value of the "customer portfolio" that that individual or group deals with each day.

The implication is clear: If you look at customers in this or a related way, you are likely to take a new view of hiring, training, compensating, and spending on tools to aid the customer-serving process. Take that waiter, managing $750,000 of your future each night. Are you still sure

121

you want to brag about the low average wages you pay? Are you certain that skimping on uniform quality makes sense? Does the investment in a small computer system to support order taking still look as expensive as it did? Suddenly, Stew Leonard's insistence that everyone in the store go through the lengthy Dale Carnegie public-speaking and attitude courses is seen in a different light. So is the high pay at Federal Express, and its seemingly lavish spending on support tools, such as the Cosmos computer system that soon will include a terminal in each delivery truck. (On the reverse side, it makes the failure of People Express to invest in service support tools incomprehensible.)

Consider another element of the pay scheme. Most firms don't discriminate between sales commissions that come from new business and those that come from repeat and add-on business. A few go so far as to pay higher commissions for new business and cut back on commissions for repeat orders, which presumably require less work. The contrary should be standard. In fact, sales commissions and/or salaries ought to be skewed substantially toward incentives for repeat and add-on business . We want our salespeople not to take today's customers for granted. Repeat and add-on business usually results from a host of small but, in total, time-consuming touches—such as acting as a go-between with the engineering or service department; our incentives should say unequivocally, "Spend that time!"

This advice is now more important than ever. With "service added" an increasingly important strategy, all sales are fast becoming "system sales." All transactions must be looked at as relationship-building opportunities.

It boils down to this: When you build a plant, it starts depreciating the day it opens. The well-served customer, on the other hand, is an appreciating asset. Every small act on her or his behalf ups the odds for repeat business, add-on business, and priceless word-of-mouth referral.

Try this calculation yourself. One hospital administrator did at a seminar of ours. Upon finding that the average nurse "managed" $2 million in business each day, he mounted an aggressive program to enhance the status of the nursing department. A European software executive did the same thing at a seminar I attended with several of his big customers present. He looked around the table, did a hasty mental calculation, and whistled: "We have 720 million guilders [$360 million] in 'lifetime' business in this room." Turning to his associates, he added, "You'd better listen to what they have to say."

Not "Gee Whiz," but a Way of Life

Thus I urge, in this prescription, that you emphasize service and, in even broader terms, the intangibles—that is, augmented and potential product traits. The overall profitability numbers and the specific cases, from high tech to low, in service and manufacturing, support me. The challenge is to view *every* element of *every* operation through the customer's lens; to constantly attempt to—literally—*redefine* each element of the business in terms of the customer's perceptions of the intangibles.

There *is* a catch. I've now been to dozens of seminars where lists of ideas for enhancing customer perceptions, often with hundreds of items, are readily made. Most of the ideas are inexpensive, so few fiscal barriers to implementation exist. Yet one of two outcomes usually ensues—only a small share of the ideas is implemented or, even if the whole list is implemented, that's the end of it.

Nordstrom's edge is that "the list," if you will, represents an attitude, a way of life. There is no end. It is always expanding. It is everyone's business. For while the attributes of service can be dissected into small and delightfully doable bits, the mind-set required to hack away, year after year, at a "service added" strategy is far from common. Preoccupation with the outer two rings in the Levitt scheme must become a lifetime affair for tomorrow's successful firms.

MEASURE CUSTOMER SATISFACTION

Measure! And reward on the basis of the measures. Quality—the poor-quality cost, customer evaluation of quality—can be measured; I emphasized that in prescription C-2. Service can be measured too. Yet few do it. And most of those who do (1) do so too infrequently, (2) don't emphasize the intangibles, and (3) haven't the confidence to pay for performance in this area.

After years of observation, I have arrived at ten considerations that are key to effective measurement of customer satisfaction:

1. **Frequency.** Formal surveys every 60 to 90 days are a must. Do informal surveys monthly at least. A major annual image survey should be the program's cornerstone. Perdue Farms and Citytrust survey daily; Domino's Pizza does so weekly—yet all too many pat themselves on the back for doing a semiannual survey. Such a low frequency doesn't cut the mustard.

2. **Format.** A third party must do the systematic annual image survey and probably should do the 60–90-day surveys. And they should be expensive—so you'll take them seriously. The results, even if embarrassing, must be widely shared. Informal "focus groups" of a few customers ought to be called in to every operation—manufacturing, distribution, accounting, not just marketing—on a biweekly or monthly basis. Debriefings with key accounts (annually or semiannually) must include formal survey questions and open-ended discussions with all levels and functions in key account operations. Mount informal (or formal) "call three customers each week" programs for senior managers in all functions, including specified rituals for sharing and discussing the data generated by the calls. Summaries of all customer complaint correspondence (statistical plus some actual letters and call transcripts) should be made available to all. Systematic "lost sale" follow-up programs are also a must.

3. **Content.** Ask some standard quantifiable questions—e.g., "How many complaints did you get in the first 90 days after the product went on sale?" "How many hours do you take to respond to customer queries of various sorts?" Put energy into devising ways to quantify the qualitative questions—e.g., "How were we to do business with?"—on a scale of one to ten. And be sure, in all such measuring, to test "us" against your "best competitor" (best overall, best in the area, newest, etc.).

4. **Design of content.** Do continual, systematic "naïve" listening from as many angles as possible (see also prescription C-7). No single measure or survey instrument is best, or even good. Coordination and cross-checking among many is essential. The chief roadblock to program success is moving beyond obvious measures to the difficult-to-articulate, controversial (especially to engineers, accountants, manufacturers, marketers, and kindred spirits) perceptual variables that ultimately determine long-term customer relations/repeat business/account growth. Take the example of the bank survey: Would your questions get at the value of "underpromising" on delivery?

5. Involve everyone. Informal focus groups must include all functions, all levels of seniority. Hold in-plant key-account reviews with all hands in attendance. Visits to customer sites should include, over time, *all* functions, *all* levels from line workers to top management. Suppliers, wholesalers, and other members of the distribution channel should also take part, formally and informally.

6. Measure everyone's satisfaction. Measure the satisfaction of all direct and indirect customers: the ultimate user and every member of the distribution channel—dealer, retailer, wholesaler, franchisee, rep, etc.

7. Combinations of measures. Reduce measures to a composite quantitative score for (a) some individuals (e.g., salespersons, service persons), (b) groups (a dispatch or reservation center team), (c) facilities (factory or operations office or store), and (d) divisions.

8. Relation to compensation and other rewards. Once measures, developed in partnership with the people being measured (ideally, everyone), are fully agreed upon and checked out for reliability over time, move to include them in compensation plans (e.g., incentive compensation for salespersons, gain-sharing programs for others). Consider making this the prime variable in sales incentive compensation (instead of volume of sales); or at least use it as a "go–no go" switch (e.g., if a person is not in the top half on the continued customer satisfaction measure, he or she is not eligible for any awards based on the volume of sales).

9. Symbolic use of measures. Key customer satisfaction measures should be publicly posted in every part of the organization.

10. Other forms of measurement. Every job description (if you have them—see S-2) should include a qualitative description of the person's "connection to the customer," and every performance evaluation should include an assessment of the person's degree of "customer orientation."

Do Something, Anything, Now!

If you're not doing anything about measurement right now (and most aren't), then consider this fallback advice. After a speech in Atlanta, a young man pulled me aside: "So what am I supposed to do?" I'd just covered the list above, and I replied: "Do those ten things." "No," he insisted, "what am I supposed to DO?" Frustrated, I thought for a moment, then blurted out: "Look, just drag fifteen customers in from somewhere, buy 'em lunch or dinner, and ask them what the heck is on their minds." "Thanks, that's great," he said, obviously satisfied, and took off.

I hope he got as much out of the exchange as I did. The measurement list is a product of a lot of work. But if it puts you off, just drag fifteen . . .

Cautionary Tales about Measurement: Tripping over Words

Seemingly innocuous terms can lead us way off course with the measurement of customer satisfaction. Here are five loaded phrases:

1. "Not symptomatic": A bank executive was discussing customer satisfaction measurement. He said that when a problem only showed up once—a particular error on a statement, for instance—then there was little or no follow-up beyond a cursory apology, because it was "not symptomatic of a larger problem."

At some of my seminars, I get detailed feedback from hundreds of people. There is invariably some criticism. Sadly, I have found every criticism symptomatic of larger issues—some continuing form of inattention or inflexibility on my part. I readily find all too sensible reasons why a particular critic reacted the way she or he did. *Every* customer complaint *is* symptomatic of a shortcoming—moreover, it usually represents a lurking improvement opportunity. Treat every snafu (a) as symptomatic of impending doom and (b) as a budding opportunity for market creation and product redefinition—and act accordingly.

2. "Objective" versus "subjective": One manager insists: "Cleanliness is subjective. By definition, it can't be measured." So what's objective? The same manager responds: "What percent of orders went out on or before the date due."

First, cleanliness can be measured. Just add a question to your next survey: "How clean was the store, on a scale of one to ten, where ten is 'like an operating room'?" Or: "Relative to fast-food places where you've eaten recently, how clean was our operation?" Choices might include "awful," "below average," "average," etc.

Second, this particular manager's example of objectivity is anything but. A high-tech firm boasted it was beating order-due dates 98 percent of the time. But customers were not knocking down the doors with repeat business. It turned out that the "due date" was actually a tortuously negotiated date: if the customer asked for the order by January 17, a harried plant manager might insist that February 25 was the best he could do. So what's the big deal in beating that kind of "due date" by even a week? When the firm switched to the "customer request date" (reasonable or not) as its measurement base, meeting or beating it slumped to a tawdry 32 percent. After a year of hard work it has climbed back to 68 percent—and repeat business has grown.*

So anything can be measured and made "objective." But measurement per se does not ensure objectivity.

3. "Ninety-seven percent satisfied": An IBM executive says, "We make 300,000 components. Don't say to me, '97 percent are okay.' Say instead, '9,000 were defective.' Sounds a little bit different, doesn't it?" He adds: "You don't really want 9,000 angry customers, do you?" A hospital administrator concurs: "Remember, 95 percent 'happy' patients in a 600-bed hospital means that 30 are thinking about suing you for malpractice at any given point!"

4. "On average": The use of averages is downright dangerous. For instance, "On average, we ship parts within 37 hours of order entry," or "The average customer requires 0.84 service visit per year." But more study reveals that the 37-hour "average" also means 89 hours for the "worst-off 10 percent"; and the 0.84 service visit translates into two or more visits for 26 percent of your customers. Gear your measures to focus attention on the worst-off 1, 5, 10, or 25 percent of customers.

5. "Unsystematic": I'm all for systematic surveys of 700 randomly selected customers or noncustomers. But I also applaud very unsystematic rituals, despite the disdain they draw from MBA analysts. Once a month, George Gendron, editor-in-chief of *Inc.* magazine, calls a half-dozen people who have not renewed their subscriptions. When I saw him last, he was flying off from the East Coast to Denver just to talk to one of those unhappy subscribers. "Her notion of what was wrong and what could be improved was positively brilliant," he said. The MBA's conception of "systematic" didn't apply in this case, but the business was well served.

Watch your language!

---

*Go back and re-read the section on customer perception, expectation, and delivery. Make sure that the denominator on the righthand side of the equation ("expectation") is the *true* customer expectation, not one that you've finagled.

THE HUMAN TOUCH IS NOT ENOUGH: TECHNOLOGY'S ROLE

It is important to conclude with a word of caution. While courtesy is powerful medicine, it is only half the story. Federal Express thrives because of its great "people orientation" (involvement, incentive compensation, empowerment to take the initiative to solve problems, etc.). But that's matched by equally great support systems. The Limited's success has resulted from the same blend of people and technology/systems. Likewise, Nordstrom matches its people emphasis with hard-dollar expenditures on inventory, salary and commissions, numerous local buying offices, and in-store amenities. American Express, McDonald's, and Frito-Lay match a people orientation with a systems emphasis too. Even grocer Stew Leonard fits this mold. His customer orientation, through people, is matchless—but he was also one of the first grocers, small or large, to do daily computer analysis of the profitability of every item he sold; Leonard was a decade ahead of Safeway on systems that are just now becoming commonplace in the industry.

On the other hand, that other express, People, is out of business. The smiles were tops. But they couldn't compensate for an awful reservation system which infuriated passengers and travel agents alike.

PUBLIC PARALLELS

With respect to those two outer rings of Levitt's, there are no limits for the imaginative public sector manager. Ron Hartman, general manager of Baltimore's Mass Transit Administration, offers up a fine example: "Two years ago we received a series of complaints on one of our premium park-and-ride express bus lines from a suburb to downtown Baltimore. Several buses were continually late. We fixed the problem, but felt we owed the riders more for the inconvenience. One day after the service got back to normal, we took advantage of the fact that it was the Christmas season. On a cold December morning, instead of the usual bus showing up, we decorated a bus with lots of crepe paper and tinsel, stuck a Christmas tree in the fare box to offer the service free, hooked up a tape recorder playing carols, and dressed the driver like Santa Claus. We offered cookies, coffee, and candy canes as commuters boarded. We still get letters from those customers and most continue to ride with us."

Sad to say, though, I can point to few public sector operations that emphasize the "outer rings," or even measure customer (constituent) satisfaction. But then all too few private firms measure it, to their detriment. On the other hand, extensive, systematic measurement is plausible and would surely be useful for any public entity—a school, a transportation or sanitation district, etc.

Many public sector managers are reluctant to seek such feedback, because they are afraid it will be too expensive to deal with, will open up a can of worms, and will result in suggestions that will be beyond their bailiwick—"Keep the library open seven days a week, twenty-four hours a day," etc. But the reality is that the lion's share of consumers of private and public services are sane and thoughtful. IBM's average customer does not respond to a survey with "Redesign the whole top of the line." The majority of suggestions will be in the line of "You always run out of soup spoons," "The towel dispenser is too high for kids to reach." If you sample regularly, and respond quickly, you will be inundated with small, practical, generally inexpensive—and implementable—ideas. Then both you and the customer/citizen win.

FIRST STEPS

1. Take one product or service that you offer. Bring in customers, informally. Spend a day working on the "two outer rings"—the augmented and the potential product. What do you offer? What do competitors offer? How do customers perceive the offering?
2. Calculate the ten-year or lifetime value of a customer. Then review, with representatives from all functions, what you do proactively to encourage relationship building. Focus especially on key front-line jobs that affect the *perception* of responsiveness to the customers. Check biases in sales and service compensation systems vis-à-vis repeat business. Perhaps start your own "Little Things Mean a Lot" program for recent purchasers and lifelong customers.

C-4

SUMMARY

Given changing technology, the opportunity granted by being close to the U.S. market, and the moves of competitors, we must:

▶ Achieve total customer responsiveness (TCR) via bold, new partnerships with suppliers/distributors/customers.

▶ Seek out and create new markets *with* our partners.

▶ Introduce "hustle" as a key strategic concept—fast moves, fast adaption, and tight linkages will become a way of life.

Adversarial relations with suppliers, distributors (and all members of the distribution channel), and ultimate end users must be quickly replaced with partnership relations. Major electronic/telecommunication linkages and other tactics to enhance speed/responsiveness must be quickly achieved. They represent the ultimate offensive strategic opportunity, but must also be done quickly for defensive reasons—others will get there first and lock in customers for years to come.

In the next 24 months, mount major partnership projects with 75 percent of your major suppliers/distributors/customers. Slash jointly held inventories and the lead time required for order fulfillment (including delivery times on new models and styles) by 90 percent. Continually add value-enhancing, ever-tighter links to every member of the distribution channel.

130

C-4

Achieve Extraordinary Responsiveness

Strategy, its high-church theologians insist, is about outflanking competitors with big plays that yield . . . a sustainable advantage. It is questionable whether this proposition is itself sustainable. . . . The competitive scriptures almost systematically ignore the importance of hustle and energy. While they preach strategic planning, competitive strategy, and competitive advantage, they overlook the record of a surprisingly large number of very successful companies that vigorously practice a different religion. These companies don't have long-term strategic plans with an obsessive preoccupation on rivalry. They concentrate on operating details and doing things well. Hustle is their style and their strategy. They move fast, and they get it right.

[H]igh profits [at top financial service institutions] stem largely from superior execution or forceful opportunism, not structural competitive barriers. Different execution styles lead to considerable variations in bottom-line results. Many wholesale banks have the same cost of funds, offer similar products and services, and use the same kinds of sales forces to reach the same customers. Yet some are more profitable than others. They "get it right." . . . They get a higher share of corporate cash balances because the account officers get and stay close to their clients. They know the clients so well that they make suggestions before the clients know they need them. . . . "Lost" wire transfers are found promptly. They're informed, fast, and available.

Amar Bhide,
"Hustle as Strategy"
Harvard Business Review,
September/October 1986

Creating well-defined market niches is not enough. Neither is TQC, total quality control. Nor is superior service with an emphasis on the intangibles. Add TCR, total customer responsiveness, to prescriptions C-1 through C-3.

LINK UP OR ELSE!

This prescription covers, for instance, extensive electronic linkups among supplier, factory, delivery truck, distributor (agent, etc.), and customer. Citicorp, Federal Express, drug distributors McKesson and Bergen Brunswig, American Airlines, American Hospital Supply, Merrill Lynch, truckers Ryder and P-I-E Nationwide, Milliken, and The Limited are typical of the pioneers here. It also means getting physically closer to your customer, with programs and resources—Campbell Soup, Frito-Lay, and PPG are among those showing the way in this. And it concerns computer-integrated manufacturing and flexible manufacturing systems in general. But it is at least as much about forming partnerships among functions within the firm and with suppliers, distributors, sales reps, and ultimate customers. Adversarial relations in these arenas, characteristic of most firms historically, spell competitive discomfort today and doom tomorrow. TCR most generally means "hustle," as Amar Bhide defined it, or "sustaining a constant sense of urgency," as Elgin Corrugated Box Company president Bob Wilson calls it.

The stakes are high—survival. The goal is breathtaking. This prescription, in a host of major areas, demands 75 to 90 percent improvements in the next 24 to 48 months. As you read this, others, possibly including your competitors, are taking on—and achieving—such goals. Winners will do it; losers won't. And once more there's a cautionary note: Though the goals must necessarily be bold, they will not be achieved by a leapfrog, big bang, or one-shot application of new technology. Change in the structure of the organization and in decades-old attitudes must precede, or at least parallel, technology's application. In the quality prescription C-2, I repeatedly warned that passion without systems was a lousy formula; so were systems without passion. The same, with minor variations, holds true of TCR.

An Alarming Contrast

It was a coincidence. My *Business Week* arrived at home on a Friday in April 1986. I came across a story about Custom Vêtement Associates, the U.S. subsidiary of French garment maker Vestra. A custom-tailored suit has always meant a ten-week wait to me. No more. U.S. retailers such as Saks have been given "terminals made for the French national Videotex system," *Business Week* reported. "These link retailers with the main manufacturing operation in Strasbourg. Tailors take key measurements from customers and plug them into a terminal. Every night the data are sent to a central computer in New York and beamed via satellite to France. In the morning, after nine inspectors look at different pieces of data, a computer-controlled laser cutter selects the appropriate material and cuts the garment. A staff of tailors does the finishing touches, and the suit is shipped within four days."

By chance, I purchased a truck for my Vermont farm the next day, Saturday. I bought American—GMC. Not until I got it home did I realize that the spare tire gobbled up almost all the truck's effective storage space. The solution was clear: buy a simple A-frame bracket to mount the tire on the rear of the vehicle. Of course, this was impossible on Saturday, when I discovered the problem, or Sunday. Very few dealers in the United States keep their parts or service operations open on weekends—that is, when customers are around. On Monday, I stayed home and went to the dealership. In place of the Custom Vêtement computer terminal was the usual parts book, several feet long and made of flimsy (and by now ragged) paper. Nonetheless, I managed to place the order. I was informed, however, that there was no way of knowing when the part might be in; I should call in "three or four days," just to find out when it might arrive. It depended on whether the regional distributor had it, and so on. To make a long story short, it took over three weeks to get the simple part (a GM part) and another week to get and complete an appointment for installation. Five weeks later and over

$400 poorer, I had a $20,000 truck that would now carry a second bag of groceries!

WAYS TO CONNECT WITH THE CUSTOMER

Going Local

High Technology editor Bob Haavind said the obvious in a recent editorial: "So where can U.S. manufacturing industry hope to gain an edge? In fact, domestic manufacturers have a tremendous potential advantage relative to offshore competitors simply by being close to the market. Amazingly, few American firms make much use of this obvious advantage."

Some, of course, do. Frito-Lay has long maintained a big lead in the snack-food business by "overspending" to get close to the customer. The $3 billion subsidiary of PepsiCo, which contributes about $350 million in pre-tax profits to its parent, sends out 10,000 route salespersons each day. And now, despite its commanding lead in market share, Frito-Lay has taken additional steps to tighten its linkages to its customers. For example, the company is moving significant marketing muscle to the field. Marketing staff members, once located in the Dallas headquarters, will now be installed in eight regional offices in an effort to make brand strategy more "bottom up than top down," according to the firm's marketing vice-president. The share of the marketing budget devoted to local needs will rise dramatically. Frito-Lay's director of field marketing declares, "Basically, there's no such thing as a national program for promotions coming out of Frito-Lay anymore. We will tailor our marketing to our prime trading areas." Frito-Lay's president, Mike Jordan, adds, "We are tailoring our program to meet the needs of individual chains. . . . That was not one of our strengths in prior years."

Frito-Lay's new approach is also being used by stablemate Pepsi-Cola. Both programs are carbon copies of an even more aggressive effort by Campbell Soup, mentioned briefly in Part I. In 1982, once stodgy and hierarchical Campbell reorganized into fifty-two business units to speed product development and niche-market creation. A fourfold increase in the pace of product development ensued. Typical of the outcome is the success of the unleashed Canadian unit. Allowed to break with the conventional wisdom of packaged-goods marketers (dominated by a mass-market, economy-of-scale mind-set), the $300 million subsidiary recently introduced, for instance, a new brand of V-8 juice for French-speaking Canadians, whose taste in tomatoes is different from that of their English-speaking counterparts. It's been a smashing success.

The second bold move at Campbell came in April 1986, when, in a break with the monolithic Procter & Gamble marketing model, it created twenty-two powerful regional marketing offices. Field brand managers, sales, and big budgets are being applied to local needs on an unprecedented scale. (Incidentally, P&G is now following suit, though at a slower pace.)

Get "Wired": Installing Electronic Linkages

Once again, Frito-Lay shows the way. Soon every one of its delivery trucks will have an onboard computer terminal, linked to the rest of the distribution system. Federal Express, with its Cosmos system (see C-3), has gained a great advantage in the same fashion.

Drug distributor McKesson's electronic linkages to its customers—independent pharmacies—*are* the successful firm's strategy. In the 1970s, Foremost-McKesson was a diversified elephant, limping along with dairies, pasta makers, and drug distributors in its portfolio. Near the end of the decade the company undertook radical surgery. It sold off virtually all nondistribution activities and invested about $125 million in a state-of-the-art computer-telecommunications system. The system not only made the renamed McKesson Corporation more profitable, but it also saved and made profitable McKesson Drug's more than 12,000 then struggling independent pharmacist customers, who can now compete with chains on price—and often beat them on availability. Orders can be placed at any time via a hand-held programmable computer that hooks up to a common phone line. Deliveries are made daily, and the rarest drugs can be readily obtained. McKesson's once imperiled independent customers have increased their business significantly in the last half dozen years and McKesson's drug distribution business has grown fourfold, from $1 billion in 1978 to almost $5 billion today, with a spiffy 20 percent return on assets to boot.

Beyond price and availability, McKesson has added numerous other features to assist—*and lock in*—its customers. Software packages, such as ECONOPRICE, ECONOCHARGE, ECONOCLAIM, ECONOPLAN, and ECONOFICHE, print continuously updated labels based on the retailer's own formula, aid in the management of accounts receivable, speed third-party (insurer) claim processing for prescription drugs, optimize the utilization of shelf space, and provide microfiche information on such things as drug interaction and Medicaid numbers. McKesson does get displaced from time to time, but all these linkages make it no mean feat to do so.

Reviewing the McKesson systems, researchers Louis Stern and Patrick Kaufmann noted these benefits from so-called Electronic Data Interchange (EDI): "(1) Reduced order lead times; (2) higher service level; (3) fewer out-of-stock situations; (4) improved communication about deals, promotions, price changes, and product availability; (5) lower inventory costs; (6) better accuracy in ordering, shipping, and receiving; and (7) a reduction in labor costs." Not bad.

Among others choosing similar strategies are McKesson's fierce rival, Bergen Brunswig, which has followed McKesson's lead; also in health care, pioneer American Hospital Supply (now owned by Baxter Travenol), which has installed supply order terminals in over 5,000 hospitals and health care establishments, sewing up this business (for now); American Airlines, which pioneered years ago with its Sabre system—now in over 10,000 travel agents' offices, and thus creating "total [customer] dependence," says *Business Week;* P-I-E Nationwide, a Jacksonville, Florida, trucking firm, which developed Shipmaster software for an IBM compatible PC and a modem linking it to carriers; and several pioneer financial service firms, such as Aetna, which have established electronic links with brokers.

Retailing has perhaps witnessed the biggest shift in this direction. In *Managing in the Service Economy,* Harvard's James Heskett comments on Italian knitwear maker Benetton, which "has pioneered a retailing approach throughout Europe that promises to influence a number of other retailers worldwide: It substitutes information for assets. Because its first retail outlet offering knitted outerwear in colorful fashions was very small, the Benetton family developed an approach to retailing that makes effective use of small spaces. Unlike its more traditional competitors with stores of perhaps 4,000 square feet, a typical Benetton outlet is not more than 600 square feet. Little space is wasted in floor selling or 'back room' storage. An electronic communications system supported by a manufacturing process allows for dyeing to order and for rapid replenishment of the items in greatest demand during a fashion season. The result is a higher rate of inventory turnover in the store and a level of sales-per-square-foot that is often several times that of Benetton's competitors. Benetton's assets support many more sales because it has injected both communications and [flexible] production technology into its service."

In fact, Benetton can make changes in inventory in ten days that take most retailers months. The only more masterful retailer may be The Limited. Its system includes the world's largest and most automated distribution center (in Columbus, Ohio), dedicated Boeing 747s bringing daily orders from over 300 factories around the world, and instantaneous data linkages among the retail outlets, the distribution centers, and the far-flung factories. All of this, for example, allowed the chain to bring a 500,000-unit order of its popular Outback Red line of sportswear to market in just ten weeks. It found the fabric, cut it, stitched it, and shipped it at a pace probably ten times faster than its competitors could have done. Sadly, The Limited stands as testimony to Bob Haavind's indictment of U.S. manufacturers. Domestic producers generally can't meet The Limited's requirements for responsiveness—which is now (spring 1987) causing special pain, since protectionist trade policies and the falling dollar are forcing the company to seek domestic suppliers as a safety valve.

TOTAL CUSTOMER RESPONSIVENESS

Manufacturing firms in general, and heavy manufacturers in particular, have been remarkably slow, as in so many other areas, to jump on this bandwagon. It surprised me to see a report in a February 1987 issue of *High Technology* commenting on a Chrysler plant which "transmits [by computer] its production schedule to the [supplier] TRW plant." This should not be news. It should be the norm.

Milliken Mounts Another Revolution

It is becoming the norm at textile manufacturer Milliken. "It's a 'bet the company' move," an executive explains. That's a startling statement.

The firm has long been its industry's leader in R&D and manufacturing technology. Finding that its traditional strengths were not adequate to meet the stepped-up challenges it faces from overseas, in 1981 Milliken mounted the all-out and successful quality improvement program discussed in C-2.

Even so, the foreign onslaught continued unabated, with most of the industry reeling from it. So Milliken mounted yet another revolution in 1985. Executives are now demanding, across the entire estimated $2.25 billion firm, nothing less than cuts of 90 percent in the time it takes to develop products and deliver them.

The first phase of Milliken's total customer responsiveness program consisted of mounting over 1,000 Customer Action Teams (CATs). Each was a self-contained effort to unearth new market opportunities in partnership with an existing customer. To launch a team, the customer had to agree to supply team members and join with Milliken representatives from manufacturing, sales, finance, and marketing in seeking creative solutions to better serving current markets or creating new ones. Each year hundreds of such projects are completed and hundreds of new ones are launched.

The details of a typical project make clear the sweeping nature of the firm's program. A two-year Partners for Profit program with apparel maker Levi Strauss has revolutionized the way the two firms do business together. First, Milliken capitalized on its unparalleled quality program. Given Milliken's flawless track record—statistically demonstrated—in the delivery of top quality, Levi agreed to omit its own inspection of inbound Milliken-supplied goods. Moreover, close cooperation between the two firms enabled Milliken to produce fabric to Levi's exacting color standards and in roll sizes that maximize Levi's ability to utilize the material.

Since the first inspection can be skipped, Milliken can ship directly to Levi's factories, eliminating the need for Levi to warehouse the material. Next, the two firms, abetted by state-of-the-art data and telecommunication linkups among numerous plants, were able to eliminate even Levi's in-plant sorting and storage. The Milliken delivery truck is now a meticulously stocked "warehouse on wheels." With exact, time-coded order information, the truck brings precisely what Levi needs to the plant entrance, and the fabric is off-loaded, in appropriate reverse order, then carried directly to the specific in-plant machine where the garments will be cut and sewn. To accomplish this ultimate reduction in work in progress, an especially complex cooperative maneuver was required. At a remote facility, Levi makes electronic tags that guide its in-plant utilization for each roll of fabric. Via yet another sophisticated, on-line hookup, the appropriate tags arrive at the Levi finishing plant just as the Milliken truck pulls up, and are attached as the truck is unloaded.

The net of all this is a monumental cost saving and reduction in delivery time for Levi Strauss. Milliken, of course, shares the dollars-and-cents benefit, but, more important, keeps an order onshore that might otherwise have been lost to overseas competition. In addition to the cost savings that come from the elimination of inspection, inventory, and warehousing, Levi achieves previously unheard-of flexibility, which, in turn, helps it respond more aggressively to today's lightning-fast changes in fashion and taste. With demonstrations of responsiveness such as this under its belt, Milliken was even able to grab some Limited Stores business that had long been filled by that firm's affiliated offshore plants.

The Milliken program is just gearing up, but cycle-shortening results are already astonishing. In a major carpet business, a six-week sample and product delivery cycle previously thought irreducible was cut to just five days. Another business's historic eighty-day cycle was reduced to three days—and twenty-four-hour response 100 percent of the time is now seen as an achievable goal.

The Basic Interactive Elements of TCR, as Demonstrated at Milliken

Several elements, working in tandem, marked this latest Milliken revolution:

▶ First, reminiscent of the quality revolution, was top management commitment. TCR was Revolution II. Letters from Roger Milliken never cease referring to the sense of urgency associated with this new operation.

▶ Second, the unparalleled success of the earlier quality program was the necessary foundation: Without it, various partners such as Levi would have had no sound basis to move forward.

▶ Third, the CATs and the projects with suppliers in the quality program paved the way for a wholesale shift from adversarial to partnership relations within and outside the firm. In 1980 Milliken epitomized

the hierarchical, authoritarian, highly functionalized corporate organization. The CATs pulled sales, marketing, and the two strongest
baronies, accounting and manufacturing, together, and this made possible the cooperation and the lowest-level, no-delay decision-making
that, much more than technology (as so many are finding out to their
dismay), are the keys to TCR.

▶ The fourth step was another breakthrough—a complete shake-up,
accomplished in 90 days across sixty plants, of the manufacturing
organization structure. In one move in 1985, the span of control in the
plants went from one supervisor for every six nonsupervisors to a ratio
of one to thirty-six. The freed-up supervisors, mostly called process
engineers, are now first-class expediters. They ensure that new product
samples are shepherded through the highly programmed system with
alacrity and that phone calls from the various functions (customers,
suppliers, etc.) are returned fast, with action taken. The increased
number of in-plant process engineers is consistent with Japanese factory organization; in fact, Milliken president Tom Malone launched
the reorganization after carefully collecting data on Japanese factory
organization in the course of over a dozen visits to that country.

Previously undreamed-of feats of multi-plant, multi-functional cooperation are now the daily norm with no letup in quality standards,
which are constantly being tightened. This last point is vital. Since
they were to be required to be so much more flexible, the company's
plant managers at first pleaded for relief from quality standards. And
indeed, the achievement of better quality and more flexibility simultaneously is a tall order. Perfection in product would seem to be at
odds with satisfying small orders on a moment's notice. But once
again, Milliken took chapters from Japan's book. Robert Hall, of
Indiana University, elaborates in *Attaining Manufacturing Excellence:*
"All Japanese motorcycle companies introduce several new models
per month into plants already producing a large mix. Each day, after
production is complete, some of the time remaining is used for trying
the new tooling and arrangements for upcoming models. When it
appears that production can go without a hitch, the new model is
inserted into the production lineup for the succeeding schedule month.
Any necessary finishing changes are incorporated at the end of the first
or second month of production." This requisite increased flexibility is
possible only because of much tighter linkages among design, engi-

neering, and manufacturing in Japan than in the United States. (This trait, also taught to the Japanese by American W. Edwards Deming, will be the subject of prescription C-8 and several others.)

Responsiveness as Competitive Edge: GE Plastics

Milliken is not alone among manufacturers in using TCR as an offensive competitive weapon. The grinding wheel (for metal finishes) division of the old-line Norton Company of Worcester, Massachusetts, has given terminals to all its distributors, which makes it "easier to do business with us and harder to leave," according to division general manager Richard Kennedy.

Or consider GE's multi-billion-dollar engineering plastics operation, built from scratch in just a couple of decades. This science-based operation was predicated on technological advantage—GE Chairman Jack Welch, who holds a Ph.D. in chemical engineering, got his start there. Today, the business sees its future strategic advantage coming from "service/responsiveness added." The new strategy's instant success brings together all of our familiar themes: (1) attitude/commitment, (2) service through people, and (3) support systems (training, computer systems, electronic linkages).

Paul Jones manages the Plastics Business Group's Sales Service Center in Albany, New York. He describes the origins of the strategy of emphasizing, then centralizing, customer service:

We were spread out—customer service was located within our marketing organizations, within the product businesses, within manufacturing, traffic, credit, collections, finance. The people in the plants were stuck in trailers. They were back in the bowels of the organization where nobody could really find them except by a telephone call. They had a 20-year-old system that we were working with; the time-sharing system badly needed upgrading. Cost is not the important thing. Customer service can be an offensive thrust for us. . . . Nobody else had done it in the industry. Somebody's gonna do it, and I want to be the first to do it. At first, [only] a very small minority of people really could understand that this is the best way to go. But as time went on, it [became] nearly unanimous. We have a showcase customer service center. We bring customers through.

We show it off as much as we can. It's a mindset throughout the whole organization to get people to see that this can be an offense. These [customer service] people can get pounds [the selling unit for plastics] for us. They can go after top line [revenue enhancement] rather than just acting as mechanics, just going through the bureaucratic procedures and telling the customer, "Well, you'll get it when we run it."

The system was centralized, and exceptional energy went into recruiting and training eighteen Customer Service Coordinators, selected from over 1,000 applicants. Jones explains the organization's approach to hiring and development: "We wanted aggressive people, we wanted ambitious people who would fight for their customer. . . . We looked for people who were very quick on their feet, very articulate. We looked for nice people. We put them through all sorts of telephone training, presentation skills, how to order wine at a restaurant, everything. We got them so involved. These people aren't just plugged into a phone; they go see their customers, they travel with the salespeople. Their jobs are to spend ten percent of the time traveling with the customers. We did all those things before we ever sat them down in front of our new computer system."

The objective—largely achieved—was to turn the new heroes, in the business's mainstream and under the close and watchful eye of top management, into true "advocates for the customer," people who, says Jones, "won't take 'no' [from some other part of the Plastics Group] for an answer."*

It's working in sales—and in attitude. The customers understand—and so does GE: "The surveys . . . will come back and say, 'Patty does an outstanding job for me, but,' and it's the 'but' that we have to focus on, the people downstream, the package that was ripped when it came in, the bag that had a tear in it, the pallet that had broken, it was the wrong color or what have you. It may have been Patty that had put the thing in with the wrong color number. The customers never believe that. Their customer service coordinator is beyond reproach. They never

---

*Domino's Pizza Distribution (Domino's $540 million [in revenues] dough, topping, and equipment supplier) is training a similar elite group of "store advocates" who will act as the franchisees' ombudsmen with the firm.

make a mistake as far as the customer's concerned. They are super people, and we've got to maintain them."

Next came the systems: "We got away from people located all the way across the country, taking orders, using this [holding up a paper tablet] as their order entry method and writing things down. Maybe it got into the system, maybe it didn't. We literally burned every bridge. We threw away the old computer system, even threw away the old computer. We went to a completely brand-new system with centralized people, brand-new people, trained, oriented solely towards servicing the customer."

Next came electronic linkages—still in an embryonic stage, but of the highest urgency, as Jones explains: "We've had to do it. We had customers . . . requesting electronic data interchange. They want to enter their orders electronically. . . . If we didn't do that, we were going to walk away from hundreds of millions of dollars a year. . . . So a very high-priority item for us right now is to go to the electronic hook-ups. We are finding that customers really want their computer to talk to ours. They don't want us to put in a little terminal, a personal computer, that they can dial up. They don't want to have a GE Order Entry Center. They just want to put their demands in—MRP [Material Requirements Planning] system, whatever you want to call it—so they can have access to us via their system, electronically. . . . They want acknowledgement electronically, they want us to tell them when we're going to ship electronically, they want us to send them shipping information electronically, invoice them electronically; they want to pay us electronically."

Taken together, these elements are starting to add up to a first-order competitive advantage. Moreover, a host of additional, unexpected advantages are popping up at every turn: "[Our average Customer Service Coordinator] will have 60 to 70 customer contacts a day apiece. They can ask all sorts of questions. They do surveys with customers on advertising. We do surveys on what other competitors are doing—'Joe, old buddy, you and I talk to each other every day. What's happening to your market? Are distributors more of a threat, are people selling direct?' It's a fantastic tool. Our customer service organization, properly trained, can gather information for us to feed back into the management of the business, and they do it in a way that leaves the customer flattered that they're asking. We're not on an intelligence-gathering mission. The customer is glad we're asking. It shows concern."

Such strategies, though far from the norm right now, will fast become the norm—or else!

Responsiveness: Training Your Customer's People

Recall, in C-1, the discussion of Milliken's shop towel business. Milliken has almost made the towel the least important part of the transaction—the company essentially provides consulting services (sales aids, advice on quality-improvement programs) which enhance its customers' overall capability.

No one understands such a strategy better than ServiceMaster, based in Downers Grove, Illinois. ServiceMaster (mentioned in Part I) manages its customers' housekeeping, food service, and maintenance operations. The heart of the firm's strategy is to train and develop the customers' workers—in jobs that are generally lightly regarded.

ServiceMaster, like McKesson et al., has numerous, highly technical support systems. But these merely complement the core program which helps the customers' people upgrade their skills, contribute ideas—and achieve extraordinary productivity and low turnover in job categories that traditionally have sky-high turnover rates.

Thus, training your customers' employees becomes yet one more opportunity to redefine responsiveness and make it an offensive marketing strategy.

Make Just-in-Time (JIT) an Offensive Strategy

Just-in-time inventory management is usually conceived of as something manufacturers do *to* their suppliers, achieving linkups "backward" toward the vendor. The Milliken idea essentially turns this on its head. Milliken proactively seeks out opportunities to assist customers, using some variant of voluntary just-in-time inventory management as a marketing strategy, linked "forward," toward the customer. Robert Hall provides another example, illustrating the attitude change that must accompany such a strategy: "A corrugated box company began thinking about providing quality JIT service to a variety of customers. A few of them were beginning to ask for it. The company's operating people could foresee considerable improvement in quality, setup times, lot sizes, and deliveries, but it immediately became obvious that the traditional sales strategy would no longer be valid. It had specialized in large, low-price orders wangled by methods occasionally employing football tickets and Christmas booze. *The sales force could no longer be box sales people but rather service representatives in the true sense—analysts of each customer's operations* [my emphasis]. How did the customers schedule? At what rate did they use boxes? What did quality mean to them? Should the company target small, short lead time orders as well as large ones?"

The ultimate expression of this TCR/JIT strategy is being applied by PPG. Without being asked, and with no assurance of a contract in perpetuity, the Coatings and Resins Division at PPG has built six satellite plants (with another four under construction) within three miles of auto assembly plants to which it is the sole supplier. Radical inventory reduction for the customer is ensured, though at least as important is the general level of responsiveness, enhanced by tight computer linkages and workers dedicated to a single customer. Though PPG has no guarantees, it's not difficult to conclude that it would be tough to displace.

The sweeping revision of the traditional new relationships is captured by Hall in *Zero Inventories:* "The development of [the] system of direct hand-off of material throughout an industry suggests many aspects of supplier relationships which do not now prevail in much of industry. Supplier-customer relationships need to extend over a period of time, and both parties need to trust each other with more details of their operations than is often true. This [also] means more faith that each will not try to invade the other's business ([a fear] usually expressed by customer companies who decide to 'pull business in-house')." In fact, most just-in-time experiments have failed to reach their potential, not because of inadequate computerization, but because of a fundamental failure on the part of participants to understand the new attitude of trust, cooperation, and mutual investment for the long haul required to make the system hum.

SUMMARY: THE NINE (AT LEAST) FACTORS NECESSARY TO ACHIEVING TCR

The sweeping nature of the change this strategy entails cannot be overestimated:

1. A wholesale change of attitude. First, the firm must replace adversarial dealings with partnership thinking, "backward" toward suppliers and "forward" toward the distribution channel and the ultimate end user, as well as among the various functions within the firm. Second, hustle and flexibility must become the norm. What has traditionally been seen as disruptive must now be seen as the chief source of opportunity —if the factory is not a hotbed of short-lead-time, customized orders, trouble is brewing.

2. Reorganization of the Milliken sort is almost imperative. Basically, reducing layers of management (flattening the organization), breaking down the barriers between functions, and upping the percentage of expediters are prerequisites to TCR.

3. The closer linkages demand a superb level of basic product quality, as at Milliken.

4. The continual interchange of electronic data, à la The Limited and McKesson, is essential.

5. People involved in managing customer contact through the new system must become company heroes and receive superb training, as at GE.

6. Forward (distribution channel, customer) and backward (supplier) integration is necessary. Though traditional economies of scale are fast disappearing and vertical de-integration (shifting operations to subcontractors) is becoming commonplace, a potent new form of vertical re-integration, via data exchange and other partnership programs (rather than ownership of assets), is partially or wholly supplanting it.

7. Co-location, electronic and physical, is important. Whether it's a terminal in the truck as at Frito-Lay, or a computer in the druggist's back room as at McKesson, or a plant two miles away as at PPG, or a regionalized marketing effort like Campbell Soup's, the smart service provider will achieve direct or indirect physical presence in the customer's operation.

8. The system must be constantly enhanced, via software packages, à la McKesson, and training of customer personnel in the use of the system.

9. TCR becomes a prime marketing tool. First, it is a defensive necessity; if you don't get your hooks into the distribution channel/customer, someone else will—and probably is doing it as you read this. Second, the strategy is ultimately offensive. An infinite stream of add-on features, like the McKesson ECONOPRICE program, can add more and more value to the provider-user relationship over time, making separation increasingly difficult. The economists have a term for this strategy—"first mover advantage." It is derived from such activities as oil or gas pipeline-building, and embodies a very simple—and powerful—idea: Whoever builds the first pipeline (or supplies the first terminal with readily usable software) will likely ship the oil for a long time to come.

New attitudes, reorganization, some form of co-location, electronic telecommunications links, and value-added software hooks add up, then, to TCR—and a monumental change in basic business relationships. In fact, there are no manufacturing or service firms anymore. Already, 70 percent of manufacturing's value-added is coming from service activities, such as research and distribution. And progressive service firms, such as McKesson or Federal Express, are more capital-intensive than manufacturers on average. This prescription, then, is really about the transformation of every product or service firm into a service-added firm. Linkages—personal, physical, and electronic—are altering the way the game of competitive business is played. Even General Motors now acknowledges this; tight customer-dealer-firm-supplier linkages are the heart of the Saturn project strategy. (GM, in fact, acquired Ross Perot's Electronic Data Systems in 1984 for the precise purpose of pursuing a link-up strategy.) And traditionally arrogant semiconductor manufacturers are turning in the same direction, providing custom chips designed in tandem with customers—and beginning by permitting customers access to what till then had been closely guarded design and production secrets.

Indeed, there are no limits to this idea. A Michigan hospital voluntarily provided all its doctors with computer terminals—to aid admissions, for example. Doctors were not compelled to use the hospital; no strings were attached. Yet once the system was in place and the doctors' staff learned to use it, admissions soared. More software hooks were then sunk into the docs—for example, the provision of overall office management accounting programs.

Use Your Imagination: Have Congress Assist with TCR!

In 1986, Deluxe Check of Minneapolis earned a whopping $121 million after-tax on $867 million in sales of, that's right, checks. Service is its hallmark (see also S-1), and it will do anything to speed an order to its customers. In fact, it went so far as to lobby Congress successfully for special legislation. Deluxe received permission to install U.S. Postal Service substations in each of its 62 plants. With such a station on the premises, the process of shipping is shortened—one more tiny step toward achieving one of the highest after-tax return on sales in the Fortune 500. Thus, there is no limit to the imagination that can be applied to the pursuit of matchless responsiveness.

FIRST STEPS

1. Take one or two major customers (end users or members of the distribution channel) and form an immediate joint task force to assess opportunities for closer linkages.
2. Mount pilots within the next 90 *days* in two or three locations at least—that is, get going! Make a plan for the achievement of such linkages a major part of your next round of strategic planning in every business unit. Consider incremental programs, to be sure, but also be careful to ensure that revolutionary thinking is a part of the process.
3. Throughout the effort, be constantly cognizant of the all-important, deep-seated attitudinal issues that underlie the "techniques." If you fail to see customers, suppliers, and members of the distribution channel as partners instead of adversaries, the rest of the program, including perhaps large dollar investments, will be more than wasted—it may well boomerang.

C-5

SUMMARY

In view of the true globalization of the economy, smaller firms as well as large ones, in service as well as manufacturing, must:

▶ Become true internationalists, at least selling to and designing in, and probably manufacturing in, Europe and Japan/Asia.

▶ Follow the unfailing international success principles: persisting, building relationships/learning the culture, choosing partners carefully/mastering the distribution system, decentralizing, and tailoring the product or service to local needs and tastes.

▶ Examine joint venture and other alliance opportunities of all sorts, though not with an expectation that such partnerships will substitute for patient market development.

Internationalism is not just for the Boeings. Smaller firms not only can succeed overseas, but must consider international opportunities in their early years. International operations must always be built upon patient market and relationship development, not an American strong suit.

Every firm over $2 million in revenues should take first steps to examine international-market-creation opportunities in the next 12 months. Every firm over $25 million should be alarmed if it is not doing 25 percent of its business overseas, including some in Japan.

C-5

Be an Internationalist

Japan Winning the [Export] Race in China: Persistence, Patience
Key

> Headline, lead article "Business Day"
> *The New York Times*
> April 29, 1987

American management in the past has been singularly blind to the
needs of human beings. Management wants to eliminate the human
equation from business. . . . That puts businessmen at a disadvantage overseas because so many businesses are based on human relations and friendship. They say, "How the hell could you do business
by making a friend? What's that got to do with the bottom line?"
As it turns out, it has everything to do with it. . . . We're impatient.
But all over the world, if you have friends, you can do anything.
That's how the system works.

> Edward T. Hall
> Author of *The Silent Language*
> and, most recently, co-author of *Hidden Differ-*
> *ences: Doing Business with the Japanese;*
> from an article in the July issue of *Science 85*

Ready or not, Americans, the global village has arrived. London's
financial market restructuring in late 1986, called "Big Bang," is only
one of the latest bits of evidence. Then, in early 1987, the value of stocks
listed on the Tokyo exchange surpassed the value of those listed on the
New York exchange. The former head of Citicorp, Walter Wriston,
describes today's reality in *Risk and Other Four-Letter Words:*

Natural gas owned by Indonesia's oil agency, Pertamina, flows out of a well discovered by Royal Dutch Shell into a liquification plant designed by French engineers and built by a Korean construction company. The liquified gas is loaded onto U.S.-flag tankers, built in U.S. yards after a Norwegian design. The ships shuttle to Japan and deliver the liquid gas to a Japanese public utility, which uses it to provide electricity that powers an electronics factory making television sets that are shipped aboard a Hong Kong–owned container ship to California for sale to American farmers in Louisiana who grow rice that is sold to Indonesia and shipped there aboard Greek bulk carriers. All of the various facilities, ships, products, and services involved in the complex series of events are financed by U.S., European, and Japanese commercial banks, working in some cases with international and local government agencies. These facilities, ships, products, and services are insured and reinsured by U.S., European, and Japanese insurance companies. Investors in these facilities, ships, products, and services are located throughout the world. This illustration is not only factual, it is typical of transactions that take place over and over again daily throughout the globe.

There is a startling paradox here: On the one hand, we are all, like it or not, participants in a single global market. Service and manufacturing firms, large and small, are exporting to the United States. Sometimes we see it: Honda, Mercedes, Heineken. And sometimes we don't: Korean construction firms are building our buildings, and there is almost no product that doesn't have some foreign subcomponents. Likewise, our smaller as well as larger firms, in service or manufacturing, are finding unique market opportunities abroad.

On the other hand, the explosion of products and the technology revolution, described in Part I, are making all international markets more local; catering to local tastes, not so-called global branding (one kind of tomato soup for 125 countries), is essential.

Yet for a host of deep-seated reasons, such as a continuing isolationist mentality and "Yankee impatience," too many of our firms are (1) either failing to consider overseas opportunities, especially in their formative years, or (2) failing at early attempts to do business offshore, then withdrawing with tail between legs.

This prescription, though broadly concerned with internationalism, emphasizes the Japanese market for three reasons. First, Japan is our bellwether competition. Second, the Japanese market is tough to crack, but (1) it has been conquered by a surprising number of American firms (though all too many give up on it) and (2) the keys to success in Japan are the keys to success in any international market. And third, I strongly believe that America must develop a "westward focus"; the Pacific Rim *is* the market of tomorrow.

A Case in Point: The United States and Japan in China

There is no love lost between Chinese and Japanese. Despite the hiatus in relations between 1949 and 1972, there is true affection between Chinese and Americans. In 1986, Japan's exports to China were valued at $12.4 billion, amounting to a 29 percent share of Chinese imports. Hong Kong came next ($5.6 billion) and the U.S. was third, with $4.7 billion—38 percent of the Japanese total.

The reasons for the sparkling Japanese success, cited in a *New York Times* (April 29, 1987) analysis, and confirmed by my own conversations with U.S. executives residing in China, go far beyond propinquity, and include the following: (1) a commitment to the market (300 Japanese firms are established there, versus 170 U.S. firms); (2) a presence, marked by offices in many cities and the initially unprofitable establishment of a strong infrastructure (e.g., spare-parts depots in numerous locations); (3) a willingness to learn the difficult Chinese language (the *Times* reports, for instance, that the big, but relatively smaller, Sanwa Bank has five offices in China, with a total of twelve Japanese employees, of whom nine speak Chinese, while huge Citicorp has three offices, with only one Chinese-speaking American); (4) a willingness in the early years to forgo profit in order to gain market share; (5) the willingness of Japanese employees to accept longer assignments (three to five years versus a U.S. average of two to four) with less lavish, closer-to-the-people living accommodations than their American counterparts; and (6) the insistence of most American firms on reams of paperwork and on the involvement of lawyers where the Japanese operate like the Chinese—more informally, creating personal bonds.

Recall that earlier, in C-4, we talked of hustle as strategy. A Western diplomat said to the *Times* of the Japanese, "[They] do better because they are better. They have a long-term perspective, they're persistent, and they're out knocking on doors." An American businessman echoes the sentiment: "They are incredibly good. If they see a possible opportunity, they go all out. They rush people in from Tokyo or Hong Kong. . . . They fight for it. The Americans are more likely to throw up their hands and walk away from it. The Americans are like fish out of water."

CRACKING THE TOUGHEST INTERNATIONAL MARKET: JAPAN

Some American firms, from some surprising quarters, are thriving overseas—and in Japan:

▶ Memphis is many people's definition of an insular town. Buckman Labs, the specialty chemical firm, is headquartered there. Though not a giant by Du Pont/Dow standards, it has been doing business offshore since 1946, when an unplanned layover in Puerto Rico started the senior Mr. Buckman down that path. The midsized firm conducts business in no fewer than sixty-seven countries, including Japan, and several of its plants are overseas. Market penetration in several countries is higher than in the United States.

▶ American Family Life Assurance of Columbus, Georgia, is not one of the insurance giants. But in 1985, selling a specialized cancer policy, the firm did $350 million in business in Japan—more than it did in the United States. And then there's Materials Research Corporation of Orangeburg, New York. It just built its second plant. This one is outside the United States, in Oita, Japan. The company sells machines that coat and etch silicon chips to Japanese firms. Or take ServiceMaster (the cleaning contractor has fifteen major hospital contracts in Japan), Loctite (adhesives maker), and Molex (electrical connector manufacturer)—all of them setting the standards *in Japan*.

Consider more broadly the supposedly toughest market for Americans, laden with pernicious systemic as well as natural barriers—Japan. In the high-tech arena, IBM makes and sells computers worth more than $3 billion in Japan. The sales in Japan of Hewlett-Packard's Japanese subsidiary top $400 million, and grew at the rate of 27 percent per year from 1980 through 1984. Xerox, NCR, and Texas Instruments are also

American high-tech giants winning on Japanese soil; the latter's semi-conductor operations in Japan are equal in quality to the best Japanese producers.

But, you say, computers and such are international by nature—what about the most American of American firms? Well, how about 7-Eleven's 2,000 stores in Japan, doing more than $250 million in sales? How about McDonald's, which sells fast food worth $400 million in Japan, enough to worry the Japanese that its next generation might lose their skill with chopsticks?

Tupperware, Kentucky Fried Chicken, Coca-Cola, Schick, 3M, S. C. Johnson (Johnson Wax), Shaklee, Bristol-Myers, Polaroid, Otis Elevator, Franklin Mint, Baskin-Robbins, Medtronic, Quaker Oats, and Johnson & Johnson also star on the Japanese scene. Estimates vary about the totals. The Japanese Ministry of International Trade and Industry (MITI) estimated that 1,000 solely or substantially owned U.S. subsidiaries in Japan had revenues there of $55 billion in 1981. A more recent estimate pegs 1984 sales from the top 200 U.S. subsidiaries on Japanese soil alone at $44 billion. That is, it can be done. (Incidentally, none of these revenues from subsidiaries producing in Japan count in the trade balance. Those who carp about closed markets conveniently ignore the success stories I've just reviewed.)

Persist!

IBM, a strong believer in internationalism from its earliest days, began doing business in Japan in the 1920s, and put a manufacturing plant there in 1939, when the firm had less than $25 million in total revenues. T. J. Watson, modern IBM's founder, lived by the creed "World Peace Through World Trade." At times he may have overdone it; he was bitterly criticized, for instance, for sticking with his German trading partners almost until the United States entered World War II.

IBM has invested heavily and, more important, become a part of Japan's and Europe's insider network through the only magic that exists in international affairs of all sorts—persistence and patience. It has continuously modified products for offshore markets and done significant basic and applied research and engineering offshore. The most recent step-up of its commitment to Japan and Asia was moving its entire

155

Pacific Basin headquarters from Mt. Pleasant, New York, to Tokyo in 1984.

The rest of the success stories bear the same stamp. Edmund Fitzgerald, chairman of Northern Telecom, commented in 1986 on the supposedly uncrackable Japanese telecommunications market: "[This is] the first time in history that American-made digital central office switches will be moving into the core network of NTT [Nippon Telephone & Telegraph]. One of our initial advisors on that told us, 'You can do business with Nippon Telephone, but you must be patient and persistent.' That was the best advice we ever got. It took a lot of patience and a lot of persistence, but it was worth it." ROLM, as a small firm (before being acquired by IBM and gaining access to its deep pockets), succeeded in Japan—but only after senior officers made twenty-odd visits, just to conclude the first, tiny sale. Similarly, American Hospital Supply worked for five years to land its first, small order. Disney spent five years negotiating the licensing agreement for its Tokyo theme park. Coca-Cola, which today has a 60 percent share of the Japanese soft-drink market, also suffered a full decade of red ink.

A small forest products company from the Northwest, without the resources of Coke et al., is now spurting ahead in Japan. But it took four years of regular visitation on the part of senior managers to get a first, small, foot-in-the-door order. The opportunity finally came when another supplier, this one Japanese, couldn't react fast enough to meet its Japanese customer's need. The American firm was given insufficient time to do the impossible—but it did it, and soon a trickle of orders became a torrent.

Build Relationships/Learn the Culture

Relationship-building among senior executives is important to international business of all sorts, but uniquely so in Japan. American impatience militates against such a major investment of time. It's no coincidence that America's top international firms—e.g., IBM, Boeing, The Morgan—are also the masters of relationship-building in our domestic markets too.

Learning the culture is essential. This starts, by definition, with language skills, another arena of unique American ineptitude and arrogance, especially when it comes to Asia. Even today, only about 10,000

Americans are studying Japanese. Worse yet, that number is only 2,000 more than in 1973. In *Second to None: American Companies in Japan,* a study of over a thousand successful subsidiaries of United States firms operating in Japan, journalist Bob Christopher recalls a highly placed Japanese official remarking that he has never met a U.S. salesperson who speaks fluent Japanese. Nearly ninety percent of U.S. executives in Japan don't even bother to try to learn the language, according to one poll. And while you might get away with doing business in English in the office during the day, real business—after-hours relationship-building—is conducted almost exclusively in Japanese; furthermore, fewer than 1 percent of Japanese wholesalers, so essential to success, speak English. Christopher also attacks the short tenure, typically two to four years, of most U.S. executives who come to Japan. Such a brief sojourn, aborts any chance of becoming an "insider." More generally, Americans' insensitivity to other cultures is demonstrated by United Nations polls which report that among citizens of developing countries, Americans place last in empathy for foreign cultures.

Choose Partners Carefully/Master the Distribution System

Dealing with local customs and institutions on local terms is vital. Take Japan's distribution system. In America, 1.5 middlemen handle the average product between producer and ultimate consumer; in Japan, that number is 4.3. The labyrinth of Japanese distributors drives Americans and Europeans crazy. An illustration of the system's complexity: Mitsubishi's consumer electronics products are distributed in Japan through 26,000 separate franchisees, three and a half times the number of outlets McDonald's has in the United States, despite a Japanese population that is just half the size of ours. Christopher calls the system "bloated," "byzantine," and "nightmarish." Nevertheless, it is there; no amount of American haranguing about market openness will change it one whit. Schick's success (70 percent of the Japanese market for stainless-steel razor blades) resulted from a consistent distribution strategy focused on one powerful partner. Gillette, which dominates the U.S. market, designed a losing strategy in the same market: It involved more than 150 distributors; the fragmentation prevented Gillette from achieving a coherent image with retailers. Apple Computer committed a cardinal sin by making a deal with a powerful distributor, then going behind its back through other channels. Apple's penalty for violating the rules where relationships are so important was a 1 percent share of the 1.2-million-unit personal computer market in 1984, despite its head start.

Many accuse the Japanese of "not letting us into the system." While this is true in some cases, there is a difference between not being allowed in and not having the patience to learn even the distribution system, though it does seem a lifetime's occupation.

For small firm or large, choosing and working with partners is a necessity almost anywhere overseas, but especially in Japan. The form of the partnership can vary. Xerox teamed up with Fuji, and Kentucky Fried Chicken in Japan is 50 percent owned by Mitsubishi. Each gained instant credibility through the partnership. IBM, though, has always gone it alone in Japan, and there are lots of possible hybrid alternatives in between. In any case, deep study and thoughtfulness are required—and once more, characteristic American impatience is completely unacceptable. Numerous hastily formed partnerships, yielding short-term financial returns, have bombed in the long run, because time-consuming relationship-building was ignored. Partnership relations are no substitute for continuous attention.

Decentralize

A decentralized organizational structure is required. Harvard's Raymond Vernon spoke frankly about our problems in a 1980 *Harvard Business Review* article. After large U.S. firms met with early success overseas, many rescinded the initial decentralization which had contributed in unseen ways to that success:

> Several factors explain the American propensity for one-way transmission [U.S. to overseas] multinational networks. Most important, [the bulk of] subsidiaries were created during a period in which U.S.-based companies characteristically had a technological lead over their competitors, generating and selling products that would represent the market of the future. As long as U.S. companies were secure in their innovative leads, there was no great need to use foreign subsidiaries as listening posts.
>
> A second factor has been the premature obliteration of international divisions in many U.S. companies. As the foreign interests of

American companies grew and flourished in the postwar period, the international divisions were often the star performers. But their success was eventually their undoing. By the middle 1960s, one American company after another reorganized itself to acknowledge the increased importance of its foreign business. According to one study undertaken in the early 1970s, the typical pattern consisted of abolishing the international division and setting up a series of so-called global product divisions to do the worrying about foreign products.

In a recent study covering a group of 57 large U.S.-based multinationals a colleague and I ran into some disturbing indications suggesting that some of these reorganizations may have been wildly counterproductive. A subset of our sample, organized along global product lines, exhibited rather striking characteristics. This group of companies seemed to show decidedly less interest in its foreign operations than those with an international division. Ten years after they had introduced their new products into the United States, the global product companies were only producing about 50 percent of their products in overseas locations. By contrast, the other companies in the sample were manufacturing more than 80 percent of their new products in foreign plants. . . .

Some companies have recognized the danger in the newer organizational form and are returning to the old way of doing things. A prime example is Westinghouse, which went from an international to a global product division and back to an international division again.

Tailor the Product or Service to Local Tastes

Finally, there's the issue of the product itself—it must be of high quality and suit local tastes and requirements. In general, given the worldwide economic recovery of the last thirty years and true globalization of the sort described by Walter Wriston, our ability to dominate through technology alone has all but disappeared. No one can succeed now except via value-added differentiation, especially on the basis of quality and service, and these have not been strong suits of the United States in the past. They must become so, but nowhere more than in

159

Europe and Japan, the world's most finicky customers when it comes to quality.

Closely related is the issue of tailoring products or services to suit customers' needs (or whims). In the easy post–World War II days, we pushed products overseas when they started to decline at home, milking them for all they were worth. Today, there usually must be substantial customizing—or even new products designed for foreign markets. Coca-Cola took the lime taste out of Sprite to cater to Japanese tastes. Kodak changed its film to adapt to Japanese notions of attractive skin tones, and also altered its graphic arts products, because most space-starved Japanese professionals don't have darkrooms.

Of course, nothing is cut-and-dried. Tupperware was told that Japanese women don't throw home parties, but it persisted and found that the party formula was uniquely suited to the norms of Japanese social intercourse. Analogously, Disney was successful even though it insisted upon maintaining its squeaky-clean image and thus ignored the Japanese convention of selling sake at recreation parks. Coca-Cola also bucked convention at least once with advertisements that featured drinking out of the bottle U.S.-style, inadvertently starting a craze labeled "drinking bugle style" (from the billboard picture of people drinking from an inverted Coke bottle). Thus, you can overdo "Japanizing" or tailoring to any nation's habits, thereby throwing away the product uniqueness that may be your primary advantage. On balance, though, I and most experts strongly come down on the side of modifying the product to suit the market.

There is a raging debate over the issue of global brands. Global-brand advocates, not the least of whom are the new monster ad agencies resulting from the recent wave of mergers, tout the power of a global image. I acknowledge their viewpoint, but my evidence weighs in strongly on the side of decentralized operations and at least some nation-by-nation product tailoring in nine cases out of ten.

Pizza Hut, for example, is known around the world—in large measure because of its flexibility, catering to the tastes of different countries. In Japan, that means squid toppings. In Mexico, jalapeños are a favorite. In Korea, it means no salt.

The stories of foul-ups—due to faulty tailoring—are numerous, and often amusing (if you're not involved). When Coca-Cola moved into China, it chose Chinese characters for its signs that sounded like "Coca-

Cola." Unfortunately, after thousands of signs went up the company discovered that the characters meant "Bites the Wax Cowboy." Coke went back to the drawing board, sorted through hundreds of additional characters, and came up with a set that had an appropriate sound, and when translated became "Makes the Mouth Rejoice." It was an important improvement—as sales increases subsequently confirmed.

"MADE IN THE U.S.A." FOR EXPORT

One Who Got It Right

Eighty miles north of Indianapolis you exit I-69 and head into Van Buren, Indiana, population 1500. Headquartered there is Weaver Popcorn, holder of sixty percent of the Japanese popcorn market.

Weaver's 59-year-old tradition is quality. Nobody does it better in the United States. Their prowess in plant genetics is well known, and they've unquestionably set the standard for excellence in this specialized industry.

With a towering reputation, and a rare American exhibition of patience (a lot of visits that others would have called fruitless), Weaver earned a few small orders in Japan.

They sallied forth with their very best, America's finest, and were rebuffed. The reason—a blow to the corporate ego: the quality wasn't right. Rather than take a few random teacup-size samples, the Japanese had hand-inspected hundreds of pounds of the popcorn—and found impurities.

Aha, you say—yet another example of Japan's closed minds and markets. But Weaver was challenged, not insulted, by the rejection. This modest-size company recalled the entire order, shelling out a substantial $65,000 without flinching. Employees were chagrined—and the Japanese were impressed. "You reacted to that problem the way a Japanese company would have," said one to Weaver's man in Japan.

Weaver did not stop there. Uniquely advanced optical inspection equipment, which cost over a half-million dollars was ordered and installed to meet Japan's standards. It was not required for the U.S. or European market that constituted the vast majority of Weaver's sales. But the smallish Weaver did it anyway—and quickly grabbed the lion's share of the Japanese market.

Many Others Who Get It Wrong

The pathetic tales of our attempts to foist nonmetric measurement, left-hand-drive cars and refrigerators as big as houses on the Japanese are too horrid to recount in greater detail. Sadly, such fiascos are anything but behind us, in products high-tech and low-, in countries from Japan to Ireland.

In *Trade War,* Steven Schlossstein, who spent six years in Japan with The Morgan, recalls a conversation with Kakimizu Koichi, executive director of Japan's Overseas Economic Cooperation Fund:

> "The Americans still talk about market access," he said, warming up. "As if Japan is still closed to the outside world, like it was over a century ago under the Tokugawas. But they forget, or do not understand, the problems that are unique to Japan. May I give you one example?"
>
> "Please," I said.
>
> He shifted his erect posture slightly and closed his eyes as he called the details into memory. "As you know, our islands sit on a deep geologic fault, and we are susceptible to severe earthquakes. Everyone remembers how Tokyo was destroyed in 1923, but we get tremors in Japan almost every day. What does that suggest to you?"
>
> "Safety in building design?" I said.
>
> "And safety in product design," he added. "The Japanese government specifies very strict standards in product design because of that fact. Like space heaters. Japanese homes and apartments do not have central heating, so we use small kerosene heaters. If they topple over during an earthquake, the fire hazard is great."
>
> He gestured dramatically with his hands, throwing them up in the air, simulating an explosion.
>
> "So when foreigners want to sell space heaters in Japan, they must conform to our standards," he said. "The Swedes make very good kerosene heaters, engineered even more stringently than we require. In all simulated tremor tests, they never tip over. They are superbly designed. The Americans, on the other hand, simply package their domestic space heaters and ship them to Japan. Now, which do you think we will approve for sale in our market?"
>
> I shook my head. "No contest," I replied. That was easy.

"So attention to precision and detail is essential if a foreign manufacturer wants to be successful in this market. Let me show you something." He reached into a drawer and withdrew a plastic picture album. Instead of vacation snapshots, it was filled with banknotes. "I used to collect foreign money when I was at the Ministry," he said. "Look at this yen note."

He handed me a standard 500-yen bill. There was Prince Itoh Hirobumi, a Meiji oligarch, with that familiar two-dollar look. I tried to make the leap from the earthquake-induced kerosene heater fires to pocket money. That was not so easy.

"Look at the white borders," he said, "how even and exact they are, on all four sides. Notice the *precision.*"

I noticed. For the first time. Who ever pays attention to the borders on greenbacks? He pulled out a handful of various yen notes. They all had identical borders and were, indeed, precise. Then he laid down some American bills. George Washington and Ben Franklin were not surrounded by a force field of identical white borders. The borders were uneven, crude by comparison.

The implication was obvious.

If our federal government was so sloppy when it made its own national currency, how could the Japanese expect American companies to be any better when they produced manufactured goods for export?

Sad to say, my partner Ian Thomson, an accountant, and I replicated Koichi's experiment. After I told Ian the story we both pulled out five-dollar bills. Sure enough, the borders varied on each bill, and between the two.

Many U.S. firms had great initial success exporting their products after World War II, when other countries' industries were flattened and few alternatives to American imports existed. We didn't have to work very hard, be very patient, or emphasize relationships—others were begging for our goods, regardless of design flaws, questionable quality, or our indifference to their culture. Not so today. Today "learn and listen" and "earn your way in" will be the only keys to lasting success. But thanks to such factors as opening financial markets, those American companies of any size and in any industry that will make the patient investment required will find boundless opportunities.

A Last, and Revealing, Case from Boeing

Perhaps a single, almost inadvertent statement captured the sense of the challenge—and the opportunity—for me. My luncheon partner was the head of helicopter operations at that masterful internationalist, Boeing. We were talking about selling capital goods overseas. "Well," he said casually, "as a rule of thumb, I expect one of my people to put in about sixty hours of specific homework to prepare for an average twenty-minute meeting with a middle-level government or industry official." That's preparation! And it is in addition to the wide experience Boeing requires of its overseas people. It is exactly such standard operating procedures which are the "secrets" of overseas commercial success, from Bahrain to Seoul—precisely the "secrets" that appear to elude so many U.S. pretenders (honorable but impatient) in the world of international markets.

Reprise

The customer responsiveness prescriptions feature the Five Value-Adding Strategies, of which this is one. That is, becoming an internationalist, regardless of firm size or product maturity, ranks on my list with the provision of superior quality and service.

This prescription is among a large set of ideas that have moved from the "nice to do" to the "must do" category. I cannot overemphasize the need for the average firm to "think (and do) international." Isolation is dead, like it or not, and regardless of any vagaries of Washington's trade policies over the next few years.

At the very least, every firm will be dealing with foreigners as suppliers (of subcomponents, for instance). Being oriented toward the markets and habits of others is a necessary defensive tactic (competitors will be doing so) as well as an extraordinary opportunity for the producer of top-quality products and services.

FIRST STEPS

1. Every $2 million firm, in service or manufacturing, has international potential. Start thinking about it early. The big-firm equiva-

lent: If you're $25 million or larger, and not doing 25 percent of your business overseas, and at least a little bit in Japan, you are avoiding today's realities and opportunities, and you risk being out of touch in general.

2. How to start: Spend time. Listen. Visit, only half purposefully at first. Make friends. Keep cool. Be patient. If you're not prepared to spend six weeks a year overseas, don't bother to start. Caution: If your first proposed product or service offering is not substantially tailored to meet the foreign market's needs—packaging, colors, instruction manual, vagaries of distribution, let alone basic function—odds are you're headed for a discouraging setback.

C-6

SUMMARY

As market fragmentation accelerates, we must:

▶ Strive more valiantly than ever to achieve uniqueness, as an organization, in the customer's mind.

▶ Get to the point where everyone in the organization can understand and state its uniqueness (strategic distinction in the marketplace).

Being unique—standing out from the growing crowd of competitors, products, and services—is an essential for survival. Such uniqueness, to be implemented, must be understood and lived by everyone in the organization. While niche-market-oriented, higher-value-added strategies are increasingly the winning hand, low-cost producers can be successful. On the other hand, an "in between" or "stuck in the middle"—i.e., not unique—strategy is unfailingly disastrous.

Can you state your "uniqueness" in twenty-five words or less? Test the level of agreement, randomly and regularly, with new and long-term employees—and with suppliers, distributors, and customers. Is your uniqueness, as practiced day to day, clear to all of these participants in your business?

C-6

Create Uniqueness

Sorting things out, for consumers of personal or industrial goods, is increasingly difficult. Markets are fragmenting. Customer choices are exploding. The strategy for success, spelled out in C-1, is differentiation and niche-market creation. But that is a product or service strategy. There is a larger question: How is the firm (or a division) positioned in the customer's mind? Sure, the ABC Company makes a terrific widget for the narrow XYZ market. But what do consumers most generally think about when they consider buying any of ABC's products? The answer to that question will determine more of your long-term success in a chaotic marketplace than any specific choice about positioning a specific service or product for a specific niche.

DON'T GET STUCK IN THE MIDDLE

I found myself nodding continuously as Mike Kami, a respected consultant on corporate strategy, stormed back and forth on the stage in front of an audience of 2,000 people from Hardee's, the restaurant chain. In a one-hour presentation, he probably used the word "uniqueness" at least thirty times. He'd shout, "What's so special about your company?" "How are you *different* from your competitors?" "Ex-act-ly how?" "What is your *uniqueness in the marketplace?*"

A 1985 *Forbes* article criticized the strategy of Federated Stores, suggesting that their approach lacked clarity. By contrast, *Forbes* applauded Federated's rival Dayton-Hudson, which is deemphasizing investment in its traditional department stores (and other off-the-main-line activities) and directing most of its energy at the relatively narrow retail segment represented by its Mervyn's and Target divisions. "The point about Dayton-Hudson's strategy," said *Forbes,* ". . . is not which segment of retailing they chose, but that they chose one." In other words, don't just stand there, be something.

Sometimes a firm loses its uniqueness. Sears lived by the slogan "Quality at a good price" for decades. In the seventies its retailing strategy became confused. Customers wondered, was it the old Sears? Or, as some of the company's activities suggested, was it becoming an upscale outfit? The customers gave Sears an unequivocal answer. As one retail executive put it: "Those who saw Sears as K Mart shopped at K Mart. Those who thought it was Macy's shopped at Macy's." Spotty retailing results, except for white goods, continue to plague the giant firm.

Substantial analytic evidence supports the importance of uniqueness in the marketplace. Strategy expert Michael Porter of Harvard contends that there are only three successful generic strategies: (1) "overall cost leadership," (2) "differentiation" (by which he means leadership in quality or service or innovation across a broadly defined market), and (3) "focus" (a niche strategy). Porter concludes:

> The three generic strategies are alternative, viable approaches to dealing with . . . competitive forces. . . . Sometimes the firm can successfully pursue more than one approach as its primary target, though this is rarely possible. . . . *Effectively implementing any of these generic strategies usually requires total commitment, and organizational arrangements are diluted if there's more than one primary target* [my emphasis]. . . . The firm failing to develop its strategy in at least one of the three directions—a firm that is "stuck in the middle"—is in an extremely poor strategic situation. The firm lacks the market share, capital investment, and resolve to play the low-cost game, the industry-wide differentiation necessary to obviate the need for a low-cost position, or the focus to create differentiation or low cost in a more limited sphere. The firm stuck in the middle is almost guaranteed low profitability. It either loses the high-volume customers who demand low prices or must bid away its profits to get this business away from low-cost firms. Yet it also loses high-margin businesses—the cream—to the firms who are focused on high-margin targets or have achieved differentiation overall. The firm stuck in the middle also probably suffers from a blurred corporate culture and a conflicting set of organizational arrangements and motivation system.

That doesn't leave much. Figure 9, adapted from Porter's *Competitive Strategy,* summarizes this point.

Empirical tests of Porter's thesis have confirmed its validity. A 1985 study, reported in the *Journal of Business Venturing,* produced dramatic results. Not surprisingly, firms classified as having "high relative quality, low relative price" led the pack with a 36 percent return on investment. However, those that rated "high on relative quality, [but also] high in relative price" fared almost as well—a 34 percent return on investment. Acceptable profitability also marked the opposite, or low-cost, outcome: Firms with "low relative quality, low relative price" had a return of 15 percent. The poorest performers by far were those stuck in the middle: The firms categorized as "middle relative quality, middle relative price" managed only a 2 percent return on investment.

This supports Porter's view—with an important modification, consistent with prescriptions C-1 through C-4. While Porter doesn't distinguish between the payoffs of low-cost and high-differentiation strategies (look at the end points of the curve in Figure 9), the study (see the details in Figure 10) decisively demonstrates that the high-differentiation strategy is more profitable. The study does strongly support the U shape of Porter's curve. However, the high-quality/high-price "end" of the curve tops the low-quality/low-price "end" by more than a two-to-one margin, 34 percent versus 15 percent.

But this analysis still fails to deal with my greatest concern: Even if

Figure 9

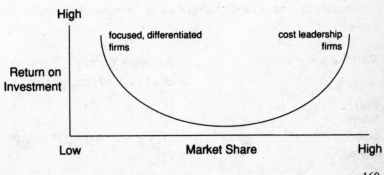

the low-price/cost, low-quality strategy is somewhat profitable, it does not appear to be sustainable. Recall the discussion in C-2 about the revision of the PIMS findings, from an emphasis on the positive relationship between market share and profit to an emphasis on sustainable market share, which is driven by high relative quality. Also see *A Passion for Excellence* for an extensive discussion of this point.

Further strong corroboration of the risk of the "in-between" or "stuck-in-the-middle" strategy comes from Dr. John Groocock's analysis of TRW, using the PIMS methodology and referred to in prescription C-2. Recall that the top third of TRW's divisions, rated on the basis of customers' perception of quality, outperformed the bottom third by three to one. In C-2 I did not report on the middle third of TRW's divisions; it turns out that these fifteen of TRW's forty-seven divisions fared far worse financially than those rated lowest. The middle third on relative quality had a 1.4 percent return on sales (compared with 2.9 percent for the bottom third and 7.7 percent for the top third) and a 5.1 percent return on assets employed (compared with 8.9 percent for the bottom third and 26.6 percent for the top third).

The study has grave implications when one looks beneath the surface. The top third in Groocock's study charged premium prices, and the product or service was usually rated "best in class." The bottom third had average quality, and was marked by a price discount. The poorly performing middle third had above-average prices and quality that was usually tied for first (Groocock calls it "joint best"). That U-shaped curve is very sensitive indeed. To take advantage of the high-differentiation/high-quality strategy, the Groocock evidence suggests, the firm/product must be perceived by customers as noticeably better, not merely

Figure 10: **Return on Investment as a Function of Quality and Price**

Relative Price	Relative Quality			
	Low	Medium	High	Average
High	17	18	34	23
Medium	9	2	16	9
Low	15	11	36	21
Average	14	10	29	17

"among the better" performers. Thence Kami's favorite word—uniqueness.

Yet another corroborating study, this one by economist William Hall, focused exclusively on mature industries. The "straddle" strategy, as he called it, proved deadly once again. Only those achieving "lowest delivered cost relative to competition coupled with an acceptable delivered quality" and those achieving "the highest product/service/quality differentials position" thrived.

The implications we can draw from these empirical tests actually square with common sense. As one seminar participant put it: "It's simple, when you think about it. The average consumer doesn't go to the yellow pages and say, 'Where can I find a product with an average number of defects at an average price?' You either want something great, and you'll pay for it. Or if you don't care excessively about the quality [or can't afford it], you want it as cheap as possible."

True as that statement has doubtless always been, it is more true than ever today. With an explosion of products and competitors, the consumer, individual or commercial, is overwhelmed by choices. Your distinction had best stand out—unequivocally.

I'm reminded of a first-rate radio ad from the stellar computer dealer, BusinessLand. A clock ticked loudly. After a few seconds an announcer came on with a message like this: "Seven seconds have passed. Somewhere, yet another software program has been introduced. BusinessLand is the expert at sorting through this jungle and giving you the most professional advice concerning the bewildering and exploding array of options out there." And, indeed, BusinessLand's profitable uniqueness is that (1) it does just that and, more important, (2) it is widely seen by customers as doing it better than anyone else.

UNIQUENESS REQUIRES CONSENSUS, NOT PERFECTION

The uniqueness idea, then, has sound analytic, anecdotal, and common-sense underpinnings. But what does it mean on a day-to-day basis? "How unique?" and "Whose definition?" are among the important questions.

Years ago, my friend Allan Kennedy, co-author of *Corporate Cultures,* and I had a lively discussion about how precise a corporate strategy has to be. Our conclusion: It must be "not wrong" and be widely "bought into" by everyone in the organization. That is, the "perfect" strategy, designed by corporate planners and altered annually in accord with minute shifts in market conditions (low cost this year, high quality the next), is worth little or nothing if it is not widely understood, accepted, and the basis for daily action throughout the firm. The fact that the team at the top supports the strategy is far less important than that the people on the loading dock support it—at 2 A.M., when no supervisor, let alone a vice-president, is around. In *Leaders,* by Warren Bennis and Burt Nanus, an exemplary chief executive makes the same point: "Leadership is heading into the wind with such knowledge of oneself and collaborative energy as to move others to wish to follow. *The angle into the wind is less important than choosing one and sticking reasonably to it.*"

So what is your organization's "uniqueness" as perceived by the marketplace? Can you state it in twenty-five words or less? Is the strategy statement printed on wallet-size cards that are given to everyone? Is it immortalized in granite—as grocer Stew Leonard's is? Leonard used to have his philosophy displayed on the store's wall—"Rule #1: The customer is always right. Rule #2: If the customer is wrong, see Rule #1." In late 1985, he went a step further, obtaining a three-ton chunk of granite and embedding it in concrete at the store's front entrance. The two rules were chiseled into the stone. Much of Leonard's reason for planting this heavy reminder is to discipline himself and the organization: "Every time a customer walks by it, they are reminded that that's how they should judge us. We'd better live up to it. There's no place to hide."

Make Uniqueness Everyone's Business

More important, would *everyone* in the organization choose roughly the same twenty-five words you chose to describe your uniqueness? The dirtiest of several tricks we sometimes play at our seminars is this: We ask each participant, "Sometime before you leave here, please call a person, at entry level, who has been on your payroll for no more than ten working days. Ask her or him to define your 'uniqueness' in twenty-five words or less. [When we're really feeling snippy, we sometimes ask for fifteen or even ten words.] If that person doesn't use virtually the same words you use, then, we contend, you have no strategy!" By that time you can hear a pin drop.

But our challenge is precisely the point. If the new receptionist doesn't understand, within hours of signing on, that you aim to be nothing less than "the most responsive temporary service agency for paralegal and paramedical needs in the Greater Milwaukee Area," you are in trouble, or at least in grave danger of not living up to your grand design.

There is much more to be said, and I will do so in the sections on people and leadership (principally L-2). But it cannot be said often enough that the deeper issue is not an ability to repeat the words (though it's a start, and most fall short even at this level), but psychological "buy-in" and commitment.

In a *Sporting News* article on the top coaches in the National Basketball Association, Coach Doug Moe of the Denver Nuggets commented, "You have to make your players believe that you believe in whatever you're doing. It doesn't matter what the style is, as long as you believe in it." While I've suggested here that the dimensions of uniqueness do matter (e.g., don't get stuck in the middle), Moe's point remains valid. Many of the people and leadership prescriptions will deal with the attributes of leadership, followership, values, and commitment which turn the stated uniqueness into a powerful driving force. That is, in summary, your statement of "what we are" has to be (1) roughly right, (2) enduring, (3) succinct, (4) memorable, (5) believable, and (6) energizing to all.

THE PRACTICAL VALUE OF UNIQUENESS

Suppliers, distributors, and customers must be in tune with your twenty-five-word statement of distinction if you are to realize the full power of your uniqueness. The one- or two-word idea or image customers have of Maytag ("Old Lonely"), Federal Express ("Absolutely, Positively, Overnight"), or Nordstrom ("No Problem at Nordstrom") is worth billions to each firm. The new three-person temporary service agency thrives or not exactly in proportion to the spread of a consistent word-of-mouth image about its uniqueness.

Suppliers have a book on your uniqueness too. No supplier tries to pull a fast one on Milliken when it comes to quality of material. If you want

Milliken's business, you know in advance that outrageous quality standards, raised each year, await you; but you also know that if you can meet those stringent standards, a lifelong relationship, perhaps as Milliken's sole source, is yours. The value to Milliken is contained in the fact that the best suppliers, knowing Milliken's uniqueness, seek it out, and are honored to have its business.

The power of this idea cannot be overstated. Mike Kami is right to rant and rave about uniqueness. From a market perspective, there are better and worse generic strategies; but above all, the numbers decisively demonstrate that mixed strategies are disastrous. And the internal value of uniqueness as a source of empowerment is the basis for that market value. If we've all learned one thing in the last decade, it's that brilliant execution is more important than a brilliant strategy. And the *sine qua non* of brilliant execution is that (1) everyone knows which way the boat is heading, (2) the course is being consistently steered, and (3) the route is an exciting one, worthy of enlistment.

PUBLIC PARALLELS

Cities are competing for employers, and are often trying to revitalize the urban core. The idea of "what's special" about Colorado Springs, or Columbus, Ohio, is decisive in determining the city's future. Likewise, the value of the empowerment of every employee—in the police department, or at P.S. 29—also derives from a feeling of uniqueness.

FIRST STEPS

Informally poll your customers (citizens, patients, commercial consumers), suppliers, and distributors. Then poll your manager colleagues, in the city planning department, the distribution center, the executive suite. Is there strong or weak agreement as to your organization's uniqueness? If it's weak (or an "in-between" strategy), put this issue at the top of your agenda, far ahead of budget preparation or strategy formulation; these latter two activities are, after all, no more than reflections of your effort to achieve uniqueness.

C-7

SUMMARY

To execute strategies C-1 through C-6, several Capability Building Blocks are essential. First, we must:

▶ Become "transparent" to (that is, listen to) customers—end users, reps, distributors, franchisees, retailers, suppliers. Listen frequently. Listen systematically—and unsystematically. Listen for facts—and for perceptions. Listen "naïvely." Use as many listening techniques as we can conjure up.

▶ Make sure that field input from those closest to the customer (e.g., sales/service/stores) gets a thorough hearing with engineers/designers/buyers—without distortion, and with immediate follow-up. (Most new product ideas are "out there," in customers' minds and practical needs, waiting for *someone* to listen—and act.)

▶ Ensure that our CIS (customer information system) is as rich and substantial—and as much discussed—as our typically inward-oriented MIS (management information system).

Listening to customers *must* become everyone's business. With most competitors moving ever faster, the race will go to those who listen (and respond) most intently.

Marketers should be in the field at least 25 percent and preferably 50 percent of the time. *Everyone* should make several customer visits per year. Add at least one new, "naïve" customer listening device to your department's repertoire (regardless of the department) each 60 days.

C-7

Become Obsessed with Listening

You can see a lot by observing.

Yogi Berra

Re "Why the Bounce at Rubbermaid?": I plan to wrap copies of your article around bricks and throw them through the office windows of selected MBA brand managers I've met. These are the guys and gals who don't believe any research results unless they're based on a sample of 10,000 questionnaires.

Now here's Mr. Gault [Rubbermaid's CEO] actually *talking* to his customers to find out how to improve his products. . . . What will American business think of next? This kind of interactive market research is said to be common practice in Japan, but many of our managers simply assume that they know—and know better than—their customers. The message on my brick will read, "Get out of your office and *meet* your buyers!"

Allyn Thompson
Letter to the Editor
Fortune, May 1987

Prescriptions C-1 through C-6 constitute the basic value-adding strategies necessary to deal with today's chaotic environment. The remainder of the prescriptions in this book deal with "how to get there from here," beginning, in this customer responsiveness section, with the first of the Capability Building Blocks.

First among equals is listening to customers, with an ear to their practical, application-oriented needs. "Listening," like so many of these apparently simple ideas, turns out to be anything but simple. Since it must be practiced if we are to survive, it will become a mindset and a way of life for everyone—or else.

Yes, even listening has changed; or, rather, must change. To be sure, traditional modalities of market research remain important. If you are launching a new line of widgets, at some stage sizable numbers of people must be brought into a room and hooked up to galvanic skin response (GSR) detectors—that is, electrodes—to get their reactions to tastes or bag colors.

But, first, even this traditional mode of market research is being drastically altered. New computer simulation models allow you to do much more with much less data, much faster. Additionally, given the widespread availability of data bases together with a host of supporting software to allow clever interpretation of what's in them, data analysis that just a few years ago only a P&G could do and pay for is now possible for small firms as well.

Even that, however, is not the real point. More important is that with product life cycles shrinking, you've got to get whiffs of new trends earlier. Moreover, everyone needs to get in on the act. The organization prepared to move fast is the listening-intense organization—not only in sales and marketing, but in engineering and manufacturing and even (see C-4) management information systems (MIS).

Most are not ready, especially the big firms. The P&Gs of the world are victims of listening that is too methodical; by the time it's done, someone else may well have stolen the market. A few of the giants (P&G itself, Campbell, Frito-Lay) are moving to address such problems through reorganizations to get closer to the market (see C-4) and through team-based product development (see I-2).

The science and engineering-driven firms are beset by worse woes: (1) an arrogance born of success in a less competitive world, and (2) an American penchant for separating the "science types" from the translators—both the sales and marketing groups and the manufacturers (see C-8, I-3). Allied-Signal's chief planner, Lee Rivers, laments, "The U.S. does more basic research than anyone else. But other people have found more effective ways to turn [U.S.-born] scientific knowledge into products, goods, and services." Those other ways, practiced especially well by the Japanese, are led by listening, always with an ear toward application. *Industry Week,* in May 1987, reported on the U.S. problem: "Take ceramics, for example, which many see as a key material for the future. While U.S. firms have set a research target of reducing the grain size of the ceramic powder, the Japanese approach has been to start at the applications stage, says advanced-materials expert Michael Eckstut at Booz, Allen & Hamilton Inc. Japanese ceramic companies work with automakers to develop useful products, he notes. 'The Japanese know that what is important to the end customer is not grain size or [process] characteristics, but a product that can withstand so many degrees for 50 hours, or something you can bang on 50 times a day. That is the technology leverage, not the grain size.' So while the U.S. outspends Japan in ceramics research, the Japanese are spending where they're more likely to get results. That's one reason Japan is faster at getting ideas to the market."

An ear for application—at Campbell Soup or Allied-Signal or Ben & Jerry's Ice Cream of Waterbury, Vermont—is an ear constantly close to the market. It's as simple, and as fundamental, as that.

WHAT IT MEANS TO REALLY LISTEN: THREE CASES

David-Edward Limited

June 13, 1985

Dear Mr. Peters,

As a manufacturer of a high-quality upholstered furniture line for the contract market, we are dependent upon design specifications generated by interior designers that we define as our customers. Like most manufacturers in our field, we have usually designed our product, our policies and our procedures and then promoted them to those people. . . .

I decided to bring together a group of 12 prominent designers in our area and ask their opinions, not of our company specifically, but of our industry in general. I . . . encourag[ed] them to talk to me

179

about their requirements, both practical and psychological. The first pilot meeting was extremely successful. . . .

With the success of the first meeting, we organized what I called the David-Edward Listening Tour. Between December 15th and April 15th, I visited 27 cities in the U.S. In each case, we invited a dozen or so prestigious designers to meet with me for two hours over breakfast. . . .

We recorded all of the sessions and I sent abstracts of these recordings to all participants. The information we received has been invaluable. We have modified products, programs, policies, and procedures to provide what our customers say they really need. . . .

Our representatives are predicting a 25 to 45 percent [sales] increase over the next six months. In addition, we were also able to reach a different audience than the one we call on in true sales calls. We got the really hard-to-see people to see us. Interesting that they wouldn't give me 15 minutes to listen to me in their offices, but would allow me two hours in my hotel if I would listen to them.

Finally, we are now perceived as an industry leader, as a firm which cares, and then does something about what we hear. A story will be written about us in an up-coming issue of our most prestigious trade magazine and our competitors are wondering how to compete with a nonrepeatable psychological coup.

> Sincerely,
> Philip C. Cooper, President
> David-Edward Limited
> Baltimore, Maryland

Pacific Presbyterian Medical Center

Robin Orr administers the thirteen-bed Planetree Model Hospital Project at San Francisco's Pacific Presbyterian Medical Center. The typical counter between the nurses and patients was the first thing to go at Planetree. The formal medical records are always open to the patient; moreover, he or she and the family are vigorously encouraged to write comments on the record. Patients are also urged to question a doctor's decision to prescribe any drug.

Interaction is further facilitated by medical library privileges and the suggestion that patients should read up on such things as their ailment, drugs, and drug side effects. The nursing arrangement provides another listening (and involvement) post. One nurse has overall responsibility for coordinating the patient's care throughout the hospital stay and afterwards. Working with the coordinating nurse, he or she makes joint decisions about every aspect of the stay and treatment. And there's a patient advocate nurse who irons out any miscommunications between doctors, nurses, and the patient—interceding long before a minor irritant festers into a full-blown problem.

Dr. Philip Lee, president of the San Francisco Health Commission (not associated with Pacific Presbyterian), says, "When patients understand the nature of their treatment, and understand how to best work with their health-care team, there is clear evidence that shows hospital stays shorten [some studies indicate a major reduction], and returns to the hospital are far less frequent."

Patients and their families rave about the program. Initially skeptical doctors are signing up in droves to take part. Orr is invited to speak about the program at meetings in cities from Dallas to Helsinki. Others are undertaking pilot projects similar to Pacific Presbyterian's. And cost per day (over and above the benefits of shorter stays and fewer repeat visits) runs no more than standard care.

The Lutheran Parish at Bendersville

Dan Biles calls the pulpit a lousy listening post. He's minister of the Lutheran parish in Bendersville, Pennsylvania (population 500). When he arrived in 1985, he astonished the local people with what he calls Ministry by Wandering Around, by being the first minister in over *twenty years* to stop by the corner coffee shop to sit down and have coffee with the local farmers in what he describes as a "one-intersection town." He concludes: "Nobody had ever thought to do something that simple—at least not for a long time. By stopping at the coffee shop, I build relationships. . . . It makes the church more visible also. It's the kiss of death for a minister to stay in his office. . . . A lot of pastors and synod staff people ought to be spending 80 percent of their time out of their office doing MBWA." Dan Biles also visits every parishioner's home at least once a year—he observes that people speak more freely on their home turf. Incidentally, attendance at Sunday services quickly shot up by 25 percent.

CHARACTERISTICS OF GOOD CUSTOMER LISTENING

After years of dealing with managers beset by turbulent conditions, my correspondence from police chiefs, mayors, school principals, hospital administrators and businesspersons occupies many a file cabinet. The most moving letters by far are the hundreds about "simple listening." In fact, if I had a file labeled "religious conversion"—that is, correspondence from those whose management practices have truly been transformed—I suspect that 50 percent of its contents would deal with just one, narrow topic: going out anew, with a "naïve" mind-set, and listening to customers. (Another 25 or so percent would be from managers who had done the same thing with their people—another version of "naïve" listening—see P-3 and L-5.)

Let's return to Philip Cooper, Robin Orr, and Dan Biles. To begin with, good listeners get out from behind the desk to where the customers are. In Cooper's case, the president of a $6 million firm visited twenty-seven cities in six months to engage in face-to-face customer contact. In Orr's situation, it was not just getting out from behind the desk, but getting rid of the desk—or clinic counter, to be precise. With Biles, the corner coffee shop was an important adjunct to the elevated pulpit.

Further, good listeners construct settings so as to maximize "naïve" listening, the undistorted sort. Cooper went one-on-twelve: one of him and a dozen of "them." He begged them to talk; he came with no slick presentation. Orr has a coordinator who is specifically charged to listen as well as a passive listening device (the chart that is to be written on), and she also provides education so that the patient will be prepared to ask wisely. Biles's frequent, leisurely, low-pressure visits to the coffee shop and parishioners' homes are a clear sign of his intent to listen, not preach—in his case, literally.

Finally, good listeners provide quick feedback and act on what they hear. Cooper sent abstracts of the talks (proof of listening, if you will) to the participants. And his company acted in short order to change a host of things on the basis of what was heard. At Planetree, the feedback is the nurses' and doctors' willingness to consider patient input in all decision making.

Don't you just wonder why no other minister bothered to hang out at the coffee shop in twenty years? I would, if that file I mentioned weren't so thick. Now I just shake my head when another letter comes in: "Dear Tom: I visited our four far west offices for the first time in five years. You wouldn't believe . . ." "Dear Tom: My ready mix [concrete] plant manager used to tell me he couldn't fit this or that into his schedule. Whenever he'd do so, I'd plop him in my truck and take him out to the customer, so he could explain face to face why he couldn't help the guy. You'd be amazed . . ." "Dear Tom: Whenever there's a customer problem, of any magnitude, we now take along an operations center person on the customer call. Their eyes really open when they hear the customer describe the consequences of what looked like a little thing to them."

So listening means: (1) hanging out (on their turf), (2) listening naïvely (comments on the patient's chart) and with intensity, and (3) providing fast feedback and taking action.

Listening with Intensity

Consider giving out home phone numbers. One division of Trus Joist, a $200 million high-technology forest products firm, has several thousand customers. A year or so ago, it sent each one a "Customer Service Card." It looks and feels like a credit card and the graphics are attractive. It prominently displays the division's toll-free customer-hot-line number. An equally well-done plastic insert for the customer's Rolodex accompanied it. Good enough, but there's more. On the back of the card and the Rolodex insert are ten home phone numbers—the division general manager, the national marketing manager, the product applications engineer, the division controller, the three plant managers in Oregon and Louisiana, and the customer service manager from each of those plants. (The general manager reports heavy use of the toll-free number—but no home phone calls.)

How about a "high roller" contest? That is, turn the tables and instead of honoring cost-cutting, honor spending—money and time in support of customer listening. Why not give an award to the factory manager who has logged the most miles and the biggest phone bill on customer calls and visits. Do the same thing among staff vice-presidents, distributors, center managers, and marketers. Present spot bonuses and/or certificates for acts of meritorious listening to customers. Make this a spirited campaign.

Spending Time and More Time "Hanging Out" in the Marketplace

Silicon Valley's Regis McKenna takes a tough-minded stance on intensity. Every marketer should be "on the road *half the time* [my emphasis]. . . . You get that . . . sixth sense only by spending time in the marketplace. You need to live and breathe the market. You need to talk to market participants on a continuing basis." McKenna concludes: "It is ironic, but true, that in this [era] of electronic communications, personal interaction is becoming more important than ever."

Japanese management expert Kenichi Ohmae sounds very much like McKenna's double:

Despite the increased ease of collecting and analyzing market data, the answer does not lie in better information systems or more corporate planners. . . . The most successful Japanese consumer-electronics companies send their product design engineers around the world for about *six months each year* [my emphasis] to study the latest customer needs and survey the competitive scene. They visit customers and dealers. They attend trade shows. They hold regional product conferences with dealers and salesmen to get direct feedback on what improvements they can make in the design and marketing of their products—a technique they regard as far superior to sending out questionnaires from corporate headquarters. In short, these people are sensitive to the *use* of the product. . . . For instance, by observing California's youngsters on roller skates, a Sony engineer came up with the concept of the Walkman, a portable cassette player. . . . The traditional approach to product development is to study the market and then have design engineers convert the marketing experts' concept into a product design. That division of labor has disappeared in many Japanese firms in recent years. . . . The engineers do the marketing in a less quantified and less sophisticated way, but move right into product design. It's more of an entrepreneurial approach where the people close to the market and product create the business. . . . Speed has become an important element of strategy.

So Ohmae and McKenna preach the six-months-in-the-field standard. This prescription is more modest: I demand "at least 25 percent" of time on the road for marketers—though I quickly add "preferably 50 percent."

Taking What You Hear Seriously—and Acting Fast

Ohmae sounds another important note, about getting information collected in the field into the design loop quickly. An emphasis on destroying functional barriers runs through many of these prescriptions (see especially C-8, P-9). In the case of this one, fewer functional barriers means that the raw listening can be translated more rapidly into new product and service ideas—essential in today's speeded-up world.

In "The New Product Learning Cycle," published in *Research Policy,* innovation experts Modesto Maidique and Billie Jo Zirger report a study of 158 products in the electronics industry, half failures and half successes. Many of the "unsuccessful products were often technological marvels that received technical excellence awards and were written up in prestigious journals." Too much exotic technology at far too high a price, they add, "is the story of virtually every one of our product failures." The successes, on the other hand, came first and foremost from intense involvement with customers. For instance: "In some cases the attempt to get customer reaction went to an extreme. . . . A test equipment manufacturer conducted design reviews for the new product at their lead customer's plants." Second, as Ohmae also observed, the successful firms had better—and faster—interaction among their "create, make, and market functions." Feedback was quick, undistorted— and taken seriously.

Taking feedback seriously remains a prime difficulty. Engineers and research scientists have long assumed that salespeople offering up customers' ideas are simply providing dream lists that would make their (the salespeople's) life easier. Senior management must intervene directly to ensure that ideas from the field are given a thorough hearing. A division of Toshiba America has turned this notion into a first-order strategic advantage. The general manager, looking for a competitive edge, realized that he was sitting on a gold mine of customer listening—the 4,000 calls a month that come into his service center. He reversed the traditional attitude of "handle this quickly and close the file," deciding instead to treat the calls as 4,000 golden opportunities to get customer ideas. To signal his seriousness, he had the service phone bank team report to top management each month on what they heard. He now considers this input—and the actions taken based upon it—to be the cornerstone of a remarkable success against larger and better-funded rivals. The story of GE's industrial plastics group, recounted in C-4, is a carbon copy—including exceptional results obtained in short order.

Involve Everyone in Customer Listening

If intensity and rapid feedback are the most important aspects of real listening, the involvement of everyone in the process follows closely. Customer listening is not just a marketing, sales, and service job. At one end of the spectrum, every clerk and machine operator should be involved. At the other end, the ivory tower researcher should also be thrown into the fray. A very high-tech firm finally cajoled its top R&D person, who epitomized the "what can I learn from these jerks" mentality, into visiting customers. He got very excited, and the president took advantage of his reaction by pushing him in front of a video camera to extol the virtues of getting out and about with customers. The tape is played in every training session.

Use Every Listening Post You Can Find

One important point, then, is not to leave listening and market research to the experts. Another deals with what constitutes "good listening." The answer is clear: any angle you can dream up. One highly successful banker is an avid reader of local banking newsletters from around the country. He's an avowed thief (see I-4). In his fast-paced world, new products are being introduced daily. He reads voraciously to get the first scent of anything that he might copy. And while he has a talented marketing department, by setting an example through his ceaseless circulation of little tidbits about this and that, he encourages everyone to get attuned to doing his or her own listening/"market research."

In *The Intuitive Manager,* Roy Rowan reports the following from a conversation with an executive of a data service firm: "I've never been surprised by research. Research is more of a confirmation tool than a discovery tool." That is, it has its place, but is no substitute for everyone's listening. Apple CEO John Sculley, who learned his craft at PepsiCo, is blunter still: "No great marketing decisions have ever been made on quantitative data."

You Must Persist

I mentioned that most of my "religious conversion" mail deals with listening. But even a genuine conversion is not enough.

A Canadian bank executive recalled a listening program that one of his regions instituted in 1986. For about two weeks, all managers spent some time each day calling customers, asking "How are we doing?" and "How can I help?" The results, he reports, were phenomenal. The customer feedback was terrific ("How magnificent that you thought to call"), morale skyrocketed, and a bushelful of new business ensued.

Yet this executive came to me in frustration. The program had been started a year earlier, and he'd just finished a review visit to the region. "The first thing I asked," he said, "was 'How's the [listening] program going?' 'Really great,' I was told. What that meant, it turned out, was that the regional manager agreed that last year's efforts had been a smashing success. But he hadn't replicated it. For the life of me, I can't figure out why he hadn't kept it up. He's not kidding me. He's a tough manager. I know it worked, and I know he genuinely thought it was a stunner. So my question is, how do we keep up the momentum?"

I had no answer, except to urge that he persist in asking "How's the listening program going?" question at every opportunity, and that he force-feed the process until it caught on. Clearly, even an earthshaking positive experience is not in and of itself enough to insure self-perpetuation.

Words: "Educate" versus "Listen"

Nothing gets my dander up faster than the numerous conversations that go something like this:

"We've really got to get in closer touch with our customers, communicate with them better."

"Yes, we have a big problem there."

"They don't understand the new features. It's all there. We just need to spend time with them."

"Yes, you're right, we've got to educate them."

Observe the quick deterioration, from (1) get in touch to (2) communicate to (3) *they* don't understand to (4) educate *them*. How quickly listening has become talking and telling.

To "educate" is to transmit our ideas to an unschooled student or neophyte. Educating presumes we know whereof we speak. Few of us do, at least when it comes to customers in today's turbulent world. Surely we know why we think our product or service or new feature is great; how we think it will help our potential customer. But can we be sure that our favorite features match the customer's perception of what he or she needs? They seldom do. The customer's perception of our product is based on a compound of history, word-of-mouth information, a bad experience five years ago (long and conveniently forgotten by us), and perhaps a competitor's recent small act of courtesy, or a "trivial" new competitor feature ("not technologically significant," sniff our engineers) that is just what the doctor ordered for this *particular* customer.

The Right Mindset: Treat the Customer as Foreigner

In fact, we'd be much better off if we could pretend that our customers are foreigners who do not speak our language. They don't. Take a person who comes from the world of commercial banking. One of his customers might come from the world of contractors; the next from the world of women's wear boutiques. The language and customs are dramatically different for each. Few of the banker's customers will speak "Banker."

Sadly, most of us don't really listen to our "foreigners." Worse still, we act as we all too frequently do when we're around a foreign person who doesn't speak our language and tries to ask us directions. As soon as it becomes clear that we aren't getting through, we shout even louder in our own tongue. He or she speaks just enough of our language (for example, the customer knows where the accelerator pedal is in the car) to convince us that if only we could yell a little louder, the advantages of the new overhead cam design would get through his or her obviously thick skull.

Each of us carries around a crippling disadvantage—we know and probably cherish our product. After all, we live with it day in and day out. But that blinds us to why the customer may hate it—or love it. Our customers see the product through an entirely different set of lenses. Education is not the answer; listening and adapting is.

Make Listening Fun

Listening can even be fun! That's the point of the VPI, or Very Promotable Item. Wal-Mart Stores' growth has been phenomenal, from $50 million per year in sales to over $15 billion in just fifteen years; from 15 to 1,000 stores in that same period. Now, in 99 out of 100 cases of such growth, executive detachment from the market follows—detachment in which lie the seeds of eventual decline. Wal-Mart, however, led by the indomitable Sam Walton, has battled the negative side effects of growth as successfully as any company I know. Executives, including Sam himself, are regularly out and about with their customers. The terrible "Taj Mahal phenomenon" has not set in: Wal-Mart's "headquarters" in Bentonville, Arkansas, are every bit as spartan as they were a decade ago.

Of all Wal-Mart's defenses against hardening of the corporate arteries, though, the VPI is my favorite. Each of the top executives (and, as of 1985, their spouses) picks out an item of store merchandise that he or she will directly sponsor throughout the year. For instance, Sam (who chooses three items instead of one in deference to his position) selected a five-gallon plastic fisherman's bait bucket in 1985. He was responsible for tracking its progress throughout the year, for pushing store managers to merchandise it aggressively, for giving those managers ideas about how to display and price the item, and for keeping tabs on it whenever he's in a store.

The most beneficial effect of the program is simply that it keeps senior management's hand in the business in a very direct way. In a word, each Wal-Mart executive remains an engaged merchant. And the hoopla that has arisen around VPIs contributes to that effect. The executives must publicly announce their choices. Moreover, they must religiously track sales and margins and—for good or ill—report on them, regularly and in full public view. The program is fun and engaging. It is humanizing—and often humbling. Some items bomb. One of Sam's did recently. The program thus effectively reminds the now-greats of a huge operation of the vagaries of the real world in which their field forces live.

YOU NEED A CUSTOMER INFORMATION SYSTEM (CIS)

A new acronym—CIS—provides a summary of this prescription. We all know about MIS, or management information system. But how's your CIS, or customer information system?

The CIS consists of formal market research and customer surveys (see C-3). It also consists of calling a couple of customers a week, of the VPIs at Wal-Mart and Listening Tours like the one at David-Edward, of giving out home phone numbers to thousands of customers, of encouraging patients to comment on their medical records, of passing articles around the office.

You see, we are what we eat. As I said, our seminars are peppered with dirty tricks; I'll share another of the nastiest. "When you get back to work," I urge, "check your in-box. Measure it, quantitatively. How many papers, or pages, deal with internal affairs such as the minutes of committee meetings or personnel actions. And how many deal directly with customers—survey results, complaints (or kudos), correspondence?" I add: "Of your 'closely watched' numbers (the half-dozen litmus test indicators that almost all effective managers seem able to recall from memory), how many are customer-centered?"

My challenge is usually met with teeth-grinding and reluctant agreement when I suggest that, for most of us, 90 percent or more of our "information flow" is internal in emphasis, not external. If that's so for you—go check your in-box—then quite simply and unequivocally you are not listening to your customers or markets. We are all victims of our in-box. We process what's there, and that's about that. If what you're processing is internally focused, then so are you.

Reprise

Listening, in sum, has three main objectives: (1) to develop, fast, an applications-oriented (practical) source of new product ideas; (2) to keep in "naïve" touch with the host of things, involving every department, that (a) bug customers and (b) simultaneously present improvement opportunities (this is the essence of C-2 through C-4); and (3) to motivate everyone in the organization through unfiltered involvement with the person who really signs the paycheck—the customer.

Furthermore, it calls for turning the organization inside out. The image in my mind's eye is a bit grotesque. I see the organization purposefully becoming a burn victim. It peels away everyone's outer, protective layers of skin and opens up more nerve cells to the painful sting of the exploding customer/competitor world. Right now our protective layers are making us noncompetitive. Too few people, at too few levels, in too few functions, listen too little and too late—and ignore what they hear too often, and act too late.

PUBLIC PARALLELS

From my colleague Jayne Pearl I gathered this gem:

How do you deliver good service when your customers are crooks and crime victims? Lieutenant Greg Stock of the Santa Barbara, California, Police Department sent his officers and himself on a "managing by wandering around" mission. Stock explains: "After my Dirty Harry stage, after I'd been an undercover cop, I was promoted and put in charge of twenty-five young officers. I realized that most of us only see crooks and jerks all day and night, or their victims. Like me, most start out with lots of vim and vigor, but we get skeptical and hardened. A lot of people out there are paying our salaries. This is a way to let them know what a good job we're doing, get a wider basis of support and experience for the officer." Not surprisingly, his idea was not eagerly embraced at first. Stock says he presented the idea as a challenge, to play up to their macho instincts. "I told them, 'Not all you guys will be able to do this, to deal with getting some doors slammed in your face.' And the general response was 'Hey, I'm not afraid of anything.' " The response was unanimously positive. The officers just ring a few doorbells every day, introduce themselves, give out a "business card" with emergency phone numbers and encourage the citizens to call for any reason. Stock says, "Our product—providing public peace and safety—will never go out of demand, and we don't have the incentive of having to be profitable. It's easy to get complacent and give rotten service—unless we keep challenging ourselves."

The device, once more, is simple—yet compelling. Beneath its simplicity, however, is the pervasive mindset that this prescription has emphasized: "I'm here to listen—and help." Not: "Let me tell you . . ."

FIRST STEPS

1. Perform the in-box test right now. How much of the content is "external"? Unless the percentage is greater than 50, go on to step 2.
2. Invent one personal listening ritual and start on it today—call three customers, follow up on one complaint, follow up one lost sale.
3. Gather a group of salespeople and bring up (or get them to bring up), and then analyze, a half dozen cases of failure to successfully transmit information collected in the field to marketers, merchants, or designers. Develop a process to shorten and upgrade that feedback loop, such as the presence of top executives at a monthly meeting where such ideas are discussed and commitments to action made.

C-8

SUMMARY

To remain competitive, the long-neglected factory must cease to be viewed as a cost center. Instead, we must:

▶ Make manufacturing or operations a—or the—prime marketing tool.

▶ Give manufacturing/operations people respect and a lead role at the firm's top decision-making table.

▶ Realize that manufacturing/operations is the prime source of: (1) superior quality, (2) day-to-day product/service innovation, and (3) responsiveness/lead-time shortening.

▶ Through new technology, increase factory flexibility; but beware that changes in organizational structure and attitudes must precede the new technology's widespread application—this means destroying traditional functional barriers and inducing a radically increased level of day-to-day, nonhierarchical interaction among factory team members, designers, engineers, marketers, and field forces—and customers and suppliers.

▶ Get customers into the factory; get factory people out to the customers.

The factory, though radically changed in shape (smaller, fewer people), is more important than ever. Though de-integration often makes sense, beware of the numerous hidden costs of subcontracting, especially overseas sourcing in pursuit of lower cost (or even higher quality). Vital day-to-day innovation, flexibility, and responsiveness come from palpable, casual, close proximity, as well as from formal interactions among internal functions (design, manufacturing, marketing, sales, service), suppliers, customers, distributors, etc.

Reassess every decision to let all or a bit of manufacturing go, especially offshore, in light of this prescription. Get all manufacturing managers into the field at least 15 percent of the time. Every production worker should make at least three customer visits per year. Get droves of customers into the factory on a regular basis. Get most engineers onto the factory floor—living there.

194

C-8

Turn Manufacturing into a Marketing Weapon

We have seen a growing number of clients in the electronics, toys, fashion, and consumer goods businesses "coming home" from abroad in 1986. The quality, supply, labor and communications issues that drove these companies offshore initially have become greatly influenced by the real need to "hang on to your valued clients." Companies that sought long-term survival with expected cost reductions and manufacturing efficiencies through foreign operations have learned the hard way that it is easier to control your own destiny through better management techniques, local manufacturing effectiveness programs, "Just-in-Time" materials scheduling efforts, subcontracting arrangements and the related training programs. The "higher-quality producer" may again be your U.S. competitor that uses these techniques.

> David M. Richardson
> Boyden International
> letter to *The Wall Street Journal,*
> November 7, 1986

Manufacturing must become a, if not the, primary marketing tool in the firm's arsenal. Quality, maintainability, responsiveness (length of lead times for delivery), flexibility, and the length of the innovation cycle (for both incremental improvement of current products and major new product development) are all controlled by the factory.

Marvin Runyon left Ford in 1980 after a distinguished career to head Nissan's new operation in Smyrna, Tennessee. His reason was the lack of respect, at the time, for the manufacturing function at Ford, as evidenced by lower salaries for factory managers and manufacturing executives than for marketing and finance people at comparable levels. Though Ford has made major progress since then, the outright disrespect for manufacturing, especially manufacturing's awesome potential marketing and market-creation power, is still typical of most old—and, more frightening, young—firms. Decisions by start-ups and old firms alike to move manufacturing offshore, or even to subcontract onshore, in the single-minded pursuit of lower labor costs are often ill conceived.

MANUFACTURING STRATEGY: AMERICAN QUICK FIX VS. JAPANESE INCREMENTALISM

In *Tales of a New America,* Robert Reich sees the current pattern as the prime threat to our future well being: "Americans have made money from transferring our Big Ideas to [the Japanese]. They have made money by selling them back to us as terrific products and parts. What is left out of this calculation is the value of experience. They learn how to organize themselves for production—integrating design, fabrication, and manufacturing; using computers to enhance their skills; developing new flexibility; creating new blends of advanced goods and services. They learn how to make the kind of small, incremental improvements in production processes and products that can make all the difference in price, quality and marketability. In short, they develop the collective capacity to transform raw ideas quickly into world-class products."

Harvard's Bob Hayes spotlights the danger of letting manufacturing slip mindlessly offshore: "When the [offshore manufacturer eventually] enters the market, he's worked with the process on a daily basis, has a sense of the wider potential of the technology, of possible applications that you wouldn't have been thinking about. . . . He who can do nothing but sell is at a great disadvantage."

So what is the problem? Reich and Hayes among others believe that it is our neglect of incremental improvements which can transform a product over time. We wait for the breakthrough idea, counting on the distant lab rather than the factory working in daily contact with the product—and customers—to save us.

That's looking at the problem from the outside in, from the market's perspective. But look at it from the inside out, from the firm's view, and exactly the same picture emerges. We denigrate labor's role, overspend on big-bang automation, remove the engineers (process and research) from the shop floor, and continue to flail away at mass production. We lose responsiveness and under-emphasize quality. And, ironically, even the cost savings that mass production and automation are supposed to abet seldom materialize. As Ross Perot puts it: "We resort too often to the unhelpful practice of trying to solve a problem with larger doses of capital. Automation can become a narcotic." In a January 1987 speech to the Detroit Economic Club, he lamented that "despite spending $40 billion for robotics-equipped plants and other capital improvements, GM lost market share and went from being the low-cost producer to the high-cost producer among the Big Three."

We Must Stop Rejecting the Simple

In his fine history of automation, *Forces of Production,* David Noble traces our passion for the complex to automation's earliest days: "The technical community [had] a preference for formal, abstract approaches . . . an obsession with control . . . an enthusiasm for computers . . . a delight in remote control, an enchantment with the notion of machines without men . . . a fetish for novelty and complexity . . . coupled with an arrogant disdain for proven, yet simpler, methods."

Indeed, there were numerous, and more basic, approaches available. However, they involved substantial machinist input. That was anathema in the anti-labor environment in America following World War II. And, of course, these rudimentary models flew in the face of inertia, bureaucracy, and the untold millions spent by big contractors to support the complex systems and military procurement specifications that effectively blocked other ways of doing things. Producers of the simpler—and proven—systems were shut out; so were smaller potential users—the independent machine shops.

All these forces were reversed in Japan. Labor organizations favored machinist input. The extensive subcontracting system and the big firms jointly encouraged small-shop use of advanced, flexible machining technology. And Japan had no military or academic bias for complex systems. Thus Noble reports that "by 1982, 90 percent of Japanese machines were of the simpler design." Moreover, two-thirds of the advanced systems in Japan itself are in small shops.

The combination of America's love of mass and complex, abstract solutions shows up in the premier customer battleground of the future—flexible manufacturing systems. Our performance has been appalling. Barnaby Feder of the *New York Times* reports on a 1986 study:

[Harvard's Ramchandran Jaikumar] studied 35 flexible manufacturing systems in the United States and 60 in Japan in 1984—a sample, he says, of more than half the installed systems in both countries. The United States came out of the comparison looking to him like "a desert of mediocrity." Rather than narrowing the competitive gap with Japan, the technology of automation is widening it further. . . . American manufacturers make and export the flexible systems. The computer-controlled machine can handle a wide variety of parts and tasks. . . . But the American manufacturers usually program the flexible systems to produce larger runs of a few products, just as if they were only current versions of the conventional machinery that has dominated assembly lines since the days of Henry Ford. . . . As a result, the average number of parts made by an American flexible manufacturing system in Jaikumar's study was 10, in contrast to the Japanese average of 93. And the Japanese used their system to handle 22 new parts for every 1 introduced by the Americans, allowing them to offer a wider variety of products more suited to the demands of individual customers. . . . The Japanese [assigned] small groups of engineers to develop flexible systems and then posted them on the factory floor where they could operate them, sometimes for years. Not surprisingly, the Japanese systems are frequently reprogrammed. . . . American manufacturers, by contrast, have tended to use fairly large engineering teams with many specialists to design and install systems. The engineers often end up building systems that are far more flexible then their intended use requires. When the engineering group is then disbanded or moved to a new project, the poorly trained and underskilled workforce that is often left behind is loath to tamper with the unnecessarily complicated systems.

This bodes poorly. It is the single most frightening instance of our strengths of yesterday becoming the burdens of today. We still rely on mass, complexity, and abstraction—in pursuit of low-cost, long-run production. Not only do we fail to achieve the low cost, but our prior rejection of simple solutions (marked by high labor involvement) and current inability to adopt such systems are crippling us in the market, where flexibility is the chief basis for future manufacturing competitiveness.

Hands Off: The Losing Marketing Strategy

In the late 1940s, General Electric led the charge in developing complex, all-encompassing automation systems, overtly aimed at eliminating as much labor as possible. Ironically, GE's chief scientist, Roland Schmitt, is now arguing in effect for amending the ivory-tower-driven approach his own company pioneered. In a 1987 editorial in *High Technology*, titled "Wanted: Hands-on Engineers," he concludes:

There's . . . the issue of effective execution—of strong performance all the way to the finish line. Here research is *not* the answer. Although we certainly need cadres of highly skilled engineering researchers, the vast majority of today's engineers need to be trained less like researchers and more like the practicing, dirt-under-the-fingernails engineers of yesteryear.

By treating everything as a research problem, we tend to devise elegant, inventive solutions without adequate attention to cost, manufacturability, and quality. Meanwhile, the Japanese exercise their skills on features that have significant customer value, while observing stringent guidelines for cost and quality.

The reason for emphasizing theory, at the expense of design and handson practice, has been to give the engineering graduate a command of the fundamentals rather than mere exposure to obsolete machines and superficial shop techniques. That objective is laudable, but its implementation has been carried too far. Students who will work in an economically competitive culture are being trained instead in a culture of research and analysis—the culture of their professors. Thus our educational system imparts mostly academic values, which emphasize optimum solutions, while putting little emphasis on such considerations as speed, cost, and customer satisfaction—the values of the marketplace.

Following the marketing and manufacturing principle of kaizen, or constant improvement, the Japanese tinker, invent, and add customer-friendly features incrementally. In *Restoring Our Competitive Edge*, Bob Hayes of Harvard and Steve Wheelwright of Stanford observe that to Americans capital investment primarily means the construction of new plants, while the Japanese principally see it as the constant improvement of machinery that they already have. Just a quarter of U.S. capital investment typically goes to improving the performance of existing machinery, while 60 percent of Japanese capital investment is devoted to that end. Likewise, a recent McKinsey & Co. study calculated that the Japanese spend just one-sixth to one-third as much as we do on big-bang automation: "The bulk of their [efficiencies] come from the home-grown approaches to design and manufacturing of production equipment."

In *World Class Manufacturing*, Richard Schonberger reports on Toyota No. 9 Kamigo engine plant, which *Automotive Industry* magazine considers ". . . the most efficient engine plant in the world." Schonberger points out that it is equipped with twenty-year-old machines from America, "retrofitted so they don't miss a beat. . . . Quality problems are nipped in the bud, so there is little rework to do, and little need to keep buffer stock. . . . Most machines can be set up in one or two minutes, so there is no reason to run large batches." The result is enhanced flexibility—and responsiveness.

In *Attaining Manufacturing Excellence*, Robert Hall observes that experts who have seen both Japanese and American plants conclude: "(1) New American plants often have excellent technology that is at least equal to Japanese and usually better. That is, any technology gap still slightly favors Americans. (2) American computer systems and software are almost always superior to Japanese. They are larger, more complex, and more powerful, but this can be a weakness as well as strength if the systems mask wasteful practices that should not exist. (3) Japanese are almost always superior in their ability to improve existing plant and equipment: tooling improvement, defect elimination, layout improvement and so forth. The conclusion is that Americans have trouble putting the pieces together and making the most of what they have." In a chapter appropriately titled "Attaining the Effect of Automation Without the Expense," he adds: "Spending big money quickly on automation is not wise. In the end, its effectiveness depends as much on organizational preparation as on money and technical prowess. Plus, equally skilled competitors cannot be beaten just by outspending them. Major automation cannot be effectively 'installed'; it must be accompanied by a way of organizational life."

Unfortunately, the phenomenon described above is not proprietary to the Japanese. The German success story is similar: Engineers live on the shop floor, and are brought up in a dirty-fingernails tradition. Investment in increasing the skills of labor is monumental. (Steelmaker Krupp spent $51 million training 4,200 would-be workers in 1986.) High quality and short production runs are the norm—success with flexible manufacturing systems has been stunning.

PHENOMENAL RESULTS FROM INCREMENTALISM IN THE UNITED STATES

What, then, is the answer for the United States? Adopt incrementalism ourselves, says Hall: "Manufacturing excellence results from a dedication to daily progress. Making something a little bit better every day, [using] every employee's skill. . . . Manufacturing excellence tries to improve activities that contribute to customer well-being in ways often unseen and frequently unappreciated."

Richard Schonberger reveals the power of these ideas when practiced in the United States. *World Class Manufacturing* ends with an Appendix titled "Honor Roll: The 5-10-20s"; that is, 84 plants he's discovered on North American soil which have been following the constant-improvement strategy and have achieved a *fivefold, tenfold, or twentifold* improvement in manufacturing lead time. Here are some representative examples:

3M, Weatherford, Oklahoma (floppy discs): WIP [work in progress inventory] cut from six hundred to six hours, space per unit cut sixfold, productivity tripled.

Omark, Guelph, Ontario (saw chain): Lead time cut from twenty-one days to one, flow distance cut from 2,620 to 173 feet.

Omark, Onalaska, Wisconsin (gun cleaning kits): Lead time cut from two weeks to one day, inventory cut 94 percent.

Omark, Woodburn, Oregon (circular saw blades): Order turnaround time cut from ten to fourteen days with 75 percent fill rate to one or two days with 97 percent fill rate, WIP cut 85 percent, flow distance cut 58 percent, cost cut 35 percent.

Hewlett-Packard, Greeley, Colorado (flexible disc drives, tape storage units): WIP cut from twenty-two days to one day, whole plant on JIT [just-in-time].

THE LOOK OF CUSTOMER-RESPONSIVE MANUFACTURING

I've come across no better American exemplars of a customer-responsive approach to manufacturing than at Worthington Industries and Elgin Corrugated Box Company. Here's what I found:

1. **Process engineers live on the shop floor,** working with line operators to extend the use of material and machines.

2. **Every machine had been modified scores of times, usually by several generations of operators.** Time and again, at Elgin, I'd hear: "This cost $1,500. Joe here did it while he was recovering from a strained back. The machine now does something that no one else [in the industry] can do. If he'd gone out to get this manufactured, it would have cost $70,000—if the big-equipment guys would even have done it." At Worthington, a spare-time project led to a component calibration task being moved in-house; what used to take up to ten days and cost $500 now takes a few hours and costs less than $10. (At Golden Needles Knitting and Glove, a jury-rigged—by people on the floor—Japanese machine does a complex, open-finger knitting job that the machine's Japanese producers still don't believe is possible. One result: Golden Needles is the just-in-time sole source for NUMMI's work gloves.)

3. **The old and new reside comfortably next to each other.** An advanced Worthington machine is powered by three U.S. Navy submarine engines, vintage 1943; it is controlled, however, by the latest computer

technology—reprogrammed by a Worthington electrician, not a computer programmer. (Similarly, Luciano Benetton brags of his old $5,000 machines, retooled and reprogrammed many times "and now valued at half a million dollars apiece.")

4. Functional barriers are virtually nonexistent. (See I-2, P-9, L-8.) All quality control at Worthington is done by the operators, who have the latest measurement equipment to aid them. They also do all except major maintenance, having wholesale access to unlocked parts and tool rooms. All salespeople train extensively on the machines. Sales reviews are held on the shop floor regularly. Order information is available to all.

Many have called the absence of functional barriers and the staff's role as support for the line keys to Japanese manufacturing success. Masanori Moritani comments in *Japanese Technology:*

> A [major] strength of Japanese [manufacturing] technology is the close connection between development, design, and the production line. In Japan this is considered simple common sense, but that is not always the case in the United States and Europe. . . .

> Outstanding college-educated engineers are assigned in large numbers to the production line, and many are given an important say in business operations. Many manufacturing-industry executives are engineers by training, and a majority have had extensive firsthand experience on the shop floor. In Japanese firms, the production department has a strong voice in development and design. In addition, engineers involved in development and design always visit the production line and talk things over with their counterparts on the floor. . . .

> In certain respects, French television manufacturers outshine their Japanese competitors in the development of top-of-the-line models. Soft-touch and remote control were introduced by the French well before the Japanese began using them. But while France may spend a great deal on producing splendid designs for their deluxe models, the quality of the actual product is inferior to Japanese sets. This is because French designers do not fully understand the problems encountered on the shop floor, and because the design work is not done from the perspective of the person who actually has to put the machine together. In short, there is a serious

gap between development and production, a product of gaps between various strata in the company hierarchy itself.

5. Process and product innovation goes on constantly. Machine operators at Elgin and Worthington routinely work with customers, in the plant, to solve problems.

6. Customers are in the plant all the time, and plant workers are out with customers all the time. I've never visited a Worthington (or Milliken) facility when customers weren't present—not just touring, but working. (Milliken sees its sparkling plants as its best sales offices. One executive flatly asserts, "We've never lost an order if we've gotten the customer to visit.") Managers in Worthington factories are routinely expected to spend about 15 percent of their time on the road with customers. The average machine operator will make two or three customer visits a year, often overnight stays. (Gene DeFouw of ALOFS, a Grand Rapids company that manufactures assemblies and stampings, describes the results of factory/customer connections: "We sent all of our people involved to see the product at work, to meet their counterparts [at GM]. Now, when a problem arises [the customer's] response is to call 'a friend,' not buck it up through the system and 'memo-ize' it. . . . And that 'friend,' I can assure you, comes running." DeFouw then half-ruefully cited several recent experiences with his own Japanese equipment suppliers. Modifying a machine for one small customer is normal behavior on their part. So is chartering a plane to bring an inexpensive spare part several thousand miles following a breakdown. "When I asked why," he recalls, "they said, 'We want you to grow so we can grow with you.' It was that simple.")

7. The plant managers have worked on the floor, modified machinery—and done a stint or two in sales. One Worthington Steel plant manager is typical. He hired on in the summer while he was an undergraduate in business at Ohio State. Turning down an offer from IBM, he went to Worthington full-time after graduation. He's been inside every machine in the plant, and once worked with Austrian equipment producers for months modifying a new machine. He talks like a Ph.D. metallurgist and/or mechanical engineer, but has no formal training in either discipline. He had a tour in sales, and was successful.

It nets out this way: (1) Elgin and Worthington are constantly innovating, with customers, in product and process; (2) their flexibility and responsiveness are unparalleled in their giant industries; (3) they produce top quality (Worthington, for instance, scores four times better than the industry average); (4) they have generally oldish machines that have been modified to achieve state-of-the-art in performance; and (5) both are low-cost producers to boot. Not a bad set of specs. Both, in sum, are brilliant market creators who use the factory as their prime marketing arm.

Market Creation Through Manufacturing at Chaparral

Chaparral Steel of Midlothian, Texas, is a pioneer in mini-mill technology. It has the lowest costs in the U.S. steel industry, and lower costs even than its Asian competitors—for instance, it can produce steel at one-half what it costs a typical Japanese mill. Founder Gordon Forward is a technologist, yet surprisingly he has no research department. He explained to the *Harvard Business Review:*

> *Our largest challenge is to cut the time it takes to get technology out of the lab and into operations* [my emphasis]. . . . Let's go back to what I think happened at some of the bigger companies in the industry. Well, nothing happened. Sure, there was research. But I often thought that those companies had research departments just so CEOs could say something nice about technology in their annual reports. The companies all put in vice presidents of research. The companies all built important-looking research centers, places with 2,000 people in a spanking new facility out in Connecticut or somewhere, with fountains and lawns and little parks. Those places were lovely, really nice. But the first time I went into one of them I thought I was entering Forest Lawn. After you spend some time there, you realize you *are* in Forest Lawn. Not because there are no good ideas there, but because the good ideas are dying there all the time. . . . Many of the ideas weren't all that hot. . . . You know, someone would come up with a harebrained scheme that would burn out the refractory lining of a furnace. Now, if this fellow had only had some production experience, he would know perfectly well that iron oxide, pure iron oxide, is a solvent for refractories. But chances are, he doesn't even talk to anybody in production. . . . I'm not arguing that pure research has no place in our industry. But

what we had was a lot of technical work that never got linked to real production needs. It was partly the fault of all those folks in the research centers, but it was also the fault of production people who were suspicious of any new ideas. They saw change as a challenge to their positions. . . . They also treated the research people as safety valves. You can guess the way they thought. "If all those smart Ph.D.'s are responsible for new ideas, we don't have to worry about them. Besides, most of the ideas are nonsense anyway. Just get out of our way and let us make the stuff we're supposed to make." It's what happens when you treat research as a staff operation.

So we've tried to bring research right into the factory and make it a line function. We make the people who are producing the steel responsible for keeping their process on the leading edge of technology worldwide. If they have to travel, they travel. If they have to figure out what the next step is, they go out and find the places where people are doing interesting things. They visit other companies. They work with universities. Working with the universities is particularly important . . . the attraction for the university people is that they get to work with Chaparral people who can go back and really make something happen. They know they're not working with someone who's just going to return to the office and write a report. . . . *The lab is the plant* [my emphasis]. Sometimes I bite my lip because it tries things that scare the daylights out of me. Of course, we don't give the whole plant over to laboratory work, but the whole plant really is a laboratory—even though it is one of the most productive steel mills in the world. We don't stop operations to try crazy things, but we do try to do our research and development right on the factory floor. You know, if you put a production fellow and a maintenance fellow and an engineer together, you're gonna find out pretty quickly whether something has a chance of getting off the ground. And if it does, having them there means that you have a pretty good chance of getting it up and working—and fast. . . .

[The manufacturing people] have to be darn good at production but also talented technologists. There are no folks in the lab somewhere backing them up. . . . We've had to create some of [these people]. . . . [For instance, there is] our sabbatical plan . . . for our people at the front line, [at] supervisor level. Some time ago, when we sat down and asked ourselves what kind of company we wanted to be, we knew we were going to have to be aggressive. We knew we had to stay on top of new technology. And we knew that the best way to get technology into the workplace is through people. Now, that may sound great, but how do we do it? We all felt that most factories stifle young people, cripple them with bureaucracy. We wanted Chaparral to give people freedom to perform, to really tap a person's ego. . . . Many of us had noticed how young people in our industry were scared stiff on the first day that they became foremen. For a year or two they would find the job exciting. They might take a management course, seek out new responsibilities, try to learn new things. But after about three years, it all became rote. . . . They could stop thinking and go get their excitement somewhere else—off the job. So we thought, let's get them out of their regular jobs and put them on a kind of sabbatical. Let's give them some special projects. . . . Sometimes we have these people travel. Or we have them visit other steel mills. . . . Or we have them look into a new kind of furnace we're considering or a new program we're working on for our computer. Sometimes they just spend time [out visiting] with customers.

Forward, too, readily sends his factory troops to the customers when the need arises:

If we have bent bars coming off our production line and they're causing problems for our customers, we might send a superintendent over with the salesperson or the person who did the bundling or somebody from production or metallurgy. It's everyone's job. We mix crews. We send off maintenance people along with some people from the melt shop and from the rolling mill. We want them to see Chaparral the way our customers do, and we also want them to be able to talk to each other. We want them to exchange information and come back with new ideas about how to make improvements or new ways to understand the problem. . . . [It's] where the issue of staff versus line comes in again. It's all a line responsibility—or should be. Everyone can help and share product quality and customer satisfaction and be held directly responsible. . . .

About four years ago, we made everyone in the company a member of the sales department. That means people in security, secretaries, everyone. When you think about who talks to customers, you realize that a lot of people do—on the phone, when customers visit on a tour, whatever.

BUILD CUSTOMER-RESPONSIVE MANUFACTURING

At Chaparral we find the same key principles described at Elgin and Worthington, and found among Japan's (and Germany's) winners: (1) destruction of functional barriers; (2) engineers on the mill floor, not detached; (3) research treated as ongoing, incremental experimenting in conjunction with manufacturing and customers; (4) an attitude of scrounge/test/modify/hustle/act; and (5) everyone's involvement with customers.

Sales, marketing, service, quality, innovation, flexibility, and responsiveness all emanate from manufacturing at Elgin, Worthington, Milliken, Chaparral, et al. It's obvious, then, why Hayes, Reich, and others dread the mindless abandonment of manufacturing in pursuit of lower costs alone. It's not only the loss of manufacturing jobs that hurts, but the loss of the ability to be market-oriented that occurs when manufacturing is either dismantled or treated as little more than a cost center.

The same factors should inject a note of caution into American manufacturing's current love affair with vertical de-integration. It is often wise, and frequently because it brings in innovation useful to customers from a host of in-tune offshore or onshore suppliers. But de-integration in the narrow-minded pursuit of low cost ignores all of the marketing attributes that the factory could and should possess.

"Feel" is a word that businesspersons find troublesome. It is too mushy. And yet "feel" is in many ways the essence of this argument. It is from hands-on interaction—among suppliers, customers, foremen, line machine operators, researchers, heads of distribution centers—that day-by-day advances in innovation and responsiveness flow. If one does de-integrate, onshore or off, the feel must be kept intact. Many have learned of late that this is easier said than done, especially with offshore producers, and even if you encourage frequent travel. The problem is that, often as not, it is chance meetings and conversations—over time—that lead to the tests of new ideas with merit. If the raw number of interactions plummets, then it becomes frighteningly unlikely that the thousands of minor, incremental innovations in product and process necessary to stay competitive will occur.

Develop a New "Model" of the Role of Manufacturing

In summary, we must shake a series of misconceptions about manufacturing, and adopt new ways of doing things:

Conventional Wisdom	*New Wisdom*
The cost advantages of our competitors force us to go offshore.	Huge productivity improvements—via people more than capital—are readily available in every industry. Models from every industry surround us, if only we will take the trouble to look. Take steel—Nucor, Worthington, and Chaparral are each three or four *times* more productive than the industry as a whole.
As long as we retain design/engineering and marketing, we keep control.	Most innovation comes from the interchange, on a daily and often unplanned basis, between those functions *and* manufacturing. Moreover, the chief American selling point should be unparalleled flexibility—this is lost when manufacturing withers.
Good people don't want to go into manufacturing.	True, given the way we have treated manufacturing over the last three decades. As some are demonstrating, though, this can be reversed in fairly short order. The factory can become the leading edge, the launching point for a brilliant career, rather than a dead end.

Conventional Wisdom	*New Wisdom*
"Comparative advantage" arguments lead us away from manufacturing and toward service activities.	It is true that not as many people will work in factories in the future, but that is not an anti-manufacturing argument. In the firm of the future, comparative advantage will come from the value added via quality, service, flexibility, responsiveness, and constant innovation. The factory, no matter how many work there, drives *all* of these attributes. This holds true for the emerging "factory" in the service businesses—trading rooms, Automatic Teller Machines, etc., in the bank; reservation systems among airlines; total systems at McKesson, The Limited, and Federal Express—see C-4. Studies now reveal that service businesses are on average *more* capital-intensive (have more "factory," if you will) than manufacturing.

FIRST STEPS

Are you working through decisions to de-integrate, to ship manufacturing offshore? These may turn out to be sound moves, but reassess them in light of the tenets presented here. Are you sure you can retain (or achieve) world-class responsiveness? constant innovation?

If you are not considering such moves, begin a thorough review of manufacturing/operations with an eye toward revenue generation rather than cost minimization. Each manufacturing activity's operating or strategic plan should be written and reviewed from a marketing perspective.

C-9

SUMMARY

To achieve the radically customer-centered strategies laid out in prescriptions C-1 through C-6, we must:

► "Overinvest"—total dollars, numbers of people and per capita—in front-line sales, service, distribution, and sales/service/distributor support people and support systems.

► Make these people the company heroes—by paying them well; training them "excessively," in class and on the job; providing them with outstanding tools; giving them the opportunity to participate in the structuring of their jobs and support systems; and listening to them.

► "Overinvest" in support for and time spent with the wholesalers, retailers, reps, franchisees, and other members of your distribution channel—select them carefully, but then regularly weed out the poorest performers.

Ironically, the most lightly regarded people in most organizations, public or private, are those who are closest to the customer (patient, citizen) and most directly responsible for the quality and responsiveness of service delivered. This tradition must be reversed with a vengeance, if total customer responsiveness is to become reality.

Consider doubling: (1) the number of salespersons, direct or in support of reps/franchisees; (2) the sales training budget; and (3) the sales support system budget.

C-9

Make Sales and Service Forces into Heroes

This prescription and the preceding one deal with the two most neglected elements of the typical American corporation: (1) manufacturing (2) sales and service. These two must simply achieve preeminence if we are to become competitive once again. They are the basic capability building blocks that permit a firm to execute the new—and necessary—strategies laid out in C-1 through C-6.

THE PAYOFF FROM PUTTING SALES AND SERVICE FIRST

The customer game is ultimately won or lost on the front lines—where the customer comes in contact with *any* member of the firm. The front-line team *is* the firm in the customer's eyes. Therefore, the front-line team must be treated as the heroes they genuinely are—and supported with tools (training, systems) that allow them to regularly serve the customer heroically. Surprisingly, all too few firms understand this:

▶ Could it be so simple? Buckman Labs thrives, despite new competitors and a relatively flat worldwide market demand for its products. Since 1980, it has more than trebled its sales force from 90 to 275; sales have increased at exactly the same rate, with a lag of about a year—which is the time it takes one of its technical salespersons to get up to speed. The chief executive officer harbors no doubts: "Sales increase at the rate of adding salespersons."

▶ The personal/home computer business—producers and distributors alike—sagged in 1985, yet retailer BusinessLand had a sales surge of almost 200 percent; today, it nears the half-billion-dollar mark in revenues. In addition to in-store personnel, it fields a 750-person sales force that has cracked the business market for personal computers wide open. That's a feat that even Apple hasn't yet accomplished. Some rate BusinessLand's sales force as one of the top three or four in the computer industry. Though recruiting top talent to begin with, the firm lavishes $600 or more a month in new training on each salesperson.

▶ Attention is showered on the mechanics at $100 million Sewell Village Cadillac. The best make upwards of $100,000 a year. The training is tops, and the computerized support systems are exceptional.

To this list add such companies as ServiceMaster, Marriott, Disney, IBM, Federal Express, Nordstrom, Stew Leonard, Safety Kleen, Snap-On Tools, and Trus Joist. These firms live for their sales, service, and customer support people. Some have unions (e.g., Frito-Lay, Disney), and some don't—it's the care, feeding, attitude, pay, and support systems that count. Regional vice-president Betsy Sanders of Nordstrom captured the spirit in a talk to a group of technology executives:

"How many of you know Nordstrom?"

All hands go up.

"How many of you have a positive image of Nordstrom?"

Once more, all hands go up.

"How many of you know me?"

No hands go up.

"How many of you know Jim or Bruce Nordstrom?"

No hands.

"How many of you know our store manager in Palo Alto, or wherever you might have visited us?"

Still no hands.

"How many of you know us via security analysts' reports?"

No hands again.

"You see, Nordstrom *is* the salesperson to you. It's not me, not Bruce Nordstrom, not a security analyst's recommendation. It is that *one* person you are in contact with when you are in the department you want."

As I've noted, Nordstrom's salespersons are paid well. There are plenty around, and management is also always on the floor to help. Moreover, the salespersons are supported by Nordstrom's high inventories, and by the phenomenal one-day turnaround time for alterations. Further, they are allowed to do almost anything—cash checks, take returns, gift-wrap.

In light of all this support, Sanders says, "We demand a lot from them!" Nordstrom, then, simultaneously dotes on and asks a lot from their front-line people. Frito-Lay does the same. In *The Marketing Edge: Making Strategies Work,* Harvard's Tom Bonoma explains that it's pay and support—and something else:

> Despite the rigidity of the [Frito] system and, indeed, some potential Mickey Mouse requirements of the system, the salesperson does things other companies can't get their salespeople to do. [Salesman Jess] Pagluica routinely took the time to "flex" each bag of Fritos or whatever he was putting on the shelf, smoothing out the wrinkles so that the display would look better. . . . He religiously counted every package of goods coming into the store, was scrupulous in crediting the customer for damaged goods, and in general was almost frighteningly zealous about what he was doing. A visitor from another planet might have thought that the display was an altar, and [Frito] his religion. Most puzzling of all, Pagluica was a union man!
>
> When [people] examine the system in detail, they come up with a number of reasons why the system works so well. Of course the commissions Jess Pagluica is paid have a lot to do with his willingness to "flex" the bags, and the training he has received allows him to understand that the neater display is likely to get more sales from the shopper than a sloppy one. There are good opportunities for advancement in the [Frito] system; the company is paying Jess's way through night school, and he has high aspirations to become a [Frito] regional manager in time. The system of multiplication tables on the backs of invoices, the optical scan invoices themselves, and account call patterns make good sense, and Jess understands how using these can help him make more money and [Frito] move more goods.
>
> But none of this . . . really explains why Jess runs. Jess runs, one comes to learn from listening to him, because he believes in Frito-Lay as a company, as a vendor of high-quality snack products, and

as a good place to work. He knows, accepts, and, best, believes the marketing theme of the firm that "we have two seconds to reach the customer with our fine line of high quality snack foods," and he wants customers, both trade and end user, to want Frito-Lay products. He understands in his belly that he is the link that makes or destroys the company's interaction with the customers.

Bonoma adds that it's top management's abiding belief in the sales forces, a belief passed on not only to the field but also to all those who support the field, which ultimately makes the difference. Former Frito-Lay president Wayne Calloway (now chairman of Frito's parent, PepsiCo) put it bluntly: " 'Service to sales' is stamped on everyone's underdrawers around here."

An emphasis on the sales and service force has served firms such as Frito-Lay well for a long time. But the Frito/Nordstrom "secret" has been oddly shielded from others, who look principally to creative buying/designing and/or low-cost production/operations for their strategic advantage. Today (and tomorrow even more so), "service added," as described in C-1, C-3, and C-4 may well be the best strategy for survival, let alone winning. The care and feeding of the sales and service force—and more, turning them into innovators—is of monumental importance. Sadly few have a tradition of such attention to fall back on.

Tom Bonoma provides another example of the compulsions of field-driven firms:

> Consider Dan Siewert, President of Cole National Corporation's Optical Division (CNCOD). CNCOD runs more than five hundred optical departments leased from Sears and other retail chains. . . . Siewert's performance since coming to the Optical Division can only be considered stunning. . . .
>
> Just one visit to Siewert's office makes the . . . culture of the division clear. . . . The district sales managers are the "heroes" of the division; it is about them that people talk and about sales increases and "small wins" in the field. The story is told repeatedly, for example, about the regional manager who did not have enough advertising money for both production costs and talent costs to make a local "spot" commercial, so dressed herself up as a television set and handled the talent problem herself. She reported a 37 percent sales gain!

As to rituals, the president (not an assistant or subordinate) reviews sales numbers with the district managers monthly; weekly reviews are held with direct supervisors, and daily sales statistics are collected.

Exceptional feats performed by sales and service people are the daily fare of hallway chatter at CNCOD, Frito-Lay, et al. But these superhuman feats have not in fact been performed by bionic men and women; they have been performed by ordinary people who have been told, in a host of ways, that the firm exists to support them.

The converse attitude, however, is the norm. Retailers skimp hopelessly on clerks. Nordstrom's Sanders concurs: "I never blame another store's salespeople for lousy service. There aren't enough of them. They get no support. They're paid miserably. They're lowest on the totem pole. What else would you expect?"

In high-technology firms, I observe a similar pattern. Salespeople, even if well paid, are psychologically neglected. Top sales management often doesn't sit on decision-making committees; top field service management almost never does. Sales is not on the fast track for hotshots, and a sales tour is not even a requisite way-stop for aspirants to general management.

Acknowledge the Role of Service and Support People in Achieving Customer Responsiveness

I am a fan of salespeople—lots of them, well paid, superbly trained, and supported by the most advanced systems, such as the intricate question-answering system, all out of the customer's view, at Disney parks. However, I want to emphasize even more strongly the potential role of service people. They suffer greater relative neglect, yet can provide even more payoff.

Service means in-the-field service personnel, but it also means others such as the people who answer the phone in the reservation or order-entry center and the personnel in the distribution center. I can only stutter my dismay at the shabby facilities, low pay, and lack of respect these people usually receive.

At Disney, the sweepers are heroes. At Marriott, the bellhops and the people in the reservation center have attention showered upon them.

217

Toshiba America made its service support phone operators into heroes—and made a strategic leap as a result.

These, however, are bright spots in a generally gloomy picture—as witness the experience of the founder of a field-service trade association representing the electronics industry. Wishing to assess the state of thinking in field-service management, he searched through the Library of Congress for texts on the subject. To his dismay, even using a liberal definition of what would qualify, he could find only two books.

We can no longer afford to neglect this increasingly crucial strategic area. While formal study is hardly the answer, we need urgently to get more organized—and especially more imaginative—about field service, service support, and service support systems management, and to develop a specific strategy for these functions (see also C-3 and C-4).

The centerpiece of such a strategy must, in turn, be a plan for upgrading the role and prestige of service and service support people in general (recall GE's newly ennobled Customer Service Coordinators—also in C-4); service management must be singled out from top to bottom. Top service management must be a part of all the firm's policy-making bodies. The service management career path must become a feeder to general management positions. And service managers must routinely become a prominent part of design teams and multi-function teams dealing with the paramount issue of enhancing overall company responsiveness.

A Strategy for Inducing Sales and Service Force Heroics

There are at least nine critical factors for enhancing attention to sales, service, and support people (see also prescriptions P-1 through P-10):

1. **Spend time with them.** If you're not visiting stores and distribution centers at 2 A.M., and dispatch offices *very* regularly, you don't care about these functions. It's that simple.

2. **Pay them well.** Are your distribution center people paid well above the norm, with gain-sharing incentives to boot? If not, fix it now.

3. **Recognize them.** The boss's time counts. So do little things. A high-technology firm held a two-day offsite meeting for distribution people, looking for new opportunities. The firm was careful to make sure that the setting and trappings were as lavish as those it provides for top management affairs.

4. **Listen to them.** Like Toshiba (see also C-7), provide regular senior

management forums in which sales and service and support people can be heard.

5. Make sales and service a feeder route to general management and/or a necessary way-stop on the path to general management.

6. Empower them. Like Nordstrom or Federal Express, give the sales and service people wide latitude to act as "the company" when they are in the field or on the phone, and especially when they are confronting a problem.

7. Train them. No firm I know has ever overtrained sales, service, and support people. And make sure it's the right kind of training. One study of retail sales training revealed that twelve times as many hours were devoted to "cash register technique" and the policy manual as to selling skills and dealing with the problems of customers.

8. Support them technically. Make sure that the systems are in place which allow them to do their job to the fullest extent possible. Federal Express people have time to spend on the customers and their needs/problems precisely because they are not burdened with a cumbersome set of forms to fill out. The system does the rote work, and provides, for example, instant information in response to any query via the truck's on-line computer system and the courier's hand-held computer.

9. Hire enough of them! Think hard about the example of Buckman Labs, about Frito-Lay, BusinessLand, and Nordstrom. All four have far too many salespeople, by industry standards. Seriously consider doubling or tripling your sales force (assuming minimal annual market growth) over the next three to five years.

As to the last point, I sadly observe that most firms' sales and service managements don't know how to dream. They are bewildered by the "what if you doubled the sales force" question. When there is a general 10 percent cutback, they automatically take a 10 percent cut too. Cost containment, not revenue enhancement, drives most firms.

When Japanese firms are faced with hard times, on the other hand, their instincts are the opposite. Assembly-line workers at automobile companies are sent out to sell. (Toyota recently sent 25,000 to the field.) Operations people in banks are sent out to seek new deposits. IBM, among U.S. firms, has followed this path, most recently in late 1986, when it moved 5,000 operations people into marketing (sales). To turn Seattle First National Bank around, chairman Richard Cooley used this Japanese tactic with great success. In fact, his temporarily unleashed "back room" people matched the firm's regular salespeople at signing up new accounts.

Then there is the "productivity increase" trap. We know that salespeople—or anyone else—can always be 10 percent more productive. If we are projecting flat or 5 percent market growth, we focus on making the salesperson 5 to 10 percent more productive, rather than adding to the force. I'm all for prudence and making sales and service people more productive. But return once again to our opening example: "We add a salesperson, and a year or so later, we've got $400,000 more revenue," says the chemical company president. No, it's not that simple. But surely it's a point well worth considering.

CATER TO DISTRIBUTORS, FRANCHISEES, WHOLESALERS, AND MANUFACTURERS' REPS

Now extend the discussion of sales and service persons to include members of the distribution channel not on the firm's payroll. The story is a carbon copy. Steelcase, a top-flight office-furniture maker, works only through dealers. McDonald's continues to soar. The dealer or franchisee is a cherished member of the family at both firms; it's almost as simple as that. Yet again, few seem to get it. Three salespeople "cover" 200 dealers or reps, or support 200 franchisees. Harvard's Bonoma has coined the revealing term "global mediocrity":

. . . Management attempts to make up for poor-quality distribution relationships with more distributors. Instead of fixing its distribution management structures and learning new . . . habits about the "partnering" aspects of distributor relationships, management often just keeps adding distributors in an attempt to get the "right" ones that will have high vendor commitment despite few signs of reciprocity on the vendor's part.

Consider . . . ten years' distribution history for a large recreational product supplier. . . . Management seems to go in "great cycles" on the distribution problem, first overrecruiting marginal distributors, then in subsequent years winnowing out marginal ones. As the list gets winnowed, however, management appears to be dissatisfied still that it has the "right" partners, and rerecruits more distributors to begin the winnowing process again. Each time this happens, distributor sales, on average, go down. . . .

Indeed, management at this company spent little to no money and gave less attention to building the dealer "commitment" it claimed it so sorely wanted. Instead, it had a total of seven salespeople to manage the entire dealer net, did little training, and gave the salespeople wide latitude in both signing up new dealers and terminating old ones. In essence management ducked the marketing "homework" of making its current distributor relations work over the years by continual distributor replacement; when it recognized this and concentrated on building the commitment it spent so much time talking about, sales per dealer went up remarkably.

Bonoma reinforces these points, describing major differences in dealing with franchisees:

Two [real] donut chains, let's call them A and B, incorporate about the same time, using similar strategies of franchising for distribution breadth. Chain A's managers, wishing to retain as much control as possible over the delivered product, implement their strategy by charging high initial and ongoing royalties from franchisees, and putting in place a rigorous system for spot-checking restaurants by corporate staff. Management in Chain A knows it is "trading off" some greater number of potential franchisees for the higher royalties and tight controls, but it does so gladly. The corporate coffers, fattened by royalties, are used for an intensive franchisee support program to aid the franchised store owners. . . .

Things go well for both chains for some period, until headquarters management at both companies becomes dissatisfied with the "share of stomach" that donuts have in the overall menu of fast foods. Looking at consumers' behavior, both managements reason that if there were a broader menu . . . customers might be more likely to stop at their outlets . . . when donut demand is low. Expanding the menu requires the addition of stoves and griddles in the franchisee outlets. . . . The question is: Which chain will have an easier time getting its franchisees to part with the incremental investment necessary to make the strategic switch?

Clearly Chain A, with its fewer but better managed and perhaps more profitable franchisees, will be more likely to be able to make the strategic move toward a full-line fast food restaurant. Chain B, with its cadre of poorly controlled, independent, and too numerous outlets, which have received little from corporate except a product recipe and a sheaf of forms, may be expected to have a much more difficult time with the strategic switch.

A Strategy for Enhancing the Role of the Members of the Distribution Channel

My observations of the good news and the bad square precisely with Bonoma's, suggesting the following strategy:

1. Once more—time and attention. For instance, are the people in the distribution channel partners and members of the family invited in to every crucial setting (and not just on a token basis), listened to long before a proposal becomes a policy, seen as the prime source of new service and product ideas?

2. Give a lot, expect a lot, and if you don't get it, prune. Recall Bonoma's Chain A/Chain B example. Chain A gave a lot and demanded a lot; Chain B gave little and got little. Be a "Chain A" type. And if the dealer/rep/franchisee doesn't eventually come through, let him go.

U.S. automakers suffer from poor service delivery by their dealers, as well as from questionable quality. Yet they steadfastly refuse to do much about the former, trapped by the "global mediocrity" syndrome. As Cadillac dealer Carl Sewell says, "If GM would just drop a couple of dealers for giving lousy service, and broadcast it on the front page of *Automotive News,* we could turn the thing around."

Similarly, I've talked with many executives of fast-food and hotel chains who haven't dropped a franchisee in years. I acknowledge that it's tough; among other things, it means forgoing immediate revenue. Moreover, if you haven't enforced your rules (or never had any), tedious, even legal, disputes can ensue.

Reps scream the loudest when I suggest that they drop suppliers who are unreliable on quality or delivery, especially well-known suppliers. Yet even a few lousy suppliers cripple the rep.

My advice: If you're not setting high standards—with reps, dealers, wholesalers, and franchisees—and then pruning the bottom 2 or so percent each year, you are in for trouble in the customer responsiveness department.

3. Provide bold—extensive, expensive—support. This suggestion exactly parallels my closing point in connection with field sales, service, and support people. Think about doubling or trebling the support force that services your dealers and reps. Don't skimp on systems support either. Be bold! When I look at Frito-Lay or Disney, for example, I simply cannot conceive of anyone, in the public or private sector, overdoing it.

The American businessperson's holy grail is cost containment. Yet the surest way to cut unit costs is to spread them over greater revenue. This entire set of customer prescriptions, but none more than this one, suggests a new premier objective: revenue enhancement. (See also C-10.) Execution of the winning strategies laid out in prescriptions C-1 through C-6 begins by turning our neglected field troops and their supporters— those closest to the customer—into the company's heroes, rather than one more "cost element" to be optimized or minimized.

PUBLIC PARALLELS

Sadly, the public sector analogue is exact regarding this prescription. The nurse in the public hospital and the elementary and secondary school classroom teacher should be the nation's heroes. They are not.

In Vermont, the people who drive the snow-clearing vehicles in the winter stand tall with their fellow citizens. Business—indeed life itself— would grind to a halt were they to give less than their all, and we know it. Likewise, the utility lineman after a storm, or the firefighter, is at least a hero during his or her short interludes of dramatic action.

But what about the garbage collectors and bus drivers? And the clerks in the planning and zoning office? And the crews that patch potholes? They are the front-line deliverers of a city's most visible day-by-day services. The public, including numerous elected officials, has a nasty habit of lumping all these people together and calling them "public dole bureaucrats."

To be sure, the public sector has its share of obfuscating, narrow-minded bureaucrats. And I'm on their case as much as I'm on the case of obfuscating, mischief-making private sector bureaucrats. But Betsy Sanders's analysis holds for the public sector too—when you see a front-line employee with a lousy attitude, and an "I just enforce the rules" mentality, it's not the clerk's fault at Podunk's City Hall any more than it's the clerk's fault at Macy's in Palo Alto.

Baltimore's transit boss, Ron Hartman, came up with an innovative answer to this. He wanted to reward good performance from bus drivers. Not fazed by the public sector's inability to give tangible rewards, he figured that downtown merchants benefited from good transit service. So he solicited gifts from them to give to top drivers (such as free meals and movie tickets) in return for free advertising space on the buses.

Every time a driver gets a positive letter from a customer, she or he gets an award. And roving supervisors carry movie tickets and restaurant chits with them. If they notice a driver performing a meritorious act, they give out an award on the spot.

FIRST STEPS

Can you answer the question: "Do my sales and service and indirect support people feel like heroes?" If not, get out and get that answer—among other things, ask customers (end users and all members of the distribution channel). Commit now to three visible activities per month with (1) field sales and service people and (2) their indirect counterparts at such places as reservation and distribution centers.

C-10

SUMMARY

With everything up for grabs in every market, we must:

▶ Become customer-obsessed.

Opportunity now lies, not with perfecting routines, but with taking advantage of instability—that is, creating opportunities from the daily discontinuities of the turbulent marketplace. To do this, the customer, in spirit and in flesh, must pervade the organization—every system in every department, every procedure, every measure, every meeting, every decision.

Make a customer-obsessed revolution. Routinely look at the smallest nuance of the tiniest program through the customer's eyes—that is, as the customer perceives it, not you. Make champions of change in support of the customer, not guardians of internal stability, the new corporate heroes in every function.

C-10

Launch a Customer Revolution

When he was mayor of Baltimore, Don Schaefer, the present governor of Maryland, had a sheet of drawing paper taped to the wall of his office, handwritten with a black felt-tipped pen. It read:

#1. PEOPLE
#2. Do It Now.
#3. Do It Right The First Time
#4. Do It Within Budget
#5. Would You Like To Live There?

If you pass the first four hurdles, but can't leap the fifth, you've missed the whole point.

That's a true customer orientation. Every action, no matter how small, and no matter how far from the firing line a department may be, must be processed through the customer's eyes. "Will this make it easier for the customer?" "Faster?" "Better?" "Less expensive?" "Will the customer be more profitable because of it?"

No department, including legal and accounting, should exist to "protect the firm." If you want to avoid badly aged receivables, there's a simple solution: Make every customer pay 100 percent of the purchase price in cash at the time of ordering. The problem, of course, is that you'll have no customers.

EMPHASIZE REVENUE ENHANCEMENT

The business equation is simple: Profit equals revenue minus cost. Or maybe it's slightly more complicated: Long-term profit equals revenue from continuously happy customer relationships minus cost.

Many firms' cost structures are out of whack, to be sure. Nonetheless, our obsession for the past few decades has been with cost containment rather than revenue enhancement. The ten prescriptions for achieving total customer responsiveness suggest shifting the focus to revenue enhancement—e.g., when times are tough, add salespersons, don't cut the sales department's travel budget.

Domino's Phil Bressler, addressing fellow franchisees, states the case for revenue enhancement in plain language:

A couple of my managers just went out and bought some nonprofitable stores. The first thing they wanted to know is how to get 'em profitable. And the first thing I said was "Forget it." When you forget profitability, it comes to you. When you worry about it, the customer invariably gets hurt. We've got one guy who took over a $6,500 [per week in revenue] store and he's got it up to $12,500 in four months. He's running horrible costs, and he's barely making money. I just keep telling him, "Forget about it," because he's going to have a $20,000-a-week store in about three months. Sales building is the way to profitability. You can only cut your costs so low before they hurt the customer. You can never raise your sales too high. Just to emphasize, we do a house-by-house analysis in our store in Towson [Maryland], which has the best market penetration of any Domino's Pizza store in the country. It does $35,000 a week, $2.00 per address, $6.49 average ticket price. So we've got a lot of customers, but we found that among the 17,000 addresses, we only have 1,700 customers. Ten percent! I felt like just going crazy. We should be doing $70,000 a week. But that's our best market penetration [among 3,800 stores] in Domino's Pizza. So look at the potential you have. You only have 10 percent of your area, at most. The sky's the limit.

Even when our theories have focused on revenue enhancement, the approach has often been flawed. We have overemphasized: (1) buying market share through low price, (2) increasing sales through marketing devices, and (3) buying and selling businesses until some on-paper Nirvana of "cash cows" and growth stars has been collected in one optimal portfolio.

The advice here is contrarian. I suggest: (1) any product can be wildly differentiated and made into a value-added winner, even—perhaps especially—in the oldest, dullest, and most ordinary commodity-like arenas; (2) not only does quality pay—everywhere—with new business, but it is better than free, actually leading to huge cost reductions as it goes up; (3) "service-added" and an emphasis on the intangibles may be an even better basis for differentiation than quality, though it does cost money; (4) radical increases in responsiveness are possible, and they, too, may save money (because they are impossible without flatter organizations with less management, they require less inventory, etc.); and (5) market creation (creating new niches) and relationship building with customers and members of the distribution channel should replace marketing gimmicks and devices as the mainstay of achieving a thoroughly customer-obsessed firm.

The above turns marketing on its ear, in big ways and small. TRW's Groocock comments on how hard it is to get a market research department to do quality-oriented market research; that is, to focus on the relative quality of your and your competitors' offerings. Silicon Valley's McKenna observes the wrenching difficulty in moving firms from a market-sharing mentality to a market-creating mind-set, from an emphasis on glitzy advertising and promotional gimmicks to an emphasis on word-of-mouth-reputation development, and from an emphasis on the tangible traits of a product or service to an emphasis on intangible traits.

All of the changes rest on the base of people's attitudes. Above all, the customer prescriptions deal with new skills, not new devices. We emphasize, in C-2 through C-4, that the passion for quality, service, and responsiveness has to be matched with world-class systems—the techniques of Crosby or Deming, the support systems that mark The Limited or Federal Express. That element is vital. Nonetheless, an overall emphasis on customer-oriented skill building is primary: (1) problem-solving skills for all to achieve consistent quality improvement; (2) naïve listening skills to understand the intangible attributes of a product in the customer's eyes; (3) a shift from adversarial to cooperative relations within the firm aimed at smashing age-old structural barriers and hierarchies in order to achieve lightning-fast responsiveness; (4) learning to work as partners with suppliers and distributors, rather than as contractually driven adversaries; (5) empowering front-line sales and service people to solve (and want to solve) most problems on the spot, rather than buck them up or blame them on "the system"; and (6) treating every customer, for groceries or a supercomputer, as (a) a "market segment" with special needs and (b) as someone with whom we wish to develop a lasting relationship.

REVOLUTION IS MANDATORY

To turn virtually all our basic assumptions upside down is a daunting task. But it is the easier of the two challenges which these prescriptions lay down. The second half of achieving a customer obsession reminds you that we are looking toward epic increases, not incremental ones:

1. In C-1, I did not ask you to "think about a value-added orientation." I asked you to shift your entire portfolio toward value-added products and services—fast. And I then insisted that every product or service can be wildly differentiated; and, further, no matter how wildly differentiated it is, you should set monthly quantitative targets for differentiating it more.

2. In C-2, I didn't ask for quality improvement, I asked for a *revolution,* carefully choosing that word. Remember Toyota's march from 5,000 to almost two million suggestions, IBM's hundredfold improvement in quality in old technologies. And remember "Old Man" Coleman's passion for perfect stoves, boilers, etc. Moreover, I offered compelling evidence that (a) the payoff in revenue enhancement from quality improvement is enormous, *and* (b) as a side benefit you can save money (remember, poor-quality costs run from 25 to 40 percent of people and assets) if you really do it right the first time.

3. In C-3, recall the Nordstrom vignettes: They, too, constitute a revolution—that is, a revolutionary attitude about the limitless possibilities for serving the customer and adding intangible benefits to your products—and reaping profits.

4. In C-4, once again revolution was the rallying cry. Slash lead times by 90 percent—and many are doing just that. Link up electronically with 75 percent of your customers in the next 24 months—or be prepared to

go broke when a competitor does so first. Smash functional factory barriers and get all functions working together to do everything several times faster than it's now being done.

Note: All of these apparently squishy traits (C-1 through C-4) can be—indeed, must be—measured: differentiators added, quality as perceived by customers and the cost of quality, the customer's perception of service and the intangibles, and response times. There is nothing "soft" about these matters.

5. Small firm as well as large: Go international. Go even to Japan, and prosper. That's what C-5 demanded. The emphasis was once again on skill building and hard work: Learn the language. Visit numerous times, only semi-purposefully, to begin to build relationships. Tailor everything to local requirements from the start. And expect years with modest returns.

6. C-6 boils down the challenges of C-1 through C-5. Develop a twenty-five-word statement of uniqueness that captures the essence of your approach to distinction in the marketplace. Make sure that the most recently hired mail-room denizen understands it, within twenty-four hours of his or her coming on board. Strategy statements which include all the "right stuff" are great, but they are useless until understood, believed, and cared about on the loading dock at 2 A.M.

7. With C-7, concerning listening skills, I began the examination of what is necessary to achieve the market survival strategies represented by C-1 through C-6. Developing a true listening orientation poses radical challenges, too: every marketer in the field 50 percent of the time; every production worker out with customers several times a year. Top it off with an attitude that says, "Treat customers as though they speak a foreign language"—they do.

8. In C-8—revolution once more. Turn manufacturing (or operations) from a "cost center" to the chief marketing weapon. Every aspect of the factory or operations center must be aligned with the customer obsession—including all hands' direct involvement with customers.

9. The idea of C-9—turning sales, service, and support people into the firm's heroes—also bespeaks revolution. And once more it's essential to quantify. Think about Nordstrom's "overstaffing" (and its sevenfold growth since 1978, in tough markets, without acquisitions), about Frito-Lay's well-equipped 10,000-person sales force (and $330 million in an-

nual profit), and the chemical firm that can't help itself—add a salesperson, and a year or so later a half million in revenues accrues. I asked you to consider doubling the sales force. And I asked you to take the top service and distribution people to the Breakers in West Palm Beach for their annual meeting, as you may have been doing with your top salespeople for years.

This last customer prescription attempts to capture the flavor of the nine *other* revolutions I've asked for so far. The sum of the nine revolutions represented by C-1 through C-9 is the customer-obsessed organization.

GET STARTED—NOW

The good news is: You have no choice. No organization, from the newest boutique on Union Street in San Francisco to Dayton, Ohio's public utility, from IBM and Du Pont to GM, is secure. Each of these prescriptions, then, is a "must-do." And no city or state is safe. Like it or not, the competition for jobs is now brutal. Employers are asking for the impossible: bigger tax breaks and better schools and highways and employee training. Moreover, cities and states are competitively selling their services to others, from energy to data systems management, in an effort to increase their revenue and spread their costs further. In health care, it's the same story: more market-driven, value-added distinctions—and simultaneously lowered costs.

To say that you have no choice is not to say, "Take on all ten at once." Recall the brief note on "patterns" at the end of C-2. I traced the evolution of five successful quality/responsiveness programs and suggested that Ford et al. had been wise not to try everything at once.

I still think that is sound advice. But the spirit of C-10 says something more. While you must wrestle with the timing of specific programs for quality and listening, you should and can get to work on shaping the organization toward a wholesale customer orientation, across the board, this afternoon.

Detailed programs, such as new training and supporting systems, are necessary parts of this revolution (see also I-1 through I-10, P-1 through P-10). But instilling a "we live for customers" attitude can become your overriding action agenda today. Tack your own version of Governor

Schaefer's chart on your real or mental wall this afternoon, and pass every action through Schaefer's sieve #5: "Would you like to live there?"—i.e., how does it feel to the customer?

FIRST STEPS

The last word is reserved for Domino's Bressler: "At the crew meetings, I get the crew together and ask each one of them, 'What have you done for the customer today?' We put up all the stories, what they've done, and then we vote. I give the manager who's done the best deed for the customer an award. And then I tell him to go give one to one of his people. So they hold the same contest at their store. That gets your people to think about what the customer is." In a way, it is that simple; this final vignette speaks a thousand words about the underlying mind-set of the customer-obsessed organization—and leader.

What ten small, measured steps will you take this week to begin to instill a "customer obsession" throughout your unit or firm?

III

PURSUING FAST-PACED
/NNOVATION

SECTION SUMMARY

If responding with almost unimaginable alacrity to customer whims (creating new, value-added markets) is the superordinate objective, fast-paced innovation is the chief enabling device—and the subject of prescriptions I-1 through I-10 (see Figure 11).

Strip away the nonessentials, and innovation—in personnel and accounting as well as in product development, in schools and police departments as well as in industry—is a numbers game. Thus, the Guiding Premise here, I-1, is: Invest in application-oriented small starts.

What turns a low-odds start into a successful innovation? There are Four Strategies: I-2, team-based product development, which involves all key functions (and key outsiders including suppliers, distributors, and customers); I-3, encouraging rapid and practical tests (pilots) in the field, instead of getting bogged down writing long proposals unsupported by hard data; I-4, the practice of "creative swiping" (and adaptation) of ideas from *anyone, anywhere,* including competitors; and I-5, selling the new product or service via systematic word-of-mouth marketing "campaigns."

Four principal Management Tactics to Encourage Innovation are next: I-6, support for persistent and passionate champions, necessary to sustain innovators in general in the face of low odds and corporate rebuffs; I-7, "managing" your daily affairs to purposefully stand up for innovation efforts (which I call "modeling innovation"); I-8, supporting thoughtful failures (from which something is learned) and defying silly rules which impede fast action-taking; and I-9, "demanding" innovation through measurement and reward systems which apply "hard"-number targets to what has been traditionally conceived as a "soft" variable.

Finally, I-10 describes the newly adaptive firm, in which the general capacity to innovate is maximized.

It is essential to note that while these prescriptions are separable, the true impact comes from all ten working to reinforce one another.

Figure 11: **Pursuing Fast-Paced Innovation**

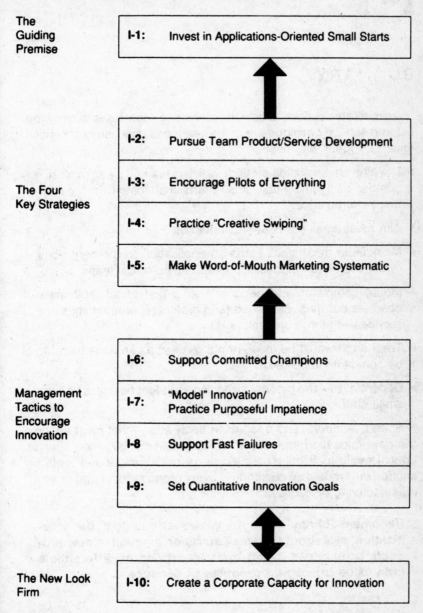

The Guiding Premise

I-1: Invest in Applications-Oriented Small Starts

The Four Key Strategies

I-2: Pursue Team Product/Service Development

I-3: Encourage Pilots of Everything

I-4: Practice "Creative Swiping"

I-5: Make Word-of-Mouth Marketing Systematic

Management Tactics to Encourage Innovation

I-6: Support Committed Champions

I-7: "Model" Innovation/ Practice Purposeful Impatience

I-8 Support Fast Failures

I-9: Set Quantitative Innovation Goals

The New Look Firm

I-10: Create a Corporate Capacity for Innovation

237

I-1

SUMMARY

As markets continue to splinter, technology continues to turn product and service development on its head, and new competitors continue to appear, we must:

▶ Develop an innovation strategy which is marked by an explosive number of lightning-fast small starts that match the environment's turbulence.

▶ Aim most small starts at small markets.

▶ Maintain in most small starts an application (customer) focus, rather than overemphasizing giant technological leaps.

▶ Mount completely independent teams that attack and make obsolete our most cherished (and profitable) product lines and services—before competitors do.

▶ Treat each would-be, new, or old product as an experiment to be constantly modified.

▶ Decentralize—the modest-sized, independent business unit *is* a small start.

Speed, numbers, and a focus on application—that must become the new innovation formula, driven by accelerating market change. Lots of small, application-oriented starts, quickly expanded or quickly snuffed out, should be occurring in every organization, large or small, manufacturing or service.

Become a Johnny-one-note: Wherever you go in the organization, ask about the small starts on innovative new products or services, or on tools to expand or differentiate (add value to) current products or services.

I-1

Invest in Applications-Oriented Small Starts

U.S. firms have a tendency to shoot for the best technology or massive markets while ignoring other, less glamorous products for which there is a market demand.

> *Industry Week*
> on Japan's success in R&D
> May 1987

You can't get the CEO of a $5 billion company excited about a $100,000 market like ceramic scissor blades or razor blades. We shoot right from the start for the ceramic [auto] engine. We don't want to go through the learning process in smaller markets.

> Dr. Lee Rivers
> Director of Corporate Planning
> Allied-Signal

Where is all this great stuff coming from? It's not really coming out of IBM. . . . It's coming out of little two- and three-man companies, because they're finding out that forty guys can't do something that three people can do. It's just the law of human nature.

> Roger Smith
> Chairman, General Motors
> on the source of innovative systems
> for the Saturn Project
> *Detroit Free Press,* March 1985

[Breakthrough] projects the entrepreneurs initiated and carried through had one essential quality. All had been thoroughly contemplated by the regnant experts and dominant companies, with their large research staffs and financial resources, and had been judged too difficult, untimely, risky, expensive and unprofitable.

George Gilder
The Spirit of Enterprise

THE UNPREDICTABILITY OF INNOVATION DEFEATS EXCESSIVE PLANNING

The essence of successful innovation is, and always has been, constant experimentation. Plans and basic research are important, but frequent tests in small markets are more important.

▶ The Sharper Image catalog is advertising Porta Copy. It's a handheld copier from Japan, measuring $6\frac{1}{4}"\times 3\frac{1}{4}"\times 1\frac{3}{4}"$ and weighing less than two pounds. It is not from Xerox, or even Fuji Xerox, and it represents a typical Japanese market foray: it is (1) customer/application-oriented; it is (2) a small product for (3) a small market (at first, anyway); and (4) the technology is not yet perfected.

▶ Japan first entered the European auto market via Finland. No one worried about a Japanese "incursion" there; it was out of sight—almost literally. In the small, "invisible" Finnish market, the Japanese experimented with new features for European consumers. Only later, with trial—and error—largely out of the way, did they launch their full-blown European "invasion."

In Part I, I discussed the systematic evidence of the dismal record of giant firms with regard to innovation: it costs them three to ten times more to develop comparable products; they are late in development or adoption of most new technologies; and they are not, as conventional wisdom has long had it, more prone to take on risky projects (in fact, they are much less prone to do so). This may have been tolerable in the past—U.S. Steel (now USX) survived for decades in our oligopolistic market despite its late adoption of every major new technology. But this will no longer do.

As McKinsey director Dick Foster argues in *Innovation: The Attacker's Advantage,* most big firms are trapped by inertia. The few that do maintain their innovative edge learn to be "close to ruthless in cannibalizing their current products and processes *just when they are most lucrative* [my emphasis] and begin the search again, over and over." The best, he adds, "abandon the skills and products that have brought them success."

This is strong language. What are the root causes of the almost inevitable loss of innovativeness in bigger firms? The list is topped by (1) slowness to move to test new ideas, (2) a bias toward conceptual research rather than application, and a concomitant overdependence on (3) ponderous planning systems and (4) Big Projects. Planning and thoughtful resource allocation surely make sense, but innovation is an inherently messy and unpredictable business, growing more so every day. And the unpredictability cannot be removed, or perhaps even substantially reduced, by excessive planning.

Patterns of Innovation: The (Typical) Case of the VCR

What do RCA, CBS, Bell & Howell, Polaroid, Magnavox, Kodak, Sears, MITI, David Sarnoff, and Bing Crosby have in common? What do Masaru Ibuka, Alexander Poniatoff, Cartridge Television Inc., Andre Blay, George Atkinson, and Stuart Karl have in common? The first set is a partial list of famous names that tried to invent or sell video recorders—and failed. The second list consists of the unknown producers and distributors who succeeded in making the VCR revolution (some subsequently also failed).

The making and marketing of the VCR in the 1970s and 1980s, as recounted in *Fast Forward* by James Lardner, is a garden-variety story of a major innovation. The mega-projects in mega-firms yielded nothing. Gut instincts prevailed. The wrong people bought the product—and then misapplied it. The wrong people sold it. A (then) young company with a small reputation (Sony) was pitted against MITI—and won. Little (then) Ampex of Redwood City, California, called "Hobby Lobby" by RCA, did in RCA, David Sarnoff, and the gigantic David Sarnoff Research Center. Then Ampex, with desks sporting signs that said "Help

241

stamp out transistors," was done in by Sony. Tiny start-up Cartridge Television Inc. of Palo Alto, California, did it even faster than Sony—but made the mistake of selling through Sears, and is now defunct. Sears et al. were usurped by Blay, Atkinson, and company, who created a whole new distribution industry—video stores. (In the end, the Betamax-format machine of now-big Sony lost out to the longer-playing VHS format of Matsushita et al.)

Listed below are four attributes of the VCR story, each of which has implications for innovation generally.

1. The "big guys" build big, non-adaptive, complex projects—and fail. RCA and CBS had head starts on video recording. Their projects were marked by (1) old ideas (RCA et al. unimaginatively saw the video recorder as just a "souped-up audio recorder"), (2) engineers in vast numbers in isolated labs, and (3) executive ego. They failed, as did Kodak, Magnavox, Bell & Howell, Zenith, et al. The big guys, with big (internal) political stakes, don't proceed by trial and error. They bet on one big project and can't afford to have it turn out poorly. Lardner reports, "[The American projects] were conceived on such an expensive scale as to leave no room for trial and error, . . . no opportunity to bring a flawed product to market (as Sony had done . . .), learn from it, and persist."

2. The "little guys" fight adversity, move fast, and often fail too—but create the revolution. Ampex, Cartridge Television Inc., and Sony did what RCA et al. could not do. Physically far from the center of things and underfunded, they thought new thoughts and moved fast. All three eventually failed.

All fought long odds. Sony, for instance, was stalled for years trying to buy, for only $25,000, the rights to use Bell Labs' transistor. MITI, carefully controlling Japan's export of then scarce funds, saw the matter as an untried company dealing with an untried technology; and besides, Toshiba, Hitachi, et al. were working with RCA on the transistor. (Sony eventually won approval and, despite the delays, beat the big guys in Japan as well as the United States by years in starting production.)

3. The winners were customer- (consumer-) oriented, though the path to the consumer was tortuous and required remarkable persistence. Ampex was engineering-driven. Sony was consumer-driven. Ampex engineers saw a market for only thirty machines; they stuck with vacuum tubes and added bells and whistles to meet every single customer's need.

Sony founder Masaru Ibuka (less well known than his partner Akio Morita) said that the U.S. players were misled by defense and space work, where money and complexity were no issue: ". . . They have no idea how to apply high technology to [the] consumer field. But I changed [the] idea. 'First for consumer' is my idea." This bias persists in Sony to this day. The firm beat Matsushita and Philips (the original inventor) with a CD player that was one-twentieth the size and one-third the cost of earlier models. Lardner reports that Sony executive Kozo Ohsone carved out a block of wood about an inch-and-a-half thick and five inches square, barely bigger than the disc itself. The idea was "to persuade the engineers. I told them we would not accept the question 'Why this size?' That was our size and that was it." (The origins of the Sony Walkman are similar—based upon consumer use; the designer observed Californians on roller skates—see C-7.)

In all these cases, Sony proudly turned its back on market research and produced simple, "user-friendly" designs by gut instinct.* Even so, the course of the revolution was not foreseen. For instance, early VCR sales were to schools, where the complex Ampex machine was intended for use by the audio-visual professional; Sony designed for the teacher or student, not the expert (Steven Jobs did something similar at Apple). Nevertheless, the early machines were still far too complex and inflexible, and Sony's breakthrough with its landmark U-matic was not a consumer sale, but a sale to CBS News, which bought a U-matic and a lightweight Japanese video camera produced by Ikegami to cover Nixon's 1974 visit to Moscow. Lardner concludes: "Decisively rejected by the [school] market for which it had been intended, the U-matic became a stunning success just the same."

4. History repeated itself in every phase of the process. The distribution drama was a replay of the saga of invention itself. While Sears et al. stumbled in normal channels, Andre Blay succeeded: outsider Blay founded the Video Club of America. Soon George Atkinson, equally unknown, made the next leap, renting to Howard Johnson, Holiday Inn, Shakey's Pizza, et al. Lardner comments: "The studios . . . found themselves dealing with the 'video software dealer,' a species of small businessperson whose existence they had never contemplated." The trend of

---

*This went too far, however, when Sony persisted with the Betamax format in the face of the even more customer-friendly design of the VHS.

hits by the "wrong" players knew no bounds in this standard story of innovation. As the initial home movie rental trend peaked, the VCR boom spawned the "how to" video boom, but, as Lardner explains, "it was not every Hollywood executive who could make the necessary mental leap." Thus, it was young Stuart Karl who turned from waterbeds to home video and created *Jane Fonda's Workout,* starting another revolution.

As usual, the big guys fought change every inch of the way. Much of Lardner's book is devoted to the studios' litigation with Sony over copying tapes. The studios also fought movie rentals, assuming it would destroy movie-going; instead, it turned out that video rental regulars were inclined to go to movies more often.

Face It, We All Guess Wrong About the Future

"For God's sake, go down to reception and get rid of a lunatic who's down there. He says he's got a machine for seeing by wireless! Watch him—he may have a razor on him."—Editor of the *Daily Express* of London, refusing to see John Baird, the inventor of television, in 1925.

"Who in the hell wants to hear actors talk?"—Harry Warner, founder of Warner Bros. Studio, in 1927.

"I think there is a world market for about five computers."—Thomas J. Watson, chairman of IBM, in 1943.

"There is no reason for any individual to have a computer in their home."—Ken Olsen, president of Digital Equipment, in 1977.

For the story of the VCR, I could have substituted the saga of upstart McDonald's and the launching of the fast-food revolution; American Express and the credit card; or Genentech (versus the big pharmaceutical houses) and the commercial application of biotechnology. The established experts and the big companies and their planners are wrong time and again. Even if they were once pioneers, they seem rapidly to become overly conservative about the future (e.g., the video recorder as just a "souped-up audio recorder") and overly optimistic once a product comes along (not foreseeing the decade or more of trial and error—twenty-five years in the case of the VCR—between the first, halting prototype and widespread use).

ACT SMALL/START SMALL/BREAK INTO SMALL UNITS OR TEAMS: A SOLUTION FOR BIG FIRMS

Big firms must act like a collection of smaller ones when it comes to innovation:

► Numerous small starts—experiments, really—must constantly be made.
► The small starts must usually be aimed at small markets.
► The small starts for small markets should have an applications orientation.
► Multiple, major, unbridled efforts must regularly be launched to knock your best products and services off their profitable perches before some new competitor does so.
► Radical, continual decentralization must be pursued—"horizontal" growth via the addition of new business units, rather than "vertical" growth by development of bigger, functionally organized units.

In short, while innovation requires thoughtfulness (I am a staunch fan of high R&D spending), it nonetheless boils down by and large to a speed and numbers game—in the marketplace, not the boardroom.

Break the "Think Big" Mind-set

Big firms have a tough time thinking small. In *The Next Economy,* economist and businessman Paul Hawken offers an insightful look at the flawed reasoning of large American enterprises, concluding with a half dozen "letters" to business chieftains in which he proposes strategies to deal with the changing nature of business. In one to Clifton Garvin, Jr., then Exxon's chairman, he observes: "Because you are a big business, you are trapped by doing things in large ways. But it is one thing to start a business that becomes large and entirely another to start things on a large scale. You should imitate nature, where meaningful beginnings are almost always unnoticeable. I suspect no one could have predicted that the commodity firm of Clark & Rockefeller [the eventual Esso/Exxon] would [become] the world's largest company."

3M does better at making small starts than any other giant firm I've come across. No project is too small for its consideration, despite its $9 billion size. Team product development (see I-2) at Procter & Gamble, Du Pont, and other firms also marks a major effort to downsize and speed up development efforts. A major reorganization at Campbell Soup in 1982 to create small business units (see Part I and C-4), IBM's formation of Independent Business Units, Milliken's launching of thousands of Customer Action Teams (see C-4), and even GM's decision to start up Saturn as a separate corporation (its first such move in over fifty years) are all part of the same effort.

Surround "Big" (if Necessary) by "Small"

The small-starts idea has endless variations. Big, hyperorganized projects must be surrounded by small-start projects and partial projects. For instance, a senior GM manager describes several innovations developed by informal groups outside the main "planning process" that paved the way for major project successes in his firm. From just one maverick band came (1) the soft bumper system for the 1973 Corvette, (2) the "friendly fender" for the Fiero, (3) fiberglass wheels for 1986 models, (4) a fiberglass spring (the invention involved "commandeering a computer"), and (5) fiberglass bumper beams for the 1980 Corvette. He concludes: "The paperless skunkwork operation gets things done in one-tenth of the time with very little money." At Pacific Bell, a system was required for automating a million transactions. Two estimates were received, one from a big, outside firm (three years, $10 million) and one from a major Pacific Bell unit (two years, $5 million). Meanwhile, three South California employees took a crack at the task—and did it in sixty days for $40,000.

Act Small/Buy Small: Another Big-Firm Solution

Still another uncharacteristic, small-start route can be followed by big firms—tiny acquisitions. For example, a few years ago, The Limited, with over 2,800 shops, bought a four-store chain, Victoria's Secret. Today they've expanded that "small start" to 160 stores—and are starting again, with the purchase of a single Manhattan store, Henri Bendel, in 1986.

The Small Start: Genuine Autonomy Required

Despite the success stories, acting small, if you are big, is much easier said than done. A new-product team in a big company has a tough time achieving true independence. *Innovation: The Attacker's Advantage* traces, for instance, Du Pont's loss of leadership to Celanese when tire cord shifted from a nylon to a polyester base. To its credit, Du Pont, with a 75 percent market share in nylon-based cord, hedged its bet by mounting experimental efforts in polyester once it learned that others were doing so. Unfortunately, however, Du Pont's start-up polyester team was forced to test its experimental product at the tire cord development center—run by the dominant (and very profitable) nylon department. Not surprisingly, the kindly advice and worldly cautions offered by the experts in that setting brought Du Pont's polyester project to a standstill. Meanwhile, Celanese, with no entrenched and profitable position in nylon to defend, entered the market for polyester tire cord with alacrity and quickly captured a 75 percent share. Thus, the small start alone is not enough. The small start unit must be truly independent of the current dominant business.

Keep the Funding Lean and the Apparatus Simple

Another big-company, big-project factor that impedes innovation bears particular mention here—too much money. In my experience, the well-funded big team seldom produces much of anything. Likewise, the small acquisition inundated with the new parent's money usually veers off course. The pressure is off. The project becomes too elaborate. Failures are met with more spending and more elaboration. Every nut, bolt, or piece of software is designed afresh, even if the project is presented as an "urgent, bet the company" move. One study cited in *The Bigness Complex* underscores this, observing that most successful innovation is the product of relatively primitive machinery—and that includes the most exotic of high-tech wizardry. Here's a description of the primitive scrounging associated with one of the most sophisticated high-energy-physics experiments ever undertaken:

At Saclay, outside Paris, the French learned that they had promised that the scintillator in their gondolas would turn out five times more light than was physically possible. They spent the next two years rethinking scintillator technology, and searching for a plastic that would give them enough light without costing more than the whole UA1 detector put together. When they found one that would do the trick, it turned out to have been purified by a German chemist in his spare time at home. So they talked the chemist's firm into developing the plastic as a research project, which meant that they could get the 12 tons they required. Then they found a shower-stall manufacturer in Belgium that would turn the German plastic into high-tech physics apparatus. They moved their computers and their sophisticated testing equipment into the shower factory to check the plastic as it rolled off the assembly lines.

The account is from *Nobel Dreams,* which describes Carlo Rubbia's winning of the 1984 Nobel Prize in physics. Rubbia's win ended years of European frustration at the hands of Americans: "Until Rubbia came along, the United States had owned high-energy physics. From 1950 through the end of the last decade, Americans had made virtually every major discovery and won nearly every Nobel Prize. . . . No matter how tough the European competition was in physics, the Americans always beat them. In the seventies, European physicists seemed to be regrouping. Yet even though CERN [the European Organization for Nuclear Research] had the most powerful accelerator in the world by a factor of ten, and a budget as great as all of the U.S. labs put together, the American physicists still somehow came up with the three most notable and clearcut discoveries of the decade, and all the Nobel prizes." Author Gary Taubes concludes that the long-frustrated Europeans "had a problem with money. Unlike the Americans, they had too much of it."

Small Starts/Small Stops: Cut It Quick if Necessary

Small starts (in small markets) can be (1) cut off quickly and (2) modified quickly. "Big" projects involve big political stakes (recall RCA and the VCR); when failure is imminent, it is (1) hidden or (2) "fixed" by further elaboration (which usually leads to bigger failures). Furthermore, "big project" failures usually lead to such a souring of attitudes toward an idea that it cannot be readily resurrected, even in an entirely new form.

Small Starts/Application Bias: Invent for the User

The small start by the small, independent team is usually application/ market/customer oriented—by definition. The emphasis on a small market means that the project is already aimed at a narrow, practical application.

"Big" projects, on the other hand, are usually driven by the science or "the big idea." Customer involvement and customer-derived content are minimal.

Small Starts: Beyond New Products

"Small starts" as an approach to innovation applies to every activity, not just new product or service development (see also I-3). *The Economist* reported on the innovation pattern of the few American firms that have been successful at adopting flexible manufacturing approaches:

> [These firms] are neither "visionaries" nor "ostriches." People in the trade call them "evolutionists." All of them have been nibbling away at computer-integrated manufacturing *without committing themselves to overly ambitious projects* [my emphasis]. As a rule, they have tended first to computerise their machine tools, creating "islands of automation." Next, they have streamlined their scheduling departments, slimming down the wadges of bumph [masses of paper] they produce. Only then have they linked the two departments together, so the machines receive their instructions and materials precisely when, and only when, they are needed.

Topping *The Economist*'s list (and my own) among those who have followed this "small starts" strategy are Hewlett-Packard, Allen-Bradley, and Chrysler. An executive of a European systems software house concurs. Successful European firms have followed what he calls a "prototype" strategy, starting small and learning one's way forward. Less successful firms have spent years and tons of money developing a rigid master plan. They have been locked in from the start, as a result of attitude and of capital expenditure, to a grand design that seldom holds up, but which they are unwilling to scuttle as implementation begins.

ACT SMALL/START SMALL: A GOOD IDEA FOR SMALL FIRMS, TOO

The small-start advice applies equally to small firms. I've observed that most initially successful small firms fail because a good *second* product or service isn't developed in a timely fashion. That's usually because a dominant founder attempts to replicate the process that brought about his or her first success. Since so many fortuitous events are involved in a success, including a raging fire in the belly, the odds of replication are slight. Seeding multiple small starts is as much a must for the three-year-old $1.5 million firm as for AT&T, though the scale of a "small start" will differ in the two cases.

NO EXCEPTIONS TO THE SMALL-START STRATEGY

What About the Japanese?

Many react to the discussion of small starts with some variation of "But aren't the hyper-organized Japanese the epitome of 'big start'/'big project' thinking?" The answer is a resounding "no." Jim Abegglen and George Stalk, Jr., in *Kaisha: The Japanese Corporation*, argue that instead, incremental improvements and rapid response to competitors, achieved through factory- and customer-driven actions, are the key to Japan's success:

> Kaisha respond and rarely leave an initiative by competitors unmet. The response is often very fast and, in the case of manufactured products, is offered with a flurry of new product introductions. . . . Western management generally prefers a more carefully considered process of responding to competitors' initiatives. Some initiatives are met and others are rationalized away. Typical rationalizations include the arguments that the new [Japanese] products are not significant improvements or that the market does not really want the product.
> The effects of these very different responses to competitive initiatives are beginning to show. For example, Japanese automobile

manufacturers are selling cars with four-valve engines, electronically controlled suspensions, ceramic engine components, turbochargers with intercoolers, lightweight nonmetallic body panels, synthesized-voice hazard and diagnostic warnings and more. Most of these innovations are unavailable in Western automobiles except, occasionally, in the highest premium optional offerings. Similar product innovation gaps are observable in Japanese air conditioning equipment, machine tools, robotics, vending machines, and parking meters, to name just a few.

The common Western response to emerging innovation gaps appears dangerously naïve. The line of reasoning goes something like this: "The Japanese competitors are not using any technology or innovation we are not already aware of. We could do the same if we wanted to. Anyway, it does not do us much good to copy them—our challenge is to 'leap frog' them." While the Western competitors consider the virtues of an appropriate response to Japanese innovation, the gap that has to be leaped continues to widen, and the probability of a successful leap continues to fall.

Thus, in the first place, the Japanese treat every product as an ongoing experiment and are constantly engaged in improving it. Second, the typical Japanese firm's close integration of design, engineering, and manufacturing induces constant experimentation. Third, Japan's big firms are less vertically integrated than ours (about half as much), and smaller subcontractors are counted on for innovation. Fourth, the Japanese have begun in almost all new markets with penetration of small, applications-oriented niches. Fifth, Japan has a small-business sector that was more vital than ours from the end of World War II until 1975. From robotics to autos, new Japanese firms have played a vital, if largely unnoticed, role in that nation's dramatic resurgence.

What About Boeing (or the U.S. Navy)?

"But you can't develop the 757 by the 'small starts' approach" is another rejoinder to the small-starts idea. "Yes and no" is my answer.

First, recall that the original Kelly Johnson Skunk Works was devoted to aircraft design. That is, moderate-sized, off-line activities can produce complex, systems-oriented projects. Second, Boeing is a perfect example of "small starts *within* big projects." Boeing's product development is driven by the close, intense, continuous involvement of its customers (e.g., airlines, national governments). Aircraft are literally designed using customers' input: prototypes of every bit and piece are presented by either side, and merits are debated constantly. Furthermore, the key to speedy aircraft design is trial and error. Parts of new aircraft are tried out as redundant systems on current aircraft. Finally, subcontractor involvement is another hallmark of aircraft development. Thus, Boeing will work with engine-makers GE, Pratt & Whitney, and Rolls Royce and with thousands of others who will design and tinker with aspects of the craft.

Thus, the effective giant project in fact epitomizes the "small starts" approach. It is blooming, buzzing confusion which eventually gets molded into a complex system. Those most open to customer/supplier involvement and innovation are most likely to succeed (see also the discussion of the Ford Taurus team development effort in I-2).

On an even larger scale, the writer and defense expert Tom Clancy contemplates treating the fleet of the U.S. Navy as a "portfolio" of experiments. Clancy (writing in *U.S. News & World Report* of June 15, 1987) contrasts the Soviet and American approaches to designing new classes of submarines:

> We shouldn't be afraid to do what the Russians do—build a few submarines with combat capacity but that are really experimental platforms. Congress won't let the Navy do that. That's stupid because that's the only way you learn. We should today have three or four boats in the fleet that are just to test out new ideas—instead of taking every new idea we come up with and putting them all in one platform at once. What the Russians do better than we do is they're willing to experiment. They are willing to make a failure once in a while just to learn. The American military is regarded by everybody in the media as the "welfare queen": They can't risk a failure, because even if they learn something from the failure, everybody's going to say they were fools for trying it. It enforces a kind of conservatism that is fundamentally unhealthy.

In other words, the small-start idea has universal application.

JUST WHAT IS A "SMALL START"?

Small-start possibilities are many. Consider:

▶ The 3M rule: Tradition demands that each scientist devote 15 percent of his or her time to projects of his or her own selection.

▶ Another longstanding 3M tradition, which ordains that each division sponsor venture-like projects by people from *other* divisions who have come to them for support.

▶ The Hewlett-Packard routine whereby most divisions have an informal list of things to work on; as teams disassemble, the next project is picked up.

▶ The Japanese strategy of entering industries via small, applications-oriented niches.

▶ That willingness of a Limited to look to tiny acquisitions as a way to test important waters.

▶ The IBM habit of funding multiple, independent, fully staffed teams to work—in parallel, with rigid separation enforced—on any big project.

▶ The slightly less formal Cray Research approach of forming duplicate entrepreneurial teams to attack big pieces of projects.

▶ The Boeing approach of inventing together with customers and suppliers who innovate in parallel on small bits and pieces.

▶ Regular "sabbaticals" for supervisors at Chaparral Steel (see C-8), during which they work on special innovation projects with universities, customers, and suppliers; researchers and production hands, too, are constantly tinkering, together, on the plant floor, which is seen as a lab.

▶ Milliken's propensity to form—at the drop of a hat and without formal charter—a dozen-person team including a customer and a supplier to ferret out or create a small new market opportunity.

▶ A less formal version of the first 3M rule—that is, managers regularly and informally supporting groups to work on alternative approaches to bits and pieces of major projects.

"Small starts," then, is principally an attitude of hustling, testing, and scrounging, aimed at shortening the development cycle by hook or by crook. It's an attitude that results in a seven-person team being pulled together and provided work space in twenty-four hours—or less—once a problem or opportunity or new competing product surfaces. And it means never betting all the chips on the Big Project or the central R&D lab—Gordon Forward of Chaparral is dead serious when he describes Big Steel's research centers as "Forest Lawns" (C-8).

The Ten Preconditions of a "Small-Starts" Approach

Achieving a small-starts approach is like making a quality revolution (see C-2). It requires a thoroughgoing revision of attitude in every element of the corporation. A small-starts approach demands:

1. Letting everyone get out with customers, listening (see C-7, C-8, I-4, P-1).

2. Getting customers into the organization, involved in the plant and lab in particular (see C-8).

3. Establishing a "do a pilot" rather than "write a proposal" mentality (see I-3, I-8).

4. Using small teams in general for almost any task (see P-2).

5. Viewing suppliers as partners—co-innovators—instead of as adversaries (see I-2).

6. Removing bureaucracy to allow teams to get on with it (see I-8, P-10, L-8).

7. Flattening the structure and working fast across functional boundaries (see P-8, P-9, L-8).

8. Developing an instinctive "market creation" rather than "market sharing" orientation (see C-1).

9. Treating the product as an experiment, to be constantly improved (see C-1, I-8, I-10).

10. Management's *living* the message of rapid tests (see I-3, I-7, L-9).

PUBLIC PARALLELS

The small-starts approach is at least as important in the public sector as in the private, because it removes the public sector's favorite excuse for inaction—the inability to gain political and fiscal support for major new programs. Here I argue that small tests and partial tests turn out to be the most efficient way to innovate, regardless of the budget climate.

Every school district (and school), every police force and transit district, should be a hotbed of little trials. Moreover, every public-sector senior manager should be, like his private-sector counterpart, on the lookout for small starts. "How many experimental classes does the principal have? Is the public works chief trying out different scheduling routines to achieve maintenance objectives with minimal service disruption?"

A specific manifestation of "small starts" has been the dramatic success in several states, such as Massachusetts, Michigan, and Pennsylvania, with new business incubator plans. Rather than putting all their eggs (their economic well-being) in the big firm/big plant basket, they are seeking to create a climate favorable to start-ups. Those choosing the big plant have often fallen victim to the vicissitudes of the quarter-to-quarter changes in capital spending plans of big firms, and the grotesque market demand fluctuations (with attendant grotesque employment fluctuations) that occur after the monster facility opens.

FIRST STEPS

1. Review your formal and informal product development budget. What share of it constitutes "big bets" and what share is aimed at small starts? Ensure that every unit's strategic plan is strongly weighted toward the latter, or at least that there is evidence of numerous small starts.
2. Beginning today, constantly talk up small starts, yours and others'. To aid this process, conduct a formal review of the almost certain explosion of new product and service offerings in your markets (odds are high that most will have come from the "wrong" place—via a small start by an unexpected player).
3. Talk these ideas up in every department; *every* activity should be engaged in small starts that will enhance and further differentiate *every* product and service offering, whether in development or mature.

I-2

SUMMARY

To speed new-product/service development to a pace approaching that dictated by new market needs, we must:

► Use multi-function teams for *all* development activities.

► Staff such new-product/service development teams almost from the outset with full-time people from all primary functions— e.g., design/engineering, marketing, manufacturing/operations, finance, and perhaps field sales/service and purchasing.

► Involve outsiders—suppliers, distributors, and customers—in new-product/service development from an early date as well.

► Be especially aware of the trap of "shared resources"—that is, partially committed people or facilities.

The use of multi-function teams is the chief tool for speeding up product development.

Use multi-function teams for all new-product/service development activities. The objective: to introduce (multiple) novel sources of innovation and reduce new-product/service development cycle times by at least 75 percent in the next two to three years.

256

Pursue Team Product/Service Development

It takes five years to develop a new car in this country. Heck, we won World War II in four years.

> H. Ross Perot,
> founder, Electronic Data System;
> former board member, GM

Lots more tries than ever are required to keep pace with changing times (I-1). But how do we ensure that the development cycle for new projects/products/services gets shortened enough to help us keep pace with new, ingenious competitors?

Recall the assertion of Chaparral Steel boss Gordon Forward that his largest challenge is to cut the time it takes to move technology from the lab into commercial use. His answer is to put the engineers and researchers on the shop floor with operators and purchasing people. The mill becomes a hotbed of experimentation, with all the principal players in minute-to-minute contact. Forward's approach is still unusual in the United States, and that's unfortunate, because the single most important reason for delays in development activities is the absence of multi-function (and outsider) representation on development projects from the start.

Rip apart a badly developed project and you will unfailingly find 75 percent of the slippage attributable to (1) "siloing," or sending memos and minutes up and down vertical organizational "silos" or "stovepipes" for decisions, and (2) sequential problem solving: design hands off to engineering, which translates the idea into detailed specifications; when engineering is finished, it passes the task on to manufacturing, which only then begins to worry about how the product is to be made; when manufacturing is finished, it passes the project to purchasing; from purchasing it goes to marketing; and from marketing to field service and sales. One group essentially finishes its "higher order" task before passing the job "down" to the next-level executor. Interaction among functions is minimal; what's done is always within the context of the hierarchy of functions—design, then engineering, at the top; manufacturing and sales at the bottom.

The answer is to commingle members of all key functions, co-opt each function's traditional feudal authority, and use teams (see also P-2, P-8). 3M has always done it; so has Hewlett-Packard. Frito-Lay slashed product development time when it adopted the team approach in the mid-seventies, a course made easier by the firm's already well-entrenched disrespect for bureaucracy and hierarchy. Today, even the most functionally oriented, hierarchical firms, such as Du Pont and Procter & Gamble, are scurrying to break down old organizational barriers and do innovation "all at once."

A CASE STUDY: FORD'S TEAM TAURUS

Among the traditional firms, none is working harder—or more effectively—at team product development than Ford. Team product development customarily features the removal of barriers between design/engineering and production and, to some extent, marketing and sales and purchasing. It can go much further. Team Taurus did, creating in the process a car that won kudos for design and quality—and coming in under the proposed product development budget by almost one-half *billion* dollars to boot.

Traditionally product development at Ford was sequential. Mary Walton describes it in *The Deming Management Method:*

[D]esigners designed a car on paper, then gave it to the engineers, who figured out how to make it. Their plans were passed along to the manufacturing and purchasing people, who respectively set up the lines and selected the suppliers on competitive bids. The next step in the process was the production plant. Then came marketing, the legal and dealer service departments, and then finally the customers. In each stage, if a major glitch developed, the car was bumped back to the design phase for changes. The farther along in the sequence, however, the more difficult it was to make changes. In manufacturing, for example, "We wouldn't see the plans until maybe a year before production started," [Taurus project leader Lew] Veraldi said. "We would go back to engineering and say can you do it this way. They'd say, 'Go peddle your papers. It's already tooled. I can't afford it.'"

That's all changed, Walton reports, again quoting project leader Veraldi:

"With Taurus . . . we brought all disciplines together, and did the whole process simultaneously as well as sequentially. The manufacturing people worked right with the design people, engineering people, sales and purchasing, legal, service, and marketing.

"In sales and marketing we had dealers come in and tell us what they wanted in a car to make it more user-friendly, to make it adapt to a customer, based on problems they saw on the floor in selling.

"We had insurance companies—Allstate, State Farm, American Road . . . [tell us] how to design a car so when accidents occur it would minimize the customer's expense in fixing it after a collision." One of the problems mentioned by insurance companies was the difficulty in realigning a car that had suffered front-end damage. As a result, Taurus and Sable have cross marks engraved on a suspension tower under the hood to define the center of gravity as an aid in front-end alignment. Team Taurus included Ford's legal and safety advisers, who advised on forthcoming trends in the laws so "we could design for them rather than patching later on."

Manufacturing was brought into the act early. Veraldi observes: "We went to all the stamping plants, assembly plants, and put layouts on the walls. We asked them how to make it easier to build. We talked to hourly people." Team Taurus collected thousands of suggestions and incorporated most of them. "It's amazing," he said, "the dedication and commitment you can get from people. . . . We will never go back to the old ways because we know so much [about] what they can bring to the party."

The Power of Supplier Involvement

Mary Walton reports that perhaps the most profound difference was in relationships with suppliers:

The common way of doing business is to choose the lowest bidder on advertised specifications. For Taurus, the company identified its highest quality suppliers and sought their advice in the beginning stages. In return for their contributions, Ford pledged to make them, as far as possible, the sole supplier.

One of those companies was A. O. Smith in Milwaukee, a family-owned corporation whose major division made automotive sub-frames, the steel structures on which were mounted the engine, the transmission, and the control arms for the wheels. The company was the world's largest manufacturer of car and truck frames. In 1980, Ford sought Smith's advice. . . . [For instance,] Ford had done the drafting in the past. But Smith offered to have its own drafting department, which was staffed by experts on that particular part of the car, do the drafts and give them to Ford for approval. "There was a willingness to accept each other's experts that had not existed before," [Ford executive vice president Paul] Smaglick said.

A. O. Smith did have to submit a bid, even after the cooperative effort, but the contract was awarded three years before production and was for five years, rather than the traditional one, another significant sign of movement toward partnership. And A. O. Smith's response was matched by others. Walton reports: "One lighting firm developed louvered interior lights that cut down on reflection on the driver's side when [they were] on elsewhere in the car. Another firm produced a carpet in which all the fibers lay in the same direction for uniform appearance. A plastics company came up with an optional fold-out tray for tailgate parties for the station wagon. Said Veraldi, 'Those are the little attention-to-detail items that we've never done before.' "

As production time neared, Walton reports, customers were given extensive sneak previews, and their ideas resulted in modifications: "In another departure, prototypes were built nine months before the first cars would come off the line. . . . [They were] tested by potential new car buyers, resulting in more changes for the better. The traditional way of making changes was to produce the car and wait for customer complaints. 'That's stupid, isn't it?' Veraldi observed, 'because the first three months, customers get something that is less than good.' "

Wholesale Involvement Yields Wholesale Success: Even Ford Was Surprised

So, from beginning to end, Walton notes, unprecedented involvement was the theme: "The prototypes were also taken to suppliers so that their workers could see the car. In the past, said Veraldi, 'The supplier would make the part, fit it to a gauge, and ship it to a plant. . . . The workers had never seen the final product they make in a car. All they do is they see a molding, or an engine, or a door. They would never see the result of their efforts in a car. . . .' When the car came to A. O. Smith, the employees got the day off to look it over. Two hundred workers at a plant that supplied exterior moldings signed a poster pledging their commitment to quality as a thank-you. . . . Framed, the poster hangs on Veraldi's office wall."

Thus the "team" in Team Taurus included, among others: (1) designers, (2) engineers, (3) manufacturing people, including hourly workers, (4) lawyers, (5) marketers, (6) dealers, (7) suppliers, including hourly workers, (8) representatives of insurance companies, and (9) customers.

Systematic studies as well as such case studies support the efficacy— actually order-of-magnitude superiority—of the team approach. For instance, Modesto Maidique and Billie Jo Zirger's study of new product launchings in high technology firms, cited earlier (C-7), determined that a critical distinguishing factor between success and failure was the "simultaneous involvement of the create, make and market functions" from the outset of the project. Similarly, analyses of Japanese successes emphasize their attention to manufacturability from the start of development efforts, the location in one place of engineers, designers, and manufacturers, and a conception of management unconstrained by traditional American functionalism (see also C-8).

TEAM DEVELOPMENT: THE SUCCESS FACTORS

The vital success factors, then, include these:

1. Multi-functional involvement. Multiple-function representation means, at best, the Ford approach: customers, dealers, suppliers, marketers, lawyers, manufacturing personnel, engineers, designers—and non-managers as well as managers; and all of these from the start.

Short of that, following the lead of Hewlett-Packard and 3M as well as lessons learned from Milliken's Customer Action Teams (see C-4), I suggest that development teams at a minimum consist of (a) a designer/ engineer, (b) a representative of manufacturing, (c) a purchaser, (d) an accountant, (e) a marketer, and (f) a field sales or service representative.

2. Simultaneous full-time involvement. Key team members—at least design, manufacturing, and marketing—must be represented full-time from the start. The involvement of others, even of lawyers, should be full-time for the duration of the most intense activity. The idea here is simple co-optation. There is no such thing as a part-time passion. The part-time team member is not really a team member. The part-timer knows where his or her bread is buttered, and is first and foremost a "functional representative," more interested in discovering reasons why things won't work than driven by the champion/entrepreneur's passion to smash down barriers and make things work. The part-timer is evaluated and paid by the "home" function; a win is seeing to it that no "surprises" occur when she or he goes back home, and the product comes their way for manufacturing, field service, etc.

Rewards should go to teams as a whole. Evaluation, even for members who are only full-time for a while, should be based principally upon team performance. This is simple to state, but tough to execute. It's a piece of a larger issue—the actual shifting of the entire focus of evaluation, including pay and promotion, from functional performance (evaluated by the next three layers of management up) to team performance, where a team leader, regardless of which function she or he comes from, dominates the evaluation process.

But what about the member of the purchasing department who may be full-time for only a few months in a multi-year process? The ideal answer is an approach like Chaparral's, where functional barriers essentially don't exist (see C-8, P-1). Short of that, it is vital that the purchasing team member be rewarded, in the short or the long run, by his contribution to the team's success, rather than the purchasing department's success. If a purchasing person was on two teams, for two months each during the year, most of his or her annual evaluation should be based upon the team leaders' appraisals, not that of the nominal boss in purchasing.

A related element is rewards for cooperation. A few pioneering firms give large and numerous awards to honor acts of cooperation. For instance, if you, the manager, give out ten dinners or $100 checks or send fifty thank-you notes this month—why not make a rule, formal or informal, that at least half of these acts of recognition must go to people in other functions who have helped you and your teams? (See also P-9, L-8.) The chief issue is attitude, but such awards can help change attitudes, over time.

3. Co-location. Walls of concrete and plaster are very important—and inimical to team work. Numerous studies chronicle the astonishing exponential decrease in communication that ensues when even thin walls or a few dozen feet of segregation are introduced. Hence all team members must "live" together. It's as simple as that. Want factory people and engineers to talk? Put them in the same room, with no dividers. Space management is yet another tough nut to crack, but I can state unequivocally that regardless of expense, you can't overdo it when it comes to putting people close together.

4. Communication. Communication is everyone's panacea for everything—but nowhere more than here. In *A Passion for Excellence,* the original Skunk Works at Lockheed was described. This renegade band regularly completed complex projects in a tenth or less of average development time, at a tiny fraction of expected cost. Tom West's Data General skunkwork (the subject of *Soul of a New Machine*) and Gerhard Neumann's exceptional General Electric aircraft engine development operation were also analyzed. Many things were special about these three leaders, but nothing more than their insistence on constant communication across typically troublesome functional boundaries. Daily meetings and brief, written status reports, circulated to everyone, were the norm in all three cases. There is no substitute.

Effective decision-making forums are a special communications consideration. It is essential that regular decision-making sessions be held, with all functions represented. More important is instituting what I call

263

the "no substitutes" rule. That is, whoever attends the meeting representing purchasing, even if it's a junior clerk who's the only one around that day, must be authorized to sign off for purchasing as a whole for whatever is on the day's agenda. Decisions subsequently undone, because a junior rep attended a meeting for his or her boss, are another leading source of project delays—and then sore feelings about wasted time, which cause further delays.

New technologies that allow machine-to-machine communication are essential; this is the essence of computer-integrated manufacturing (CIM), for instance. Yet this software, especially if developed by a central and detached engineering group, can do more harm than good. Most CIM failures (which means most CIM projects at this point) result from not taking into sufficient account issues of organization/people/attitude, and in particular from designing systems too complex to allow constant adjusting and tweaking on the factory floor.

5. The "shared resource" trap. Recall, in I-1, the discussion of Du Pont's loss of the tire cord market to Celanese. The problem was shared resources—a tire cord development center that reported to the established nylon department; it slowed the powerless polyester team's test efforts. I can hardly in good faith urge duplication of every resource for every development project. On the other hand, the Du Pont story is the norm, not the exception. In fact, recent research reported in the *Journal of Business Venturing* concludes that the sharing of resources between new-product/service teams and main-line activities—including manufacturing, marketing, and sales—is a leading cause of sandbagged product development and introduction efforts.

My best advice is to urge that you at least try to wholly dedicate bits of labs or factories, or parts of marketing or field service operations, to the new-product efforts when you feel you can't afford full duplication. That is, approximate duplication as best you can, even if the costs seem high. They usually aren't when measured in retrospect.

6. Outside Involvement. Suppliers, dealers (or other distribution channel members), and ultimate customers must become partners in the development process from the start. Much, if not most, innovation will come from these constituents, if you trust them (i.e., show them all information from the start) and they trust you. This is one of the most important instances of the urgent need for a shift from adversarial to cooperative relationships.

THE INNOVATIVE MIND-SET: BEWARE OF INCREMENTALIST THINKING

New car model development cycles used to be six or seven years. Now they're down to about four to five years in the United States, and three to four in Japan. Not good enough, say the Japanese, who are shooting for one to two years.

Their approach? They determine not what "can be" but what "must be": The cycle *will* be one to two years. The question then becomes: How do we organize to accomplish it?

The difference between the formulations "can be" and "must be" turns out to be profound. In May 1987 I had discussions with a highly successful Swedish firm on this subject. They have reduced new product development cycle times by about 50 percent, using many of the tools Ford used, including Computer Aided Engineering (CAE) systems, simultaneous rather than sequential product development, and partnership relations with suppliers. But now Japanese corporations, large and small, are showering their market with new products. Can the Swedes make another cut of 50 to 75 percent?

The first answer was tentatively "no." They went through each element that influenced the cycle—new tooling, design, etc. They could foresee a 25 percent reduction here, maybe 50 percent there, and very little in a few places—nothing approaching 75 percent overall (or even 50).

Then we shifted the fundamental premise of the discussion: "Given: You *must* cut product development cycle time by 75 percent. How do you organize to do so?"

Recall the determination of Milliken & Company to cut its lead time by 90 percent, discussed in C-4: The key was an earth-shaking reorganization. This, I proposed, was the way the Swedish firm must think. This is the way their Japanese competitors are thinking.

The solution thus begins with a whole new mind-set, and involves radical new ways of organizing (e.g., *much* flatter organizations, with a total transformation of middle management's role—see P-8, P-9). With a revolutionary mind-set, the firm is now more confident of success—any number of radical organizational ideas were indeed brought to the surface.

265

FIRST STEPS

1. Immediately re-assess one critical development project that's in its early phases—are suppliers, distributors, customers, purchasing, manufacturing, field sales and service, and marketing deeply involved, along with design/engineering? If not, experiment with involvement of each of these groups. Launch a radical experiment in team/simultaneous development with a forthcoming new product venture.

2. Consider radical organizational/relationship options needed to slash product cycle time drastically (75 percent at least) in the next couple of years.

3. Bite the bullet, if you are a functional manager. Start proactively lending your people, full-time at critical junctures, to project teams—whether you are an accountant or a purchasing manager. When you form your next team, isolate it physically, and attempt to get full-time help, at least for short periods of time, from the two or three most important contributing functions.

Shift the basis of evaluating your people to focus on their contribution to others' teams. Reward those who did well in team settings, even or especially if it caused some pain to your function. Likewise, go out of your way to honor those who aided your teams, and especially their bosses, who allowed them to do so.

I-3

SUMMARY

With ever more confusion in the market, it becomes increasingly important to replace talk with tests; we must:

▶ Substitute pilots and prototypes for proposals.

▶ Find trial sites and field champions for new programs/projects/products as far from headquarters as possible.

"Piloting," rather than the constant rehashing of abstract proposals, must become a way of life. We need to dramatically speed up the first test or partial test of the first prototype, subassembly, store within a store, training module, software subsystem, pre-test market.

Cut your average "time to first tangible test" of everything by 75 percent, in every arena, in the next 24 months.

Encourage Pilots of Everything

[D]on't get too prepared. . . . A lot of people who want to go into business want to know everything. They never do anything. My idea . . . is get out on the damn field and start kicking that ball. . . . All I had was the inspiration. I didn't know that much about soccer. I didn't know there were even two sizes of soccer balls. . . . So the next thing with the inspiration is "get out and start doing something." The doing part of it is picking up a phone, calling a few friends, and saying, "Why don't you meet me over on Mercer Island and I've got an idea here. I really feel it." So when they come over, I pull out a soccer ball. They already have their crutches, and we start kicking it. . . . Then things start happening.

> Don Bennett, businessman
> and first amputee to climb
> Mount Rainier, on the founding
> of the Amputee Soccer League;
> from *The Leadership Challenge*

The first EDSer to see a snake kills it. At GM, the first thing you do is organize a committee on snakes. Then you bring in a consultant who knows a lot about snakes. Third thing you do is talk about it for a year.

> H. Ross Perot,
> founder, Electronic Data Systems;
> former board member, GM

The formula implied by the above—test it now, at least some piece of it, in the real world—has always been a key to success. Now it's much more. It's become a key to survival.

PILOTING YOUR WAY TO (RAPID) SUCCESS

Take an innovation in a staff department. You are the head of training in a $150 million firm, which urgently needs a spanking-new, high-visibility international management program. The president has been after you to get going for six months. What is the fastest and most effective way to move toward development and large-scale implementation?

You've been chatting about the subject around the office. Now a vigorous young woman comes to you with her strongly held idea for such a program. What do you do? One course is to ask her to write a proposal to float with the executive committee. Another is to bring it up casually at a meeting with your peers or seniors to see how it flies. The second approach is better than the first, but it's still dumb. There's a much better answer.

First, forget the international headquarters staff three doors down. They've fought this idea for years on the pretext that "if it ain't entirely broke, why try to fix it"—in other words, hands off! Instead, sit down with your young would-be champion and go through a list of the international line managers whom you know best, or better yet, whom she knows. Pick out a couple. The persons you've identified should not be skeptical about trying something new. They probably should not even be very senior. They should be people who you or your champion know will be excited about this topic. They must be line managers.

Find some pretext to send the young champion off on a brief field trip to visit with the foreign managers you've identified—to gather live, raw, far-awayfrom-headquarters input from them at the outset. And then the proposal? Not yet. When your eager champion gets back, have her write up three or four pages of rough notes. Fewer and rougher is better; high polish puts people off. Then, the next time you're meeting with international managers (perhaps you could stop in for lunch or coffee during a training session), pull out those unimposing notes. Chat about a couple of the key points with several of the managers—once again, those most likely to be friends instead of foes. Have your champion do the same sort of thing as opportunities present themselves. Then gather a little more data. Perhaps send your champion off to a couple of companies you've heard about that have interesting new international training programs. Circulate notes from those visits to the people you've both talked with.

And so on. The objective is to strike some sparks—to get several committed champions to own the idea. Not you or even your senior international counterparts, but your young champion and a few enthusiastic mid-level line persons in the field.

Test Bits and Pieces Unobtrusively

Can you segment, or "chunk," the project? That is, can you find a little piece of it that can be 75 percent developed in the field by one of your new field champions? If so, get on with it posthaste, and test it casually. That is, stuff some of the partially developed new material into an ongoing training program, perhaps as an extra half-day or a substitute half-day. Have the field champions run through the program with a few of their people. As the opportunity arises, expand the network of champions. By now, pilots of chunks should be popping up in various places, and word should be leaking out. After some months of this, it is finally time to float the proposal more formally.

Piloting Shortens the Process

Some of you are by now saying that this takes longer than making proposals to senior management. That's a typical rejoinder. I beg to differ.

The process is best represented by an exponential curve. There is a slow, low-level, virtually invisible start, followed by a wildly efficient takeoff as word of mouth, led by the *field* rather than by headquarters, starts to do the selling for you. Most pieces of the program have been tested (piloted) by the *field,* refined by the *field*—and are working and getting better and more *field*-oriented daily. Other managers have begun to insist that their operation be the next pilot site for this exciting, new, *field*-designed course.

Mastering the Quick Pilot Mentality

I've chosen an innocent training program as my example. The process is precisely the same with a new product or service, a new accounting procedure, a new distribution procedure, a new factory layout, a new partnership program with a supplier, a new approach to a union.

Traits of pilot-driven innovation include: (1) test sites in the field; (2) a committed champion or two at home; (3) some carefully nurtured line champions far from home; (4) network building via word-of-mouth reports of experience with pilots; (5) chunking the project into small parts for the most rapid testing; (6) casual introduction of chunks into ongoing routines, so as not to prematurely upset the status quo; (7) rapid sharing of the precious bits of real, test-generated data as they accumulate; (8) field design and ownership of the chunks; and (9) protection of the champions by you, the senior manager.

The beginning of the process—the time when commitment can be killed—is most crucial. Most significantly, no valid market data exist at first—none can exist about something untried. So it is precisely at the outset that proposals get shot down or become the topic of endless, hypothetical debate. Any new idea is, by definition, disruptive. It also automatically challenges the wisdom of seniors who have been in place a long time and who didn't think of it in the first place. Building a ground swell, through pilot projects in the field, with line operators as champions, simply turns out to be the most effective—and efficient—way to implement anything.

I acknowledge the dogmatic nature of the previous statement. "Most effective" and "efficient" are strong words in a complex world. I generally avoid them like the plague. But not this time. The stakes are too high. We must learn to innovate fast. "Try," "test," "adjust," "try again," "fail," "modify," "scrap," "start over"—this must become the normal pattern. Regis McKenna calls all products continuous experiments. The Japanese view manufacturing (indeed, life) as a battle to achieve constant improvement. I see life in business analogously, as a series of pilots—committed people, on the nearby shop floor or 6,000 miles away, constantly performing real-world tests on small chunks of the new.

If you walk through a store or distribution center and you can't find a dozen tests of systems or partial systems going on, you should worry.

If you find a senior engineer or buyer or MIS manager wasting most of his or her time "working up the chain" with proposals, rather than "working down"—that is, seeking pilot sites and champions far away from headquarters—you should worry even more.

We don't need proposals. Or, rather, we need a new form of proposal. The most useful proposal aimed at an executive committee is one that has been thoroughly presold to everyone on the basis of hard evidence in support of the new, evidence gained in numerous pilot projects designed by and contributed to by each key executive's own field people.

The piloting mentality is best fostered by chatting it up. When any idea surfaces, instinctively ask these questions: (1) Where are you going to test it? (2) Who is the field-test sponsor? (3) Who "owns" it, you or the field sponsor? (4) Are you sure? (5) When are you going to test it? (6) Can't you test a piece of it sooner? (7) Can't you do the first test in less time? (8) Can't you chunk it more? Later, the questioning shifts: (1) What did you learn from this pilot or that? (2) What have you done with that learning? (3) How's your network growing? (4) Is someone from X or Y function part of it? (5) Does the field still own it?

"Soft" Analysis versus "Hard" Pilots

Is this approach "soft"? No! It is hard—the very hardest. It is rational, and it is "scientific." In fact, it amounts to the organization's embracing the essence of the scientific method—empiricism and the experimental method. Piloting is the data-based approach. By contrast, decision making by proposal churning is whistling in the wind; it is the truly soft and ultimately less rational route.

Piloting Is Dirt-Cheap!

The best news of all is that this piloting/chunking/testing mind-set, far from creating expensive and time-consuming chaos, actually creates inexpensive order and powers the way to rapid success. That is, the whole firm becomes engaged in collecting real-world data from real-world tests as fast as possible. People are not wasting time speculating and posturing and politicizing and proposal writing. When they talk in the halls, they talk of data and evidence. Further, those who are making tests and learning on the firing line, instead of speculating at staff meetings, are the new, honored elite. In fact, staff people generally are no longer around headquarters all that much in the fast-learning organization—their role is now to be out and about, seeking field champions and sponsors and test sites and spreading information about pilot successes throughout the network, in hopes of starting a bandwagon in the *field* for an idea.

The simple historical point is this: In every arena, from Citicorp and PepsiCo and GE at their best, to Lockheed's Skunk Works over a forty-four-year period, we find some organizations, big and small, that do things, not "a little faster," but five or ten or twenty or fifty times faster. Their secret is encompassed by this prescription: Move forward on the basis of hard facts and quick testing, not speculation.

But that's history. The difference between yesterday and today is dramatic: Now, there is no choice. A host of new or downsized competitors are working to undermine your defenses. Many are small and unencumbered by bureaucracy. The small players are also no longer handicapped by traditional diseconomies of scale, thanks to the technology revolution. You are vulnerable. The smaller firms are, in a sense, pilots. You will either answer their challenge—and the challenge mounted by the faster-moving teams at Campbell Soup and Du Pont and Milliken and Procter & Gamble—or lose much of your business in short order.

A CASE STUDY: HOW TO FOSTER A QUICK-TEST ENVIRONMENT

Most ad industry experts are in agreement: the "noise" (volume of competing advertising messages) is so high today that to be a success, one's message must increasingly be startling, outrageous, or "intrusive," to use the insiders' term.

Such a proposition didn't sit well at conservative Young & Rubicam ($4.2 billion in billings), long known for its methodical research. But Y&R is shedding its stodgy image (witness its stellar new campaign for Colgate's low-tartar toothpaste). Much of the credit goes to a systematic program to induce risk-taking via quick tests, launched in 1984 by the creative director of the New York office, John Ferrell. Here are several of the steps Ferrell took:

(1) He began with a pep talk to all 300 employees in the creative department. The new message: Take risks. Such an exhortation, of course, would have had little effect without numerous reinforcements.

(2) A key to the transformation was creation of The Risk Lab. Its objective is to provide a chance for creative people to test far-out ideas early in the ad development process, rather than late, when much is at stake with bosses, account executives (ad agencies' senior sales people), and client officials. (a) Ferrell gave the director of creative research, Stephanie Kugelman, a new title, Dr. Risk. (b) Kugelman moved out of the 18th-floor research department offices, and camped out, a week at a time, on various floors in the creative department; when she was in residence, the floor's reception area even sported a sign, "The Doctor Is In." (c) Kugelman would give an instant reaction, on behalf of the research community, to wild and woolly ideas; moreover, in a major departure from conventional practice, she would hastily pull together a panel of consumers to provide a "quick and dirty" test for a new idea (again, without risking supervisor or client opprobrium). (d) Kugelman's role is now being institutionalized; she and five researchers are moving permanently out of the research department and into offices in the creative area.

(3) Procedures were modified, too. Before, all research pro and con (and confusing and equivocal), would be packaged in an imposing document. Now, research information is boiled down to one summary page. None of this denigrates the role of research, but it does mute its overpowering influence on the decision-making process. As Ferrell remarked to *The New York Times,* "So many research methods are designed to say don't take any risks at all."

Thus, between exhortation, some fun, co-location of warring functions, de-bureaucratizing, purposeful reduction of a dominant function's influence, and devices to aid fast tests before an idea gets politically "locked in," Y&R is waking up.

TEST IT FAST: A QUANTITATIVE TARGET

Time is short. Aim for a 75 percent reduction in "time to first tangible test" for the average project, achieved over the next 24 months. Smaller and midsized firms are doing it as a matter of course. Team product development and the nurturing of champions (prescriptions I-2 and I-6) are powerful aids in this effort. But both of those tools lose most of their potency if you fail to pilot in accordance with the guidelines established here.

PUBLIC PARALLELS

This prescription is even more applicable to the public than to the private sector. I remember chiding a city's middle managers. Most were spending the majority of their time floating proposals for this or that, trying to stretch an already badly stretched budget.

"But why," I said, "should anyone support this or that new program? You have no evidence that it works." "Precisely" was the reply. "We need demonstration money to try it." In one case, demonstration money meant $250,000 for a nine-month test, with a formal evaluation due six months later. After some heated debate, we came to agree that a "quick and dirty" test could be performed in 90 days in the field (out of sight of top management) for $5,000 to $20,000; moreover, there was a champion already out there, a person who'd wanted to have a go at it for years.

In fact, there is always someone "out there" ready to take a whack at it, whether we're talking about a school district or a complex military technology project. Furthermore, almost anything can be subjected to a partial test in 90 days for $25,000 or less. (This is not speculation. I've repeatedly seen it done in supercomputers and financial services alike.)

"Devote 100 percent of your time (or 50 percent, to be realistic) to getting that one, real, first piece of test-generated evidence," I counsel public managers. "Then float the $250,000 proposal." Even better, try several partial pilots before going to the trough to try to pry loose the scarce resources.

Another part of the conversation goes like this: "But what if the little one blows up? The whole deal will be scotched before we've even tried to get the money." You can probably guess my answer: "Better to know now, and get a little egg on your face, than to find out later, at great expense, and get the frying pan thrown at you too."

FIRST STEPS

1. Ensure, through every form of recognition you can dream up, that the organization's heroes are those who are piloting, not merely speculating.
2. Formally (and informally) ask at each staff meeting, on each visit, in each performance appraisal: What are you testing? Where are the pilots?
3. Always be on the lookout for pilots and tests, as you walk through the hotel or purchasing office, review major account sales programs, visit customers and suppliers. Commend them on the spot, including any interesting failures (see prescription I-8).

I-4

SUMMARY

In today's ever-accelerating business environment, you must:

▶ Put NIH (Not Invented Here) behind you—and learn to copy (with unique adaptation/enhancement) from the best! Do so by aggressively seeking out the knowledge of competitors (small and overseas, not just tired old foes) and interesting noncompetitors.

Become a "learning organization." Shuck your arrogance—"if it isn't our idea, it can't be that good"—and become a determined copycat/adapter/enhancer.

What *ten* ideas have you swiped—and implemented with appropriate enhancement—from competitors and noncompetitors in the last 60 days? If you've adopted/adapted fewer than ten, beef up your "creative swiping" program immediately.

Practice "Creative Swiping"

Kobayashi: When we want to do something, we just try to learn and absorb all the possible answers, alternatives and developments not only in Japan, but in Europe, in developing countries and in the U.S. Then, by combining and by evaluating the best of all this, we try to come up with the optimum combinations which are available. For instance, we are very sophisticated copycats. I have accompanied many executives, many union people going abroad to study—groups, of course. All top executives of chain stores, for instance, make two or three trips a year to Europe or to the U.S. . . .

Interviewer: To do what?

K: To learn something. To get something new.

I: Are you saying, then, that one of the secrets of Japanese success has to do with their desire, their urge to get the best . . .

K: . . . to collect information from all parts of the world. If any Japanese manager wants to develop a new product, he likes to find out all the possible seeds—instead of the needs, here.

I: Seeds?

K: Seeds-oriented. Try to find a good seed rather than try to identify the needs here. For instance, the transistor—when the former chairman of Sony saw the article in *Fortune* magazine about the transistor, he imported it. I have been speaking over and over again of the obsession; the urge to absorb is quite high and intensified here.

Interview with Professor
Kaoru Kobayashi, from
*Japan: The Most Misunderstood
Country*

The Presidio Theaters in Austin, Texas, have been a spectacular success. Presidio's flagship Arbor Cinema Four, though in the ninety-eighth-largest market in the country, regularly places among the ten top-drawing theaters in America for any given movie. From theater seats found in France to a sound system developed by Lucasfilm, Presidio prides itself on having stolen the seeds of virtually every idea it's implemented. But the chain is careful to steal only from the best! Charlie Chick, Presidio's president, calls it "creative swiping."

Only the best steal from the best. When Honda launched the upscale Acura project, it picked BMW as its principal competitor—Best in Class. The Acura design team was given just one year to beat BMW. Early signs suggest that they either succeeded or came remarkably close.

BECOMING OBSESSED WITH COMPETITORS

Americans, in semiconductors and retailing alike, are generally terrible at analyzing their competitors, especially in comparison with our competitor-obsessed Japanese rivals. We don't do enough of it, and if we do do it, we usually relegate it to an egghead "competitive analysis" unit, stuck on a hilltop light-years from our centers of operations. Directly related is our cherished go-it-alone, pioneer spirit which leads us to look down our noses at *any* copying. It's the NIH [Not Invented Here] syndrome and it can be deadly.

Challenge Number One: Determining Who the Competition Is

The first question is: *Who,* exactly, is the competition? Too often, firms have focused on old rivalries. Sears worried about Penney, Ford worried about GM, and Xerox studied Kodak—and vice versa. Sears's real problem is K Mart and Wal-Mart at the low end, Mervyn's in the middle,

Nordstrom at the high end, and cataloguers from Spiegel to Banana Republic.

A California department-store merchandising executive stunned me. When talking about competitors, she restricted her remarks to other department stores. "But what about The Limited, Victoria's Secret, The Limited Express, The Gap?" said I, no expert. "Aren't they the real source of your woes?" The executive's information on any competitor was weak; it was especially superficial concerning these newer and more venomous ones.

Xerox's obsession in the mid-seventies with crosstown rival Kodak's new (and good) high-price copiers effectively led it to ignore the little stings from Savin, Canon, et al. in pipsqueak market segments. Then, suddenly (or so it seemed), these mice moved out of their corners and became lions; Xerox lost more than half its market share before it stemmed the tide.

On the other hand, a Ford executive delighted me recently when he said, "Our competitor is Toyota." For too long, Detroit's leaders ignored the hard data and continued to focus on the current enactment of the old rivalry between Barney Olds and Henry Ford, Sr. In fact, some Detroit sources say that GM really began to panic only when Ford's Taurus and Sable took America by storm—that is, when a fellow denizen of Detroit had clearly captured the buying public's imagination.

So determining the "who" is no trivial task. You must check out: (1) foreign firms, with special emphasis on the first, unobtrusive entry into small niches (this has been a favored Japanese tactic, in everything from small engines to machine tools to copiers); (2) small domestic firms, especially their entries into tiny, premium (and profitable) niches; (3) new, big domestic rivals trying to shed their troubles by intruding on your patch; (4) the very best competition, region by region (even stellar firms such as Frito-Lay have a relatively small share of the market in large parts of the United States); and (5) oddball forays through distribution channels and from competitors you wouldn't expect (e.g., TV home shopping, and the explosion of cataloguers in retailing).

Analyzing the Competition: The Obvious and Beyond

Even gross indicators, such as market share by segment, relative revenue, and relative earnings, can give you a good start on competitive analysis. These are crude measures, yet I am surprised at how few (1) collect the data, (2) update them regularly, and (3) share them widely within the firm. Every person in the company should have ready, visible access to the numbers on market share—yours and your competitors'—updated weekly; it is a good first step toward getting the competitors "in the air." (Once again, beware of new incursions. Gross share data is less important than share by segment. A loss of one-quarter share point overall might be mainly attributable to a 20 percent share loss in an unobtrusive but important niche.)

But even the best numeric analysis is not without pitfalls, as one expert on competitive analysis ruefully acknowledges. *Fortune* profiled Wall Street analyst Maryann Keller, the most respected follower of the auto industry. Despite a high batting average, "Keller's record has not been flawless. As a stockbroker, she missed a great opportunity Chrysler offered in 1982, arguing for GM instead. 'Chrysler was a disaster financially, and I believed that GM, with all its financial power, would prevail,' she says. 'After all, how could a company that has everything going for it blow it? It's the one time in my life where I let the numbers rule my judgment. I will never make that mistake again.' "

The next level of analysis focuses on the technical traits of your competitors' products, as gleaned from "reverse engineering" (ripping apart their products) and studies of comparative cost structures. This is a big step beyond market-share analysis, but there is a trap in overemphasizing a comparison of generic product traits too (see C-3). Such analysis can obscure factors that may be more important in predicting the outcome of future marketplace skirmishes. Frankly, Coca-Cola can learn more about the course of its future wars with PepsiCo by thoroughly studying Pepsi's nonbureaucratic, no-nonsense, "test it, try it . . . now" environment than by chemical analysis of any soft drink.

Thus, at yet a third level, it is essential to focus on common-sense business queries: How do the competitors organize for R&D? How high in the pecking order are the service managers and sales managers? How much and what kind of training is given to the people who answer the phones? How high is the division manager's spending authority? The answers to such questions are terrific indicators of a potential competitor's responsiveness. For instance, if a competitor has an organizational structure with only three layers and gives great spending authority to general managers, it is likely to be quick to respond to change.

MAKE COMPETITIVE ANALYSIS
EVERYONE'S BUSINESS

After the "who" and the various levels of "what" comes the "how." I support having expert technicians doing "reverse engineering," and I do think there's a place for small economics units churning out world-wide competitive analysis statistics. But there is a more basic dimension.

Competitive analysis should be everyone's business. The objective is to turn everyone on to it—service people, check-processing people, MIS people. There are two reasons to do so. First, they can be exceptionally good sources. At conventions, or in chats with friends and neighbors, they can pick up a great deal of information, if they are tuned in to the general process—and then listened to. That is, the MIS professional will be the first to hear that a competitor is developing a sweeping new electronic linkup with hundreds of major customers. He or she will hear it (1) from their computer service/salesperson, (2) from a customer, (3) from an MIS person in a bank who heard about it from a friend, (4) from a former employee now at a software house who heard it from a friend, or, most likely, (5) from a braggart who's doing the software in the competitor's MIS department! The pressing question is: Will he or she merely "be fascinated" by the tidbit? Or are there ready channels, formal and informal, for swapping the information fast, getting it to the right division, or marketer, or whomever? Most such intelligence goes no-where because of conventional barriers to communication or, worse yet, because of an attitude of nonurgency, which means no alarm bell is tripped in the back of the MIS person's head.

Take the simplest case. Does the average retail salesperson look at other retailers' ads or arrangements in the mall on the way to work? Why not start a monthly contest, with $100 (or $50 or $500, or dinner for two at the best restaurant in town) going to whoever picks up the best "I walked by Saks and saw" idea? You could design a full-fledged sugges-tion system devoted exclusively to ideas from competitors.

So the average person can be of great service, if he or she is given a mission, a sense of urgency, and a forum in which to be heard.

Competitive Analysis as Motivation

The second, and perhaps more important, benefit of getting every employee to think about the competition is the effect upon general readiness to accept change. I've heard GM executives flatly deny the extent of the erosion of GM's market share within hours of my talking to a leading analyst. Their retort is some dubious, oddball interpretation that makes "awful" look merely "bad."

If GM's executives are trying to confuse me, think what they must do to their employees. If you want to induce a sense of urgency, share the gory details of any loss of market share (especially big losses in tiny segments), of polls that show the extent to which customers prefer the vehicles or traveler's checks of others. Almost all employees are smart. If they are inundated with the unvarnished news, the odds that even onerous change will look acceptable go way up.

FIGHTING NIH ("NOT INVENTED HERE")

As a manager, trade in "Not Invented Here" for "Not Invented Here, But Swiped from the Best with Pride."

The best leaders (see L-5) are the best note-takers, the best "askers," the best learners. They are shameless thieves. Grocer Stew Leonard heard a great little idea from an executive in the Department of Defense at a meeting I attended in late 1986; he implemented it within the week. There was no NIH. No "Gee, if it's DOD, it must be bad." The only operative question was: "Will it work [with a twist or two] for us?"

For Leonard this is second nature; in fact, *A Passion for Excellence* highlighted his One Idea Club and One Idea Club van—a device for transporting a dozen people to a competitor's (or interesting noncompetitor's) operation, nearby or far away, to look for small, good, immediately implementable ideas.

Citytrust prospered under former president Jon Topham, who had the same passion. His attitude is: "Somebody, somewhere, big or small, near or far, has introduced a service we could copy with enhancements—today."

Above all, keep it simple. Competitive analysis buffs have made a mess of competitive analysis. They brought the term to our vocabulary, which was a fine service. But then they did what most experts do with good ideas, turning the process into an arcane discipline and quasi-science which can be understood and conducted only by a mandarin class— namely, them, and for a high fee.

There is, as noted, a place for ultrasophisticated competitive analysis. But the prime objective of this prescription is to turn *everyone* into a vacuum cleaner, trying to understand—and often copy—the best of what our new and most thirsty competitors are up to.

NIH is marked by an endless number of denials: (1) We can't copy old rivals because "if they did it, (a) it must be dumb or (b) we wouldn't want to look like them." (2) We can't copy new rivals, especially foreign ones, because "we're not Japanese, you know." (3) We can't copy small rivals if we're big, because "you can't do that sort of thing if there are more than 500 people on the payroll." (4) Or big ones if we're small— "Hey, we don't have AT&T's deep pockets." (5) And we can't copy from nonrivals because "that stuff will only work in (a) groceries, (b) semiconductors [or any other industry except ours]."

As usual, the problem is attitude, and the solution lies in changing it to: (1) being positive rather than negative about competitors' products, especially tiny features (after all, you couldn't have invented everything first); (2) being positive about other industries' products and services from which you can learn; and (3) opening up the organization, at all levels and in all functions, to the buzz of "what's going on out there that's interesting."

In the successful Taurus/Sable program, Ford bought cars from around the globe. They assessed over 400 features, from major performance parameters to the ease with which the gas cap could be removed. The objective was to become Best in Class (BIC) on most of these features; with a creative mix of copying *and* marginal improvement, Ford feels it reached BIC status on 80 percent of the 400.

COPYING AND UNIQUENESS

Prescription C-6 was unequivocal: Success depends on uniqueness. How do you square that with being a copycat?

The answer is threefold. First, every idea you "steal" should be adapted and enhanced to fit your special circumstances. Second, though

285

your goal should remain the achievement of uniqueness, uniqueness most often comes not from a breakthrough idea, but from the accumulation of thousands of tiny enhancements (the Milliken shop towel—see C-1) that utterly transform the product and create new markets in the process. Most of these enhancements will have been done first by somebody else in some other market—e.g., those who are linking up electronically with customers are, at one level, "swiping" from American Airlines' Sabre system. In particular, tiny companies are, de facto, experiments worth watching.

Third, copying does not interfere with breakthrough thinking; to the contrary, it improves the chances of achieving a breakthrough. For instance, the most creative scientists are synthesizers. They pull together disparate ideas and reshape them to solve a current conundrum. Thus, Charles Darwin's "breakthrough" formulation about evolution came after reading Thomas Malthus, whose 60-year-old ideas on overpopulation meshed in Darwin's mind with his original data from the Galápagos Islands. *The Origin of Species* is at once "unique" and a first-rate example of creative swiping.

In business, this process generally means the ability, for example, of drug distributor McKesson to learn about electronic linkages from American Airlines—and to uniquely apply the concept to achieve commanding strategic advantages in a different industry.

Note, however, that such creative swiping is by no means plain copying, which in a fast-moving world is increasingly useless. Simply copying a competitor today precludes creating your own unique basis for advantage. Creative swiping, which amounts to adapting ideas from unconventional sources, aims solely at creating uniqueness.

In sum, I continue to counsel an urgent quest for uniqueness. The overall vision/positioning of a firm in the marketplace should not be copied from anyone. But the enhancement of each tiny element of the vision can greatly benefit from the hard work that others, in almost any organization, are doing to improve quality, service, responsiveness, etc.

REMINDER: CUSTOMERS' PERCEPTIONS ARE WHAT COUNT

I conclude with a reminder about a critical word from the prescription dealing with listening to customers (C-7)—naïve. Customers like our competitor's products for whatever reason *they* choose. On *our* tests, we might seem better than the competitor on eight out of eleven traits; but if our market share is 15 percent, we're obviously missing something. As a friend at Ford put it: "I remind [my colleagues] that despite our improved quality, design, and profitability, each and every minute, over four out of five car buyers worldwide decide that they don't like Fords, vis-à-vis *some* competitor. Why?"

Why? What can we learn? What can we copy and enhance? These are critical questions.

PUBLIC PARALLELS

The Venture Project was a model study in competitive analysis in the public sector. A Participative Management Project was launched in Walnut Creek, California. One result was an awareness that the city could learn from others.

In 1986 four California cities—Walnut Creek, Irvine, Palo Alto, and Palm Springs—joined in a learning (competitive analysis) venture. Venture Teams from each city spent an intense week visiting the other three cities. The observations were written up and widely shared, resulting in the implementation of a raft of practical ideas. While acknowledging that some programs are unique to a particular city, one participant quickly added: "In most cases there is a product that can be used either socially, organizationally, or economically to benefit others."

Most significant was the underlying spur to action described in the project's summary report: "City managers can no longer act as caretakers of their cities' resources, but must act as entrepreneurs to guide their cities to be more efficient and productive." (The project's first round was so successful that it was continued, with participants visiting private-sector organizations in search of new ideas.)

Some private operation, some entrepreneur somewhere, is doing just about everything any city is doing. What does the best private firm picking up garbage charge and what is the quality of its service? Precisely this sort of comparison, of course, has been a major impetus to the growing "privatization" of public services.

You can also consider every neighboring city a competitor. How is it that XYZ makes a profit on its airport while you must subsidize yours to the tune of tens of millions? Maybe the reason is different labor conditions beyond your control (watch out for the old enemy, NIH)—but then again, maybe it's not. Maybe it's an accumulation of a thousand factors, the majority of which are under your control.

Most important, any public sector operation can mount its version of the One Idea Club and turn the organization into a hotbed of learning and swiping. What city, county, state is doing what about X or Y? What are schools in East Oshkosh doing about ABC? The public sector consists of thousands of schools, sanitation departments, and fire and police operations. Some are lousy, as some firms in the private sector are lousy. But surely the best 10 percent have something (lots, I'd judge) to teach each and every one of us.

FIRST STEPS

In the next 90 days, mount a contest in each department, including accounting and personnel. Which one can come up with the most implementable ideas? Awards might be for (1) best idea overall, (2) most ideas from outside the organization, (3) highest percentage of participation, (4) best idea from a small competitor, (5) best idea from a big competitor, (6) best idea from a foreign competitor, (7) best idea from a noncompetitor. The emphasis should be on quantity, not the magnitude of any idea, since the aim is to get everyone looking for tiny differences.

Consider institutionalizing such a program through a "swiped-idea fair" (once or twice a year) or a special Not-Invented-Here-But-Swiped-with-Pride suggestion system.

I-5

SUMMARY

Since the exploding array of new products and services is causing more and more confusion in the marketplace, and in the minds of early buyers of industrial or consumer goods, we should:

▶ Organize new-product/service marketing efforts around explicit, systematic, extensive word-of-mouth campaigns.

Purchasers buy the new based principally upon the perceptions of respected peers who have already purchased or tried the product. The twist this prescription adds is the idea that word-of-mouth campaigns for the new and untried can be as systematically pursued as can the use of traditional marketing tools, such as advertising. Such programs are increasingly important, as the number of competitors and their offerings increase exponentially, and their products' life cycles decrease dramatically. Influencing the early sorting-out process must be managed with great skill.

Use *systematic* word-of-mouth campaigns as the keystone for launching all new products and services. The campaign should include specific and detailed strategies to land a half-dozen progressive (probably not big) customers prior to full-bore roll-out.

Make Word-of-Mouth Marketing Systematic

Buying a new personal computer? Trying to figure your way through the jungle of new personal financial services? Where are you likely to go for counsel? Certainly you don't sit in front of the TV waiting for an ad to appear. And you're not likely to "let your fingers do the walking." You probably ask a respected friend, neighbor, or colleague who's been down the same route recently.

Now switch sides. If you were the would-be seller of a new service or product, how could you tie into that network of friends and experts who advise potential buyers? Most sales of services, complex products, and especially new products and services, come via word of mouth. As a seller, you need not passively sit by. <u>You can be just as organized, thoughtful, and systematic about "word-of-mouth advertising" as about media buys.</u>

However, marketers tend to over-rely on mass media advertising and under-rely on the careful development of reputational campaigns, according to Regis McKenna. He goes on:

> Word-of-mouth communication can take on many different forms. Industry participants form "old-boy networks" to keep each other informed about new developments. One recent market-research report showed that such a network plays a key role in the telecommunications industry. Gaining access to the network is critical to success. . . .
>
> Word of mouth is so obvious a communications medium that

most people do not take time to analyze or understand its structure. To many people, it is like the weather. Sure, it is important. But you can't do much about it. You never see a "word-of-mouth communications" section in marketing plans. . . .

Of course, much of the word-of-mouth communication about a company and its products is beyond the company's control. But a company can take steps to put word of mouth to its advantage. It can even organize a "word-of-mouth campaign."

. . . [T]he company must decide who should receive the message—and who from within the company should deliver it. By the nature of word-of-mouth communications, it is not possible to spread the message too widely. Luckily, there is no need to. Word of mouth is governed by the 90-10 rule: "90 percent of the world is influenced by the other 10 percent." . . . A word-of-mouth campaign should be based on targeted communication. Word of mouth is not an efficient means for distributing information widely. . . .

The targets for a word-of-mouth campaign fall into several categories:

The financial community. Who backs a company is often more important than how much money is behind it. . . . A company's initial backers can use word of mouth to spread the company's message.

Industry-watchers. Rapid-growth industries are filled with consultants, interpreters, futurists, and soothsayers who sort out and publish information through word-of-mouth. . . .

Customers. Companies can use word of mouth to reach customers at trade shows, technical conferences, training programs, and customer organizations. [New-product test] sites and early customers become especially important.

The press. More than 90 percent of the major news stories in the business and technical press come from direct conversations. All journalists have networks of sources they use for background, opinions, and verifications. It is valuable to become part of this word-of-mouth network.

The selling chain. The selling network includes sales representatives, distributors, and retailers. . . . word of mouth is needed to generate enthusiasm and commitment toward the product.

The community. Every person who is interviewed, or delivers a package, or visits a company walks away with an impression. If company employees communicate properly, every person who comes in contact with the company becomes a salesperson for the company, a carrier of good will about the company.

Ev Rogers of the University of Southern California is the leading expert on "diffusion of innovation." He has examined how new ideas and new products spread. His dozens of studies have analyzed new commercial products, the adoption of birth control techniques, and agricultural technology to determine the reasons behind the typical thirty-year and forty-year delays in the widespread dissemination of innovations—delays which mark even products and services which demonstrate crystal-clear, decisive advantages from the start.

Rogers, like McKenna, emphasizes the overriding power of networks: "Most individuals do not evaluate an innovation on the basis of scientific study of its consequences. Most depend mainly upon a subjective evaluation of an innovation that is conveyed to them from other individuals like themselves who have previously adopted the innovation. This dependence on the communicated experience of near-peers suggests that the heart of the diffusion process is the imitation by potential adopters of their network partners who have adopted previously." Study after study that Rogers reviews reveals that: (1) an innovation takes off only after "interpersonal networks have become activated in spreading subjective evaluations" and (2) "success is related to the extent that the change agent or marketer worked through opinion leaders."

I write, I must admit, with the zeal of a true believer. My first book, *In Search of Excellence,* was launched by an unsystematic (but, in retrospect, thorough) word-of-mouth campaign. A 125-page presentation of what became the book's principal findings was first bound in 1980, fully two years before the book was published, and circulated surreptitiously among business executives. My co-author, Bob Waterman, and I eventually printed 15,000 presentation copies to meet the underground demand, much to the misguided consternation of our publisher, who was certain we were giving away most of our future sales. We also assiduously courted opinion leaders in the media over a period of several years. Thus, within days of the book's launching, supportive reviews appeared, and the network of 15,000 (plus at least an equal number of photocopied knockoffs) hurried to buy the real thing, often in bulk for their subordinates. We could not have more effectively marketed the book if we had planned the process meticulously.

GETTING WORD OF MOUTH ORGANIZED

The important point, to which McKenna speaks so passionately, is that the process can be systematized. For instance:

▶ Careful charting of official and unofficial opinion leaders can be conducted.
▶ Disproportionate selling time can and should be aimed at highly reputable, would-be early adopters.
▶ Sales incentives should encourage working with early adopters.
▶ Events that pair happy new customers with a wider audience can be staged on both a one-shot and an ongoing basis.
▶ User newsletters can be established, then circulated to targeted nonusers.
▶ Testimonials can be systematically gathered and circulated.
▶ All of these programs and others can be put together in a detailed, written, step-by-step "word-of-mouth" campaign plan.

THE SEARCH FOR SMALL, PROGRESSIVE BUYERS

The most critical word-of-mouth activity is, of course, targeting early adopters. Above all, look for the innovative adopters, not necessarily the big ones. Sure, you'd like to launch your new workstation by signing up GM. Yes, you'd like the chairman of the town's biggest firm to be the first to buy your new personal financial planning service. But such giants, though certainly helpful to word-of-mouth diffusion, are usually laggards when it comes to adopting new products and services. Therefore, you'd be wise to look to smaller firms or individuals with a reputation for progressiveness; they're much more likely to become early adopters. Pouring almost all of your energy into getting a couple of these leaders on board is usually a worthwhile strategy.

FIRST STEPS

Take one new product and ask these questions: (1) Am I devoting 75 percent of my marketing effort—dollars and energy—to activating a word-of-mouth network? (2) Are all of my salespersons devoting a specific—and sizable—share of time (and money) to user network development and expansion? Are they compensated for doing so? (3) Is *every* employee a conscientious network developer among his or her colleagues? Based upon the answers, develop a sixty-day word-of-mouth blitz (targeted very precisely on a few key progressive customers) to re-launch or enhance product/service acceptance.

I-6

SUMMARY

To match the accelerating rate of change in the environment, numerous innovation projects must be mounted, which requires us to:

▶ Encourage as many "determined beyond reason" (though pragmatic if you look more closely) champions to come forth.

▶ Accept some level of champion-induced disruption, far beyond the traditional norm.

▶ Draw out champions in personnel as well as engineering, around the edges of big and well-planned projects as well as in independent ventures.

Any one innovation project, whether in accounting or in new-product development, has low odds of success. We must learn to cherish those with a passionate enough attachment to a new idea to push for it, though most such people will be rough around the edges and most of the projects will fail.

Each *day,* find one or two specific opportunities to publicly applaud/guard/clear the way for champions. Let no visit to any unit, especially support functions, go by without taking the opportunity to cheer at least one new-project champion and one audacious, but hitherto unnoticed, supporter of that champion.

Support Committed Champions

I used to think that anyone doing anything weird was weird. I suddenly realized that anyone doing anything weird wasn't weird at all and that it was the people saying they were weird that were weird.

Paul McCartney
original Beatle

The reasonable man adapts himself to the world; the unreasonable one persists in trying to adapt the world to himself. Therefore, all progress depends on the unreasonable man.

George Bernard Shaw
Man and Superman

CHAMPIONS ARE REQUIRED

What are the management tactics that allow us to achieve the thoroughgoing innovative attitude described in I-1 through I-5? The need for spirited champions inside the firm heads the list.

▶ In *The Spirit of Enterprise,* George Gilder pays tribute to the entrepreneur: "[T]he entrepreneurs sustain the world. In their careers, there is little of optimizing calculation, nothing of delicate balance of markets. They overthrow establishments rather than establish equilibria.

They are the heroes of economic life." He viciously attacks conventional economic theory, which, he insists, denies their role: "The prevailing theory of capitalism suffers from one central and disabling flaw: a profound distrust and incomprehension of capitalists. With its circular flows of purchasing power, its invisible-handed markets, its intricate interplays of goods and moneys, all modern economics, in fact, resembles a vast mathematical drama, on an elaborate stage of theory, without a protagonist to animate the play."

▶ America's premier expert on small business, David Birch of MIT, notes in the same vein that small businesses are uniquely successful at innovating and meeting market needs, in part because of "their [leaders'] unfettered and somewhat undisciplined efforts."

▶ In *Star Warriors*, science reporter William Broad quotes a Lawrence Livermore Labs manager concerning the development of a supercomputer by a tiny team there: "Curt and Tom were considered off-the-wall crazy because it was well known that the big computer companies would have done it if it had been possible. The fact that it hadn't been done meant that it was foredoomed—they were absolutely wasting their time. They got an enormous amount of ridicule. Just because people say you're crazy doesn't mean you're going to win, but sometimes it sure looks like a necessary condition for success."

All of the above support this prescription: Learn to acknowledge—and love—those protagonists.

Inside the firm or outside it, the product/project champion *is* special. He or she is a dreamer, and also a scrounging pragmatist. The champion takes on activities that have low odds for success but are high-odds matters to him or her precisely because of the passionate attachment.

By any rational analysis, the odds of any project's success are low. The barriers are monumental: As if low odds based on technology, manufacturability, and the explosive market where everyone is trying everything weren't enough, everyone inside the firm is out to get the champion of a new product—or a new accounting technique. Machiavelli spoke of the champion's plight in *The Prince:* "It ought to be remembered that there is nothing more difficult to take in hand, more perilous to conduct, or more uncertain in its success, than to take the lead in the introduction of a new order of things. Because the innovator has for enemies all those who have done well under the old conditions, and lukewarm defenders among those who may do well under the new."

Those who attack the innovator, moreover, have a seemingly valid point. Why, they ask, should we disrupt a production line to test a device which has little likelihood of succeeding? Why divert precious equipment in the R&D lab to a flaky project? Why work overtime in the purchasing office to procure a new epoxy resin for some oddball with a wacko idea, using up credibility with a supplier in the process? Why burden a marketer, on a stretched three-man marketing staff, with a two-week assignment to check out a woolly notion?

So this is the *logical* response to the champion in pursuit of a low-odds venture. It thereupon induces a self-fulfilling prophecy: Only the sort of person who is passionately committed to stand up to all this static and ridicule is likely to succeed. Such a person is almost a sure bet to be egotistical, impatient, and disruptive. And those traits in turn further enhance the odds of stiff rebuffs from any establishment's managers.

Only the "Unreasonable" Champion Can Succeed

Richard Pascale, co-author of *The Art of Japanese Management,* describes a unique Japanese entrepreneur: "Any account of Honda's successes must grasp at the outset the unusual character of its founder, Soichiro Honda. . . . Honda was an inventive genius with a large ego and mercurial temperament, given to bouts of 'philandering' (to use his expression). In the formative stages of his company, Honda is variously reported to have tossed a geisha out a second-story window, climbed inside a septic tank to retrieve a visiting supplier's false teeth (and subsequently placed the teeth in his mouth), appeared inebriated and in costume before a formal presentation to Honda's bankers requesting financing vital to the firm's survival (the loan was denied), hit a worker on the head with a wrench, and stripped naked before his engineers to assemble a motorcycle engine."

Gary Taubes reports in *Nobel Dreams* on Carlo Rubbia:

> On December 10, 1984, Carlo Rubbia finally got his Nobel Prize.
> . . . Rubbia is arguably the most powerful man in high-energy physics. . . . His is a discipline in which political savvy, physical endurance, money, and maybe guts, can be as important as scientific

insight. . . . [H]e is renowned for his frenetic energy and his inability to sit still—or even to stay in one city or one country for more than a week—as much as for his physics and his political acumen.

Rubbia had an incurable passion for physics. If his proposals were rejected by the management, he would do experiments under the table. He would set up his equipment on test beams and, if questioned, explain that he had only been checking his apparatus. . . .

He was considered one of the three toughest men to work for at CERN, and as far as I can tell, few physicists who worked for him liked him. . . . He was unsteadfast. Frequently he failed to finish what he had started. He tended to create extravagant experiments, then leave them for other extravagant experiments as soon as they showed signs of coming up with unextravagant results. He had a reputation for impetuosity, for lacking the patience to do the kind of excruciatingly careful analysis high-energy physics demands. And physicists who knew Rubbia at the time suggested that, as a result, his numbers were inaccurate as often as not. "I would feel badly if I did something wrong," explained one senior physicist who worked with Rubbia in the sixties. "For Carlo, that's not what counts. Clearly, he has a different kind of thing that drives him." Bernard Sadoulet, who first met Rubbia in 1969, put it more bluntly: "His numbers are what they are. They are usually wrong—but if they suit his purpose, nothing is wrong."

Rubbia's career faced ruin several times in the 1970s because of questionable data. Yet he fought back. Because of his reputation, he was at times pushed to the back of the line, but that just created another barrier to batter down: "Rubbia went through contortions to get precedence. He tried to have detecting equipment built quickly in the machine shops at CERN, but was informed that his competitors had priority there, too. He then borrowed some equipment from a Harvard colleague, flew it from Boston to Geneva checked as luggage, and rolled it into the path of the colliding beams while the technicians were taking a half-hour tea break. He took the first pictures of protons in collision and showed them a few weeks later at the American Physical Society meeting in New York. It was called a tour de force."

When he got support for his vital experiment, which eventually led to the prize, he and a partner went out in search of a team: "One physicist described [the recruiting process] as the Rubbia roadshow: polished transparencies, lots of hyperbole, plenty of striding back and forth and gesticulating, and remarkable amounts of enthusiasm." And once the team was assembled, Rubbia pushed. "[H]e would control the detector to the best of his paranoid abilities. 'Paranoid' is the word Rubbia himself uses. He would push his physicists to work on a timescale that they considered impossible. He would tell them he wanted some device in a weekend that they thought would need three months, and they would eventually get it to him in two weeks. They would never know quite how they were able to do it so fast. But Rubbia expected it, and it wasn't worthwhile giving him another reason to scream, since he found so many without their help."

In Rubbia we see all the successful champion's characteristics writ large: (1) energy, (2) passion, (3) idealism, (4) pragmatism, (5) cunning, (6) towering impatience, (7) an unrealistic unwillingness to allow any barrier to set him back, and (8) love-hate relationships among his subordinates.

Would you hire Soichiro Honda? Would you hire Carlo Rubbia? If you had hired them, would you have kept them on when even their integrity was under attack? Be honest with yourself.

The role of the absurdly committed champion is an established fact, from the battlefield to the fast-food industry. Yet historically, the pace of change was such that you could survive, at least, without many champions.

Not so today. Today we are confronted by a brutal conundrum. Because of all the interacting sources of uncertainty described in Part I, the odds for the success of any one project are going down fast—after all, twenty-seven firms in your market are trying the same thing you are, with new ones added every day. Increasingly, then, we need to innovate faster just to survive; put another way, we need many *more* people to sign up for projects with much *lower* odds for success just to stay even. In short, we need impassioned champions by the thousands. Yet the impassioned champion is anathema to everything that traditional, civil, organized corporate endeavor stands for. But we must hire him, even though he will alienate some good people, irritate almost everyone, and in the end fail anyway more often than not. The picture is not meant to be pretty. Rubbia hardly comes across as a "nice guy." Neither did Honda in his inventive days. But in saying that, I steadfastly refuse to sugarcoat the truth: Most successful innovators, in training departments, factories, and labs, have a bit of the Rubbia in them. If they didn't, they'd never have had the gumption to start—and never, never have had the will to stay the course.

THE MISSING LINK: MANAGERS MUST
ACT AS EXECUTIVE CHAMPIONS

So what's the manager to do? <u>You must become what I call an executive champion—a nurturer, protector, facilitator, and interference runner for as many energetic champions as you can induce to sally forth.</u> Moreover, if you are a senior executive, you must encourage other managers also to view their role, in large measure, as that of executive champion.

You must individually and collectively dance a tightrope: (1) hire your Rubbias, (2) provide them with pillows rather than accountants to punch when things are at a low ebb, (3) protect others from them and them from others, often for long periods of time, and (4) occasionally fire them if they do stray too far off the reservation.

EVERYBODY CAN (MUST) BE A CHAMPION

So far, I have dealt only with the gloomy half of the story, with the oddballs who must be kept from self-destructing before the job is done. The deeper issue is how to elicit something only a little short of Rubbia's energy from larger numbers of people already on the payroll—in the operations center even!

Take this story from Ford, reported by William Allan of Scripps Howard in 1986:

> A few months ago, Ford Motor Co. gave up on the EXP, its two-seat sports car. Two seaters—MR2, Fiero, Civic, 300ZX— are so popular even Cadillac is planning one, but EXP sales were sluggish. Its styling was stale, and for a sports car it was plain lazy. . . .

But when the news of EXP's planned demise reached Ford's Wayne, Michigan, assembly plant, there was a revolution of sorts. . . . Losing an entire model line sent visions of layoffs through the plant. "We hated to lose a whole model. Building another car line gives the plant security," said John Latini, plant manager.

The employees, with a bit of assistance from Latini, went down to the body shop and pirated parts from the other models and put together what they thought was a much better-looking EXP. "Ford had actually canceled the EXP, but we took the front end and both bumpers off a prototype of the current Escort GT. We had to smooth some sheet metal back along the body, but it looked real good," Latini said. . . . The employee pumpkin wasn't ready for the big dance just yet. Detroit doesn't work that way. But the plant's version was good enough to be shipped to Ford's Design Center, where the pros smoothed out some rough edges.

The result is the 1986 Escort EXP. During its first three months it posted steadily increasing sales. . . .

I contend, then, that many average people have a lot of the Rubbia in them, and we must find ways to unleash it. Several prescriptions in this book will focus on how to do so—to engender commitment and passion in everyone for constant improvement of everything. The trick is not mere exhortation to "become an impassioned champion." We must do many things right, in tandem, to up the odds of champions coming forth to take on risky projects—and even moving a filing cabinet ten feet is a risky act in many places (see C-2).

Among them, we must: encourage rapid testing of everything in small pilot projects (I-3); model innovation ourselves (I-7); proactively support failure and defiance of the rules, as long as core values are not violated (I-8); train the daylights out of people (P-4); rid the organization of senseless bureaucracy (P-10) and excess layers of management (P-8); reconceive every manager's role as one of facilitator rather than cop (P-9); and give people a stake in the action when their taking the initiative works out (P-6).

PUBLIC PARALLELS

It should go without saying that the passionate champion is the engine of innovation in the public sector as well, from the army in battle to the neighborhood school. Moreover, he or she shows all the "difficult" traits exhibited by champions in the private sector. Thus, the role of executive champion in the public sector requires even more deftness because of public scrutiny. The executive champion must provide succor for both the champion and the aldermen the champion offends.

FIRST STEPS

1. Whenever a project team is about to be formed, do you instinctively think first of the passion of the champion or would-be champion when you are searching for a project leader, or do you focus on other skills? I suggest the former. Regardless of your level in management, do you think of yourself as facilitator (or nurturer, protector) of champions? Or do you think of yourself as master project administrator, managing other plan-driven project administrators? Keep the distinctions at the front of your mind when it's time to appoint the next team or project leader.
2. Each day, give yourself a grade on how well, as evidenced by specific actions, you have defended, guarded, and made things easier for champions. If you can't point to specific actions taken each day, you are simply not engendering innovative activity at the pace required for survival.

I-7

SUMMARY

To get the constant innovation necessary for survival, managers must:

▶ Personally symbolize innovativeness in their daily affairs.

▶ Seek out opportunities to stand foursquare with innovators.

Seeing is believing! Would-be champions will be encouraged to come forth when senior managers demonstrate, by their actions, that they support constant innovation, even when it's a bit disruptive. It is essential that managers make a constant effort to recognize innovators (and applaud the details of their victories over organizational inertia), at all levels and in all functions.

Each *day*, seek out at least one opportunity to stand on the side of innovation and innovators. Practice "purposeful impatience" daily: applaud the new, rough-cut or not, and yawn at even good performance that involves no bold moves and no fast-paced experiments. Create an Innovators Hall of Fame, and include members from support functions in at least equal numbers to those from the engineering, design, or merchandising function.

I-7

"Model" Innovation/Practice Purposeful Impatience

A wonderful story is told about Lee Iacocca when he wanted to add a convertible to Chrysler's line. Following standard operating procedures, he asked his chief engineer to craft a model. The engineer, consistent with (actually better than) industry standards, replied, "Certainly. We can put together a prototype in nine months." Several bystanders report Iacocca's furious response: "You just don't understand. Go find a car and saw the top off the damn thing!" Iacocca got his prototype—and in short order. He then proceeded, so the story goes, to engage in some "systematic" market research. He drove around Detroit with the top down on the new prototype, and when the number of people waving at him reached a level he thought satisfactory, he ordered the car built—and it's a fact that a big success ensued.

Is the tale apocryphal? Parts of it surely aren't, as I've heard the story confirmed again and again. In any event, it has given rise to the two key terms in this prescription: "purposeful impatience" and "model innovation in your daily affairs."

A MANAGER'S DAY-TO-DAY ACTIVITIES: SYMBOLS OF SUPPORT FOR (OR REJECTION OF) INNOVATION

1. Be careful of your mundane actions. Do your office routines, whether you are in the executive suite or the supervisor of the seven-person accounts receivable department, exhibit the "saw the top off the damn thing" attitude that you are asking of others? Or are you inconsistent? Do you encourage people to bypass functional barriers and deal directly with their counterparts in other functions, but then get bent out of shape when someone does this and gets you in hot water with a fellow vice-president? Do you encourage cutting the paperwork to speed the pace of action, but continue to spew out twenty-three memos per day?

Do you applaud when someone scrounges computer time, breaking a little china, and succeeds in speeding up a project? And do you continue to applaud—or at least shrug it off—if the effort fails and it turns out that the scrounged computer time means a delay in receiving a 275-page report you've anxiously been awaiting because the president wants it?

You want committees sharply reduced. But have you appointed any new ones lately? You want product development teams to have a full-time operations person on them from the start. But do you then scream when an operations snafu arises, attributable (it is said) to the fact that Ms. Jones was detailed to one of those teams?

The new rules for innovation that these prescriptions propose controvert most conventional wisdom. You, the boss, must live up to them—especially the small, but symbolically significant, ones.

2. Behave with purposeful impatience. I believe in civility—most of the time. But not when it comes to an exercise like this: "We need three more days to get the computer run on the cost buildup from the division controller's office; they're tied up with the corporate monthly operating review." Don't put up with it. Ever again.

That is, you must make it clear that people are paid to beat down functional barriers—preferably by building solid relationships in every function. They are not being paid to guard turf and process "cover your tail" memos up and down the organization (see also P-8, P-9).

So the answer to the plea for "three more days" is: "Uh-huh. Well, you've got forty-five minutes to get the numbers; that's when the presentation starts." Or: "You've been involved with this project for eleven months. You should know the numbers we need from memory." Or: "Fine. We'll sit here in the boardroom and wait. Anybody know a good carry-out restaurant?"

It is essential—today more than ever—not to put up with traditional excuses that come from the victory of boardroom-brand civility and functional primacy over taking action.

3. You want innovation? Just ask for it. A bank president called a two-day meeting at a remote location to work with his top forty officers on some strategic issues. The group trundled off at one point for a "breakout session," where teams traditionally get together to noodle over some key issue, coming back with a vague report about "the important parameters." This time the president's guidance was unconventional: "You've got two hours to come up with big savings, without layoffs. . . . See you in 120 minutes." They did return—and with the savings. A significant share of the ideas were implementable. One group brought $700,000 back to the table, and exceeded that brash target in practice.

At Milliken's four-day annual retreat for top managers, I've seen groups of twenty from disparate functions and businesses wrestle with a thorny issue for two hours, knowing they had to come up with a lengthy action list, to be implemented—and reported on—in 30 days. They unfailingly do it. No one says, "But my boss is not here, I can't commit our group to that." It's your job as a senior manager, says Milliken, to know what you can and can't commit to—and you'd better be able to offer a lot, or you and your boss are both going to be in hot water. Little time is spent on nuances, less on bureaucratic bickering. The issue is: "We're going to crack this nut," and that's that. They quickly go around the table; each participant has a minute or two to discuss her or his idea—*and* to propose a 30-day action plan, such as "Meet with X at plant Y and shorten this step in the paper processing. Due date 3/18/87." The meeting chairman nods quickly, the item is duly recorded, and on they go: "Fine. . . . Okay, Dave, what does the New York sales office have to say about the new product sample preparation process?" Bang. Bang.

It may sound impossible. I couldn't believe my own eyes at first. But I've seen it at Milliken four years running, and at a number of other firms as well. It can be done.

4. Seek out and celebrate the innovators. There are mavericks who do the impossible in support departments such as MIS—for instance, a software code writer who finishes what's typically a month-long debugging task in a weekend. It turns out that although he's in North Dakota, he has scrounged computer time from a little-used mainframe in Barcelona, then cajoled a couple of vendor people into helping out, too.

Somehow, you must develop routines that aid you, as boss, in hearing about him. It's not easy, since he generally works from midnight until 10 a.m. in a hidden corner of a faraway building (most computer installations are in low-rent neighborhoods or rural states). Once he surfaces, call immediately (or fly in) and make a fuss over his herculean effort. (One California bank executive gives awards to persons who tell her about innovators that are almost equal to those she gives the innovator per se. It's a great strategy for unearthing unsung stars in faraway places.)

5. Establish a Hall of Fame in every unit—and insist that it be full. And though big annual innovation awards are desirable, a month is probably the longest you should go without some sort of award. Even on-the-spot awards should be more or less formalized. Give all managers an informal quota. I don't favor a rigid target like "four per month." But I do recommend that you carefully track the results and cajole those who seem to be reluctant to give out such awards: "No innovations in purchasing again this month, I see. Could that be right, John?" Or include in the monthly operations review a brief "Innovation Report" that lists the innovations, innovators, and innovators' bosses; the repeated absence of any executive's name adds to the pressure on him/her to produce.

6. Reward small innovations as well as large ones. Wholesale participation in innovating is essential. This will be spurred by vigorously celebrating small innovations, not just breakthroughs. (Interestingly, American financial awards for suggestions average ten percent of the savings that the suggestions subsequently generate. Japan's far more numerous awards average only one percent of savings. The Japanese reason—correctly—that lots of small awards induce more tries.)

7. Support the supporting cast. Be sure that those in the support functions who help the innovators get about as much credit, in both fanfare and dollars, as the hotshot software engineer or children's wear merchant. We need to replace buck-passing with rapid action. One vital aid is ensuring that the Hall of Fame trophy for the beat-the-competition introduction of the 2938R test machine, the Fangouli line of women's wear, or the new salad-bar format includes the names of the people who helped out from purchasing, accounting, training, and the like—and includes them prominently, not in a footnote.

The reasoning is straightforward. <u>Most improvements and time reductions in the product/service development process will come from turning the largely unseen supporting cast into committed champions.</u> Therefore, treat them that way. Consider, for example, George, the accountant who voluntarily goes all out doing a complex cost analysis in three days that usually takes two weeks. He turns a touted designer into a hero, but misses his son's first Little League game in the process, and gets his immediate boss's nose bent out of shape to boot, because the boss's pet project slipped a bit. George deserves a medal, and more than a bronze one. But—and here I repeat, but this is vital—you must first work like the devil to find him! The chief engineer never fails to bring around "Jane the genius circuit designer," but George never gets to tag along. If you are really wired in, you'll personally send Joey, George's boy, two box-seat tickets—for Joey and George—for a game during the Padres' next home stand. The plaque in the Hall of Fame gallery should prominently feature George too.

I've seen all of these management spurs to innovation in action. They are individually powerful, and collectively dynamite. However, they require a thoroughgoing penchant for innovation and close attention to its outcroppings—on a day-to-day basis.

FIRST STEPS

1. Get a close associate to act as your conscience. He or she should let you know, bluntly, each time you start acting like the problem rather than the solution—that is, fostering inertia and barrier-building rather than action-taking and barrier destruction.
2. Simply demand action without muss and fuss. Raise a big rumpus—that is, walk out—the next time you hear "X couldn't get the data because . . ."
3. Seek at least one opportunity each day to say in effect, "Saw the top off the damn thing"—that is, do a quick modification, don't reinvent the wheel.

4. Go out of your way to publicly pat an innovator on the back. Recognize at least one innovator a week, even if only with a simple note.

5. Be relentless in systematically seeking out and celebrating the invisible supporters of the successful project team, especially those from off-line functions who helped out at some peril to themselves. Make sure that you reward at least two supporters for every front-line innovator; do some personal digging to get at these supporters.

I-8

SUMMARY

To speed action-taking—and reduce innovation cycle time—as necessary to be competitive requires us to make *more* mistakes, *faster;* we must:

▶ Support *failure* by actively and publicly rewarding mistakes—failed efforts that were well thought out, executed with alacrity, quickly adjusted, and thoroughly learned from.

▶ Actively and publicly reward defiance of our own often inhibiting regulations.

▶ Personally seek out and directly batter down irritating obstacles—often as not small ones—that cumulatively cause debilitating delays and which champions cannot readily clear from their own paths.

Inaction is the chief enemy of speedy innovation. These prescriptions, as a whole, are designed to induce faster action-taking. This necessarily translates into making *more* mistakes and defying silly bureaucratic rules and traditions.

Revel in thoughtful failures that result from fast action-taking. If you haven't yet cheered at least one interesting failure today, applauded an act of defiance, and removed one tiny hurdle from a champion's path, you are not four-square behind fast innovation.

I-8

Support Fast Failures

You've got to have an atmosphere where people can make mistakes. If we're not making mistakes, we're not going anywhere. The scientific method is designed for mistakes.

> Gordon Forward
> President, Chaparral Steel

Many people dream of success. To me success can only be achieved through repeated failure and introspection. In fact, success represents the 1 percent of your work which results only from the 99 percent that is called failure.

> Soichiro Honda
> founder, Honda Motor

[Limited founder Les Wexner] actually likes mistakes; buyers are graded not only on their successes, but also on their failures. Too many hits means the buyer isn't taking enough chances. . . .

This is not a company that lingers over its mistakes. Wexner's divisions dump tons of [unsalable] clothing into the off-price and bargain-basement market each year. "When you eat like an elephant, you s—— like an elephant," Wexner has said.

> *Forbes,* April 1987

Gordon Forward worships at the altar of science—and cherishes mistakes. Honda says he mucks up 99 percent of the time. Wexner goes further and rewards failures, and is wary of too much success. What is the meaning of so much passion for failure by well-known superachievers?

COMPLEXITY + NEED FOR SPEED = MAKE MORE MISTAKES (OR ELSE)

There's little that is more important to tomorrow's managers than failure. We need lots more of it. We need faster failure. It is fair to say that if we can't increase the gross national failure rate, we're in for a very rough ride indeed. (Actually, the economy's brightest star is the increase in failures. That is, our accelerated rate of business start-ups has brought record levels of job creation—and an accompanying record rate of failures.)

After a speech I gave in April 1987, a bank executive from Colorado urged me to "title your next book *How to Learn to Love Failure.*" Nothing, he avowed, is more vital in financial services, where new products are introduced daily, new competitors emerge weekly (recall Eastern Airlines' MasterCard in C-1), and product life cycles are shrinking dramatically.

The logic is simple: (1) We must innovate, in every department, faster. (2) Innovation obviously means dealing with the new—i.e., the untested. (3) Uncertainty is rising. (4) Complexity is rising. (5) Uncertainty is only removed and complexity dealt with by action. (6) To act on the new in the face of increasing complexity yields failure. (7) To act speedily yields speedy failure. (8) Rx for speedy innovation: More failure, faster. (9) Rx for dramatically speeded-up innovation: Dramatically increased rates and amounts of failure.

Plans can only go so far, and not very far at that. Literally thousands of variables—people (you, your boss, your champion, your accountant, etc.), technology, competitors (and their people, technology . . .), timing, macro-economic forces, random external events—are at play in successfully introducing the most basic training course, let alone a new computer, a memory chip, a fashion line, a menu change at a 100-restaurant chain, or a consulting service. Those variables, beyond the few that any formal plan covers, can only be addressed (and then tinkered with) when the project sees at least the partial light of day (this was the main message of I-3).

Perhaps a 750-page plan can anticipate 10 percent of the possible snafus. But it takes nine months to prepare. Those nine months are an eternally lost opportunity to do real-world testing, failing, and adjusting.

A 25-page plan anticipates 8 percent of the problems, and can be completed in a tenth of the time. The point is this: There is an almost irreducible number of failures associated with launching anything new. For heaven's sake, hurry up and get them over with!

Get Over the "F-Word" Hurdle

When I talk with businesspersons I find they certainly understand, and sign up for the obvious logic of, the discussion above. Yet they have a terrible time coming to grips with the word "failure." In fact, several people, when asked in a seminar to discuss the role of fast failure in speeding up innovation, could not bring themselves to do so directly. The closest they could get was "the hated 'F' word" and "outcomes of the other variety."

To increase the speed of innovation and dramatically accelerate product development cycles as required by competitive conditions, we must quickly come to grips with the word "failure" and the issue of failure. The timely achievement of anything new entails vigorous public support of failure—not just support for "good tries," but public support for failures themselves.

Talk Up Failure

The goal is to be more than tolerant of slip-ups. You must be like Wexner and actively encourage failure. Talk it up. Laugh about it. Go around the table at a project group meeting or morning staff meeting: Start with your own most interesting foul-up. Then have everyone follow suit. What mistakes did you make this week? What were the most interesting ones? How can we help you make more mistakes, faster?

Literally give awards, perhaps fun ones—a bent golf putter, an old tennis shoe (bronzed), or a model of two cars crashing into one another—for the most interesting/creative/useful/fastest failure. Ask everyone to repeat this exercise with his or her people, weekly or monthly. Have an annual "Hall of Shame" banquet where you give awards for the fastest/most useful—and the dumbest and most embarrassing—foul-ups. Also include "interesting fast failures" as a regular category in your newsletter.

On the informal side, add a leaf to the one-minute manager's ritual:

317

instead of looking to "catch someone doing something right," <u>look to catch someone doing something wrong</u>! Make it a habit to send thank-you notes to people who make innovative, fast failures; send such a note around the office when an interesting, fast failure comes to your attention.

"Fail Forward"

To be sure, pay attention to Mr. Honda's formulation—"failure and introspection." To support speedy failure is not to support (or tolerate) sloppiness. It is imperative to demand (1) that something be learned from each failure, and (2) that it be quickly followed with a new modification.

Dave Boyer is president of Teleflex, a profitable maker of high-tech control systems, based in Limerick, Pennsylvania. The firm's automotive division has rapidly grown from $10 million to $60 million, attributable to a rate of new-product introduction which has resulted in 50 percent of sales coming from products launched in the last year. The key to that success rate is what Boyer calls "failing forward." That is, failing fast—and learning from it so as to make the next and smarter step quickly. The Teleflex team talks openly about "failing forward," and sees this openness as a prime ingredient in their success.

You Can't Wait to Dot All the "i's"

There is an important caveat to the above. I said that supporting fast and useful failure does not imply supporting sloppiness. That's true only to a point. Sloppiness could be interpreted to mean not tying up every loose end, not waiting until all the data are in. But the fact is that we can't afford to wait until all the data are in because by then the market will be lost. We must trust instinct, and we must launch tests with only some of the data in. So be careful to tolerate fast-paced moves (and subsequent failures) when only some of the answers are available, and when the fastest way to get more of the answers is to test, not talk (it usually is the fastest way).

"Fast Failure" and "Do It Right the First Time": No Conflict

How do you reconcile the inevitability of failure and the quality gurus' plea that you "do it right the first time"? Aren't the two ideas at odds?

To begin with, so far I've been dealing with the introduction of a new product or service or training program or accounting software package; the emphasis has been on addressing the vagaries of the market (including the internal-to-the-firm market for, say, a new training program). Introducing the new, which by definition goes beyond the routine and accepted, will be accompanied by failure—period.

More generally, though, the "do it right the first time" philosophy rests squarely on the acknowledgment of failure and the need for constant tinkering. That is, we are presumably not now doing it up to maximum potential (not doing it right the first time) because we haven't: (1) worked with suppliers on problems, (2) trained and encouraged our people to analyze existing problems, and (3) assessed and updated systems which cause bottlenecks.

So implementing "do it right the first time" means acknowledging that each job, routine, and system is a hotbed of endless opportunities for improvement. The simple definition of an "opportunity" is that something is now broken, regularly failing, or at least not working as it might. Furthermore, new and improvement-conscious competitors are constantly making their product better; if we are not constantly improving (which means testing and adjusting—and failing, since each test deals with the novel), we are by definition falling behind, relatively—and relatively is what counts.

So "do it right the first time" and the quest for constant improvement depend on (1) acknowledging current failures, and (2) making lots of fast failures as we constantly experiment with new ways of doing things.

Seek Out "Little" Failures: Become a "Failure Fanatic"

Today's essential quest for constant improvement of everything only comes from constant adjustment of routines, both trivial and great. To adjust any process means dealing with new conditions—which means (once again) failing ("if you're not falling down, you're not learning" is the skier's dictum). It is impossible to overstate the degree to which tiny failures (minuscule errors resulting from trying new things—e.g., changing the way an order entry form is handled) feel like big ones on the front line in most companies.

To induce constant improvement, *everyone* must be failing faster, including the newest mail clerk, trying to improve his or her method of sorting the mail. The idea of supporting—seeking out and vigorously applauding—numerous little failures is essential. For the littlest novel effort feels like a huge risk to most, and it traditionally has been ("we don't pay people to screw things up, Ms. Jones"). We must, then, especially on the front line, become "failure fanatics," constantly in search of a little mistake to applaud, even a dumb one made in an effort to improve something.

THE DIRE RESULTS OF FAILING TO SUPPORT FAILURE

It is so frightening to observe, as I repeatedly do, organizations where the fear of revealing the tiniest of errors is sky-high. Here's what ensues: (1) Small failures are individually hidden and fester until they accumulate, causing big failures much further down the line; (2) small failures, since they are unacceptable, do not quickly lead to adjustments, but are followed by a huge effort to fit a square peg into a round hole; (3) data are faked (or very liberally or partially interpreted) so that failures can be seen as successes; (4) data are hidden from those in other functions who could help, because the lead function's boss doesn't want to lose face with his or her peers; (5) those at the top are kept in the dark and partially misled (at least by omission), and then commit themselves further and further on the basis of incorrect knowledge—which makes subsequent exposure of failure even harder; (6) no learning takes place, especially among politicized seniors, because no failures ever come to the surface, and normal human give-and-take, chiding and crowing, is replaced by stilted posturing; (7) real tests are delayed and delayed as more and more simulations are done, in a panicky, time-consuming effort to make sure that no failure occurs on the first test—now highly visible and expensive; and, finally, (8) truth, fun, and speed all go down the drain.

SUPPORT DEFIANCE OF REGULATIONS
THAT SLOW THINGS DOWN

The innovation prescriptions boil down to tactics for speeding up the pace of action-taking. And there is an even more audacious requirement than the last one (support for fast failure): <u>Actively and publicly hail defiance of the rules, many of which you doubtless labored mightily to construct in the first place.</u>

To be sure, this does not mean condoning lawbreaking, abusing a fellow employee (or customer or supplier), or allowing shoddy products to go out the door, even to a test market. These few core values should not be defied.

Here I refer to lauding the breaking of bureaucratic rules, regulations, and conventions which, even when written out, unnecessarily slow down action-taking. But how can you teach respect for the law and individuals, promote perfection in quality and service, and then race around cheering out-and-out defiance?

In a perfect world, there'd be no Mickey Mouse rules, written or otherwise (see P-10, L-8 for my suggestions on getting rid of such nuisances). Furthermore, you'd have no functional jealousies and turf-guarding to clog up the works. But the world of sizable organizations is not perfect and won't be, no matter how hard we work at eliminating bureaucracy. So it is not inconsistent to urge an obsession with quality and at the same time to cheer on someone who ignores petty rules and traditions in order to scrounge some parts or commandeer a computer or 250 square feet of factory space to quickly knock out a prototype. The process of seeking constant quality improvement or enhanced flexibility requires us to break silly rules that impede communication and fast action.

Telling Stories About "Constructive Defiance"

The leader's chief tool here is storytelling (see also L-3). Storytelling allows you to make your point with precision—to distinguish precisely, through example, between "good defiance" and the unacceptable violation of core values. So I suggest that you use storytelling (in person at all-hands meetings, in newsletters, on videotape) to laud innovators' appropriate defiance and, at the same time, their adherence to shared values. Thus, you can publicly laugh at the details of their scrounging of this and that, and at the same time applaud the quality of their work and their respect for their teammates. More specifically, I propose that you go out of your way to recount at least one vignette which illustrates constructive defiance, as I call it, in pursuit of speedy innovation each time you give a little talk; include at least one story of constructive defiance in each newsletter.

Few Rules Should Be Inviolable: "Place Your Waterline Low"

The late Bill Gore (founder of W. L. Gore & Associates, makers of Gore-Tex and medical products) had a superb metaphor for managing risk-taking. "You can try anything, as long as it's above the 'waterline,' " he'd say. "Above the waterline" meant anything that didn't affect the basic integrity of the organization. "If you want to drill holes below the waterline," he'd add, "you need to check with your sponsor [the W. L. Gore equivalent of boss]."

I've found that metaphor useful—to a point. That is, the practical issue becomes where management places the waterline. Bill Gore placed it as shown in Figure 12A; very little was below it. You were encouraged to try almost anything. In fact, the last time I saw him, in 1986, he bragged that a European associate had bought a plant (albeit for a song) without telling him!

Figure 12

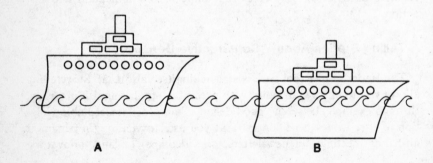

A   B

I find that the conventional listener is enamored with the waterline metaphor. However, in his or her mind, it's placed as shown in Figure 12B. Virtually nothing is above it. The message: Experiment (and risk failure) as long as the issue is trivial. While I can't provide exact advice on waterline placement, I can urge you to edge toward Bill Gore's version. Constant risk-taking and experimentation are required today simply to survive.

CLEAR AWAY THE HURDLES THAT IMPEDE INNOVATORS' PROGRESS

The final element of this prescription is a suggestion that you adopt a "running the copier" mentality. Innovation project teams get bogged down for numerous reasons, and most of them turn out to be trivial: The team is unable to cadge an extra 100 square feet of office space, even though the project has a high priority. They have to go through a lengthy capital appropriations ritual to get a personal computer. As boss, often the biggest boost you can give your innovation teams comes from seeking out opportunities to knock down these small hurdles, the ones that people are not likely to talk to you about because they are so mundane they don't merit "bothering you." Take heed of the words of Fred Brooks, legendary chief designer of IBM's pathbreaking System 360: "How does a project get to be a year behind schedule? One day at a time." The accumulation of little items, each too "trivial" to trouble the boss with, is a prime cause of miss-the-market delays. As boss, you must consciously seek out opportunities to help in little ways. You must view yourself as basher-in-chief of small barriers and facilitator-in-chief of trivial aids to action rather than "the great planner."

Performing this barrier-bashing activity also presents one more opportunity to symbolize innovation (see I-7). When you, as chief, directly intervene to clear the "little stuff" out of the way, you are not just being helpful to the team. You are also sending a powerful message to all involved that you don't want such barriers to interfere with innovation-minded project teams in the first place. Flailing away at the little hurdles—and publicly clucking at the hurdle-makers—is all part of the process of upping the pace of activity.

PUBLIC PARALLELS

"But we're under the microscope of constant public scrutiny." If I've heard that once, I've heard it a hundred times from my public sector colleagues. Therefore, it's implied, we can't abide failure.

Utter nonsense! The public scrutiny makes support for failing *more* important in the public sector. The best—and only—way to avoid the embarrassment of big program failures is to encourage little ones.

The best approach to a major reform in, say, police practice is to test bits of it in one neighborhood, for a few weeks or months. Small-scale tests, and accompanying small-scale failures, are the only building blocks for efficient and effective long-term, full-scale success. "All at once" implementation, without such tests and failures, is a recipe for disaster—and true public embarrassment.

FIRST STEPS

I suggest that you (1) publicly applaud at least one fast failure, (2) reward at least one act of constructive defiance, (3) knock down at least one seemingly trivial barrier in a team's way, and (4) perform at least one small facilitating act this week. Insist that each of your subordinate managers do the same.

I-9

SUMMARY

Since a stepped-up rate of innovation has become essential, we must:

▶ Measure innovation.

What gets measured gets done. While there are difficult issues of specification and definition, innovation can be measured. Even imperfect measures provide an accurate strategic indication of progress, or lack thereof.

For every profit center, fast-growing or stagnant, establish a uniform and tough quantitative target for the percentage of revenues stemming from new products and services introduced in the previous 24 months; be liberal in your definition of what constitutes "new." As a starting point, consider a target of 50 percent; this is far too low for some industries, and perhaps too high for others.

I-9

Set Quantitative Innovation Goals

Business Week proclaimed in mid-1986 that Digital Equipment's resurgence could be measured by the 85 percent of sales coming from products introduced in the last 18 months—and contrasted it with IBM's 40 percent over a comparable period. The magazine added that the Digital figure has become an obsession in IBM's executive suite. There's doubtless more to the current state of the ongoing contest between IBM and Digital, but this simple analysis does get directly to the heart of the matter: Innovation can be measured, and thought about—quantitatively.

As usual in these prescriptions, attitude is the root issue—in this instance, getting innovation "in the air." But also as usual, I've discovered no better way to get at these "soft" concerns than by measuring what most consider impossible-to-quantify phenomena. Precise measurement involves sticky matters of definition, as we shall see. However, even crude measures focus the debate. *Business Week*'s crude 85 percent versus 40 percent turns out to be a pretty good indication of IBM's nagging sluggishness in an ever accelerating marketplace.

MEASURING INNOVATION: FIVE KEY FACTORS

You must consider five key factors when measuring innovation:

1. Definition: What constitutes an innovation. It *is* difficult to define innovation. I acknowledge that, and suggest that you worry about it. But then I also suggest that you reach a quick compromise and move to action—in this case, measurement.

Just what is a new product? Surely it's Apple's new Macintosh SE computer. But what about a new cable for that computer? It's the addition of a breakfast menu at a fast-food chain. But is it the addition of a new jelly for morning muffins at the same chain? It's a new photo-finishing kiosk in a retail store, but is it the availability of a new extra-large or extra-small size in one line of shoes?

My strong bias is toward a broadly inclusive definition of what constitutes a new product, for at least three reasons. First, small can turn out to be big. In the early seventies Frito-Lay went after big wins, focusing new-product development energy on whole new categories. Its batting average was low. A new emphasis on "line extensions" marked the late seventies. Line extension connotes small changes in general. But Frito-Lay found out that small was often big. A new bag size opened the market to new customers with new needs. The addition of a new flavor in an old product created a new market.

The story is repeated in other arenas. A building material is repackaged to make it easier for construction workers to handle it on the job. The small change creates new and growing demand for the product. Even in very high technology, a small, user-friendly twist creates unexpected new uses and new customers, and thence new markets.

The second reason for a broad definition of innovation is that the accumulation of small innovations is the premier source of big innovations. The objective is to create history fast—the rapid transformation of every product and service. This was the essence of C-1 through C-4. And recall, from prescription I-1, Regis McKenna's concept of a product as a continuous experiment. Apple has changed the bellwether Apple II dozens of times in a few short years. Each change creates new uses, and over time total transformation has occurred. So, too, has any given department in Nieman-Marcus been modified time and again until it bears only superficial resemblance to its original form.

In fact, research concludes that most landmark products (called "technological guideposts" in engineering- and science-based firms) do not involve breakthroughs. Instead, they are the culmination of many changes, each small, which eventually lead to wholesale user adoption of the product.

The final reason to emphasize small innovations is psychological. "Have innovation on the mind" and "act fast everywhere" are the underlying imperatives of all ten of these prescriptions. Focusing on small innovations improves the odds of generating lots of wins and greater involvement in and enthusiasm for innovation in general.

But isn't there a danger in ignoring the breakthroughs and working far too long on buggy whips and vacuum tubes? Of course there is. But in general, overemphasizing the search for the miracle solution is more dangerous than overemphasizing day-to-day, user-friendly improvements.

2. Rewards: Linked to the innovation goal. Tie compensation and evaluation to the quantitative innovation goal. Measurement stirs up discussion, but the clincher is tying evaluation to it. That was the message on quality (prescription C-2) and service (C-3); the same tune is being hummed here.

3M has pioneered. Compensation, especially at senior levels, has been linked to the percentage of sales that come from new products introduced in the previous couple of years. We urge that you move in the same direction, once you put the issue of definition behind you.

I don't want to make this seem easy. It's not. The aim of measuring innovation is to foster more action, faster, and there is a danger—and this applies to quality measurement schemes as well. The main objective might be derailed if measuring ends up creating bureaucratic pettifogging—for example, if it leads people to revise catalogues weekly to make more colors available on a particular product in order to satisfy the innovation measurement system's appetite. That's obviously not the point.

To beat back the chances of such a bureaucratic drift, arrive at a broadly agreed-upon definition of what constitutes innovation. Then rate executives and others on the basis of the definition, sorting them into three or four broad categories; reward on that basis. And if the definition you chose leads to nitpicks and dysfunctional behavior, change it.

3. Uniform innovation targets. The most important nuance again comes courtesy of 3M: Consider making every business unit's innovation target exactly the same. The theory is simple. Every division, old and mature or new and exotic, should be responsible for regular regeneration. The sandpaper gang should not be let off the hook, or treated as a "cash cow," to use that unfortunate term from the 1970s.

I can't overemphasize the importance of this. In C-1, I presented decisive evidence that (1) all markets, including mature ones, are fragmenting and becoming increasingly dominated by value-adding specialists; (2) highly differentiated mature products are the biggest moneymakers; and (3) any product can be fundamentally differentiated/transformed—a store is no longer "a store," but becomes an "experience," etc. Were I not for target uniformity, I would be led to suggest tougher innovation targets for older and more sluggish divisions or units. The divisions involved in new markets will be forced automatically by competition to act fast. The units with older, established markets can easily (1) become complacent if they are doing well or (2) fall into the "it's a commodity, so only price/cost counts" mind-set.

4. Widespread use of the innovation target. Once more, an atmosphere with chatter about innovation is the central objective. Track and measure innovation, quantitatively and qualitatively. Put innovation goals in every manager's set of objectives. Have quarterly or monthly innovation review meetings in every function, including training and accounting. Start each weekly or monthly staff or operations review meeting with five minutes on innovation programs. Get innovation measures into the formal accounting system. Share information on innovation with everyone. Post measurements of progress conspicuously.

Talk it up!

5. The involvement of all hands. Finally, this measurement process should include everyone. You should emphasize a single, big measurement (e.g., IBM's 40 percent versus Digital's 85 percent and 3M's single target). But at a secondary level, performance evaluation criteria should have "innovation requirements" (note that there's an analogy here to the "customer connection" proposed in C-3). And this should be as true for cash register clerks as for bench scientists and division general managers (see also I-10, L-9).

FIRST STEPS

1. Do immediate, rough-cut measurement of innovation. Define it loosely and tightly and compare the numbers. Let each department or division do it themselves; *don't let central accounting run the*

show! Try some rough comparisons with competitors. Get customers into the act, for they usually give more weight than insiders to minor innovation—and customeroriented—advances.

2. After observing the stability and usefulness of the measure, move to include it in evaluation and compensation within 18 months from now.

I-10

SUMMARY

The turbulent marketplace demands that we:

► Make innovation a way of life for everyone.

We must learn—individually and as organizations—to welcome change and innovation as vigorously as we have fought it in the past, in accounting as well as in new-product development. The corporate capacity for continuous change must be dramatically increased.

Assess each and every action in light of its contribution to an increased corporate capacity for change.

I-10

Create a Corporate Capacity for Innovation

BUILDING INNOVATION SKILLS IS
A LONG-TERM COMMITMENT

I concur with strategy expert Mike Porter's condemnation of mergers, either to diversify or to acquire market share. They are "a drug," he says, "which makes managers feel good in the short term, but ultimately saps the energy and creativity of the firm." Most so-called strategic alliances, so popular these days, don't work either. Porter goes so far as to say they "are never the solution to a company's strategic dilemma." The alliance is usually aimed at papering over a severe weakness rather than working to correct it; the flaw usually becomes more pronounced, not less, when the teammates attempt to work together. Restructuring, in its conventional guise, comes in for severe criticism, too. Porter agrees that it may be necessary and useful as far as it goes. "But restructuring," he observes, "is not a strategy." It atones for past sins (e.g., excessive layers of management); it does not build for the future (i.e., create new and necessary skills). He faults imitation, too. Imitators, unlike innovators, "lack the conviction to set themselves apart."

All of these commonplace approaches to dealing with today's business environment have one thing in common: they are attempted short cuts. All share a fatal flaw. They sidestep the painstaking effort required to create the core capabilities necessary to achieve sustainable competitive advantage in a turbulent setting. No skill is more important than the corporate capacity to change per se. The company's most urgent task, then, is to learn to welcome—beg for, demand—innovation from everyone. This is the prerequisite for basic capability-building of any sort and for subsequent continuous improvement.

Elicit Innovation from Everyone

Creating a basic innovative capacity means inducing a steady, high-volume flow of new projects, products, and services (I-1, I-9). It requires nurturing and ensuring an adequate number of passionate and at times disruptive champions (I-6). It means measuring managers on how much innovation they've induced (I-9). But the challenge ends up being much more broad-based. Everyone, in every function, must constantly pursue innovation; the average firm's overall capacity for innovation must increase dramatically.

It is ironic that we usually argue that Americans are innovators while the Japanese are copycats. There is a good case for the opposite conclusion. To be sure, we Americans love our cowboy entrepreneur heroes, our touted buyers in retailing, our engineers and deal-makers, and our matchless stream of Nobel Prize winners. But we are the ones who treat our workers as rote executors. And our first-line supervisors too. We even treat our middle managers as administrators—not creators of a new (or constantly improving) order. The Japanese, on the other hand, have created a corporate capacity for innovation. They are the ones who insist that every person be constantly involved in improvement projects—every boss, every nonboss, every salesperson and researcher and supplier and subcontractor. Consultant Masaaki Imai even quantifies the trait for managers: "Japanese management generally believes that a manager should spend at least 50 percent of his time on improvement."

The best American firms and leaders, without reference to Japan (to them it's neither Eastern nor Western, but a simple matter of common sense), live the same doctrine. At W. L. Gore & Associates, for instance, the principal success measure for every job—from the mail room to the lab—is innovation, the degree to which the worker (or manager) has changed/improved things. The operative question is: "How is your twenty square feet of the accounts receivable department different (and better) from the way it was ninety days ago?"

334

The Constant Search for New Ideas

In a related vein, I have long observed that one of the primary distinguishing characteristics of the best leaders is their personal thirst for and continued quest for new/small/practical ideas. The two people to whom this book is dedicated, Governor Don Schaefer of Maryland and Roger Milliken, are voracious note-takers (see L-5). Certainly neither one, nor their kindred spirits, ever turned his back on a so-called breakthrough idea. It's just that they long ago gave up believing in miracles; instead, they depend on a mass of small innovations—from everyone—to raise every element of their operations to stratospheric levels of performance.

The idea of being in touch (C-7), swapping and swiping ideas (I-4), and testing them without muss and fuss (I-3) is central. As we saw in prescription C-8, the Japanese and Germans and the best American manufacturers insist that engineers live on the factory floor, getting a feel for the action and being immediately available to assist workers in improvement projects. Being in touch also means breaking down functional barriers. I have emphasized this in relation to new products in prescription I-2, which urges multi-function staffing for newproduct teams.

And being in touch and swapping ideas also mean customers, suppliers, and distributors wandering the company's hallways and plants; and everyone from the company wandering the customers' operations. All of this is more important than ever, because the world-class manufacturing or service firm will be more highly integrated than before, albeit in new ways. Just-in-time inventory management will apply "backward" to vendors and "forward" to distributors and end users. Computerized design tools will link buyers and engineers to plants and operations centers—and to the customer, too. That is, everyone in every function will be a full-scale partner in the value-adding team. Therefore constant innovation by everyone will be requisite.

OWN UP TO THE MAGNITUDE OF THE TASK

"Improvement" is an innocuous term. Even "innovation" is fairly innocuous. "Change" is not. Change means disruption, by definition. Whether it's holding a welding torch at a slightly different angle, moving a file cabinet ten feet, or installing just-in-time inventory management across ten plants, change *is* disruptive. <u>Constant change by everyone requires a dramatic increase in the capacity to accept disruption.</u> Consider our daily affairs: When a road on the way to work is under repair for sixty days, it's a pain in the neck to search out a new route, especially if you were used to stopping at a particular deli on the old route for the world's best cappuccino and buttermilk doughnuts.

I use this trivial example because we should not downplay what a tall order this prescription, I-10, amounts to. This is especially so given the traditional American mechanical model of management derived from mass production, in which disruption of any sort has been a very dirty word. In fact, in seminars the most common rejoinder that I get to the idea of constant innovation is: "But isn't there a high cost to this chaos and anarchy that you're proposing? Surely we don't want that mail-room clerk you talk about being inventive! We want the damned mail on our desks by 9:30 A.M. For heaven's sake, when do you get any work done with all this 'innovation' going on about you?"

The question is fair only in the context of the old model, in which the worker is seen as a pair of hands, with the head a necessary evil. <u>The reality is that millions—*literally* an unlimited number—of innovation/improvement opportunities lie within any factory, distribution center, store, or operations center. And you can multiply that by more millions when you can involve the factory and distribution center and store working together as a team. And multiply again when you add in involvement in innovation by suppliers and customers.</u>

Only when we come to understand that the ideas are principally on the front line (or in the supplier's operation), not in R&D or "higher up," will the fear of disruption recede. For when the new understanding is stamped in, we will begin to search for ways to give workers more time to work at innovation, rather than threatening them at every turn.

Learning to See Disruptions as Opportunities

At Milliken, slipping in an urgently needed new-product sample used to be the ultimate disruption to the very orderly—"rigid" is not an unfair term—factory production environment. Top management became painfully aware that a much higher rate of such "disruptions" (that is, more new products) was its sole path to survival. The firm's major reorganization described in prescription C-4 was aimed at turning former disruptions into a normal way of life, with no loss of efficiency or diminution in quality.

Turning Adversaries into Partners

Most innovation in the future will demand that historically adversarial relations—(1) between many functions in the firm, (2) between labor and management, (3) between suppliers and the firm, (4) between the firm and its distributors/customers—be replaced by cooperative relations. (See, for instance, C-2 on working with suppliers and on the use of cross-functional teams in quality improvement efforts, and I-2 on speedy team product development.)

Establishing new relationships requires listening, creating a climate of respect and trust (P-1 through P-10, S-4, S-5), and coming to understand the mutual benefits that will ensue if partnership relationships are firmly established.

Creating Innovation Capacity

Creating a corporate capacity for constant innovation is a staggering task, the antithesis of the short-cut approach discussed at the beginning of this prescription. It requires all of the skills covered in the nine innovation prescriptions immediately preceding. Further, I-10 provides an ideal introduction to the next twenty prescriptions. Constant innovation, from everyone in every function, can only occur if each person is uniquely valued for—and trained to make and paid for—her or his potentially awesome contribution (P-1 through P-10). The capacity for change (a shift from love of stability to love of change) is also the implicit topic of all ten leadership prescriptions (L-1 through L-10).

FIRST STEPS

1. I-10 is different from the other innovation prescriptions, and therefore the first step is different—it calls for reflection. Think beyond the practical steps, such as inducing pilots of everything (I-3). Focus on the overall capacity (willingness) of your organization to embrace innovation. Subject every personal

action, especially small ones, to this acid test: Does the action increase or decrease the corporate capacity for change? That is, is it on the side of increasing risk-taking and piloting, of encouraging champions to come out of the woodwork? Does it help reduce the fear of the unknown (through kidding about useful failure, for instance)? Or is it on the side of encouraging over-analysis and inaction? If you can't fill in the blank in the following sentence, "This specifically fosters a greater willingness to innovate (especially on the usually fearful front line) because _____," then modify the action you were about to take. Encourage each person working for you to pass every minute daily action through the same filter.

2. Begin to emphasize the shift from adversary to partner by watching your language: How do you describe people in other functions, union leadership (if applicable), suppliers, franchisees? Begin by ensuring that your language toward the traditionally adversarial group is the language of a partner. And, as in Step #1 above, pass each small act through a filtering operation: Does this impede or accelerate the shift from adversary to partner?

IV

ACHIEVING FLEXIBILITY BY EMPOWERING *P*EOPLE

SECTION SUMMARY

The first twenty prescriptions depict a newly flexible, responsive, and adaptive organization. The implicit, and at times explicit, theme has been "through people"—people *must* become the primary source of value added, not a "factor of production" to be optimized, minimized, and/or eliminated.

The first two of the ten prescriptions here (see Figure 13) constitute the Basic Premise: P-1 boldly asserts that there is no limit to what the average person can accomplish if thoroughly involved; P-2 adds that this power can most effectively be tapped when people are gathered in human-scale groupings—that is, teams, or, more precisely, self-managing teams.

The next prescriptions, the Five Supports, are the tools required to achieve wholesale involvement by everyone: P-3, an atmosphere marked by constant opportunities (both formal and informal) for everyone to be listened to—and then recognized for their smallest accomplishments; P-4, substantial line effort devoted to recruiting that focuses explicitly on desired values and qualities (ability to work on teams, for instance); P-5, a radical emphasis on training and retraining—that is, constant upgrading of skills; P-6, incentive pay, based upon contribution and performance, for everyone; and P-7, provision of some form of employment guarantee for a major part of the work force, assuming acceptable individual performance.

These supports can assist in achieving P-1 and P-2 only if the Three Inhibitors are removed: P-8, simplifying structure by reducing layers and eliminating all front-line supervision as we know it; P-9, changing the role of middle managers from cop and guardian of functional fiefdoms to basher of barriers between functions in order to induce true autonomy and speed action-taking at the front line; and P-10, eliminating silly bureaucratic procedures and, worse still, demeaning regulations and dispiriting work conditions.

A 1985 study by consultants at A. T. Kearney discovered that some 80 percent of Fortune 500 firms had started some type of quality circle program since 1980; unfortunately, 83 percent had dropped the effort within 18 months of its inception. Why?

The principal reason is a tendency simply to form "teams" and in effect tell their members to "get interested and participate." The remedy is to work on all ten of these prescriptions at once. I admit that doing it "all at once" is a tall order. Yet accomplishing the objectives of this set of prescriptions—upon which all else (e.g., C-1 through C-10) depends—is uniquely resistant to piecemeal implementation. Obviously, progress and breadth of implementation will vary from prescription to prescription. But you must at least get started on all ten more or less simultaneously. That is, involvement means nothing without training; involvement and training mean nothing unless overly complex, bureaucratic procedures are eliminated; and so on.

When General Motors and Toyota joined together in the NUMMI venture described in prescription P-1 and referred to elsewhere in these pages, a formal, guiding philosophy was developed. It included these elements: (1) "Kaizen, the never-ending quest for perfection"; (2) "the development of full human potential"; (3) "Jidoka, the pursuit of superior quality"; (4) "build mutual trust"; (5) "develop team performance"; (6) "every employee as manager"; and (7) "provide a stable livelihood for all employees." These seven features, supported by simple systems, extensive training, and a host of other devices, have resulted in startling performance improvement in short order. One *can* break NUMMI's success into a series of discrete factors—but although each *is* essential, it is the interaction among all of them, at work simultaneously, which has proved to be NUMMI's secret.

Figure 13: **Achieving Flexibility by Empowering People**

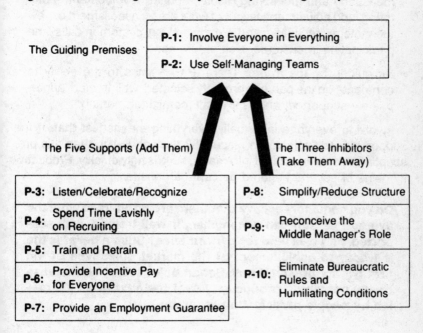

The Guiding Premises

P-1: Involve Everyone in Everything

P-2: Use Self-Managing Teams

The Five Supports (Add Them)

P-3:	Listen/Celebrate/Recognize
P-4:	Spend Time Lavishly on Recruiting
P-5:	Train and Retrain
P-6:	Provide Incentive Pay for Everyone
P-7:	Provide an Employment Guarantee

The Three Inhibitors (Take Them Away)

P-8:	Simplify/Reduce Structure
P-9:	Reconceive the Middle Manager's Role
P-10:	Eliminate Bureaucratic Rules and Humiliating Conditions

P-1

SUMMARY

Executing the business strategies laid out in the first two sets of prescriptions (C-1 through C-10, I-1 through I-10) requires the unstinting involvement of everyone in the firm. Therefore, we must:

▶ Involve all personnel at all levels in all functions in virtually everything: for example, quality improvement programs and 100 percent self-inspection; productivity improvement programs; measuring and monitoring results; budget development, monitoring, and adjustment; layout of work areas; assessment of new technology; recruiting and hiring; making customer calls and participating in customer visit programs.

▶ Be guided by the axiom: There are no limits to the ability to contribute on the part of a properly selected, well-trained, appropriately supported, and, above all, committed person.

Involving everyone in virtually everything means just that. If the supporting elements are in place (P-2 through P-10), then this prescription can be translated into reality, surprisingly quickly. Productivity gains of several hundred percent can ensue.

Do you genuinely believe that there are no limits to what the average person can accomplish, if well trained, well supported, and well paid for performance? Such a belief is the #1 spur to achievement of the market objectives of the first twenty prescriptions. Set an objective of an increase of 100 percent in productivity over the next three years—led by people-participation programs.

Involve Everyone
in Everything

Powerlessness corrupts. Absolute powerlessness corrupts absolutely.

> Rosabeth Moss Kanter
> Harvard Business School

Something happened that must not happen again. Somewhere, somehow, the employees got the idea that they were in the driver's seat. That they had control in their hands. This is an attitude, gentlemen, that must be reversed. This is the fantasy that must be eradicated.

> Lemuel Bouleware
> GE industrial relations executive
> commenting to top management
> after a 1946 strike

I'm not going to have the monkeys running the zoo.
> Frank Borman
> former chairman, Eastern Airlines,
> discussing worker participation,
> *The Washington Monthly,* June 1986

The customer prescriptions emphasized quality, service, quick response, and heretofore unheard-of flexibility. The innovation prescriptions demanded numerous champion-powered small starts, team product development, and making innovation everyone's responsibility.

Execution of these two sets of prescriptions is impossible without the wholesale involvement mandated by P-1. In fact, despite the accelerating technology/automation revolution, our organizations must become more dependent on people (line workers). To be sure, fewer people will work on the line in a given factory or operations center, but those who do will be more important to and responsible for the company's success than ever before. Prescription C-8 noted the problems American firms have had in implementing flexible systems. All too often we throw money at the wall in the form of overly complex automation schemes designed in some ivory tower and hope it sticks. More important, the successful manufacturing firm is turning to a "service-added"/"responsiveness-added" strategy that is people-intensive.

Thus, we turn to the people prescriptions as a practical matter, in order to execute the strategies laid out in C-1 through C-10 and I-1 through I-10. And once again, this set of prescriptions is "must-do," not a "nice-to-do." Surviving depends upon quality, flexibility, and constant innovation, which in turn depend upon people.

ACKNOWLEDGING THE ROOT OF THE PROBLEM: ATTITUDES OF MANAGEMENT

It's absurd! We don't want for evidence that the average worker is capable of moving mountains—if only we'll ask him or her to do so, and construct a supportive environment. So why don't we do it?

Why do we mindlessly ship jobs offshore, when evidence surrounds us—even from the toughest industries—that we can compete on quality and cost, despite our high wages, if only we take advantage of the work force's potential?

Harvard economist Robert Reich, as noted in Part I, puts the blame on our 150-year love affair with mass production. We, alone, have consistently tried to make labor ever more narrowly specialized and, in the end, to eliminate it. When automation was introduced by U.S. firms such as General Electric, the ad copy made it clear that the objective was (1) to get tighter control over labor and then (2) to eliminate as many people as possible as fast as possible through all-encompassing "big bang" systems.

In my view this mind-set has proved disastrous, especially of late. Indeed, the chief reason for our failure in world-class competition is our failure to tap our work force's potential. By contrast, as discussed in Part I, Japan and Germany, among others: (1) have always had a craft labor tradition and thus have not ceaselessly pursued the narrowing and specialization of job content; (2) have on the contrary looked to automation to enhance labor's value, utilizing labor's input to program simpler and more flexible machines (designed in the United States, but rejected by Americans in favor of complex systems—see C-8); and (3) have sought competitive advantage through constant, rapid refinement of products via a philosophy of constant improvement.

I am frustrated to the point of rage—my files bulge with letters about the power of involvement. Sometimes it's planned, and I'll talk about that. Sometimes it's inadvertent. But the result is always the same: Truly involved people can do anything!

Consider this statement from Nucor Corporation's president, Ken Iverson: "I've heard people say that Nucor is proof that unions per se have a negative impact on worker productivity. That's nonsense! That conveniently ignores vital questions like: What's the quality of direction being given the workers? Where are the resources the workers need to get the job done efficiently? Where's the opportunity for workers to contribute ideas about how to do the job better? The real impediment to producing a higher-quality product more efficiently isn't the workers, union or nonunion; it's management." W. Edwards Deming is a little kinder, insisting that management is merely 90 percent of the problem.

Ralph Stayer is president of Johnsonville Sausage of Sheboygan Falls, Wisconsin. Recall that the firm, mentioned in Part I, has increased its share of the greater Milwaukee market from 7 to over 50 percent since 1978. How? Stayer explains: "Workers felt here's where I get my money and I have fun elsewhere. In the final analysis, a person's work determines what they are in life. I can tolerate being a mediocre golfer, but not a mediocre human being. I didn't really change stuff to get a better product [though that's what ensued]. What I decided to do, if I take my business and turn it this way and that, I can bring out the greatness in people. . . . I listened to people more, asked them how they do things. . . . I didn't find much resistance, but I did find inertia. Their lifelong learning was to take directions and orders, not to be asked questions. I wanted to help people become the instrument of their own destiny."

Tennant executives (see C-2) were proud of their long-standing tradition of being "people-focused." Yet in looking back at the start of their exceptional quality improvement program in 1979, they realized that even their assumptions had been askew: "We frowned on any activity *except* the job. We didn't ask production employees to help design new products or improve procedures. But the quality emphasis gave us an opportunity to tap the knowledge and skill of the people who do the production work."

And yet, a poll of post–World War II graduates of leading business schools done in late 1986 produced these results: 98 percent of the MBAs felt that "Japan's blue-collar workers work harder than their American counterparts." Do they see management as at all responsible for this "fact"? Apparently not. In answer to the next question, 69 percent of the MBAs swore allegiance to themselves, signing up for this statement: "The United States has more capable managers in business and industry than the Japanese."

THE POWER OF INVOLVEMENT—EVEN IF INADVERTENT

Let me begin again, more systematically, with three cases illustrating the astonishing effects of worker participation. None of the three involves training, structural change, pay incentives, or any of the other supports that I'll recommend in this section on people. They simply offer a glimpse of what I believe is the compelling, natural human thirst to be engaged:

▶ Pieter Martin, manufacturing manager of Buckman Labs' plant in Ghent, Belgium, wanted to improve communication between departments. When he installed what he thought would be a perfect communications system, he noticed an unintended result. Martin had invested $5,000 in walkie-talkies for eighteen employees that would allow the warehouse workers to contact the shipping department, for instance, or the lab supervisor to call the production line without bothering the maintenance crew. But the walkie-talkies of two of the workers didn't work right—they picked up all the interdepartmental chatter. Martin says, "They didn't tell us. And eventually I noticed that at meetings those two were so involved, asking lots of questions and offering solutions to problems in other departments." When he discovered the reason was the "flawed" walkie-talkies, he didn't try to get them fixed. Instead, he traded them in for a downgraded system to allow everyone to listen in on everyone else.

▶ The $25 million video products firm was growing, but its operations department was fast slipping out of control. The groups involved in purchasing, scheduling, order entry, packaging/labeling, and shipping were always at odds. Foul-ups were costing millions. The operations vice president tried everything. He had an outside systems expert look at the difficulties. He dove in himself. He called in each of the dozen key people for individual counseling. Defeated, he decided that hiring a full-time "coordinator" would be the only lasting solution.

But, in a Catch-22 twist, the problem was so advanced that there were no funds for hiring the coordinator. So, on an interim basis, he pulled the dozen together, unloaded his continuing frustrations, and simply begged them to meet once a week and talk about the problems. It couldn't hurt. He informed them that he would be available to give advice, as needed. He then effectively washed his hands of the discouraging mess, even turning over to the leaderless "group" the authority to sign off on items worth tens of thousands of dollars.

It didn't take a genius to see that things started to improve within just a couple of weeks. And the nagging problems didn't just get better, they began to disappear. Another few weeks went by; he was surprised that no one had called to ask his advice.

Some time later he received the long-awaited tap and was asked to show up at a meeting the following week to provide some expert counsel on a technical issue. Upon arrival, he found a formal, professional agenda at his assigned seat, and discovered that he—the nominal boss—was on call for item number six. The pace was brisk and the handling of items was efficient. A couple of other outside experts appeared before he did, including the local UPS manager, who had been asked by the committee to solve a nagging distribution coordination problem.

The VP's turn routinely came and went. As the meeting moved along, his only irritation was somewhat minor. The youngest and only female participant was taking notes. "Just one more example of delegating the crummy task to the junior woman," he grumbled to himself. Then, as the meeting ended, she raised her head from her note-taking and commented: "Well, that will do it for this week. I pass along my role as chairman. Whose turn is it to run the show next week?"

▶ The AMAX coal mine was about to run out of material at its main operating face. Three expert studies, one by an outside consultant, demonstrated decisively that extension of the current operation was uneconomic. A $24 million project was required to extend the mine's life.

A new engineer, who didn't know any better, broke tradition by going underground and wandering the face, chatting with miners. One old-timer, a member of the United Mine Workers, was perplexed at the impending shutdown of the current face. He laid out a relatively inexpensive approach to keeping it open. The green engineer allowed as how the scheme sounded plausible to him.

The engineer quickly put together a proposal triggered by the miner's idea. It costed out at $4.8 million, and management was grudgingly convinced it was worth a try, if the engineer could get volunteers. He asked, and thirty UMW members came forward, along with a handful of supervisors and engineers.

The project immediately ran into trouble; a roof caved in as the group began a tricky attempt to drill through a fault. The mine boss, a skeptic to begin with, gave the young engineer a weekend to fix the problem or "pack up your gear and get out." On Saturday, the engineer met with the entire team all day, laying out the situation and soliciting ideas. A revised scheme was quickly concocted. It worked superbly.

The project became a model of participation in any number of ways. For example, after the first emergency session, the entire team adopted the habit of meeting every Saturday to discuss progress and problems. Team involvement included equipment reclamation too. Given top management's skepticism, the group was allotted the two worst machines for the job—machines ticketed for the scrapheap at project's end. The miners—UMW stalwarts all—entirely reconfigured the old equipment in the course of the project. The two worst machines emerged as the best pieces of equipment in the mine's inventory, far superior to much newer models.

At one level, then, the message of this prescription is involvement by hook or by crook. That is, do it! Of course, the more systematic questions are: How much? At what pace? With what tools?

MANAGING THE WORKPLACE TO
MAXIMIZE INVOLVEMENT

Worthington Industries and Chaparral Steel produce steel of superb quality—but have *no* quality inspectors. "Our people in the plants are responsible for their own product and its quality," says Chaparral's Gordon Forward. "We expect them to act like owners." Forward goes on:

> It's really amazing what people can do when you let them. Take our security guards, for example. Normally, when you think of security guards at four o'clock in the morning, they're doing everything they can just to stay awake. Well, ours also enter data into our computer—order entry, things like that. They put the day's quality results into the computer system each night. We upgraded the job and made a very clear decision not to hire some sleepy old guy to sit and stare at the factory gate all night. Our guards are paramedics; they run the ambulance; they fill up the fire extinguishers; they do the checks on the plant; now we're even considering some accounting functions.
>
> In the plant, our supervisors do their own hiring. The two people we have in personnel [for a 1,000-person operation] do some initial screening and look after group health insurance and a few other things. But the supervisors run their own shows. They're responsible for training their people and for their safety. They have room to grow. Every time a new piece of equipment comes into the plant, the foremen and their crews decide how we are going to operate it. Or if we upgrade some equipment and find a new, better way to operate it, those people make those decisions too.

It should be evident that the removal of barriers between functions and the abolition of nitpicking job specialization are essential to such involvement. Certainly it has been near the heart of the success at NUMMI. The landmark UAW-NUMMI agreement reduced job categories from eighty to four. A parallel plan encourages workers to learn upwards of a dozen jobs. The practical consequences are, of course, considerable. But the psychological ones are even more important. One worker, who was employed at GM's operation in Fremont, California, before it shut down and reopened as NUMMI, explains his liberation: "For six years, all I did was ashtrays. Now I don't know which of the nineteen things I'm trained for so far I'll be doing." That sounds rather innocuous. But think about your day. It may go well or poorly, but it's not likely to be boring or mind-numbing. Problems will arise that will keep you engaged. Engagement is the point.

And what have been the results? The same UAW workers who were disaffected GM employees in 1981 are now producing what some statistics confirm is the top-quality car made in the United States.* Productivity quickly became tops among GM's plants, despite a below-average level of automation. An absenteeism record and a grievance rate that were among the worst in GM in 1981 are now among the best—with those same people.

GM has taken its lumps in this book. But its vast operation also includes models of the best of what can be; the firm's problem has been a failure to implement widely the lessons learned from its best operations. One bellwether is its successful Delco-Remy plant in Fitzgerald, Georgia, which provides a good laundry list of just how far involvement can go. The *average* workers there:

▶ handle all quality control (experts are on tap only if needed in specific cases)
▶ do all maintenance and make minor repairs on machines
▶ keep track of their own time; there are no time cards (no clock)
▶ handle the "housekeeping" (no janitors)
▶ participate in a pay-for-knowledge program (for learning almost every job in the plant)
▶ are organized in teams which engage in regular problem-solving activities
▶ are responsible for safety
▶ have full-time access to the lock-free tool room
▶ do budget preparation and review (capital and operating)
▶ help determine staffing levels
▶ advise management on equipment layout and generate requirements for new equipment

*NUMMI alternates production of the Toyota FX and Chevrolet Nova. The former is selling. The latter, still burdened with lackluster design and a lingering perception of shoddy GM quality, has not done well. (No layoffs are in the works, however.)

▶ are in charge of all recruiting and run the assessment center for new recruits

▶ decide on layoff patterns (whether to lay people off or have everybody work shorter hours, for example)

▶ rotate as leaders of work teams

Sadly, NUMMI and Fitzgerald, with their extraordinary records for low absenteeism, high quality, and high productivity, are still far from the norm, at GM and elsewhere.

CREATING A CLIMATE THAT ENCOURAGES SPONTANEOUS INITIATIVE-TAKING

The ultimate stage of involvement is the regular, spontaneous taking of initiative. For instance, Tennant Company executives brag about their welders in *Quest for Quality:* "Traditionally, the welding department's procedure was to weld several individual machine parts . . . then send them to the stockroom, where they were stored until the department had an order to produce a particular machine. The company's engineers wanted to streamline the operation by welding more and storing fewer units. They devised a system with a $100,000 price tag that was rejected by management as too expensive. Even a scaled-down, $25,000 version was deemed too costly. A small group of welders tackled the problem. They designed an overhead monorail that could carry welded parts from one station to another so a frame could be welded together from start to finish without leaving the department. The welders weren't deterred by cost. They discovered a supply of I-beams in a local junkyard and bought them for less than $2,000. In *two days* [my emphasis] they installed the monorail. In the first year of its use, the new system saved . . . more than $29,000 in time and storage space."

Service firms have the same opportunities as do manufacturers. Consider the case of a janitor, the sole person on duty at a commissary of Domino's Pizza Distribution Company. He took an off-hours call from a franchisee about to run out of pepperoni. (Having a franchisee run out of anything is the cardinal sin at Domino's Distribution.) On his own initiative, he located keys to a truck, loaded the vehicle with one small box of pepperoni, and drove hundreds of miles to keep the franchisee from closing down. It never occurred to him that Distribution, as the subsidiary is called, would want him to do anything else—and he was right.

And how about the relatively junior telecommunications expert at Federal Express who, following a blizzard in the California Sierras, was faced with the prospect of having no phone service for several days? With no coaching—and no need to seek approval from above—he rented a helicopter (using his personal American Express card), was dropped onto a snowbound mountaintop, trudged three-quarters of a mile in chest-deep snow, and fixed the line to get Fed Ex back in business. This occurrence, though spontaneous, was hardly accidental. Federal Express, like Domino's, constantly emphasizes (through management example, the absence of stifling bureaucracy and structure, exhortation, recognition, and formal training) that all workers are routinely expected to take whatever initiative is required to fix problems and/or extend first-rate service to a customer. In fact, not to act this "outrageously" (by the standards of others) is cause for a poor evaluation.

The question confronting us in the remainder of this section is how to induce such involvement and initiative-taking as a matter of course.

Sometimes some seem to be learning. I'll stumble across an article, such as one in a late 1986 issue of the San Jose *Mercury News,* titled, "McDonnell Looks to Rank and File to Help Set Management Strategy." It reports: "In a departure from its traditional top-down management style, the St. Louis aerospace giant is trying a new tactic: It's asking some of the company's lowest-paid workers how to run the business better."

But then a few days later I hear two different sorts of tales. A family friend works in a New Jersey construction products plant. To cut costs, they removed *all* the pay phones. She had a father who was desperately ill, and was infuriated. Another friend does duty on the swing shift in a midwestern chemical plant. "They out and out told us," he says, " 'You're not here to use your heads.' " The plant's products are used in medical procedures, and when he went into the hospital last year, my friend asked a nurse if a particular procedure involved his company's product. "She said it didn't," he reports. "If it had been our stuff, I wouldn't have let them do the procedure. I'd have demanded [a competitor's product]." Is that damning?

I conclude with a simple and heartfelt request: Spend some time by a lake and just think about all of this. Recall the extraordinary feats of Domino's janitor and the junior telecommunications expert at Federal Express. Recall the effects of the inadvertent involvement of the two people tied into the walkie-talkie system at Buckman Labs, and what happens routinely at Worthington, Johnsonville, and Nordstrom. Recall the welders at Tennant, the AMAX miners, the Chaparral night watchman, the turnaround at NUMMI—with the union involved—and the long list of normal worker activities in Fitzgerald, Georgia.

Do you really think the average worker can become so engaged? Can earn his or her salary several times over? Let me remind you that the increases in productivity associated with my examples, not to mention the improved quality, often amount to a hundred percent or more (the national average, remember, is less than 2 percent a year). That is why I demand, in this prescription, that over the next 36 months you shoot for an increase of 100 percent in productivity via participation-led programs.

Yes, we are fighting 150 years of converse assumptions about specialization, jurisdiction, participation, skill enhancement, and initiative taking—and the will of the worker. But the eleventh hour is upon us. Just what do I, and Chaparral's Gordon Forward, and Buckman's Pieter Martin, and Johnsonville's Ralph Stayer, Worthington's John McConnell, and Fred Smith of Federal Express, have to do to convince you?

DO SOMETHING!

Involvement can start with anything. Maybe even a party. The point is to find *some* window into the process. GM's pioneering efforts at Buick City provide a good example of seeking an opening, any opening:

The QWL [Quality of Work Life] process began in Buick in 1975. The general manager provided the initial impetus based upon his participation in a union-management QWL seminar sponsored by the GM-UAW National Quality of Work Life Committee. This meeting so impressed him that he encouraged his staff to participate in a similar seminar with the leadership of UAW Local 599, which represents the 16,000 production and maintenance workers at Buick in Flint, Michigan.

353

The first meeting was held in October 1975. Among other accomplishments, a joint committee was established to oversee the QWL process. After about a half dozen off-site meetings, the third of which was held at the UAW Family Education Center as guests of the union, a decision was made to provide an opportunity for the workers to become involved in some form or fashion. Since neither party was quite sure of how the process might work and how people might react to the joint invitation, they agreed upon the safe step of an open house. The voluntary participation of employees was sought in the planning, organization, and administration of a division-wide open house for Buick families and friends. The open house was so successful that it was followed over the next two years by a bond drive, a blood donor campaign, a hospital fund-raising, and a United Way of Michigan campaign.

Because the people so impressed management with their talents, their eagerness, and their desire to become more involved, the manufacturing manager began to look for a way to institutionalize the high level of involvement.

And, indeed, much has happened since. Yet the opening was critical. Having a party is surely not the only way to begin. But it's a pretty good one, it turns out.

PUBLIC PARALLELS

The public parallels are exact, with one possible catch: union-management tension. Sadly, most management-union agreements to do such things as reduce job specialization categories have been made with a gun to the heads of both parties—the threat of going bust. Perhaps a stringent budgetary environment in the public sector will lead to the same sorts of useful pressure—on both unions *and* management.

Despite this, it remains a fact that W. Edwards Deming's assessment of management as 90 percent to blame for lack of enthusiastic participation among front-line employees applies to the public as well as the private sector. Any manager, low-level or high-, in a union or nonunion environment, can accomplish 75 percent of what's advocated here, regardless of the setting. As usual with our prescriptions, attitudes are fundamental.

FIRST STEPS

1. Spend a week or two working a regular shift in a factory or operations center. Make a list of the tasks that the first two levels of supervision are now doing. Talk with colleagues. Think about inadvertent or planned acts of front-line initiative-taking in your past experience. How many of the tasks that supervisors perform could be done by first-line people?

2. Experiment with some enhanced, new skill training for first-line people, starting in the next 60 to 120 days. Bring informal groups together to talk about job redefinition. If you can do it in the context of competitive necessity, so much the better. Involve first- and second-line supervisors in your frightening (to them— see P-2) deliberations from the start.

3. In the course of the next six months, form a study group of fifteen (principally line managers at all levels). Visit at least ten American factories or operations centers which are undertaking dramatic participation-led programs. At the end of that study, consider committing to the quantitative productivity improvement goal established above.

P-2

SUMMARY

To achieve the level of involvement described in P-1, which is necessary to become appropriately flexible, quality-conscious, and thence competitive, we must:

▶ Organize as much as possible around teams, to achieve enhanced focus, task orientation, innovativeness, and individual commitment.

The modest-sized, task-oriented, semi-autonomous, mainly self-managing team should be the basic organization building block. Be aware that the wholesale use of a self-managing team structure probably calls for elimination of the traditional first-line supervisor's job.

Regardless of whether or not the fit is perfect, organize *every function* into ten- to thirty-person, largely self-managing teams. Eliminate all first-line supervision as we know it (see also P-8).

P-2

Use Self-Managing Teams

P-1 set the stage. Wholesale worker involvement must become a national priority if we are to create the competitive strengths necessary just to maintain, let alone improve, our national economic well-being. The next nine prescriptions address how to achieve this goal. At the top of the list is the use of teams, variously called quality circles, semi-autonomous work groups, and self-managing teams.

Use them. That's the first piece of advice. The self-managing team should become the basic organizational building block. Train them; recruit on the basis of teamwork potential; pay them for performance; and clean up the bureaucracy around them, dramatically changing the roles of middle managers and staff experts (these are topics of subsequent prescriptions).

Team-based organization, though not widespread in American business, is hardly a new idea. And it is certainly not Japanese-inspired or some product of a mysterious Asian group mentality. True, the twelve-person section is the basic Japanese organizational unit, but teams, in the form of eight-person squads, have been the bedrock of Western military organization, for instance, for hundreds of years.

357

EXAMPLES TO LEARN FROM

The good news is that numerous examples are available for observation and analysis. General Motors, for instance, has been experimenting for a dozen years now, at a host of union and nonunion sites. One early experiment, at the Delco-Remy plant in Fitzgerald, Georgia, was described in P-1, where the subject was the exceptional involvement of individual workers. The Fitzgerald plant is entirely team-based. Figure 14 shows the interlocking nature of operating and support teams, all the way to the top of the organization chart.

But, you say, what can I learn about team-based organizations from a new, nonunion plant like Fitzgerald? Consider, then, GM's Cadillac engine plant in Livonia, Michigan, which was reorganized in the early 1980s. Fundamental to the transformation were these elements: (1) A planning team, consisting of (2) management and union leaders, as well as (3) several hourly employees, worked (4) full-time for (5) almost a year on plant organization and operation. (6) Visits to other sites were made. (7) The previously secret account books were opened up. (8) An operating philosophy was hammered out, called the Livonia Engine Plant Operating Philosophy. (9) A team structure was arrived at. Former plant manager Bob Stramy and two colleagues report the planning team's principal finding in *Transforming the Workplace:* "The most powerful and influential conclusion concerns the Livonia Planning Team's unqualified support and promotion of the team concept as a central and unifying force throughout the new organization. So urgent and prominent was this ideal, moreover, that it immediately became the recurrent main theme of the evolving operating plan and its orchestration over the months of planned implementation."

The team focus at Livonia meant that (10) every person in the organization became part of a group of eight to fifteen people. (11) Importantly—and appropriately—the groups came to be called, not work groups, but business teams.* (12) The "business team" is a highly autonomous group (especially by prior standards), responsible for scheduling, training, problem solving, and many other activities. The teams, for

---

*Goodyear's most successful plant, in Lawton, Oklahoma, has chosen a similar designation. Each of 164 teams of five to twenty-seven people is a "Business Center," responsible for quality control and productivity measurement and enhancement.

Figure 14: **The Fitzgerald Plant Organization**

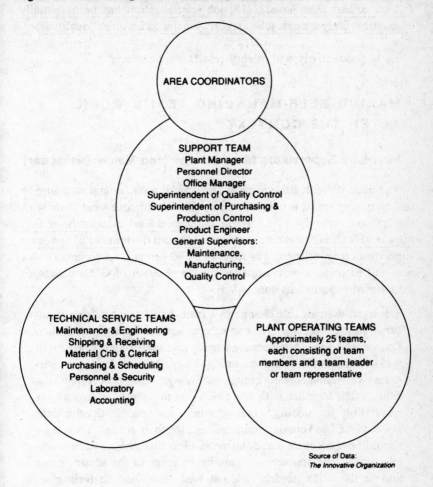

AREA COORDINATORS

SUPPORT TEAM
Plant Manager
Personnel Director
Office Manager
Superintendent of Quality Control
Superintendent of Purchasing &
Production Control
Product Engineer
General Supervisors:
Maintenance,
Manufacturing,
Quality Control

TECHNICAL SERVICE TEAMS
Maintenance & Engineering
Shipping & Receiving
Material Crib & Clerical
Purchasing & Scheduling
Personnel & Security
Laboratory
Accounting

PLANT OPERATING TEAMS
Approximately 25 teams,
each consisting of team
members and a team leader
or team representative

Source of Data:
The Innovative Organization

instance, (13) developed their own quantitative performance indicators. (14) They meet at least once a week as a group. (15) Pay-for-knowledge, as at Fitzgerald, encourages everyone (16) to learn virtually every job in the plant. (17) Most awards for suggestions are team-based (this is yet another commonplace Japanese practice), and (18) individual performance appraisals emphasize support for the business team. As at NUMMI (which is also team-based), (19) job specialization has been virtually eliminated. Only a single job category remains at Livonia: "quality operator."

Early productivity and quality results were exciting.

MAKING SELF-MANAGING TEAMS WORK: ALTER THE CONTEXT

First-Line Supervisors Must Change (and Mainly Disappear)

The most difficult issue in most shifts from a traditional structure to self-managing teams is not the worker. It's figuring out what to do with the first-line supervisor. At Livonia, the second level of supervision, that of general foreman, was entirely eliminated, and the number of first-level supervisors (the foremen) was reduced by 40 percent; the foreman's role was retitled team coordinator. An outside observer of GM's numerous team-based experiments concluded:

The most difficult role change in a team-based plant is from traditional production supervisor to an area advisor for a group of shop floor work teams. Advisors are usually chosen through a process of self-selection and careful screening. They are then trained in participative management, group facilitation, and problem-solving skills, often together with the union committeemen. Advisors are responsible for quality, cost, schedule, and people development goals, as well as boundary management for their groups. Their style should become more participative and less directive as work teams gain skills. The dramatic increase in the scope of the advisor's role and in the skills needed to do it well often lead to feelings of ambiguity and confusion. In this area, as in so many others, top plant management must provide a flexible support system for advisors which is designed to help them grow into their roles.

Ford's extensive Employee Involvement (EI) programs have been headed in the same direction. For instance, at Sharonville, Ohio, "a decision [was reached in 1981] by the plant manager, supported by the division, to reorganize the plant hierarchy. *The general supervisor level was completely eliminated* [my emphasis]. In its place, each zone superintendent was assigned an assistant known as a manufacturing planning specialist who, as the name implies, was to provide planning and coordinating assistance to each superintendent. The individual was not to be in a position of line authority. His position description called for another responsibility which was to have a profound effect on the future 'management' and growth of the EI process. He was to act as the departmental coordinator for all present and future EI problem-solving groups, working closely with his own superintendent and the plant co-coordinators."

By 1987, several of the most advanced Ford and GM experiments had removed all formal supervisor designations, except for plant manager, in operations of up to 1,000 people. At Johnsonville Sausage, mentioned in prescription P-1, all formal supervision has been eliminated from its four plants; even the plant manager position has been eliminated. Teams (called Pride Teams) manage almost everything.

Where the first-line supervisor's job is not being de facto eliminated, it is being changed. Training expert Jack Zenger reports that his phone has been ringing off the hook. Hundreds of firms have consulted him about increasing spans of control from, say, one supervisor to ten non-supervisors to one supervisor to 50 to 75 workers (see P-8).

With such a shift in span of control, the job goes through an automatic and radical adjustment. An over-the-shoulder style of management is not even physically possible under the new circumstances—see Figure 15. However, the casualty rate among efforts to retrain and transform the supervisor from detail person/cop to facilitator is very high, especially in traditional firms.

In conclusion, if you do not drastically widen the span of control, and shift the supervisor's job content, the self-managing team concept will not work—period.

Pitfalls on the Road to Self-Managing Teams

One way to sidle toward team organization is to install quality circles, which were also discussed in prescription C-2. The route is not easy, however, for a well-functioning circle program requires changes in traditional supervisorial attitudes and practices almost as radical as those demanded by total team-based management. And the pitfalls are similar.

One recent assessment based upon extensive experience throughout Martin-Marietta listed these problems:

► misunderstanding of the concept and process by upper and middle management, creating false expectations
► resistance to the concept and process by middle managers and supervisors, often verging on outright sabotage
► empire-building by the quality circle office, substituting the illusion of immediate success for the long-term goal of institutionalizing the quality circle process
► poor and "one-shot" training for circle members, supervisor-leaders, and managers
► failure to prepare the organization to provide incentives for participation in quality circles
► failure to prepare the organization to provide the information and support necessary for members to solve problems
► failure of the organization to implement circle proposals
► failure of the organization to measure the impact of quality circle participation—on defect rates, productivity rates, attrition rates, accident rates, scrap rates, grievance rates, lost-time rates, and so on
► failure to develop and codify a set of process rules prior to forming the first circles
► moving too fast—forming more circles than the quality circle office or the organization can deal with adequately

THE MARKET WILL DEMAND A SELF-MANAGING TEAM STRUCTURE

New flexible manufacturing systems and the decentralized availability of the information needed for fast product changeover are leading to the wholesale adoption of cellular manufacturing, which essentially concentrates all the physical assets needed for making a product in a self-contained configuration which is tailor-made for team organization.

Participants in these increasingly fast-paced settings have no choice but to depend upon each other. Moreover, because of just-in-time inventory management and other techniques, it is essential that the teams/

Figure 15: **The Changing Nature of First-Level Supervision**

Old	New
• 10 people reporting to him or her	• 50 to 75 "direct reports"
• scheduler of work	• coach and sounding board for self-managing team leaders/coordinators, working on training to emphasize skill development
• rule enforcer ("manager" of the union contract on management's behalf, if applicable)	• facilitator, getting experts to help the teams as needed
• lots of planning	• lots of wandering
• focused "down" (or "up") the structure	• focused "horizontally," working with other functions to speed action-taking
• transmitting middle/top management's needs "down"	• selling teams' ideas/needs "up"
• providing new ideas for workers	• helping workers/teams develop their own ideas; providing ideas for cross-functional systems improvement

work groups be in constant, nonabrasive contact with all the operation's other functions. Thus the transformation of the traditional, internally directed first-line supervisor/cop into the externally directed coordinator/facilitator is a must, not a "nice-to-do."

The power of self-managing teams has been demonstrated in numerous settings. Why do they work? Quite simply, people of groups of ten to thirty can get to know one another well, can learn virtually every one else's tasks, can be gotten together with little fuss, and under enlightened leadership can readily achieve unit cohesion and esprit.

Team-Based Structures Work Everywhere

At the highest level of abstraction, this prescription constitutes one more attack on vertical, functional organizational structures, and on big scale in general. The evidence from watching well-trained teams perform is that extreme specialization was always dumb. Maintenance, budgeting, inventory management, and even customer contact can all be done by the twenty-five-person group. More generally, I urge you to emphasize mainly self-sufficient units, or what I call the small-within-big principle, throughout the organization. Even traditionally centralized activities, such as MIS, purchasing, and accounting, can be radically decentralized; I will say more about this in prescription P-8, which deals exclusively with structure.

Are there any limits to the use of teams? Can we find places or circumstances where a team structure doesn't make sense? Answer: No, as far as I can determine.

That's unequivocal, and meant to be. Some situations may seem to lend themselves more to team-based management than others. Nonetheless, I observe that the power of the team is so great that it is often wise to violate apparent common sense and force a team structure on almost anything. Even if a store or factory or distribution activity doesn't neatly break down into bands of ten to thirty, shift layouts around, "inefficiently" if necessary, to gain the potential power of a self-managing team structure. There is ample evidence that American economic performance will increasingly depend on quality, service, constant innovation/improvement, and enhanced flexibility/responsiveness. Committed, flexible, multi-skilled, constantly retrained people, joined together in self-managing teams, are the only possible implementers of this strategy.

FIRST STEPS

1. Start a test with a team structure in one facility within the next 180 days. The steps should be a small-scale version of the Livonia experience described above.
2. If you are already a user of teams (in the factory, say), develop an action plan for expanding the idea to all operations. Pick one department (MIS, for instance) and get going in the next 90 days.

3. Home in immediately on the crucial role of the first two levels of supervision. Can the supervisors be retrained or shifted to purely support jobs if you adopt some form of self-managing team structure? At the very least, the supervisor will undergo a traumatic shift of role (assuming you keep the role); don't let this surprise you—or dissuade you from proceeding. Above all, don't evade the issue. The failure to dramatically change the roles and numbers of supervisors has torpedoed the lion's share of self-managing team experiments.

P-3

SUMMARY

Wholesale involvement is necessary to engender the level of quality, service, and flexibility required by today's markets (P-1). Intense communication is required to foster that involvement; we rnust:

▶ Listen constantly, congregate, or share ideas/information, and recognize achievement.

▶ Celebrate—informally and formally—the "small wins" that are indicative of the solid day-to-day performance turned in by more than 90 percent of your work force.

Unprecedented information-sharing, interaction, and recognition are required to induce the attitude change and horizontal communication necessary to foster widespread involvement and commitment.

Develop formal and informal devices aimed at spurring intense, proactive listening—these should range from "chats with the chairman" to extensive formal surveys. Invest lavishly in regular get-togethers—at least bimonthly, for all hands, in each facility. Support this with ancillary devices—such as weekly (or more frequent) newsletters, videos, or audios. Hold a minimum of five celebratory "events," small or large, each month; top this off with a minimum of ten thank-you notes per week for jobs—particularly small ones—well done.

P-3

Listen/Celebrate/
Recognize

The first two prescriptions in this section stressed the involvement of everyone in virtually everything. End specialization. Use self-managing work groups as the basic structural unit in the organization. All this, however, requires new attitudes. How do we foster them?

CREATE A LISTENING ENVIRONMENT

Create an environment where listening is cherished—and opportunities for structured *and* unstructured listening are rife. Listening means managers listening to their people, of course. And it means teammates listening to each other—recall in the previous prescription that in several cases a major portion of each worker's evaluation rested upon his or her contribution to the team as a whole. Listening also means people paying attention to those in other functions, battering down the time-honored, action-slowing functional boundaries at every opportunity.

Informal Listening

Listening can be informal; for instance, the daily "kaffeeklatsch" tradition in each work area at giant Hewlett-Packard. It is the weekly breakfast of the president and twenty randomly selected employees which was used to stimulate a transformation at Rockwell's Semiconductor Division.

The top managers of a Canadian forest products company felt they were top-flight communicators until a survey revealed that employees felt they stank—at listening. Solution? The two owners undertook a series of thirty dinners in the course of the next year. Ten employees and their spouses, eventually including everyone at the mill, went to dinner with the bosses. After the meal, there was a sociable and often long and intense question-and-answer session. "We all want to be listened to," says the president. "By the end of the evening I'd often see a remarkable change in attitude on the part of even the crustiest of the union guys."

Formal Listening

Casual get-togethers, then, are an essential part of listening—coffee klatches, breakfasts, dinners. So are more formal affairs. The president of Rockwell Semiconductor also devotes one day each month to tours of his major facilities, making sophisticated, no-holds-barred, no-information-withheld presentations to all hands. Our friends in the forest products company topped off their dinner routine with an informative weekly newsletter. It, too, holds back nothing, covering last week's affairs and next week's; delivery comes punctually at the end of the day shift on Fridays.

More? Tandem Computer's Friday Beer Busts, described in *A Passion for Excellence*. They sound like fun, and are, often involving a theme or a special food. But the activity, held religiously at each Tandem facility around the world at four o'clock each Friday, is also a deadly serious opportunity to break down barriers in what is already a remarkably informal, communication-intense environment.

More extreme? Federal Express brings all 3,000 managers together about once every eighteen months for several days to meet, talk, clear the air.

How about such listening "devices" as surveys? Some—such as IBM, for example—use them as a primary feedback (listening) device. The key is the feedback. IBM spends lavishly on the questionnaires, but so do many others. IBM departs from the norm in using the surveys as a basis for the evaluation of managers. Furthermore, when surveys indicate a major problem, a SWAT team from division headquarters is often on the site almost instantaneously. The whole process feeds on itself: Since employees know that action will result, they take the survey very seriously.

The Essentials of a Listening Environment

Here are some key factors in the creation of a listening environment.

1. The bare-bones essential, not to be underrated, is provision of a forum per se in which eventually you can talk and listen in a nonthreatening environment. I add the word "eventually," because putting listening programs in place does not ensure instant "straight talk." There must also be a sincere desire to listen—and hear—and the patience to persevere until the floodgates open. But without a "listening opportunity structure," probably including several of the informal and formal devices described above, little or no progress toward participation and enhanced commitment will ensue.

2. Next is a physical location—a place to listen. The most successful experiments with self-managing teams almost always include the provision of well-equipped rooms where teams can meet for problem-solving. At Chaparral Steel, each operation has a problem-solving room—with an added fillip: it is equipped exactly like the corporate boardroom. As the president says, the decisions being made in the plants are at least as important as those being made in the boardroom—shouldn't the setting and amenities reflect that?

3. Feedback and action reinforce the intent. Remember that these are forums for listening, not preaching. The breakfast meetings at Rockwell were stilted at first, until attendees realized that (a) they weren't going to get in trouble with their bosses by talking and (b) the president was acting on what they were saying. At that point, the dam broke and ideas poured in not only at the meetings but in general. Likewise, as noted, the power of IBM's surveys lies in the fact that they elicit active responses.

4. Training is essential. I spoke of "listening training" for everyone at Tennant (see C-2). One suggestion program has a "writer" assigned to it who helps sometimes inarticulate people translate their ideas onto a form; another uses audiotapes similarly as a vehicle for making suggestions. Training in group problem-solving and in the identification of problem causes and effects (see C-2) is also essential. Supervisors are especially in need of help; in traditional settings, the supervisor plays a talking role, not a listening role.

5. Opportunities must be frequent. Here are several possibilities: (a) set aside work hours for team meetings (a ten- or fifteen-minute meeting each day at the start of the shift, an hour at the end of the shift once a week) for problem-solving, and also encourage employees to call after-hours meetings with pay as needed; (b) as at Tandem, hold informal weekly sessions that involve others beyond the immediate work group; (c) issue a weekly, or at least biweekly, rough-and-tumble, no-holds-barred newsletter; (d) hold a monthly or bimonthly, no-holds-barred, state-of-the-plant/operations center/division/company (as appropriate, but the more inclusive, the better) session, during working hours, with at least 50 percent of the time devoted to questions and answers; (e) make formal annual surveys involving a quick-action feedback routine; and (f) establish some set of systematic rituals, such as the boss hanging out in the cafeteria two mornings a week.

6. Attitude is vital. The last point, of course, deserves to be first. Recall prescription P-1. If you don't believe there's much worth listening to, you'll make a mess of this. Remember, this prescription is a *tool* in service to a much larger idea.

How much time does it take? Lots. Does it cost a lot? Quite often the answer is yes, in terms of hard dollars for shipping thousands of people to the site of the annual get-together and soft, "opportunity cost" dollars associated with having people meet with each other regularly during working hours.

CREATE PUBLIC FORUMS FOR RECOGNITION (TEACHING)

The construction of public forums for the recognition of achievement is closely entwined with listening. Among other things, well-constructed recognition settings provide the single most important opportunity to parade and reinforce the specific kinds of new behavior one hopes others will emulate. Thus, recognition activities become a key listening and communication device, beyond their straightforward motivational influence on those being recognized.

Begin with an elementary question. Exactly how much recognition is desirable? To survive a day in the average check-processing or factory operation, or in the dispatch office, is tough. A machine breaks down. A customer unexpectedly demands a rescheduling. The colleague next to you has two kids sick with German measles and is distracted all day. That is to say, survival—for the average person on the average day—is not easy. Making it through five such days in a row is heroic. That's why my least favorite phrase is "a fair day's work for a fair day's pay." An informal poll of friends unearthed not one who had done merely a fair day's work for a fair day's pay. Our own, albeit self-centered, view of our performance is that we always do more than required, surmounting those numerous—but very real—daily and daunting hurdles with élan and dispatch. This seemingly high self-assessment is shared by almost 100 percent of the working population. And it is, by and large, a correct assessment.

I therefore believe that substantial recognition for fairly mundane actions—which are never really mundane—as well as for truly exceptional performance is called for, and is usually markedly absent.

Recognition: "Little Things" with High Impact

Consider this. A new owner of Fletcher Granite Company in Westford, Massachusetts, observed a record-breaking productivity effort by one of his employees. On impulse, he grabbed a two-way radio and publicly lauded this prodigious feat, with everyone listening in. A colleague of the worker later reported to the president: "Lou is walking on cloud nine. He's been here thirty-five years, and it's the first time the boss has recognized his work." What a sad-happy story! Want to hear another 200 to 300 like it? I've got them in my files. Here's just one more.

Sam Preston recently retired as executive vice-president of S. C. Johnson (Johnson Wax, etc.). He had a habit of sending little notes, with a bold "DWD" scrawled across the top, after coming across a sparkling effort. The "DWD" stands for "Damned Well Done." At his retirement party, Preston was stunned. People came up and thanked him for DWDs sent fifteen years before. Recognition is that memorable and that infrequent—even at S. C. Johnson, which has been one of America's top people-oriented companies for decades.

A Menu of Recognition Devices

Start with informal recognition:

▶ Keep mental or calendar notes of informal, semi-spontaneous celebratory events. Plan to do a minimum of five each month. Begin by stopping at the bakery on the way to work and picking up two dozen doughnuts to "award" at coffee break to a project team that passed a minor milestone—on schedule—the day before yesterday.

▶ Have a special meal at the distribution center cafeteria to celebrate ninety days of meeting the promise of "95 percent fulfillment within 24 hours of receiving the order." Have hamburgers made of top sirloin—and have management do the cooking and serving and cleaning up. "Ninety days at 95 percent" hats or T-shirts wouldn't hurt either. P.S.: Recalling one of the other major themes in this book—be sure to invite people from outside the center who helped you reach the goal, such as the three people in MIS who worked three straight weekends to help you simplify a critical, bottleneck-creating system.

▶ Consider a ritual like that of the top property manager of Marriott's in Albuquerque, New Mexico. He makes it a rigorous habit to send out at least 100 thank-you notes a month to his staff for jobs well done. You don't think you can find a hundred things worth saying thank you for? That's a prime indicator that you are out of touch.

▶ Trinkets. Simple observation suggests that most of us are trinket freaks—if they represent a genuine thanks for a genuine assist. A very successful Skunk Works manager sends skunk-adorned mugs, belt buckles, etc., to those in *other* functions who have stuck their necks out and helped his woefully undermanned operation.

Recognition on a grand scale: The Domino's Pizza Distribution Olympics are a fine example. The second annual Olympics were held in Dearborn, Michigan, on May 13, 1986. As usual, the games did not begin until the tripod (its bowl in the shape of a pizza) was ignited. But the torchbearers were no ordinary athletes. They were Domino's Pizza president, Tom Monaghan, a rags-to-riches entrepreneur, and Anthony Scales, a double amputee, who is "fast, does his job as a tray scraper and dough maker extremely well," according to his boss.

Distribution's compound annual growth over the last eight years has been 75 percent. Employment has soared to well over 1,700 people at 35 commissaries across the United States, Canada, and West Germany. How does Domino's manage such extraordinary growth, especially with its unusually young work force (the average age is 28)? The Olympics, brainchild of Distribution president Don Vlcek, is part of the answer.

The Olympics provide a showcase for the skills that underpin Distribution's success. Management obsessively measures and regularly rewards good job performance and customer satisfaction (customers in this case are Domino's franchisees), but the games may be even more memorable than Distribution's monthly bonuses. Moreover, they help maintain the company's focus and cohesiveness in the face of extremely rapid growth.

Competition for the May 1986 Olympics started in September 1985. The first round took place in each of the commissaries. At the beginning of the next year, about 650 local winners proceeded to the three regional rounds, which spawned 78 regional winners. Finally, the regional winners and their spouses moved on to Dearborn for the "national games," covering fourteen areas of competition. The "veggie slicing" contest emphasizes quantity and quality of vegetables, individual appearance, and sanitation. "Traffic management" measures skills at routing and coordinating team members and their delivery vehicles. Other categories include "dough making and catching," "store delivery," "driving," "loading," and "maintenance."

Less predictable contests involve the accountants, testing not only their speed and accuracy in bookkeeping and reporting but their interpersonal skills as well. For instance, in one contest, the accountant must handle a simulated phone call from a franchisee who is very late in paying his bill. Phone skills are also tested in contests among customer service reps and receptionists. Other contests rate team leadership.

One particularly nice touch is the involvement of Distribution's franchisee-customers, who comprise the majority of the judging panels. But most significant is the fact that the lead-up to the event has become a year-long process, not just a one-shot deal that is quickly forgotten. The first year's pizza "athletes," especially the runners-up, went home to their commissaries determined to "go for the gold" next year.

The stakes in Dearborn in 1986 were high. Sixteen winners in the fourteen main categories received top prizes of either $4,000 each or a lavish vacation for two.

The Olympics thus represent a serious commitment by management. Counting the prizes, Distribution spends $800,000 on the regional and final games, and that excludes the unrecorded costs of local competitions. But the investment has an invaluable return—honed skills plus a powerful sense of camaraderie and overall excitement that propels mostly young, inexperienced people through a system in which there is great potential for stress.

The Essentials of Successful Recognition Programs

Factors that make the difference between success and failure in granting recognition include these:

1. All recognition for acts of special merit must be heartfelt. Though, as noted, I define "special merit" more broadly than most, promiscuous recognition is self-defeating. I observe that great managers, like great teachers, are themselves most highly rewarded by the accomplishments of their employees. The best teachers say, "Look at what Andrea or Cliff did. Isn't that incredible?" The not-so-good ones talk about how they are being innovative in their lesson plans. In other words, if the accomplishments of your team are not really a source of excitement to you, don't engage in what will come across as patently phony acts of recognition, whether as simple as "DWD" or as grand as Distribution's Olympics.

2. Big awards for herculean efforts are a must, perhaps limited to 2 to 5 percent of the work force. But numerous awards for small acts of heroism are at least as important.

3. You can think systematically about all this. Domino's carefully designed Distribution Olympics is a case in point. Moreover, Distribution's management sits down after each year's programs and carefully assesses details and major themes, making numerous modifications for the next year. Here's another: The president of a forest products company instituted annual recognition dinners at each of his facilities last year. He sent me a copy of the detailed twenty-page "critique" he distributed to each operations manager after the entire round was complete (he attended every one). The document assessed everything from treatment of spouses, to table settings, to length of speeches, to procedures for picking people to be recognized, and the observations were carefully considered in planning the next year's event.

4. Celebrate what you want to see more of. Obvious as this dictum is, we ignore it too often. If you want more cross-functional barrier-breaking, make sure that every celebration includes hitherto unsung helpmates from other functions. Or, to the same end, do what one insurance company did—at least 50 percent of each manager's awards for good performance went to those in *other* functions who helped his or her team.

Likewise, if you want to build team spirit, make sure that the gala for the gang at the distribution center is equal in lavishness to that for the top sales people; and make sure that most of the awards go to teams of people, not individuals.

Celebrate. Recognize. Communicate. Teach.

Inc. magazine called "Stew's News," the Stew Leonard's dairy store newsletter, "the ultimate company newsletter." I'd have to agree. I'll let the content do the talking. The November–December 1986 issue had 42 overflowing pages and over 300 pictures:

Cover: "This year's Hall of Fame winners!"—large photo.

Page 2: An editorial by Stew, Sr., on recognition given by outsiders to the dairy, ending with a strongly worded admonition: "Guard against being lulled to sleep."

Page 4: Story about employee Art Rosenblatt's idea that increased clam chowder sales by 30 percent; he designed a container so "it looked more homemade."

Page 5: A peppy article, "Come on, Stew, is the customer ever wrong?" Answer: No (with numerous specific supporting examples).

Page 8: Poem by an employee: "Ode to my Stew Leonard's fellow employees."

Page 9: 44 customer comments from the thousands per month that are popped into the store's suggestion box. About one-third were suggestions, one-third criticisms ("Your veal chops are cut too thin"), and one-third praise ("My therapist suggested I come here to cure my depression. It worked!! I love Stew Leonard's").

Page 10: Article on customers; headline: "Thanks, Dody Forrest [the writer, an employee], for the Great Article."

Page 11: "What's new at Stew's," reviewing new features around the store.

Pages 15–16: Awards being given out at the Christmas party, with photos.

Page 18: Large star symbol at the top, feature on "Two Stars in Fresh Products," with big picture and description of what they did.

Page 20: Article by an employee on teamwork.

Pages 21–22: Dozens of birthday and work anniversary pictures.

Page 35: "Dairy Personals"; e.g., "D.T. I love you. Signed your assistant carpenter."

Page 37: "Let's welcome our new employees," with list of names.

Back Cover: "Super Star of the Month," featuring big photos and detailed write-up of accomplishments.

What's going on here? (1) Celebration and recognition galore; (2) detailed teaching/feedback via descriptions of specifics as to why people won awards, quotes from customer suggestion slips; (3) precise communication of the spirit, cooperativeness, and all-hands participation that mark Stew Leonard's. The newsletter, produced by employees, is itself a model of participation. It also achieves a nice blend of formality and informality. The paper stock is of high quality and the printing is tops. But it is done in typescript, with lots of fairly rough sketches; you'd be proud to take it home and keep it, but it completely avoids any suggestion of PR department glitz.

PUBLIC PARALLELS

My public sector friends are quick to point out that their elected aldermen would scream bloody murder if they took the fifty top performers to Disney World for a four-day annual recognition event, or even downtown to Hardee's.

True—and irrelevant. Obviously, thank-you notes are possible. So are plaques, Halls of Fame, mugs, and T-shirts. Beyond that, let your imagination guide you. In 1986 I spoke at a dinner meeting honoring the teachers of Irving, Texas. An aggressive superintendent had worked with an aggressive school board chairman to raise private funds to celebrate the teachers' efforts.

As for petty cash, if the city won't let you buy doughnuts for the gang that worked overtime to get the budget presentation for the supervisors ready on time, dip into your own pocket. The spontaneous "I care"/ "Thank you" act, at a cost of $17.95, is worth as much to the people recognized as many a stilted corporate affair costing $225,000.

FIRST STEPS

1. Mount at least a Rockwell-variety, informal breakfast program. Immediately. The first step is to get a firsthand feel as to whether or not people think they are being listened to.
2. Start observing your own meetings, and ask a colleague to observe you. How much listening and open exchange takes place within your organization?
3. Don't run out and launch a major recognition program! Chew the recognition idea over first, with great concern for genuineness. Also review prescription P-7, which deals with compensation: *I am pointedly not proposing coffee mugs with decals as a substitute for profit distribution or a decent wage.* After you've thought through these things, then consider a major affair—in the context of your overall people program.

P-4

SUMMARY

Prescriptions P-3 through P-10 are supports for P-1 and P-2, which in turn are necessary for survival in the current environment. The process of engendering commitment, the first step toward involvement, and organization featuring self-managing teams can be radically enhanced (or detracted from) by the recruiting process. To get off on the right foot, we must:

▶ Invest heavily—in line persons' time—in recruiting.

▶ Avoid psychological testing and interviewing by staff psychologists like the plague—hiring is a line responsibility, too important by far to delegate to "experts."

▶ Use selection criteria which emphasize appropriate "soft stuff" that will be directly important to the company in the future—teamwork potential, customer orientation—as much as or more than "hard stuff."

Per P-5, for instance, we must invest substantially more money in training people than ever before. Per P-1, we will ask people to give more of themselves. Per P-2, we will put people into arenas with modest numbers of formal supervisors compared to the past. For all these reasons and more, which add up to more autonomy and the need for mutual trust, the recruitment process takes on added significance.

Interviewees for all jobs who pass initial screening should spend a day or two in at least a half dozen lengthy interviews. Senior line people, peers, and even potential subordinates, starting with the receptionist, should be part of the formal evaluation system. The interview should unequivocally stress the attitudes and skills necessary to thrive, for cashier and bench scientist, in an ever more ambiguous and fast-changing world.

P-4

Spend Time Lavishly on Recruiting

It's a simple fact. The average person, in the bank operations center or factory, will be supported by much more capital equipment in the future. All of these prescriptions have had one underlying theme: The average person will be asked to contribute much more than in the past. It doesn't follow that we need all be bionic people, but it does mean that we'd better worry about issues such as commitment from the outset.

The task of transforming raw recruits into committed stars, able to cope with the pace of change that is becoming normal, begins with the recruiting process per se. The best follow three tenets, unfortunately ignored by most: (1) spend time, and lots of it; (2) insist that line people dominate the process; and (3) don't waffle about the qualities you are looking for in candidates. These practices join the long list of those that must move from the nice-to-do to the must-do category.

LOOK FOR WHAT YOU VALUE

The most effective recruiting processes are intense, and straightforward in their objectives:

▶ As an applicant for a job at Hewlett-Packard, if you pass an initial screening, you're in for at least a dozen long interviews. A division general manager of a $75 million operation will likely spend an hour or so with final candidates for a first-line purchasing job. Other interviewers include bosses at two or three levels and numerous peers and potential subordinates; each also spends an hour or more. They make the time. Daily committee meetings can wait.

Moreover, each of the interviewers zeroes in on the traits that most people would call mushy and unmeasurable. When I taught in Stanford University's MBA program, I observed students returning from a long day of interviewing at HP, baffled that the interviewer seemed to take little interest in their ability to manipulate a balance sheet or understand which direction electrons flow in. Instead, HP interviewers were determined to figure out whether or not they'd be good team players. A typical "question" might go like this: "Describe in detail an experience you had working in an intense, long-lasting small group." It makes sense, of course, given that so much of HP's work is carried out by small teams engaged in high-pressure projects.

▶ Grocer Stew Leonard considers retailing experience or skills at the cash register secondary. First, he seeks outgoing people who are likely to be genuinely friendly toward colleagues and customers. "We can teach cash register. We can't teach nice," says Stew. And as at HP, judgments about these traits start with the receptionist.

Similarly, at retailer Nordstrom, regional vice-president Betsy Sanders reports that the chief criterion is not prior retailing experience, but "friendliness." And retailer Luciano Benetton uses virtually the same guidelines for selecting Benetton franchisees; he doesn't demand any merchandising experience, but asks that the operators have what he calls "the right spirit" to run one of his thousands of shops. A chief bellman at Marriott—who is involved in recruiting—adds: "I don't want them if they've worked at other hotels. Too many bad habits. I want them to be friendly and outgoing. I'll teach them how to be a good bellhop."

Most people argue that it is impossible to judge such squishy "soft" traits accurately; hence, while acknowledging their importance, they fail to give them a decisive role in candidate evaluation.

However, the companies cited here have become just as adept at judging an applicant's potential courtesy or teamwork skills as they are at assessing mathematical, accounting, or other so-called hard competencies. It's simply a matter of painstakingly zeroing in on specific behaviors and asking detailed questions whose answers reveal the presence or absence of these vital attributes. Tom Melohn, co-owner of North American Tool & Die (NAT&D), an exceptionally profitable $10 million firm, recalling interviews with several candidates for one clerical job, explains: Most applicants began by asking about hours, money, and other mechanics. The one he picked, however, "asked all kinds of questions about our approaches and procedures. Clearly, she wanted to understand the business. She was also able to handle complex tasks and seemed genuinely excited at the end of the [trial] half day."

GREAT ON PAPER IS NO GUARANTEE

In the recruiting process, beware of credentials. Education is a source of much of the nation's productivity increase over the decades. I acknowledge that, and I am an advocate of more, not less. On the other hand, American firms tend to overemphasize not only the MBA (to a disgraceful degree) but technical diplomas as well.

In *Kaizen*, Maasaki Imai reports that innovative Honda Motor, responsible for a disproportionate share of automotive technical breakthroughs in its short history in that business, "has only three Ph.D.s on its engineering staff. . . . One is founder Soichiro Honda, whose Ph.D. is an honorary degree, and the other two are no longer active in the company. At Honda," Imai concludes, "technological input does not seem to require a Ph.D." That's some contrast to GM. Remember that the same philosophy of developing technical skills on the job is followed by steel's high-tech star, Chaparral; Worthington Industries, and many if not most of the other stellar manufacturers mentioned in prescription C-8, follow the same path.

By deemphasizing paper credentials, the Japanese and Chaparral et al. encounter much less static when they attempt to assign engineers to the plant. A much higher share of Japanese than American engineers work in the plant on projects that at first blush appear to be rather mundane, and far from the exotic design chores that highly trained engineers think should be their lot.

"Great People" Don't Equal "Great Teams"

Do wall-to-wall great people—on paper—make great teams? Not necessarily. In the first twelve years of their existence, the National Football

League's Tampa Bay Buccaneers have had an unprecedented six first choices in the college draft. First choice in the draft is awarded to the team with the past season's worst record among the NFL's twenty-seven members; overall, Tampa's twelve-year record is worst by far.

WHY INTENSIVE RECRUITING WORKS

The recruiting process followed by HP, Nordstrom, et al. has such an impact for a series of reasons, some quite subtle:

▶ A lengthy set of interviews unmistakably demonstrates that the firm cares enough about the candidate and the working environment to get people at all levels deeply involved in recruitment. Those who are hired start with the key values of HP or Nordstrom instilled by the recruiting process itself. And since those firms live their values so openly, if the person is going to be uncomfortable, he or she will probably become so during the lengthy courtship—and drop out then. (Most of those who do so nonetheless become fast friends of the firm, as a result of the obvious care and concern lavished on them.)

▶ The heavy investment of time by line managers and peers has an even more significant outcome. It puts the monkey squarely on the backs of the bosses and colleagues of the new hire. It's up to them to look directly for what they want (e.g., "good with customers") and then to affirm their choice by making the new person into a partner and a success. Their judgment is on the line. They can't blame any problems on "the jerk recruiters who only care about grade-point averages."

Tom Melohn of NAT&D, which has reduced turnover from 27 percent to 4 percent since 1978, sums it up nicely: "I strongly believe in the importance of having a work force that shares the same values. For that reason, I interview each candidate before other managers do. That takes time, obviously." And that's demonstrating commitment—from the top.

A corollary is the virtual noninvolvement of personnel or human resource departments. After an initial screening, recruiting should be considered far too important to delegate to any staff "experts." In this vein, I strongly oppose the use of a company psychologist to interview candidates, and the use of psychological testing in general. These devices impart precisely the wrong message about the company's value system. They suggest you are looking for flaws rather than strengths, and for pat "personality profiles" rather than interesting human beings. Further, it is an unequivocal indicator to the candidate that you value staff experts over line input. It also makes it darned tough for line managers, no matter how highly they esteem a candidate, to overrule a negative evaluation by the highly paid, jargon-spouting psychologist.

Finally, the use of such techniques suggests that there *are* pat answers, and evades the hard work of really figuring out what you (line person) want and how to discern whether it's present.* (That is, the judgments that Nordstrom is making are much more subtle—and thoughtful—than anything that could be provided by a given profile on the Minnesota Multiphasic Personality Inventory test.)

In the course of a year and a half, one professional service firm's managing partner reduced turnover from 30 percent a year to zero in a critical professional-skill area in which the local labor pool suffered a chronic shortage. He attributes the dramatic turnabout to the transfer of the entire recruiting process from the "pros" (human resource people, psychological testers, and the company psychologist) to the line. Similar results are occurring even in auto plants, where first-line people are being given wholesale responsibility for running in-plant assessment centers (see the story of GM's Delco-Remy plant in prescription P-1).

DO YOU KNOW YOUR VALUES?

The recruiting message is simple: line people looking for no-nonsense traits that will be of use in the world of tomorrow. There's an unspoken assumption behind this—that you know what your values are, or must be.

Most don't. Most recruiting practices, which mirror the firm's values, for better or for worse, are reflections of yesterday's needs; and bureaucratic (overly complex) reflections to boot.

---

*I have no problem with using the personnel department to provide extensive training in the interview process, to help the line interviewers figure out how to get at indications of the traits they are looking for.

"To get your recruiting straight, you'd best have your values straight," says Melohn of NAT&D. I talk so frequently in these prescriptions about the need to welcome change rather than fight it. Do you look for "flexible people"? Would you know how to screen or ask questions based on that criterion? (Without a doubt, in this area at least, the best predictor of the future is the past. "Flexible people" tomorrow will have been flexible yesterday—will have sparkled in ill-defined assignments, contributed to the creation of new ventures, such as a new college periodical. Substantial research, for instance, has been devoted to discerning who is likely to be "entrepreneurial." It turns out that tomorrow's entrepreneurs will have been entrepreneurial from the start—e.g., will have figured out a new technique for selling Girl Scout cookies at age 12.)

PUBLIC PARALLELS

Many of my public sector colleagues applaud these ideas, but inform me that the public's idea of fairness requires them to use extensive written tests and to depend heavily on credentials (a minimum of seven courses on the theory of elementary-grade lesson plans are required for a teaching certificate, etc.).

I certainly acknowledge the abuses of nepotism and politically inspired hiring that these rules were designed to prevent. However, I believe that even written tests, and especially written interview protocols, can at least be substantially tailored to allow you to look for the kinds of criteria that I've suggested drive Hewlett-Packard or Nordstrom.

In particular, look at your district's best teachers or your city's best police sergeants, and extract success criteria from that review in an objective manner. My bet is that the best will be light on credentials and heavy on other, so-called softer factors. Use these as a basis for your written selection process.

FIRST STEPS

1. Look at your stars: in engineering, in accounting, in the operations center—especially those best adapting to the environment's fast-paced needs. What makes them tick? What is their

background? Have any group that's recruiting begin the process by working up a practical list of "what works with that job," based upon the traits of these top performers. Have the group work to turn that list into a series of practical, desirable traits; then create a set of interview questions around those traits. Above all, the traits and questions should pass the "common sense" test and be free of theoretical, "ought to need" attributes.

2. Do you specifically emphasize "soft" values (e.g., teamwork potential) in your recruitment process? Take one job designation you are about to start recruiting for and think through what the values are. Write them down, and write down a series of questions that would help you determine their presence or absence in an interview. Add these questions to your next round of recruitment interviews. Again, make sure they are in common-sense language, not boilerplate or psycho-babble.

3. Recall P-1: Consider turning the front-line recruiting process over to the front line! Begin by involving front-line employees in interviews, and gradually give them full responsibility. Further consider, as some have done, giving sizable bonuses for bringing in candidates who are hired and are subsequently successful. (Review I-5: Word of mouth is as powerful in recruiting, especially in tight labor markets, as it is in new product sales.)

4. Have you canceled any recruiting interviews in the last three months because you were unexpectedly harried? What does that say to the recruit—and everybody you work with—about your valuation of the hiring process and people in general?

P-5

SUMMARY

The need for involvement—and flexibility—has an obvious corollary: Train and retrain. We must:

▶ Invest in human capital as much as in hardware.

▶ Train entry-level people; retrain them as necessary.

▶ Train everyone in problem-solving techniques to contribute to quality improvement.

▶ Train extensively following promotion to the first managerial job; then train managers every time they advance.

▶ Use training as a vehicle for instilling a strategic thrust.

▶ Insist that all training be line-driven—radically so; all programs should consist primarily of input from the line, be piloted in several line locations, and be taught substantially by line people.

Work-force training and constant retraining—and the larger idea of the work force as an appreciating (or depreciating) package of appropriate (or inappropriate) skills—must climb to the top of the agenda of the individual firm and the nation. Value added will increasingly come through people, for the winners. Only highly skilled—that is, trained and continuously retrained—people will be able to add value.

Consider doubling or tripling your training and retraining budget in the course of the next 24 to 36 months. Less serious consideration means a failure to come to grips with both the nature of the problem—and the magnitude of the opportunity.

P-5

Train and Retrain

Above all, [IBM's Thomas] Watson trained, and trained, and trained.

Peter Drucker, *Management*

We've documented the savings from the statistical process control methods and problem-solving methods we've trained our people in. We're running a rate of return of about 30 times the dollars invested—which is why we've gotten pretty good support from senior management.

Bill Wiggenhorn
Director of Training, Motorola
June 1987

BEATING THE COMPETITION THROUGH SKILL ENHANCEMENT

Recall from prescription C-2 that success requires increasing the relative quality of a firm's product or service—relative, of course, to the competition. When we think of our work force, we should emphasize the same word, "relative," also vis-à-vis the competition.

The work force is indisputably our principal asset. Each day its overall level of useful skills (as well as its commitment and energy) is either increasing or decreasing relative to that of the competition. The operative strategic question, then, is obvious: What have you done today to enhance (or at least insure against the decline of) the relative overall useful-skill level of your work force vis-à-vis competitors?

Much of the answer lies in your response to a series of questions about training: Who? How much? How relevant to tomorrow's needs? And how would the competition answer these same questions?

Work-force training must become a corporate (and indeed national) obsession. It is not. And it is on this variable that the outcome of the overall competitive struggle may most strongly depend.

A National Disgrace, An Epic Opportunity

Our investment in training is a national disgrace. That should come as no surprise. Despite lip service about people-as-our-most-important-asset, we value hardware assets over people, and have done so for the last century.

The ideas in the people prescriptions are not startling—or, at least, should not be. Involved and committed people can move mountains. Yet the fact that this set of prescriptions needs to be presented at all speaks to our longtime national deemphasis on human capital. Ross Perot once said that "brains and wits will beat capital spending ten times out of ten"; he was referring to the production line, not just the laboratory. TRW policy analyst Pat Choate estimated in 1986 that "The federal government contributes $3,200 to plants and technology for every dollar it chips in for employee training through tax incentives."

Even when we do train, we get it backwards. *Training* magazine's 1986 survey reports that while 69 percent of organizations with over 50 people on the payroll provide training for their middle managers and 70 percent train their execs, only 25 percent train production people, 30 percent train salespeople, and 34 percent train customer service people. Digging deeper, *Training* finds that for those who do provide training, much more (in terms of time spent per person) goes to managers than to nonmanagers.

Analyze the competition, and the story gets grimmer. The Japanese, Germans, and others outspend us wildly on training, especially in-company skill refurbishment and upgrading.

In short, our training track record is pathetic. Worse, it's getting worse. That is, as the pace of change picks up, the rate at which skills become obsolete—for scientist, machine operator, and actuary alike—is quickening. The customer prescriptions featured value added through quality, service, and responsiveness; factory/operations center hands and

388

sales and service people are the necessary heroes. The innovation prescriptions were clear—*everyone* must innovate. Everyone *must* be prepared (1) to contribute ideas and (2) to work together with less supervision (see P-2). And only constant training will provide the basis for constant adaptation.

TRAIN EVERYONE—LAVISHLY

Some few American firms learned the training secret long ago:

▶ Training has been IBM's secret weapon for decades. At one point, the senior Watson had just a one-person staff—an education director. An ad last year featured an IBM worker at the company's Lexington, Kentucky, site who had undergone major retraining a half-dozen times in a twenty-five-year career to fend off technical obsolescence. IBM pioneered in training women for service jobs in the 1920s. Its sales training course is still arguably the best in the land. And its training for entry-level managers is legendary—the firm is one of the rare ones that do not assume that supervising "comes naturally."

Training immediately follows each promotion at IBM. Everyone must spend at least 40 hours in the classroom each year. When IBM moved into alternate distribution channels a few years ago, all of its employees received a basic course in retailing. And when it launched its quality program (C-2), it formed Quality Institutes (special training schools) in the early 1980s as the spearhead of its remarkable quality improvement program; over 150,000 people were trained in quality control during the first five years of the program. Today IBM is facing major problems in many of its markets. It is doing many things to turn the tide, but none more important than massive retraining aimed at equipping the work force for the new challenge.

▶ Federal Express and Disney have thrived with similar training rigor. Unlike IBM, both firms have a large number of employees who are unlikely to spend their careers with the firm. Nonetheless, both treat everyone as a potential career employee. The training Federal Express gives its customer service people in Memphis and Disney's training of a 17-year-old would-be jungle boat driver far surpass the training many technical firms give their machinists.

Others have turned to training in a time of need, or to pursue new opportunities. Recall Milliken's 22 weeks of in-class training for its rag (shop towel) salespersons, and Tennant's training, used to push its top-drawer quality program along. As the second epigraph at the beginning of this prescription suggests, Motorola has turned to training to stay competitive in its high-tech markets. The firm's leadership in U.S. semiconductor products is supported by an allocation of over 2.5 percent of its payroll to training; in addition, it extensively trains suppliers, including Japanese firms.

Consider these additional examples as well:

► In four short years beginning in 1982, Pat Carrigan, the first woman to manage an assembly plant at GM, turned around a horrid situation at Lakewood, Georgia. Her strategy? A partnership with people. She cited three principal tactics: (1) a two-week pre-start-up training program for everyone, following a long shutdown during the depths of the 1981–83 recession; (2) an ongoing training program that gave 3,000 people some 360,000 hours of training in 24 months; (3) establishment of some 133 work groups, covering 90 percent of the work force—the only tactic that did not involve training. Overall success indicators at Lakewood include a drop in absenteeism at the troubled plant from 25 percent to 9 percent between 1981 and 1985. A moving, formal union tribute to Carrigan marked the end of her term at Lakewood.

► When Nissan moved to Smyrna, Tennessee, it started right—or average, by Japanese best-company practice. It spent $63 million ($7 million courtesy of the state of Tennessee) training about 2,000 workers, or over $30,000 per person, before the plant started operation. Not only does that ensure well-trained people; it also sends a "you're important to us" message to each and every individual. Sadly, the typical American manager's response to the Nissan story is some variation of "They're nuts. Give 'em that much training and they're sure to leave." People will hasten to leave if you treat them well? Some logic! Neither common sense nor the hard evidence supports this view.

► Computer maker Amdahl of Sunnyvale, California, took a chance with something akin to the Nissan approach. In 1981 line workers asked management how they could get a leg up in the company. The director of manufacturing and operations, Bernie Sussman, responded by offering employees who never went to college a chance at higher education. Amdahl's program, designed with local De Anza Junior

College, offers courses such as quality assurance, materials in process, production and inventory control, management principles and accounting. Students who complete the two years earn 41 college credits, which can be applied to an Associate Arts (AA) degree. Bill Flanagan, vice-president of manufacturing, notes that classes are taught on site and employees can attend up to five hours of class a week on company time. Amdahl also picks up the tab for books. Total cost: $125,000 a year. In early 1987, 58 employees were enrolled. Of the 40 who have completed the program, 38 are still working at Amdahl; in fact, the turnover rate among participants (5 percent) is half the company's overall turnover rate. Furthermore, 30 of the "graduates" have been promoted. After completing the program, Flanagan's secretary went on to earn a business administration degree; another woman who worked on the wiring assembly line for more than two years is currently a staff assistant in the finance department.

▶ Grocer Stew Leonard swears by Dale Carnegie training. That's hardly surprising, since his customer-first philosophy stresses warmth and courtesy. His seriousness is demonstrated by the offer to send anyone—including a 20-hour-a-week high school part-timer—to a full 14-week, $600 Dale Carnegie course. One wall at Leonard's displays photos of the 800-plus graduates of the course; Leonard's overall training tab of $1,000 per employee per year is four times the grocery industry average. With this kind concern so evident, Leonard has a long waiting list for every job in the store. His turnover is tiny by industry standards, and his talent pool for promotion is unsurpassed.

Each of these examples illustrates an instinctive "training first" approach to (1) jumping off to a good start (IBM, Fed Ex, Disney, Leonard, Nissan) or (2) responding to crisis/opportunity (Motorola, GM/Lakewood, Tennant, Milliken). Sadly, such instincts are unusual in America.

ELEMENTS OF A GOOD TRAINING PROGRAM

The following attributes will mark successful training programs for the future:

1. Extensive entry-level training that focuses on exactly the skills in which you wish to be distinctive. Disney, IBM, Federal Express, Stew

Leonard, and Nissan provide models: their training "overemphasizes" the skills that define their uniqueness. Leonard focuses on courtesy and communication skills; the shoddy training of most retail clerks focuses on how to run the cash register—and what a message that sends! Disney teaches Walt's vision directly, as well as acting and atmospherics; it sends another clear message through its extensive training—in customer servicing skills—for sweepers, parking-lot attendants, and ticket sellers. Federal Express has made a science of training its Memphis-based customer service force in how to deal with antsy customers.

2. All employees are treated as potential career employees. One might not ordinarily think of a cleaning contractor like ServiceMaster as a place for people to have careers. But ServiceMaster is different. Promotion from within is its invariable policy, and its training is offered in the context of career development. Retailer Nordstrom takes exactly the same view, in another industry that traditionally has low company loyalty. The Amdahl example above is illustrative of the payoff that can come from shifting to a "career" attitude toward employees, in that case with production people.

3. Regular retraining is required. IBM, as noted, and Milliken are among those who force everyone into the classroom each year. This is a must. Moreover, constant skill broadening should be everyone's goal. Pay-for-knowledge programs, discussed in P-1 and P-2 (see also P-6), are an important and too often overlooked ingredient.

4. Both time and money are generously expended. Regular time off from work, as in the Amdahl program (which, remember, was not directly related to the participants' current job), is a signal of serious interest in the worker's development. Generous tuition contributions are another vital sign of interest.

You can't overspend on training. At least, the odds are very low. Recall prescription C-9, where I encouraged you to consider doubling the sales force. Take the same approach to training: What could you accomplish if you doubled or tripled the training budget? Keep Nissan's $63-million-and-over-$30,000-per-person pre-start-up figure in mind—it's unlikely that you'll be pushing beyond that benchmark.

But a word of caution: Throwing money at a problem is unfailingly stupid, be it training, automation, or basic research. Most training is now ill conceived. Many training departments are not run by highly respected executives. So, take it a step at a time, with quality the goal—but think very boldly too.

5. On-the-job training counts too. Nordstrom provides what's possibly the best training program among retailers. Yet very little takes place in the classroom. The Nordstrom "trick" is "overstaffing"—salespersons *and* managers, on the sales floor. There is always a manager available to help. And since the firm's emphasis is on careers, each employee is encouraged to act as a coach from the start; success at doing so is a component of everyone's evaluation. Nordstrom is a living classroom, every day.

6. There are no limits to the skills that can profitably be taught to everyone. Johnsonville Sausage, in conjunction with a local community college, and Worthington Industries, courtesy of the finance department, teach basic, but complex and not sugarcoated, economics to everyone. Tennant, Motorola, and others, in their quest for quality improvement, have learned that over time almost everyone can absorb well-conceived courses in complex problem analysis and statistical process control.

7. Training is used to herald a commitment to a new strategic thrust. In the 1960s and 1970s, General Electric used training as the flagship for strategic change on several occasions. Inflation accounting, strategic planning, and technology management courses spearheaded major strategic programs in each area. Almost 100,000 managers and service professionals went through programs lasting several days in each case. Senior executives devoted enormous amounts of time to course development and teaching per se. Hewlett-Packard successfully followed a similar approach with manufacturing, marketing, and strategic planning in the early 1980s.

8. Training is emphasized at a time of crisis. Don't cut the training budget when crises come; increase it! That's what Carrigan did at Lakewood, Georgia (GM). It's also the logic of the path chosen by Motorola, Tennant, and IBM when mounting their respective quality revolutions. Massive and lengthy retraining to aid redeployment at times of technological change or wrenching competitive dislocation is another aspect; Digital Equipment, IBM, Ford, and GM are learning this skill (see P-7, on employment security, for more detail).

9. All training is line-driven. Even when the skill to be taught is a new one, the line must take the lead in developing program input, and then again in the teaching. Without these ingredients, the line has no personal stake in the program, and it is soon discovered that the would-be student is "too busy to spare three days" for training. Senior and junior line people must be temporarily assigned to training to work out the details of course content. The training department person is the pedagogy expert, but not the content leader. Some firms have gone the final step—to insist that the line pay for all training programs. That puts extraordinary pressure on the training department to listen. The objection is that more conservative programs will result, and this is doubtless true to a certain extent; but a conservative program "owned" by the line is far more useful than a radically innovative program written off as "the training department's fantasy after they consulted with academics."

10. Training is used to teach the organization's vision and values. "Control" and "management" in the future will flow through an empowering vision and shared values (see both the leadership and systems prescriptions). The best training programs, at all levels, from beginner to brush-up, must be seen as a prime opportunity to underscore these values. Top management must be involved in every training program as teachers, using the opportunity to discuss and transmit the vision that holds the firm together in turbulent times.

Training Supervisors: Now More than Ever

Supervising is a skill. Of course it is, you say, nodding. Yet most first-level managerial training courses are awful. There's no urgency in getting the new supervisor to attend: "We're stretched as it is; wait until the ABC project is beyond the critical stage"—but somehow it never quite is, or there's a DEF project that follows. Moreover, the content of these courses, like the courses for retail clerks that primarily teach how to use a cash register, typically emphasizes mechanics—the twenty-three official preliminaries to firing someone—and seldom stresses leadership or coaching. When the next promotion comes, the story is repeated; the far different task of managing managers is all but ignored. All of the above amounts to a frightening omission—and lost opportunity. There is no more difficult transition in a career than the one from nonboss to boss; the second-toughest is to boss of bosses. These passages should be marked by programs commensurate with their significance.

The historic de-emphasis of these transitions has been unfortunate. The future consequences of such neglect are unacceptable. The first-line supervisory and middle-management job must change dramatically (see P-2, P-9, especially). Timely training in the newly required skills is essential.

Consider Revolution

The ten elements of a good training program and the suggestions about management training add up to a tall order. Most firms are "working on" all of them to some extent. The prescription here, though, asks you to consider a revolution: (1) Review the training budget *before* the capital budget. (2) Do a thorough competitive assessment of your investment in skill development and career enhancement (for the work force as a whole) vis-à-vis domestic and foreign competitors. (3) Evaluate the content of every course relative to the opportunities suggested, especially in prescriptions C-1 through C-10. (4) Do a "zero base" assessment of your training department; you are probably not a fan of training, because you've mixed line rejects and detached "training professionals" together, creating courses that smart line operators avoid sending people to like the plague. (5) Consistent with the first four points, treat your training (skill level) assessment as the essence of strategic opportunity. If you don't spend as much time on this assessment as on the evaluation of the capital (hardware) budget, you have entirely missed the point of all ten of the prescriptions in this section.

The "revolutionary decision," following the sort of assessment just suggested, may well require the establishment of a rather grand "corporate university." Many are turning in this direction—especially to remedy deficiencies in the skills of high school graduates. Note, however, that there is a great opportunity to do this wrong: (1) to emphasize the glitz and glamour of a new facility, filled with computer-controlled audio/video monster machines; (2) to fail to tie the curriculum directly to the firm's key strategic needs; and (3) to emphasize executive training at the expense of total corporate skill enhancement. If you can avoid these pitfalls, the opportunity is both strategic and limitless.

FIRST STEPS

1. Go out and survey the five very best first-line training programs you can find. Do it in the next 60 days, and make sure the survey team has no controllers, and no more than one trainer, and is dominated by highly respected line people.

2. Next, insist that each top manager attend a large share (at least three or four days' worth) of one front-line training program as it is currently provided.

3. Presuming that steps one and two suggest vast opportunity, do not immediately retool the training department; instead, start by thoroughly revamping *one* entry-level course in the next four months. The project leader should be a respected line person, with a trainer as deputy.

4. Following step #3 above, move to include a "zero-base" assessment of the current training staff and the magnitude of the opportunity in next year's strategic plan. The strategic assessment task should be handled by division general managers (or the equivalent), with trainers as "staff" to the assessment group. A major part of the group's work should consist in overall measurement of your total corporate skill pool/skill level—make it quantitative, and in contrast to your competition's. (If such an assessment does not unearth dramatic opportunities, you've probably done it wrong, or else your overall vision is too limited— i.e., it does not sufficiently emphasize the value-adding, market-creation objectives that are discussed most fully in C-1 through C-6.)

P-6

SUMMARY

Involvement of skilled workers on a grand scale (see P-1, P-2, P-4 especially) is essential to achieving future competitiveness. To further enhance worker commitment to proactively seeking constant improvement, we must:

▶ Provide bold financial incentives for everyone. Incentive pay for everyone is the "clincher," the ultimate recognition for a contribution to improved company performance—and not widely used. But incentives programs must be accompanied by a genuine and clearly perceived opportunity to influence the results. Incentives should focus on the ten- to thirty-person work group.

Above-average pay yields above-average work—or at least the converse is true. Consider putting everyone on salary. Pay-for-knowledge incentives to learn several jobs are a must. Include everyone in a profit-distribution/gain-sharing incentive pay scheme. A variable target of at least 25 percent of base pay is reasonable. Feedback (performance pay) should be quick—monthly at least. Employee share ownership should be strongly encouraged, through an Employee Stock Ownership Plan (ESOP) or similar program.

P-6

Provide Incentive Pay for Everyone

A Yankelovich poll of Japanese and American workers is illuminating. On the statement "I have an inner need to be the best I can, regardless of pay," American workers, maligned by so many (especially American managers), surprisingly outscored the Japanese. On the much more practical question concerning "who would benefit most from an increase in [worker] productivity," the tables were turned. Some 93 percent of Japanese workers thought that they would benefit, while only 9 percent of American workers felt that way. Self-interest probably rules in both countries, but our workers keenly believe that increased productivity and self-interest don't go hand in glove. Japanese workers' traditional 25 to 50 percent bonus after a good year doubtless helps induce the feeling that there is a direct link between contribution and outcome.*
In fact, in Japan the total sum distributed as bonuses usually exceeds a firm's after-bonus profit.

PROFIT DISTRIBUTION: AN OLD IDEA IN NEED OF DUSTING OFF

The idea of incentive pay for everyone is hardly new to Americans. A century ago, in 1887, Procter & Gamble installed a profit-sharing plan that divided profits between the company and its workers in the same

*From 1970 through 1980, the average bonus was 4.52 months' pay for people in firms of over 500 employees, 3.21 months' pay for those in firms of 30 to 100 employees.

proportion that labor costs bore to total costs (in an era, remember, when labor costs were a much bigger slice of the pie than today). That is, if wages were 50 percent of all costs, the workers' bonus would be one-half of profits. President Cooper Procter stated at the time: "The chief problem of big business today is to shape its policies so that each worker will feel that he is a vital part of his company with a personal responsibility for its success *and a chance to share in that success* [my emphasis]."

Sadly, Procter's statement is equally apt today. A century later, it is still less than 20 percent of the U.S. work force that participates in a profit distribution plan or other productivity-based gain-sharing plan. Furthermore, just 10 percent own shares of stock in their company, despite the generous incentives granted by the historic Employee Share Ownership Plan (ESOP) legislation passed in 1974.

As prescription P-1 and several of its successors suggest, I observe that America's productivity and quality problems—for the individual firm and for the nation—are directly linked to a failure to involve people in their jobs, and a failure to seek their assistance in the achievement of consistent quality and productivity improvement.

Such involvement is the paramount step. But if managers ask people to give of their creative talents and commitment, and to take apparent risks by doing such things as proposing labor-saving ideas, those people should share handsomely in any profit that results. The widespread failure to reward people for higher involvement is a missed opportunity of the first order.

A FIVE-PART INCENTIVE PAY PROGRAM

Base Pay Above the Norm

It is commonly assumed that the high wages of unionized steelworkers doomed integrated steel manufacturing in this country. The high pay at Nucor, Chaparral, and Worthington Steel makes a mockery of this. All three firms are several times more productive than average, with superb quality and responsiveness to boot. Yet Worthington, for instance, sets its base wage within the top 25 percent of local wages, and then adds to that with a profit-distribution formula that usually averages 80 percent of the base wage each 90 days.

Retailing is notorious for low pay. But Nordstrom soars in an increasingly competitive market with superb service—and wages that are pegged about $2.00 per hour above retail's average in a given area; the premium wage is then further enhanced by an unusual 6.75 percent sales commission. Top salespersons can clear $70,000. Federal Express pays very well too. A part-time Courier-Pak sorter in the Memphis Hub started at $9.75 an hour in 1986 and received a profit-sharing bonus and a sizable tuition refund.

University National Bank & Trust of Palo Alto is a top-performing example of the new brand of relatively small specialist banks. In 1986 the fast-growing institution earned three times more (on assets of $180 million) than the average California bank (1.27 percent versus 0.43 percent). Chairman Carl Schmitt explains his approach to pay: "It's one thing to have a strategy, but you have to also make it work. To do that, you have to hire good people. Then you gotta pay them." UNB&T's average salary and benefits per employee rank seventy-sixth out of seventy-eight California banks (with total deposits between $100 million and $500 million). "That sounds terrible!" says Schmitt. "But the way they rank it, the lowest-paying banks are at the top [of the list]. Now that's an interesting window to the industry's attitude—that it's better to have lower salaries, to keep costs down. That's not how we think and that's not our practice."

In general, I recommend: (1) base pay somewhat above the geographic area average for comparable jobs—which means that total pay, with incentives added, will be substantially above average. I also urge (2) that everyone be put on salary.

Pay-for-Knowledge

Prescriptions P-1 and P-2 discussed pay-for-knowledge, including the specifics of several programs.

Since only the employee trained in a number of skills will provide the bedrock for the constant adaptation that will mark the new breed of winners, such programs are a must. Incentives might encourage learning the jobs of at least two teams in an average factory or operations center setting; that would amount to twenty to twenty-five jobs. Three to five significant pay incentive steps should be associated with the progression of skill acquisition.

Productivity and Profit-Based Incentive Pay

▶ Lincoln Electric is a Cleveland-based manufacturer of welding machines and induction motors. It suffered over a 40 percent decline in revenues during the 1981–83 recession, yet it laid no one off, and has not done so since the early 1940s (see also P-7).

Lincoln was an early adopter of the Scanlon Plan, named after Joe Scanlon, a USW worker who developed the incentive scheme in an effort to save La Pointe Steel during the Great Depression. The original Scanlon Plan splits profits and cost savings from suggestions with the work force. At Lincoln, each employee gets a semi-annual "Merit Rating," which results in the addition or subtraction of "points" from a starting score of 100, based on "ideas and cooperation, output, dependability, and quality." The points are then valued according to the firm's current profit level. From 40 to 55 percent of pre-tax profits go into the bonus pot. The bonus has averaged 95 percent of base wages each year, since 1940. With sales back up to pre-recession heights in 1984, some 2,405 workers split $42 million—about $15,000 per person. Employees also own 40 percent of the firm's stock.

The payoff for Lincoln is productivity that is 250 percent above industry average, making it possible for the firm to continue to be the world's low-cost producer in a tough industry.

▶ Nucor's team-based bonus system is key to its astounding productivity, which keeps it ahead of even foreign producers on costs. The firm's production people are grouped into units of fifteen to thirty-five people. The principal incentive program works like this: A standard for an activity is set at 90 percent of the average time historically required to do the task,* and the team bonus is determined by how much the team beats the standard. For instance, if the team does 60 percent better than the standard, its members get a 60 percent bonus, *paid the next week.* The resulting compensation is exceptional. For instance, the average pay in recessionary 1983 for an hourly worker at Nucor's 525-person mill in Darlington, South Carolina, ran over $30,000; more than 75 percent of the workers had been unskilled when hired just a few years before.

---

*It is vital that the standard be based on past averages, and devised in cooperation with the workers. "Merit pay" plans in which the standard is some shifting "optimum" mandated by a stopwatch or the boss's whim foster suspicion, not commitment.

▶ Worthington Industries follows another, equally successful formula to keep its productivity, quality, and responsiveness tops. It distributes 17 percent of pre-tax profits each quarter on the basis of divisional performance (e.g., the steel operations). This translates into about 80 percent of the already high base wage, as noted. Attaining membership in the plan works this way: Each facility has an elected committee of nonmanagers. After a ninety-day probationary period, a worker is eligible to become "permanent" and join the profit-distribution plan. The committee of peers at the facility votes the person in or out, or calls for additional probationary time. Employees also own over 30 percent of Worthington's stock, and stock awards are granted for such things as superior attendance. Everyone at Worthington is on salary, and is therefore not docked for absenteeism, which runs only 1 percent. Productivity is about 200 percent better than the industry average.

▶ At Steelcase, tools for maintaining top market share in an increasingly competitive market include profit- and productivity-based bonuses averaging 60 percent of base pay. On top of that, the firm invariably contributes 15 percent of total compensation (the maximum allowable by the IRS) to a deferred profit-sharing plan. Bonuses are based in part on individual performance, and also include quarterly and annual profit distribution.

▶ At Publix, a Florida grocer, where employees own 100 percent of the stock: (1) each store pays a quarterly cash bonus equal to 20 percent of its profits; (2) there is a standard Christmas bonus equal to two weeks' pay; and (3) 10 percent of profits (in addition to the 20 percent for the quarterly bonuses) goes into a deferred profit-sharing plan, divided among all employees with over 1,000 hours per year.

▶ Andersen Corporation of Bayport, Minnesota, continues to be the nation's largest and most successful manufacturer of windows and patio doors. A mundane product? Don't tell that to the firm's work force of 3,500 or to its customers, for whom Andersen provides high-quality, customized products. In 1986, the workers divided up a profit-distribution bonus—a tradition since 1914—of $72 *million,* coming in *one* check and equivalent to eight months and three weeks' pay! (If they invest the bonus money, in a home for instance, they get the further assistance of a Thrift Bonus Program.) The employees, called "working partners," also own 30 percent of the firm's stock, and are eligible for a substantial personal productivity bonus. The Andersen approach is straightforward. The Minneapolis *Star and Tribune* summarizes: "[The three basic] principles are to make products that are different from, and better than, others in the marketplace; to hire the best people *and pay the top wages in the industry* [my emphasis], and to provide full employment year-round." The last-mentioned, in a notoriously cyclical business, is a bold objective indeed—but with rare exceptions, it has been faithfully followed by the firm, which has grown from $50 million in revenue in 1966 to $790 million in 1986. Productivity at Andersen runs at twice the industry average.

These few examples are typical of the most progressive profit-distribution plans. Each, moreover, comes from a tough industry, where keeping pace with the competition is difficult indeed. Drawing on them and many others, here's what I recommend:

1. Productivity-and-quality-based incentives that emphasize team performance and profit-distribution incentives based upon the performance of the facility, division, and, to some extent, the corporation as a whole. The team and the facility/division are the basic building blocks (see also P-2); identification with these groups should be maximized, and the lion's share of variable compensation should follow from team/facility/division performance. Individual incentives are fine as long as they are not too complicated. However, I urge that specifically suggestion-based individual incentives be handled outside the normal incentive compensation system, as a special case. Furthermore, suggestion-based incentives should emphasize numerous small awards, rather than big ones.

2. A variable incentive bonus level that works out to a minimum of 20 percent of the total paycheck.

3. Monthly distribution of bonus money, separate from the regular paycheck.

4. A simple and understandable bonus formula. Worthington's chief financial officer, Joe Stegmayer, shakes his head in dismay when he talks of the people who visit his company to learn about their plan: "They call back to tell us what they're doing. And if they're doing anything, it's usually '7.33 percent of pre-tax profits, above $100,000 per facility, if a target return on adjusted net assets of 12.6 percent is also reached.' No one can figure it out. That means people's motivation to increase profits will not improve." Worthington's formula, 17 percent of pre-tax profits, has stayed the same since the plan began in 1966. (One thing has changed at Worthington. Profit distribution used to be based on facility rather than divisional performance. The firm shifted to the latter so that fully booked plant managers would have an incentive to shift orders to other plants more able to meet them rather than hoard them at their own operation—adding unnecessary costs through overtime pay—in hopes of gaining higher profits for their own facility.)

A Time of Trouble: The Best Time for Incentive Pay

Business Week in late 1986 reported a save-the-business agreement reached by grocer A&P. The Philadelphia local of the United Food & Commercial Workers (UFCW) agreed to a 25 percent pay cut in exchange for participation in a major incentive scheme: "If a store's employees could keep labor costs at 10 percent of sales—by working more efficiently or by boosting store traffic—they'd get a cash bonus equal to one percent of the store's sales. They'd get an 0.5 percent bonus at 11 percent of sales or 1.5 percent at 9.5 percent of sales. It was a gamble in the low margin supermarket business, but it worked. . . . Philadelphia A&P workers now earn $10.40 an hour in base wages plus an average of eighty-five cents an hour in one-time bonuses. The average food store wage in Philadelphia is $10.60. . . . Overall labor costs have been cut from 13 percent to 11 percent, versus an industry average of 12 percent."

Business Week adds: "Just as important is the effect of the bonus incentive on per-store sales, which have jumped 24 percent since 1984, to $7 million a year. With a vested interest in improving the way their stores are run, workers have made useful suggestions in bi-monthly meetings with store managers and at the regional level. In Richmond, Virginia, employees suggested that the pathway between the checkout lanes and the store shelves be widened, because in peak times the checkout lines stretched into the aisles, and customers would leave rather than fight the crowd. In one black and Italian neighborhood in Philadelphia, employees suggested adding large sections of popular ethnic food. Previously all A&P stores had to carry the same items. 'You'd be amazed at the willingness of people to participate when they can say anything without fear of reprisal,' says Thomas R. McNutt, president of UFCW Local 400 in Landover, Maryland. . . . A&P's rivals said [it was] crazy to offer one percent bonuses in a business where profit margins aren't much larger. But the dividends from the Philadelphia experience have silenced them."

Employee Share Ownership

Lowe's Companies is the biggest U.S. lumber and hardware retailer, with 309 stores in 21 states. It has been a model of the power of ESOPs to add to a firm's strength in a fragmented, competitive market. Workers at Lowe's own 25 percent of the company. The firm contributes 12 to 15 percent of payroll to its plan each year. Ownership is taken seriously at Lowe's. Each store elects a representative to an advisory committee, which hears management reports and makes recommendations. Each store holds a monthly meeting, where employees discuss changes in such things as operating procedures and merchandising. Against this backdrop, Lowe's has achieved productivity 200 to 300 percent above industry average, while employee theft is less than one-sixth of normal.

In 1974, fewer than 500,000 American workers owned stock in their companies. Now, over 8,000 ESOPs involve 8 million workers. The great explosion was fueled by the 1974 legislation that allows employers tax deductions for up to 25 percent of payroll that they contribute to an ESOP. In *Employee Ownership in America,* Corey Rosen, Katherine Klein, and Karen Young make the first comprehensive analysis of ESOPs, assessing some thirty-seven plans in depth. They review prior studies that sometimes demonstrate productivity increases of 200 to 300 percent following installment of an ESOP.

Averages aren't really the point, though. After extensive analysis, the authors home in on several possible factors that could determine the success or failure of an ESOP. Three, in combination, determine effectiveness: (1) employer contribution has to be high (at least 8 to 10 percent of payroll); (2) a true philosophy of employee-as-partner has to exist (this is the topic of the ten prescriptions in their section, taken together); and (3) multiple mechanisms for worker participation must be in place and actively used.

Among the factors that, perhaps surprisingly, were *not* decisive contributors to success were: (1) percentage of the company stock owned by employees; (2) extent of voting rights (which can range from virtually none to normal shareholder rights); (3) the reason for installing the plan (altruism versus a leveraged buyout, for instance); and (4) stock price performance following the installation of the ESOP. I find the insignificance of that last factor of special importance. The immediate rebuttal I hear to the ESOP idea from executives is: "Sounds great when the stock price is soaring. But what about lousy years and bear markets?" As usual, this is a residue of our insulting view of workers' intelligence. Executives with stock options understand that markets go up and that markets come down. Why do the same executives suppose that the people who work for them can't understand such things? The study by Rosen et al. suggests decisively that they do.

In summary, I strongly urge consideration of an ESOP, with a contribution of at least 8 to 10 percent of payroll—as long as the factors that Rosen et al. found important are also in place.

Executive Incentives

The suggestions here are simple: (1) very low base pay compared to very high incentive pay and (2) rewards based upon what you want to happen.

I am mindful of the critics' continuing concern about American management's obsession with short-term profitability. Nonetheless, especially in big firms, I observe the opposite phenomenon: executives have huge salaries that don't tumble when performance tumbles.

In a bad year, Nucor's Ken Iverson bragged that he was the lowest-paid of the Fortune 500 chiefs. I heartily applaud such bragging. The partners in the Trammell Crow real estate company draw a minimal base salary of less than $20,000; the rest of their compensation depends upon performance in the course of the year.

Here's what can happen. A bank's subsidiary was struggling. The parent devised a clever incentive scheme to perk things up. It capitalized the unit with $2.5 million in preferred stock and $500,000 in common stock. Then 40 percent of the common was given outright to the unit's managers. They were allowed to pocket dividends and stock appreciation, after profit was used to pay dividends on all the preferred stock.

Suddenly, the newly enfranchised and recently voracious-for-more-capital managers decided they had too much money. They returned $1.5 million, or 60 percent, of the preferred immediately, reducing preferred equity to $1 million. They gave up cars and perks as well, and even tried to move the unit's office to a low-rent neighborhood (the corporate parent intervened). Profits in the previously somnolent unit quintupled in the first year.

I don't particularly recommend such a plan, and perhaps in time it could lead to an excessive focus on the short term. It is, however, a dramatic illustration of the power of a clear executive incentive.

I propose base salaries of $200,000 or less for all corporate chiefs (and $75,000 or less in firms of $25 million or less), with incentives based on a mix of short- and long-term performance. And when times are tough, managers, especially top executives, should take the first and hardest hits. In a bad year, the pay of Nucor's workers will plunge 20 percent on average; executive pay will drop 70 percent.

Second, base bonuses upon the strategic skills you want to improve or emphasize. Once again, if you want to underscore the importance of superior quality, base your incentives on some measurement of quality and the improvement thereof. Ford, Tennant, Perdue Farms, and others do. If you want to emphasize customer service, pay on the basis of customer service ratings; IBM does, all the way to the top. If increased innovation is your target, reward executives, as 3M does, on the basis of the share of revenues stemming from recently introduced new products. If you want inter-unit cooperation, award big bonuses for bold acts of inter-unit support.

A Gigantic Opportunity

This Five-Part Incentive-Pay Program could add up to a lot of bucks. And it does at Steelcase, Nucor, Worthington, Lincoln Electric, Publix, Nordstrom, et al. But then, and this has been the point of all of these prescriptions, there's an enormous gain to be had: Nordstrom—200 percent above the industry average in sales per square foot; Lowe's—productivity 200 to 300 percent above average, with little shrinkage; Lincoln Electric—productivity running 250 percent above average; Nucor—productivity 300 percent above average; Worthington—productivity 200 percent above the norm, quality 300 percent above average; Andersen—productivity that's 100 percent above standard. And all of these firms are in markets growing more competitive each day.

It is distressing to see jobs mindlessly shipped offshore, and then to learn that Lincoln, in a violently competitive market from which most Americans have withdrawn, is the world's low-cost producer, while paying its average employee in excess of $40,000 a year in a merely okay year. When will the rest of us learn to "get revolutionary" about the people involvement/pay issues?

WARNING: INCENTIVES WITHOUT INVOLVEMENT WILL BACKFIRE

There are several caveats to consider before mounting a radical performance incentive plan. The worst possible thing you can do is to accept some of these suggestions without opening the doors to involvement—that is, without giving the person who is part of an incentive scheme access to the financial numbers, to training, and to the opportunity to influence the now variable pay outcome. To do otherwise is maddening; it says, in effect, "Here you are, chum. Look at the carrot [big variable incentive]. But—ha! ha!—you have no tools to reach out for it." The way to increase productivity is to allow access to an unlocked tool room, so the modem can be obtained when needed; to train extensively in cause-and-effect problem analysis; to give access to a meeting room where the team can do analysis and implementation planning. If these tools (and a host of others) are absent, the effect of the incentive is to underscore the worker's impotence. It will backfire badly.

Moreover, let me make clear what this prescription is *not.* It is *not* a reversion to the old saw: "In the end, money is the only incentive that counts." No! Involvement and the opportunity to influence the outcome come first; the money is a fine form of recognition for the help rendered. In fact, John McConnell of Worthington Industries calls his firm's generous incentive programs "just one more form of recognition." So it is, then, the coupling that counts: Involvement is important. Control over the outcome (e.g., minimum bureaucracy and supervision) is essential. And incentive pay confirms that the worker has done well using the tools and freedom thus granted.

There is, I earnestly believe, no downside. There is no evidence that workers are incapable of comprehending or bearing the pain of a poor year if (1) they have a chance to do very well in a good year and (2) they were involved in the decisions and actions that led to the outcome.

PUBLIC PARALLELS

First, there are public parallels. All levels of government are now experimenting vigorously with pay-for-performance programs. A pilot project in the U.S. Navy at China Lake, California, for instance, has sharply reduced the number of pay bands, and has dramatically increased the share of wage increases awarded on the basis of merit.

None of these programs, that I know of, approaches the radical proportions of Lincoln Electric's. On the other hand, the public pay system has been so constrained for so long that even small changes have dramatic impact. Pay-for-performance programs should also be on every public manager's agenda.

FIRST STEPS

In the next 60 days, study ten radical incentive schemes, inside and outside your industry. After day 60, consider (1) a radical scheme and (2) a three-to-five-year process for phasing it in. (This is the only prescription where I don't recommend an incremental/pilot approach. Pay is too sensitive an issue, psychologically. Once you commit, you must follow through, or suffer a very great loss of credibility.)

P-7

SUMMARY

In order to demand constant risk-taking from everyone for the sake of continuous improvement; and in order to pave the way for flexible response and constant change/reorganization, we should:

▶ provide a guarantee of continuous employment for a large share of the work force (subject to acceptable individual performance)

▶ develop a wide range of tactics, from retraining (see P-5) to short-term redeployment to understaffing by 5 or 10 percent, to ensure that layoffs rarely if ever occur.

Instability of circumstance requires constant change in technology, work procedures, structures; the formation of joint ventures and alliances; the drastic shortening of product life cycles; the institution of such procedures as just-in-time inventory management. To deal with all this turmoil, the worker must embrace change and flexibility to a previously unimaginable degree. While training and changes in attitude will help, some form (sweeping, I believe) of employment guarantee is necessary to certify management's intent to place primary emphasis on its skilled work force.

After a probationary period of 6 to 18 months, provide a guarantee of continuous employment to your permanent work force (where "permanent" is defined as enough people to handle 90 percent of normal demand). Develop, ahead of time, a specific strategy for dealing with precipitous drops in demand, including major redeployment (to maintenance, sales). Develop an ongoing retraining program to precede/accompany the introduction of, say, new technology.

P-7

Provide an Employment Guarantee

If we have too many people, we consider it a management problem, not an employee problem.

> Lowell Mayone
> Vice-President,
> Hallmark
> May 1987

When a company has a layoff, it's most often the management's fault. . . . In a recession people want to test me, to see if I'm brave enough to have a layoff. I'm willing to take that ridicule because it's paid off to hold on to our people. I don't have layoffs to see how brave I am. . . . We have a big investment in the people. . . . It's also good business for our people to have confidence that we will not lay them off just to help our profit short-term. This faith in the company is important.

> Ken Olsen
> President, Digital Equipment,
> in a 1982 speech to Wall
> Street analysts,
> 1982

In May 1987, UAW vice-president Bill Casstevens announced ratification of an agreement with Case-IH (Tenneco's farm equipment subsidiary) that "marks the first time the UAW has negotiated full employment protection in a major contract."

413

Case-IH won numerous provisions for job flexibility (a two-thirds reduction in job classifications, the ability to require more overtime) and a 39-month wage freeze in return for guaranteed employment levels (GELs) that cover 3,500 employed and 1,600 laid-off Case-IH workers. The base of 3,500 will be maintained with a guarantee of 40 hours of pay per week, regardless of changes in technology or market conditions. Moreover, when normal attrition occurs, for every two "quits" (retirements, etc.) one worker will be brought back from layoff. If increasing demand leads to sustained higher employment, the prevalent GEL will automatically go up. The landmark agreement also includes such provisions as earmarking a substantial portion of any future increase in the employees' cost-of-living allowance (COLA) to a major retraining program (this will represent the employees' contribution to the program, which may be added to by the company if necessary).

The pact follows the UAW's historic 1984 agreement with GM that included a "no layoff" provision protecting all workers with more than a year's seniority from unemployment due to the introduction of new technology, outsourcing decisions, and negotiated productivity improvements.

Critics call such agreements no more than a flurry of defensive actions on the part of floundering manufacturing unions—last-ditch attempts to protect a few overpaid jobs at the expense of (1) competitiveness (competitive wage rates) and (2) future/new workers. The hue and cry about the latter reached epic proportions when the pilots' and flight attendants' unions accepted American Airlines' landmark two-tier wage structure (significantly lower pay for entering employees) in return for lifetime employment guarantees for current workers.

Doubtless there is some truth to such claims. The numbers alone suggest that union strength is waning in the U.S. as competition surges and many basic worker rights are assured by legislation and judicial decisions. But be that as it may, guaranteed employment (1) has non-union origins that are over 175 years old and (2) is an idea whose time has come—i.e., it's yet another of the "nice to do's" turned "must do."

Not a New Idea

Most trace the idea of employment security back to 1806 and the cotton mill owned by Robert Owen in New Lanark, Scotland. Faced with an abrupt reduction in the supply of raw materials (an American embargo), almost all millers shut down and fired their workers. Owen stopped the machinery, but kept paying full wages and turned people to maintenance tasks during the four-month crisis.

Owen reaped the reward that is, today, the heart of the matter. His workforce was subsequently much more amenable to managerial, organizational, and technological changes. Constant innovation, supported by workers, led to extraordinary long-term profitability relative to competitors.

The U.S. has a long tradition of enlightened firms offering employment security. Though no written provision (other than to do the utmost to avoid layoffs) has ever existed at non-union IBM, the company has followed a de facto no-layoff policy for over 60 years. It has used a series of tactics (to be discussed below) to avoid layoffs. Procter & Gamble (largely non-union) introduced a minimum 48-weeks-per-year "guarantee" for production people back in 1923.

Other venerable and new guarantors include S. C. Johnson (Johnson Wax), Hewlett-Packard, Hallmark, Digital Equipment, Federal Express, Worthington Industries, Nucor Corporation, and Lincoln Electric. The last-named, for instance, guarantees 30 hours of pay a week minimum for every employee who has been on the payroll for two years.

THE POWER OF EMPLOYMENT GUARANTEES

The Work in America Institute is the foremost proponent of guaranty programs, having studied hundreds of creative experiments throughout the country. Its list of advantages is consistent with my own observations, and includes increased employee willingness to:

1. Accept management-proposed changes that might otherwise threaten security.
2. Volunteer ideas for improving performance and productivity, even when labor-saving changes may result.
3. Maintain an optimal pace of work, without fear that the job may run out.
4. Give up restrictive practices (such as jurisdictional lines and obsolete work rules), which are designed to protect jobs.

415

5. Agree to perform tasks outside their normal job definition, when there is need to do so.
6. Accept inconveniences, such as mandatory overtime, when persuaded of the need.
7. Volunteer for, and profit from, training that expands the boundaries of their job.

Other benefits to employers that the Institute observes include:

1. Maintenance of productivity because of higher morale and preservation of employee skills.
2. Retention of skilled workers.
3. Reduction or elimination of the large costs associated with layoffs, particularly where "bumping" occurs—for example, distorted production scheduling, delayed start-ups when recession ends, retraining of bumped employees.
4. Greater flexibility in deploying human resources to keep operations going.
5. Savings in employer costs associated with severance pay, early-retirement incentives, and other layoff schemes requiring substantial financing.
6. Avoidance of post-recession costs of hiring and training new workers to replace those who find other jobs during layoff.
7. Reinforcement of group loyalties and strengthening of employee loyalty to the firm.

These substantial benefits have long been affirmed by pioneers such as IBM, P&G, and Lincoln. But that's not the point. The point is that the preceding list reads like a summary of the tactics necessary to implement the survival strategies laid out in this book (see especially C-1 through C-10, I-1, I-10, P-1), namely that firms must, above all, (1) become more flexible and (2) achieve the benefit of constant, employee-driven improvements in quality, service, and productivity.

It is almost a psychological truism to state that *only* some guarantee of security will enable firms to induce employees to (1) constantly take risks (improve things, add new skills), and (2) be flexible enough to deal with constant change. This is the principal paradox with which management must deal (see also L-1): the engendering of heretofore unheard-of flexibility requires an equally heightened level of underlying stability—

but a stability born of trust and the shared understanding of a vision, not stability based on tedious contracts and lengthy procedure manuals. Trust comes from the heart, from attitude—and from a guarantee that the newly empowered risk-taker in the maintenance shop has a relatively safe nest to which he may return.

WHAT IS A GUARANTEE?

"Lifetime employment" as practiced in Japan is the image that usually springs to mind. But the Japanese guarantee is less of a model than it seems. For one thing, "lifetime employment" covers, according to most estimates, just 15 to 35 percent of the work force, and applies almost exclusively to males in big firms. Furthermore, it is maintained through a series of strong-arm tactics such as (1) pulling in subcontract work, on short notice, from small firms, (2) using women in temporary, unprotected roles to absorb peak demand, and (3) massive redeployment of people to sales, for instance, in troubled times.

"Guarantee" turns out to be an elastic term in general. Except for those in union contracts, few guarantees are given in writing. Most, including IBM's, are oral agreements to move heaven and earth to avoid layoffs, backed up by what really counts—a decades-long track record of having done precisely that. Even Lincoln Electric's "guarantee," sustained through the toughest of times for over 50 consecutive years (with the exception of layoffs required by the return to normal production at the end of World War II), is not hard and fast; it can be changed, with six months' advance notice, by a vote of the firm's board of directors.

Here are a few of the variables that are often used to define whose employment is guaranteed, and some of the tactics used to maintain the guarantee. First, the who. Once again, the Work in America Institute provides a useful laundry list of practices:

1. *Different classes of employees* may enjoy different degrees of employment security. For example, managers normally have greater security than blue-collar employees.
2. *Permanent* employees have more employment security than temporary employees.

3. *Length of service* may determine the degree of security.

4. *Certain changes,* but not others, may be covered. For example, employees may be secure against technological changes, but not against plant closures.

5. *Occupation and wages may be altered.* Employees may be assured of permanent employment, but not necessarily in the current position or occupation or at the current wage level, and not necessarily with the current employer.

6. *Employment may be offered in a different location.* For example, a displaced employee may be transferred to a different job in the same community by outplacement to a different employer.

7. *Certain aspects of employment* may be protected and not others, such as weekly earnings, an hourly rate, a minimum number of working hours per year, and so on. Thus, the job is protected, but the terms of employment are modified temporarily.

8. Security may be contingent on *acceptance of certain conditions,* such as mandatory overtime, internal transfer at management's discretion, and blurring of jurisdictional lines.

9. *Negotiated concessions* may be required, such as wage reductions, benefit modifications, and work-rule relaxations.

10. Security may apply for a *limited period of time* (such as for the duration of a collective agreement), or for the work life of the employee (as in the case of the newspaper typographers, longshoremen, and others).

In general, the more restrictive the definition of "guarantee," the less trust is engendered and the less the benefit to the firm. I strongly recommend a broad definition—accompanied by the adoption of certain tactics designed to make sure the firm can live up to its promise.

MAKING A GUARANTEE FEASIBLE

There are three primary tactics that enable a firm to offer a guarantee—and stick with it:

1. Careful hiring (understaffing) and extensive use of overtime/

temporaries/subcontractors. Most "guarantee" firms purposefully understaff with permanent (guaranteed) employees—often by a considerable number.

This in turn requires very tight control over hiring. For example, at Lincoln Electric every new hire must be approved by four vice-presidents. A more common device is granting permanent employment to the numbers needed to handle less than normal market demand. Thus, IBM's giant typewriter operation in Lexington, Kentucky, is staffed to meet 85 percent of normal demand. Overtime is used to make up about 10 percent of the remainder (ten to twelve Saturdays per year are expected as a condition of employment, and up to twenty-two Saturdays per year can be required as a matter of course in times of high demand). For the final 5 percent or so, subcontracting and temporary help are used.

Motorola, in its semiconductor operation, also staffs for 80 to 85 percent of normal demand, but rather than extensive overtime or subcontracting, the firm uses "contract workers" to meet shortfalls; they are hired on six-month contracts, at the same pay as permanent workers. Control Data (which targets for just 70 percent of normal demand), Hewlett-Packard (a major user of subcontractors), and Nucor are others who staff their facilities with fewer permanent employees than required to meet normal demand.

It is imperative to add that such "lean" permanent staffing can only be effective if work practices are nonrestrictive, with everyone trained to perform multiple tasks—the second primary tactic.

2. Redeployment and retraining. From Japan to Kansas City, redeployment and retraining is a conventional tactic for those who guarantee employment.

Hallmark, which is also a very cautious hirer, (a) switches assignments (in stark times, factory workers take on maintenance and housekeeping jobs), and (b) lends employees to the community (for instance, in the 1981–82 recession, several factory workers weatherproofed houses).

Shifting people to sales in tough times is a common Japanese practice, which IBM has followed, too. In 1981–82, Lincoln increased revenues by $10 million by shifting factory and office workers temporarily to sales. Kimberly Clark used the same tactic with seventy-five factory workers—and reports an added benefit: After returning to the factory, the seventy-five had a much greater appreciation of the importance of quality to customers.

During the same slump, semiconductor equipment-maker Materials Research Corporation had scientists and engineers call on customers. They also had factory and office crews perform housekeeping, security, and maintenance functions; groups, including supervisors, rotated through the tasks on ninety-day assignments. MRC's overall responsiveness to the slump proceeded in stages: (a) attrition, which was unsuccessful (it works notoriously poorly during general downturns), (b) redeployment, as noted above, and, finally, (c) generic education. That is, people, with full pay, were encouraged to go to school to upgrade skills that would be useful to them and the firm over the long haul.

Retraining has long been IBM's middle name (see P-5). Digital Equipment has undertaken massive retraining/redeployment of factory workers more recently, offering such options to 4,500 workers between 1984 and 1987; some 3,800 have accepted. For instance, about 100 supervisors have moved into sales. Because of automation, retraining and redeployment at Digital are expected to continue at the rate of 2,200 to 2,500 factory people per year for the foreseeable future—despite booming demand.

Buick is using retraining/redeployment as a major tool to deal with technological change. Its Employee Development Center in Flint, Michigan, guarantees a minimum one-year stay to each person displaced by technological development, regardless of seniority. While retaining full pay and fringe benefits, the worker is retrained for other Buick jobs.

Pacific Bell, faced with massive overstaffing following the breakup of the Bell System in 1984, has cut employment from about 100,000 to 70,000 with no layoffs. The reduction, induced by programs such as sweet early-retirement packages, has caused uneven staffing shortages. Redeployment and retraining have been potent tools to ease the adjustments. Overall, the program has been so effective that despite the cuts, grievances have fallen from nearly 5,000 per year to less than 100 in the six months through May 1987.

3. **Work sharing and short work weeks.** If cautious hiring, conscious understaffing, cutting back on temps, pulling in subcontracting, working at discretionary tasks (e.g., performing deferred maintenance), shifting to revenue enhancement activities (sales calls by engineers, factory

hands, et al.), and retraining fail, firms that guarantee employment use shortened workweeks and work-sharing. Nucor, Lincoln, and Hewlett-Packard have been among those who cut back substantially on hours. At Nucor in bad times, three- or four-day weeks are not uncommon (executives incur bigger penalties, via cuts in compensation); in good times, six-day weeks are common.

Job-sharing is still not legal in many states, but is increasingly being used where allowed.* The case of Motorola's semiconductor operation is typical. In the 1981–83 recession it took four successive steps: (1) a hiring freeze, (2) elimination of all overtime, (3) the pulling in of virtually all subcontracting, and, finally, (4) job-sharing.

THE COSTS OF RENEGING ON A GUARANTEE

Though few non-union guarantees are in writing, most have been effective by dint of long practice. But what if times change drastically, and layoffs become a must? That's happened at such venerable firms as Kodak.

The story is mixed, and depends on the firm's approach. Meatpacker Hormel's guaranteed-hours program was considered a landmark, especially in a highly seasonal industry. However, faced with very tough competitive conditions, management invoked a narrow interpretation of its contract with the union, demanding substantial wage cuts. The result was a rancorous, sometimes violent, nine-month strike, in which faith was shattered on both sides.

The other side of the coin is represented by Advanced Micro Devices (AMD), a semiconductor-maker forced to renege on a hard-and-fast no-layoff promise. Since the company (1) genuinely tried many alternatives, and (2) was so much more generous than its industry neighbors such as National Semiconductor, the breach of promise was not met with an outcry.

---

*In job- or work-sharing, an employer spreads unemployment, via reduced hours, over the whole work force. In some cases, state law allows compensation via unemployment insurance for the hours lost.

DEALING WITH MANAGERS

The organizational structures of U.S. corporations continue to feature bloated management ranks, with reductions of 50 to 80 percent still required at many firms (see P-8). How does an employment guarantee square with the need for continued management-pruning?

First, the thrust of this prescription is directed to the nonmanagerial work force. Our managerial population, in big firms at least, has been until recently, de facto, guaranteed employment. With rare exceptions, managers have stayed on even as downturns required huge non-managerial layoffs, often of long duration.

So management must be cut back. However, I applaud the efforts of Digital Equipment (et al.) to redeploy supervisors. Retraining, redeployment, and lavish early-retirement programs should be used to accomplish as much as possible of the management cutback without firings.

If these tactics don't work (and managers are generally more reluctant than workers to accept redeployment), make the necessary cuts in one step, rather than extending the process. The latter induces perpetual fear (and risk aversion) throughout the firm. After the cut, extend the guarantee to managers as well as nonmanagers.

THE LARGER CONTEXT

An employment guarantee involves three major issues: (1) providing security in return for flexibility/risk-taking on everyone's part, (2) treating the work force as a long-term "asset" worthy of constant re-investment (e.g., retraining), and (3) shifting from a mind-set that sees cost reduction as a primary goal (with labor a "factor of production") to a revenue enhancement strategy.

Pragmatically, the first issue governs. We must achieve more flexibility and a willingness not only to accept change, but to wholeheartedly participate in its speedy implementation.

The second issue, discussed in Part I, represents a monumental shift in attitude to perceiving the work force as the prime source of value added—via quality, service, responsiveness, and constant improvement of everything by everyone. This strategy is a must (see C-1 through

C-10), and guaranteed employment—and attendant continual retraining (see P-5)—is a cornerstone of its execution.

Finally, I can only wish that American managers will come to consider job creation (or maintenance) as one of their chief obligations. As noted, this suggestion does not fly in the face of pleas to cut overstaffing. It does suggest that the firm's long-term goal and guiding premise should be to maintain current employment levels or increase them via revenue enhancement. Revenue maximization, not short-term cost minimization, should become the new lodestar (see C-10).

FIRST STEPS

Develop a plan for using temporaries, subcontractors, and overtime in conjunction with staffing at 85 to 90 percent of normal demand requirements. Consider what retraining and redeployment needs would have to accompany a no-layoff guarantee. After a thorough review, begin a program of attrition and the use of, say, temporaries (perhaps as Motorola does, with a six-month contract at wages equal to those of permanent employees) before committing to the guarantee. If you do commit to a guarantee, phase it in over a one-to-five year period, with new features predicated upon the achievement of various growth and productivity improvement goals.

P-8

SUMMARY

Excessive organizational structure is a principal cause of slow corporate response to changed circumstances. We must:

▶ Radically reduce layers of management.

▶ Assign most "support" staff—in accounting, personnel, purchasing, etc.—to the field, reporting to site (line) managers.

▶ Establish a radically increased ratio of non-supervisors to supervisors—a "wide span of control"—at the organization's front line.

Structure kills. Most are moving to reduce it. Few are moving fast enough. Excess middle management staff—often to the tune of several hundred percent—still exists in most big firms and even in many smaller and midsized firms.

No more than five layers of management are necessary, regardless of firm size; limit layers in any facility to three at most. Get staffs out in the field, and encourage them to be "business team members" rather than narrow functional specialists (see also P-9). Minimum spans of control at the front line should be one supervisor for every 25 to 75 non-supervisors.

P-8

Simplify/Reduce Structure

The most important thing American industry needs to do is reduce the number of management layers. . . . [It's] one thing we're really fanatical about. We have four management layers. We have a foreman, and the foreman goes directly to a department head, and the department head goes directly to the general manager, and he goes directly to this office.

> F. Kenneth Iverson, chairman
> Nucor Corporation
> (1986 sales: $755 million)

We have the poorest productivity growth in any Western industrialized country. And managerial ineptitude has put us into this box. The way to get higher productivity is to train better managers and have fewer of them. Four years ago we had more than 1,200 people at corporate headquarters. We're coming down to 250.

> William Woodside, chairman,
> Primerica
> (formerly American Can)
> February 1987

MANAGEMENT'S TIME BOMB:
EXCESSIVE STRUCTURE

We are being strangled by bloated staffs, made up of carping experts and filling too many layers on the organization chart. Today's structures were designed for controlling turn-of-the-century mass-production operations under stable conditions, with primitive technologies. They have become perverse, action-destroying devices, completely at odds with current competitive needs.

The consultants McKinsey & Company recently examined thirty-eight advanced manufacturing technology systems; they concluded, according to *Boardroom Reports:* "The first step in accomplishing successful plant floor implementation of new manufacturing approaches is the clearing out of *all* [my emphasis] the middle managers and support service layers that clog the wheels of change. These salaried people are often the real barriers to productivity improvement, not the hourly workers on the floor." Similarly, the Yankee Group (a Boston consulting firm) concluded, as I did in P-2, that there will be no need for foremen in future factories; information technology will provide all the data needed, and routines for digesting it, to the front-line worker.

James O'Toole, professor of corporate strategy at the University of Southern California, in a study of "span of control," has observed that it averages one supervisor to ten nonsupervisors in the United States. The Japanese ratio runs 1:100, often 1:200. Not surprisingly, O'Toole concludes: "In general, American workers appear to be oversupervised."

Review the discussion above: (1) Iverson says structure is the primary management issue, and makes do with four layers (and a headquarters complement of a little over a dozen) to run a firm with almost a billion dollars in assets—and to make a profit, in steel. (2) The chairman of Primerica, a manufacturing firm (American Can) turned service company with $5 billion in revenues at the end of 1986, finds he can cut central staff by 80 percent. (3) Normally conservative McKinsey & Company, reviewing the disastrous results of attempts to install new and flexible manufacturing systems in the United States, says get rid of all middle management; and the Yankee Group contends that we soon won't need foremen. (4) Researcher Jim O'Toole says the ratio of supervisors to workers on America's industrial front lines may be out of whack by a factor of ten.

Treat people well, involve them in everything (P-1). Put them on self-managing teams (P-2). Make a "customer-oriented revolution" (C-10). Nurture volatile champions in every function (I-6). Do all these things and more, and still you will be doomed to suffer the failure of or unmercifully slow implementation of your strategy if you are saddled with a ten-layer organizational structure.

My co-authors and I downplayed the importance of structure in *In Search of Excellence* and again in *A Passion for Excellence.* We were terribly mistaken. Good intentions and brilliant proposals will be dead-ended, delayed, sabotaged, massaged to death, or revised beyond recognition or usefulness by the over-layered structures at most large and all too many smaller firms.

THE ORIGINS OF STRUCTURAL BLOAT

Almost seventy-five years ago, Du Pont created what may have been the first modern divisionalized organization structure, with separate units containing all the functions necessary to do business (R&D, engineering, purchasing, manufacturing, distribution, sales). General Motors soon followed suit. It has been estimated that between the end of World War II and 1970, 90 percent of the Fortune 500 decentralized into divisional structures.

Decentralization was the right strategy—it still is. But the "clean," business-minded structures envisioned by the pioneers lost their zip over time, and success didn't help. Many decentralized units grew big, with some divisions encumbered by ten or more layers of management.

Decentralization Is Reversed

But worse was to come. The "operations research paradigm" appeared during World War II; optimization of everything (e.g., manufacturing, engineering) became the cry. The optimizer is by definition a centralizer, a hyper-organizer. Function after function—purchasing, for example—was de facto recentralized at such companies as GM, despite the nominal retention (on paper) of the decentralized divisional structure. Then came the new marketing theories, which required central coordination of ad budgets, for instance; then the dominance of finance people, with their complex centralized control systems. The enormous increases in trans-

427

portation costs in the 1970s led the centralizers to take over distribution, too, in the name of "optimal efficiency." New requirements in personnel (resulting from equal opportunity and safety legislation) led to big, central personnel staffs. New sensitivities—the environmental and consumer movements, for example—led to centralized approaches to the outside world via massive public relations and lobbying operations that attempted to control the "decentralized" division's outside contacts, even with local press. Each development, sensible in itself, fostered the further growth of expert central staffs. Each central staff addition meant (1) more requests to the line for reports, and (2) more requests that this or that report be coordinated with numerous others; moreover, each staff was increasingly requested to coordinate almost everything with every other central staff. The mess (and resultant inertia) increased exponentially.

To deal with the mess, still more layers and "offices of" were added— the idea of the group executive, the office of the chairman; and each of these in turn developed private staffs (1) to consolidate their power and (2) to deal professionally with the queries of other staffs. Even Kafka would have been challenged to describe the situation adequately.

The Final Blow: Matrix's "Dotted Lines"

Meanwhile, the thrilling early successes of NASA's project organization structure brought us a new idea, the "matrix"—yet another form of de facto centralization. Every group was to be "wired" to every other group (organization charts show dense clouds of dotted lines going this way and that) to gain "synergies" that would come from coordinating everything and everyone with everything else and everyone else. In the mid-seventies, new marketing themes developed, wedded to the matrix concept. For instance, "global branding" became an excuse for gutting international divisions of the authority that had devolved to them in their glory years; recentralization left the illusion of local control intact, but in reality put New York–based, English-only-speaking, MBA-toting market modelers in charge of Thailand and Luxembourg and all stops in between.

Stir in the mainframe computer, central data banks, instant telecommunications, and exploding global financial networks calling for centralized cash management—and by 1975, anything approaching true decentralization was dead in most sizable firms. At about that time, the competitive crunch hit. And the first response was? You guessed it—*more* centralization, this time in the name of centralized control over costs ("rationalization") to achieve efficiency.

Structural Weaknesses Become Apparent—but Are Tough to Fix

Increasingly, the new competitors that most effectively started chipping away at the giant firms' profitable niches were smaller, less complicated, and more focused—Honda nibbled at GM, Nucor at U.S. Steel, Digital at IBM, Federal Express at the U.S. Postal Service, and so on (see Part I). It is now all too apparent that our overly centralized, over-layered organizations are dysfunctional. But saying that, even understanding it, and doing something about it are two different things. We are so hooked on the tools, logic, and false comfort of expert staffs and centralized systems that the task is an enormous one. Furthermore, we have developed a generation of big business managers (and continue to develop them in our MBA factories) who have become so dependent on these systems that they have lost all feel for the totality of a business operation. It is a travesty even to call them "businessmen," in any historic sense of that term.

Thus, we must change habits developed over several decades—at a time when certain tools such as telecommunications networks are becoming more powerful. Such tools *can* be used in the service of an autonomous unit (see C-4); whether or not they will be so used by more than a few is an altogether different matter. The danger is that they will be used, as so often in the past, to further centralize operations once more in the name of the great management deity, "synergy."

Logic Will Not Help

Suppose you agree with all this, and are ready to move forward. You may (probably will) be ensnared by a last irony. Each isolated element of the overdetermined structure looks necessary—on paper. Every job in the "charts and boxes" structures makes sense; you and your predecessors weren't fools. You didn't add staff jobs capriciously. Far from it; you were always reluctant to add to "headquarters headcount." And yet it's still two or three or five times too high. Bellwether firms are developing new products five times faster than you are. And your sluggishness, make no mistake, is chiefly attributable to all those layers.

CREATING THE STRUCTURE OF THE FUTURE

Limit Management Layers to Five

Peter Drucker in his classic book *The Practice of Management* recommends seven layers as the maximum necessary for any organization. But that was in 1954, a more placid era. I insist on five layers as the maximum. Incidentally, that's the number of layers with which the Catholic Church makes do to oversee 800 million members. As Eli Ginzberg and George Vojta observe in *Beyond Human Scale: The Large Corporation at Risk:* "Many writers on organization have termed the Catholic Church the most venerable large institution in the West, as it has achieved and maintained a position of leadership and power for over a millennium and a half. A key organizational characteristic of the Church is that despite its size it has avoided excessive layering."

In fact, even the five-layer limit should apply only to very complex organizations such as multi-division firms. Three layers—supervisor (with the job redefined to deal with a span of control no smaller than one supervisor for twenty-five to seventy-five people), department head, and unit boss—should be tops for any single facility, such as a plant or operations or distribution center. That's about the way Nucor does it: foreman (wide span of control), department head, general (facility) manager, president. Chaparral Steel makes do with a similar arrangement: foreman/general manager (who is highly empowered to make decisions and cross functional boundaries), superintendent, vice-president, president.

Put Staff in the Field

Much of the problem of sluggishness, it is true, comes from sheer excess of staff and layers of staff. On the other hand, where the staff is located and what they do are as important as how many there are. Colleagues from several firms, such as Mars, Inc., where a thirty-person headquarters guides a $7 billion company, say that they're not altogether sure they have fewer staff people per revenue dollar than other firms do. Their companies' effectiveness, they suggest, stems from the placement of virtually all staff people in factories, sales branches, and distribution centers. They do not populate corporate or other central headquarters. And indeed, I regularly observe that when you put an accountant (or someone from "personnel") in the field, as a member of a business unit of manageable size, she or he automatically and almost instantaneously changes. Ginzberg and Vojta invented the term "business-mindedness" to describe the shift in such managers' perspectives from "inward" to "outward":

> The overall aim is to create a climate of "business-mindedness" in the large corporation. In other words, the behavior of managers must be primarily geared to success in the marketplace over the long pull, in contrast to their current preoccupation with fighting their way up the corporate hierarchy through alliances and maneuvering. . . .
>
> In corporations in which power-related behavior patterns are well established, which means in almost all large corporations, managers spend a great deal of their time and energy trying to keep informed of developments that can affect the future of their groups. They attend many meetings for the sole purpose of insuring that the group's franchise or turf is not reduced. The extent to which they find it necessary to expend energy in such defensive tactics means that they can direct less effort to improving the group's business performance and, ultimately, the profitability of the corporation as a whole.
>
> The moral of such behavior is not lost on junior and middle managers. They soon realize that the evaluation of their work by supervisors, peers, and subordinates depends as much upon how they are perceived as on how competently they perform, on politics rather than performance. Such a climate favors cautious organizational maneuvering rather than business risk-taking. . . .
>
> The long-range impact of such risk-avoiding behavior can have devastating effects. If young managers are shielded from having to operate in an entrepreneurial environment in which they are held accountable for the resources under their command as well as for

the consequences of their decisions, they will move up the hierarchy without ever having been forced to operate in an exposed business setting, in which the market calls the shots.

The Effect of Fewer Layers: Less Is More

The good news from those who are experimenting radically is that less is more:

▶ A meticulous 1985 study of forty-one large companies by management consultants A. T. Kearney contrasted winning and losing companies on the basis of long-term financial performance. Winners had 3.9 fewer layers of management than losers (7.2 versus 11.1) and 500 fewer central staff specialists per $1 billion in sales.

▶ In *World Class Manufacturing,* Richard Schonberger returns time and again to the topic of "better support with [fewer] people," based upon his extensive observations of hundreds of revolutions in structure at the factory level of organization. One chapter on staff roles, for instance, discusses "better maintenance with fewer people in the plant maintenance department" (operators do their own maintenance, faster—and cheaper, when prevention of failure is considered), "better quality with fewer people in the quality department" (self-inspection, with appropriate training, becomes the norm), "better accounting with fewer accountants" (for instance, direct costing replaces cumbersome overhead allocations when just-in-time inventory management and operator maintenance take place), "better production control with fewer production controllers" (self-contained, so-called cellular manu- facturing units abet this), "better material management with fewer materials staff" (just-in-time leads to less complex processes in the factory), and "better information with less data processing" (again, simplification is the cause).

▶ The Brunswick Corporation cut its layers by 40 percent—and turned a losing situation around in short order. At first, the expectation was that expert staff in the divisions would have to be increased to take up the tasks previously performed by those now cut from corporate staffs. It didn't work out that way. What all frustrated businesspersons joke about turned out to be hard fact. The division staffs were immediately able to reduce their numbers, too. That is, it turned out that much of what the division staffs had been doing was not productive work, but simply generating responses to requests flowing down from the corporate center and group-lead staffs.

► *Industry Week* conducted a special study in late 1986 on the realigning of middle management in big firms:

> William Dowdell, a 45-year-old manager of printing-plate systems for Du Pont, . . . heads an experimental operating unit created 18 months ago. [He] is a perfect example of how companies are restructuring managerial responsibility. Before the new unit was formed, Mr. Dowdell managed the marketing arm of the photo products division. . . . That unit found it difficult to make money, because decisions on pricing . . . new products rarely kept up with the competition. *Indeed, major decisions required between 30 and 40 signatures for approval* [my emphasis]. "It was incredibly frustrating," Mr. Dowdell recalls. "That kind of bureaucracy just stifles creativity." In the old structure the photo products division consisted of three subunits, each of which reported to a vice president. Under the experimental arrangement, Mr. Dowdell was put in charge of the entire $45-million-a-year division and given responsibility for all marketing, manufacturing, and research and development work. And, since Mr. Dowdell no longer has to obtain all those approvals for a project, the bureaucratic paper shuffling has stopped. . . . "It's amazing to see the change in people—the enthusiasm they have—when we released them from the paper chase and made them part of the process," Mr. Dowdell says. Not only have the profits of the photo products division firmed up—since it now meets competition head on—but improvements in printing-plate technology have enabled the unit to produce a magazine for the industry. That project would never have got off the ground under the old structure, Mr. Dowdell says.

► A small example from Mountain Bell is also instructive at the microlevel. A new manager in a town of 20,000 was determined to emphasize customer service. The problem, as he quickly saw it, was that "there was no one person any customer could turn to. No one was really responsible for anything." The group closest to the action was hopelessly factionalized. Thirty nonmanagers were overseen by seven first-line supervisors, each of whom guarded his functional turf jealously. The new manager rapidly concluded that "there was no horizontal communication." Moreover, at the top of the already overorganized heap sat yet another two managers (second-line supervisors). The new boss acted swiftly, clearing out five of the seven first-line bosses and one of the two at the next level up. Even the two first-line supervisors no longer managed separate functions; the thirty non-managers were reorganized into one, undifferentiated team. Communication improved dramatically—and customer service along with it: complaints per hundred subscribers per month rapidly dropped by 75 percent.

These examples, and a host more like them, are staggering in their implications—not merely that "less is more," but that "a lot less is a lot more." Pruning central staff/layers by 50 to 90 percent leads to more responsiveness and better staff work. It all adds up to this: If you have more than a handful of people at headquarters, if you have more than a few layers, you are in trouble—or fast heading for it. It's as simple and stark as that.

CHANGING CORPORATE STRUCTURES: ISSUES AND (SOME) ANSWERS

Slash the central staff and layers. Then slash the decentralized staffs and layers. Assign the staff work to the line. And things get better. But there's more to it than that. Attacking the issue of structure requires us to take on a bewildering array of difficult issues:

1. Powerful forces still apparently push toward centralization. Many—such as transportation network optimization, telecommunications linkups, common data base management—are actually on the rise. Only an abiding contrary belief in the observed power of the smaller, niche-creating unit (see Part I, C-1, and I-1) will help you deal with these forces. Examine your company's problems vis-à-vis foreign competitors, and consider experimenting somewhere with a new structure (for instance, despite its current problems, GM deserves lots of credit for the radical nature—structurally—of the new Saturn operation).

2. Most senior managers have developed a psychological dependence

on the instant—if irrelevant—answers to everything that are provided by big central staff groups. Examples such as Dowdell of Du Pont suggest that top management can go from thirty signatures to one, but it is painful, which is why most move so slowly. Perhaps only radical experiments such as Du Pont's will wean top management from its past. But a failure or two (which is guaranteed to occur), even a small one, can stall progress.

3. **What do we do, as a firm or nation, with the huge excess of middle managers?** There's no easy answer here either. Many can be devolved to the field, but many will not survive the transition. Extensive retraining is a minimum (see P-5, P-6). But a whole generation who did their jobs well and a new generation of women and minorities finally making it into management's lower and middle ranks have been cast adrift—and we must continue the shift, faster still. (Part I hints at some of the adjustment assistance that is needed as a matter of policy; but most proposals, mine and others', still don't deal adequately with the immensity of this problem.)

4. **What do we do with the first-line supervisor population, of whom 90 percent are redundant?** Retraining for a new role may, again, help some (see P-5, P-6, P-7); but there are no easy answers. Demotions back to nonsupervisorial status seldom work out. The harsh truth, though, is that line jobs will not be salvageable unless the excess hierarchy at the crucial front line is moved out.

5. **True decentralization will require such things as order-of-magnitude increases in the spending authority of unit managers.** How can we quickly develop general managers whom we trust with such large sums? Once more, no easy solutions are on the horizon. As noted, most of today's functional experts are not "businessmen." For every Dowdell of Du Pont there are several who fail as managers of newly autonomous units. Training doesn't seem to help much, either, for those who have spent a lifetime climbing the ladder at headquarters. Sadly, the most practical solution is a kind of musical chairs—move 'em in and move 'em out, and hope that one out of several will rise to the challenge.

6. **How can we develop alternative control schemes when the complement of intervening, inherently conservative staff layers virtually disappears?** Here there are some answers, though once again not easy ones, since they come up against deep-seated attitudes. When I suggest that you slash the layers, I'm not asking you to slash away, lay off 75 percent

of the staff, expand the span of control from 1:7 to 1:50—and then wash your hands of the whole mess. New controls must replace the old ones. What will they be? Customer contact, the subject of several of the first set of prescriptions, for one. True closeness to the market and constant commerce with customers and suppliers turns out to be an amazingly effective control device. The power of the market (i.e., angry customers constantly visiting) is more of a disciplining force than a passel of visiting staff managers with a 2,000-page analysis. Likewise, the people prescriptions are aimed at substituting a new form of control—self-control born of the involvement and ownership that follows from, among other things, training people on the line to take on many traditionally supervisory roles. Being fully responsible for results will concentrate the mind more effectively than any out-of-touch cop on the staff. Finally, the leadership prescriptions also spell out new roles and new forms of control. Getting out and about to listen, concentrating on shaping and clarifying your vision, and the like are alternatives to the feeling (usually an illusion today) of control that exists when you are in the boardroom surrounded by clever MBAs whose glowing lap-top computers can spew forth multicolored contingency answers to any question in seconds. None of this, however, will turn out to be easy. And making senior management comfortable with these arrangements—that's an especially tough nut to crack; only successful experience will crack it.

7. **How can we deal with the apparent turmoil of some inevitable duplication that results from the creation of independent business units working in closely related markets**—e.g., several (uncoordinated) sales calls on the same customer, products from different divisions that at least partially compete with one another, incompatible computer systems and data bases? Once more, we must experiment. Some duplication, in practice, will occur; but accumulating evidence suggests it will fall far short of our worst fears. (And even if it is fearsome, we must still move. The embarrassment of a few snafus with multiple sales calls is a lot less than the embarrassment of losing your market to five mid-sized competitors, each of whom is five to ten times faster than you.)

Fighting Your Instincts

This list of seven presents a nightmarish challenge—and an absence of comforting answers. Your firm's competitive position is probably declining. Every instinct, honed over decades, says crack down, grasp the reins more tightly, opt for the always impressive paper efficiencies of more centralization. But following your instincts here can be catastrophic. Just look who's killing you—a firm which is a tiny fraction of your size. (GM is five times bigger than Honda, for instance. IBM is 25 times bigger than Apple, and six times bigger than DEC.)

You must, sad to say, bite the bullet, and take drastic action (or at least experiment boldly)—without good answers to most of the basic questions posed above. But you can choose among an increasing number of places to visit—ongoing experiments of the most radical sort. Visit Nucor or Chaparral and see how to live with four layers of management. Visit Mars to observe how a thirty-person group runs a giant firm. Visit the new-look Ford or GM plants, to observe how union and management have dealt with the demise of job specialization and the elimination of supervisors. See how Brunswick makes do with half the layers it had. Find out how Johnsonville Sausage (see prescription P-2) gets on without even facility managers. Or how half-billion-dollar Lincoln Electric makes do with a span of control of 1:100—and yet achieves productivity that's several times the industry average.

Here, as elsewhere, you are asked to consider radical steps. But I am not speaking as a theorist, only urging in the strongest terms that you consider what others have done.

FIRST STEPS

1. Don't hire a consultant to help you with this!
2. Visit: Schedule at least 5–10 trips in the next 6–12 months to interesting companies experimenting with radically new structural configurations. On each trip, stay for several days. Do this by yourself, or put together a line-dominated team to study 5–15 interesting firms.
3. Consider taking radical action—fast. A policy of letting people go a few at a time, day by day and year by year, is aborting the transformation of many companies, since every remaining person lives in terror of the other shoe dropping.
4. *Structure and the unit manager:* If you are in the middle of the pyramid, I'll spell out a new role in the next prescription, P-9. But

let me make a few suggestions here. Get out of the office and into the field. Get every person in your unit out into the field. If this is a physical impossibility (you run central computing), get everyone in regular touch by phone with his or her "customers" before problems arise; induce your "customers" to visit you. Also, make sure that every person is working on at least one special project in the field, that everyone on your staff is assigned to a field operation for at least one specific project of 30 to 60 days' duration each year. You can do these things, and they will help.

P-9

SUMMARY

One of the most dramatic requirements associated with increasing responsiveness is to shift the organization's entire "way of being" from a "vertical" (hierarchical) to a "horizontal" (fast, cross-functional cooperation) orientation. To do that, we must:

▶ Reconceive the middle management job as one of facilitator and functional-boundary smasher, instead of expert and guardian of functional units.

▶ Use a "reverse pyramid" organization chart, with front-line people "on top" and supervisors and middle managers below them in a support-and-facilitation role.

The middle manager, apparently in the way of the required organizational revolution, *can* become the most important player in the newly conceived structure—but his or her role must be wholly changed from the traditional one.

Dramatically shift reward (formal and informal) and evaluation systems for middle managers in order to emphasize "making things happen" across formerly sacred functional boundaries.

P-9

Reconceive the Middle Manager's Role

Management excellence cannot come from fragmented contributions by various functional staffs; that is, if quality assurance has exclusive jurisdiction over a quality program, if production control has an inventory program, and so on. Each staff seeks to impose another set of techniques, each set demanding adjustments and attention from an already choked line organization. Only so much can be assimilated at a time, and it should be cohesive. . . . Japanese are good integrators. . . . Americans are accustomed to thinking that integration of a company is only in one place—at the top, where strategy is made.

Robert Hall
Attaining Manufacturing Excellence

Perhaps the biggest change of all for manufacturing engineering is getting used to the idea that the best way to make a contribution is found on the factory floor, not in the equipment manufacturers' catalogs. The [manufacturing engineer] must spend some time with equipment sales reps but should spend more with machine operators, setup crews, maintenance technicians, and supervisors. Most of the tangible wealth of industry is in old equipment that is falling apart fast. Most of it is worth rescuing.

Richard Schonberger
World Class Manufacturing

I, like many others, have repeatedly attacked middle managers. And we do indeed have too many layers, too much staff. Yet the leanest of sizable organizations does need *some* middle managers. What should their role be?

We must start by acknowledging the problem. Jan Carlzon dramatically reversed the fortunes of the Scandinavian Air System (SAS) in the early 1980s. It lost millions in 1979–80, but achieved high profitability and won "Airline of the Year" status just twenty-four months later, while the rest of the European airline industry lost billions.

Carlzon accomplished his miracle through an extraordinary improvement in service. The new company heroes were the first-line service providers. Carlzon explicitly ordered them to go around their managers, right to the top if necessary, to clear hurdles out of the way. He acknowledges that he "hot-wired the system" to achieve immediate results.

Now he sees the need for a second, more lasting and more profound revolution. In his first effort, which he now calls the First Wave, he was dismissive of middle managers—the "layer of insulation," as he described them. He admits he gave them "no viable alternative" to their old and traditional role as "rule interpreters." They were the scapegoats. Now, in the Second Wave, he believes, that must be changed. Middle managers are to be autonomous—but no longer as rule interpreters or as protectors of "functional integrity" in the traditional, vertical, "functional stovepipe," "functional silo" organizational structure. Instead, middle managers are to be responsible for seeking out and battering down the very functional barriers that they were formerly paid to protect. They are to be charged with making things happen, come hell or high water. In other words, as Carlzon concludes in his book *Riv Pyramiderna!* (Flatten the Pyramids),* "the distribution of roles is radically different."

MAKING THE MIDDLE MANAGER PART OF THE SOLUTION

It would be impossible to overestimate what a profound shift this constitutes for Western management. British researcher Malcolm Trevor

*The title of the English translation is *Moments of Truth.*

442

and his associates studied Japanese and European managers in European settings, and summarized their research in *The Japanese Management Development System*. Their conclusion about British managers applies to the United States as well: "As a country, the UK is cursed by [managerial job] specialisms. . . . [The] Japanese expected that managers would not stick to functional boundaries. . . . British managers were over-concerned with a formal chain of command but little concerned with horizontal communication. . . . British managers hoarded information that [the Japanese] managers [in Japanese-owned operations] intended them to share. . . . For British managers, sharing information can be seen as a danger to their own career prospects."

For the Japanese, the authors add, "jobs are ambiguous, are roughly defined. . . . Job contents change all the time. . . . [There are] no divisional fences." This connotes no lack of discipline on the part of the Japanese, to be sure, but a different interpretation of what the managerial job is all about. A typical Japanese manager, they continue, "follows company rules and procedures very strictly, but . . . his job area is very flexible." There is no sense of contradiction between rule-following and job flexibility. In the West, managements at firms such as Chaparral, Worthington, and Hewlett-Packard historically, and Ford, Du Pont, Omark, P&G, and Milliken have been experimenting with lower-level integration of functions. The emphasis has been on team-level, multi-function coordination, not on the several (at least two or three) layers of management immediately above the team. None has gone as far as the Japanese; none except Carlzon has so precisely defined the revolutionary shift in the role of middle management that would be required to do so.

Back in the 1940s, Rensis Likert developed a "linking pin" idea of organization; Herman-Miller implemented it, and GM experimented with it in several places. The core idea is that each level of management is a member of a multi-functional team that includes the next level up.

But Likert's essential idea doesn't go far enough. For one thing, it focuses on coordination, and "coordination" *as it is practiced* emphasizes that horrid role of protecting one's function. While coordination does include "getting together," to "coordinate," often as not in practice, is to stall in the name of "checking this out three layers up" before acting. The objective here is to go one giant step further, as Carlzon suggests. Every middle manager should spring out of the gate each morning as a dedicated, proactive boundary basher. He or she is not just passively "coordinating" but is aggressively seeking ways to force activity that involves multiple functions to occur faster. In this new role, the middle manager must become: (1) expeditor/barrier destroyer/facilitator, (2) on-call expert, and (3) diffuser of good news. In short, the middle manager must practice fast-paced "horizontal management," not traditional, delaying, "vertical management."

Task #1: Turning the Organization Upside Down—and Sideways

The organization chart must be turned upside down. Carlzon did it; so does retailer Nordstrom (Figure 16, p. 370). First-line management's role is to support the front-line people. Middle management's role is to act largely as facilitator, greasing the skids and speeding up actions, especially those actions (most) requiring cross-functional, multi-unit cooperation. Middle management is no longer to be the umpire, in charge of constraining, preventing, or slowing action in the name of turf, rights, or integrity. As you can see, the Nordstrom organization chart even includes the idea of a "helping hand" aimed "upward."

What precisely does this mean? At Milliken, close on the heels of SAS in moving this idea forward, the new breed of middle manager is becoming an out-and-out expediter (see C-8 also). Days are spent on the phone, inducing faster interaction among functions, in an all-out attempt to shorten product development time, for instance. No longer does the manager conceive of his or her job as protecting the well-oiled factory mechanism from disruptions caused by the aggressive New York sales team, who in the past were generally seen as "playing lapdog to customers with unreasonable demands." The idea now is to welcome those demands, no matter how "unreasonable" at first blush.

It's essential to connect this idea to prescriptions P-1 and P-2. That is, the new breed of middle (or even first-level) managers, per our model, will have turned over the lion's share of their traditional tasks as experts and referees—their responsibility for maintenance, inspection, score-keeping, scheduling, hiring, etc.—to the self-managing team structure "below" them. Thus they are less concerned on a minute-to-minute basis with the quality of the widgets flowing past them. Instead they (1) make sure that their work teams are trained and equipped to do their own inspection, (2) then turn their attention to eliminating crossfunctional bottlenecks that cause quality and scheduling—and cost—problems, and

Figure 16: **Nordstrom Organization Chart**

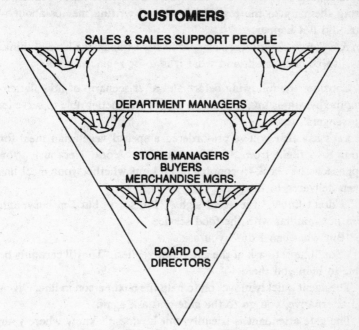

CUSTOMERS

SALES & SALES SUPPORT PEOPLE

DEPARTMENT MANAGERS

STORE MANAGERS
BUYERS
MERCHANDISE MGRS.

BOARD OF DIRECTORS

finally, (3) proactively seek ways for the operating unit as a whole to increase responsiveness. Evidence suggests that 75 percent of middle managers' time must be spent on horizontal rather than vertical (down or up) communication.

The SAS Example

In this role, the middle manager is given a new life—the power and incentive to say "yes," and make things happen, rather than merely the negative power to say "no," and delay/stop things. At SAS, for instance, the middle manager in maintenance at a geographic location is asked to proactively seek out his or her counterpart in baggage-handling to try to create projects that cross functional barriers and make things work better, rather than act as the simple guardian of maintenance's rule book. The manager's duty is to solve problems—now, on the spot—rather than passing them up to the regional level and writing memos about why things did not happen.

In *Riv Pyramiderna!* Carlzon specifically explains the kind of thinking that is to be eliminated, and what it is to be replaced with:

> Consider the following before-and-after scenario of how flattening the pyramids might make an airline staff better able to serve its passengers' needs.
>
> Let's say that you've pre-ordered a special vegetarian meal for your SAS flight from Stockholm to New York. Nervously, you approach the check-in counter to find out whether your meal has been delivered to the plane.
>
> "I don't know," the agent sighs. "I'm sorry, but I'm busy, and I'm not familiar with the food service."
>
> "But what can I do?" you ask.
>
> "You'll have to ask at the gate," she replies. "They'll certainly be able to help you there."
>
> The agent quickly moves on to help the next person in line. Given no alternative, you go to the gate and ask again.
>
> The gate attendant is friendly, but he doesn't know where your meal is either. "I wish I could help, but I don't have anything to do with food service. Just check with the stewardess when you get on board and things should certainly work out."
>
> Reluctantly, you board the plane. When you ask the stewardess about your vegetarian meal, she is bewildered. She hasn't heard anything about special food orders, but the plane is about to take off and nothing can be done now. "You should have contacted us earlier," she reprimands. "There would have been no problem if only we had known in time."
>
> In this situation, the hierarchical organizational structure has caused the airline to ruin three "moments of truth" [Carlzon's term for fleeting contacts with a customer]. No one the passenger encountered had the authority to handle the specific problem, and no one dared step out of his normal role to try to solve it.
>
> Let's now suppose that the organization has changed its structure

by flattening the pyramid and putting a team of people in charge of the Stockholm-New York flight from start to finish.

The team has 15 members, two of whom function as "coaches," one indoors and one out by the plane. The indoor coach sits in on the flight crew's briefing and consults with them about pre-flight information such as the appropriate time to begin boarding, whether any infants . . . are on the passenger list, and whether anyone has ordered a special meal.

In the morning, the indoor team assembles at the check-in counters to solve passengers' ticketing problems, assign seats, handle fragile baggage, and so forth. When a mother arrives with her baby, she is . . . told that a suspended cradle has already been put on board and that the seat beside hers will be kept free if at all possible.

When you arrive at check-in and ask about your vegetarian meal, you won't be hurriedly dismissed by the agent behind the counter. Thanks to the new team arrangement, your meal request becomes that agent's responsibility. She can confirm that it is already on board—or take steps to make sure it's loaded by the time you step into the plane.

As more and more passengers check in, the SAS team gradually moves to the departure gate, where they nod to their passengers in recognition. They are well acquainted with the flight to New York and can answer all the usual questions: how to transfer from JFK to La Guardia, why there is a stopover in Oslo, the actual flight time, and whether the captain will announce when they are flying over Greenland.

Problems are solved on the spot, as soon as they arise. No front-line employee has to wait for a supervisor's permission. No passenger boards the plane while still worried or dissatisfied.

In some few, critical areas, the new conception of the middle manager's role may even result in more middle management jobs, not fewer. Robert Hall, for instance, observes in *Attaining Manufacturing Excellence* that "the need for manufacturing engineers to unplug work flow may call for greater staffing in that area." When one starts thinking of managers as expediters, it is no longer so obvious that their numbers should always be minimized.

Task #2: To Be an Expert on Call

In *World Class Manufacturing,* Richard Schonberger identified staff experts on call to support the line—when requested—as a key attribute of the best manufacturing settings. He observed:

Having salaried people (engineers, schedulers, buyers, plant managers—everybody) on call is common in Japan and also seems to be ingrained in Japanese subsidiary plants outside of Japan. The concept was in place at Kawasaki in Nebraska *circa* 1981. . . . Doug Sutton, chief of scheduling, told me, "Boy, is it ever different at Kawasaki than when I worked at [U.S. firm]. I hardly spend any time in my office." Doug was out on the floor solving problems much of the time during the work day. Most were probably not scheduling problems. They were problems of all kinds. In the JIT [just-in-time] concept, job titles mean little and responsibilities blur. One American company, Hewlett-Packard, has a tradition of having salaried support people's desks on the factory floor, intermingled with work stations. That is part of the fabled "HP Way." In my judgment Hewlett-Packard is further along in implementing JIT than any other non-Japanese-owned company except, perhaps, Omark Industries. And why not? HP had a head start, since the problem-solvers were already located in the right place next to where the production problems occur.

There is no question that special expertise is needed, but now the provider plays the role of consultant to teams doing their own problem analysis, rather than holder of the stopwatch. The command to which our new managers must learn to respond is: "Don't call us. We'll call you." It suggests that if they wish to justify their existence, they'd better have something valuable—to the line—to offer.

Task #3: Passing on the Good News

The final new and revolutionary role of middle management is to spend more than half its time on the road, passing on news of the experiments in plant X or distribution center Y to others throughout the system. (Dana Corporation is typical of those who have done this with senior staff.) "Passing on" rather than "shoving down the throat of" is an essential distinction. The newly conceived middle manager/senior staff expert is a clearinghouse and walking/flying newsletter, not an arbiter of taste who *tells* operating people what's good and that "distribution center A and B *shall* implement the idea that was so successful at center C." The distinction is vital.

Getting Started

All the above is easy to say, exceedingly difficult to implement. In effect, we are calling for a reversal of a hundred years of tradition and a 180 degree shift of attitude among people who were originally "hired to make sure that instructions are followed," to use Carlzon's language. Hired and promoted, often several times, I'd add—because, by definition, these managers have been the very best at making sure that instructions are followed to the letter, and that their bosses farther up the functional stovepipe are never held to account for a foul-up. "Blame the other function first, before they blame you," has been the operative rule. Now we are asking these master corporate politicians and memo writers to seek out minute-to-minute opportunities to transcend the rules (that is, break them, at the margin) and make things happen. Wrenching change after wrenching change is required—to begin with, the visit and the phone call replace the "memorandum for the record" as the prime mode of communication. The requirements will include:

▶ Extensive training, (with heavy executive involvement) to underscore the firm's serious commitment to the new conception of the role and to teach practical skills, such as team-building.
▶ Performance evaluation and compensation systems that emphasize teamwork across functions and enhanced action and risk-taking, rather than the creation of tidy audit trails that show that the XYZ function was "within its rights to slow thus and such down."
▶ Physical relocation, to get middle managers out of their departmental centers and into operations centers and distribution centers (see also P-8).

Most important, the managers of staff managers and the firm's top executives must seek out daily opportunities to pat the newly reminted managers on the back for acting as facilitators rather than cops. This, too, will be difficult, because the managers of managers, former cops themselves, have long operated successfully in an environment of safe and orderly inaction, rather than proactive problem-solving, with its inherent (by past standards) untidiness.

FIRST STEPS

1. Begin the process with some subtlety. Focus, without fanfare, on rewarding (pat on the back, mention in the newsletter) facilitation of the most minor sorts between functions. Assiduously seek out examples of multi-plant, multi-function affairs that went smoothly and fast, under ordinarily trying circumstances; find out who provided the lubricant, and praise him or her to the skies— especially if the managers in question took proactive action to prevent a slowdown or to meet an impossible customer demand. Set quantitative goals for yourself—a pat a day for an act of skid-greasing.

   Also, practice the reverse of this: (a) Don't accept any more memos (or even oral reports at staff meetings) that are basically excuses for inaction, or that blame other functions for foul-ups. (b) Spot-check to see how many action items on a typical meeting's agenda are being solved on the spot, versus how many stay unresolved ("I'll have to check 'up the line' on that and get back to you"); raise hell about the latter.

2. Move to include proactive cross-functional facilitation as a *major* element in performance evaluation systems and objective-setting routines for managers at all levels (see also P-10).

3. I hate to be nasty, but ceremoniously fire or demote an upper middle manager who, after training and coaching, still flagrantly puts roadblocks in the way of critical tasks in the name of functional integrity, and then tries to cast the blame on others.

P-10

SUMMARY

Even the use of self-managing teams, training, and the radical shift in structures and management roles are not enough to ensure the level of involvement described in P-1. We must go further:

▶ De-bureaucratize: radically reduce and simplify paperwork and unnecessary procedures.

▶ "De-humiliate": eliminate policies and practices (almost always tiny) of the organization which demean and belittle human dignity.

▶ Become a housekeeping fanatic.

Directly attacking the "Mickey Mouse" of excessive paperwork and demeaning rules is required to take the lid off the organization—and genuinely invite wholesale participation and commitment necessary for survival.

Reduce all manuals by 50 to 75 percent this year (and then do the same thing next year). Stamp out memos! Send none. Respond to none. Send back all memos sent to you with a "received but not read" stamp. Rid yourself immediately of obvious and nauseous insults such as executive parking spaces. Eliminate ten "demeaners" every 60 days. Ask lots of questions such as: Do you really need an office? Do you really need a policy manual? Keep stores (including their back rooms), plants, distribution centers, sales branches, etc., spotless. Keep rest rooms shining and graffiti-free, and don't skimp on dollars for the enhancement of personal space on the line; plan to introduce five new "housekeeping" improvements every 90 days at every facility.

P-10

Eliminate Bureaucratic Rules and Humiliating Conditions

I find it mind-boggling. We do not shoot paper at the enemy.
> Admiral Joseph Metcalf
> on the 20 tons of paper and file cabinets
> aboard the Navy's newest frigates
> *Newsweek,* May 1987

Quick response to perpetual turmoil is now a competitive necessity. People's involvement, commitment, and empowerment, in turn, are the keys to speedy organizational action. Training, team configuration, reduced structure, and new roles for middle managers aid speedy action-taking. But if the bureaucratic rigmarole remains, all of the above add up to naught.

Moaning about bureaucracy is a time-honored management prerogative. Now, however, bureaucracy is beyond moaning about; it is a block to survival. The campaigns against bureaucracy must become strategic priorities of the first order.

SIGNS OF HOPE

There are people and firms which have beaten back bureaucracy's seemingly inevitable encroachment:

▶ *The New York Times* recently reported that anti-bureaucrat Ken Iverson of Nucor Corporation maintains an "executive dining room": "[He] has designated as the executive dining room the Chinese restaurant and the delicatessen—usually the deli—in the shopping center across the street from Nucor's headquarters in Charlotte, N.C."

▶ A division general manager in a large high-technology firm raised spending authority, without approvals, for his engineers—from $25 to $200. The accountants screamed. Following imposition of the new standard, spending plummeted by 60 percent. He explains: "That wasn't the point, cutting costs. It was to quit treating them like kids. But you know what happened, of course. With the $25 limit, it's 'Let's see how many $24.99s we can tack together, without authorization.' It was a time-consuming game—'We can out-Mickey Mouse you, boss.' Now, with the $200, people say, in effect, 'Hey, that's a lot of money I'm responsible for.' They look at it as theirs."

▶ In *The Intuitive Manager,* journalist Roy Rowan reports: "[Ross] Perot claims he operated a memo-less company. Like Napoleon, who reputedly tossed out all written reports from his generals, figuring he'd already heard the important news, Perot prefers to conduct all of his business by personal contact. 'Written reports stifle creativity,' he says."

▶ *Fortune* reports on James Reid, running an exceptionally profitable auto-components firm, Standard Products: "He drives a compact Oldsmobile. His company, on the verge of the *Fortune 500* (sales in fiscal 1986: $433 million), is still run from a drab two-story brick building in Cleveland's warehouse district. Reid's 15-by-20 office will never adorn the pages of *Architectural Digest.* But, he says, 'I can do as much thinking here as in an office 50 times this size.' "

▶ $1.9 billion retailer Nordstrom gets by with a one-sentence policy manual: "Use your own best judgment at all times."

Bureaucracy—excessive rules, regulations, and paperwork—is not a must. Ross Perot ran a company worth several billion dollars without writing memos. By raising spending limits and thus cutting down on game playing, an executive cuts spending—and improves morale and speeds action-taking. A billion-dollar company finds that a corner deli makes a great executive dining room, and so on.

Everyone talks about cutting the red tape. A few do it. Why not the rest of us? How do you reduce the policy manual to just a single sentence? Or raise engineers' spending limits, in one step, by almost a factor of ten? Or stop sending *any* memos?

I cannot provide you with the will to do these things. I can simply tell you (1) that they can be done, (2) that they must be done if we are to (a) move faster and (b) liberate people—managers and nonmanagers alike—to perform up to their potential, and (3) that they have been done, with gusto, by others like you.

LIBERATION THROUGH THE ELIMINATION OF EXCESSIVE PROCEDURES

Start with the voluminous rules. Nordstrom V.P. Betsy Sanders acknowledges that the one-line "policy manual" drives Nordstrom's lawyers crazy. So be it, she adds.

The point is that it frees Nordstrom employees from an astonishing amount of Mickey Mouse. Sad to say, rule books are only referred to in order to slow action, defend turf, and assign blame. Have you ever heard of anyone going to a rule book to figure out how to speed things up?

University of Chicago philosopher Ted Cohen has commented that since sports are so rule-driven, most innovation revolves around how to be ingenious at cheating without getting caught: "How *much* of a head slap is legal for a defensive end trying to slow down a tight end?" How far can Reggie Jackson "stick his fanny in front of a ball [to deliberately get hit and be awarded first base] in the World Series?" Moreover, says Cohen, it's precisely because there are so many rules and rule enforcers (umpires and referees in sports, supervisors in business) that "the player feels he may abandon the responsibility for decent conduct because someone is around."

Less Is More (Again)

At Nordstrom, the absence of manuals is anything but an invitation to chaos. Nordstrom supervisors are always coaching and teaching. Indeed, says Sanders, their chief duty is to coach salespersons on "*exactly* what it means to 'use your own best judgment.' " The absence of childish rules shifts the employee's focus of innovation to precisely where the firm wishes it to be: in pursuit of serving the customer better, rather than in pursuit of evasion of the rules about toilet breaks. In fact, self-control is such a powerful control that entry-level turnover is high.

At a Mars, Inc., subsidiary, fewer rules means less fuss—and more emphasis on the business task at hand. A principal labor contract was up for renewal. A rookie management negotiator set an objective about which most of his peers were highly skeptical—to replace the inch-thick document with one of five pages or less. He was successful, and as a result of his efforts, among other things a grievance record that had been about average was cut to a trickle. There are simply no little nitpicking details—"subparagraph 7.13.b.2.ii"—left for either side to get hot and bothered about on a day-to-day basis. Dayton Power & Light followed a similar path. The firm opened negotiations early, and worked for six months with the union to define the nature of the changing, ever more competitive business environment for utilities. The upshot, another twelve months later, was a reduction in the length of the contract from 200 pages to 14, the first being their statement of shared philosophy. In short order a profound change in attitude has ensued, with people working together to confront problems. NUMMI and the UAW also forged a streamlined contract, starting with a statement of philosophy; similar positive results have followed (see the section summary preceding P-1, and P-2).

Or consider Worthington. No union has ever organized one of its field start-up operations, but it has acquired several unionized companies. Though top management strongly discourages applying pressure to decertify, five operations have done so. Worthington senior managers observe that front-line employees have little problem living without the protection of a union contract. But first-line supervisors have had the devil of a time adjusting. One executive notes: "You just took away their reason for being. They were there, as they saw it, to administer the contract on management's behalf. They were there to catch guys goofing off. Now, suddenly, no rule book, no time clocks, no scheduled breaks [you take a break when you conveniently can], no locks on the tool-room door, no forms to be signed to check out a tool or a spare part. What's left for them to do? Very little, by the old standards. Some don't make the transition."

A Practical Agenda

Here's an approach to getting on with the task of reducing bureaucracy:

1. As a manager, "model" nonbureaucratic behavior. (Also see L-3, L-8.) Demand that any report sent to you be reduced to, say, three pages or less. Starting today, do not send memos to anyone for any reason. Use the phone or personal contact. Also, prune the number of reports you receive by 50 to 80 percent in the next six to twelve months. Further, send back without comment—and repeatedly if necessary—all "information copies" of memos. (I studied this at one point. The conventional humorous wisdom turned out to be hard truth. Well over 90 percent of several hundred memos I analyzed were of the "cover your ass" variety—designed only to clear the writer of any hint of blame should anything subsequently go awry.) Finally, send back, without comment and repeatedly, any decision documents that should not be addressed to your level. One senior political appointee within the Department of Defense, in the Installation and Logistics secretariat, arrived on the job to find that tiny architectural changes were sent all the way to Washington for his approval. He put no comment on them whatsoever, but just started sending them back. People eventually caught on, and the flow stopped.

And if you're a lower-level manager? All of this can at least be done "downward"—that is, eliminate the rules you can control and refuse to be nitpicky about enforcing the ones you can't control. But a surprising amount of bureaucracy fighting can be done "upward." When you get a memo from your boss, pop into his or her office with an answer—don't call your staff to general quarters and retire to your office for three days to write a treatise in response.

2. Announce and implement your own "stamp out the silly [and action slowing] regulations" operation. One manager, for instance, designed an engaging ritual to involve all his group in eliminating irritating rules and regulations: "I bought a bright red mailbox and placed it in the division hallway. I commissioned a cartoon around the theme 'Send back to Mickey Mouse.'" He acts within a week on the suggestions about what regulations should be cut, and awards a porcelain Mickey Mouse statue each month to the person who identifies the biggest nuisance. A U.S. Army brigadier general who attended one of our seminars picked up on this idea and is implementing it vigorously and with great effect—and fun—in a large command.

3. Cut every procedure manual within your bailiwick in half over the next twelve months. Then do the same thing again in the following year. Sure, you're not chairman, chief executive officer, mayor, or general. But at least get your own house in order and stop being the principal cause of spreading havoc and wasting your people's time.

4. Urge the lawyers or contracts department—none too gently—to experiment with handshake agreements or contracts of no more than two pages. It can be done.

Roots of a Bureaucracy-Free Environment

I would be greatly remiss if I failed to note a caveat here. This business of eliminating rules and regulations is a big deal—a matter of replacing detailed, written "what if" strictures with trust (see S-4, S-5 also). Take the last suggestion. The way to eliminate lengthy supplier contracts is to join in long-term partnerships with a much smaller than normal number of quality suppliers. The same thing applies to all the others. You won't reduce the paperwork in a lasting fashion until you remove the underlying cause for it—mistrust and adversarial relations. This is why 9.9 out of 10 "paperwork reduction" committees fail to achieve any lasting change.

STOP TREATING PEOPLE WITH CONTEMPT

Knocking off humiliating practices is the second part of this prescription. A blast from Ross Perot, while at GM, captures the spirit: "In Pontiac [Michigan], GM executive parking garages are heated, while the poor guys who work in the plant freeze their tails off walking to work in the snow. It costs $140,000 a year to heat one parking garage. I'd shut that thing down. It has nothing to do with cars."

U.S. Steel ignominiously became USX in 1986; it has reduced its USW worker population from 94,000 in 1974 to less than 30,000 today. Yet *Business Week* reported acidly in 1985: "On the 61st floor [of the firm's headquarters] in Pittsburgh, uniformed stewards deliver coffee on silver trays to executive suites."

During a visit I made to Columbus in 1986, a Worthington employee and I struck up a conversation about the American steel industry. It was right after LTV had declared bankruptcy. The guy just couldn't fathom how the chairman of that company had the nerve to bring home a $700,000 salary, and pay himself a whopping bonus to boot, for driving a firm over the edge. Neither could I. In fact, the final break between Ross Perot and GM came when that firm's problematic performance in 1986 led it to decline to pay a profit-sharing bonuses of $1,000 to hourly workers—while giving executives all they were "entitled" to by traditional practice. "You can't look the troops in the eye and say, 'It's been a bad year; we can't do anything for you,' but then say, 'By the way, we're going to pay ourselves a $1 million bonus,' " Perot said.

I suspect that Perot would have been equally peeved at Lee Iacocca. Upon being questioned by the press as to how he reconciled his $20.6 million total compensation in 1986 with Chrysler's cuts in merit pay for other employees, he replied, "That's the American way. If little kids don't aspire to make money like I did, what the hell good is this country?"*

This is difficult material to talk about. How does one remain calm? Each of these examples is mind-numbing. So humiliating to the very work force whose renewed energy, talent, and flexible response to change we need for survival. So easy to avoid—in theory. So revealing of dysfunctional, age-old assumptions—in practice.

We insult employees with executive parking spots, heated, no less; with executive dining rooms; with bonuses and "strategy meetings" in lavish settings for the top 100 officers and their spouses even after lousy years. Roger Smith announces eleven plant closings and 27,000 more potential layoffs—then retreats behind double-locked—or triple-locked (depending on whose story you believe)—glass doors to contemplate the wasteland he's created (his $1.4 million in compensation in 1986 doubtless eased the pain a bit).

Stop! I want to scream. It's dumb. I don't say this for humanitarian

*It might be the American way—and important to our entrepreneurial vitality. But as we consider the more important role of the work force in the future, we should at least acknowledge that it's not the only capitalist way. The compensation ratio between labor and top management runs 1 to 80 in the United States, versus 1 to 25 in West Germany and 1 to 7 in Japan.

reasons, much as I believe in such reasons. My point is pragmatic: How do you humiliate and demean someone and then expect him or her to care about product quality and constant improvement?

Nucor's Ken Iverson found multicolored hard hats when he arrived at the company: white for workers, blue for foremen, green for department heads. He replaced them with one color—green—for everyone.

At NUMMI the separate entrances for managers and workers were eliminated, as was the executive lunchroom. The brother of the president of Toyota was the first NUMMI chief; many remarked that they were stunned to see him eating regularly with line workers in the common cafeteria. Perhaps the importance of eliminating humiliating practices is underscored by the very fact that so many, from both inside and outside the industry, noted his presence in the cafeteria; it stood out among the many positive things NUMMI had done.

Other humiliations are more subtle. Psychological assessment tests (see prescription P-4) and, certainly, urinalysis are demeaning. A Boise Cascade worker was recently suspended for smashing a camera hidden in the ceiling of a locker room to detect theft from lockers; employees hadn't been consulted on its installation. Can you imagine what would have happened if the firm's security chief had secretly installed a hidden camera in the executive washroom?

The Mickey Mouse rules that smell of contempt and distrust are part of the negative signals we send. By a great deal of our entry-testing, we make it clear that we assume the candidate is a misfit or a thief or drug addict or all three. Then we confirm it daily after he or she comes aboard. For instance, do you want a dollar's worth of stamps in a hurry to get a customer letter out in a timely fashion? It is presumed you are a cheat, and want them for personal use, so you have to fill out a fifteen-line form to get them. Need a spare part to fix a broken machine? Fill out a two-page form, get two supervisors to sign it (if the part costs more than $2.95), and then pass through the double-locked door to the supply room. And then we turn around and have the nerve to ask people to "do it right the first time," to take an interest in the machine. How absurd!

It goes from top to bottom. The "hourly" can't check out a screwdriver. The engineer is trusted with only $25 (though you're "betting the company" on his or her design skills). And the division general manager, overseeing 700 people and $25 million in assets, has a signature authority of $1,000. The message sent could not be more clear if it were printed on a banner dragged behind a plane flying over the Super Bowl.

Start Now—Do SOMETHING Fast

There are two answers to the above. One is removing the "humiliators." Start with the physical stuff, such as executive parking spots, executive dining rooms, separate entrances for managers and nonmanagers, the use of limos—right now. Next, scour every procedure book, looking—with the help of those being demeaned—for the small and large put-downs and irritants. Consider a team effort such as the Gnat Patrol from a BFG operation in Oklahoma that seeks out and swats petty annoyances. I propose that you go so far as to set quantitative goals: For instance, remove ten procedural "demeaners" every 60 days.

BECOME A HOUSEKEEPING FANATIC

Despite the best efforts of a professional photographer, the photo appearing in *Fortune* in mid-1986 of a Japanese-owned and -managed auto-component factory in the Midwest was somewhat washed out. Washing out occurs when there is too much reflected light. In this case, the reflected light came from the mirror-like, highly polished floors and the metal fittings. There go the Japanese, cheating again. This time it's unreasonably clean plants—on U.S. soil.

I shouldn't have to say this. There should be no more obvious point. If the workplace looks shabby, if the toilets are foul, with graffiti on the walls, how can you *dare* preach about commitment, participation, quality, and service? Worthington Industries founder John McConnell was considering buying a company a while ago. One of his acid, pre-acquisition tests is a tour of the facilities. In the employee cafeteria, he found netting temporarily rigged beneath the ceiling—to catch the crumbling plaster and keep it out of the food. It led him to question the whole deal. If management was that insensitive to its work force, could the company be salvageable?

In the spring of 1985, British coal miners went back to work after a year-long strike. *Newsweek* reported: "The miners filed into the pit baths to change for work. They found the floor sprinkled with paint chips from the peeling walls. There was no hot water, and the pipes, after a year's neglect, needed repair. 'To see this is an insult,' said . . . an official of the local. 'It's degrading.' " The strike had been rancorous, the worst of this century. When it ended, the objective for both sides should have been to get on with the job at hand, to seek both the efficiencies and the increased cooperation necessary if the coal industry is to survive. One way not to up the odds of the industry's survival is to insult the miners. Yet by allowing the miners to return to filthy conditions, British coal management, intentionally or not, did exactly that.

I wonder about these things a lot. How can you possibly preach service to your fast-food franchise employees and then not have an unlimited supply of clean uniforms ready, so that they can change whenever they spill something? It's so obvious: It is psychologically impossible to deliver good service in a dirty uniform. Don't you suppose, on a gray day, that the cleanliness of the Fed Ex truck peps the driver up? You bet it does.

And what's so very obvious for service employees, or any employees in contact with customers, goes double in the factory. How can you ask a quality circle to deliberate seriously in a cramped, noisy corner of a filthy cafeteria? How can you allow grime to collect on the floor of the auto dealership's service bay and then send directives to mechanics on the importance of customer service? How can you possibly chide a distribution center team for a high error rate on deliveries and ignore the fact that the toilets are foul, that the employees' locker room hasn't been painted for ages, that the saltshakers on the canteen tables don't work, that one vending machine (out of only three to serve 125 people) is chronically out of order, that the controller reduced the number of pay phones in the break area from four to two?

There is so much you can do. Perhaps fresh flowers on cafeteria tables. Will tough factory hands respond? Answer, without exception in my experience: yes. Don't expect thank-you notes. But do expect such small touches to pay off many times over. Spend money on this kind of improvement. Most of it doesn't cost much—flowers and paint, for example. Some amenities do cost more: brighter lights in the parking lots or better landscaping. But if you're smart, this part of the facilities budget will be the last to feel the cost cutter's ax. Delay purchasing a new piece of machinery if you must—but don't delay refurbishing the chairs and tables in the cafeteria—and start eating there yourself, regularly.

Heroes with Paint Buckets and Washrags

▶ Ron Kowal, director of manufacturing and purchasing at Tennant, talks about a very special painter:

Frank Smith is a good example of an employee who takes quality seriously. Frank is one of the people responsible for making sure the Tennant Company factory has the reputation of being one of the cleanest in the country. A painter in the maintenance department, he has been painting interior and exterior walls and ceilings at Tennant Company for years. Frank has applied hundreds of gallons of white paint each year at the request of department managers, who remembered once in a while to thank him for the good job. Nevertheless, Frank knew he was doing an important job. And there is no doubt in our minds that a clean plant is one of the highest priority objectives in any quality process. When people take pride in work areas, they will also take pride in their work.

About six years ago, as part of the quality emphasis, Frank decided to put a little extra into his job. He began creating wall murals—pictures of fish, grouse, or deer, paintings of Tennant company products, slogans about quality, or whatever the people who work in the area requested. Every year, requests for his work increase, along with the positive comments on what a great job he is doing. Frank proves that quality can be achieved in more ways than assembling products. He achieves quality with a brush, a ladder, a bucket of paint, and a fertile imagination.

▶ The authors of *The 100 Best Companies to Work for in America* report on the billion-dollar maker of office furniture:

The emphasis on quality and pride in workmanship extends to Steelcase's truck fleet, which comprises 97 tractors and 213 trailers. It's one of the largest truck fleets in the country—and it boasts the best safety record of any private fleet. Steelcase has such a rigorous maintenance program that some of its trucks last one million miles. Its vehicles are kept in spotless condition. New drivers are required to spend their first six months on the job doing nothing but washing trucks. Drivers have their names on door panels. In 1984, a new driver, 30-year-old Paul Rosendahl, was so impressed with the pride and the spit and polish that he recorded a song, "Blue and Chrome," to salute the Steelcase trucks.

PUBLIC PARALLELS

Reducing bureaucracy: Maryland governor Don Schaefer provides eloquent testimony: "It is strange to see sometimes how our elected officials change. When they run for the first time for a major office . . . for example, mayor of a large city—they are in shirtsleeves. They have some crudely made banners (prepared, of course, by your average citizen). They virtually demand of the people they meet while campaigning that they be called by their first name or nickname. They shout to the rooftops that if you have a problem—call me.

"Yet, what happens after they are elected? Dare you still call them Bob or Bill or Don? How do they respond to your problem (if you can ever get to them)? Do they simply just waltz past you now as you wait in a line at a restaurant? And do they wave to you through the tinted-glass back window of their chauffeur-driven limousine as they splash backed-up gutter water all over your clothes?"

The new Model Installation Program of the Department of Defense, brainchild of Deputy Assistant Secretary of Defense Bob Stone, is another effort making a difference. Its bulletin, the "Graduate Journal," subtitled "Turning Writers into Fighters," chronicles success at reducing bureaucracy. Here are some snippets from a recent issue collected by a staff dedicated to making visits to the MIP sites and spreading the good news (see P-9, Task #3):

▶ The 200-page construction manual will be replaced by a four-page guide that removes detailed restrictions, emphasizes quality, and gives installation commanders more influence over what gets built.
▶ Eighteen housing regulations will be replaced by one that gives lots more authority to commanders.

▶ Commanders will be able to buy locally when it's smart to do so; when [the Government Services Agency] has the best deal, we're making it easier for commanders to buy from them.

▶ DOD can now buy the cheapest airline ticket available rather than pay a more expensive government rate.

The task is daunting, but the philosophy is now taking hold. Thousands of accumulating success stories, spurred by the development of a word-of-mouth network, are increasing efficiency and responsiveness, and returning control to the field.

De-humiliating: Go back and reread this prescription. About nine-tenths of the suggestions concern things that are inexpensive or free, so there is no financial bar to implementation. And if you instill the attitude this prescription aims at, employees, public or private, will often chip in themselves. In several crippled firms, following a new boss's obvious determination to put workers first, I've seen the most incredible outpouring of plants from home, and after-hours repair projects sprout up overnight.

FIRST STEPS

I don't care if you've waited twenty-seven years for it, get rid of the damned reserved parking spot right this bloody minute. (*Then* you can consider asking "them" to "do it right the first time.")

Actually, dozens of inexpensive (in terms of money or time) First Step suggestions are contained in this prescription. What's holding you up?

V

LEARNING TO LOVE CHANGE: A NEW VIEW OF *L*EADERSHIP AT ALL LEVELS

SECTION SUMMARY

The dictionary defines "axiom" as "a statement universally accepted as true." Management, as it has been professionalized and systematized, has developed many axioms over the past century. But in the past twenty years, the stable conditions (large-scale mass production) that led to the slow emergence of these universals have blown apart. So now the chief job of the leader, at all levels, is to oversee the dismantling of dysfunctional old truths and to prepare people and organizations to deal with— to love, to develop affection for—change per se, as innovations are proposed, tested, rejected, modified and adopted.

This set of prescriptions (see Figure 17) begins with the Guiding Premise, L-1, that leaders must above all confront—and master—a series of paradoxes—that is, willingly embrace (test, learn about) across-the-board challenges to conventional wisdom.

Mastering the paradoxes and what they stand for (L-1) requires the Three Leadership Tools for Establishing Direction: L-2, developing and preaching a vision which clearly sets your direction, yet at the same time encourages initiatives from everyone to perfect and elaborate the challenge that vision lays out; L-3, channeling interest by living the vision via your calendar (what you do—and do not—spend time on), which is the single most effective tool for establishing faith in the vision amidst otherwise debilitating uncertainty; and L-4, practicing visible management, for the purpose of preaching the message and enhancing the leader's understanding of the context where it counts—on the front line, where true implementation takes place.

The principal challenge is to empower people (everyone) to take new initiatives—that is, risks (as they see it)—on a day-to-day basis, aimed at improving and eventually transforming every routine in the firm. Of course, prescriptions P-1 through P-10 addressed this. But there are four enabling leadership prescriptions (Leading by Empowering People) as well: L-5, on becoming a compulsive listener, since listening (especially to those at the front) remains the truest signal that "I take you seriously"; L-6, on cherishing the people at the front—demonstrated in a host of ways, from pay scales to invitations to staff meetings; L-7, on delegating "authority" in a way that truly empowers; and L-8, vigorous and visible pursuit of bureaucracy bashing.

The last two leadership prescriptions urge you to get directly on with the new "it": L-9 proposes that everyone be evaluated on the simple but revolutionary question: "What have you changed lately?" L-10 suggests that leaders must epitomize change in every action in order to create an overwhelming sense of urgency throughout the organization.

As in the prior sections, the leadership prescriptions, though separable, should be considered as a whole. While you can't do "everything at once," no one prescription makes much sense in a vacuum.

Figure 17: **Learning to Love Change: A New View of Leadership at All Levels**

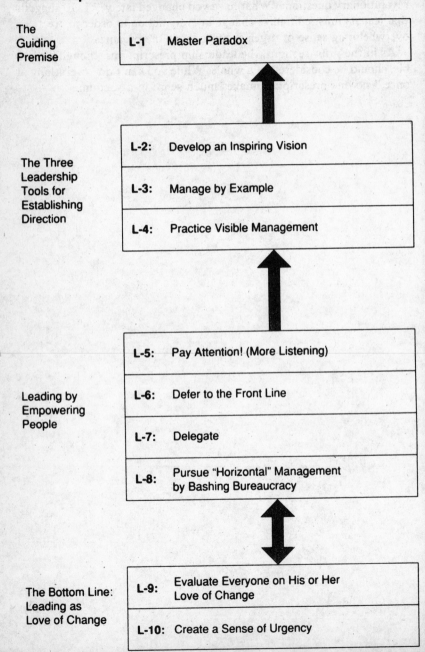

The
Guiding
Premise

L-1 Master Paradox

The Three
Leadership
Tools for
Establishing
Direction

L-2: Develop an Inspiring Vision

L-3: Manage by Example

L-4: Practice Visible Management

Leading by
Empowering
People

L-5: Pay Attention! (More Listening)

L-6: Defer to the Front Line

L-7: Delegate

L-8: Pursue "Horizontal" Management by Bashing Bureaucracy

The Bottom Line:
Leading as
Love of Change

L-9: Evaluate Everyone on His or Her Love of Change

L-10: Create a Sense of Urgency

L-1

SUMMARY

To adapt to tomorrow's fast-unfolding world, leaders at all levels must:

▶ Come to grips with a series of paradoxes that have set almost all conventional management wisdom on its ear.

The management principles we have held dear are undergoing relentless attack—and succumbing. Most of the cause-and-effect relationships we have cherished have been found wanting.

Each day, each manager must practically challenge conventional wisdom, especially cause and effect relations that have been considered axiomatic. Since new truths are not yet clear, the manager must become "master empiricist," asking each day: What new experiments have been mounted today to test new principles (in the market, in the accounting department, etc.)?

Master Paradox

Perhaps we would be well advised at this juncture, since formal knowledge can no longer help us to understand a world in which the pace of change and development is so great, to think of the jester's role in relation to the king. Since the jester did not speak on behalf of any respectable body, he was able with impunity to draw attention to abuses which the king should suppress, to raise uncertain matters in an admonishing tone, to be receptive to things which the established authorities were either unwilling or unable to see. The contrast is thus between the perception of the jester and the knowledge of the authorities. Is there a similar contrast between perception and scientific thought? . . . Science makes progress by distinguishing between what it regards as meaningful and what it considers to be merely static, i.e., a disruptive factor which can be ignored. Perceptiveness on the other hand deals with problems which as yet have no significance but which acquire significance in the future.

> Isabelle Stengers*
> "Order Through Chaos"
> May 1987

Paradox: A statement that seems contradictory, unbelievable or absurd but that may actually be true in fact.

> *Webster's New World Dictionary*

*Isabelle Stengers is co-author, along with Nobel Laureate (Chemistry) Ilya Prigogine, of *Order Out of Chaos*. The quotation here is from an essay in the 1987 Annual Report of Buro voor Systeemontwikkeling bv, the Netherlands' largest systems software house.

Today's successful business leaders will be those who are most flexible of mind. An ability to embrace new ideas, routinely challenge old ones, and live with paradox will be the effective leader's premier trait. Further, the challenge is for a lifetime. New truths will not emerge easily. Leaders will have to guide the ship while simultaneously putting everything up for grabs (see L-2), which is itself a fundamental paradox.

Here are eighteen paradoxes, large and small, which are indicative of the chaotic business environment now unfolding:

1. More stability of purpose/employment is necessary to deal with less stability in the environment. More flexibility and responsiveness are the survivors' watchwords. However, more flexibility will only be engendered when there is a clearer vision (see L-2), more trust, and fewer adversarial dealings. That is, you can't ask a fearful person to break all the conventional rules and regularly take what feel like (and are, by past standards) risky initiatives.

2. More competition requires more cooperation. More competitors and competitors' products require more flexibility/responsiveness and higher quality, for instance. This in turn means supporting partnerships between: (a) companies and their (often sole source) suppliers, (b) companies and other companies that can bring in critical new skills needed in a market area (especially overseas), (c) the performers of various functions, to speed action-taking where it counts, at the front line, (d) management and the work force (and the union, if applicable), and (e) the company and its distributors/franchisees/reps. If we are to compete effectively, we must learn to cooperate with all these sets of partners.

3. More productivity will come through more people—not fewer. Winners will learn to add value through the work force (its attention to quality, service, and responsiveness). Losers will continue to willy-nilly replace people with machines, in the vain hope of competing with Brazil or Indonesia on cost. More sales and service people and expediters in the factory will be needed to add more value—i.e., to enhance revenue. Better-trained people in the factory will provide massive productivity improvements over time. While I acknowledge corporate bloat (see P-8, for instance), sensible job creation in pursuit of revenue enhancement must nonetheless replace today's most frequent management boast: the number of people cut in the last eighteen months.

4. Success will stem from more love of the product—and less attachment to it. To get everyone enthusiastic about constantly improving the product requires commitment to it as well as to them (see C-2). On the other hand, products will be made obsolete more frequently by competitors' offerings or by our own, competing efforts (see I-1). Thus, a commitment to ceaseless improvement of the product must reside side by side with a willingness to scrap it when we develop a replacement (or someone else does).

5. **We must be wary of the economics of scale—but create more complex alliances.** Efficiencies of scale in the traditional sense are going—or already gone—for a host of reasons (see Part I). On the other hand, more joint ventures and partnership arrangements are required to thrive, especially overseas.

6. **More de-integration goes hand-in-hand with more re-integration (on new dimensions).** Vertical integration is fast being reduced; subcontracting of anything and everything is becoming routine. Yet closer linkages, via electronic/telecommunication channels, for instance (see C-4), are a must. Thus while one (traditional) form of "big scale" (vertical integration) is being undone, another form (electronic linkages and new partnerships) is emerging.

7. **"Big yields low cost" can and must rapidly give way to "small yields low cost."** New, miniaturized technology and the adoption of techniques such as cellular manufacturing and just-in-time inventory management are leading to lower costs from smaller units that feature short production runs and great flexibility. Smaller units also may have much less overhead, and they are more likely to subcontract services such as accounting—yielding still more cost reduction.

8. **More productivity ensues from having fewer suppliers.** Conventional wisdom pits suppliers against one another to obtain low-bid contracts. Success now will stem from high quality (lifetime cost of product, not initial contract cost—see C-2) and supplier responsiveness to constantly shifting customer/market demands; this, in turn, will come only from partnership relations, based on trust, with a few suppliers.

9. **The more a market seems "commodity-like," the more adding small increments of value pays off.** Adding numerous small increments in service, quality, and responsiveness actually makes a bigger difference—is more valuable—in mature markets than in growth markets. Surprisingly, the low-price strategy is the weapon of last resort in all markets; adding value is the first choice—regardless of market circumstance.

10. More products (with shorter production runs) does not mean lower quality. The necessary reorganization of the plant into manufacturing cells, for instance, and much greater involvement of the work force—plus appropriate automation to support (not supplant) people—allow more complex production scheduling (short runs, fast responses) to coincide with higher quality. There need not be (and cannot be, given the competitive situation) any tradeoff between quality and flexibility.

11. High quality yields lower costs. Quality and cost, within a wide performance range, are not part of a "tradeoff" equation. Increasing quality, which generally results from simplification of design and manufacture, radically reduces costs.

12. Higher quality comes with fewer inspectors. Once again, people are the key. Virtually all inspection should be self-inspection—and this can be accomplished if the work force is involved, committed, trained, supported with appropriate tools, relieved of bureaucratic Mickey Mouse, and paid for performance.

13. Accelerating the success rate comes only from accelerating the failure rate. Revolutionary improvement in quality, service, and responsiveness will only occur when all are participating in the day-to-day enhancement of the product/service; that is, when all are taking risks to try new methods. Numerous failures always (according to the laws of science) precede any success. Therefore, speeding up the success rate requires speeding up the failure rate.

14. Tighter control can be achieved through more decentralization. The new, decentralized organization features (1) well trained and highly involved people (everyone) and (2) units "transparent to" (permeated by) the customer. Truly decentralized, externally (customer-) obsessed units, with a clear vision and high involvement, are more under control in today's volatile environment than traditional, centrally controlled units—which are inflexible and more out of touch by definition. The latter focus on slow, power-driven, "vertical" decision-making; the former emphasize market-driven decision-making and fast adaptation.

15. Tighter adherence to policy is accomplished when less time is spent in the office. Proactive adaptation to a volatile environment comes when people are both inspired by a useful vision and empowered to act. These two traits follow from visible management—not hierarchical, committee-driven, out-of-touch management. The old form of organization via rulebook and policy manual is not able to keep up today. Teaching flexibility (and modeling it) is an out-of-the-office task (see L-3, L-4); flexibility in turn engenders control—empowered people pursuing (and elaborating) a clearly transmitted vision.

16. Strategic planning exercises led by staffs are being supplanted by strategic capability building led by the line. The long-range strategic plan, of voluminous length, is less useful than before. But a strategic "mind-set," which focuses on skill/capability-building (e.g., adding value to the work force via training to prepare it to respond more flexibly and be more quality-conscious), is more important than ever.

17. More appropriate measurement is achieved with fewer measures. Anything can be measured. The winners' measures will emphasize the vital performance parameters—e.g., quality, service, flexibility, responsiveness, and employee skills/capabilities (see S-1). True control stems from a very few, simple measures of high integrity, understood by all (also covered in S-1). More flip charts measuring the important variables and fewer 800-page printouts dealing with arcane cost information are the success prescription.

18. Success will come to those who love chaos—constant change—not those who attempt to eliminate it. The fleet-of-foot, value-adding, niche-market creator (see C-1) thrives on the very uncertainty that drives others to distraction. Stability and predictability are gone for good—and therefore must not be the implicit or explicit goals of organizational design, the layout of factory or operations center, pay schemes, strategic planning, objective-setting exercises, accounting systems, or job evaluations. Victory will go to those who master instability by constantly working on responsiveness-enhancing capabilities.

THE LEADER AS EMPIRICIST

These eighteen paradoxes are but a small sample—yet they violate all the core organizing assumptions of the last hundred or more years. Consequently, the leader at any level will not convince his or her boss (traditional middle manager or outsider members of the board) of these still heretical ideas through argument. His or her role must therefore become that of "empiricist in chief" (see also I-3, on "piloting"). That is, the firm must become a hotbed of tests of the unconventional. It must become an experimenting (and learning), adaptive, change-seeking organization. It must ceaselessly send its people, at all levels and in all functions, out to visit other interesting firms, universities, customers, suppliers, distributors, competitors (see C-7, I-4). The unit manager willingly lends people to project teams full-time and other functions for lengthy assignments, so that they can learn more faster, and be part of useful tests aimed at dealing proactively with change. The organization learns from the best, swipes from the best, adapts, tests, risks, fails, and adjusts—over and over.

Recall that Chaparral Steel president Gordon Forward calls his mill a laboratory. That is the right image. Every person becomes an empiricist and every department becomes a laboratory. The experiments deal with procedures and rules and forms of supervision and communication patterns, as well as with new products and services.

Nothing can be "institutionalized." All products not being rapidly improved are, ipso facto, falling rapidly behind. This morning's new widget is being made obsolete by two early-afternoon start-ups. A fast failure—followed by a fast adjustment—becomes the organization's most cherished event, demanded from everyone, daily.

THE CORE PARADOX

The core paradox, then, that all leaders at all levels must contend with is fostering (creating) internal stability in order to encourage the pursuit of constant change. The vision must be clear enough (consistent, etc.—see L-2) to encourage continual risk-taking and failing, or else the continual testing and stretching and enhancing—changing—of everything will not occur, or not occur fast enough.

This dichotomous task has not been imposed upon leaders before. They must preach the vision with verve—over and over. And at the same time, they must insist upon and then revel in the constant tests that re-form (expand, contract, destroy) the very same vision. The ship will seem somewhat out of control by the old standards. That is, the madness of thousands of simultaneous experiments—including some by the newly hired reservations clerk—is the only plausible path to survival. What once amounted to being "in control" (i.e., being guided by a plodding hierarchy of bureaucrats, conservators of the past) is a design for disaster today. <u>"In control" by the old standards is "out of control" (fast slipping behind) by the new standards.</u>

TIPS FOR THE PARADOX-LOVING MANAGER

Here are a few tips to deal with the task of simultaneously nurturing stability and instability:

1. Be out and about (see L-4). Only by being "at the front" will you be able to "feel" the pace and progress—and the problems—where it counts, on the line.

2. Demand empiricism. Demand hard tests and fast tests and partial tests of everything, by everyone (see I-3).

3. Listen and provide listening forums. Everyone must be listening, sharing, recognizing small successes, laughing at small failures (see P-3, for instance), and urging even faster tries.

4. Learn to love and laud failures. As previously mentioned, one seminar participant proposed that *How to Learn to Love Failure* be this book's subtitle. It's a good idea: "test fast, fail fast, adjust fast" must become the organization's battlecry (see I-8).

5. Proclaim the virtues of speedy "horizontal" action-taking. Be vociferous in support of tests and fast failures that have resulted from eschewing excessive "vertical" decision-making and instead foster fast "horizontal" action-taking, i.e., involving multiple functions at the front line (see P-9, L-8).

6. Define and chat up the common denominators. I suspect that superb quality, flexibility, and everyone's wholesale participation will top most firms' menus. Define these constants through "preaching"—and especially through example (see L-3). Tie this idea to #2 above (empiricism); that is, preach principally by using examples of nifty, somewhat risky experiments that seem to be forwarding the new cause—especially experiments conducted on the front line, by front-line people and multifunction teams.

7. Let customers—and soaring goals—do the "teaching." The most effective control in the midst of madness is control which is externally inspired. Constant customer listening, coupled with a vision that proclaims the goal of being the very best in the customer's terms will act as an almost moral context for (and control over) the firm's ongoing revolution—that is, the firm that is engaged in continual experiments with everything, by everyone. If customers populate every cranny of the organization, literally (and symbolically), the sense of urgency and the basis for self-control will increase immeasurably, and fast—and never slip (see C-10 also).

8. Make it fun. Only fun—in the sense of taking pleasure in accomplishment and interesting foul-up alike—will allow you to thrive amidst the ravages of change in a world turned upside down. It's the basis for yet one more paradox: The economic stakes have never been higher; therefore, it's never been more important not to take yourself too seriously. "We are in the midst of a great and crazy adventure, creating our brave new rulebook by error and trial as we go along"—that must be the tone (see L-10).

9. Promote those who deal best with paradox. Perhaps this goes without saying: If the ability to deal with these paradoxes is the key to success, then we should promote, at all levels, those who show the greatest facility in doing so. A new breed of managers is required. Full-speed execution will not occur until the new breed is in place. It is imperative to dig into the ranks, or do whatever else is necessary, to get them in place as rapidly as possible.

FIRST STEPS

Openly address and discuss, in every forum, the practical implications of the paradoxes described above. Make sure that you find at least one excuse per day to raise issues surrounding at least one of these paradoxes. And then mount a quick test. And then talk about that test, whether successful or not.

L-2

SUMMARY

In a time of turbulence and uncertainty, we must be able to take instant action on the front line. But to support such action-taking at the front, everyone must have a clear understanding about what the organization is trying to achieve. We must:

▶ Develop and live an enabling and empowering vision. Effective leadership—at all levels—is marked by a core philosophy (values) and a vision of how the enterprise (or department) wishes to make its mark. Look inward, work with colleagues, work with customers, work with everyone to develop and instill such a philosophy and vision.

▶ Ensure that the vision is at once (1) specific enough to act as a "tie breaker" (e.g., quality is more important than volume) and (2) general enough to leave room for the taking of bold initiatives in today's ever-changing environment.

▶ Become the vision's foremost itinerant preacher: Do not let a single day pass without taking at least two or three opportunities to deliver your three-minute "stump speech" on the vision and to "showcase" events and people (small events and front-line people rather than big events and senior executives) that are illustrative of initiatives which support the vision. When it comes to vision and philosophy: (1) consistency is not the hobgoblin of small minds, and (2) God is in the details.

Quite simply, the vision must supplant the rule book and the policy manual. "Hustle" in service to the customer was the message of C-1 through C-10. "People's involvement is everything" was the rallying cry of P-1 through P-10. How does the leader direct this front-line energy and quick initiative-taking? A soaring purpose—a vision and corporate values responsive to today's and to-morrow's needs—is the answer. Day-to-day flexibility and innovation by every-onecan only occur if the outline/charter/vision is unmistakable—and exciting.

Via soul-searching listening, assessment of the external situation, and solicitation of all points of view, develop a succinct vision that is clear and exciting, and at the same time leaves wide latitude for the pursuit of new opportunities.

L-2

Develop an Inspiring Vision

> The very essence of leadership is [that] you have to have a vision.
> It's got to be a vision you articulate clearly and forcefully on every
> occasion. You can't blow an uncertain trumpet.
>
> Father Theodore Hesburgh
> former president, Notre Dame University
> *Time,* May 1987

The corporation has shared information widely (S-3); you understand you are in a competitive pickle. You're part of a profit-distribution plan (P-6), you've been well trained (P-5), and the unnecessary
structure has been removed (P-8); there are no supervisors around.
But it's 2:35 A.M. The truck is almost loaded. The last order comes
out on the dock, and the deliverer scoots off into the shadows. Something is amiss, you feel (but you're not sure), as you go over the pack-
ing label. What do you do?

The driver is chomping at the bit, and costing a fortune. The guy who
passed the order on to you is senior to you by two years, supposed to
know what he's doing. Odds are high you're all wet. Do you give in to
your suspicion, and push the red button—or do you let it go?

To survive in today's quality-conscious environment, the answer had
better be "push the panic button." But it will be only if the firm's vision
and values are unmistakable; if they make what's of overarching importance clear, and at the same time leave vast latitude for initiative-taking—by everyone.

Some understand the role of vision in the brave, new, turbulent world:

483

▶ In *Leaders,* Warren Bennis and Burt Nanus conclude: "Leaders articulate and define what has previously remained implicit or unsaid; then
they invent images, metaphors, and models that provide a focus for
new attention. By so doing, they consolidate or challenge prevailing
wisdom. In short, an *essential* factor in leadership is the capacity to
influence and *organize meaning* for the members of the organization.
. . . Managers are people who do things right and leaders are people
who do the right thing. The difference may be summarized as activities
of vision and judgment—*effectiveness* versus activities of mastering
routine—*efficiency.* . . . [The subjects in our study] viewed themselves
as leaders, not managers. This is to say that they concerned themselves
with their organizations' basic purposes and general direction. Their
perspective was 'vision-oriented.' . . . There were no 'incrementalists.'
These were people creating new ideas, new policies, new methodolo-
gies. They changed the basic metabolism of their organizations. These
leaders were, in Camus' phrase, 'creating dangerously,' not simply
mastering basic routines. . . . Their visions or intentions were compelling, and pulled people toward them. Intensity coupled with commitment is magnetic. And these intense personalities do not have to
coerce people to pay attention; they are so intent on what they are
doing that, like a child completely absorbed with creating a sand castle
in a sandbox, they draw others in."

▶ In *The Leadership Challenge,* Jim Kouzes and Barry Posner discuss
Phil Turner, facilities manager for Raychem Corporation (he has since
been promoted to plant manager for the company's Wire and Cable
Division): "We had the chance to sit in with him one day when he was
talking with his supervisors. Phil was describing the daily life of the
people who work in facilities. A typical day-in-the-life might begin
with this phone call: 'Phil, the toilet is overflowing in the men's room.
Would you send somebody over to fix it?' Or, 'Phil, the air-conditioner
is broken in our building. It feels like it's 110 degrees in this place.
Would you send someone over to fix it?' . . .

"Phil related to his managers how one could get the impression that
the people who work for Raychem were ungrateful. . . . 'But . . . I don't
think that's what they are trying to tell us at all. I think what they are
trying to tell us is that they care about their space. I have a vision for
this department. I got the idea from [an executive vice-president]. The
other day, [he] came by my office. The door was open and he walked

in. He put his hand on my shoulder and said, "Phil, I want to thank you for planting those flowers outside my office window. They make me feel good." So I think our job is to make people feel good,' declared Phil."

Developing a vision and, more important, living it vigorously are essential elements of leadership. And they are not, as the case of Phil Turner shows, the exclusive province of mayors, governors, and chief executives. Vision occupies an equally important place of honor in the supervisor's or middle manager's world.

"CREATE DANGEROUSLY"—OR GO BELLY UP

The leaders Bennis and Nanus describe were "creating dangerously," "chang[ing] the basic metabolism of their organization." This radical definition of leadership must become the norm today. A supervisor or the chief executive of a big firm not bent upon "creating dangerously" is apt to lose his or her job and go out of business. It's as simple and as grim as that.

Following and administering rules might have been dandy in the placid environments of yesteryear. Not today. Managers must create new worlds. And then destroy them; and then create anew. Such brave acts of creation must begin with a vision that not only inspires, ennobles, empowers, and challenges, but at the same time provokes confidence enough, in the midst of a perpetual competitive hurricane, to encourage people to take the day-to-day risks involved in testing and adapting and extending the vision.

Don't Let It Become a Fad

Failure, today, is failure to change. The leader's vision is at once the license to dare to be better and the beacon and "control system" which keeps the process of mastering new worlds from deteriorating into direc-tionless anarchy.

Sadly, "visioning" has become a fad in business circles. The idea of an effective enterprise being energized and guided by a succinct and uplift-ing philosophy that dares everyone to take risks to realize its challenge

is a compelling one—especially as an alternative to guidance via necessarily static, 300-page strategic plans and 1,700-page policy manuals
written for yesterday's placid conditions. And, indeed, this alternative
form of control/motivation is essential in a setting where, for survival's
sake, flexibility and constant change must replace rigidity. For this very
reason, the idea of developing a vision is too important to be trivialized
by the explosion of handbooks on "how to get vision" in twenty-seven
easy steps. Thus, the line I tread here is a thin one. No leadership topic
is more important. There are some things that can be said based on
others' experience. But no precise path to "finding one" can—or
should—be described. The process of discovery is personal, and the
essence of the art of managing/leading in chaotic times.

Visions: A Broad Definition

Visions are aesthetic and moral—as well as strategically sound. Visions come from within—as well as from outside. They are personal—
and group-centered. Developing a vision and values is a messy, artistic
process. Living it convincingly is a passionate one, beyond any doubt.
Posters and wallet-sized cards declaring the vision and corporate values
may be helpful, but they may not be. In fact, they can hinder and make
a mockery of the process if the vision and values are merely proclaimed,
but not lived convincingly.

The "What" of Visions

1. Effective visions are inspiring. Steve Jobs, at Apple, wanted no less
than to start a revolution in the way the average person processes information, thinks, and deals with his or her world. Fred Smith, founder of
Federal Express, had a vision of truly reliable mail service. The Nordstrom family seeks to create "an experience" with their stores. And
Raychem's Phil Turner, cited above, wants to create revolution, too,
through an uplifting idea about what the maintenance of facilities can
accomplish for all his fellow workers.

These leaders were not simply engaging in "market creation," as
important as that is (see C-1). They were engaged in a crusade, and asked
employees with nerve and verve, and customers and suppliers, to join
them. To experience Apple or Fed Ex or Nordstrom, even as a customer,
is to have your world changed permanently.

By contrast, inspiring visions rarely (I'm tempted to say never) include numbers. Earnings-per-share targets, however inspiring to the chief's pocketbook and the stockholders, are seldom uplifting to 10 or 10,000 people. While the numbers are important—especially in a world where corporate raiders await in every alleyway—they are a by-product of spirited performance, not its cause. Rather than numbers, the most effective visions ask for the best in one way or another—the highest-quality widgets, the best service ever in retailing history, the best customer relations in banking, the widest selection of clothing ever, a life-transforming experience for customers (of Apple or Outward Bound or Mrs. Field's Cookies); furthermore, they make it clear that "the best" will only be attained by the willing risk-taking of everyone on the payroll, starting with the just-hired teller or bellhop.

   2. **Effective visions are clear and challenging—and about excellence.** One of Bennis and Nanus's leaders was Sergiu Comissionà, renowned conductor of the Houston Symphony: "When asked what he was like, his musicians answered, 'Terrific.' But when asked why, they wavered. Finally they said, 'Because he doesn't waste our time.' That simple declarative sentence at first seemed insignificant. But when we finally watched him conduct and teach his master classes we began to understand the full meaning of that phrase. . . . *It became clear that Comissioná transmits an unbridled clarity about what he wants from the players. He knows precisely and emphatically what he wants to hear at any given time. This fixation with and undeviating attention to outcome—some would call it an obsession—is only possible if one knows what he wants* [my emphasis]. And that can come only from vision, or as one member of Comissionà's orchestra referred to it, from 'the maestro's tapestry of intentions.' There is a high, intense filament, we noticed in our leaders—similar to Comissionà's passion about the 'right' tone—and in any person impassioned with an idea. . . . The visions these various leaders conveyed seemed to bring about a confidence on the part of the employees, a confidence that instilled in them a belief that they were capable of performing the necessary acts. *These leaders were challengers, not coddlers* [my emphasis]. Edwin H. Land, founder of Polaroid, said: 'The first thing you naturally do is teach the person to feel that the undertaking is manifestly important and nearly impossible. That draws out the kind of drives that make people strong.' "

   3. **Effective visions make sense in the marketplace, and, by stressing flexibility and execution, stand the test of time in a turbulent world.**

Prescription C-6 emphasized "uniqueness." How does the firm position itself—make itself distinctly different from all its competitors? Further, C-6 said that some forms of uniqueness were better than others, emphasizing a limited number of effective, generic strategies: Quality, service, responsiveness, and constant creation of new niche markets, even for seemingly mundane products, are the essence of a market-oriented strategy that has high odds of success over time. <u>The vision that will be effective in the marketplace emphasizes the creation of enduring capabilities that will allow the organization to execute the strategy</u>. The vision is thus paradoxical: It is relatively *stable*—focusing on superior quality and service, for instance. But it is *dynamic* in that it underscores the constant improvement (individual skill-building, for instance) and constant try-fail-adjust cycles that keep the skills/capabilities up to date. (See also L-1 and S-3, on strategic planning.)

4. Effective visions must be stable but constantly challenged—and changed at the margin. Johnson & Johnson's simple credo has served it well. Yet J&J has a periodic, highly articulated Credo Challenge. Key ideas seldom if ever change, but minor alterations add up to substantial adaptation over time. Kodak's smooth-running machine served it well for decades—while no effective competition was on the horizon. In the late 1970s, battered by newer film and camera makers, it had to renew its commitment to old tenets grown flabby, and make adjustments for tomorrow as well.

The vision must act as a compass in a wild and stormy sea and, like a compass, it loses its value if it's not adjusted to take account of its surroundings. People Express, for example, confused its early success as a "phenomenon" with the requirements of long-term customer satisfaction. When the firm was no longer a "phenomenon"—as others matched People's prices and then their costs—the bases for sustained attractiveness to customers, such as an adequate reservation system, were found to be sadly lacking. The very arrogance which led to the firm's bold start blinded it to a changed world.

5. Effective visions are beacons and controls when all else is up for grabs. Only fast-moving, structurally trim, action-oriented firms will survive. They will be populated by self-managing teams and marked by the total absence of first-line supervisors and fewer middle managers. So who's in charge? As a Tandem Computer executive puts it: "The controls are not a lot of reviews or meetings or reports, but rather the control is understanding the basic concept and philosophy of the company." The immense effort involved to achieve "buy-in" by everyone and the discipline required to live the vision with unswerving consistency are what transform this single sentence from Tandem into practical reality.

To turn the vision into a beacon, leaders at all levels must model behavior consistent with the vision at all times (see L-3 and L-4 especially). Bennis and Nanus are once again instructive: "Trust is the lubrication that makes it possible for organizations to work. Trust implies accountability, predictability, reliability. . . . The truth is that we trust people who are predictable, whose positions are known and who keep at it."

Jim Kouzes and Barry Posner heard a slightly different, somewhat broader statement of this same idea from Stanford University president Donald Kennedy, who says:

> The leader's job is to energetically mirror back to the institution how it best thinks of itself. I just try to keep reminding students of certain things . . . about their opportunities, their obligations about public service and the like. And I try to pick what [the dean of students] calls "teachable moments." Like the recent honor code violations. This strikes me as a moment to use to try to get people to understand what we are doing. People say, "You've got a massive cheating incident, the honor code doesn't work." I say, "Wait a minute, what do you think the honor code is for?" "Well, the honor code is to prevent cheating." "Gee, are you sure about that? If the honor code is to prevent cheating, there are surely better ways. Give me a lot of police and I'll end it around here. And you think everyone will cheer about that?" "Well, no." And so you start talking about what the honor code is for. And about responsibility.

6. Effective visions are aimed at empowering our own people first, customers second. As mentioned, visions must be consistent with market realities—and to be sure, the vision of a Federal Express, for example, attracts customers. But the first task of the vision is to call forth the best from the company's own people.

7. Effective visions prepare for the future, but honor the past. A contemporary German philosopher has stated: "Whoever supplies memory, shapes concepts, and interprets the past will win the future." Oddly, visions are about the past as much as about the future. Ronald Reagan, whatever his faults, called upon us to create new opportunities for the future by recalling our entrepreneurial, high-spirited past. The most effective visions draw upon enduring themes to make us feel more confident about stepping out in new directions to deal with a brave new world. Thus, a call for renewed emphasis on quality may be rooted in the tradition of craftsmanship of the firm's honored founder. A call to shed slovenly ways and innovate rapidly can be tied to the organization's early and glorious entrepreneurial days, when it succeeded by catching then established firms napping. A call for greater work-force involvement and less bureaucracy may be related to the company's and the nation's pioneer days when self-reliance reigned.

The continuity is stressed for the very purpose of paving the way for change: "As you seek to change every procedure and job description to aid responsiveness, remember the bygone days when *we* whipped big competitors by being faster and fleeter of foot." That is: "You are safe in that you honor our most cherished traditions as you seek to break out of today's constraining bonds."

8. Effective visions are lived in details, not broad strokes. A vision is concise, encompassing, a picture of sustaining excellence in a major market. But, as in the example of Stanford president Donald Kennedy using honor code violations as a "teachable moment," or Phil Turner's planting a few flowers at Raychem, the vision lives mainly in the details of its execution. This is the theme of L-3 and L-4. Calendars, notes on memos, and who gets invited to meetings are the "stuff" of visions on a moment-to-moment basis. They form the basis for reliability and trust as nothing else can.

Getting a Vision

To describe the eight key traits of an effective vision is not to describe how to get one. You've just been promoted to your first supervisory job or to chairman of the board, or founded a small company, or become head of New York's Eastern Regional Boy Scout Commission—and you realize the unique opportunity such a moment presents to shape your part of the organization. You want to present a compelling vision. So what do you do? Do you go to the mountaintop? Can you hire a consultant to give you one? (If so, how much does it cost?) Do you form a team to hammer one out? Do you solicit "vision input" from the front line? From customers?

All of these and none is the confusing answer. Here are a few ideas about how you might proceed:

1. Look to your prior experiences. You don't come to the table cold. You've been part of the organization (or some organization) for years, starting with Sunday school or a Brownie troop. What have you learned? What really bugs you the most about such groups? What's been nifty? What's been memorable? What seems to have been going on at work when people were really soaring? When they were at each other's throats?

A vision and a set of values come first from these past experiences. Here's your chance—first-line supervisor or chairman. Fix what's been wrong in every place you've been before: Not enough communication? Set up daily, informal rap sessions. Too much politics? Stamp out incipient politics by pouncing on those who attempt to butter you up—begin this on hour one of day one in the new job. Too much bureaucracy gumming up the works? Cut out five reports right now, and stop all memo writing. Lousy attitudes toward customers? Insist that any customer call be put through to you instantly, even if you are in a closed-door meeting with your boss or your boss's boss.

2. Fiddle around, but make haste. Make lists. Doodle. Write ideas on index cards. Talk with others—from all walks of life—and seek their advice. Reflect on all such numerous inputs—but move fast. The organization is most malleable on day one; it becomes less so with each passing hour. The metaphor, from national politics, of a president's "honeymoon" is apt; term after term it's proved accurate. That is, you've got about a hundred days to get on with it.

Set down your ideas, loosely or precisely. Take some immediate steps of the sort described above. Begin in a fairly dramatic fashion, albeit using small events as your fodder.

3. Try some participation. After noodling a bit, you might schedule fifteen meetings in the next thirty days with disparate groups—first-line people from each function, first-line supervisors from each function, first-line supervisors from a mixture of all functions, suppliers, customers, wholesalers, community leaders. Chat about your ideas. Seek their list of top-ten irritants, their ten best experiences in the company or function; and keep on scratching away.

4. Clarify over time. Perhaps a two- or three-day session with those who report directly to you is in order. Again, swap stories, dreams, precise internal and market assessments, wallow in the data (mainly anecdotes). Ask them to come to the party with lots of data, gathered by doing their own smaller-scale version of what you've been up to. Maybe the result will be a formal declaration of values, maybe not. Maybe it will be two flip charts' worth of handwritten ideas that everybody sticks up in his or her own office. Perhaps it will eventually be turned over to a printer and circulated to everyone on wallet-sized cards and posters alike. But then again, maybe it never will.

5. Remember, listening is basic. Paradoxically, visions are seldom original. Bennis and Nanus observe: "The leader may have been the one who chose the image from those available at the moment, articulated it, gave it form and legitimacy, and focused attention on it, but the leader only rarely was the one who conceived of the vision in the first place. Therefore, the leader must be a superb listener, particularly to those advocating new or different images of the emerging reality. . . . Successful leaders, we have found, are *great askers,* and they do pay attention."

Living the Vision First

The printing of the cards and slogans is the least important part of all this. By then, if the process is to work, it's a done deal, bought into, already being lived. The most important part is wallowing in the ideas and then, as they become increasingly clear, living them.

1. "Live, then post." In fact, if you began with a formal declaration, you are probably doomed. You don't know what it really means, let alone anyone else. You are likely to be continually trapped by a thousand tiny inconsistencies as you wobble toward clarity. That is, some small personnel decision or some small customer decision requires you to do the thinking you should have done before turning on the printing press. Such inconsistencies, after a formal declaration, convict you of hypocrisy and set the process back, perhaps derailing it forever. Remember, honeymoons are not very long; you seldom get a second chance. So, in the end, act fast when it comes to living the emerging eternal values; go slow when it comes to sloganeering.

2. Preaching it: The Stump Speech. Part of living the vision is in the details that will mark prescriptions L-3 and L-4—paying attention via time spent and getting out to the front line, where true implementation occurs. But there is a "preaching" element too, which I call developing a "stump speech," a term whose origins are, of course, political. The boss with a vision—supervisor or chairman—is political, in the very best and purest sense of that word. He or she, running an accounting department or a police department, is constantly out "campaigning"—campaigning for the support, energy, and whole-hearted participation of everyone in the organization.

I suggest a three- to five-minute "stump speech," with many variations. Use it at least a couple of times a day, almost regardless of setting. No opportunity is, in fact, inappropriate for reiterating the vision, using a pertinent detail that happens to be at hand. If possible, end the speech with a couple of examples of people in the ranks living the vision in their daily affairs—not in a dramatic fashion, but in a small way that illustrates the way the vision affects daily operating routines; try harder still to have that example encompass a small risk (not small to him or her) that someone took to enact the vision.

3. **Another part of living the vision is pure emotion.** One crew member said of Dennis Conner, the winning skipper in the 1986 America's Cup race, "He gives confidence to the whole crew." Los Angeles Ram running back Eric Dickerson said of his coach, John Robinson, "He makes you think you're invincible." Football commentator John Madden reports a comment by a Chicago Bears lineman on the team's quarterback, Jim McMahon, "In the huddle, your eyes just glue into him. I'd jump out in front of a bus and block it for him."

This brings us back full circle to the paragraph from Bennis and Nanus's *Leaders* that prefaced this prescription. The vision lives in the intensity of the leader, an intensity that in itself draws in others. This is the final ingredient.

Caveat: Beware of Stasis

The very purpose of the vision is to provide the bedrock upon which constant evolutionary, opportunistic change can take place. However, it is all too easy for even the most compelling vision (initially) to become static, impeding the very change it is meant to induce.

IBM's main premise, to provide the best service of any firm in the world, has gotten a bit tattered in recent years. It often came to mean, as a by-product of IBM's success, the best service to the managers of central information systems. When information processing began to be radically decentralized, IBM's tough account managers often joined with the client MIS director in rearguard actions to fight change. The vision had come to be interpreted in a limited—and limiting—way.

The vision must provide stability—it inspires the confidence necessary to induce constant risk-taking in pursuit of its execution/perfection/expansion. But it must not become constrained by yesterday's success pattern, or by a narrow interpretation of market need. The vision must be infused with no-holds-barred customer/competitor listening (see C-7, I-4); it must be coupled with stringent innovation goals (see I-1, I-9); and it must be abetted by flat, nonbureaucratic, close-to-the-market organization (see P-8)—all of which in themselves encourage initiative-taking which will over time change the operational definition of the vision at the margin or, eventually, dramatically. It is true, nonetheless, that despite all these spurs, the vision still stands a good chance of getting rusty, and even enlightened exercises such as Johnson & Johnson's Credo Challenge are not likely to stave off some narrowing over time.

"Beware" is hardly practical advice, but it is a first step. The absence of bold new initiatives, in pursuit of objectives that may seem somewhat contrary to the vision, should be cause for alarm. Don't let the vision be shot through with holes, but be damned sure some of your best and brightest are shooting at it—with bazookas as well as snipers' rifles. Recall the advice of Richard Foster, from *Innovation: The Attacker's Advantage*—winners, he says, are those who have constantly attempted to make obsolete their most cherished skills and products. While always true to some degree (Foster reviews centuries of history), the implications of his analysis are stunning as we look to the breathtakingly more turbulent future.

FIRST STEPS

The process of developing a vision, though it represents the "highest level of abstraction," is quintessentially a trial-and-error process. Reread this prescription; take any angle on the process you can think of—but start today.

L-3

SUMMARY

In these uncertain times, when the need to accelerate the pace of change is paramount, we must:

▶ Lead, as never before, by personal example—in particular, calling attention to the new by means of our primary leadership tool: our calendars; that is, the way we spend our time.

▶ Reinforce attention to the new direction by the second most powerful day-to-day leadership tool—promotion decisions.

▶ Understand the power of our smallest actions: Amidst uncertainty, when people are grasping at straws in an effort to understand the topsy-turvy world about them, their symbolic significance is monumental.

People in organizations are all boss-watchers, especially when external conditions are ambiguous. For better or worse, what you spend your *time* on (not what you sermonize about) will become the organization's preoccupation. Likewise, the proactive use of symbols, such as the sorts of stories you tell and the people you invite to meetings, sends powerful signals to the organization about what's important. The final confirmation of "what really counts around here," when things are changing, is who gets promoted—risk-takers and harbingers of the new, or "the same old crowd."

Modify your calendar by 15 percent in the next six weeks to call attention *quantitatively* to your top priority. Eventually, spend no less than 50 percent of your time, visibly and directly, on your top priority. Dip down in the organization and intrude in *every* promotion decision; keep a *quantitative* scorecard on the degree to which promotions reflect the top strategic priority. Pause briefly and consider the symbolic significance of *every* act, given that others are especially thirsty today for clues about your organization's priorities.

L-3

Manage by Example

Example is leadership.
> Albert Schweitzer

My moment of truth came toward the end of my first ten months. It was one of those nights in the office. The clock was moving toward four in the morning, and I was still not through with the incredible mass of paper stacked before me. I was bone weary and soul weary, and I found myself muttering, "Either I can't manage this place, or it's unmanageable." I reached for my calendar and ran my eyes down each hour, half-hour, quarter-hour to see where my time had gone that day, the day before, the month before. . . . My discovery was this: I had become the victim of a vast, amorphous, unwitting, unconscious conspiracy to prevent me from doing anything whatever to change the university's status quo.
> Warren Bennis
> while president of the
> University of Cincinnati,
> as reported in *The Leadership Challenge*

I did the thirty-day [calendar] review and a general review of the last six months. I became shocked and then saddened as the truth [about how I was spending my time] slowly sank in.
> Hospitality industry executive
> Skunk Camp participant, 1985

I started by delivering on my number one promise—I have cleared my calendar so that about 60 percent of my time is available for listening, walking around, etc. I have even set aside all airplane travel time for "innovative dreaming," in fact that's where I am now. I previously used this time for "in-basket clearing."

> Senior civilian executive
> U.S. Army Corps of Engineers
> Skunk Camp participant, 1986

ATTENTION GETTER #1: A CHANGE IN YOUR CALENDAR

I have studied leadership and strategy implementation for over twenty years, reviewing hundreds of books, thousands of studies, and observing a host of effective and ineffective leaders. Literature on management style is best measured by the ton, as is true for topics such as conflict resolution, consensus-building, "forging a team at the top," choosing an optimal structure, and goal-setting techniques. More recently "how to create the 'right' culture" seems almost to have become a boardroom obsession.

To be sure, many sound ideas have surfaced concerning each of these important topics. Yet I am willing to stick my neck out and state unequivocally that all of them, taken together, pale by comparison to the power of this one: changing your calendar.

Changing your calendar is not sufficient to bring about desired organizational change. But it is necessary. It is quite simply impossible to conceive of a change in any direction, minor or major, that is not preceded by—and then sustained by—major changes, noticeable to all, in the way you spend your time.

At one level, this prescription seems almost tautological. As managers, we don't do the business of the enterprise anymore—drive the municipal bus, patrol the beat, sell the shoes or computer. Therefore, *we are our calendar,* the signals we send about what's important and what isn't. That seems to be what Warren Bennis found out in the course of trying to institute changes at the University of Cincinnati.

At another level, the power of the calendar exists because virtually everyone is a boss-watcher. In ways both direct and convoluted, the agenda of others soon come to mirror that of the boss. And this is true—to the point of being a truism—on the shop floor, in the elementary school, on the garbage route, and in the executive suite.

Why, then, since the powers of example (that is, the calendar) are both ageless and indisputable, do we stress them here? Quite simply because their creative use is more essential today than ever before.

All organizations must now be jerked rapidly in new directions. Moreover, the requisite change in direction is taking place against a backdrop of ever more confusing messages from the environment—cut costs but achieve better quality; decentralize and recentralize. Even if conventional planning tools were once effective as direction setters (a questionable assertion), they are much too slow—and not blunt enough—for today's needs.

Telecommunications engineers have a precise term for all this: "signal-to-noise ratio." When you are transmitting through the air, or via a transatlantic cable, there is lots of interference or "noise," such as random electromagnetic signals. Your transmitted signal must be strong enough (i.e., of great enough amplitude, distinct from all others) to override the noise—in other words, the signal-to-noise ratio must be high enough—so that the signal arrives clear and unequivocal at the receiving location.

Turbulence in the environment is now causing unprecedented noise. If the organization is to be led clearly to implement its vision (see L-2), our "signal amplitude" had better be great indeed. Only when the front line receives crystal-clear signals that leaders, at all levels, are foursquare behind them will they be comfortable enough to take the risks necessary to make the far-reaching changes required. And the only for-certain confirmation of the commitment of leaders is the way they spend their time. In summary, to signal the need for dramatic change, the calendar must be altered dramatically—unmistakably enough and visibly enough to overwhelm the growing noise level.

So it boils down to this: Want to call attention to your new quality program, or your new people participation program, or your new innovation program? There's only one way that counts with the organization's members: Spend time on it—lots of it.

A Possible Scenario: Making Your Calendar Send Your Message

Is quality your necessary and consuming passion?

▶ Start *every* meeting—even if the topic is a new computer for the Düsseldorf office—with a quality review.

▶ Schedule a full-dress quality review once a month with those who report directly to you and an informal report on quality at the start of each week's routine staff meeting.

▶ Go outside the firm to a number of seminars on the topic—even if you're chairman of a $20 billion company—and let everybody know you went, and took notes.

▶ Meet once or twice a week with longtime customers or suppliers, on their turf, to discuss quality; then circulate detailed notes on the meeting.

▶ Make sure your desk is stacked high with books on quality—for all to see.

▶ Regularly call people at all levels of the organization to ask questions about quality.

▶ Circulate dozens of articles on the topic—to hundreds of people, with a simple note appended, such as "Can we make use of this? Let me know."

▶ Have a three-day "off-site session" with front-line quality managers from each facility.

▶ Start routinely poking around—in person—in the bowels of the organization, even in functions outside your own; chat up everyone who's willing to discuss the topic with you; mainly ask questions at first.

▶ Get anyone and everyone to send you reports on some aspect of quality in their operation.

And then, and here's the rub, add up all this activity to determine, exactly and quantitatively, just how much gross calendar time you are spending on the matter. You simply must have at least one daily activity that is clearly—i.e., visibly (stands out against the background "noise")—devoted to it. You should set a bold, quantitative weekly and monthly target as well, and then track your progress, and publicize your schedule (and schedule changes) for everyone to see.

The Message Is in the *Amount* of Time Spent

Though the issue might well be quality, you need not spend so-called "quality time" on it. That is, you don't need to get everything right at first; you simply need to get quality demonstrably on your agenda. No doubt you will be at sea in the beginning; implementing a new strategic thrust is not easy: "Just what the hell *is* quality anyway?" You won't know whom to meet with, whom to call, what to ask or talk about, whom to believe. The odd thing is that it really doesn't matter. What matters is that everyone who works for and with you observes you embracing the topic with both arms—and your calendar. What they need to observe is your obvious, visible and dramatic, determination to batter down all barriers to understanding, and then implementation.

Your energy and intensity—as shown chiefly by your time spent—will signal everyone who comes in contact with you, directly and indirectly, that you are in dead earnest, which is really the point. In surprisingly short order, even if the organization is a big one, their calendars will mysteriously start to match yours. The firm will slowly begin to come to life around the issue. Many efforts will be misdirected or useless. A few may even be harmful. No matter. Slowly the lumbering beast called the unit or organization (whether with 17 or 17,000 occupants, whether public sector or private) will shift its sights. And if you sustain your effort—as proved by that damnable calendar—attention to, and experimentation with, the new strategic thrust will be sustained as well. Over time, you and the obviously sensible people on your payroll will inexorably begin to do more things "right."

Creative Uses of the Calendar: (1) Turning Any Occasion into a Soapbox Opportunity and (2) Self-Cooptation

Is it as easy as just changing your calendar? Yes. And no. It is that easy—after the fact. But it's no easier than losing weight and then keeping it off. After all, your calendar, as it is now, is not the calendar of an idiot. It was "chosen" by you. Perhaps you feel it was foisted on you by superiors, or just grew topsy-turvy, like Bennis's, out of maliciousness or mindlessness. And it is true, you are in part a victim—but never, I contend, decisively so. You may well be forced to go to meeting X and declaim on topic Y. But even in that extreme case, you can always—yes, always—turn the presentation into a soapbox opportunity to preach the quality (or service, or participation, or innovation) gospel: "Let me begin my discussion of European computer selection with a review of its impact on quality as perceived by our customers." It would be darned tough to stop you from doing that!

Another example: Former Secretary of Health, Education, and Welfare John Gardner had a number of pet projects, but the "system" stymied him. He broke somewhat free when he started to schedule seemingly insignificant speeches, a year in advance, on one of those pet topics. Suppose he had a keen interest in cancer research. In February of one year, he might schedule a speech to an obscure cancer research consortium for March of the following year. Once on the master calendar, the event becomes "real" to the bureaucracy. About six to eight weeks before the speech, the system starts to cough up papers and speech drafts on the subject, and meetings automatically get scheduled to discuss the forthcoming event; in other words, Gardner would grab hold of the "mindless system," and use this subtle lever to make it attend to his desires.

In less august surroundings, we all have similar opportunities. Each year, for instance, I deliberately schedule about ten or fifteen speeches to groups that will force me to think about new topics I'm interested in. As the day approaches, I'm often mad as the dickens at myself for having scheduled such a "disruption." But I know I've got to show up, so I start working on the new topic; the result is that a small number of what I call "self-cooptation" events often set the tone for the rest of my work.

Measure (Quantify) Your Progress

Specifically, I propose that you begin by shifting at least 15 percent of your time toward your top priority in the next six weeks, and follow up with another 15 percent (for a total of 30 percent) in the six weeks after that. Indeed, it is certain that the first figure can be 25 percent, or even higher. I have seen any number of superb leaders almost totally clear the decks to get on with a new agenda. Remember the busy executive from the U.S. Army Corps of Engineers who quickly shifted 60 percent of his normal working time, and then his airplane time too.

In the face of most organizations' need for revolutionary change, this shift in the use of your time must soon add up to even more than I've suggested so far—to fully 50 percent of your time devoted to the new, revolutionary strategic priority. Nothing less will shake most organizations from their lethargy fast enough to restore competitiveness.

Bob Townsend, author of *Up the Organization* and *Further Up the Organization,* offers even more dramatic counsel, based upon the turnaround he engineered at Avis. He urges you to devote 100 percent of your time to the critical issue. For instance, at one point Townsend determined that Avis's financial reporting was a mess. He was unable to measure anything accurately, or even know how he stood at the end of the day. He relieved the controller, and then, over the furious objections of the board of directors, formally appointed himself full-time controller. He moved out of the president's office and into the controller's office for several months, until the problem was in hand and a replacement had been selected. As he says, the extreme demonstration of concern sent "a darned clear message." Talk about a high "signal-to-noise ratio"!

There Can Be No Surrogates

There is in fact no alternative to you acting as standard bearer for a dramatic strategic shift. You may, if you are chief executive, appoint a "representative"—a "quality czar," for example. But beware. He or she can be no more than your point person, and never a true surrogate. There can be no substitutes when it comes to the way the members of the organization assess your priorities and the seriousness of your intent. You are either "on" the topic—or you are not.

ATTENTION GETTER #2: PROMOTING CONVERTS TO THE NEW PROGRAM

For us boss watchers (all of us, that is) the way our bosses spend their time, not what they say, is the top attention director. Ultimate confirmation of the seriousness of the intent signaled by a change in the calendar is who gets promoted—attention getter #2.

For example: The firm must shift from an inward-looking to an outward-looking focus. The process started a year ago. The calendar of the unit chief, or the top executives, says, "This is for real." Now a general management job pops open in the second most important unit in the company. Who gets it?

The three most obvious candidates are all longtime toilers in the trenches, several times promoted, talented beyond doubt. But all three have been lukewarm about the new thrust. Their backgrounds are all oriented heavily toward finance (rather than sales or marketing).

Does one of the three get the job, or does the person at the top dip down and anoint a somewhat younger line marketer who has been out front, at no small personal risk, on the new strategy? Everyone in the firm, from junior distribution supervisor to the crusty old director of MIS and the corporate sales VP, is focused on this bellwether appointment. It is the acid test.

The picture need not be so stark. It need not be "marketers" versus "finance persons." Suppose one of the three finance people, by chance the most junior, had taken to the new program like a duck takes to water, long before even the chief had demonstrated he would stay the course. Or suppose it's an old tiger, the oldest of the three, with only eighteen months to go to retirement—but he got out in front while the relative youngsters lay back, testing the chief's mettle.

The latter two examples are taken from personal observation. A big firm undertook a shift to a quality-before-cost-and-volume orientation. The "old boys" were certain that when push came to shove the chairman would return to penny-pinching, "cost is what really counts around here" ways. Then, two years into the program, the chairman confounded the reluctant dragons by appointing someone fifteen years their junior as chief operating officer—and heir apparent. He came from a relatively small division—but he had been the most energetic by far in implementing the quality thrust. In the second case, a 63-year-old was named vice-chairman of a big firm for precisely the same reason. He, at age 61, had far surpassed those fifteen years his junior in his zeal for a new, customer-oriented strategy in an operation that had been primarily numbers-oriented—and he had previously been a card-carrying member of the inward-looking finance fraternity.

In both instances, those on the scene, from top to bottom, describe the surprising promotion as decisive proof that the new strategy was no flash in the pan.

I am not suggesting that you mindlessly scour the woods for some boot-licking youngster who has taken to the new approach for the purpose of self-aggrandizement. But zeal for the new will always vary among candidates for a key job. Make sure that you pick a convert; at least don't pick someone, regardless of past loyalty, whom everyone judges to have been dragging his or her heels.

Go one step further. Though I am an avowed fan of decentralized organizations and delegating authority, I strongly urge that any boss get personally involved in every promotion in his organization, even those three or four layers down. There aren't all that many promotions per year in firms of ordinary size, particularly in a division or in an operations center. Each one is a precious item, a signal of matchless amplitude. Autonomy be damned—you can't let those gems slip through your fingers. Scream about "quality over volume" as a division general manager, but then permit three of the next six first-line supervisor promotions to go to "ship the product" fanatics, and you can effectively kiss your strategically crucial program goodbye. Down on the line, where it counts, you are a dead duck—and a hypocrite.

And, as usual, quantify. Keep a running scorecard on promotions. What's your overall batting average? E.g.: "Six first-line promotions— four filled with converts or zealots; none filled with heel draggers."

MANAGING (LEADING) AS SYMBOLIC ACTION

Len Bias was not just another drug-overdose victim. Rock Hudson was not just another AIDS victim. The arrival of the planet's five-billionth human citizen is not just another birth.

On the other hand, we don't even know who that five-billionth person was, or, in fact, whether he or she was born in 1986 or 1987. And the deaths of Bias and Hudson rate only routine entries in the dusty record books of Maryland's Prince Georges County and Los Angeles County. Nonetheless, each of these occasions has a significance far beyond the simple statistical one, affecting the broader and graver issues of drug abuse, AIDS, and overpopulation.

Storytelling

People, including managers, do not live by pie charts alone—or by bar graphs or three-inch statistical appendices to 300-page reports. People live, reason, and are moved by symbols and stories.

We read ceaselessly about President Reagan's talent as a storyteller. Even his most stalwart fans regularly blush at the gap between statistical reality and his chosen story. But no one, friend or foe, snickers at the skill and power with which he has created compelling images that have moved the nation and defined controversial policies.

Researchers, somewhat ruefully to be sure, attest to the power of stories. One study involving MBAs—those persons more likely than almost any others to profess devotion to pie charts—is illuminating. Stanford researcher Joanne Martin attempted to convince a number of Stanford MBA students of the sincerity of a firm's policy of avoiding layoffs. Dividing them into separate groups, she presented one group with an illustrative story; another group received a wealth of statistical evidence indicating the firm had far less involuntary turnover than normal for the industry; a third group got both story and stats; a fourth group was given an executive's statement about the firm's policy. The most convinced group? The "story only" one—even more than the group that got both the story and the statistics.

Managing at any time, but more than ever today, is a symbolic activity. It involves energizing people, often large numbers of people, to do new things they previously had not thought important. Building a compelling case—to really deliver a quality product, to double investment in research and development, to step out and take risks each day (e.g., make suggestions about cost-cutting when you are already afraid of losing your job)—is an emotional process at least as much as it is a rational one.

It requires us, as managers, to persuade people quickly to share our sense of urgency about new priorities (see L-10); to develop a personal, soul-deep animus toward things as they are; to get up the nerve and energy to take on the forces of inertia that work against any significant program for change. The best leaders, especially in chaotic conditions (effective generals, leaders of revolutions), almost without exception and at every level, are master users of stories and symbols.

Furthermore, they are not ashamed of it. Martin Luther King talked openly about creating "a sense of drama" at crucial moments. Douglas

MacArthur's first actions upon arriving in Japan at the end of W~
War II (such as landing unarmed) were masterpieces of the use of
symbols. So was the carefully orchestrated arrival in France following
the Allied landings on D-Day of the officially powerless Brigadier General Charles de Gaulle: within days he established dominance amidst
total chaos through the skillful use of symbols representing the glory of
France. And to jolt a quality program into gear, numerous managers I
know have saved up defective products for a week and piled them on the
factory floor in plain view of all involved; or even carried them by the
bucketful into a board-of-directors meeting.

I am not suggesting that you quit collecting statistics. Numbers are
important. Moreover, you should make sure that your "story of the
week" bears a strong relation to overall developments, that it is a valid
outcropping of an emerging trend.

Fortunately, or unfortunately, the average day or week serves up a set
of good-news and bad-news stories that are plausible and that conform
to systematically collected data. Resolve to collect three good-news and
two bad-news stories concerning your top strategic priority within the
next week. Talk about them, write about them. Ask others to collect—
and use—good-news/bad-news stories in a similar fashion.

Everything Is Symbolic: Some Questions to Ask Yourself

A hundred forms of symbolic action add up to the clearest of pictures
of the firm's (and leader's) true, rather than espoused, concerns:

1. What questions are asked first? You talk quality, but you always
have the volume/cost report come first. Priorities are clear to one and
all.

2. Where do you visit? You say partnerships with suppliers are the
key to quality. Yet your calendar shows that of your sixty-five formal
visits outside the firm this year (to attend outside board meetings, for
example), only one has been to a supplier; moreover, three visits to
suppliers were canceled at the last moment because of "pressing priorities."

3. Is there a pattern to the notes you pen on memos? Many reply to
memos by penning notes in the margins. Are yours always merely topi-
cal, or do they have an overall theme? For instance, no matter what the

topic, do you use your notes as reminders about innovation opportunities (if that's your theme)?

4. What does the "look" of the business reveal? You talk austerity and openness, yet hide behind your secretary and continue to allow officers to fly first-class "because of their burdensome schedules." What's on the menu in the executive dining room or corporate cafeteria? What's on the menu in the plant cafeteria?

The Manager as Pattern, Like It or Not

In the end, the manager's minute-to-minute actions provide a living model of his or her strategic vision. "Modeling," the behavioral scientists tell us with rare accord, is the chief way people learn. This is true in general, but now more than ever, when the search for themes by people beset with uncertainty and fear is at an unprecedented level.

Studies show that each day, like it or not, is marked by thousands of symbolic acts. Your personal note on a memo will be copied by hundreds and deciphered by thousands before nightfall. Your seemingly minor personnel decision will be debated in every outpost of the company, within minutes of your "secretly" making it. Your candid conversation with a salesperson during a customer call you made together flashes through the grapevine. Your inadvertent decision to park in a different slot this morning is causing reverberations of 5.9 on the Richter scale: "What's it mean?" You are spewing forth signals by the thousand, to thousands, each day. This is a plain fact. Whether or not you approach this inevitable set of signals opportunistically is up to you. But never doubt that you will send them—or that others will make a pattern from them, no matter what you do. What this pattern will suggest to those others, however, can be influenced dramatically. Grab hold of these opportunities. You *are* a rich, daily pattern to others. You *must* manage it in today's environment, when the conventional systems (such as policy proclamations and strategic planning) are overwhelmed by the pace of change and proving to be wholly inadequate. Only proactive management of the torrent of signaling activities can create the pace of implementation necessary for business survival.

There are those who object that a manager such as I describe is paying too much attention to style, not enough to substance. This is nonsense. Because the fact is, there is no perceived substance without symbols.

Trust and credibility come through everyone's observation of the manager's symbolic integrity, not his or her "policy documents."

FIRST STEPS

1. Change that calendar—this afternoon. Change just one hour this week (surely you can do that). Change six days in the next six weeks to unmistakably reflect your top strategic priority.
2. Watch your symbols! Perhaps with the help of a friend, assess the degree to which your minute-to-minute behaviors closely reflect (or contradict) your strategic themes. Make this assessment daily, or at least weekly—starting right now.
3. Can you, without hesitation, point to one symbolic activity *each day* which not only showed you foursquare in support of your top priority, but also showed you making a tough choice that demonstrably placed yesteryear's top priority in second place?
4. Stop, right now, a mindless decision about a promotion, about to go to someone everyone assumes is the "best person for the job." Make sure the next promotion decision sends an unequivocal message throughout the unit or firm as a whole about your commitment to your top priority.

L-4

SUMMARY

To deal with a world turned upside down for everyone, a world in which clear guidance is hard to come by, and where rules and paper no longer reign supreme, we must:

► Practice visible management.

► Act to reduce information distortion.

► Get rid of our offices, or take several steps in that direction.

Visible management is a requisite today. All are confronted with change. Change is the only source of opportunity—and yet change has been anathema, especially to American organizations designed for stability and mass production of goods and services. To enable all organization members to get comfortable with change and constant risk-taking, management must be ever present, training, coaching, cajoling—and caring and comforting. A prime side-benefit of such a direct presence is a radical reduction in information distortion, which is now more dangerous than ever (delusion has a higher-than-ever price tag).

You are out of tune with the times if you are in the office more than one-third of the time.

L-4

Practice Visible Management

The most effective leaders, from Mohandas Gandhi to Sam Walton of Wal-Mart, have always led from the front line, where the action is. Today, any leader, at any level, who hopes for even limited success must likewise lead from the trenches. The changes are first discovered out where the customer is, where the small new competitor is, and where the disgruntled dealer is, not in the stillness of the meeting room on an overhead transparency.

When a trend, in today's world, is well enough known to put on paper, it's too late; the market is lost.

Furthermore, today's requisite flexibility will, as the people prescriptions argued, only come when every person is, and feels, empowered to take action at the front line. We, as leaders, will only know if they are so empowered (or still encumbered by silly, action-stifling rules) by being there.

So you be the judge:

Case One:

Dear Mr. Peters,

I have just completed perhaps the most educational month of my business career (including four years of business school).

I am responsible for the parts department of a large Caterpillar dealership. As part of a renewed emphasis on customer service, I spent a week working in the warehouse of one of our largest customers. What an eye opener! Being on the receiving end of one of our

Caterpillar parts shipments rather than the shipping end was informative, to say the least. I learned firsthand why this customer was complaining about certain aspects of our parts service, because *I* was the one who had to open the boxes, sort through the parts, and process the paperwork. Now I believe this customer, and will act on his concerns, where before, I would tend to shrug off his complaints as "just part of doing business." Actually working *with* customers is the key to finding out what they *really* think of our company.

To follow that up, I have spent two days a week working as a warehouseman on our day and night shifts. Again, my eyes were opened. Not only did I find out how our warehouse really operated, I found out that our warehouse people are genuine *heroes!* They have a hard, monotonous job, but they show up day after day, year after year, with smiles on their faces and willing to do their best. I can't tell you how impressed I was with their professionalism, dedication, and willingness to work with me. Before, I viewed them as employees on the low end of the pay scale. Now I view them as friends, worthy of all the respect and support our company can provide.

[These activities have] opened my eyes to the obvious—that my job is to learn to think as our customers think, and to provide the kind of environment that will let the people I work with think, innovate, make mistakes, have fun, and do their very best.

Sincerely,
General Parts Manager
(February 1987)

Case Two:

Although I will almost always be in my office not later than 7:30 in the morning, I do not want to see anyone until approximately eight o'clock, nor do I want people hanging around in the outer office. Again, because of the time demands on everyone, if you want to see me about a particular subject, call [my secretary] and leave a message as to the subject matter. It is my intention to see you as quickly as possible to resolve the problem or discuss the matter at hand. But I want no one just drifting around the office to visit or address a particular problem.

> Excerpt from a memo to all
> vice-presidents by a new chief
> executive officer of a
> multibillion-dollar service company

Between the two, who would you bet on?

Getting out and about is a dandy idea. But it is more than that. It is an attitude toward managing and leading. It is a way of life. It is virtually a theory of organization unto itself. That is, it deals with the fundamental way in which communication, including executive communication, takes place in and among collectivities called organizations—communication that deals with gathering the information necessary for decision-making, with making a vision concrete, with engendering commitment and risk-taking, with caring about people beset with an unprecedented disruption of normal routines.

Getting away with not getting out may have been possible yesterday. It is not today.

THE PERILS OF INFORMATION DISTORTION

I was appalled by a feature in the January 12, 1987, issue of the Detroit *News* titled "The Hazards of Business Fads." In it the president of the American Management Association, Tom Horton, took on "managing by wandering around" with a vengeance. Or, the paper reports, "by stumbling around, as Horton says. It's his nomination for most ridiculous recent management fad." The article quotes Horton's argument: " 'The theory is that the captain needs to get away from the bridge and roam the ship. But somebody's got to be steering the ship.' Good managers, he points out, don't wander aimlessly; their visits are planned and purposeful."

This is utter nonsense, for several reasons:

▶ Management enemy number one, perhaps at all times but today for certain, is information distortion, especially when the information comes professionally packaged, accompanied by computer-generated sixteen-color graphics. As a longtime consultant, I know almost every trick of the trade when it comes to distorting information behind crisp logic and clever schematics.

The world today is uniquely "messy," with a host of new variables surfacing at lightning speed. The manager had better be as "messy" as the world; that is, she or he must have an undistorted feel for the uncertainties out there on the line. Information-processing scientists even have a term to describe this need: requisite variety. That is, the variety of your sources must match the complexity of the real problem, or you will be led to erroneous conclusions.

In the office, whether you are chief of a big organization or a small one, you are shielded from the truth by a bewildering array of devices, prudent or malicious, all designed to "save" you from trivia and complexity so that your mind can be clear as you confront the "big picture" decisions. Instead, your mind is all too likely to be empty of all but prepackaged data, leading you to make uninformed decisions.

▶ The action and the information necessary for implementation are on the front line, as the parts manager from Caterpillar quoted above learned so swiftly. The team plugging away in the distribution center on the 11 P.M. to 7 A.M. "graveyard" shift knows more about the company's problems with quality and service and about new competitors than the bosses do, all nine levels of them, from center supervisor to CEO. But to get at that information, and to "feel" what is keeping people from acting on it, you must visit and chat with these knowledgeable people where and when the action is—at 3 A.M., on the loading dock.

▶ Ambling must be semi-aimless to ensure numerous sources and perspectives. Psychologists used to preach to guilty dads: "It doesn't matter how much time you spend with your kids, it's the quality of the time that counts." Common sense, as well as subsequent studies, says that's bunk. Most good experiences with kids (or anybody else) are inadvertent, a sideshow to the planned purpose of an activity. As philosopher Vilfredo Pareto put it: "Logic is useful for proof, but almost never for making discoveries." That meticulously planned state visit by the chief of the 16- or 16,000-person unit or firm will be fashioned by subordinates to ensure that the views they've espoused to the boss before won't be distorted by, say, an irate customer.

▶ The distortion of information is everyone's problem. It is worse in the White House than in the corner store. But not by as much as you'd think. Distortion in the ten-person outfit can be mind-boggling. Oddly enough, if you're a "good guy" or "good gal," it doesn't help either. That is, if you're well liked, easy to get along with, committed to service, you're still in trouble—because the gems whom you've hired don't want to disappoint you. They therefore unintentionally shade the truth. Three or four sequential, little shadings rout veracity. So no matter what your style, Simon Legree in pinstripes and vest or warm and tender in shirt sleeves, you've got a problem.

But let's return to Horton's bridge. I think he means "someone's got to be in charge." I half agree. Recall prescription L-2; the leader in turbulent times must articulate a vision that others (1) sign up for and (2) are empowered by. But stamping in the vision, the essence of the new leadership, is not best done from the bridge. It is best done on the front line, where exemplars who are taking "little" risks to implement the new way can be found and singled out for all to see. Moreover, it's out there where the leader finds answers to the more fundamental question: Does the vision make sense in its implementation?

Furthermore, the main reasons a captain gets stuck on the bridge add up to a frightening Catch-22: (1) his vision is muddy, (2) he doesn't dramatize examples of effective initiative-taking, (3) he fails to break down functional barriers to action-taking, and (4) he doesn't effect true delegation. Thus, even minor decisions flow up to the top—and the captain gets ever more firmly stuck on the bridge (1) deciding about trivial affairs (2) based upon distorted information (3) provided by equally out-of-touch staffs who (4) stay at home themselves to await the boss's call for more overhead transparencies.

Visible Management: A Return to the Old School?

Horton's objection about aimlessness is one of two principal gripes about "managing by wandering around." The second is the polar opposite—some see it as a repudiation of the delegation of responsibility through management by objectives. They contend that visible management can be a return to close, over-the-shoulder, KITA (kick them in the ass) supervision. While I'd admit that such an interpretation is plausible, the point of being out and about, as I conceive it and observe it at its best, is the antithesis of KITA—it is to listen and facilitate, not give commands and inspect. That's easy to say, but recall that a major thrust of the people prescriptions dealt with a revolution in the first-line supervisor's role. Extensive training and coaching are required to shift an old-timer from out-and-about-as-KITA to out-and-about-as-facilitator-and-listener.

The Special Case of Offices

Consider the all-too-characteristic course of a mom-and-pop enterprise. Years ago, when the company was founded, the owner sat in a chair at a little desk out on the shop floor. Then he moved into a cubicle with a three-foot partition around it. Later the walls were extended up to the ceiling. Then a door was added. More and more frequently it was observed to be closed. Next came a secretary's desk outside his office. Then she was given a cubicle, then high walls, then a door. An executive row began to form.

And now you check in with a security guard and get a plastic card. Then, escorted, you ride an elevator to the middle floor. Next, you shift to another elevator for the trip to the top floor. Then you check in a second time at a reception desk on the top floor. You wait, and a new escort appears. You are taken down a long, imposing hall with a fourteen-foot-high ceiling, punctuated by dark oak doors on either side— almost all of them closed. At the end of the hall, you enter *his* door and are passed off to his personal secretary, who seats you in the anteroom. Eventually, his door opens. . . .

And this man, I invariably find, wonders why he has gotten out of touch. He doubtless believes he stays close to his company's product by using it. But each nut and bolt in his edition of the product has, of course, been inspected ten times before it gets to him.

This sort of detachment plagues most of us, not only chairmen of Fortune 500 companies. It starts with that initial shift from the plain desk to the cubicle, and occurs one step at a time, mostly invisible, through a 100-step (or, more likely, 1,000-step) process. I observe the problem in corner stores, in restaurants, in twenty-five-person shops, in schools, in hospitals, in municipal offices.

One executive reversed the process. During a Skunk Camp, Ted Santo, a senior manager from Dayton Power & Light, called home to order a drastic step: he had his office dismantled. Several months later he wrote:

My office is indeed gone. I wanted to wait a while before describing the effects to you so I could be sure of my feelings and to be sure my feelings wouldn't change over time. It has been seven months now and I still don't miss it. I love the "freedom" it has given me to move about or wander. I find myself meeting people more often and on their turf.

As luck would have it, I have been promoted recently and have gained the responsibility for three new departments. Fortunately, without a "large stuffy office," I have the freedom to jump around all four work areas. My former office would have been even more of a hindrance to me now then it was before.

The reaction to the demolition of my office was profound. People genuinely thought I had gone off the deep end. Also, people thought I had worked years for my beautiful office and that I had earned it. Besides, they were looking forward (especially my staff) to their big office someday. Since then, they have accepted it, although I still catch a fair amount of ribbing over it.

I do maintain a small work area in two departments: a round table with three chairs and a file cabinet in an open area by the entrance door. This allows me to correspond with my secretarial support, correspond on the phone and handle my mail efficiently. However, I am in full view of everyone, and, therefore, I am more accessible to all. I love it!

Consider the two cases carefully. I strongly urge you to turn back the clock as far as you can. If you don't go so far as to dismantle your office, at least consider:

▶ dispensing with all executive secretaries, and sharing a secretary with three or four other executives. ("The world" will adjust—the flow of paperwork to you will actually go down to match the newly diminished secretarial capacity; I guarantee it.)

▶ dispensing with the secretary's office, and the door to your office.

▶ ensuring that your office is no bigger or better appointed (if you're chief) than the office of the manager of the factory/operations center.

▶ starting to answer your own phone, all the time when you're in (when you're out—which, remember, should be at least two-thirds of the time—let the overall office secretary take messages).

GETTING ON WITH VISIBLE MANAGEMENT

Ten Steps:

1. Put a note card in your pocket and write on it: "Remember, I'm out here to listen." I don't carry such a card, but I used to. I've now got the habit down to the point where I can merely say to myself before each meeting, "Shut up. Shut up. You are here to listen." In two-person sessions, I sometimes informally keep track of the time I talk versus the time I spend listening.

2. Take notes, promise feedback—and deliver. Fix small things on the spot, or within twenty-four hours. Send thank-you notes to individuals or small groups, perhaps summarizing what you thought you heard, within twenty-four hours of the meeting. Listening is abetted by note-taking; note-taking also lets the other persons know you are serious. But the clearest indicator is that something happens—either on the spot or soon after you get back to the dreaded office: A directive is issued wiping out a silly regulation you found was irritating everyone; or a faulty toilet is fixed up in three hours; or new lights are installed in the parking lot within the week. (Recall the discussion about the role of symbols in L-3. Make sure that two or three "little" things like this happen fast.)

3. Cycle your actions through the chain of command. Do it, yes—that is, take direct action on some small stuff (or maybe large, if you're sure you understand the issue). But tell the chain of command what you are up to; let them take—and take credit for—the bulk of your follow-up actions.

4. Protect informants. As you demonstrate your commitment by listening and fixing things, you will hear more and more unvarnished truth, often drifting in through side channels. Use it with care, and make sure, by using your own network, that no informant gets burned by an irate supervisor. And if a supervisor ever comes down on someone who was candid with you about a problem, remove him or her from managerial responsibility on the spot.

5. Be patient. When you start to wander, even in a ten-person purchasing operation, you will be treated cautiously and as if you were a bit mad. You are sometimes challenging a decades-long routine of comfortable, if nonproductive, noncommunication. Only repetition, and lots of it, will lead to opening up. Only repeated instances of swift follow-up and action by you will make it worthwhile for them to talk freely. Only evidence that you will protect informants will turn the tide. It takes time to demonstrate all these things.

6. Listen, yes; but preach a little too. Don't preach as in sermonize, but use tiny, concrete opportunities—dealing with housekeeping, or excessive paperwork—to preach, via example, your guiding theme. Don't scream at too much paperwork. Laugh at it, instead: "Why, surely this is a mistake—a two-page form requiring three signatures to requisition a $17.95 spare part for this machine, so you can repair it before it breaks and stops the line?" Then declare that form dead as of that moment— and check next week to make damn sure that it did, in fact, die.

7. Give some, but not much, advance notice, and travel alone. The limited advance notice is not meant to "catch" people; it is meant to head off the truth-inhibiting trappings of state visits that accrue to the hinterlands forays of even middle managers, especially from corporate "headquarters." And whatever your "management level," don't bring a staffer/note-taker with you. Take your own damn notes!

8. Work some night shifts, take a basic training course. Follow the path of the parts manager from Caterpillar. Of course you might be treated "oddly." But if your commitment is sincere, you will be responded to genuinely. You cared enough to try, awkwardly or not, and that trying sets you apart. Human beings respect human acts, and even respect the awkwardness, because we've all been odd man out ourselves on numerous occasions.

9. Watch out for the subtle demands that you put on others which cut down on their practice of visible management. You may preach getting out and about for all, but then you call for some data "right away, I've got a meeting with the investment bankers in two hours." You have just sent a bulletin, printed in six-inch-high red letters: "Getting out is great, but be in the office whenever I capriciously beckon." Bye-bye, visible management.

10. Use rituals to help force yourself and your colleagues to get out and about. Ask numerous, pointed questions that can only be answered through firsthand knowledge: "You know, we have an awful lot of errors in shipping. How does the system work? What do the people on the night shift think about the new computer? Let's go through a couple of individual orders in detail. How does the paper actually get transmitted from Joe to Jane? Does it come to Joe's desk? Who brings it? How long does it take?" Keep homing in until subordinates have no choice but to go out and find out for themselves. But watch out for gimmicks doomed to fail. I used to believe in "meeting-free days" that would allow people to get out and about. It never works, given the perceived crises that always arise (and seem to demand a meeting).

The primary tool for inducing visible management, recalling L-3, is the behavior you model. You planned a visit to a distribution center on the other side of the country, your first in eighteen months. A minor crisis arises. Cancel or not? Don't cancel. Let your able team handle the crisis. Go on with the visit. That sends an unmistakable message.

What If Your Boss Is an Ogre?

My file has more than one like this: "My boss is in the office 90 percent of the time. He expects me to be at the ready when a question arises, as it often does, before or during one of his endless meetings. So how am I supposed to be out and about with my seven-person economics forecasting group and our 'customers' throughout the firm?"

It won't be easy, I'd be the first to agree. But here are three possible strategies:

▶ Chronicle your three worst failures in the last year. Odds are, they occurred because you were out of touch. Admit your guilt to the boss, and propose a plan, including visits to your customers, as a way to avoid repeating the sin this year.

▶ Build customers' demand for your services. When a line executive vice-president comes to your boss, a staff vice-president, and asks for you to visit the Rubber Products Division in Sacramento, he'll have little choice but to acquiesce.

▶ At least you can get your gang of seven out of their offices. They, after all, are probably mimicking your behavior. Don't let them. Force them out, and their real-world contacts will doubtless enhance your work product—and maybe induce your boss to see the merit of your getting out.

Pay special attention to the last of the three strategies. Our bosses may be able to force us to do dumb things, but they can't force us to transmit the dumb things on down to our people. Manage down, not up—always begin by cleaning up your act in those areas where you clearly do have discretion.

The Power of Very Visible Management:
The Revolution at Valley Medical

The Association of Western Hospitals gave one of its prized Innovation Awards (sponsored jointly with 3M) for 1986 to Valley Medical Center, in the Seattle area. The association's magazine reports on the turnaround:

[CEO Richard Roodman explains:] "Valley Medical Center developed a very poor reputation in the Seattle community for the quality of care delivered. In fact, it was known as 'Death Valley.' . . . The night I was hired there were 150 protesters outside a room where a public session was going on and they were carrying pickets and banners that said 'It's cheaper to die.' The press had a field day."

Indecision, lethargy, demoralization, insecurity, feelings of betrayal—these were some of the conditions that the VMC medical staff and employees were experiencing when [Roodman] came on board. "The culture was one in which there was a total absence of pride," he said. "The employees basically felt left out. No one had seen the administrator in five or six years . . . they had *heard* there was a guy there. . . ."

To further complicate the situation, the community "hated" VMC. . . . *Within approximately two weeks [of being hired], Roodman visited nearly 700 employees* [my emphasis]. He wrote each of them a letter and mailed it to his or her home, and met with medical staff and formal and informal leaders. . . . "What we decided to do was develop a skeleton of what we wanted to accomplish and then we asked for *their* ideas," he said. "We got close to 600 people— union representatives, department managers, members of the community—and we went around the area and met with the chambers of commerce, the elected officials, the mayors. We tried to work the formal and informal structure of the medical staff into the process. We went to the volunteers, the auxiliary . . . we tapped the chaplains . . . we did all this in about three months."

The result of these and other innovative approaches to the web of problems at VMC was a long-range plan that involved *people* in a variety of ways. The plan focused on five different areas: patient

521

and community responsiveness (quality issues), medical staff relations, human resources, marketing, and financial management.

The article concludes with an impressive array of statistics attesting to VMC's subsequent success. It all started with a powerful dose of getting out and about.

FIRST STEPS

1. Take ten small steps in the next ten days to get closer to raw information. Take one step before the sun sets today!
2. Starting today, have all customer calls put through to you directly. Is your theme quality? If so, put a red "quality" phone on your desk. Publish the phone number; anyone with a good-news or bad-news quality story is to call you directly (your secretary mustn't even have the number on his or her phone console).
3. The next time you pick up the phone to ask someone to stop by and see you, check yourself. Go visit the person instead—it is precisely by such (individually) "small" actions that you get your time in your office down to one-third—or less.

L-5

SUMMARY

While keeping in touch with the first winds of the new has always distinguished superior leaders, it is now a necessity. Today's effective leader must:

▶ Become a compulsive listener.

Today's successful leaders will work diligently to engage others in their cause. Oddly enough, the best way, by far, to engage others is by listening—seriously listening—to them. If talking and giving orders was the administrative model of the last fifty years, listening (to lots of people near the action), is the model of the 1980s and beyond.

Rip one front-line job apart: Listen to those who hold it. Learn their frustrations. Then act to clean up the mess and encourage them to do what must be done to react to today's volatile environment. Repeat with another job every 120 days.

L-5

Pay Attention! (More Listening)

Continuous improvement and flexibility—those are words that can't be repeated enough. What do they mean, practically? Turning over "control" and responsibility for action (test, modify, improve, repeat the cycle) to the front line, shifting the bulk of communication from "vertical" (up and down the hierarchy) to "horizontal" (people from multiple functions working together at the front line to do/create new, rapid responses to every customer need).

"Empowering" really boils down to "taking seriously." No one denies where the answers are: on the firing line. How do we get people to come forth and give the answers, to take risks by trying new things bound to fail at times? Near the top of the list is listening—that is, taking people seriously by the act of listening per se, and making it clear that you do take people seriously by what you do with what you hear.

The most effective leaders, political or corporate, empower others to act—and grow—in support of a course that both leaders and followers find worthy. The leader's job is at once to articulate the empowering vision (L-2), and to stay in touch with followers to ensure that she or he is in tune with the needs of the real world where the vision is implemented. Studies of effective leaders demonstrate that they do not induce narrow obedience to a precise objective among followers. To the contrary, powerful leaders make followers more powerful in pursuit of a commonly held dream, jointly defined. Furthermore, the listening leader inspires other leaders (managers at all levels) to be listeners too. The listening organization is in turn the one most likely to pick up quickly on changes in its environment.

Listening and Visible Management

Visible management (see L-4) involves listening, too, of course. What's the difference here? First, the prime "listening objective" put forth in L-4 was to reduce the distortion of information flowing to the boss, to enable him or her to make better decisions, for instance. Second, visible management is also about parading and symbolizing the vision—it has a "telling" component. Third, and most important, listening to the front line, in particular, is too important to be a subsidiary point. There are many who would say that unvarnished listening is the chief distinguisher between leadership success and failure, especially in times such as these when the empowerment of everyone is paramount. Oddly enough, to listen, per se, is the single best "tool" for empowering large numbers of others.

THE LISTENERS

There's a certain image of Roger Milliken that I keep in my mind's eye. It's from his firm's annual strategy meeting at Calloway Gardens, Georgia, in 1986. Four grueling, down-to-the-wee-hours-of-the-morning sessions, no recreation—this is a survival exercise, as Roger sees it. He's just come out of a meeting with his company presidents and a few handpicked outsiders, in this case from Dana, IBM, and Du Pont (and me). At the meeting, he probably asked sixty questions an hour. Each principal question was followed by five or ten more to get at the details, always the details—the real implementation story, not the gloss. In two-and-a-half hours he probably filled a quarter of a yellow legal pad with notes. (The next morning he'll turn the copious notes from this and other such sessions into his traditional meeting's-end speech—at which time he will announce a score of specific programs that will set the tone for the next twelve months.)

The participants of the meeting are exhausted from the intensity of this tireless 70-year-old, who's held the chief executive's job for over forty tumultuous years. We race back to our rooms for a fifteen-minute breather before the next grueling session commences—twenty-five action-packed small-group reports in ninety minutes. I happen to look up. There is Roger, pacing the corridor in front of his room, dictating at a staccato pace—yet more notes.

Listen. I don't know when it first occurred to me that I was observing a pattern. At our first Skunk Camp I watched Frank Perdue, the chicken king, and grocer *sans pareil* Stew Leonard engage in an Olympian struggle: Who would take the most notes?

Leonard won hands down, but even runner-up Perdue topped the rest of us put together, I'd bet. Both have been at their jobs, engaged, for decades. What was the subject? Milliken's president, Tom Malone, was describing the firm's quality program. Perdue, Mr. Quality to me already, rudely interrupted him dozens of times. He wanted clarification. Malone, a scientist, is as clear a speaker as I've heard, but he wasn't concrete enough for Frank. The reason quickly became clear. The next morning Perdue was up at 3 a.m. discussing with his people on the East Coast the implementation of the stuff he'd heard the day before. A major new executive compensation plan focused on quality and a landmark corporate training center were among the big ideas Perdue took from the seminar—and implemented in short order.

Stew Leonard didn't wait until 3 A.M. He was on the phone at lunch break. "Are you sure you know what this means?" I asked. "It makes sense, doesn't it?" was Stew's reply. Well, yes, I agreed. "So why wait?" Leonard snapped back. I had no rebuttal to that one.

Another time, I gave a talk to a civic group in Baltimore. Mayor Don Schaefer attended. My speech lasted two and a half hours. I've had Fortune 500 CEOs and governors attend my sessions. Most come for the opening remarks and to be seen, then scoot out as soon as the lights are dimmed, or fidget endlessly and talk to a stream of aides rushing in and out half bent over so as not to disturb others in the front row—and doing so all the more because of their pronounced scurrying. Well, Schaefer sat there for two and a half hours, and he took as many notes as I used to take in a semester-length engineering course. I next saw him at a purely social occasion, a 1987 Toast honoring his over fifteen years as Baltimore's mayor. Several speakers appeared at the event—and true to form, Schaefer took copious notes, on napkins, on the menu, on various scraps of paper. The results of Schaefer's scribbling were legend in Baltimore—

when the mayor took notes, action memos were sure to follow, including very pointed advice.

EFFECTIVE LISTENING IS ENGAGED LISTENING

There's an important emotional component to this. There's listening, and then there's engaged listening. The note-taking habit is a tip-off to the latter, but there's more to it than that. Engaged listening may be the principal mark of concern that one human being can evince for another, in any setting.

Once more, Roger Milliken provides a role model. Despite his decades in the business—to be sure, he's "seen it all"—he's like a kid when attending a session with dozens of team presentations from the front line. He'll turn to me with stunned amazement: "Can you believe that? Look at what they did." All news from the front is engaging to him, and especially if it comes from junior people who've caught fire and pushed Roger's vision further than anyone had a right to expect.

We've all been victims of the other side of the story. The vice-president goes on a field trip. He's been isolated for so many years that he really doesn't have, or feel he has, anything to talk to that truck driver about. After all, he's just reviewed twenty-three pages of "driver productivity indicators" with the boss of the driver's boss's boss. Why bother with the driver herself? Questions at best are brief and pro forma. The boss hasn't got the inclination, or nerve, to really dig in and ask about the forms and procedures. Trucks sure as heck don't interest him; he has a limousine. In fact, I'm not being fair. Down deep he's probably greatly embarrassed that he doesn't have anything to say or ask. He's scared to death of revealing his ignorance (especially to her), though to do so would doubt-less break the logjam.

Prescription C-9, among others, made it clear: The drivers and the dispatchers will become the heroes of the newly responsive organization—or else. Leaders are only as good as they are: *They* have the answers to *your* problems. You must get passionately interested in the view, and the impediments, as seen from the dispatch center and rolling along I-80 with your products jostling in the back of the vehicle.

Engaged Listening Is Strategic!

When I deal with this issue of "engaged listening" in seminars, I'm at a loss to give prescriptive advice. It's not possible to prescribe "engagement" in any direct way. I can, however, give you a tip that will help. This "stuff" is strategic. If you can muster the nerve (that is what it takes) to get engaged with that truck driver (or reservations center person), I guarantee you that a lengthy discussion of the "little things" that rule their lives in your organization will collectively reveal the *strategic* stumbling blocks to higher quality, more responsiveness, etc. Wonder why your $80 million investment in a new reservations (or distribution) computer system is not reaping the benefits promised by senior staff experts? The people in the reservations center know. If you can stomach the repeated "You should've asked us about———" (to which you reply, stunned, "They didn't ask you?" . . . "No"), you'll end up with an earful.

Listen because they are your heroes; but if that's not your view, listen because the answer to strategic conundrums lies within the "little" roadblocks to their executing the vision.

You Must Have the Guts to Ask Dumb Questions

I was blessed early in my consulting career at McKinsey & Company. My first boss, Allen Puckett, is one of the smartest people I know. He was smart enough and comfortable enough with himself to ask really elementary (some would say dumb) questions.

He'd be with an oil executive from Getty who was paying us a bundle to be there. The fellow would, unself-consciously, be talking a private language: rigs, wildcatters, landsmen, scouts, stepouts, tertiary recovery. Whenever Allen would hear a word he didn't understand, he'd ask. "What's tertiary recovery?" he'd say. "Stepouts?" The rest of us were scared stiff; we assumed that since we were being paid an exorbitant fee, we shouldn't ask dumb questions. But the result was we'd lose 90 percent of the strategic value of the interview because we were afraid to display our ignorance by asking, "What's a barrel of oil?"

Mostly, it's the "dumb," elementary questions, followed up by a dozen even more elementary questions, that yield the pay dirt. "Why in the heck does this form go *there* next?" and "Who has to sign it?" are probably the two most vital questions when it comes to discussing the reason a firm is slow to act on something. "Experts" are those who don't need to bother with elementary questions anymore—thus, they fail to "bother" with the true sources of bottlenecks, buried deep in the habitual routines of the firm, labeled "we've always done it that way."

BREAKING DOWN FUNCTIONAL BARRIERS BETWEEN WARRING FIEFDOMS: THE POWER OF PATIENT LISTENING

Numerous scholarly monographs and case studies offer complex theories about ingrained stereotypical assumptions and resistance to change, the principal bases for the incessant battles that take place between major functions in any organization. But the most effective tactic I have observed for overcoming these stereotypes is the manager at the local level taking the initiative and offering, in a nonthreatening way, to sit down and chat with everyone involved; that is, from all functions. It takes a while—perhaps a long time—for any noticeable change to occur. But with lots of patience, the results can be startling. Here are two typical cases:

▶ During a seminar a debate about why doctors and administrators seem unable to cooperate bogged down. A woman who had crafted a brilliant turnaround of a troubled hospital in the Boston area proclaimed, "Look, we just assume that doctors don't want to cooperate and we treat them based on that assumption. I simply declared that I was going to be in my office on the same morning each week, with coffee and Danish, and I'd be pleased if any of the medical staff would drop by and join me toward no particular end. It was slow to catch on, I'd be the first to admit it. There were a lot of lonely breakfasts, but now it's the most important and real 'staff meeting' of the week."

A young man chimed in with another, equally pointed anecdote. He said he held an informal staff meeting every two weeks with a group in his hospital. They went to a local pub for burgers and shop talk. For no particular reason, a year or so into the process, he invited some doctors to attend. They did. He was surprised, and asked one why he'd showed up. "Why not?" came the reply. "You always have this lunch, and no one ever invites us. Why do you think we wouldn't want to attend whenever we can?" Decades of stereotyping was the clear reason.

In fact, over the course of several seminars with several hundred senior hospital managers, we collected a list of dozens of ways of breaking down the barriers. They almost all had the same theme: Find a setting that is not charged with tension and invite voluntary participation at some form of "let's chat" get-togethers. My favorite was the administrator who reported this strategy: "Eat your way through the medical staff." During a year's time, she had scheduled about seventy-five lunches, never with more than one doctor at a time; the cumulative outcome was a revolution in relations between the medical staff and the rest of the hospital.

▶ Les Wexner, founder of The Limited, provides corroboration. After acquiring the Lerner store chain in 1986, he cut off a host of hard-nosed suppliers in order to deal with bloated and outdated inventory. Naturally, the suppliers responded with a passel of lawsuits. The Limited's Bob Grayson, who is now chief executive of Lerner, was tossed into the wolf pack of New York garment makers. Grayson, whom Wexner calls "a good Iowa farm kid" and a hell of a merchant, discovered the power of the kaffeeklatsch. He said he'd show up at Lerner's midtown Manhattan headquarters at the crack of dawn each morning to read *Women's Wear Daily* and be available to discuss the business with anyone who cared to come. It started small—very, very small—but it's still growing to this day. Suppliers, with whom relations started so poorly, are there in droves. The Limited's once very strained relations with suppliers, in the toughest environment imaginable, were substantially reversed.

After careful consideration, I conclude that this is an especially good tactic for breaking the stereotypical images that keep warring functions apart, in all organizations. Some manager must take the lead to disarm, sit down, listen, and accept repeated rebuffs. After all, she is often facing decades of bruised feelings. More important, she must wait it out until it becomes clear to her "adversaries," not that she is in any way a "good gal," but that she has the conviction to sit quietly, to start a dialogue, in order to salvage or enhance the increasingly threatened organization on whose payroll all "sides" depend for bread, butter, and recognition.

The only danger, and it is a grim one, is a badly damaged ego. Sitting

and sitting and waiting and waiting for the first coffee-and-Danish atten-
dee is the ultimate in passivity if being out in front leading the charge
is your style.

FIRST STEPS

1. Develop some personal listening ritual immediately. For instance, once every couple of weeks have an hour-long discussion with some first-line person. Think of yourself as a consultant
   called in on a nitty-gritty systems improvement assignment.
   Track down, in great detail, the nature of one or two critical tasks
   the person performs—precisely what's done, why it doesn't get
   done faster, and so on. (Use the outcome as you wish. This little
   listening device, repeated regularly, will unfailingly yield strategic
   insights.)
2. Start some form of "coffee and Danish" in the next 30 days.

L-6

SUMMARY

The flexible organization's leaders will put a disproportionate emphasis on the care and feeding of front-line people (see also C-8, C-9, P-1 through P-10). We must:

▶ Ensure that the front-line people—the implementers, the executors—know that they are the organization's heroes.

▶ Honor staff people to the extent that they support line people, not on the basis of the beauty or the elegance of their paper solutions to intractable problems.

▶ Promote managers (or promote to manager)—of line and staff functions alike—only those who create excitement among their people and colleagues from other functions; do not promote dull ducks, turf guardians, or those who do not take their greatest pleasure in the accomplishments of others, particularly their subordinates.

Success in today's environment will come when those on the front line are honored as heroes, and empowered to act—period. A prime leadership task is to ensure that honor goes to the line and those who support it most vigorously.

Review your actions at the end of each day. Have you made your "bias" for front-line operators—and for those on staffs who support them most vigorously—unmistakably clear?

L-6

Defer to the Front Line

Harvard Business Review: Everybody talks about ["Celtics Pride"].
It's at the heart of the Celtics' mystique. What is it?
Boston Celtics President Red Auerbach: It's the whole idea of caring.

> From an interview in the
> *Harvard Business Review,* March/April 1987

The "visible" half of execution—the marketing professionals—can
perform only as well as the "invisible" operations area allows it to.
Moreover, the quality of operations can also determine an institution's ability to innovate. . . . Executives can promote quality operations by giving that area an independent identity . . . [and] status
along with identity. "Class" divisions between lending officers and
backroom operators are crippling. Institutions that are serious
about the quality of their operations give employees compensation,
recognition and opportunities for advancement comparable to what
they offer marketing professionals. Citibank made John Reed [now
chairman] its youngest senior vice president [in 1969] largely due
to his role in operations. At Goldman Sachs, the partner in charge
of operations is widely regarded as the third most powerful person
in the firm, and the firm actually recruits promising business school
graduates for that function.

> Amar Bhide
> "Hustle as Strategy"
> a *Harvard Business Review* article
> on financial service institutions

I love 'em all. [The offensive linemen are] my guys. Anytime I felt bad about something, . . . I always went over to where they were warming up at practice. We would always warm up in groups— offensive linemen here, wide receivers there, running backs over here. . . . Somehow, just being with the offensive linemen always made me feel better. Maybe it was because they were such solid guys—solid as rocks.

> John Madden
> Football commentator
> former NFL coach

John Sculley has masterminded a remarkable turnaround at Apple Computer. The nature of it is nicely captured in one comment: "Implementers aren't considered bozos anymore." That is, those who write the manuals, answer the phones, sell the product, spend time with dealers, build the product, and are engaged in constant improvement of the product are the new Apple heroes. There's nothing wrong with talented designers, to be sure. They are essential. But there is something very wrong with any company that is over-dependent upon talented designers to pull its bacon out of the fire.

Bacon will increasingly be pulled out of the fire at 2 A.M. on the loading dock and at the reservation center. That is, it is pulled out of the fire by the people who work on the firing line. The role of everyone else—from president to junior accountant—is to enhance the ability of the front line to do its job.

ARE YOU LINE-ORIENTED?

Here are a few of the indicators that reveal the status of line personnel:

1. **Pay.** There are two key indicators here—entry-level pay and managerial pay. Prescription P-6 and others described the high front-line pay at Andersen Corporation, Lincoln Electric, Federal Express, Worthington, Nucor, Nordstrom, and others. Pay was often "off the scale" by others' standards—and so was productivity—several *hundred* percent above average.

From my days at McKinsey & Co., I remember one study especially well. Over a fifteen-year period, senior staff executives at an old-line manufacturing firm came to be paid almost 60 percent more than senior line executives (with comparable titles). That is, an accounting boss, sitting on the corporate staff at Level 4, made half again as much as a manufacturing boss at the same level. What was important in this firm? It was clear as day—how close your office was to the chairman's, and the brilliance and beauty of your paper solutions. The staff ran the line. The bright young men and women on the way up wanted to get on that staff, and not get stuck in isolated factories, distribution centers, sales branches, or any other kind of operational function.

Managerial pay is a dead giveaway. To underscore the line's role, line managers (operations, sales, distribution) should be paid somewhat more than their staff (personnel, accounting) counterparts—or at least not paid less.

2. What's hot? What do the best and the brightest head for? Operations or the corporate controller's staff? The line-oriented firm's objective must be enhancement of the line jobs. Over the long haul, this can be best accomplished via the promotion pattern ("three of the last five general manager promotions went to people who spent most of their careers in the line functions"). The problem can be addressed immediately by: (1) insisting that entry-level college graduates or MBA recruits start on the line (those that don't buy in aren't hired), and (2) offering better pay and a clearer career track to those who start on the line, and (3) lavishing symbolic attention on line people.

3. Where the action is. Do people in your firm blanch at the prospect of a three-year tour as deputy director of the Spanish affiliate? Or distribution manager for the southwestern United States? Making "boondocks" operating jobs the plums (a chance to demonstrate independent initiative), rather than those closest to the throne, is essential to achieving a line orientation.

4. Who calls the shots. Does the operating review consist of a parade of lonely line people called in one by one for a ritual grilling by three top executives and twenty staffers—with another twenty staffers, with "backup data" by the pound, sitting in the anteroom? Or is the line "overrepresented," with a few key staff people in attendance? This indicator—attendance at decision-making forums—is a first-rate tip-off of a firm's orientation.

5. What the calendar says. Recall L-3 (leading by example) and L-4 (visible management). Quite simply, does senior management spend more time with customers, suppliers, and line operators—especially front-line people—than huddled in session with staffers?

This means both the chairman and the president. In some firms, the chairman is "Mr. Outside"—dealing with analysts, the board, etc.—and the president is "Mr. Operations." This is the GM pattern, for instance. It doesn't cut the mustard. The top gun must demonstrate commitment to the line—by time spent. This is especially so in this era of uncertainty, when the firm's top priority is often retooling line skills and reestablishing contact with long-neglected customers and distributors.

6. Who gets the recognition. Does the boss send notes congratulating young staffers on superb presentations, but fail to discover and praise similar accomplishments in the field—25, 250, or 2,500 miles away? The lion's share of recognition should go to line people; measure this *quantitatively*—track yourself by the week.

7. The language you use. Recall John Sculley's remark. Hang out at most corporate headquarters and you soon come to believe that in most firms everyone on the line is considered a "bozo." As one (line) friend put it to me: "They've never met a dumb marketing staffer or a smart sales manager in their lives." That's precisely the wrong feel. Linguistic disrespect leads to subtle—and not so subtle—denigration when decisions are being made and pay/honors are being apportioned.

8. What the "little things" reveal. Would a vice-president turn down an invitation to the chairman's dinner party at his Long Island estate in order to visit a new plant in County Cork, Ireland, because he wants to be with his newest troops on Christmas Eve? Would the chairman publicly applaud the decision? Or ignore it? Or would the hallway talk be about "naïve Joe"? "He'll learn. The rough edges wear off in time. He's spent too many years away from the pulsebeat [the halls of power]."

These and a host of other indicators provide clear evidence of the organization's concerns. The good news is that each of the eight can be managed. The first step is to take the list seriously, do an assessment of your own firm using a list like this—and then get meticulously to work reversing the polarity of the firm's interests, if it is not line-oriented.

LEADERSHIP THAT HONORS THE LINE

Pride in the Accomplishments of Others

A related trait is taking obvious pride in the work of others, especially people on the firing line. In *20 Teachers,* author Ken Macrorie talks about an extraordinary high school woodworking teacher, Sam Bush. Bush spent most of his time with Macrorie bragging about his charges: "Isn't this beautiful work?" "Do you see this mirror?" "Isn't that turning done beautifully?" "And the way that design is laid on there?" "That piece means something special to me because it was done by a boy who was falling apart in life and couldn't get it together in the shop either."

Bush takes genuine pride in his students' work. He describes his accomplishments, not in terms of techniques taught, but in terms of his genuine and transparent thrill at *their* accomplishments. Obvious as this may sound, it is at once unusual and a trait of exceptional leaders in all walks of life. (A psychologist's recent study of child-rearing practices employed by the parents of successful businesspersons concluded that constant, outright—and often public and obnoxious—bragging about the child's accomplishments topped the list of successful parenting traits.)

Bragging about the achievements of the front-line troops can rekindle long dormant spirits; it is also a matter of increasing importance, given the demand of the times for stellar contributions from every front-line person.

This idea can readily be turned into hard-boiled management advice: Only promote people whose greatest pleasure is bragging about the accomplishments of their front-line troops.

"Measuring" Managers' Attention to the Line

How do you "measure" it? Simple. Suppose you're a regional vice-president making a site visit to a hotel. Where does the property manager take you first? To her office to review "the numbers" or a "summary presentation"? Or is she bubbling with energy and determined to make you walk every inch of the property looking at tiny touches and meeting the people responsible for them?

Does she introduce you only to the four assistant managers, including one who finished the night shift three hours ago, whom she ordered to stay around? Or does she introduce you to everyone (and know them by name), beginning with the bellhops and housekeepers? Does she have them explain to you what they're doing, while she glows with pride? Or does she explain, while they hover in the background?

It's easy to make judgments, once you start focusing on these differences, which usually are this extreme. Be careful, though. You might have brought this on yourself. You, and perhaps several of your predecessors, may have clearly signaled that "I've seen a million hotels in my time"—and that you are interested in skipping the umpteenth tour of the scullery in favor of "getting into the numbers." That is, the first task is to get your own priorities straight and signal them unequivocally.

Incidentally, this same advice holds for the evaluation of staff managers. Do they bubble on about great analyses and paper coups? Or do they brag about Judy, who is on temporary assignment to Brazil for ninety days, to work on implementing a just-in-time inventory management system with the operations manager there? That is, do they brag about (1) their people and (2) their support for the line? Or do they emphasize their central watchdog-analyst's role?

Promotion Priority: Creating Excitement as a "Hard" Leadership Trait

Promote those people who create excitement, zest, and enthusiasm among their colleagues (before they become a boss), subordinates (after they become a boss), and even their peers in other functions (see also L-10). This applies to accounting or personnel supervisors as well as shift foreman in the factory and engineering section heads.

I clearly remember the advice my first boss gave me when I became a consultant at McKinsey & Company. The organization, on any given day, is divided into project teams. Selecting your next project makes or breaks your career—and your mental well-being. How do you select that next project? "It's simple," said my mentor. "Choose somebody you'd like to work with, whom you'd learn from, who would be fun to be around in a tense situation." He shocked me by adding: "Don't worry *at all* about the content of the project." He was so right. An uninspiring boss can turn the most exciting strategic project into a dispiriting exercise. The genuinely engaged and enthusiastic boss can turn a dull inventory management problem into the most exciting thing since NASA put Neil Armstrong on the moon.

The key is to trust your judgment, not psychobabble spewed forth by the Ph.D.s in the personnel department. Promote people who love people, who cherish their subordinates' accomplishments, and who create excitement. It's easy. People with these traits usually show their mettle about midway through their first week on the job. They're talented, fun to be around—and they bring the place to a high pitch of spirited performance, years before the mantle of manager is first placed upon them.

Promote Leaders Who Lead

This prescription epitomizes the common-sense underpinnings of the entire set. Great football franchises—Pittsburgh, Oakland/Los Angeles, Washington, Chicago, Miami, Dallas—are marked, over the course of decades, less by Hall of Fame quarterbacks and halfbacks than by top-flight nose tackles, free safeties, linebackers, centers, and special teams. It's not that marketers and engineers (quarterbacks and fullbacks) aren't important. They are. It's just that the emphasis must be placed—especially today, when all competition is as intense as NFL competition—on the people who more fully determine the outcome *over time*—those troops on the line. In fact, each of these teams has had great "marketers" (Roger Staubach of Dallas, Ken Stabler of Oakland) from time to time. But the basis for sustaining performance has been year-in-and-year-out front-line brilliance.

Basically, I'm asking that you take leadership seriously. Promote into leadership positions those who perform like leaders. That sounds silly—at first. But we too often give our support chiefly to the "squared away" young man or woman who gives brilliant presentations, who is terrific to be around at lunch or dinner with an important client. I'm not against analysis and good presentations and social graces in front of clients. But I am in favor of understanding that success ultimately comes from making the implementers into heroes.

The point, as always it seems, is a "must-do." Executing the winning customer strategies (C-1 through C-4 especially) requires line leadership—the willingness of front-line people to take the initiative, to listen to customers, to act fast. The desirability of great quarterbacks and marketers is not diminished. However, the presence of great linemen and nursing staff is decisive for future success.

FIRST STEPS

1. Go back to the eight questions that determine a line-versus-staff mind-set. How do you stack up? Use your next visit as fodder: Change your routine in five ways that enhance the line, not at the expense of staff, but to make it first among equals.

2. Hold off and reflect upon a current promotion decision. Are you evaluating the candidate on the basis of (a) his or her attitudes toward subordinates' accomplishments and (b) his or her ability to create excitement? That is, are you really looking at *leadership?* Or are you using technical traits as the primary determinant?

3. I can give no advice on making yourself care and enhancing your desire to be around offensive linemen, except for one small thing: Spend time with them. They're the greatest. I think you'll soon see that. If you don't, I sincerely propose that you quit and become a management consultant.

L-7

SUMMARY

Delegation of responsibility has been a central topic in management texts through the ages. But today's marketplace, which demands heretofore unheard-of front-line freedom to initiate far-reaching actions, propels the subject toward the top of the list. To be responsive, we must:

▶ Examine each act of delegation through the lenses of (1) really letting go, (2) not inadvertently "taking back," and (3) carefully setting the context for delegation by (a) establishing high standards, (b) developing commitment to a jointly shared vision, and (c) encouraging mutual faith and respect.

Delegation is "hot"! We must learn to let go, or suffer the consequences of unacceptably slow action-taking. Other prescriptions, such as P-8, have urged the elimination of most traditional forms of control. So we must learn the subtle art of delegation anew—more delegation than ever with fewer than normal formal controls.

Increase true delegation—radically. But first institute a new and paperless form of control—a shared vision (L-2) and remarkably high standards. Review every act of delegation, assuming such alternate controls have been established, to see if you are "really letting go" to the extent required to inspire others to take true and vigorous responsibility. Carefully monitor your casual remarks to those to whom you've delegated, ensuring that you don't inadvertently rescind the grant of autonomy.

L-7

Delegate

The Tower Board Report issued early in 1987 on the Iran-Contra affair gave delegation in general a black eye. That's unfortunate. The thrust of virtually all of these prescriptions is freeing up the organization to work faster and with less traditional hierarchy and supervision. That is, much more delegation is required today than ever before.

DELEGATION: THE SINE QUA NON OF EMPOWERMENT

Even without considering today's stepped-up need for delegation, the plain fact is that nine of ten managers haven't delegated enough. Oh, yes, they think they have. They hand over tasks and pass out assignments routinely. But only rarely does the "delegate" really catch fire and become empowered with true ownership—and its concomitant, the true burden of responsibility.

What goes wrong? To begin with, there's the difference between letting go and Really Letting Go. But wait, you say, doesn't Really Letting Go mean anarchy, chaos, and confusion, i.e., of the Iran-Contra sort?

Effective delegation does mean Really Letting Go—for instance, high spending authority (outrageously high, by old standards), relatively infrequent formal reporting, geographic separation, and, above all, psychological distancing—in other words, the works. But . . .

There is a big, qualifying "but"—true delegation, of the Really Letting Go variety, will result in superb performance only if these four counterforces are simultaneously at play:

► The boss (that is, delegator) has ridiculously high standards, which she or he lives, transmits, and uniformly demands.

► The boss has a crystal-clear vision about where the ship's headed (see L-2) in which she or he and the delegate have faith (in fact, the delegate is made the living embodiment of the vision).

► The boss wholeheartedly believes in people, and will be deeply disappointed, as a mentor, if the delegate fails or at least fails to make a herculean effort—all the more so since the boss has made it clear (albeit indirectly) how far out on a limb she or he has gone to let the delegate take on this task.

► The boss lets the delegate bite off a lot more than he can chew if he is insistent upon doing so, but stops just a touch short of letting him bite off an absurd amount.

Subtle Cues Add Up to Really Letting Go: Four Cases

Take this seemingly simple case. British mystery writer P. D. James is also a superb management analyst; here's an apparently innocuous passage from her 1986–87 best-seller, *A Taste for Death:*

Dalgliesh had accepted that the agreement must be kept; [Kate Miskin] would meet Carole Washburn alone. He had given her no instruction and offered no advice. Other senior officers would have been tempted to remind her of the importance of the meeting, but this wasn't his way. She respected him for it, but it increased her burden of responsibility. Everything might depend on how she handled the encounter. [Adam Dalgliesh is James's Sherlock Holmes, a respected senior detective. Kate Miskin is the only woman in Dalgliesh's new, elite unit. Carole Washburn is a murder suspect.]

That single paragraph, within the novel's context, reveals most of the attributes of successful delegation. Dalgliesh really does let go—on several levels. Most obviously, he lets the relatively junior Miskin go alone to a most crucial meeting. But there are several additional levels of letting go involved. To begin with, Dalgliesh's elite unit is new, and has been formed despite political objections. This is its first "visible" case. Moreover, the case is dragging, and Dalgliesh is being sniped at by the press and entrenched political enemies. Under these circumstances, to allow the youthful Miskin to go ahead, alone, takes on added significance.

Dalgliesh is risking opprobrium from the press, from his own bosses, and from within his team as well—his seasoned colleagues are perturbed at his appointment of a relatively young woman. Finally, at the deepest, though seemingly most insignificant, level of letting go—that is, the Really Letting Go level—Dalgliesh pointedly has not reminded Miskin of the meeting's importance, a fact that she is well aware of (as you and I would be).

What does she doubtless feel? Terror, along with pride, at being on Dalgliesh's team. He is a stern taskmaster, seldom given to praise. His standards are widely known to be Olympian. But she also knows that he has faith in her. The meeting sequence is just the most recent indication. Dalgliesh is not sentimental, and certainly no radical feminist. She has been chosen early in her career because he thinks she's darned good.

In sum, we see the full-blown paradox of true delegation in this brief vignette. On the one hand, the boss lets go: (1) formal delegation, (2) a monumentally important task, (3) he is sticking his neck way out by delegating (both internal and external foes are sharpening their knives), and (4) he ups the ante by pointedly not reminding her of all of the above.

On the other hand, she has hardly been sent on an anarchist's mission. That is: (1) the boss is a commanding professional and has made it clear that she's in this position because she's talented and he trusts her skills, even though he knows it will force her to test the limit of her capabilities, and (2) his standards are extremely high. The autonomy granted is real and significant, but it is matched by the psychological pressure to perform up to one's limits and to the highest standards.

Consider three shorter cases. Two involve me, the third a close friend. I began to learn to "really" delegate only after being forced into it. Ten years ago I was heading a small unit that was doing quite well. I had a stellar supporting cast. Yet, when crucial presentations came, I made them. And why not, since I'd been on board since the beginning—and my superiors had made it clear to me that it was my show—and my neck.

As the unit was approaching its third anniversary, I was in a severe automobile accident—knocked completely out of action for two or three months. My major interest became soap operas and midday TV game shows. Then, as the reports began to come in, it became abundantly clear what a talented team I had. It was disconcerting, but one heck of a learning experience. Rather than behave decently (as I would have put it then) and cancel the numerous engagements that I had booked, every single activity had been taken on by a team member. And while, a decade later, I still harbor the suspicion that I might have done any one activity 2 percent better than they, the reality is that a dozen people caught fire—all at once.

In the fall of 1986, a similar event occurred. A colleague had made a promise years before to contribute to a significant project that I too was interested in. She never quite got around to it. I kept my hand in, often bailing out the project before an about-to-pass deadline with last-minute heroics, all the while wondering why my colleague's promise remained unfulfilled. Then a family tragedy caused me to be unavoidably out of touch as a critical project deadline approached. Without a word from me, my long-dormant associate grabbed the reins. Once more, I'd like to believe that I could have done the task 1 percent better—we all hold such rationalizations dear. What I do know is that out of the woodwork she came, and the task was brilliantly done. Now her superb contributions are routine. We've still never discussed any of this.

A close friend had a similar experience. He had been letting go of a big operation of his making for about two years. Rather, he had been "sorta letting go." Suddenly, he was gone—on a long-planned trip, 10,-000 miles from home. His interests didn't change entirely, however, and just three weeks after departing he called to get an update—and discovered that once it had become clear that he had "really gone," a series of hitherto unthinkable things had occurred. One senior colleague, in particular, had suddenly become wholly engaged in the operation—and effectively so, to the point of patching up a very frayed relationship with another principal player.

Each of these three examples involves some subtle attributes of Really Letting Go. "Sorta letting go," it's clear, doesn't work. It took a life-threatening accident, an unequivocally about-to-be-missed deadline, and a several-month-long, 10,000-mile journey to do the trick. In every instance there was not a shred of doubt on the part of the newly inspired participants that the "boss" had let go.

Beware the Subtle Cues That Add Up to "Really Taking Back"

The process is extremely delicate, which explains why so few do really catch fire as we'd hoped at the time of the act of delegation. Bob Townsend relates a cautionary tale: "You tell a guy to get on with it. He's on his own. You make that clear. Two days later, on the way out at about seven in the evening, you poke your head into his office ever so briefly. You say, as a last, inadvertent aside, 'Have you checked with Bernie on your plans?' If you had stuck around another ten seconds to watch his reaction, you would have seen physical deflation, like a balloon when its air is let out. And his color fades, too. You just stole the whole damn thing back from him, and in about five seconds. And worst of all, you didn't mean it. Or even know it, for that matter. I mean, he would have checked with Bernie anyway!"

The first four "case studies" related above all suggested that moving to true delegation means crossing an imaginary line which transfers psychological ownership to the delegates: This is the real thing, there's no going back. Recall the example from *A Taste for Death:* The apparently trivial act of refraining from reminding Kate Miskin that an important meeting was, in fact, important (nothing, it would seem, could be more trivial) was the key to upping the ante and putting the monkey squarely on her back. Townsend's caveat is frightening—how easy it is to then grab the whole thing back.

Checklist: Are You Letting Go?

Whenever you are delegating, then, you must address a lengthy series of questions:

▶ Have you first transmitted the overarching vision with clarity? That is, does the delegate, through demonstrated behavior, clearly "buy in"?

▶ Have you set high standards in the past that make it clear what level of performance you demand?

▶ Have you demonstrated in the past, in small ways, that you trust the delegate's judgment?

▶ Do you have a track record for jumping in at the last moment (before a deadline) to pull the irons of others (to whom you've delegated) out of the fire?

▶ Do you consciously avoid attending meetings (i.e., avoid the seemingly innocuous excuse for attending: "just to be informed; it's your show") when the delegate is meeting with (a) his or her team, (b) outsiders, such as customers or vendors, (c) more senior people (including your own boss)?

▶ Have you bitten your tongue and stayed out of the delegate's hair when "back channel" reports (i.e., gossip) inform you that "Joe's in over his head," "Joe didn't check with me on thus and such"?

▶ Have you staved off your boss (or staff experts) who want status reports ("He's awfully young, I assume you're on top of this")?

▶ Have you avoided excessive reporting (a paragraph a week is okay—preferably handwritten; 10 pages is not okay)?

▶ Have you given the manager formal authority (a high dollar sign-off level) to insure he doesn't need to come running every five minutes?

▶ Have you provided (in most cases) a separate physical location for his/her team (at least an enclosed, separate space; at best a grubby space in another building—even a block away helps)?

▶ When she or he calls (or stops by) for advice or to "touch bases," do you (a) avoid giving direct orders ("Hey, I'm rusty on that, you might go see Mary or Jean" is the best response) and (b) keep the "touch bases" conversation from being an approval-granting (by you) session (practice the art of the slightly disengaged "uh huh," rather than "sounds good" or "good work")?

▶ Have you made it clear, by your total (and visible) inaction as a critical deadline approaches that (a) you are not going to jump in and (b) you are not even going to raise the volume of questions ("uh, Joe, uh, three days to the presentation, huh?" He knows that!)?

ESTABLISHING THE CONTEXT FOR DELEGATION

I've pounded on the idea of letting go, and its subtlety and fragility. Let's take a closer look at the issues of faith, mutual respect, and high standards. Napoleon and Moshe Dayan had something in common. Napoleon made it clear, in word and in deed, that he would not leave wounded soldiers behind to be savaged by the enemy. A crucial part of the Dayan legend likewise involves the lengths to which he went to ensure that his wounded Israeli soldiers would not be picked up by their foes.

The same chord was struck by legendary Green Bay Packer coach Vince Lombardi. He said that you didn't have to like your football players but you must love them and respect them. The University of Alabama's equally legendary coach, Bear Bryant, was in the same mold. Former Oakland Raider quarterback Ken Stabler said that Bryant was indeed a tough son-of-a-gun; but he quickly added that you could abide it, because Bryant made it abundantly clear that he had total respect for you.

Napoleon, Dayan, Lombardi, and Bryant asked their soldiers and players, time and again, to do the impossible, to do more than they had ever dreamed they were capable of. And time and again, to the dismay of so many enemies and opponents, the people responded. The bosses were tough. But beneath it was abiding love and respect for the people who were asked to go out and meet a challenge greater than they had ever met before.

Management expert Karl Weick studied musicians. In one experiment, he gave a talented jazz ensemble a new piece of music that no member had ever seen. He told them it was a little-known piece by a famous composer. Then he gave them a second novel piece, which was in fact by the same composer; this time, however, he told them it was by Joe Doaks. The experiment was repeated numerous times with several groups to ensure the validity of the results.

When musicians played the new (to them) work of the unknown (Doaks) the first few times, they made numerous mistakes. However, their first attempt with the new (to them) piece by the "renowned composer" resulted in far fewer mistakes. That is, the confidence induced by the famous name alone led to substantially more competence on the part of the musicians from the outset.

Why include Napoleon, Dayan, Lombardi, Bryant, and a jazz ensemble in a discussion of delegation? Most treatments of delegation focus almost exclusively on the letting go, with a bit on formal controls needed to keep track. Few discussions of delegation emphasize the role of faith, belief, vision, caring, intensity, and the psychodynamics that the effective leader sets up with his followers. To discuss delegation without this misses the point.

Small things enhance delegation. Even smaller things destroy it. It happens in a context. Paradoxes abound, such as really letting go, but establishing an inspiring moral context for the importance of the task—including the leader's obvious confidence and caring.

The Mayor Believes in You

Laurie Schwartz had worked for Mayor Don Schaefer but had taken off to pursue a career in the private sector. After a chance get-together at a Christmas party, he once again tapped her. She had indicated that she might be available for one of his famous "special projects." Without another word, he invited her to a meeting. He didn't tell her what it was about, even after she joined a confab of senior business people from Charles Street.

With amenities quickly out of the way, the mayor got down to business. "I want you to meet Laurie Schwartz. She," he declared, "is now Ms. Charles Street. She's going to get us going here." (Baltimore's main business street was not being transformed at a pace that was up to Schaefer's soaring standards.) And that was that. Charles Street was Schwartz's. The mayor dragged her back down to City Hall, where the city's department heads were assembled. "Laurie's back," the mayor announced. "She's running Charles Street, and you're to do whatever she says."

The charge was about that simple, though the execution obviously was not. A couple of years later, Charles Street was fast becoming a gem, with over 100 million new dollars invested in it. Laurie Schwartz was the cheerleader, the quarterback, the de facto chairman of the board.

Did Schaefer really believe that she could pull off this miracle? One suspects he did. It is clear that he delegated the responsibility to her unequivocally. She was out on a limb. She had said she was somewhat interested in doing something for him; in return, he had lobbed a key part of the city her way.

Schaefer had done a frightening thing to her. She believed in him, believed in his compelling vision, believed in his track record of making the impossible seem almost routine. Moreover, she believed that he believed in her, and that he wouldn't have done this "to her" unless he thought she *could* pull it off. So she now had the monkey on her back for a piece of his—their—vision. It was her ball, in her court. Deliver or else, her psyche said; and that's precisely what His Honor had intended.

DELEGATE TO ACT "HORIZONTALLY"

Delegation has traditionally meant "pushing decision-making to the lowest level." That has been the thrust of this prescription, too. The implicit (or explicit) target is the individual and his or her work group (see P-2 on self-managing teams, for instance).

But there is another "half" of delegation, growing in importance. That is, delegation to the front line and self-managing group to act "horizontally," to seek out fast connections with other functions, without checking "up."

This "horizontal" delegation was a theme of P-8 and P-9. It is also the theme of the next prescription, L-8, which urges nothing less than a full-blown "horizontal style" of management.

FIRST STEPS

1. Make it a habit to examine and reexamine regularly every important act of delegation. Have you really snipped all the strings—physical, psychological, etc.—necessary to transfer psychological ownership? While I believe as a rule in spontaneity, also take care that your language in chance encounters doesn't make that monkey jump back your way.
2. But examine the context equally carefully. Is there real agreement about the vision? Are your standards known to be high?

L-8

SUMMARY

We must pursue fast-paced action at all costs, and therefore:

▶ Vigorously and gleefully, with all hands participating, take the lead in destroying the trappings of bureaucracy.

▶ Manage the organization "horizontally"—that is, insist that "vertical" obfuscating be replaced with proactive (no checking "up"), "horizontal," front-line cooperation in pursuit of fast action.

Test. Try. Modify. Test. Act. Or: Act, act, act. To do so means to become an avowed and public hater of bureaucracy, and to ceaselessly pursue more spontaneous communication among functions (at the front line).

Let no day pass without acting as a visible model by engaging in at least one feat of bureaucracy destruction. Ensure that most of these publicized feats of bureaucracy-bashing are in service to a "horizontal style" of management, which minimizes up and down (vertical) communication and replaces it with fast, front-line cooperation across functional boundaries.

L-8

Pursue "Horizontal" Management by Bashing Bureaucracy

In December 1986, I gave a speech to young graduates of the U.S. Navy's Civil Engineer Corps Officers School. The centerpiece was a list of ten suggestions. At the top: "I beg each and every one of you to develop a passionate and public hatred for bureaucracy." I meant it.

The central point of this prescription is its proactive nature. Don't appoint a paperwork reduction committee (see P-10). Such an approach might be dandy, but I mean something much more proactive. Become an emotional, vociferous, repetitive, public hater of bureaucracy. Become a nuisance!

ENERGETIC BUREAUCRACY-BASHING

Rant and rave. Tear up papers. Refuse to read them. Don't attend meetings. You may put your career in jeopardy in the short run, for having a lousy attendance record. But if you don't put it in jeopardy for that, it will likely be in jeopardy in the long run, when the business goes bust or the city can't pay its debts or the weapons system won't work.

Be outrageous. Get rid of all your file cabinets—think of it as the white-collar equivalent of installing a just-in-time inventory management system. Put big cardboard boxes around your desk, and throw all the junk you receive into them—unread. Put a big red label on the boxes: "This week's unread paperwork."

Whenever you get a report, read only the first two pages. Call the sender: "I didn't understand your report."

"I'll come down to your office and explain."

Your office, a short time later:

"Of course you didn't understand it, you only read the first two pages of my thirty-nine-page report."

"My eyes tire. I can't read anything longer than two pages. It's age, I'm sure. I'm thirty-eight [or twenty-six or fifty-two] now."

"I think I get the point. Shorten it up."

"No, you don't get it at all. Next time, just come down and explain—like you did just now. Don't write a damn report!"

Be colorful. Have a Friday afternoon ceremony, once a month at 4 P.M. Bring beer and invite your people out to the incinerator. Burn all the paper you received but did not read.

Invite them next month to a spot in the woods. Bring beer and shovels. Dig a hole. Tote out a small wooden casket. In it place all the forms and rules and discontinued reports that you and they have tagged for immediate elimination. If you've got real nerve, bury the office copier next to the casket. Wear mad garb. Lead a chant as the casket and copier are lowered into the ground: "No more paper, no more forms."

(Yes, I know you may be the highly respectable chairman of a staid $1.5 billion company. "Antic" is not exactly your middle name. But then what's so bloody honorable about your miserable earnings record and the 4,000 jobs you've shipped offshore in the last six years?)

You've got two choices: (1) find your own style of doing this or (2) go broke. I realize the danger of losing the reader here: "You can't do that around here." "It's not me." I urge you to reassess those oh-so-reasonable responses: (1) We all agree that urgency is essential to survival today. (2) We all agree that getting rid of "bureaucracy" induces urgency (no number of "motivational devices," including gobs of incentive money, will overcome our petrified forest of barriers). (3) And, sadly, we all agree (those of us who are honest, anyway) that we don't know what to do about the problem, other than rail at it. (4) Therefore, I am merely suggesting that we match the need to address these radically shifting times with a radical and proactive strategy: fun, energy, anger, participation, vigor—and time and attention—in urgent pursuit of demolishing the barriers, especially the excessive "vertical processing" of information that slows action down among functions at the front by orders of magnitude.

Involvement and Celebration: Part and Parcel of Bureaucracy-Bashing

Make bureaucracy-demolition fun—and participative. Get everyone to nominate forms and procedures for elimination. Have a committee, made up principally of junior line people, assess the suggestions and act on them within a week. Insist that they accept at least 50 percent.

Give an award to every individual who makes a nomination, a bigger award for every nomination accepted—then group and unit awards. Perhaps even put "anti-bureaucracy effectiveness" in your performance evaluation scheme.

Have a semiannual or annual luncheon or dinner, labeled: "Beating Back Bureaucracy: Luncheon of Irate Red-Tape Cutters." (Bronze shears of various sizes would make nice trophies.)

Formalize a separate, anti-bureaucracy suggestion system, individual- or group-based. There's no end to such ideas. Fun and participation are the keys. A more serious matter—survival—is the goal.

Is a project stuck at a fairly important milestone? A negotiation with a supplier bogging down? Spend lavishly on airfare (and long-distance phone calls). Get on the plane, visit with the supplier or customer or project team—and don't leave until the darn thing is fixed. Forget the committee meetings that you missed in the process—most of them were to worry about how to deal with other project teams around the company that were stuck or with other negotiations that were bogged down.

In fact, go a step further. Give awards to the persons who spent the most money (or logged the most miles) in pursuit of unblocking stalled projects or negotiations; give a concomitant award to the person who missed the most meetings while in pursuit of speeding up stalled affairs. (See L-10 for a broader discussion of inducing a sense of urgency.)

INSTALLING A "HORIZONTAL STYLE"
OF MANAGEMENT

Consider your group to be a company. Every other function is, by definition, either a vendor or a customer. Treat them with the respect and care with which you'd deal with outsiders. Practice relationship management, customer listening, customer visiting, and, mainly, reward your "salespersons"—i.e., everyone—for getting and keeping your "customers" happy. Hold "vendor"/"customer"-appreciation days and open houses.

Suppose you are in manufacturing. Invite the division controller's staff to your next beer bust. Send one of your shift foremen to the chief cost accountant's office on a sixty-day temporary assignment. Teach "customer-serving" habits—accounting in this case—to your supervisors. Send thank-you notes to an accountant who did a job swiftly for you, with a copy to his or her boss and boss's boss.

Devote 15 percent of your monthly operations presentation to specific examples of smooth cross-functional cooperation. Devote 20 percent of your discretionary bonus money to awards for those in other functions who have assisted you; devote another 20 percent to rewarding your own people for meritorious acts of proactive skid greasing.

Hold a surprise party for a team from MIS that took the trouble to spend a weekend getting bugs ironed out of a new program's software—to help your unit. Send one of your machine operators to a full-blown, twenty-week information systems department training program so that he or she can be a well-schooled prime contact when the next new manufacturing software package is on the drawing boards.

Keep daily or weekly score for yourself or your unit: For instance, perform a dozen "barrier bashers" each month.

Poke fun at the bureaucracy, bureaucrats, and barriers that interfere with "horizontal" management. Regardless of how deeply you buy and live this message, you will still act like a bureaucrat and turf guardian several times a day. That's wonderful news, because it means you can unfailingly preface an attack on others with an attack on yourself!

At each weekly staff meeting, consider including a "report card" on yourself. Cite your violations: paperwork excess, turf guardianship, and so on. Have a half-dozen such categories. Give yourself a grade on each one—a bureaucrat's grade on your dealings with each key "customer"/ "vendor" functions you work with—and an overall grade. Then post the results. Give people hell, lightheartedly (present a duncecap) or in earnest, who have "checked in" with you on a horizontal-action issue instead of acting on their own.

Have a different person present a report card on your function as a whole each week. Anybody who has the temerity to give the function an A on anything buys lunch for everyone and makes coffee all the next week. The chosen report-card preparer should be encouraged to spend several hours collecting instructive stories and preparing the report card.

The logic is impeccable: Two towering hindrances to quality, service, responsiveness, fast innovation, and people involvement are functional barriers—"vertical" management—and bureaucracy. Therefore, it follows logically that two of the leader's top strategic priorities ought to be proactively attacking bureaucracy and working at that "horizontal style."

"Hot Buttons"

In *The Leadership Challenge,* Jim Kouzes and Barry Posner tell of a productive barrier-bashing device that was also great fun: "At Sequent Computer, company president Casey Powell at one critical point handed out buttons. Most of the company would wear green 'How Can I Help?' buttons, but people on the critical path would get red 'Priority' buttons. People with green buttons were to do anything to remove obstacles for those people with the red buttons. Powell wore a green button. . . ."

FIRST STEPS

Review the numerous practical, and participative, devices for establishing "horizontal" management included in this prescription. In the next thirty days, select two activities and begin to implement them.

L-9

SUMMARY

To up the odds of survival, leaders at all levels must become obsessive about change. They must:

▶ In the matter of formal and informal evaluations of leaders (managers at all levels), focus less on measures that deal with such things as budgets, and more on the explicit questions: "What, exactly, have you changed lately? What, exactly, have your subordinates changed lately?" Additionally, every meeting should commence with a rapid, explicit review of exactly what has been changed since the last session, even if it was yesterday; every newsletter should emphasize change; and so on.

Change must become the norm, not cause for alarm. The bottom line: If you can't point to something specific that's being done differently from the way it was done when you came to work this morning, you have not "lived," for all intents and purposes; you surely have not earned your paycheck by any stretch of the imagination. Furthermore, the incremental changes of today must almost unfailingly be in support of non-incremental change—that is, a bold goal to be achieved in record time.

Make "What, exactly, have you changed?" the most common question in the organization. Ask it a dozen times a day, at least.

L-9

Evaluate Everyone on His or Her Love of Change

Are sales consistent with your forecast? Did you exceed budget? These are reasonable and important questions. They are standard fare for performance appraisals or quarterly or monthly reviews. They deal, as the experts say they should, with results that presumably are more or less under the manager's control.

But I believe these are the wrong questions for the times. They are tangential to the main event. We should be asking something more fundamental: "What, precisely, exactly, unequivocally, have your changed—today?" And: "Are you sure?" And: "What's next?" And: "Exactly what bold goal does the change support?"

The questions are deceptively simple. Most often they go unasked. Yet I firmly believe they are far and away the most crucial questions for all today's managers, at all levels.

A vice-president from IBM said flatly that this question—What have you changed?—has become the most frequent query at all levels throughout his firm. Discussions with IBMers down the line confirm his assertion. And well they should. IBM's industry is in chaos—and will remain so for years—and there is mounting evidence that on some dimensions the giant company has not been keeping pace.

From computers to retailing to health care to government, managers of all functions and at all levels are confronted with an unprecedented amount of turmoil. Just over a dozen years ago, when I was working with McKinsey & Co., my colleagues and I didn't even bother to take inflation into account while making twenty-year cash-flow projections for quarter-billion-dollar petrochemical facilities. Moreover, we were confident in our ability to predict supply, demand, and commodity prices for wheat and corn (we were concerned with a fertilizer facility) with a fine degree of accuracy, over a twenty-year period. Feedstock (oil and gas) prices, we felt, were also predictable. As for the value of the dollar compared to other currencies—it never crossed our minds to consider wide fluctuations.

Today all of those variables—and a host of others—are just that: highly variable (see Part I). Nothing is "for sure" over a *three-month* time horizon, let alone one of *twenty years.*

NEW TIMES DEMAND NEW QUESTIONS

This radically new environment demands radically new forms of organization and radically new forms of evaluation of those who manage. To be sure, making budget remains a valid aim. But while it may be a necessary condition for survival, it is no longer even close to a sufficient one—for the shift supervisor, let alone the division general manager.

The IBM executive continues: "We must reexamine every relationship, every element of doing business, every process, every procedure. The only plausible criterion for success is: 'Are you changing enough, rapidly enough, to successfully confront the future?' "

To adapt to a radically altered environment, each procedure—in MIS, accounting, personnel, manufacturing, product development, distribution—that links up with other functions, each relationship with suppliers and distributors, must be "zero-based," that is, wholly reassessed and, in nine cases out of ten, changed in its essentials. We must, then, measure each manager directly on his or her ability to change things dramatically.

How Many? How Much? How Fast? How Bold?

Are you looking for new opportunities to exploit technology? Opportunities to, say, link your data base electronically with that of your key—and probably even smaller—suppliers and middlemen and customers? Have you launched a new training program to expose all hands to one or another aspect of an altered future? Are front-line people being empowered to change things and cross traditional functional boundaries at a moment's notice without checking "up" first? Are temporary organizations being created on twenty-four hours' notice, and then scrubbed fifteen or thirty days later when the task is done?

It's no longer adequate to ask: "How many people, up from whatever last year, did you process in basic sales training?" It's necessary to ask:

▶ "How, *exactly*, have you changed basic sales training to match possible future scenarios—within the last three months?"

▶ "How much material in the sales refresher course has been updated in the last six months?"

▶ "How many new case studies are you using?"

▶ "Why *these* new cases?"

▶ "Whom have you recently asked to advise you on course content whom you *never* asked before?"

▶ "Are you *sure* that your advisers—from inside and outside the firm—are diverse enough to mirror the changing conditions in the real world?"

▶ Is all of this change dramatic enough/fast enough to allow us to surge ahead of our competitors—or at least keep pace with the new ones entering the market each day?

CREATING NEW RITUALS

"What have you changed lately?," "How fast are you changing?," and "Are you pursuing bold enough change goals?" must become pressing questions asked of any manager, at any level, in any function, as a matter of course. For instance, during each staff meeting, go around the table posing the question to each colleague. Don't spend much time, perhaps no more than ten minutes for ten people. But do it, ritualistically. Make the simple question a prime element in your formal performance appraisal system, as well as in your informal monthly sit-down appraisal: "What have you changed? How much have you changed? What are you planning to change next? What are your direct-reports changing? What have they changed in the last two days, two weeks, two months? How bold are the goals of your change program?"

My assessment of the surprising continued vitality of 3M, PepsiCo, and Citicorp, arguably three of the fastest-moving giant firms in the

United States, is that they are, above all, impatient. They'll reorganize on a dime, while others barely have the energy to do so every half-dozen years. In fact, my own measure is that if you aren't reorganizing, pretty substantially, once every six to twelve months, you're probably out of step with the times. These firms don't stand on ceremony. They never stop exploring ways to get it right—for now. And they don't fret much about getting it wrong—as long as it's fixed fast. They are brash experimenters, moving in tandem—through error and trial—with the pace of the dynamic markets in which they participate. And yet even they are showing signs of slippage; remember the opening sentence of this book: There are no excellent companies. No one big (almost no one at all), in my judgment, is changing fast enough.

DEALING WITH THE ARGUMENTS OF NAYSAYERS

There are three routine rebuttals to this idea. The first is: "Aren't you advocating wheel-spinning? You don't really want change for change's sake, now, do you?"

I'd be the first to acknowledge that I've seen many instances of very unproductive, frenzied behavior. I don't support that. The manager's job is to make sure that frenzy for frenzy's sake does not occur. On the other hand, I'm not a Pollyanna. I don't believe in pure win-win situations. There is something to be traded off. In today's environment, when you boil it all down, the principal enemy is inertia, in smaller firms as well as in large ones. Thus, on net, a fair dose of change for change's sake, even including some wheel spinning, is preferable to continued inertia.

The second argument is more fundamental: "You've gone on and on about work-force commitment and achieving the highest level of quality and service. Don't these things, which by their nature suggest stability (how can anything be better than best?), fly in the face of 'changing everything'?" Once more, the answer is not simple. Constant change programs surely do threaten many people, especially traditional supervisors and middle managers. But constant change is thoroughly consistent with pursuing perfection in quality and service. Indeed, it is a must, for no one among the increasing array of competitors is standing pat. In the time it takes to read this prescription, Toyota will have implemented another fifty suggestions—that is, will have gotten better (there is no best for long).

But the threat posed to stability by constant, incremental changes is the least of it. For I have just proposed radically changing the organization's structure annually or even more frequently—it's a must. Changing all the procedures and then changing them again—another must. Smashing the market into bits, and then smashing it into even finer bits—a must as well. Restlessly altering the structures and markets and procedures depends upon keeping the vision and value system constant, more constant and more prominent than ever before—replacing control by procedure with control by vision and trust. The vision and managers' consistent, daily actions in support of it is the sea anchor, the basis for keeping people from running aground as the waves of change toss them to and fro.

Yes, it is a paradox (see also L-1): In the face of more change, more stability (but not the paper-driven kind) is essential. Charts and boxes and stability based upon lengthy job descriptions and your place in the organizational structure must be replaced by vision, values, and stability based on trust.

The final argument: "You keep asking for pursuit of incremental change; now you're saying 'dramatic change,' 'bold goals.' Can you reconcile the two?" Yes, on two scores. First, there is no choice. The goals must be bold, even to stand still. Hence incrementalism must always be in pursuit of the dramatic minimum improvements set out in these prescriptions.

Moreover, the most efficient and effective route to bold change is the participation of everyone, every day, in incremental change (see I-1 on small starts and I-3 on pilots, especially). Most bold change is the result of a hundred thousand tiny changes that culminate in a bold product or procedure or structure. The dramatic success symbol is usually just that, a symbol. The road to it is paved with a million experiments, a million false steps—and the wholehearted participation of everyone.

THE ACID TEST: CHANGE IS THE MANAGER'S DAY-TO-DAY BOTTOM LINE

Lately I've been ending my speeches with a snide observation which directly concerns this prescription: "If you are interested in keeping your jobs, ask yourself at the end of the day, every day, 'What exactly and precisely and explicitly is being done in my work area differently from the way it was done when I came to work in the morning?' The average manager starts each and every day as an expense item ('wealth dissipator,' in the words of Brunswick's Jack Reichert), not a revenue enhancer. You must earn the right to draw your substantial managerial salaries. The only way to do so is by making things different and better. Different and better today can only mean—changed, acted upon. If you can't put your hands on something—a coaching session that's leading to demonstrably new behavior, a changed form or eliminated rule—that's being done differently in the afternoon from the way it was done in the morning, then you haven't been alive." Furthermore, that specific something changed today had better have been changed in pursuit of a very bold goal (i.e., a 90 percent decrease in defects in the next thirty-six months). That is, the moment's tangible change must be in pursuit of dramatic change.

It's tough medicine. The manager, in today's world, doesn't get paid to be a "steward of resources," a favored term not so many years ago. He or she gets paid for one and only one thing—to make things better (incrementally and dramatically), make things different (incrementally and dramatically), to change things, to act—today.

FIRST STEPS

What exactly, precisely, have you changed today? What precise bold goal is that change connected with? Ask yourself. Ask everyone, junior or senior, with whom you came in contact this very day. Repeat, daily, for the rest of your career!

L-10

SUMMARY

Since our foremost need is to change more, faster, we must:

▶ Induce a sense of urgency and hustle throughout the organization.

▶ Seek to minimize potentially paralyzing fears, despite the uncertainty which makes fearfulness legitimate.

To achieve the awesome but minimum acceptable agenda laid out in the thirty-nine previous prescriptions, the organization must be energetic, from stem to stern. A principal leadership challenge, then, is to go all out to create a sense of urgency.

Every managerial act must be seen as an unequivocal support for urgency in pursuit of constant testing, change, and improvement.

L-10

Create a Sense of Urgency

George Washington University business researcher Peter Vaill, the pioneer scholar of a field called "high performing systems," says that the stellar outfits—whether Brownie troops or factories—all have a certain feel, or "aesthetic motivation." A U.S. Air Force general I know insists that the best air squadrons "hum." Similar words or expressions include "electric," "electricity in the air," "in synch."

Most of us "learned" about this phenomenon in grade school. Some classrooms "hum," are "electric," are "in synch." Most lack any such spark. So, too, with training departments, retail buying offices, and software development groups.

The challenge this book lays down is all about "hustle" (see C-4 and Amar Bhide's superb description of "hustle as strategy"). We must challenge everything, change everything, improve everything. We must cut this cycle time and that by 75 to 90 percent (and do it fast), become orders-of-magnitude more responsive, implement thousands of individual and team suggestions each day just to keep up with the Joneses (the Hondas, Electroluxes, Limiteds).

The necessity of learning to love change permeates this book. Most of the prescriptions, sometimes indirectly, have taken aim at inducing flexibility and minute-to-minute risk-taking. Figure 18 is a partial listing, some forty key factors whose primary effect, working in tandem, is to create organizational fluidity—i.e., love of change (and the ability to make changes) by everyone. They range from the power of information provided to the front line (detailed knowledge of competitors, for instance, is an unsurpassed spur to action) and the removal of excessive "layers" of structure, to extensive worker training in how to solve problems and a straightforward call to evaluate everyone on the basis of how much he or she has, in fact, changed (I-9, I-10, L-9)—and lately, to boot.

But even if you do all these things (an imposing challenge), there will still be something missing—an intangible (that maligned "soft" word) "X-factor": electricity, hum, hustle, or whatever else you choose to call it. This prescription urges you to add the "X-factor" to your organization, whether it's a small team in the loan department or a large multinational institution.

Well, just what is it? After all, this is a book of practical suggestions. Allied-Signal, a then-sluggish firm embarking on a turnaround, ran advertisements a couple of years ago that featured otherwise stodgy-looking executives without suit jackets and with their shirt sleeves rolled up; the inscription read: "We mean business." I don't know what the ad's effect was (on customers or employees), but its flavor is to the point here. We must break out of the old molds, and fast. Rolled-up sleeves are hardly the whole answer, but they do provide a hint.

Figure 18: 40 Factors That, Reinforcing One Another, Induce Flexibility

1. The visible presence of new, flexible competitors
2. Visible display of the exploding array of new products
3. Talking up sales lost to revolutionary new technologies
4. Spruced-up old competitors intruding into your market
5. Business failures and restructurings in your industry
6. Good competitor analysis available to all
7. A belief that new market creation is the premier business success strategy
8. A belief that any product can be constantly improved
9. Unvarnished customer listening programs of every description
10. Constant measurement of customer satisfaction
11. Unadulterated feedback from sales and service forces
12. Customer (and supplier and distributor) visits by everyone: us to them, them to us
13. An environment that encourages numerous "small starts" and instant pilot tests of everything

14. Vociferous support for fast, thoughtful failures
15. Encouragement to fight NIH (not invented here) and "swipe" ideas from anywhere
16. Support for somewhat eccentric champions at all levels who may break the rules (who exhibit "constructive defiance"); praise of risk-taking supporters of champions
17. The use of "fully staffed," self-sufficient product development teams
18. Skill training and constant retraining; training in jobs in other functions; training in problem-solving techniques (cause and effect analysis)
19. Involvement in a "pay for performance" plan
20. Membership on a self-managing team, responsible for most of its own support activities such as budgeting and capital planning
21. A chance to be a team leader
22. Removal of bureaucratic impediments
23. Removal of humiliating rules
24. Provision of an attractive (clean and peppy) work environment
25. Constant rewards and celebrations for small accomplishments
26. Guaranteed employment
27. Fewer (or no) first-line supervisors
28. Middle managers who encourage constant front-line contact among functions
29. Middle managers who act as "on call" experts, spending most of their time helping teams; likewise, middle managers (experts) living "on the floor" of the factory or operations center, or distribution center
30. No more than five layers of structure
31. The use of small units, "small within big" configurations, everywhere
32. Senior management in touch with the line; strong, demonstrated top management support for the front line
33. Encouragement to "be the best" and "be unique" on some important performance dimension
34. Supervisors (and others) who are promoted on the basis of their ability to create an exciting work environment
35. Suggestions systems, reward systems, and other devices that invite zestful bureaucracy-bashing and constant cross-functional contact

36. Everyone evaluated on what/how much they have changed/improved
37. Wholesale information availability to everyone
38. Basic business forecasting and evaluation systems that emphasize trust, fairness, and integrity
39. People evaluation systems that emphasize "degrees of winning"
40. Genuine "bottom-up" setting of objectives and appraisal of performance

CREATING A SENSE OF URGENCY

How do you create urgency, hustle, and electricity? Part of the answer, of course, lies in a review of Figure 18; are you making use of all of these factors—at once? The rest involves management (leadership) by example—but example that doesn't so much emphasize, for instance, the quantity of time spent on your top priority (see L-3) as it does the presence of that intangible "X-factor." That is, if you want hustle—well, hustle yourself:

1. Cut out excessive trappings of office. Begin at home. Answer your own phone. Damp down the regal splendor of the office (regal is relative; this applies equally to first-line supervisors and chairmen of $10 billion firms). Don't travel with executive assistants. Etc. (See P-10, L-8.)

2. Follow a spartan routine. Give up executive perks and increase your people's perks. I can't tell you to fly coach or drive a 1965 pickup; I can tell you that doing so helps others take your "lean, mean, and urgent" speech seriously.

3. Be enchanted by the product or service. Want others to be excited about the 2379B widget, or the new "home bakery" you've added to your 125 supermarkets? The answer is simple (to state): *you* must be—and act—excited. If it's not crystal-clear to all that you love "it" (and "it" may be a new training program), then it's hard to imagine that "they" will love it.

Love it? How? I can't say how, as in how to love; but I can say what, as in what love means. The what is—being fascinated by it; asking questions about it; showing it off to everyone; displaying it everywhere; bragging about it (and its creators); examining it regularly; using it (if possible). It is, yes, intangible, but it boils down to engagement. If you're not engaged, others' sense of urgency will be damped immeasurably. (See C-2.)

4. "Go to the sound of the guns" (customers). The late Lieutenant General Melvin Zais (featured in *A Passion for Excellence*) advised would-be generals to do this—to seek the center of the maelstrom. Maryland's Governor Don Schaefer, a World War II Army veteran, puts this near the top of his list. When he was Baltimore's mayor, "go to the sound of the guns" meant go to the neighborhoods.

In business, the sound of the guns is wherever the customer is. Again, recall L-3 (Manage by Example). Want others to become obsessed with customers? You go first, Ms./Mr. Leader. A big (and longtime) customer calls from the other side of the country with a "little problem" with the first shipment of a new product. The board meeting is only forty-eight hours away. You've got very tough queries coming. So what do you do? Call the sales vice-president and order him to "get on it"? No. You go to the sound of the gun/customer. With some public fanfare, you toss your board presentation out, order up a charter jet (charters are okay when a big customer is involved), and *you* go there. Buy a clean shirt when you arrive; don't wait to pack a bag. It's almost that simple: Become a "hustling fool" (as a friend calls it) when the customer beckons; a whole lot of other such "hustling fools" will quickly be born in your organization.

This suggestion also applies, without modification, to lower-level managers and staff managers. Be observed (by your people) canceling an important meeting with the boss in order to rush to a customer's side (which, if you are in a staff job such as MIS, may mean a factory manager for whom you are installing a new CAM system). Yes, it is risky; but the risk you take as well as the nature of the act itself will go a long way toward instilling that "X-factor."

5. Redouble your commitment to "symbolic management." Much of L-3 (and L-4, L-6) was about symbols. All of this, the last leadership prescription, is about symbols. Creating a sense of urgency is, make no mistake, a symbolic exercise. It may come naturally. But it may not. If not, there is good news: You can learn to think symbolically—in fact, you must.

The most important step is heightened self-awareness: Put each small action through an "X-factor" filter. Does it foster or impede a sense of urgency? A perfectly reasonable decision, such as sending a proposal for a new product back for more staff work, when put through the "X-factor" sieve, should be reversed. Yes, you could learn more from another six weeks of study; but the presenter, a staff manager, said he was ready to charge ahead. Even though you're not sure, throw caution to the winds (at the margin) and tell him to proceed.

The more subtle trick is achieving a "bottom-up" perspective on urgency. What looks eminently reasonable to you often as not looks from below like waffling based upon power politics or mistrust of the line.

6. Laugh/cry/smile. "Hustle" and "electricity" are purely emotional. The era of the effective but detached manager, supervisor, or chief executive is gone. Necessary urgency throughout the organization and detachment at the top (or in any managerial post) cannot coexist.

This is not a "style tip." Former Oakland Raider football coach John Madden was a screamer, shouter, and arm-waver. Dallas Cowboy coach Tom Landry has a contained style. But talk to their players, as I have; both are paragons of emotionality. That is, both are transparently intense; their will to win and their passion for flawless execution are unmistakable.

I am not, then, urging you to be more extroverted or introverted. I am advising you that involvement, especially with the work of the front line (see also L-6), is a must for survival in a world where the front line's willingness to take spontaneous initiatives counts for more with each passing day.

One form of emotional involvement, laughter, deserves a special comment. Urgency and laughter go hand in glove. "Get going" and "try something" are among this book's central tenets. To speed action-taking, we simply must learn to laugh at our own (personal, organizational) bureaucratic, action-delaying foibles (L-8); and we must learn to laugh at interesting and useful mistakes (or "fast failures"—see I-8). In general, a spirited environment is marked by laughter—enthusiasm for being on a team and trying darn near anything to make the service or product better.

7. Be the first to get in to work. I have some qualms about this one because of the possibility of a "macho" misinterpretation. But I believe it is essential. Let me indulge once more in a sports analogy. My memory reaches back to the great Oakland Athletics team of 1972 (few now recall that Oakland is the only team in the last thirty years to win three consecutive world series, starting in 1972). Young Vida Blue pitched for the A's and was a whirlwind. Blue did a lot well, but I vividly recall one of his habits in particular. Pitchers are in general cerebral sorts by baseball standards and march to the tune of a different drummer; among other things, they walk, often with studied slowness, off the mound at the end of an inning. Not Blue. He trotted off. And that simple trot came to symbolize the hustling, scrounging, brilliantly successful A's.

I urge you, then, to come to work first, and trot off and onto the mound. Your personal display of spunk, of energy and zest for your task and life in general, especially if you are visible to the line, will be the single most important determinant of the organization's energy.

URGENCY AND FEAR

The fearful organization is not a hustling organization. Fear, of tiny failure or impending layoff (management or non-management), is the chief enemy of urgent action and flexibility. Unfortunately, in many of our biggest firms, the middle or first-level manager, on whom we must ultimately depend for survival, has lots to fear. Until that fear is erased or minimized, hustle—urgent testing of the untried—will not become common. Information hoarding rather than sharing (information is power, after all) and action-delaying tactics (not to act is not to risk failure) become the norm in fearful organizations. Political maneuvering (in an effort to make oneself apparently valuable to someone who looks like a survivor) goes up too.

Dealing with fearfulness requires any number of strategies, which either have already been discussed (see C-10 on establishing a revenue-enhancing attitude, I-8 on supporting failures, P-7 on tactics to accompany guaranteed employment, and P-4 on retraining managers and others) or will be discussed (see S-4 and S-5 on integrity and trust).

But beyond all these is yet another leadership "X-factor." Wartime military leadership provides the best and most obvious analogue. By definition, wartime command involves, day in and day out, the ultimate source of fear—sudden death for those in the prime of life. Military leadership offers two answers: confidence and accessibility.

Confidence means non-paralysis, a willingness to act, and act decisively; to start new things and cut failing ventures off. It does not mean false confidence about the future—complacency or unwarranted certainty about the correctness of the organization's strategy. Such false confidence, amidst obvious turmoil, is correctly read as foolishness, inducing more fearfulness—i.e., loss of confidence—rather than less. (The continued unwillingness of many corporate chieftains to face up to reality in the face of plummeting market share provides ample demonstration of complacency, and of its dire consequences—a continued lack of a sense of urgency on the part of the rest of the organization. GM in 1986 and Xerox and Kodak in the mid- and late seventies come to mind.)

So demonstrating confidence means demonstrating self-awareness of the competitive problems (which we all have) and then exhibiting a willingness to move fast to test strategies that will lead to fast adaptation. Move fast, above all, does not mean "get it right"—it does mean experiment fast, bravely, and continually. (And, I reiterate, it means having the guts to cut off the failed experiment before it becomes an elephantine disaster, then plunging ahead with a new one posthaste.)

I cannot, obviously, provide a formula for "getting confident." I can suggest that confidence only comes not when you are rolling the dice on a "big idea," but when you know you're working successfully at implanting the basic skills which will turn the organization into a hotbed of experiments aimed at improving everything dramatically and creating little new markets at a record clip.

The second tactic for fighting fear is accessibility, discussed in L-4 and L-6 as well. When times are chaotic, in war or in an increasingly crowded marketplace, just to *see* the leadership, to be around the leaders, to observe their humanity, is a tonic. (Even the leader who appears appropriately fearful helps instill confidence—if he or she is still willing to act boldly.) To "stand beside" at time of need is the best killer of fear. It doesn't necessarily lead to acts of extraordinary bravery (or risk-taking in the market), but it does induce a willingness to shed paralyzing fright and move forward, begin acting (testing). And to act, to have everyone taking those minuscule moment-to-moment risks (which are, of course, not cumulatively minuscule at all) is the essence of urgency and, ultimately, success.

FIRST STEPS

Pass every action, starting now, through the "scullery filter": That is, "Will the new worker in the scullery (or housekeeping or accounting department) view this as an example of our organization's new sense of urgency, will it be viewed neutrally, or will it look like delay and 'business as usual'?" If you cannot decisively answer "foster a sense of urgency, readily apparent to all," then the act is a step back, not even neutral. You have no time to waste; every tiny act must be an unmistakable demonstration to the scullery crew that a newfound sense of urgency has been unleashed.

VI

BUILDING *S*YSTEMS
FOR A WORLD TURNED
UPSIDE DOWN

SECTION SUMMARY

Systems are more important than ever, principally because today's systems cause real harm. For starters, if the market logic set forth in Part I and in prescriptions C-1 through C-10 is valid, we are measuring the wrong things. Second, our systems, as conventionally conceived, channel information narrowly and restrict the power to act. Thus the systems prescriptions (see Figure 19), like the leadership prescriptions, are aimed at both controlling (directing attention to appropriate strategic concerns) and decontrolling (empowering everyone to act).

The Guiding Premise, prescription S-1, is a paradox: Measure more by measuring less. That is, simplify systems (in some instances replace computer printouts with flip charts), but make sure that they measure "the right stuff"—e.g., quality, innovation, flexibility, and even such especially "soft" traits as effectiveness at bureaucracy-bashing.

Reconceiving the System Tools of Control and Empowerment is the topic of the next two, enabling prescriptions: S-2, revising performance appraisal, management by objectives, and job descriptions through simplification (or elimination in the case of job descriptions) and redirection toward what's important; S-3, sharing information (and power, since information is power) widely, increasing spending authority, and instituting simplified, relevant, nonbureaucratic, "bottom-up" strategic planning.

The "glue" that binds a company together in an uncertain world, and provides the stability necessary to encourage constant experimentation, is trust, which can be abetted by systems. The last two prescriptions address this central topic of Establishing Trust via Systems: S-4 makes the case for conservative financial and nonfinancial goal-setting; and S-5 focuses on maintaining total integrity.

The fifteen leadership and system prescriptions (1) revise the nature of control, (2) radically decentralize the power to take action, and (3) come to grips with the stability-instability paradox—the need to provide more stability in order to encourage the greatly increased day-to-day risk-taking necessary to deal with that instability in a world turned upside down.

Figure 19: **Building Systems for a World Turned Upside Down**

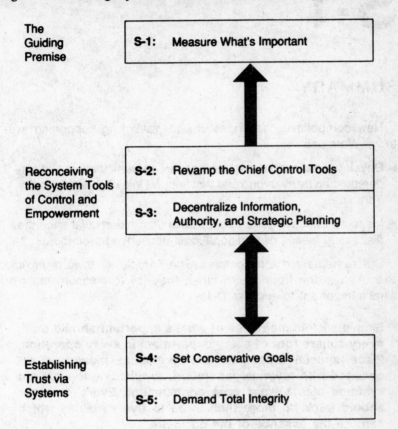

S-1

SUMMARY

New competitive challenges call for rethinking supporting systems. We must:

▶ Develop simple systems that encourage participation and understanding by everyone and that support initiative-taking on the front line.

▶ Measure what's important to the business; in particular shed the distracting biases of traditional cost-accounting procedures.

Our systems are too complex. The complexity thwarts flexible execution at the front line. Further, they fail to measure most of what's important to success today.

Simple, visible measures of what's important should mark every square foot of every department in every operation. Place special emphasis on developing measures associated with revenue generation, supplanting the current systems bias toward cost containment. Every manager should track no more than three to five variables which capture the essence of the business.

S-1

Measure What's Important

Measurement is too often equated with how many pounds of numerical indicators the senior manager receives weekly. There is little feel for the data at any level. Line—especially front-line—involvement in its use or formulation is limited. Ironically, the need for flexibility in an increasingly complex environment requires systems to be made less complex.

In addition, our systems invariably measure "the wrong stuff." We know how to measure costs—using models whose assumptions were created decades ago for a much different world. Sources of long-term revenue enhancement—such as quality, service, flexibility—are virtually absent from most measurement systems.

KEEP IT SIMPLE (AND VISIBLE)

Keep It Simple: Flip Charts and Line Involvement

Flip charts, two-variable management, back-of-the-envelope calculations—surely these were yesteryear's way of life, inappropriate to today's complex setting.

Not so. An accounting firm executive recalls his surprise at the "systems" used by NUMMI (the GM-Toyota venture). He had expected state-of-the-art—that is, complex—measurement techniques. "Instead," he says, laughing, "it was flip charts, red and green lights depicting a system's status . . . absurdly simple, but to the point."

A primary test of a sharp manufacturing operation, according to Richard Schonberger in *World Class Manufacturing,* is the presence of living, and simple, measures: charts on the wall assessing the causes of delay, updated hourly by crayon or marker pen; physical space for teams to meet near the line, equipped with blackboards that can be covered with simple, to-the-point analyses.

Schonberger makes no bones about the method: "Data recording comes first. The tools are cheap and simple: pencils and chalk. Give those simple tools for recording data to each operator. Then make it a natural part of the operator's job to record disturbances and measurements on charts and blackboards. The person who records data is inclined to analyze, and the analyzer is inclined to think of solutions." He goes on to describe the feel of a pragmatic, measurement-happy environment:

> . . . One [plant] stands out for its attention to keeping the walls covered with measured data on the basics. It is the Hewlett-Packard plant making the HP-3000 series 500 minicomputer. . . . [Simple] charts are everywhere in the California plant where the 3000-500 is produced. The charts have been in use for several years with excellent results. . . .
>
> A main wall near the center of the manufacturing floor has three large charts posted on it. One shows the JIT [just-in-time] material flow. Another chart shows the total quality control process. The third, centered between the other two, contains a wealth of data plotted on graphs and charts, mostly on performance in printed circuit assembly (PCA). One graph plots PCA throughput time: down from fifteen days in 1982 to 1.5 days in 1984. Another shows WIP [work-in-progress] inventory: down from $676,000 in 1983 to $200,000 in 1984 to $20,000 in 1985. Three more graphs show scrap, floor space, and labor hours in PCA—all cut roughly in half. Several more graphs show declining defects. . . . Every day PCA people post detail sheets showing number of bent leads, missing parts, and other nonconformities, and they plot defect total on the graphs weekly. . . .
>
> In short, the plant is set up for *visual management* [my emphasis]. A manager, a quality engineer, a supplier, a customer, or a visiting class from a college campus can make a circle tour of the compact facility in an hour or two and know what is right and what is wrong.

Compared with this, managing a plant by examining periodic reports seems like looking through binoculars the wrong way. . . .

World-class manufacturing surely does require strategic leadership. I am convinced that the best strategy is doing things better and better in the trenches. The best leadership is that which insists on visible measures of what is going on in the trenches and on action there to achieve a high rate of improvement.

The essential variables are these: (1) simplicity of presentation, (2) visibility of measurements, (3) everyone's involvement, (4) undistorted collection of primary information throughout the operations area, (5) the straightforward measurement of what's important, and (6) achievement of an overall feel of urgency and perpetual improvement. Unfortunately, all six of these elements are missing in systems that govern the average operation I've observed.

Getting started on achieving this sort of environment involves all of the activities covered in the people prescriptions (P-1 through P-10). Once more, the outcomes are readily describable, but they hinge on attitude—a belief that people can accomplish their tasks and that they wish to accomplish them.

Of special importance, recalling previous discussions (especially P-8), is the idea of staff on call. The information-intense environment—with the information used by those who collect it—is based upon "bottom up" initiative. Decisions on what to collect, when to collect it, how to record it, and how to use it must remain the almost exclusive province of well-trained front-line people, aided only on an "as needed" basis by the experts.

Keep It Simple: One or Two Measures That Count

. . . the manager good at monitoring has at his fingertips [a few general measures] with which—he or she feels—the pulse of the business can be tracked. Whether or not the variables identified are causally related to the effects measured in a scientific sense is immaterial; the point is, the manager has driven his or her understanding of the business to such a fine point that he or she has isolated the two or three really useful measures about the products, company, and industry and religiously tracks these as a test of progress and a barometer of change.

Tom Bonoma
The Marketing Edge

For senior managers, the idea of simplicity, as captured in this comment by Tom Bonoma, means boiling what's important down to a couple of variables that capture the strategic essence of the unit or firm.

The uniqueness of wildly profitable Deluxe Check (see C-4) lies in remarkable customer responsiveness, going back to an "order" written by founder W. R. Hotchkiss on August 18, 1936. He declared that henceforth all orders would go out no later than the day after they were received, adding that "no money should be spared" to achieve this end.

This dictum still drives the firm, and the two simple service statistics measuring their success are prominently reported in the firm's annual report. In 1986, Deluxe shipped 97.1 percent of orders in accordance with its promise; 99.6 percent of those orders were error-free.

How is this achieved? While appropriate automation marks Deluxe's sixty-two plants, simple, visible systems are the essence of success. For instance, each day's order slip is a different color. Tuesday's is orange, and one plant manager comments: "At 4:30 Wednesday, I don't want to see any orange around here."

Detailed, computerized data collection systems are a must, but operating managers must also "know the [essential] numbers" from memory. "No orange by late Wednesday afternoon" is easy to remember. And the greater the complexity swirling around us, the more important it is to maintain this kind of grasp on reality. The operating manager must not slip into a morass of complexity, answering every question, as so many do, with: "I'll have accounting run the numbers, and we'll get an estimate in four or five days." Requisite lightning-fast responses demand keeping a feel for things at all times.

Thinking About Vision, Symbolic Action, and Recognition as a "Control System"

Recall the discussion of managing as symbolic action (see L-4). In particular, I stressed the role of stories in guiding an institution. Analogously, prescription L-2 emphasized the role of a succinct vision. In an ambiguous environment, people need something to provide day-to-day guidelines in handling an endless series of novel circumstances.

The old hierarchical organization provided a simple answer: Buck everything up the line for decision. We no longer can afford the luxury of such time-consuming deliberations. We must increasingly depend on front-line people to make the right choices. Further up the line, but far short of corporate staffs, we must depend on senior functional or general managers to make decisions on strategic affairs.

The best "systems" to ensure correct choices are (1) a clear vision, (2) sharing stories that illustrate how others, at all levels, have reacted to novel situations consistent with the vision, and (3) recognition for jobs well done, those that illustrate imaginative responses in the face of numbing uncertainty.

These devices—vision, symbolic action, recognition—are a *control system,* in the truest sense of that term. The manager's task is to conceive of them as such, and to consciously use them. There is nothing soft about a Federal Express, Domino's, Nordstrom, or Deluxe Check "story" or recognition affair. It purposefully defines what each firm means by "go the limit to serve the customer."

MEASURING WHAT'S IMPORTANT

Current Systems Mislead

Our traditional measurement systems are dangerously misleading. Take the standard cost-accounting system. It "allocates" overhead costs such as the accounting department, engineering, utilities, machinery, and management to direct labor. That is, direct labor "hours" are the most readily counted indicator; all of the other expenses are appended to this one, visible expense. In fact, each typical "direct labor hour" may carry an overhead "burden," as the accountants call it, of as much as 1,000 percent. That's why, when a manager is pushed by higher-ups to cut costs, there is but one sensible target under this accounting regimen: to cut direct labor, which, on the books, includes that huge "burden." Thus, for accounting purposes, when he cuts a direct labor hour, he will usually be credited with the reduction in the "burden" as well, whether it actually occurs or not.

Suppose the manager decides to subcontract production of a labor-intensive part. He saves 100 hours of direct labor a month at $20 per hour ($2,000 in all). But on the books, he saves not only the direct labor costs but the 1,000 percent burden (worth ten times the labor) as well—for credited monthly savings of $22,000. The subcontract to a smaller, low-overhead, perhaps offshore operation costs, say, $5,000 a month. The net "booked" saving, then, is $17,000 a month. Much applause goes to the plant manager.

Unfortunately, the real story is different from the accounting story. In fact, actual factory overhead is not reduced much or at all by the act of subcontracting (you can't shut off the heat around one idle machine). Most likely, overhead is increased, because the plant manager (or someone, somewhere) has to negotiate and administer a contract with the new supplier and handle the incoming components. Not to mention the increased uncertainty of delivery and quality in the early days of dealing with any supplier—that also carries real costs. So the true net saving is the $2,000 saving in direct labor minus the $5,000 subcontract cost minus, say, $1,000 in real, added overhead—or a loss of $4,000. Nonetheless, thanks to the miracle of "modern" accounting, the plant manager still takes that bow.

Such perverse outcomes are standard, according to H. Thomas Johnson and Robert S. Kaplan in *Relevance Lost: The Rise and Fall of Management Accounting.* In fact, the authors report, some experts claim that "cost accounting is the number one enemy of productivity." Industrialists trained in engineering, such as Andrew Carnegie, used accounting to assist line managers in decision-making on the factory floor. But slowly, as professionally trained accountants began to take control of the system, accounting's emphasis shifted from being a management tool for the factory floor to financial reporting. And it's those oh so frequent financial reporting requirements laid on by agencies such as the SEC and the IRS that necessitate, for instance, allocating all overhead costs to direct labor and the cost of goods sold—which in time leads to the kind of flawed decision-making described above. That is, to determine profit for the fleeting "accounting period" across numerous products in a factory (a meaningless number from a proactive managerial standpoint), you must, by hook or by crook, assign every dollar of expense to something. Direct labor is the easiest "something," even though the result misdirects decision-makers.

The "expensing" of activities such as research, worker-skill upgrading, and process improvement is another prime example of a traditional cost-accounting device that can have a deleterious effect on performance. Since these investments in the future are treated, *for accounting purposes,* as "expenses of the period" (wholly written off each thirty days, for instance), they fall prey to the short-term cost cutter. That is, cutting R&D is a 100 percent cut—you get full credit; thus it's a fat target. Were it "capitalized" as a building is, when you cut it you'd only get a few percent credit in the short term—and the temptation would be reduced accordingly.

Another error of this sort involves hidden cross-subsidies among products that make it difficult, especially with today's conventions, to measure true product profitability—a particularly dangerous problem in these times, when short production runs for an ever wider variety of products are becoming the norm. You must know whether a product is making money or not; our present systems cloud the issue. A related sin is our fixation on short-term measures, which makes it almost impossible, for instance, to assess the long-term costs of developing a product.

A last example involves purchasing: Most purchasing departments still are evaluated principally on the contract cost of procurement. Almost always, however, they fail to factor into these "contract costs" how the poor quality of purchased goods can diminish final product quality—tarnishing the ultimate producer's reputation and driving up other, hard-dollar costs (fixing defective supplier material, warranty work).

The Essential Variables Are Ignored—But Can Be Measured

Bad as these problems are, however, there are sins of outright omission in traditional accounting that are far worse. Our fixation with financial measures leads us to downplay or ignore less tangible nonfinancial measures, such as product quality, customer satisfaction, order lead time, factory flexibility, the time it takes to launch a new product, and the accumulation of skills by labor over time. Yet these are increasingly the real drivers of corporate success over the middle to long term, as emphasized in the first forty prescriptions in this book.

The good news is that nontraditional measures are popping up. Prescription C-2 offered several examples of the thoughtful measurement of poor-quality cost, for instance, at Tennant, IBM, and Milliken. Firms such as Ford, Tennant, and Perdue Farms use quality objectives as a basis for compensation. IBM continues to refine the measurement of quality, most recently devoting substantial effort to the quantitative measurement of business systems (see C-2); that firm also uses direct incentives (rewards and penalties for quality) in supplier contracts.

Quality is slowly becoming a basis for purchasing department evaluation. For instance, Schonberger reports on Uniroyal's Rubber Division, which adopted a scheme in which quality accounted for 40 percent of its Vendor Service Rating; price carried a 25 percent weight, on-time delivery 20 percent, and service 15 percent. But obvious as such schemes might seem, they are still very rare. A discussion with acquisition quality managers at the Department of Defense underscored the point. Quality is receiving lip service at DOD these days, but one frustrated senior civilian executive reported: "The files are filled with vendors who've delivered 20 to 30 percent defective parts for years; yet we still won't cut them off."

Getting quality into the routine measurement system is not easy. In *The Chain of Quality*, TRW's John Groocock (see also C-2) describes the effort he made when he took on his first quality assignment at ITT Europe. In Harold Geneen's ITT, nothing was taken seriously until it was measured and included in the intricate financial review process. If quality were to be a priority, Groocock reasoned, it would have to edge its way into that all-consuming system. So early on he sought an accountant as an ally:

> He was responsible for accounting systems throughout the company, and reported to the controller. He showed me how to write a controller's procedure and together we did so. He suggested we should make quality costs a quarterly report instead of a monthly report. That seemed rational. Quality costs do not change all that rapidly, and he said it would save the divisional controllers, who were already greatly overworked, a substantial amount of effort. I had never asked a senior accountant for anything before in my life and was surprised that he was taking my request so seriously. However, I felt intuitively that, as most of the financial system was on a monthly reporting, a quarterly measure would always be a low-prestige bother (it would never become institutionalized). . . . So I kept my nerve, dug my heels in, and got away with monthly

reporting. . . . We circulated the draft controller's procedure to the division quality managers and controllers and quickly incorporated their comments. Most of them felt it was not serious and that it would not really happen. Early in December the controller's procedure was signed off. People had been surprised to find that they could not think of any good reason for disapproving it. No one had stood up and shouted "Nonsense!" during my presentation at the conference. The division people had their chance to table rational objections, and these were taken into account. My colleague in accounting devoted so much personal effort that he was becoming a champion himself. Suddenly, it was no longer an academic exercise, and amazingly at the end of February, most of the required reports for January 1967 came in (January is a quiet month for accountants). The delinquents were a minority and were exposed to the pressure that minorities suffer, and soon came into line. I nursed the fledgling system for three years, and after I went to Brussels as Director of Quality ITT Europe (ITTE) in 1969, I championed the system throughout Europe for the next eleven years.

Other prescriptions supply other examples of companies that are measuring "the right stuff." McKesson (C-4) measures its responsiveness to its customers. Schonberger's *World Class Manufacturing* underscores the importance of measuring responsiveness, which he calls lead time: "The number of believers in zero lead time as a superordinate target is still small but growing fast. One by one, top companies are coming to the conclusion that reducing lead time is a simple and powerful measure of how well you are doing. The manufacturing people at both Motorola and Westinghouse have chosen lead time reduction as a dominant measure; various divisions of Hewlett-Packard and General Electric have too. Lead time is a sure and truthful measure, because a plant can reduce it only by solving problems that cause delays. Those cover the gamut: order-entry delays and errors, wrong blueprints or specifications, long setup times and large lots, high-defect counts, machines that break down, operators who are not well trained, supervisors who do not coordinate schedules, suppliers that are not dependable, long waits for inspectors or repair people, long transport distances, multiple handling steps, and stock record inaccuracies. Lead times drop when those problems are solved. Lead times drop fast when they are solved fast."

The innovation prescriptions also emphasize measurement. Prescription I-9, for instance, features 3M's measurement of innovation, and its linkage between executive pay and a precise, quantitative innovation target. The people prescriptions, especially P-6, advise rewarding everyone on the basis of measured quality and/or productivity improvement, and present many novel schemes for doing so. The people prescriptions also emphasize the need to foster cross-functional cooperation. We aren't used to measuring or rewarding on this basis, but a 1986 story in *Fortune* about American Express suggests it can be done:

> [Chairman Jim Robinson] started preaching the virtues of intramural cooperation. Amex, he said, is "one enterprise." . . . He then reinforced his pitch with steel rods, requiring senior executives to identify two or three promising One Enterprise synergy projects in their annual strategic plans and work on them during the year. He made it corporate policy to evaluate every manager and professional employee on their contributions to One Enterprise, and then he handed out extra bonuses to senior executives who did their bit for the cause.
>
> One of the two bonuses paid in 1985 went to [the] chairman of American Express Bank. He received $80,000 because the bank had worked on a dozen or so successful synergy projects, including introducing Shearson investment bankers to its overseas clients and selling $240 million of money orders and traveler's checks for the card division. . . .
>
> In addition to providing his senior executives with financial incentives to cooperate, Robinson relies on a watchdog to make sure the middle managers do so too. [The manager of corporate strategy] issues . . . a monthly report on the status of each One Enterprise project, which [is] circulated among the company's top 100 executives. The report gives managers collaborating with other managers unusual visibility; it also turns the high beams on task forces that get bogged down in internal politics. In those cases [the report indicates] "no progress" in the Project Status column: "After two or three months of that kind of attention . . . people start finding ways to resolve their differences."

I have, in fact, attempted to provide quantitative measures for most of these prescriptions. Figure 20 summarizes several of them. Unfortunately, the course is largely uncharted. There are a few, pioneering examples, such as those just mentioned. In most instances, however, you are on your own, with my sketchy outline as guidance. But the issue is of the utmost significance. "What gets measured gets done" has never been so powerful a truth.

Figure 20: A Sample of Unconventional Measures Proposed in This Book

Prescription	Measure
C-1: Niche Creation	Number of "differentiators" added to each product every 90 days.
C-2: Quality	Relative perceived product quality; poor- quality cost; rewards based on quality goals. Devise quality measures in every unit. Evaluate suppliers on the basis of quality.
C-3: Service	The ten attributes of customer satisfaction; customer evaluation of the intangibles; the lifetime value of a customer.
C-4: Responsiveness	Speed of response to customer needs; percentage of customers covered by tight (electronic or other) linkages; new links (electronic or other) added to each product each 90 days.
C-7: Listening	Informal listening ("call three customers per week").
C-8: Factory as Marketing Arm	Customer visits to factory; factory manager and nonmanager visits to customers.

(continued on next page)

593

Prescription	Measure
C-9: Sales, Service, and Distribution	Time spent with sales and service people; rate at which additions are made to sales and service force; number of franchisees/distributors pruned.
I-1: Small Starts	Number of small starts; percentage of time/R&D budget devoted to small starts.
I-3: Pilots	Number of pilot tests of anything going on in each area.
I-4: Competitive Analysis	Number of ideas "swiped" from competitors per month.
I-5: Word of Mouth	Percentage of ad/marketing budget devoted to word of mouth.
I-6: Support Innovators	Number of awards to innovators; number/percentage of awards to unsung supporters of innovators per month.
I-8: Support Fast Failure	Number of awards for interesting failures, constructive defiance of rules.
I-9: Share of Revenue from New Products	Percentage of sales coming from new products introduced in the last 12, 24, 36 months.
P-2: Teams	Percentage of people in team configurations.
P-3: Recognition	Number of recognition acts/events per month.
P-5: Training	Hours/dollars devoted to skill upgrading.
P-6: Compensation	Percentage of total compensation from profit-distribution bonus plan/ pay-for-knowledge program.

Figure 20 *(continued)*

Prescription	Measure
P-9: Middle Management Role	Number of acts of boundary-bashing; number of awards going to boundary-bashers.
P-10: De-bureaucratize	Number of demeaning and debilitating regulations renounced per month; number of amenities added to each facility per month; your "housekeeping," scored vis-à-vis competitors.
L-3: Manage by Example	Time spent per day/week on top priority.
L-4: Visible Management	Percentage of time out of the office; percentage of time with customers, front-line people.
L-6: Line Focus	Number of line versus number of staff at meetings; line versus staff salaries; time spent with line people.
L-9: "What Have You Changed?"	Amount of things changed; formally evaluate everyone accordingly.

FIRST STEPS

1. Assign each business unit and department the task of developing in 30 days five rough, unconventional, paper-and-pencil measures of what's going to be important to their unit's ability to support the firm's mission.
2. Use the measures, in rough form, in formal reviews. Insist that two-thirds of the new measures emphasize (a) customers (e.g., quality, service, listening), (b) flexibility/responsiveness, (c) innovativeness, and (d) the relative increase/decrease in the value of the workforce's skills, taken as a whole.

595

S-2

SUMMARY

In an effort to induce flexibility, we must turn our backs on, or radically redefine, the three staples of control over individuals— performance appraisals, the setting of objectives, and job descriptions. We must:

▶ Simplify these three primary control systems.

▶ Focus on what's important (e.g., flexibility rather than rigidity).

▶ Make the process of developing objectives, etc., truly "bottom up."

▶ Make the documents "living" ones, subject to constant discussion rather than infrequent, pro forma review.

These three control systems, like the measurement systems just discussed in S-1, are increasingly doing more harm than good. As typically constituted, they attempt to achieve a specificity of result inconsistent with today's fluid, competitive environment. If we can't fix them, we should scrap them.

Performance appraisals should be ongoing, based upon a simple, written "contract" between the person being appraised and his/her boss. Limit objectives to no more than three per period (quarter, year). Eliminate job descriptions.

Revamp the Chief Control Tools

W. Edwards Deming has contended that performance appraisal is the number one American management problem. He says it takes the average employee (manager or nonmanager) six months to recover from it.

I think Dr. Deming is about right, though I'd add the setting of objectives and job descriptions to the list of personnel control devices that are downright dangerous—as currently constituted.

Like the cost-accounting systems described in S-1, these are systems started for useful reasons which (1) have become increasingly bureaucratic, run by "experts" (often personnel departments in this case, rather than accountants as in S-1), and (2) are frighteningly out of touch with today's and tomorrow's needs. They are stability-inducing systems at odds with a world where flexibility is the chief survival requirement.

PERFORMANCE EVALUATION AND PAY SCHEMES THAT ARE SIMPLE AND TO THE POINT

Performance evaluation is essential—more than ever, in fact. It is a tool for directing attention, and attention today must be directed to new targets (see C-1 through C-4, for instance). Throughout the first forty prescriptions, I implicitly endorsed performance appraisal—at various times suggesting that it emphasize quality, constant innovation, and functional-barrier destruction.

The following attributes can turn performance appraisal from a minus to a plus:

1. **"Appraisal" must be constant,** not focused principally on the big annual (or semiannual) appraisal "event." (Dr. Deming points out that, in contrast to American dependence on the one or two big events, specific feedback to the average Japanese employee comes daily.) To ensure this, middle managers should evaluate first-level managers on the degree to which the first-level managers give their people constant feedback, both good and bad.

Above all, the annual (or quarterly or semiannual) appraisal review should never come as a surprise. The employee should be fully aware of his or her status and progress throughout the year.

2. **Appraisal is—and should be—very time-consuming.** We usually fail to give regular and direct feedback (painful negative feedback in particular) in the course of day-to-day affairs. Now it's time to fill out the semiannual appraisal form. We put it off until late on Sunday afternoon prior to "appraisal meeting week." Then we hurry through it, accompanied by a stiff scotch or two. Likewise, we rush through the scheduled meetings at the rate of seven or eight a day. (We hold them—as opposed to slipping the form under the door—only because the personnel department representative says we must.) Then the office is a shambles for the next few weeks. A few find their superb self-images confirmed; most are stunned, hurt, and disappointed. In no case has the meeting been a useful one for either the appraiser or the target.

Successful appraisal requires four different sorts of time: (a) day-to-day time spent giving constant feedback; (b) preparation time for the annual or semiannual evaluation; (c) execution time for the appraisal meetings, which should be spread out rather than bunched by the dozens in a single week; and (d) group time, during which fellow managers are consulted and appraisal criteria coordinated. (This last category not only provides the manager with input, but also engenders a sense of fairness and equity throughout the organization.)

3. **There should be a small number of performance categories, and no forced ranking.** I'm well aware of "category inflation," in which 90 percent of the people end up being graded as nine or ten on a one-to-ten scale. Nonetheless, there is simply nothing dumber (and more debilitating) than labeling one-third to one-half of your people losers, which is exactly what virtually all forced-ranking systems do. Surely, all the time

you've spent recruiting and coaching has resulted in a work force more than half of which is doing an adequate job. Label an individual a loser and you will induce that person to behave like a loser. In particular, the person so labeled will work at keeping out of sight, and therefore cease to take even small risks, which is intolerable in today's environment.

This is not a plea to go easy on your "problem" people. They deserve counseling and a second and third chance, to be sure; given that nod to genuine due process, I am behind you when you make the necessary decision to demote or let go. But forced ranking doesn't help you go after those who need serious help, and its unintended fallout creates a large number of unnecessarily disaffected employees.

I suggest a system in which about 10 to 20 percent receive a "superior" evaluation; another 70 to 85 percent are satisfactory; and no more than 5 to 10 percent or so are in a questionable/unsatisfactory status. The lumping of 70 to 85 percent in one "grade" does not in any way limit your ability to pay tribute to jobs well done by individuals and groups. Recognition (see P-3, L-6) and group/team financial and other awards (see P-2, P-6) are the heart of the true evaluation—and motivation—system. Bob Townsend, in *Further Up the Organization,* urges just three categories, with attendant bonuses: "unsatisfactory (no bonus), satisfactory (bonus of X, on average), outstanding . . . equal to 2X or greater." Townsend adds ruefully: "Keeping it simple means fighting the experts. . . . [Yet] every change [of rules or percentages] means loss of understanding, loss of trust, loss of motivation."

4. Minimize the complexity of formal evaluation procedures and forms. I am against complexity. I am not against putting comments in writing. You, as manager, and each subordinate should jointly and literally sign off on a one-to-two-page written "contract," drafted initially by the subordinate, that includes the following: (a) one or two specific annual or semiannual objectives; (b) one or two personal/group/team growth or career-enhancement objectives; (c) one or two objectives for skill improvement in deficit areas; and (d) one objective that relates to the group's (or team's) overarching strategic theme—such as quality improvement. The format should be open-ended prose. Formal reviews of progress should be scheduled at least bimonthly, and informal reviews should be more frequent. You (the manager) should be able to recall—from memory—the content of each and every contract.

One executive, in a financial services firm, responded to this idea with:

"Aren't you catering to your bias—after all, you're a writer, and prose seems natural. I'm a numbers guy."

I objected vigorously. First, I'm an engineer by training—and disposition. And a measurement fanatic, as this book demonstrates (see S-1). My point, I said, was that numbers too often focus on highly abstract outcomes. We need, instead, to emphasize capability building—developing the skills that will give us strategic advantage over the long haul. We need to talk about "building sales-force capability and support systems," "achieving flexibility," and "cutting product development time" more than about achieving "15 percent earnings-per-share growth." The latter target may be admirable, but is not much related to the skill enhancement necessary for adjusting to the changing world.

Of course, I have no objection to quantitative indicators of the enhancement of the skills of the sales force or the shortening of development cycles, for instance. But I'd also want to see an objective statement such as "be rated, by 1989, by third-party survey as having the premier sales force in the region."

5. Performance appraisal goals ought to be straightforward, emphasizing what you want to happen. You want quality improvement to rank as number one for your group? Rank it number one in the performance evaluation, and ask each manager to have one key objective—the first one—dealing with it directly (recall that Tennent did this—C-2). If barrier-dismemberment is the key for a middle manager, put it first in the jointly edited "contract."

Grocer Stew Leonard doesn't beat about the bush: Everyone's evaluation asks of them how they contributed to "STEW." The "S" stands for customer satisfaction, the "T" for teamwork, the "E" for excellence, and the "W" for Wow! The last is Leonard's favorite word, referring to the sense of excitement which he believes is the essence of the store's achievement. In other words, Leonard's evaluation is unequivocal about what he deems important to the business's continuing success.

6. Make the pay decisions public. Most bridle at this, but the benefits are several. In the absence of public disclosure, speculation is rife, and the picture it paints usually distorts or darkens the truth. More important, public disclosure causes embarrassment only if there truly is an inequity, about which, regardless of its convoluted historical basis, you should be embarrassed.

7. Make formal appraisal a small part of overall recognition. I have argued vociferously here for appropriate use of appraisal, especially to direct attention to new concerns. I even stated it was more important than ever before. That said, the thrust of the first forty prescriptions is clear—recognition (listening, celebration, pay, involvement) should/ must come from a host of ongoing activities, of which performance evaluation is but one.

Together the seven attributes of performance appraisal outlined here add up to a common-sense approach. The rejoinder I most frequently get is: "But how can you not resort to complex categories—level 9 [of 23], pay step 7 [of 10]"—in a complex organization?"

The answer harks back to prescription P-8:

▶ First, keep the organization simple, with few layers. That is, there should be only a handful of managerial and nonmanagerial (professional, scientific) categories, or levels.

▶ Second, each should have a small number of wide, overlapping steps for pay purposes.

▶ Third, fight conventional wisdom in one last way—allow stellar professionals (salespersons, engineers) to outearn, sometimes by a wide margin, their bosses. I'll go a step further: 10 to 25 percent of each sales manager's salespersons and 10 to 25 percent of each R&D manager's engineers/scientists should be outearning their boss. "Let the top pros remain pros" (if they wish) is the guiding advice—don't force them to become frustrated managers.

▶ Fourth, "spend time." Managers develop a sense of what's equitable on the basis of hours and hours of discussion—at the time of formal reviews, when opportunities for promotions arise, etc.

OBJECTIVES THAT EMPHASIZE THE ACHIEVABLE

Put a 5-foot-10-inch person into 6 feet 3 inches of water, and odds are he'll learn to swim. He may sputter and spit a bit, but he can always hop up off the bottom and get air. Put that same person in 7 feet 4 inches of water, and you may have a dead body on your hands.

In any managerial forum, the topic turns at some point to goal-setting. Most American managers seem all too ready to toss the people who report to them into the 7-foot-4-inch-deep tank. This is what I hear: "You've got to push your people. Shoot for the moon. That's what motivates 'em. Give 'em half a chance and they'll sign up for a goal 10 percent less than last year's, even though the market is way up." And so on.

I have come to hate the term "stretch target," as it is commonly used. Yet I fervently believe in "stretch." I believe, however, in the 6-foot-3-inch variety for the 5-foot-10-inch participant. There is an attribute of goal-setting that stands out in creating a highly charged environment—teaching people that they are winners and that they can succeed, which in turn induces them to take on more, risk more. Thus, the prime objective of goal-setting should be to turn 90 percent of the people in your firm into confident winners who will take the new and always greater risks required by the chaotic times we live in.

That does leave room for "stretch"—it's a must. Without it, there is no sense of accomplishment. But the real art for the manager lies in creating challenging but achievable targets. That may mean, for example, creating just a two-inch hurdle to "teach" a previously demoralized individual (or group) that she or he (or it) is a winner.

This is not just theoretical speculation. I am an inveterate reader of biographies. Consider Field Marshal Bernard Montgomery and General George Patton; the two have something surprising in common. In North Africa, both (at different times) launched their careers in the limelight after inheriting winless and dispirited armies. And both rapidly reversed these armies' fortunes—using exactly the same technique to begin the turnaround. Both focused on the instantly "doable"—pushing their men to achieve *something,* and thereby leading them to realize they weren't born losers. In both cases, appearance and fitness were the chosen vehicles. A first "stretch target" (of the two-inch variety) was to demand spotless uniforms and to launch an intensive physical fitness program. A study titled "Excellence in the Surface Navy" describes a similar turnaround by a successful ship captain: "He began by 'planning victories for the ship.' By this he means that he was constantly on guard, looking for competition that the ship could enter into reasonably sure that it would emerge victorious. This could be something as trivial as challenging other ships in the task group to a sailing competition, knowing full well that their ship was the only one that had any sailboats, to seeking recognition as the top ship to complete refresher training in a given year.

In either case, the crew's image of itself was enhanced by such actions."

The right attitude is one I call "degrees of winning," rather than "winners and losers." This is especially important today. We are required to teach so many fundamentally new things—how a manager can be a facilitator instead of a cop, how to stop emphasizing volume and enhance quality, how to manage a flexible organization instead of a stable one, how to make everyone rather than a handpicked few an agent for change and a risk taker responsible for constant improvement. Building new skills, when large numbers of people are involved, depends above all on generating momentum and commitment. Momentum and commitment come from learning that you can act as needed in—and succeed in—the brave new world. "Punishment," the behavioral scientists have long told us (with compelling documentation), is a futile strategy in general, but especially when new behaviors are required, as they are today. Punishment drives us to hide and be even more averse to risk.

A final word and pleasant surprise: If you work with your team to set achievable goals, you may find yourself managing goals downward—and "unstretching" them, if you will. Social psychology experiments reveal time and again that once people (singly or in groups) get on a roll, they set their objectives too high! They rapidly come to believe they can leap any building of any height in a single bound; by overreaching, they set themselves up for demotivating disappointments. The best route to long-term success, especially where new skills need to be learned, is therefore to meticulously set tailor-made targets that do indeed stretch, but which can be hurdled by almost everyone.

A Comment on Management by Objectives

Management by objectives (MBO) is one more great idea that has been neutered by bureaucrats in nine out of ten applications. That is, MBO (like performance appraisal) is a superb tool if the objectives are (1) simple, (2) focused on what's important, (3) genuinely created from the bottom up (the objectives are drafted by the person who must live up to them, with no constraining guides), and (4) a "living" contract, not a form-driven exercise.

Peter Drucker "invented" MBO in 1954, in *The Practice of Management.* Interestingly, Drucker never capitalized the words, nor did he use the three words by themselves. He spoke of (lowercase) "management by objectives *and self-control* [my emphasis]"—that is, nonbureaucratic self-management was the avowed purpose. The antithesis, an accountant-driven extra layer of bureaucracy, was what usually ensued, as the fine idea became encumbered over time by complex top-down techniques.

So by all means keep MBO—but get rid of the capital letters, restore Drucker's "and self-control," and follow the four rules proposed above. Once more, the point is underscored by the times—we can't afford systems that implicitly abet inflexibility, as most MBO routines do today.

SCRAP JOB DESCRIPTIONS

Who would fight "you gotta know what you're supposed to do"? No one, until the job description starts to constrict options—which is almost inevitable. Perhaps a case could be made for job descriptions in a stable, predictable, very vertically oriented (functional) organization. Today, in all cases the "j.d." is a loser.

Begin by answering this question: Have you—the average reader has been successful—ever read your job description? Most, if they're honest, will admit that they haven't. If you haven't read your job description, yet have had a successful career as a nonmanager and manager, what's the big deal about job descriptions? I have never read a job description in any of my incarnations. I've done stints as a U.S. Navy Seabee battalion operations officer and a detachment commander (overseas); a Pentagon junior assistant (in the Office of the Chief of Naval Operations); the President's senior drug abuse adviser; and a junior consultant, senior consultant, and partner at McKinsey & Co. My failure to read my job descriptions has never been a handicap. In fact, it doubtless helped me from time to time. By not reading my job descriptions, I've never been burdened by knowing exactly what I'm officially *not* allowed to do or with whom exactly I am required to "interface" on a project. (To be very honest, and this speaks volumes, I'm not sure whether any of my jobs, even in the Navy, had a job description.)

In the typical job description, with the stroke of a pen the boss sets all her or his managerial worries to rest. She or he conjures up the tasks that need completing (however impossible they may be), and then sets any nasty worries about coordination aside by endlessly listing all the groups that are to be "interfaced with" in the process of executing the "wish list."

This misleading comfort is, in my experience, unavoidable in written job descriptions. The only solution therefore is to scrap them.

While I am an archenemy of job descriptions, I am an unabashed supporter of great coaching as the alternative. That is, I wholeheartedly acknowledge the validity of "you gotta know what you're supposed to do." Especially today. I was blessed with uncommonly good coaches throughout the formative years of my career. I've found those who rely on job descriptions to be those who, in general, favor paper over people. In contrast, great coaches put in grueling hours teaching values—and, most important, they teach the "how-to's" of successful day-to-day risk-taking; that is, their coaching emphasizes flexibility under fire, not in-flexibility. They do not try to replace that painstaking coaching effort with the typical job description, a four-page document which "covers all the bases."

The job description is a cop-out, pure and simple. But it is more (or less) than that. It is imperative today that managers and nonmanagers be induced to cross "uncrossable" boundaries as a matter of course, day after day. Standing on the formality of a written job description (as an excuse for inaction, or the reason you have to "check up—and up and up—the line") is a guaranteed strategy for disaster.

NEW SYSTEMS IN SUPPORT OF FLEXIBILITY

Performance evaluations, objective setting, and job descriptions are three staples of management "control." All, though sound of purpose, typically become bureaucratic. They stamp in distinctions and rigidity, rather than stamping them out. They impede fluidity.

To throw them out (job descriptions) or revamp them (performance evaluations, objective setting) is not to promote anarchy. Control, in service to the new business requirements, is brought about through a shared and inspiring vision (see L-2), by coaching—and by treating people as fully participating parties (P-1 through P-10). The contract for performance evaluation, for instance, must be as fluid as the fluid, highly competitive system in which it exists.

PUBLIC PARALLELS

The worst offenders on performance appraisals and job descriptions are in the public sector. The reasons, as usual, are sound. The turn-of-the-century reform movement, led by Teddy Roosevelt and others, struck at the caprice, favoritism, and corruption of the political machines. They replaced hooliganism with professionalism.

As with most movements, this one went too far. Today, there is an especially virulent form of corruption induced by overly rigid systems. This new corruption, in service to the "system's imperative," is nonresponsiveness to constituent needs. A second form of corruption is the shocking waste of time and talent poured into beating the system. In my public sector incarnations, I saw that the master job description writer was prized indeed; she or he could make almost anything come to pass, through painstaking construction of job requirements that would jump scores of regulated hurdles and end up with the desired placement of Ms. X in job Y.

I have no illusion about the elimination of job descriptions in the public sector. I do believe, on the basis of my observations, that such systems can be greatly simplified. Most regulations, written in response to legislation or executive orders, amount to killing gnats with a sledgehammers. The average public sector operation is choked on bureaucratic garbage of its own design, not that of misguided legislation. Goals of 75 to 95 percent reduction in system complexity (including all those described in this prescription) are within the domain of the *average* mid-level or senior public sector manager.

A promise to ask, at least five times each day, "Who says we have to do it this [complicated] way?" will launch the attack on systems gridlock—especially if you create an environment where everyone starts asking such questions.

FIRST STEPS

1. In one division or department, replace a complex system of performance appraisal with a contract written in plain prose. (Invest heavily in group discussion with those affected before

doing so. It is essential that the "security" of the current, complex, objective-appearing system not be wholly compromised; the people to be evaluated must "buy in" and understand why the new system does not mean they will be prey to the whims of their managers.)

2. In conjunction with the establishment of a vision (L-2), eliminate job descriptions entirely or in one part of the organization this year. Again, substantial discussion, involving everyone, must accompany this move.

S-3

SUMMARY

To deal with the new strategic requirements for success, all the tools to induce and support action-taking must be available at the front line. Therefore, we must:

▶ Share virtually all information with everyone.

▶ Decentralize control systems, and decentralize the accountants/systems people who oversee them.

▶ Provide very high levels of expenditure authority for division general managers—and all other levels as well.

▶ Decentralize strategic planning.

The ability to take action close to the market—and fast—is the first requirement for competing. Therefore both information availability and the authority to move forward at the front line are musts.

Share, publicly and visibly, virtually all information about operating results—with everyone. Provide training to abet understanding this newly available information. Spending authority for business unit managers should be $20,000 to $50,000 (in a $25 million unit); spending authority for facility heads (and all others) should be proportionately as high. Make strategic planning an exclusively "bottom up" activity, with two-thirds of the content focusing on skill/capability-building rather than prediction of the future.

S-3

Decentralize Information, Authority, and Strategic Planning

An individual without information cannot take responsibility; an individual who is given information cannot help but take responsibility.

Jan Carlzon
from *Riv Pyramiderna!*

Promoting information exchange . . . was the original purpose of Quality Control circles in Japan, and it still is probably the most valuable use of circles.

Richard Schonberger
World Class Manufacturing

UNLEASH INFORMATION POWER

There are few greater liberating forces than the sharing of information. There is no such thing as "delegation" or "motivation" without extensive information.

Knowledge is power—it always has been; it always will be. Power—at the front line—is one more "must-do," not a "nice-to-do." Without power, there will be no (or, at least, no timely) action.

One stutters with amazement: The meeting is with executives of a food-processing company in the Midwest, over one billion dollars in size, privately held. The discussions turn to the distribution of profit-based bonuses, and the ins and outs of the facility (such as a factory) versus the division as the basis for distribution. A plant manager, who would be among those most affected by any scheme, has surprisingly little to say. I probe, and am stunned to learn that he has never been privy to data on the profitability of the facility he runs.

How can he manage? How can he be "motivated" to improve? How can he cope at all? A twenty-year veteran (and obviously successful), he acknowledges that there's "lots of conventional wisdom about individual product profitability" but no one really knows the score. In fact, a detailed corporate study had just revealed that an all-time favorite, a product thought to be a "cash cow," had in fact been losing money for years. This was clearly seen when costs were allocated more logically (see S-1).

This story is bad enough in any circumstance. It is terrifying in this case. New competitors are offering a bewildering array of new products. If the firm can't figure out what it takes in the plant to profit on a given product, it is doomed.

Information hoarding, especially by politically motivated, power-seeking staffs, has been commonplace throughout American industry, service and manufacturing alike. It will be an impossible millstone around the neck of tomorrow's organization. Sharing is a must.

Sharing means, apropos the preceding vignette, the availability of all data to facility managers. Equally important, it means availability of virtually all data to everyone, all the time.

"Everyone" includes the front-line team. Moreover, much of the most important information should be posted.

Yes, post the quality, scrap rate, and efficiency statistics. Let the whole factory team know—and visiting customers and vendors too. First Chicago, a bank with $40 billion in assets, worked with customers to develop some 700 performance measures (encompassing a large number of business units); these are the spearhead of its highly touted quality improvement program. Charts track progress on each of the indicators. Weekly performance reviews depict progress, or lack thereof, on each measure in terms of a stringent goal. The reviews, with dirty and clean linen alike aired, are always attended by customers and suppliers. The bank's executives believe that being publicly "on report" on what were previously the most confidential (or simply not tracked) measures is a great spur to performance. As they see it, there is no downside risk.

Leaks: The Phony Threat

The possibility that information will slip into the hands of competitors is the chief objection to widespread information sharing. It is a phony excuse on several scores.

First, there is no evidence that people on the line do leak the information. Firms such as Tandem Computer and Herman-Miller have long shared their corporate secrets—with everyone. More recently, firms such as GM have been sharing previously sacrosanct cost and operating performance data with front-line employees. There is just not a shred of evidence that such information gets leaked. (As one executive wryly observed: "If there's any evidence of leaking in general, it's usually vice-presidents who are the culprits.")

Second, determined competitors will have ferreted out, indirectly, what's important anyway—so you end up hiding the data only from those who could best use it on a day-to-day basis, the machine operators or first-line supervisors.

Finally, the specter of leaks is beside the point. Even if they were to occur, the value, for motivation and fast decision-making, of making information available to all is so high as to make any debate meaningless.

Is there any information that shouldn't be shared? Not much. Certainly patent information, confidential personnel records, and information about would-be acquisitions are off limits—for legal as well as common-sense reasons. But that's about all.

The evidence is unequivocal. People's thirst for understanding, especially amidst the new and permanent turbulence we now face, is unlimited; and with some training, their skill in interpretation is always extremely high, according to those who have been the most liberal sharers.

The Multiple Facets of the Power of Information

Information motivates in several ways:
1. It provides critical confirmation that the firm sees the worker as

a partner and problem solver. The absence of such information confirms the worker's impotence.

2. **The widespread availability of information is the only basis for effective day-to-day problem solving, which abets continuous improvement programs.** Recall Jan Carlzon's comment at the beginning of this prescription: Without information, taking responsibility for improvement is highly unlikely.

3. **Sharing information on the front line inhibits the upper-level power game playing that is the prime enemy of flexibility and moving fast.** Basically, most power plays (and thence delays) are born of information hoarding. One group doesn't want to share a problem it may have caused. Another sees its unique data base as a way to control or delay action on a proposal it doesn't favor. Make information available to all, and most such behavior disappears—fast.

4. **Visible posting of information radically speeds problem solving and action taking.** There is an inherent human tendency to "butt in"—and it's great in this case. Post information on something, and a million experts bloom; most are helpful. Information—charts, graphs, operating data—is the organization's lubricant. When the plant or distribution center becomes one big billboard, a thousand chance interactions are triggered.

5. **Information sharing stirs the competitive juices.** Unit-versus-unit comparisons do this. But so do simple charts and graphs, even without such comparisons. Just about everyone would rather get better than get worse, especially when spurred by the increasingly intense competitive environment. Put a chart on the wall, and you've upped the odds that the suggestion box under it will be filled with ideas on how to make the performance curve go up.

6. **(Useful) information begets more (useful) information.** When information is "around"—a lot of it, publicly posted—people start asking all sorts of useful questions, and require more (and more relevant) information. Time and again, new measures are invented by groups close to a machine or process who have finally been let in on its secrets.

7. **Information abets flattening the organizational pyramid (see P-8 and P-9).** Information availability inherently shifts skill and responsibility to the front line and facilitates front-line communications across functional barriers ("horizontal management"). Information in and of itself is the chief substitute for first-line supervisors—and many staff experts too.

Training in the Use of Information

But information availability is not enough. It must be accompanied by extensive training in ways to develop the information, record it, analyze it, and act upon it. Successful firms such as Worthington Industries and Johnsonville Sausage go so far as to provide extensive training in economics and accounting for everyone (see P-4). All the best-quality programs involve training in problem analysis and data collection and interpretation, as well as in group problem-solving skills to promote the interchange of information and speed implementation (see also C-2, C-8).

HIGH SPENDING AUTHORITY

This prescription is really about the nuts and bolts of systems-induced autonomy. Information is a primary source of power, and a major stimulant of initiative- and risk-taking close to the action. Ranked right along with it is spending authority.

Again and again I find the most insultingly low spending authority granted to people—at all levels. It is especially self-defeating in a setting where everyone is being asked to act fast and take the initiative. All too commonplace is (1) the division general manager with $5,000 in "sign-off" authority (despite "control" over $40 million in assets), (2) the factory or operations center manager (600 employees) with $1,000 in authority, (3) the shift site manager or functional boss with $250 in authority, (4) the engineer or supervisor with $50 in authority, and (5) the first-line employee who must fill out a page-long form, with a supervisor's signature, to buy a $2.95 roll of tape needed in a practical problem-solving venture.

First, such low spending authority is demeaning and demotivating. We "trust" people to take the initiative and "make things happen," but give them no authority to do so. Second, it is self-defeating to that essential strategic need—hustle. Speed of execution depends not on big leaps, but on a million tiny actions taking a fraction of the time they used to. These in turn are driven by the ability to buy a roll of tape, a $100 tool off the shelf from Sears (rather than spending six weeks and $300 to "procure it" through channels), and take a $1,000 visit to a remote site, at a moment's notice, to speed up a project or move a new customer or supplier relation along another inch or two.

Here are the spending authorities I support:

▶ Front-line employee—$250
▶ First-line supervisor—$2,000
▶ Bench scientist or engineer—$2,000 to $10,000 (depending on seniority)
▶ Plant or operations center manager (two hundred people)—$5,000 to $25,000
▶ Division general manager ($25 million operation)—$20,000 to $50,-000

The guidelines at Worthington are close to this, though much higher at the "lowest" level—$2,000 for a first-line employee (typical is the employee who went out and hired people and bought equipment to remove snow, making it easier for everyone to come to work). Chief Financial Officer Joe Stegmayer adds that "Nowhere is any of this written. . . . we want people to think, do it, and worry about it later. A person is never disciplined or chastised for spending money. In fact, we want people to make mistakes or they aren't being aggressive enough. If a person continues to make mistakes, however, then there's a problem."

More Control with Higher Spending Authority

Increasing spending authority does not entail a loss of control. To the contrary, it begets more control of the most powerful sort—self-control. Low spending authority leads to shenanigans—avoid a $1,000 limit by making an endless stream of $999.95 requisitions. High spending authority says to the worker, or unit boss, "I take you seriously." The monkey is on his or her back to live up to the trust.

And, to be sure, those who abuse the trust badly should be severely disciplined. Of course, it's not quite that easy; the leadership prescriptions come into play here. That is, the out-and-about leader (L-4), preaching the vision (L-2) and reinforcing it with stories about appropriate behavior (L-3), is essential to true delegation (L-7). Once more, I remind you that we are talking about substituting one form of control (vision, values, and visible management) for another (control by demeaning, voluminous rules).

The Leader's Job: Teaching About Limits

As a new consultant at McKinsey & Co. in 1974, I was immediately assigned to a team evaluating a huge addition to a southwestern petrochemical facility. An early task (second week) was to "check out supply and demand for [certain agricultural chemicals] in Canada over the next twenty years."

Arriving in Calgary, I soon decided that *I* needed a consultant. So I hired a Canadian energy specialist, for about $5,000, to do an analysis for me. No one told me to do it; nor did anyone approve my move. As a matter of fact, other than understanding that "you do whatever it takes to get an answer, fast," I don't know what led me to make such a bold (for a newcomer) move.

Sure enough, the answer helped the project along, but I also got a "coaching" lesson from my boss. He lavishly applauded my initiative as "good McKinsey tradition," but allowed as how I might have given him a jingle before doing the deal. He assured me he would have approved my effort, and I'm sure to this day that he would have.

The story is a fine example of how to teach initiative-taking—and limits. There was no spending limit imposed and in a similar crunch I would have done what I did again (I subsequently did many times), yet I also learned a lesson about touching bases first (which I subsequently also did). Thus my zest for reaching out—and the firm's support for such initiatives—was left intact, and, if anything, enhanced, while controls were maintained. This is all just common sense, not mysterious at all—and organizations can (and must) be run this way.

GENUINE "BOTTOM UP" STRATEGIC PLANNING

Sound strategic direction has never been more important—which is why the strategic planning process must be truly decentralized. Yet strategic planning, as we conventionally conceive of it, has become irrelevant, or worse, damaging.

What is a good strategic *plan*? There is none. But there is a good strategic planning process. A good strategic planning process (1) gets everyone involved, (2) is not constrained by overall corporate "assumptions" (e.g., about the general economics picture), (3) is perpetually fresh, forcing the asking of new questions, (4) is not to be left to planners, and (5) requires lots of noodling time and vigorous debate. As for the document per se, it (1) is succinct, (2) emphasizes the development of strategic skills, and (3) is burned the day before it is to go to the printer—that is, it is a living document, not an icon.

Flexibility is the necessary watchword. Sound thinking and debate about the future, marked by the asking of novel questions, foster flexibility of thought and action. Two-hundred-page plans do not. Moreover, flexibility is made possible by strategic capabilities and the habit of hustle (the ability to execute strategies quickly); strategic plans can address these topics, but seldom do.

. Tomorrow's successful corporation will be a collection of skills and capabilities ever ready to pounce on brief market anomalies. Any useful strategic plan, or planning process, must focus upon the development and honing of these skills (which translates into readiness to seek and exploit opportunities), rather than emphasize static approaches to market development. That is, the strategy should focus primarily on such things as the time and energy to be devoted to creating revolutionary quality improvement (see C-2) or getting linked up fast with almost all of our customers (see C-4).

The "new" strategic plan, and planning process, must necessarily be "bottom-up." Assessing the ability (and necessary skills) to execute—to be responsive, flexible, attentive to customers—starts on the front line. Obviously, as the process moves forward, it will involve debate among senior officers, and compromise. But it should never lose touch with or sight of the front line, where execution takes place.

In fact, each facility, as well as each business unit and function, should have a strategic plan. The plan should not exceed a dozen pages, and perhaps two-thirds of it should be devoted to strategic skill/capability development in the context of the corporation/business unit's vision and the most significant external forces at work.

The plan, whose development involves everyone, should be shared with everyone after completion. At that point, there is a serious case to be made for destroying it—if not in practice, at least in spirit. Its value is as an assemblage of thoughts, not constraints. The process of developing it is close to 100 percent of its value—or perhaps more than 100 percent of its value. Slavishly following the plan despite changing conditions (now the norm), because of the time and political capital spent in assembling it, is counterproductive.

Finally, the content and format of the plan and the planning process should be modified substantially every year. Most plans and planning processes readily become bureaucratic (within two years), whereas the sole purpose is to be thought-provoking. Only changes in process which demand wholly new questions—from near the front line especially—will ensure vitality and usefulness.

FIRST STEPS

1. Do not hesitate or equivocate. Schedule an "all hands" meeting with your small or large group in the next 30 days. Share all operating information with them, leaving behind a printed version. Insist that every manager post key indicator charts, developed by front-line people, in every work area within the next 60 days.
2. Institute a thoroughgoing review of all spending authorities—this should not be an accountant-led review, but should be line-led, focusing on specific instances of delays in operations caused by limited spending authority.
3. Scrap your current strategic planning process—now. Burn your current strategic plan. Announce, in the next 30 days, that first-line input to the new process will be actively solicited—and demanded.

S-4

SUMMARY

Given the rising uncertainty that surrounds each project, and the firm as a whole, we must:

▶ Set conservative financial targets in all arenas—revenue, earnings, depreciation.

▶ Develop a true "appeal" system, which allows line managers ultimately to reject, if necessary, targets handed down to them.

▶ Set conservative growth targets, insisting in particular that infrastructure development—e.g., distribution networks, sales and service forces, the management talent bank—lead, not lag behind, projected revenue growth.

Above all, in an increasingly volatile environment, financial systems must have integrity and not be marred by unrealistic estimates. Likewise, if in a growth situation, we must be sure that the basic skills (e.g., distribution) are in place to support the exploitation of the opportunity.

Financial objectives should be small in number and conservative—only rarely should a manager fail to meet his or her objectives. Every growth plan must be backed up by the near-certainty of available supporting infrastructure.

S-4

Set Conservative Goals

This prescription is part of a paradox. The world is uncertain; so we must move at the snap of a finger to exploit any opportunity. To be ready and capable of this, however, we must be able to rely absolutely on our financial control systems and on the projections and promises we make. That is, the system must thrive on integrity and trust (see S-5). These two traits demand conservatism, not puffery, in our objective setting and budget promises.

Likewise, in order to grow through instant response to any opportunity, we must be certain that our execution skills—e.g., trained workers and managers, a well-oiled distribution system—are firmly established. To support aggressiveness in pursuit of new markets, then, we need conservatism of underlying systems.

There is an analogy in sports. A former all-pro defensive back, who once led the National Football League in interceptions, attributed his success to being the first to start and the last to finish the boring drills that make up everyday practice. "Any one interception," he said, "is just luck. But to increase the odds of 'getting lucky,' I needed to study and study the film and run and run with our guys who were running my [opponent's] patterns. I then stand a better chance of being in the right place any time the ball is a little bit off target."

Similarly, the most daring musicians are the ones who have mastered the basics so well that they can step out and try, at the margin, new variations. The boldest generals are invariably the truest masters of logistics; boldness under fire can only occur if the refueling operation runs like clockwork.

619

"SIGN UP"—AND DELIVER

In too many firms, budget drills, though nominally bottom-up, are in fact top-down. Targets are sent down, and you sign up—or else. So you do sign up, and some succeed. Many more fall short, and given the generally unrealistic nature of the estimates, you can't punish those who fail (that is, you can't punish 70 percent of all managers). More important, no one at any level can depend upon anyone else; the "numbers" are jokes. And when "numbers discipline" goes, so does the rest of discipline. Milestones are not met. Promises in general are not kept. Bad news is hidden or distorted. Blaming takes up most of the time, with little time left for doing.

Budgets, revenue projections, milestones, and objectives should be simplified (see S-1 and S-2). But what there is should be (1) prepared at the bottom and passed up, (2) believed in, (3) publicly committed to, and (4) subject to severe discipline if missed.

To move fast requires trust—period. Trust, though essentially interpersonal or one-on-one, is exhibited on a day-to-day basis by not signing up for what you can't deliver on.

Not a Plea for Timidity

The times do not permit timidity. They demand a new aggressiveness. So the conservatism I suggest does not mean setting unchallenging goals. To the contrary, goal setting should involve all sorts of peer pressure, and be done in the context of understanding the programs of competitors, which require us to respond energetically in return.

"Stretch" (within limits; see S-2) and fast movement are a must. But then when you commit to support manufacturing by April 27, at a cost of $70,000, with an installed system, you'd best deliver a working system—on April 27, for $70,000. And if you don't, there should be some substantial consequence, regardless of the reason for the miss.

Appeals

To support the integrity of goal setting, there must be a genuine, not phony or "paper only," opportunity for the manager to appeal any objective shoved down his or her throat.

You, as training officer, "get" an objective to support 50 percent growth in the minicomputer segment aimed at financial service institutions. You meet with the sales boss and come to understand the request. You go through several possible ramp-up scenarios, but you just can't do what's demanded in the next 120 days.

There must be, this prescription urges, a genuine, semi-formal (or formal) channel for you to appeal the request, up the line two or three levels if necessary. Ninety percent of the success of execution depends on commitment to the goal. If it is truly not achievable, commitment will not be there, and perhaps the whole plan will collapse like a house of cards.

Such an appeals process is not, as some suggest, tantamount to letting people off the hook. To the contrary, it puts them squarely on the hook. First, no manager will use it often (unless he or she has a very bad—unrealistic—boss); one does not lightly go over the heads of one or two bosses to challenge a target. More important, the system is a symbol of the overall seriousness with which the process of goal setting—and accepting—is taken. It says, in effect: "Don't sign up for what you can't do. If you do sign up for an undoable chore, you are a lousy manager, and you probably won't be with us long."

INFRASTRUCTURE MUST LEAD GROWTH

"We must take advantage of this narrow window of opportunity to launch the [new product or service]." That's an increasingly common statement. And it's true. Yet there is a major caveat. If the machine doesn't quite work yet, if the sales force isn't well trained in its special features, if distributors have been chosen promiscuously, if adequate spares are not appropriately positioned—well, not only will the product launch go poorly, but the firm's reputation will be set back immeasurably, perhaps irreparably if it is a small firm.

Thus, there is a second form of conservatism—ensuring that growth at any cost and opportunity at any cost does not become the company's watchword. Growth (new-product launches, etc.) must be preceded by skills/capabilities development.

All too many firms—Atari is a recent example—take advantage of what they see as a once-in-a-lifetime opportunity; they pour the product out upon the world, then play catch-up with sales training, distribution center development, and distributor selection. It doesn't work.

Indeed, this strategy of conservatism, which demands that basic skills/ capabilities development precedes growth, is more important in these volatile times than ever before. First, there are more temptations (little windows of opportunity) than ever before. You must regularly seize them; but if you get into the habit of doing so without doing your sales and service development homework, you are doomed to short-term project failure and long-term loss of reputation.

Second, with more products and services—and more good ones— available to the consumer, quality, service, and reliability/responsiveness (C-2 through C-4) are increasingly the only effective differentiating strategies; you can't play catch-up on quality and service. Given competitive alternatives, the customer will not let you get away with more than one lapse. That is, the skills/capabilities, per se, are *the* most valuable strategic weapons—they can't be "assumed" to follow a clever product's launch.

Loving Growth—with Good Sense

Let me reiterate that all of the above is not a plea for slow growth, or a rejection of opportunism. Opportunistic growth is increasingly essential to any organization's health. A firm is never static—it is either growing or stagnating. While growth for growth's sake at the extreme is silly, growth alone provides an expanding opportunity structure for everyone in the firm. Moreover, stagnation, absolute or relative, is enervating, negatively affecting every element of the firm. Excitement (growth) spurs performance; contraction doesn't.

I am simply insisting in this part of the prescription that the growth should be led by, and governed by, infrastructure development:

► Lead with upgrading the skills of the work force. Teach factory people to be flexible; invest in equipment that abets that flexibility *before* you need it.

► Upgrade the skills of the sales force continuously—*before* the need arises; provide the sales force with tools ahead of the market need.

► Engage in distribution system/distributor upgrading *before* the specific market requirement arises.

▶ Budgets should emphasize ongoing skill/capability development as the essential strategy (also see the section in S-3 dealing with strategy).

The firm should be looked at as an ever-improving packet of necessary capabilities. If this conception becomes second nature, then the company will indeed be ready to take advantage of almost any market opportunity that comes along, with foreknowledge that it can execute to support the idea.

A WORLD TURNED UPSIDE DOWN

This prescription constitutes a new view of organizing and of strategy development in particular: the company as a set of skills being continuously elaborated, to be applied as needed to market opportunities. The traditional view of strategy is to let the product, product family, or market drive all thinking, with skills in a secondary or supporting role. One does "what makes sense" based upon a static market analysis— filling in behind market opportunities with requisite support skills.

Paradoxically the "rightness" of that idea—conquering or reconceiving markets—is precisely what requires us to reject a "market conception" approach today. The company simply must be ahead of itself in capabilities in order to exploit these fast-appearing/fast-disappearing market/product opportunities. Essential skills must be in place before the fact.

3M has epitomized such an approach. It is a finely tuned machine designed to invent new markets. All of its organizational paraphernalia, from incentive schemes to management development techniques to approaches to factory development, constitute one giant exercise in skill/capability development—which is then directed opportunistically at fast market creation. Likewise, the development of responsive, field-centered marketing mechanisms at Frito-Lay and Campbell Soup (see C-4) is a strategy of "skill development in search of market enhancement opportunities."

The pragmatic implications are twofold. First, as observed, budgets and strategies—and individual evaluations—should emphasize capability development. Second, growth targets for products/markets should be

623

conservative—that is, governed by the status of skill development/readiness.

FIRST STEPS

1. Ensure that each formal and informal review (operations reviews, performance evaluations) emphasizes promises kept—for instance, budget targets, milestones. No small breach of promise can go unnoted, regardless of extenuating circumstances (see also S-5). (In today's world "business as usual" has become a meaningless phrase; every circumstance is an extenuating circumstance—*promises must be made in light of expected extenuating circumstances.*) After due process is observed, fire those who don't get this message, especially those who don't come through on acts of cross-functional support, major or minor (if a pattern exists).

2. Devote two-thirds of budget preparation and strategy formulation/review to skill/capability/infrastructure development. Consider a single forthcoming product. Are growth projections driven by the availability of needed skills/capabilities/infrastructure or by "window of opportunity" logic? Reassess the project in light of an "infrastructure-driven" approach.

S-5

SUMMARY

Today's new realities (let alone common sense) require us to:

► Demand total integrity—of the Boy Scout/Girl Scout/"squeaky clean" sort—in all dealings, with people and systems, inside the firm and out.

► Eliminate Mickey Mouse rules and regulations (see also P-10, L-8) that induce cheating and game playing, which then spread to all the firm's affairs.

Integrity has been the hallmark of the superior organization through the ages. Be that as it may, today's accelerating uncertainty gives the issue new importance. People on the front line must be able to deal quickly across traditional functional barriers; sole-source arrangements must be made with suppliers in the face of uncertain future demands. Successful organizations must shift from an age dominated by contracts and litigiousness to an age of handshakes and trust.

Set absurdly high standards for integrity—and then live them, with no fuzzy margins. A deal made on a milestone (see S-4) which is subsequently missed is grounds for dismissal, especially when it involves support for another function or a vendor/customer. A person who is genuinely—and legitimately—surprised by his or her annual performance appraisal provides grounds for dismissal of the person's boss.

S-5

Demand Total Integrity

Without doubt, honesty has always been the best policy. The best firms on this score have long had the best track records overall—Johnson & Johnson, IBM, S. C. Johnson (Johnson Wax), Hewlett-Packard, Merck, Digital Equipment.

Yet once more, this very-nice-to-do for all times is a must-do for tomorrow. Quality and flexibility—and constant innovation—are chief among the new winner's watchwords. These traits require wholesale involvement by employees and a willingness to work together. Barriers between functions must fall, as must adversarial relations between labor and management, suppliers and buyers, sellers and distributors, sellers and customers.

Involvement by all and nonadversarial relations must necessarily rest on a cornerstone of trust, which in turn can only be engendered by total integrity. If a promise (even a minor one) is not kept, if ethics are compromised, and if management behaves inconsistently, then the strategies necessary to survival today (see C-1 through C-4, for instance) simply can't be executed.

This prescription once more reveals a paradox—namely, that the uncertainty of the environment can be swiftly dealt with only if the firm can fall back upon the certainty of relationships among people and among groups—in other words, upon trust and integrity.

INTEGRITY IN DEALINGS WITH
THE FRONT LINE

Integrity means living up to commitments, inside and outside the firm. As discussed in C-3, in a world of exploding product and service offerings, keeping your word takes on added significance. It might at first seem that, faced with stiff new competition, you must make outrageous promises to get the deal. While I hardly advocate being the slowest in town, I do urge very conservative—high-integrity—behavior. With more, often newer, firms, there is more uncertainty surrounding the buyer's purchase, regardless of the offsetting joy of having more choices. With more uncertainty the norm, reliability is worth more than ever, especially when it comes to that all-important repeat business.

Routinely "over-delivering" to the customer cannot be achieved without more cooperation (among functions in a firm) and greater commitment within the firm—which again stems from integrity. Engendering wholesale commitment from everyone involves making "deals" (compacts) and living up to them. Chief among the "deals" is a commitment to lifetime employment (if performance remains acceptable) for some substantial share of the work force (see P-7). The vendor equivalent is sole-sourcing, as long as performance meets agreed-upon goals.

Quite simply, if we are going to ask people to be flexible (C-4), be responsible for constant innovation (I-10), take risks, and perform a host of tasks (P-1), we must provide a relatively certain future. It is inconsistent—or a pipe dream—to ask people to "step out and take risks" (speak up, change things, blow the whistle on poor quality or service) and then confront them with a capricious, never-ending, nickel-and-dime pattern of layoffs or force reductions.

Likewise (see P-10, L-8), it is inconsistent to ensnare people via Mickey Mouse and demeaning rules, and hogtie them with voluminous procedures—and then ask them to take responsibility for quality, maintenance, housekeeping, etc. And it is inconsistent to require much higher commitment and involvement without offering a dollar payoff if the performance is positive (P-6).

All such inconsistencies are abrogations of integrity—that is, they don't amount to a sensible and fair compact between the employee and the firm—especially the firm beset by uncertainty (as almost all are).

Integrity and Quality

High quality of product and high quality of service demand absolute integrity. Providing a superior-quality product or service is a moral and aesthetic act (see C-2), as well as an act that "conforms to specifications." Superior quality stems from pride and enthusiasm for the product or service as much as from good measurement instruments. Top quality also means, of course, not skimping or taking shortcuts in order to meet a production schedule, especially during the last week of the financial reporting period.

Superior quality simply cannot be extracted from a low-integrity organization. That is, unfairness in personnel policies, for instance, directly affects the quality of the product over time. To be treated capriciously by the firm is incompatible with caring about the product religiously.

Integrity and Perks

To use the psychologists' terms, integrity is not only absolute (stealing is bad, period), but it involves "perceived equity." That is, fairness is in the eye of the beholder. Paying bonuses to management and withholding worker bonuses in a problematic year is perceived to be unfair, regardless of the extenuating circumstances (the executive bonuses may have come from cashing in years-old stock options, or be due to extremely good performance in one small part of the business).

In general, the wisest firms avoid excessive executive perks and even the appearance of minor impropriety (an executive "off-site" at a lavish resort following a not-great year). Mars, Inc., is among those paying its managers very well, but avoiding almost all perks, including lavish offices. (It is the officers' special dental plan, covering orthodontics for kids, that causes more anguish on the line than their six-figure salaries. Somehow, the former is more tangible than the latter.)

"SMALL" INJUSTICES—BIG IMPLICATIONS

Integrity may be about little things as much as or more than big ones. It's about executives taking friends, rather than customers, to sit in the company's box seats at the ballpark. It's about pushing salespeople at the end of a quarter to place orders, knowing that many will be canceled within the week—but that the cancellations will count in the next period for accounting purposes.

These "minor" lapses set a tone of disrespect for people, products, systems, customers, distributors, and relationships that can readily become pervasive. That is, there is no such thing as a minor lapse in integrity.

"Squeaky Clean"

IBM has been known to fire an employee for accepting a gratuity from a supplier (a pen set), and then discipline the employee's boss severely as well. As a vendor to Stew Leonard's (he and others have attended our seminars), I am on a mailing list that includes a letter before Christmas asking me not to send any gratuities to anyone in the store. I believe that such rigid behavior around "little" integrity issues is a must.

Go a step further. An employee receives an annual performance evaluation, and is genuinely surprised by his or her low rating. Delve into it, and if it turns out that the supervisor misled the employee, or failed to communicate displeasure along the way, that supervisor should be severely (and officially) warned, and let go if there is a pattern of such behavior.

"Overdoing it" on "little" breaches of integrity pays big dividends as long as you are perfectly consistent (perceived to be even-handed). It pays with people in the firm—it induces integrity in general (living up to all commitments). And it pays with outsiders—suppliers, customers, communities, and even governments.

For example, Milliken's and IBM's squeaky-clean reputations make both firms very desirable to suppliers. Both are downright tough—but also unquestionably fair. You will not lose business for a capricious reason, though you might well lose it for a "minor" breach of promise (by the standards of others), such as a "slightly" missed schedule.

INTEGRITY IS CONSISTENCY

In *Leaders*, when Warren Bennis and Burt Nanus say they observed the highest integrity among their many heroes, they are referring especially to consistency. Visions were clear—and lived with almost frightening consistency, in small as well as in large ways.

Once again, this is a timely issue as well as an issue for the ages. All people must take risks and welcome change, if the firm is to survive. They will only do so when the larger picture (the firm's vision—L-2) is unmistakable.

If it is unmistakable (that is, consistent), then they can take small chances with impunity, knowing that these "tries," successful or not, are consistent with moving the execution of the vision forward. Conversely, if there is no vision, or if the edges of the vision are blurred, you don't know what is "risk in pursuit of the vision" as opposed to "risk for risk's sake." Few of us, mavericks or not, are willing to chance the latter. And a few risk-takers are decisively not the point anyway. We need everyone to be taking risks all the time within the context of the vision.

Hypocrisy: Enemy #1 of Integrity

The boss who preaches quality, but puts wholly unrealistic schedule demands on the plant or operations center, is seen as a hypocrite. Trust, integrity, fairness in dealing with others (all under the gun to do unrealistic things and sign up for unrealistic promises), and quality/service all go kaput.

SYSTEMS SUPPORTS FOR INTEGRITY

Many of the prescriptions in this book, especially those dealing with people and leadership, are enhancers of integrity. Chief among these is removal of bureaucracy and demeaning rules. Silly and demeaning rules invite game playing; it's as simple as that. Likewise, reduction of "layers" on the organization chart (P-8) helps integrity too. In the absence of a lot of paper-pushing middle managers, there's likely to be less delayed action, which is always viewed on the line as being the result of political power plays made for personal reasons—that is, the antithesis of integrity in support of people and quality.

Widespread information sharing (S-3), wholesale people involvement (P-1), and extensive training (P-5) all foster integrity by making front-line people powerful themselves—full-scale, fully informed, participating partners.

Visible management (L-4) is chief among the leadership prescriptions that foster integrity. Integrity, that is, also means "knowing the score." When leaders are perceived to be out of touch (not out and about regularly, for instance), they cannot, in the view of the line, behave with integrity—that is, with consistency or realism. Since they don't know what's going on (in the line's view), their "orders" and policies and nifty new programs often look downright foolish.

Prescriptions S-1 and S-2 touted simplicity—in measures, goals, plans. Simplicity and integrity go hand in hand. If objectives are limited in number and thoughtfully negotiated, the odds of their being meaningful skyrocket. Complex and lengthy skeins of objectives are less well understood, are less likely to be carefully negotiated, and are therefore taken less seriously; in other words, the system lacks integrity.

REPRISE

The systems prescriptions are not a matter of some generic "good practice." They are all in service to the violently changed competitive conditions that now surround us. Moreover, they directly support the other four sets of prescriptions. Without these last five systems prescriptions, much of the power of the first forty will be lost. Though each prescription lays down a major challenge, it is vital to remember that each of the forty-five supports the others; you must somehow address all forty-five at once, even though specific programs will emphasize one or another. That is, the forty-five taken together, and nothing less, constitute the elements of tomorrow's surviving organization.

FIRST STEPS

1. Do not make any commitment, starting right now, internal or external, that you can't live up to (with room to spare)—large or, especially, small.
2. Review delivery promises to ten key customers. Review objectives for the next 90 days that you have agreed to or that you

have negotiated with people who report to you, focusing on simplicity—and achievability. Review the achievability of commitments to other functions. Make such reviews a commonplace part of staff meetings, operations reviews, and managerial evaluations, informal as well as formal.

3. Seek out at least one symbolic opportunity each week (preferably small) to emphasize the simplicity/achievability of commitments—to a supplier, to a customer, to another function, to an employee.

Second Thoughts

Thriving on Chaos was published on October 19, 1987, the day of the crash that sent the stock market tumbling 508 points. Of course I didn't know it was coming. But the book is concerned with precisely such turmoil. In many ways, the crash certified ours as the age of uncertainty.

As MIT professors Michael Piore and Charles Sabel point out in *The Second Industrial Divide,* predictability is the chief premise underlying the operations of our biggest business organizations, from their "charts and boxes" management structures to the size of their factories. But the continued gyrations in the value of the dollar and in international trade balances, as well as in the stock and bond markets, mark the end of predictability. And there is no sense in pining for the past; the stability we took for granted for so long will not return.

The chief axiom of *Thriving on Chaos* is the necessity of attaining, and then maintaining, heretofore undreamed-of flexibility. Each of the forty-five prescriptions, and especially the forty-five taken together, is explicitly and implicitly aimed at advancing the cause of achieving flexibility, and the centrality of this requirement is clearer now than it was two years ago when I began to work on the book.

"Flexibility" rolls off the tongue easily. Attaining it in big firms or maintaining it in small ones is not so easy. I was rebuked by some reviewers of *Thriving* for providing long, long lists of things to do—followed by an uncompromising dictum: Do it all; do it all now. But I stand by my demand. Without a doubt, we are facing a once-in-a-century (or more) sea change in the management environment. There is little that we knew "for sure" about managing fifteen years ago that is true today, much less that will remain in place fifteen years from now. Yes, the agenda prescribed in *Thriving* is daunting. But as the rapid shifts even in the membership of the Fortune 500 attest, those who don't sign up for dramatic change, along multiple dimensions, may not be around for long.

NEW CONCERNS

Here are some of the stunning changes that are easier to see now than they were a couple of years ago.

1. *Technology's vast sweep. Thriving* does not sufficiently emphasize the impact of the new technologies. Were I to rewrite the book today, I would include an entirely new section of prescriptions on dealing with what is, unquestionably, the technology *revolution*. Look at Citicorp, Federal Express, The Limited, The Benetton Group, Turner Broadcasting, or Wal-Mart. Each is a service company. Yet through the pioneering use of information technology, more than any other single factor, each has literally remade a huge industry. (In some cases, such as Citicorp, the impact has been global.) Each of these firms has essentially "bet the company" on the new technologies; the strategic use of information technology is defining each firm's future.

Every industry is affected. In writing the foreword to *The Rise of the Expert Company* by artificial intelligence pioneer Ed Feigenbaum and his colleagues Pamela McCorduck and Penny Nii, I was brought up short by their case study of Navistar (the old International Harvester). Thanks to a new "expert system," it will soon offer every truck purchaser a fully customized vehicle, from the innards of the engine to styling features. The terms "software added" and "service added" hold the key to the future for almost all manufacturing. Learning that manufacturing is not just—or even mainly—about "making things" is the toughest transition for the managers of that troubled sector to make.

In *Thriving*'s Prescription C-4, I did write about Electronic Data Interchange, the linking of everything to most everything else. I said that those who weren't hooked up electronically to customers at one end of the business system and suppliers at the other could be in for big trouble. I would underscore those remarks today. Suppliers, purchasing officers, designers, engineers, manufacturing (or operations) shops, marketers, sales offices, distribution centers, wholesalers, franchisees, and ultimate end users will all be "on line" with one another before you know it, and in all businesses, from fast food and insurance to autos and steel. If you don't believe me, check with the managers of The Benetton Group, which is a pioneer in this area, or General Motors, where, after a slow start, such linkages are now being established at a pace that is surprising even optimistic experts.

My advice is meant to suggest an unparalleled opportunity (competitive necessity is more like it) and to provide the sternest warning possible. As to the opportunity, mastering the new technology quickly provides an enormous leg up on the competition. That is proving to be as true for Mrs. Fields Cookies, Ryder System, and Avis as for Citicorp, Federal Express, and Navistar. On the warning side, implementation of the new integrated information technology–based systems is much more difficult than anyone dreamed. For one thing, it turns out that the installation of such systems is not primarily a matter of technology. It is a matter of organization. *Every power relationship, inside and outside the firm, is affected by the installation of the new information technology systems.* The failure of so many elaborate new systems (in many arenas the failure rate is estimated at well over 90 percent) typically results from a failure to think through the bare-knuckle issues of power redistribution. In a word, to implement such systems, hierarchical organizational structures must be destroyed.

2. *The destruction of hierarchy (and its replacement by fully empowered, continuously reeducated work teams).* Some critics attacked my shrillness in *Thriving.* But if I could write it again, I would be more shrill, not less. Take the demand that you "reduce hierarchy" and "flatten the organization pyramid." Forget such mellow propositions, which appear again and again in *Thriving.* Substitute "destroy the hierarchy," for destruction is exactly what must transpire.

Why have The Limited, Federal Express, The Benetton Group, Citicorp, and Wal-Mart thrived as they applied the full power of new technologies, while GM's $50–$75 billion outlay in high-tech manufacturing over the last decade seems largely wasted—or at least has fallen so far short of its promise? The answer is that key word "hierarchy"—and the lack thereof. The Limited et al. have used new technologies to achieve startling reductions in the time it takes to respond to market demands— often doing things a dozen times faster than the prior industry norm—

precisely because the new technology has been installed in conjunction with the minimizing of management layers and the abolition of the time-consuming traditional decision-making apparatus. It turns out that the speed and flexibility necessary to compete can only be achieved by eliminating the wasteful process of passing information back and forth, up and down a steep, functionally arranged hierarchy.

But there is a very big catch. The management "pyramid" can only be destroyed if managers are willing to share authority, responsibility, *and* power with the front ranks of the firm, and to do so enthusiastically. The destruction of the hierarchy must be accompanied by a level of training, information sharing, and empowerment in general that adds a new emphasis to the already strong words in support of the "people prescriptions" in this book. In particular, I would now upgrade Prescriptions P-1, P-2, and P-5, which deal with fundamental beliefs about capabilities of people, the use of work teams, and training.

I thought I knew what believing in people's capabilities meant. But this past year I was reeducated by a visit to Harley-Davidson's motorcycle assembly plant in York, Pennsylvania. Harley was on the brink of financial collapse just a half dozen years ago, thanks to the pathetic quality of its product and the fine competitive offerings of such firms as Kawasaki and Honda. Today, Harley is grabbing market share back with abandon, and doing especially well in an export program—to Japan.

The principal reason for Harley's success has been the improved quality of their products—the result primarily of a new obsession with quality among the company's fully empowered frontline employees. After my visit, the term "fully empowered" took on new meaning for me, far beyond the admittedly aggressive definition in *Thriving*. The new attitude was captured most exactly when, during a discussion with a group of work-team members, I heard one fellow mutter to a friend, "I'm really uptight. I've got to give a presentation to top management on Friday." This was not a high-powered consultant talking, but a twenty-year veteran, an hourly worker who belongs to the union. It turns out that, having completed a thoroughgoing statistical analysis and several off-site vendor visits, he was about to present a proposal for a $250,000 line-reconfiguration scheme, directly to top management. Five years ago, his sort suffered from what one called "that hourly feeling." Five years ago, he wouldn't have been allowed within a country mile of the numbers needed to do such an analysis, let alone be asked to present it to anyone.

To be sure, such things are not everyday affairs. Still, this one was an undeniable indicator of just how much people can do, when given the wherewithal and a genuine green light.

But there was more redefinition in store for me. The year also included a visit to Johnsonville Foods, which has grown twenty-fold in revenues since 1980, to about $100 million. The firm was mentioned briefly in the hardback edition of *Thriving*. I have begged that more attention be given to training; after my visit to Johnsonville, I decided to toss the word "training" out of my vocabulary for good. I am substituting "continuous learning," which encompasses much more.

Johnsonville president Ralph Stayer goes on and on about people becoming "the instrument of their own destiny." When you talk with employees, you think you've made a wrong turn and ended up in an army recruiting office, as you hear them discuss the firm's desire that everyone "be all that they can be." The funny thing is, they really mean it.

A typical Johnsonville work team: (1) does its own recruiting, hiring, personnel evaluation, and firing; (2) regularly acquires new skills and then conducts training sessions for everyone else on the team; (3) formulates and tracks its own budgets; (4) makes capital-investment proposals as needed (doing all the supporting analysis, making appropriate site visits to vendors, etc.); (5) is responsible for all quality control, inspection, and subsequent trouble shooting and problem solving, as required; (6) suggests and then develops prototypes for possible new products or packaging (or even, in a few instances, new businesses); (7) works on improvements in every area, all the time; and (8) develops its own quantitative standards for productivity and quality, as well as goals for improvement, which are mercilessly tough, according to Stayer. This doesn't leave much for management to do. But then there's almost no management (or hierarchy) at Johnsonville.

Impressive as the above list is, the fundamental belief in continuous learning is what really stands out. For instance, Stayer, who appears to be such a humanitarian, has granted no general raises since 1982. All raises are based on merit, and most are tied directly to additional education and demonstrated new skills. It's an extra fifteen or twenty-five cents an hour if you take on leadership of the team's budgeting effort, an extra fifteen or twenty-five cents if you work on a so-called Pride Team (tackling a special improvement project), fifteen or twenty-five cents if you take an outside course to be a trainer and then take over leadership of your team's training activities, and so on.

Continuous learning, with the sky as the limit, is a religion at Johnsonville. You are encouraged, with company support, to study anything, job related or not. As one employee (or "member," to use Johnsonville's term) explained to me, "Look, anything you learn means you're using your head more. You're engaged. And if you're more engaged, then the chances are you'll make better sausage."

Continuous learning—not just "x hours per year of training"—marks darned few companies, and it entails a lot more than a few more bucks in the training budget or enhancing trainer skills, important as such factors are. The rule is that top-management philosophy must make it clear, as at Johnsonville, that continuous learning is the primary source of ongoing value-adding for the corporation. It must be a consuming marketplace strategy, not just a tactical program. Nothing less will do.

Replace "involvement" with limitless involvement. Replace "training" with continuous learning. And, third, replace "more teamwork" with the wholesale use of the autonomous work team. Yet another memorable stop in 1988 was at a decrepit, seventy-year-old, wood-floor GM components plant in Bay City, Michigan. I was talking with members of the "135 Group" (one of a number of self-managing teams in the plant), when I noticed the phone in the midst of their work area. As any wanderer through industrial America knows, phones are not usually found on the production line. I asked what it was for. The answer was commonsensical—but also revolutionary.

The phone is a direct line between the Bay City work team and its chief "customer," a work team at an assembly plant in Toledo, Ohio. Despite a continuing budget crunch that has everyone counting pennies, team members from Bay City (all in the union) were vigorously encouraged by enlightened local leadership to visit the work teams that use their products on the Toledo assembly line. When the two groups got together, they made an "obvious" decision—obvious if you're a normal human being, not so obvious if you have been schooled in traditional professional management and pyramidal organization structure.

These workers in Bay City (where average seniority is more than twenty years as a result of prior layoffs) wanted to keep their jobs—and they know what that means, thanks to the thorough management-union program of continuous information exchange. Exacting delivery schedules must be met, and without fail. Matchless quality goes without saying. So in the midst of the meeting, the Bay City team members turned to their "customers" in Toledo and said, "Let's install a 'hot line' between us. If you have a problem with anything we send you, call us—we'll fix it, quickly, with no muss, fuss, or memos."

And that was that. Problem solving now takes place on a real-time basis—and a couple of thousand people in Bay City (and a couple of thousand more in Toledo) have upped the odds of keeping their jobs.

The power and scope of the work team, illustrated here and in the two examples from Harley-Davidson and Johnsonville, are unlimited. I knew work teams were important (see P-2). But I severely underestimated their potential. I hope you don't. (And, as in my warning on technology, also don't underestimate the difficulty of implementation. Power—and lots of it—must be devolved from middle- and first-level management. There are, as usual, no easy answers.)

So the destruction of hierarchy means just that. Not reduction, but destruction. It is a competitive must, not an option, to achieve what I call appropriate flexibility. But, to reiterate, the destruction of hierarchy must be accompanied by the wholesale empowerment of virtually everyone. Empower, as to *give power to.* To describe these ideas more fully, I have included as an appendix a discussion of two sharply contrasting organization "charts," which define the difference between yesterday's and tomorrow's needs.

3. *The demise of huge scale.* Big is not dead. Giant firms will continue to play a leading role in our own economy and the economies of others. But acting big—that is, sluggish—is a guaranteed loser's strategy.

A discussion of bigness occupies some of the introductory chapter of *Thriving.* But once again, I want to take a moderately controversial issue and turn the heat up, not down. Upon retiring from Westinghouse, after years as one of America's most highly regarded strategic planners, Don Povejsil told *Fortune* (in February 1988), "The classical justifications of large size have proved to be of minimal value, or counterproductive or fallacious." At about the same time, one of the latest and most vitriolic attacks on bigness appeared, written by a conservative—former *Fortune* writer and Ford public relations executive Paul Weaver. The title? *The Suicidal Corporation: How Big Business Fails America.*

So the attacks on bigness are now coming with increasing regularity. But the most important evidence of our awakening from giantism's long spell can be observed in the daily reports in the business press of big-firm restructuring. Virtually all of the megafirms are rationalizing to reduce the monumental costs of bigness gone awry, which were conveniently ignored in the absence of real competition for America's big firms that followed World War II.

Our most famous names are routinely: (1) casting adrift numerous businesses that don't clearly match core corporate skills (i.e., they are deconglomerating); (2) savagely reducing hierarchy (levels and absolute numbers of middle managers), often by 50 to 75 percent or even more; (3) establishing many more highly autonomous small and mid-size business units; (4) dramatically reducing factory size; (5) enhancing the role of small, autonomous work teams on the factory or operations center floor, and adopting the idea of "small factories within a factory," or "small within big" as I call it; (6) forming more alliances with smaller, innovative firms and turning their backs on vertical integration by using more and more subcontractors (usually of modest or moderate size) for anything and everything, from watering the greenery to tackling the most sophisticated technical and legal projects—subcontracting by big firms has increased three-fold in just the last five years; (7) linking incentive pay for everyone to his or her small unit's success or failure; (8) turning to smaller, more coherent multifunctional teams (which are closer to the market and driven by customer need) to do most product development; and (9) from a strategic perspective, emphasizing moderate-size, "value-added" niche markets, while reducing dependency on mass manufacturing.

But this "downsizing" revolution is just half the story of bigness losing its grip. The parallel entrepreneurial explosion is the other half. It can be readily observed in service and manufacturing, in high tech and low, from the Silicon Valley to the Monongahela Valley, from Milan to Canton.

In the struggle for national comprehension of and political legitimacy for the entrepreneurial phenomenon, MIT economist David Birch's recent book *Job Creation in America* is a landmark. It's the product of a meticulous, ten-year research program that tracked the growing and declining fortunes of some twelve million American firms of all sizes. Birch claims, with a wealth of supporting evidence, that the smaller firms are creating all the net new jobs—and doing most of the innovation in every area, from banking to steel, computers, and superconductivity (in this vital arena, nineteen of the forty-eight firms, worldwide, are recent American start-ups).

The reasons for the explosion of private entrepreneurship in the United States at this time are many. Technology, especially information-based technology, is playing the lead role. On the demand side, markets are fragmenting as the technology revolutionizes design and distribution, abetting product customization and allowing unprecedented targeting of ever narrower markets. Technology further spurs market fragmentation by making vast storehouses of previously sacrosanct big-producer knowledge available to suppliers and distributors and consumers of all sizes at affordable prices. On the supply side, again in every arena, from autos and steel to fashion goods, increasing miniaturization and the rapid development of flexible manufacturing systems are fast erasing any former advantages of very large-scale production.

Then add the impact of new competitors from around the globe to technology's explosive role. As postwar oligopolies have crumbled, giant firms have been slow to adapt to change—both in matching others' efficiency and in innovation. Smaller and mid-sized firms have rushed in to fill the void. Moreover, as nations such as Taiwan and Korea have challenged the Japanese on high-quality mass production, the Japanese have joined the race for value-added niche markets with a vengeance. It is a simple fact that the smaller (and more flexible) firm has a big, inherent advantage in the emerging customized world (as even the Japanese are now acknowledging).

Next, stir in radical change in financial markets: globalization of financing means more access to more funds via a wider array of instruments for everyone. So-called junk bonds were invented in response to the observation that the financial paper of smaller firms is underrated, and that of the largest firms is overrated. The availability of venture capital has soared, too, even from conservative sources. And the stock market, despite postcrash jitters, is favorably disposed to initial public offerings (IPOs). The so-called "market for corporate control" (the activity of the raiders) also takes deadly aim at slovenly big-firm management. The financial markets' own brash new competitiveness and their fascination with scale are both effect and cause of the rapid reassessment of the roles of small, mid-size, and large firms.

Another factor is especially difficult to describe, yet of the utmost importance—America's entrepreneurial bent. Some call it a fourth factor of production, to go along with land, labor, and capital. Somewhat dormant in the face of the last seventy-five years of giant-firm dominance, it has returned with a flourish.

Bigness is also under attack in the public sector, in the military, for example (where our continuing attraction to high-tech super weapons has resulted in highly questionable readiness, particularly among conventional forces); and in the school system (where teachers' lack of classroom autonomy is as bad as workers' lack of autonomy in the factory, with perhaps even grimmer results for the nation). In fact, you can't turn around without running into evidence of failures of our largest operations, private or public—and parallel successes of smaller, more decentralized and entrepreneurial alternatives, public or private.

It is increasingly clear, then, that to a considerable degree the root cause of our public and private performance problems is size per se. Of course, criticism of giant private enterprises and public agencies is hardly new. But the intrusive presence of serious alternatives to giantism is new. That is, the entrepreneurial burst—smaller scale within a big activity or in a stand-alone configuration, and more competition in the private and public sector—is now seen by more and more governors, federal and state legislators, public administrators, academics, financiers, and even big business leaders as not just a complement or a poor relation to the giantism that has been our bent for so long, but the wave of the future. In short, the age of the elephant is passing. We are now entering the age of the gazelle.

4. *Pacific Basin, here we all come.* Several executives from a large French high-technology conglomerate visited me in Palo Alto in the spring of 1988 to talk about the West, or was it the East? Well, it was *our* West (California et al.), but *the* East (Japan, China, Korea, Taiwan, Hong Kong, et al.). In a rewrite of this book, I'd be inclined to replace Prescription C-5 ("Be an Internationalist") with a full section of prescriptions on internationalism. Moreover, several of those prescriptions would deal directly with Asia. We've simply got to put foreign business dealings, especially with Asia, at the top of our national economic—and managerial—agenda.

My advice to my French colleagues: Get your hooks into Silicon Valley or the Los Angeles Basin *and* Japan or Hong Kong—fast. Even if you lose money for years, at least establish a presence there. With the production of top-drawer Ralph Lauren garments in Hong Kong and the boom in low-tech (as well as high) manufacturing in the Los Angeles area, the Pacific is increasingly where the world's leading-edge economic action is. The talk of the coming Pacific Century is not hype.

I now often wear a California booster pin in the lapel of my suit coat. But I'm no booster (and I happily spend half my days in Vermont). Rather, the pin is a spur to talk about the Pacific with anyone who asks why I'm wearing it. California, with a population of twenty-eight million and a "GNP" of $550 billion, is also the receiving point for over $70 billion a year in goods from Asia. In the Los Angeles Basin are the U.S. headquarters of almost all Japanese and Korean car companies, as well as those of many of Japan's major banks. Los Angeles also has become the number one manufacturing center in America—with manufacturing jobs growing fast in industries of all description.

All of this may be a partial tribute to California's continuing entre-preneurial spirit, but it's more the reflection of the surprisingly rapid shift of our economic axis from the Atlantic (New York and London) to the Pacific (Los Angeles, Tokyo, and Hong Kong).

I must reluctantly admit that I don't always practice what I preach. Two years ago, my little firm, deciding to go international (as I advise small firms to do in *Thriving*), opened its first offshore office—in Stock-holm. Why? A talented colleague from Sweden became available to run it. And Europe is more comfortable for non-Asian Americans. But while I'm glad we're there, I knew at the time that we should have taken the more uncomfortable step of starting our offshore activities in Asia, and having visited mainland China for five weeks in early 1988, I now intend to rectify the oversight with dispatch; a Hong Kong office is in the offing.

Americans are not instinctively internationalists. And we especially shy away from Asia. Yet as Prescription C-5 shows, many of our firms, even smaller ones, have done very well overseas, including in Japan. An extensive study by the American Business Conference (an association of mid-size growth firms) appeared last year. It confirmed the export poten-tial of smaller firms in all industries; our best such firms are outperform-ing the giants overseas.

There are no shortcuts to international (and especially Asian) success, as I say in Prescription C-5 and said to my French friends. The Eastern languages are especially daunting. It takes forever and a day—and lots of personal top management presence—to even begin to form the necessary associations in Asia. But it is still worth it. More than worth it, it's another of those new necessities.

5. *The primacy of design.* The strategic use of technology, the destruction of hierarchy (and accompanying attention to continuous learning), a reversal of our fascination with bigness, the coming of internationalization, and the Pacific Century—these are four areas that I believe demand major reassessment in light of the changes since *Thriving* was written. Does product design fit on such an imposing list? My unequivocal answer is yes.

In early 1988, *Business Week* and *Forbes,* within a few weeks of each other, became the first national news magazines to put product design on their covers. And not a moment too soon. In *Thriving,* as a subtopic to quality (Prescription C-2), I give a nod to design. But that nod is not enough. Since then (and before *Business Week* and *Forbes!*), I've written about design extensively. Were I to amend the basic text of *Thriving* today, design would merit a prescription to itself, subsidiary to no other.

In *The Design Dimension,* Chris Lorenz, management editor of the *Financial Times* (London), contends that design merits a seat at the head table of any business strategy. Presenting evidence from around the globe, he argues persuasively that the "industrial design vision" deserves equal billing with the "engineering vision" and "marketing vision" in the process of product development. That is, design, technology, and marketing should be equivalent determinants of product strategy.

Surely leading European firms (Olivetti et al.) and Japanese firms (Sony is the most obvious) would agree (a senior design position at Sony underscores the importance of design to that firm's strategy). Moreover, in many Japanese and European firms, industrial design takes the lead in product development. Design conceives and passes its output on to engineering and marketing. In the typical American firm (albeit with sterling exceptions such as Apple, Herman Miller, and A. T. Cross), engineering does its bit, marketing does its bit—and only after that is the output passed to design, to "round off the rough corners." Design is a frivol, a poor relation.

It must not remain so. Design, flair, personal signature: as all of the most industrialized countries increasingly race up the value-added chain, and as technology permits more and more customization of everything, design becomes yet another of those new "musts" for the strategic arsenal of almost any firm of any size.

Furthermore, as many experts point out, design is far more than product prettiness. It's the company's signature, from order forms to packaging to the look of the reception area, as well as the physical appearance of the product or service itself. As American designer Michael Shannon puts it, "Design is the company's strategic objective made buyable, made real in customer terms. It is how the company looks, feels, tastes, wears, rides—what the company is that customers care about."

When lecturing in China in the spring of 1988, I described Japan's passion for industrial excellence by talking about my flight from San Francisco to Tokyo on Japan Airlines. I had saved the little plastic bottle (about an inch and a half long) in which the soy sauce that accompanied the dinner had come. Though clearly disposable, the plastic bottle was well worth saving. It is not unfair to declare that it was a work of art, as was the delicate little box (two inches by three inches—also saved) that had contained my peanuts. Though the first-class airfare across the Pacific runs $2,000, it was the soy bottle and peanut box that became JAL's signature in my mind, memorable enough to use as a preaching and teaching device throughout China. The careful attention to their design became a symbol of the airline's care for its customers.

Design is also symbolically important to this discussion. It is typical of what we have neglected in the past, and must now attend to in every nook and cranny of the economy. When industry's emphasis was on mass production, a few rough corners didn't matter. Now, when so many have mastered mass production (the Koreans being perhaps the latest), "the difference" is what matters to any product or service offering.

ALL BETS REALLY ARE OFF

The rapidity with which we are acknowledging that "all bets *really* are off" stuns even me. Practitioners, pundits, and reporters alike are now homing in on the models of management required for the new shape of competition—in utilities, financial services, and health care, as well as in steel, autos, computing, and retailing.

The new concord about ideas that until recently would have been deemed heretical was illustrated when a half dozen sober articles on these ideas appeared within a few days of one another in the winter of 1988. The first was about so-called vertical integration (owning all the elements of production, from the iron mine to the auto assembly plant, for example). Its desirability has long been a bedrock belief of American business. Yet the cover story in the January 4, 1988, issue of *Industry Week* magazine was titled "Doing It All Yourself . . . and Ensuring Worldclass 'Under Performance.' " The article leads off with this: "The demise of highly vertically integrated manufacturing companies is upon us. The wisdom within industry is that the failure to dis-integrate could lead to real disintegration. Now, less is more. Minimization is in."

That is, inefficiency, not efficiency, turns out to accompany owning too big a chunk of the action. The article goes on to quote a senior security analyst: "When manufacturers were in oligopolies or monopolies, they didn't have to worry about cost as much as they do when there's loads of competition. . . . Now, those companies that are highly integrated have an inherent disadvantage. Their costs are typically higher." That's far from the logic of yesteryear, when vertical integration was undertaken specifically to yield cost efficiencies. Moreover, *Industry Week* says that the trend in manufacturing is toward developing a competitive niche, which is related to less vertical integration.

But de-integration, in many minds, means shipping jobs offshore, probably to Asia. That is not necessarily the case, as Joel Kotkin made clear in the February 1988 issue of *Inc.* magazine. In "The Great American Revival," Kotkin observes that big manufacturing has indeed been in precipitous decline, shucking 1.4 million jobs between 1974 and 1984. At the same time, however, small manufacturing outfits with fewer than 250 people have grown in number by 41,000, and more than offset the others' loss. "People have developed a mythology about size," notes one venture capitalist Kotkin quotes. "In sharp contrast to the mass production-oriented giants of the last industrial era," Kotkin adds, "the new stars in manufacturing are small, highly focused companies whose fortes are flexibility, customization and market sensitivity."

As if these two coincident, unconventional assessments of management practice weren't enough, turn to Peter Drucker's provocative "The Coming of the New Organization," which appeared as the lead article in the January/February 1988 *Harvard Business Review*. Drucker, too, now turns his back on the excesses of bigness. He touts flexibility and the mid-size firm, even suggesting that the new organization, featuring new information technologies, may have almost no middle management at all.

But the most unsettling assessment of management practice comes from another article in that February 1988 *Inc.* magazine; this one discussed several management gurus' favorite business biographies. Among others, University of Southern California professor Jim O'Toole, who also is editor of a magazine appropriately called *New Management,* explained why Alfred Sloan's *My Years with General Motors* is his favorite: "[It] is internally so consistent, so well argued, so convincing that it became the model for how managers should think. . . . And the intriguing thing is that it's *all wrong.* For example: For the first 300 pages or so, Sloan seems oblivious to the fact that there are any *employees* in the company. . . . [The book] helps me understand what's wrong with management of large companies in America. . . . By reading this book, [my business students] learn which management practices to avoid."

If such an assessment seems too far out, read the coincident cover story of *Fortune*'s February 15, 1988, issue—a haymaker aimed at General Motors by former director Ross Perot. Before launching his litany of charges, including inflexibility and inattention to people and customers, Perot blurted, "We've got to nuke the GM system. We've got to throw away Sloan's book."

Any one of these out-and-out attacks on core management beliefs by respected commentators would have raised eyebrows not so many months ago. To have them all besiege us in the space of a week or two is startling confirmation that the for-so-long comfortable world of management practice has truly been turned upside down.

The real world simultaneously chimed in with clear-cut evidence, providing icing on the cake. On January 28, 1988, IBM announced a reorganization that chairman John Akers described as "a fundamental change . . . as significant as any we've ever made." The reason, said *The Wall Street Journal,* was IBM's "being too unwieldy to exploit market niches and develop new products quickly." The hallmark of the new IBM organization will be radical (by past standards) decentralization.

ADVICE TO OUR COMMANDER IN CHIEF

Since this edition of *Thriving* is being released around the time of a presidential election, it seems appropriate to make a comment or two about the tasks facing our next commander in chief. Is he to be confronted with an exorable American decline? Or is the best still to come?

Many responded to *Thriving on Chaos* by saying that Tom Peters, the happy warrior who brought you good news in *In Search of Excellence* (with Bob Waterman), has become a cynic. That's exactly half right—and therefore exactly half wrong.

The agenda of American business is staggering. Consider the greater (much greater) attention to quality, design, fast-paced innovation, and the frontline worker. Then add in the need to assimilate revolutionary technologies and to develop into an internationalist (with a special emphasis on the Mysterious East). Top that with the need to question the very nature of traditional organization structures—and the fact that those who don't question it, and act decisively, will simply not be around for long.

The bad news is that far too many of our biggest firms, from GM and Sears to IBM and Pan Am, are having a devil of a time addressing the changes with the necessary alacrity. The worse news is that many experts, including important economic advisers to both presidential candidates, insist that the problems are not structural, that solving them requires only the tweaking of traditional macroeconomic levers.

On the other hand, the offsetting good news is that everyone—including the Japanese—is struggling to figure out how to adapt to radically altered economic and organizational circumstances. And the best news of all is that we have more role models illustrating how the Brave New World can be addressed than any other kid on the global block—from computer and semiconductor firms to finance houses and retailers. Stodgy Europe, which is responding to its version of competitive change—the true opening of the European market in 1992—by reverting to thoroughly discredited sixties-style American conglomeration, shows virtually no entrepreneurial vitality. Japan lags badly on this essential dimension as well.

We are in the midst of a stunning transition. And though we must do much, much more to smooth the transition for the all-too-many workers who are the victims of shabby management, our chief policy approach, beyond reining in the deficit and increasing savings, must be to markedly upgrade work force skills, provide new forms of assistance for those who are dislocated or are in smaller firms, spur domestic R & D—and then *let the competitive juices flow*. Though lots of statistical indices in the United States look foreboding, we are arguably further along than any other nation in addressing the altered environment. We are shaking up our firms faster than anyone else, and this is thanks largely to unleashed competitive forces—from entrepreneurs and their financiers to, yes, the raiders. These groups are collectively shoving change down the throats of even the most complacent managers. Are we moving fast enough? Of course not. In some industries, dominated by older firms, progress is downright depressing.

But the policy choice, as it is emerging, is to turn up the heat (let competition loose) or turn it down (muffle the raiders, discourage risky investments, support creeping protectionism). It should not be viewed as a choice. Only the former offers hope of success for America.

BOLD GOALS NOW (AND YES, I REALLY MEAN IT)

I begin many seminars these days by presenting a list of "absurd" goals. The problem is that I didn't make any of them up. And *I* don't think they're absurd. Others, more often than not in "mature" industries, have already achieved these heights. Moreover, such heights are consistent with emerging ideas about work force participation and the use of new technology—that is, consistent with survival in the brave new competitive world.

I begin by flatly asserting that *productivity* must be increased by 100 to 200 percent in the next two to four years. My evidence? Much of it is scattered throughout the pages of *Thriving*. Productivity that's several hundred percent above average is a fact of life at steel makers Nucor, Worthington, and Chapparal, at Andersen (windows), and at retailers Lowe's and Nordstrom. Yet I am still routinely challenged. "Peters has flipped out" is not an uncommon response. I recall the hard facts from hard settings, and then usually refer to the November 9, 1987, issue of *Fortune* magazine, which featured an analysis of the Harvard Business School. That article garnered most readers' attention, so many probably missed the most surprising news, contained in an unobtrusive sidebar way back on page 88. It capsulized an interview with Honda's president, who matter-of-factly stated that Honda, which is probably already 100 percent ahead of most of its American competitors on productivity, intends to increase its productivity by 300 percent in the next few years.

Such objectives may be evidence of flipped lids to some, but not to Honda and other worthy competitors.

Then take *quality*. I propose a defect reduction target of 95 percent in the next three years or so. Once again, the pages of *Thriving* are studded with those who have achieved such improvements, from Milliken in textiles to Tennant in the manufacture of floor-cleaning equipment. Next I "suggest" that *product development cycles* be cut by 75 to 90 percent. Well, why not? Development cycles at garment maker/retailers such as The Limited and The Benetton Group are often only one-fifth to one-tenth as long as that of competitors. New-car development in the Japanese firms, especially Honda, may take as little as a fifth of the time it takes in the United States. Yes, these numbers *are* staggering. But others are achieving them: there's not a slice of pie in this sky.

A 90 percent reduction in the lead time required to fill orders is demanded. Orders from retailers or wholesalers took about twenty days to fulfill at U.S. Shoe in Cincinnati until recently. Now orders take only four or five days to turn out. In Prescription C-8, I offer examples from Richard Schonberger's "honor roll" of over 80 domestic manufacturers who have cut such lead times by factors of 5, 10, or even 20 in low- and high-tech arenas alike. *Inventory* reduction of 90 percent or more is also urged; once again, Schonberger's list (partially excerpted in *Thriving*) provides exemplars of those who have already done this.

Figure 21: **Eight Bold Goals***

Productivity	Increased by 100% to 200%
Quality	Defects reduced by 95%
Product Development Cycles	Shortened 75% to 90%
Order Lead Time	Reduced 90%
Inventory	Reduced 90%
Layers of Management	Reduced 75%
Span of Control	Increased by a factor of 5 to 10
Continuous Learning	Training budget increased by 200% to 300%

*Within the next 24–60 months, depending upon the industry.

And cut the *layers of management* by 75 percent, I plead. Once more, stories from Nordstrom, The Limited, Wal-Mart, Nucor, Worthington, et al. show the way, demonstrating that much, much less is much, much more when it comes to organization structure. Along with that, increase *the span of control* by a factor of 5 to 10, from today's average of one supervisor for ten nonsupervisors to one supervisor for fifty to one hundred workers, especially through the utilization of self-managed work teams. Examples in these pages are numerous, but once again the practice is far from the norm.

I conclude by urging that *continuous learning* be abetted by tripling or quadrupling the training budget in the next handful of years. While I don't believe in throwing money at any problem, the level of resource support that we give to training is intolerable right now. Once more, those who are doing it right dot the landscape (and the book), though they decidedly represent the tiniest minority.

Any one of these objectives is daunting. All of them together (summarized in Figure 21) may give one a true fright. And yet others, at home and abroad, are getting there—and have gotten there, but have not stopped. Goals like this are not a matter of choice in most industries. The serious question should be how quickly you'll get on with it.

There's a special significance in thinking about improvements of 100 to 200 percent in key business variables. You can't "increment your way" into change of this magnitude. Thinking about how to make an improvement of 10 or even 15 percent next year and then the next is simply not the same thing as thinking about "what the organization would look like if we were 300 percent more productive three (or five) years from now." It turns out that a 300 percent increase in a key variable is seldom the product of a bunch of 10 percent increases. It's more likely the product of adopting a whole new way of doing things. Of course, you will move ahead one step at a time. But we only move with dispatch toward the implementation of dramatic goals, like "destruction of hierarchy" discussed above, when we work at the complete reconceptualization of the process of organizing. "Radical incrementalism" is the paradoxical term I use to describe the process you must undertake. Get on with it, now, to be sure. Take an experimental approach—that's the incremental part. But make sure that these quick-fire steps and constant experiments are aimed at implementing a revolutionary future.

Appendix

We need entirely new ways of thinking about organizations if we are to respond to wildly altered circumstances. The familiar "military model," the hierarchical or "charts and boxes" structure, is not bearing up. It was developed when we knew who the enemy was (and he was neither a Libyan terrorist nor a crazy old man sitting in Tehran), and had time to prepare a response (it took Americans several years to gear up to win World War II, a nonaffordable luxury in the event of nuclear exchange, to put it mildly). Likewise, in the peacetime "economic wars," the days of old were marked by near certainty. Americans brought cheap energy to the contest and were blessed by a vast, "free trade" home market. And for the first six decades of this century, for instance, we knew who our competitors were—a few big domestic concerns. We knew where their leaders went to school, what cereals they ate for breakfast.

Today, almost every industry has competitors everywhere, from low-cost Malaysia to high-cost Switzerland, and including tiny domestic competitors by the score. Every industry now has—and keeps getting—new, previously unknown competitors. Moreover, the reality of fluctuating exchange rates, interest rates, rates of inflation, and energy prices, as well as the ever-reconfigured microprocessor, means that everything is changing, constantly gyrating.

But remember that colonial America broke away from its British masters via a guerrilla army victory. The popular mythology has it that the British insisted upon lining up in straight-line formations to do battle, sporting bright red coats, while the likes of Ethan Allen and his fabled Green Mountain Boys eschewed formations, hid behind trees, and used their skill as crack shots to achieve victory in the icy woods of the Hampshire Grants (now Vermont). Perhaps we need—again—organizations that evince the spunk and agility of the Green Mountain Boys, rather than the formality of the British—a formality that was out of touch then, in the new competitive reality in eighteenth-century colonial wars, and that is out of touch now, in the reality of our new economic wars.

A picture, so it is said, is worth a thousand words. I believe that, and this appendix is devoted to describing two pictures. Both purport to be "organizational maps." Neither looks much like a traditional organization chart. There is no square box at the top labeled "Chairman" (or "Vice Chairman," or "Chief Executive Officer," or "President," or "Chief Operating Officer," or "Executive Vice President," or "Office of the Chairman," or "Office of the Vice Chairman," or "Office of the President," or "Office of the Chief Operating Officer"). Both organization "charts" break tradition in that they include—can you believe it?—customers and suppliers, as well as distributors and franchisees. And both layouts are circular, moving from customers in toward the corporate chieftains at each circle's center. But beyond the circular scheme, the two bear little resemblance to each other.

THE INFLEXIBLE, RULE-DETERMINED, MASS PRODUCER OF THE PAST: ALL PERSONS KNOW THEIR PLACE

Let's begin with an assessment of Figure 22. *Start with* a, *the corporate center/policy.* The corporate center is purposefully conveyed by a very tiny circle. This is the traditional, largely invisible, impersonal, generally out-of-direct-touch corporate hub. The smallness of the circle suggests both tightness and narrowness of scope. Communication is downward and via the chain of command. Formal declarations are the norm—the policy manual and the multivolume strategic plan, by and large determined on high, are favored devices. Within this tiny circle lie the "brains of the organization." Here, almost exclusively, the long-term thinking, planning, and peering into the future take place.

Move on to b,· one-way, functionally narrow communication via rules

Figure 22: **The Inflexible, Rule-Determined, Mass Producer of the Past: All Persons Know Their Place**

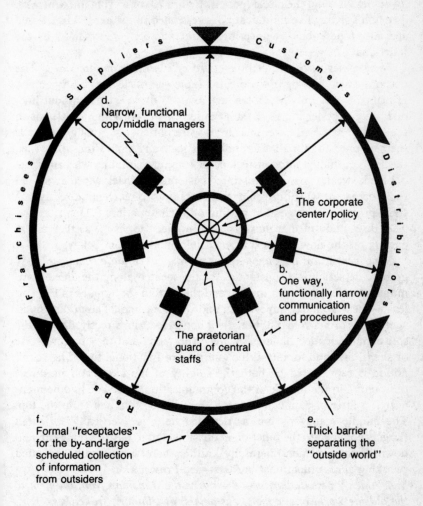

and procedures. Most communication in this generic organization type is highly channeled (thence the straight lines), top-down (note the direction of the arrowheads). So communication and "control" are principally via rule book, procedure manual, union contract, and the endless stream of memos providing guidance and demanding another endless stream of microinformation from the line. Moreover, the communication rarely "wobbles" around the circle (peek at Figure 23 for a dramatic contrast). The lion's share of communication is restricted to the narrow functional specialty (operations, engineering, marketing, etc.), represented by the individual arrows.

Then comes c, *the praetorian guard of central corporate staffs.* The corporate center is tightly protected (note the thick line) by a phalanx of brilliant, generally MBA-trained, analysis-driven staffs without line-operating experience. As if the isolation of the corporate chieftains in their plush-carpeted executive suites were not enough, this group seals them off once and for all. The staffs masticate any input from below (i.e., the field), turning it into fourteen-color computer graphics with all traces of blood, sweat, tears, and frustrated customer feedback wiped away. On those occasions when the senior team attempts to reach out directly, the staffs prove to be as good at cutting off their superiors ("Don't bother, we'll do a study of that marketplace—no need to visit") as they are at cutting off the flow of unexpurgated information from below.

Next, per d, *are the functionally narrow cop/middle managers.* My graphic depiction is a substantial square, located along the linear communication flow between the top and the bottom (bottom, as in last and least—the first line of supervision and the front line). The middle manager, as his or her role traditionally is conceived, sits directly athwart the sole communication channel between the "top" and the "bottom." He or she is, first and foremost, the guardian of functional turf. The "cop" notion is represented by both the solidity of the block and its direct positioning in the middle of the communication flow. The middle manager is a filter of data coming both from the bottom and from the top. The middle manager's job, as depicted here, is "vertically" oriented (largely confined to the function in question and to passing things up and down the management hierarchy), rather than "horizontally" oriented (working across functional borders—see Prescription L-8).

*A "thick," opaque barrier—*e—*marks the transition from the firm to the outside world of suppliers, customers, distributors, franchisees, reps, etc.* The barrier is very nearly impermeable. Communication, especially informal communication, does not flow readily across it, neither from the customer "in" nor from the front line of the organization "out." *Which leads directly to* f, *formal "receptacles" for the scheduled collection of* *information from outsiders.* Of course, old-style, inflexible mass production organizations do communicate with the outside world. But the communication tends to be formal, coming mainly from formal market research, or from orderly interaction via sales people. Both the timing and the format of the communication is largely predetermined. Even competitive analysis is rigid, hierarchical, and focused—by a formal competitive analysis unit that audits known competitors, mainly on a scheduled basis.

These six attributes hardly constitute an exhaustive description of the "old-style" organization. But they do give the gist: the old-style organization is static, formal, top-down oriented, rule-and-policy determined, and orderly to a fault (a dandy trait in a different, calmer world). To be sure, this depiction is stylized, and therefore somewhat unfair. However, it captures a frightening amount of the "truth" about today's larger organizations.

THE FLEXIBLE, POROUS, ADAPTIVE, FLEET-OF-FOOT ORGANIZATION OF THE FUTURE: EVERY PERSON IS "PAID" TO BE OBSTREPEROUS, A DISRESPECTER OF FORMAL BOUNDARIES, TO HUSTLE AND TO BE FULLY ENGAGED WITH ENGENDERING SWIFT ACTION AND CONSTANTLY IMPROVING EVERYTHING

It takes but a glance to appreciate the radically different nature of the organization depicted in Figure 23. It's a mess! Welcome to the real world in today's more innovative businesses: start-ups, mid-sized firms, slimmed-down business units of bigger firms. Welcome to the world of The Limited, Benetton, and The Gap in retailing. The world of Compaq, Sun Microsystems, the ASIC divisions of Intel and Motorola. The world of steel makers Worthington Industries, Chaparral, and Nucor. The world of Weaver Popcorn, Sandwich Chef, Johnsonville Foods, Neutrogena, ServiceMaster, and University National Bank & Trust of Palo Alto, California. Welcome to the world of somewhat ordered chaos, somewhat purposeful confusion; the world, above all, of flexibility, adaptiveness, and action taking. Welcome to a world turned upside down.

Start with a: *the new-look corporate guidance system—a vision, philosophy, set of core values (and an out-and-about senior team—also see* b *and* c *below).* First, the innermost circle depicting the corporate center in Figure 23 is considerably bigger than its counterpart in Figure 22. I pictured the traditional corporate center, in Figure 22, as out of touch, shriveled, and formalistic; ruled by very "tight" policy and a constraining rather than opportunistic strategic plan, with "contacts" inside and outside the enterprise made largely in a written format, usually via brisk, impatient, bloodless staffers. By contrast, the image that comes to mind for Figure 23 is a glowing, healthy, breathing corporate center.

People from below regularly wander in without muss or fuss. Those at the top are more often than not out wandering. Customers and suppliers are as likely to be "members" of the "executive floor" (which, happily, doesn't really exist as a physical entity) as are the official members of the senior team. But, above all, the glow comes from management's availability, informality, energy, and hustle—and the clarity of (and excitement associated with) the competitive vision, philosophy, or core values. "Rule" here does not usually proceed through written directives; rather it is rule by example, role model, spirited behavior—and fun. At the corporate center, you can "feel" or "smell" or literally see the vigorous pursuit of a worthwhile competitive idea, whether the firm is a bank, local insurance agency, or superconductor outfit.

Next comes b—*top management "wandering" across functional barriers and out to the front lines of the firm.* First, all of the "communication lines" in Figure 23 are zigzagging and wavy. The point is this: to be as flexible and adaptive as required by tomorrow's competitive situation demands the wholesale smashing of traditional barriers and functional walls, both "up and down" and "from side to side." Furthermore, this particular wavy line not only depicts the chief and his senior cohorts wandering about, but it also shows them purposefully disrespecting those functional dividing lines (in fact there are no formal functional dividing lines in this "organization chart"). Even more significant, the wanderings of the chief (and his lieutenants) regularly take him out to where the action is—at the front line, in the distribution center at 2:00 A.M., at the reservation center or the night clerk's desk, in the factory or the lab, or on the floor of the operations center.

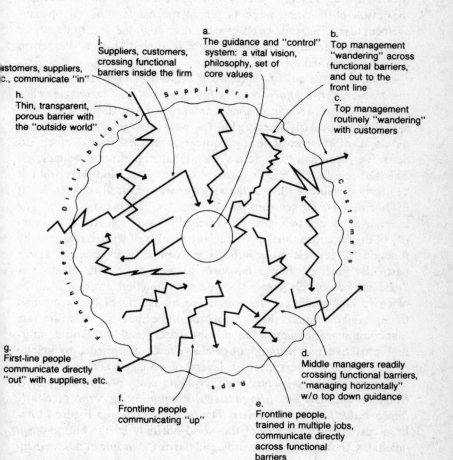

Figure 23: The Flexible, Porous, Adaptive, Fleet-of-Foot Organization of the Future: Every Person is "Paid" to Be Obstreperous, a Disrespecter of Formal Boundaries, to Hustle and to Be Fully Engaged with Engendering Swift Action and Constantly Improving Everything

j.
Suppliers, customers, crossing functional barriers inside the firm

a.
The guidance and "control" system: a vital vision, philosophy, set of core values

b.
Top management "wandering" across functional barriers, and out to the front line

stomers, suppliers, c., communicate "in"

h.
Thin, transparent, porous barrier with the "outside world"

c.
Top management routinely "wandering" with customers

Suppliers

Distributors

Customers

Franchisees

Reps

g.
First-line people communicate directly "out" with suppliers, etc.

f.
Frontline people communicating "up"

e.
Frontline people, trained in multiple jobs, communicate directly across functional barriers

d.
Middle managers readily crossing functional barriers, "managing horizontally" w/o top down guidance

Top management's "somewhat aimless ambling," as I call it, is not just restricted to the "inside" portion of the "chart." *So* c *depicts top management "wandering" with customers, too.* Top management is out and about—in the dealerships, hanging out with suppliers and with customers, big and small. And again, the irregularity of the line suggests the clarification that the visits of senior management to these settings are not restricted to the stilted, formal "Visit-a-Customer Day" affairs that mark the outside-of-the-company contacts of all too many traditional top management teams. Instead, we observe the drop-in to the dealer or supplier or customer, the largely unscheduled "ride around" with a salesperson on her normal, daily route.

As important as any of the contrasts between Figures 22 and 23 is d: *middle managers routinely crossing functional barriers, "managing horizontally," without specific top-down guidance.* To move fast to implement anything, particularly to engage in fast-paced new product and service development, there must be much quicker, much less formal, much less defensive communication across traditional organization boundaries. The lead role for the middle manager of the future (and there will not be nearly as many of them as in today's characteristically bloated firms) is "horizontal management," rather than "vertical management." The latter, as suggested by Figure 22, principally involves guarding the sanctity of the functional turf, providing any number of written reasons why function "X" is already overburdened and can't help function "Y" at this particular juncture. In the new arrangement, the middle manager is "paid" to proactively grease skids between functions, to be out of the office working with other functions to accomplish, not block, swift action taking. And once more, the zigzag nature of the line is meant to illustrate that communication *across* functional barriers should be natural, informal, proactive, and helpful; not defensive and not preceded by infinite checking with the next layer (or layers) of managers above.

But perhaps an even bigger difference involves e—*frontline people, trained in multiple jobs, also routinely communicating across previously impenetrable functional barriers.* The frontline person in Figure 22 has been cut off from the rest of the world not only by the button-down chieftains, those praetorian guards, and the turf-guarding middle managers, but also by a lack of training and cross-training, a history of not being listened to, and the "lowest" layer of cop—an old-school first-line supervisor. The role of the "new look" frontline person is very different. First, she is "controlled" not by a middle-management supervisor and a lengthy procedure book, but by the clarity and excitement of the corporate vision, its daily embodiment by wandering senior managers, an extraordinary level of training, the obvious respect she is given, and the self-discipline that almost automatically accompanies exceptional grants of autonomy.

Not only is the frontline person encouraged to learn numerous jobs within the context of his work team, but he is also regularly encouraged—at the front line—to cross funtional boundaries. Only regular, uninhibited frontline boundary crossing will induce the pace of action necessary for survival today. Formally, in the new regime, you would expect to see frontline people as regular members of quality or productivity improvement teams that involve four or five functions. Informally, you would routinely observe the frontline person talking with the purchasing officer, a quality expert, or an industrial engineer (whom she has called in for advice, not vice versa), or simply chatting with members of the team seventy-five feet down the line—always at work on improvement projects that disdain old divisions of labor/task.

Move on to *f* and *g,* which take this frontline person two nontraditional steps further. *First,* f: *frontline people communicating "up."* The key to unlocking extraordinary productivity and quality improvements lies within the heads of the persons who live closest to the task, those on the firing line. In the new-look organization, it becomes commonplace for the frontline person to be communicating "up," perhaps up even two or three levels of management (and one prays that there are not many more than that in toto), and all the way to the top on occasion.

And then, virtually unheard of today outside of sales and service departments, the "average" person, per g, will routinely be out and about—that is, first-line people communicating directly with suppliers, customers, etc. Who is the person who best knows what's wrong with defective supplies? Obviously, the frontline person who lives with the defective item eight hours a day, whether it's a computer system, a machine tool, or a sheet of steel or paper. With some advice and counsel from team members, and perhaps some help from a middle manager on occasion (and following a bushel of training), who is the best person to visit that supplier—yes, to take on a multiday visit that includes discussions with senior supplier management? Answer: It's again obvious—the first-line person or persons who suffer daily on the line as a result of the supplier's "crime."

Now let's turn to the organizational boundary, h: *a thin, almost transparent, permeable "barrier" between the organization and the outside world.* This is yet another extraordinary distinction between the "old-style" and the "new-look" outfit. Recall Figure 22: the outer barrier was thick, impermeable, except at designated "receptacles." The new "barrier" is thin and irregular. Both the thinness and the irregularity suggest that there will be frequent movement across it, anywhere and in both directions. Frontline people, and senior people without prior notification, will be heading out with only partially planned routines. Likewise, "external" colleagues will regularly hang out inside the firm (also see i and j below). To be sure, the firm exists as a legal entity. It is incorporated. People are on its payroll. But the image I'm trying to convey is one of the firm turned inside out, with the tough, recalcitrant hide that separates it from "them" (customers, suppliers, etc.) peeled away. NIH (not invented here) is no longer tolerable. The firm must be permeable. It must readily seek out, listen to, and act upon ideas gleaned from competitors, small and large, foreign and domestic; from interesting noncompetitors; from suppliers and subcontractors; from customers; from franchisees; from reps; from dealers; from frontline people; from suppliers' frontline people; from joint venture partners. It should be virtually impossible to put a finger on the "outside" organization boundary. Passage to and fro by virtually everyone, all the time and largely informal, leading to fast improvement without muss, fuss, and memos, must become the norm.

Next we move to i—*customers, suppliers, etc., communicating (talking, hanging out, and participating) "in."* The movement from adversarial to new nonadversarial/partnership relations with outsiders of all stripes is one of the biggest shifts required of American firms. Right now, the big (or even small) business organization is typically the site of unabated warfare: top management versus lower management, management versus the union, function versus function, and, relative to outsiders, company versus customers, company versus franchisees, company versus dealers, and, above all, company versus suppliers. This must stop. Cleaning out the bulk of the distracting praetorian guard and middle management will obviously help. But achieving an attitude of partnership is at the top of the list of requirements; that is, "living" a permeable organizational barrier. Customers and suppliers (and their employees at all levels) must be part of any new product or service design team. Even more routinely, customers and suppliers and franchisees and reps must be part of day-to-day productivity and quality improvement teams. Once again, to compete today means to improve constantly, to invent fast; virtually eliminating the barrier with the outside is the *sine qua non* of the speedy implementation of improvement projects.

Which leads directly to j—suppliers, customers, etc., crossing functional barriers to work—and help—inside the firm. The idea behind *i* is dandy, but not enough. Customers and other outsiders shouldn't just be "in" the firm; they must be part of its most strategic internal dealings. The supplier executive shouldn't be shunted off to the purchasing person. He or she should, instead, be working with cost accountants, factory or operations center people, marketing teams, new product and service design teams. Moreover, the jagged line suggests that the communication will be informal.

There is no doubt that Figure 23, taken as a whole, appears anarchic. To a large extent, this must be so—and we must not try to evade this truth. To move faster in the face of radical uncertainty (about competitors, energy costs, money costs, currency costs), revolutionary technologies, political instability, etc., requires more chaos, more anarchy in the organization.* But that is only half the story. Return to Figure 23, idea *a*—the corporate guidance system in the new-look firm. Recall my halting effort to describe it as a glowing sun, an energy center. In fact, the "control" in Figure 23 may be much "tighter" than in the traditional organization. Instead of stilted, formalistic baloney issued by out-of-touch leaders, the new "control," as noted, is the energy, excitement, spirit, hustle—and clarity of the competitive vision—that emanate from the corporate center. So when the newly empowered frontline person goes out to "experiment"—e.g., to work with a supplier or on a mul-

---

*There is a compelling theoretical, as well as pragmatic, basis for this idea. In 1970, R. C. Conant and R. W. Ashby posited the Law of Requisite Variety ("Every good regulator of a system must be a model of that system," *International Journal of Systems Science*). It has become the cornerstone of information theory. In laymen's terms, it means that you have to be as messy as the surrounding situation. In a volatile world, we must have more sensors processing information faster and leading to faster (and by definition more informal) action taking.

tifunction, internal team on quality or productivity improvement—he or she is, in fact, *tightly* "controlled" or "guided" by the attitudes, beliefs, energy, spirit, and so on of the vital competitive vision and the leaders who embody it. Moreover, that frontline person is extraordinarily well trained compared with his or her counterpart of the past, and remarkably well informed (for example, almost all performance information is available to him or her). So it's not a matter of tossing people into the supplier's operation and saying, "Go be a partner, now." The frontline person "out there" is someone who has seen senior management face to face (and felt their enthusiasm); a person who has already served on numerous multifunction teams; a person whose learning (training) has been continuous; a person who has just reviewed last month's divisional P & L in all its gory (or glorious) detail (after having taken an accounting course for all frontline "hands"). Thus, we can readily envision an astonishingly high degree of "controlled" flexibility and informality, starting with the front line and outsiders, in our "new-look" organization. But there is also an astonishing amount of hard work required—e.g., perpetually clarifying the vision, living the vision, wandering, chatting, listening, *and* providing extraordinary and continuous learning opportunities—that must precede and/or accompany all this. So perhaps "purposeful chaos" is the best description of the new-look firm.

Acknowledgments

A nonfiction book is as good as the stories people share. I am first and foremost indebted to the experimenting, risk-taking men and women who are trying (sometimes successfully, sometimes not) to restore American competitiveness and who have let me glimpse their efforts. Likewise I am indebted to the talented reporters for such publications as the *Wall Street Journal, The New York Times, Business Week, Inc., Fortune,* and *Forbes,* and many local papers and journals. I am an inveterate—and unrepentant—user of secondary sources, either directly or as leads for my own investigations; I find the quality of reporting generally to be high—i.e., the facts are straight.

This book grew out of our Skunk Camps. I gratefully acknowledge the role of our participant-customers who kept carping, "Get prescriptive." Well, I've tried—and this book is a work in progress toward that end. I'm also indebted to my close Skunk Camp colleagues, especially Bob Le Duc and Reuben Harris; they are both superb teachers, and our continual reshaping of the seminars together provided another major assist to this effort. Finally, the seminar participants, as mentioned in Part I, more often than not represent America's vital mid-sized ($75 million to $750 million) companies; it was my experience with executives from such firms that triggered my study of these firms' overall contribution to the economy. There is no doubt that these are the bellwether organizations.

I also heartily acknowledge a series of intellectual debts. In this book, I have explored numerous avenues that were new to me, from the history of automation to the history of employment guarantees. Perhaps because of my earlier academic training, I am only comfortable with my empirical efforts when I can find some leading-edge thinkers who are mining the same veins. Among others, then, I doff my cap to James Abegglen, Walter Adams, Warren Bennis, David Birch, Tom Bonoma, James Brock, Dick Cavanagh, Bob Christopher, Dick Foster, Brad Gale, George Gendron, George Gilder, John Groocock, Robert Hall, Jim Harrington, Bob Hayes, Masaaki Imai, Robert Kaplan, Jim Kouzes, Regis McKenna, David Noble, Michael Piore, Brian Quinn, Robert Reich, Charles Sabel, Richard Schonberger, Pat Townsend, Martin Weitzman—and Karl Weick, whose highly original conception of organizational structure remains the single most important influence on my thinking over the years. ("This fits with the unique way Karl sees organizations" is my ultimate test of any idea.)

Another group of people is far too large for me to mention individually—those who have supported me through the years such as Stew Leonard, who exhorts, at exactly the right moment (after I've suffered my tenth consecutive delayed flight), "Keep it up. Keep yelling. Keep talking. Keep writing." Stew will have to stand in for the hundreds I know well, and the thousands who write each year with kind letters of encouragement.

Last but not least are friends closer to home. At the top of the list is my friend (and spouse) Kate Abbe. She believes that there is nothing in life that counts except writing. Her continual and ungentle reminders of that, and support in a million ways, are invaluable. Also invaluable is the contribution of my friend and editor at Alfred A. Knopf, Corona Machemer. Her mastery of detail is impressive, and her damnable questions in the margin have simply reshaped this book several times. Her grasp of the content is at least as good as mine, and her innocent six-word queries have sent many a chapter back to the drawing board (or into the wastebasket); there is no higher tribute.

Kathy Dalle-Molle has checked almost every fact in this manuscript, and has devoted passion and awesome energy to tracing down the most obscure references (and people) imaginable; many of her queries have resulted in valuable elaborations as well. Susan Bright Winn typed and retyped (usually by "yesterday") the formidable manuscript from which this book emerged at least six times—wow!

Jayne Pearl, whose principal activity is the editing of our newsletter, has also been a constant source of creative needling. Jayne and I struggle weekly with my syndicated column, where many of the themes in this book have been born or honed.

Many at Knopf have bent over backwards to bring this book to life in very short order, among them designer Peter Andersen, production manager Andy Hughes, Corona Machemer's assistant, Ann Kraybill, and production editor Melvin Rosenthal. The indexer, Maro Riofrancos, and the compositors at ComCom also did superior jobs under pressure.

My partners, Debbie Kaplan, Bob Le Duc (mentioned before), and Ian Thomson, continue to encourage and cajole. Debbie, I think, works for Knopf—at least she's asked, "How's the manuscript coming?" many more times than they did.

Finally, one last thanks to the two people to whom this book is dedicated, Roger Milliken and Don Schaefer. When I come across an especially bold idea, one that I think is necessary to our economic survival, I always ask myself, "But could anybody in the real world ever pull this off?" And then I think of Roger and Don—oh yes, it can all be done!

T.P.

Notes

Facing Up to the Need for Revolution

page 3   "Can America make it?": "Rebuilding the US Model," *Financial Times,* May 9, 1987, p. 26.

This is the General Electric idea: Edwin A. Finn Jr., "General Eclectic," *Forbes,* March 23, 1987, p. 75.

6   A formidable $41 billion positive trade balance: James Brian Quinn and Christopher Gagnon, "Will Service Follow Manufacturing into Decline," *Harvard Business Review,* November/December 1986, p. 95.

6   "It will take hard and": Ibid., p. 103.

8   On the one hand: James R. Norman, "General Electric Is Stalking Big Game Again," *Business Week,* March 16, 1987, p. 113.

"Certainly most studies suggest that": Michael Porter, "The State of Strategic Thinking," *The Economist,* May 23, 1987, pp. 18, 22.

9   "Current 'merger mania' notwithstanding": Raymond E. Miles and Charles C. Snow, "Network Organizations: New Concepts for New Forms," *California Management Review,* Spring 1986, p. 62.

"Restructuring. The magic word": John Heins, "But the Grass Looked Greener over There," *Forbes,* April 27, 1987, p. 54.

14   "Henry Ford made great contributions": "Business Guru Finds a Following," San Jose *Mercury News,* April 17, 1987, p. 13D.

17   "they preferred Japanese suppliers": Sylvia Nasar, "Competitiveness: Getting It Back," *Fortune,* April 27, 1987, p. 223.

GE chairman Jack Welch: Finn, p. 75.

18   Lee does a thorough: O-Young Lee, *Smaller Is Better: Japan's Mastery of the Miniature* (New York: Kodansha International, 1984), p. 19.

The folding fan: Ibid., p. 35.

"Nothing comes harder": Ibid., p. 87.

19   Though it was a: Ibid., pp. 154–6.

page   Lee concludes: "That reduction": Ibid., p. 156.

In summary, says Lee: Ibid., p. 169.

20   "Bigness has not delivered": Walter Adams and James W. Brock, *The Bigness Complex: Industry, Labor and Government in the American Economy* (New York: Pantheon Books, 1986), p. xi.

"Scientific evidence has not": Ibid., p. 46.

"a big, sprawling, inert giant": Ibid., p. 35.

21   "in practically all our activities": Ibid., pp. 39–40.

In a classic 1956 study: Ibid., pp. 45–6.

"Cost-cutting opportunities": Ibid., pp. 44–5.

"the Milwaukee-based firm": Jack Thornton, "New Marketing Muscle," *Industry Week,* May 4, 1987, p. 38.

22   "Some 90 percent of those": "California Doing Its Own Thing," *U.S. News & World Report,* December 22, 1986, p. 25.

23   "Ostensibly, giant firms might": Adams and Brock, p. 50.

"reality and the available": Ibid., p. 52.

24   "Nor do giant firms": Ibid., p. 54.

Yet another study: Ibid., p. 55.

"A study . . . found the": Ibid., p. 52.

24–5   "The large corporation at risk . . .": Eli Ginzberg and George Vojta, *Beyond Human Scale: The Large Corporation at Risk* (New York: Basic Books Inc., 1985), pp. 218–19.

26–7   ". . . high wage economies can": Robert B. Reich, *Tales of a New America* (New York: Times Books, 1987), pp. 118, 119, 120, 121, 147, 148.

28   "Uniformity has given way": Martin Davis, "Two Plus Two Doesn't Equal Five," *Fortune,* December 9, 1985, p. 175.

30   In September 1986: "Chipping Away," *Financial World,* September 30, 1986, p. 4.

"The way in which market": "IBM Humbled," *The Economist,* January 31, 1987, p. 17.

". . . parallel/multiprocessor computers" market: Dwight B. Davis, "Parallel Computers Diverge," *High Technology,* February 1987, p. 20.

31   The greater good news story: Michael S. Malone, "America's New-Wave Chip Firms," *Wall Street Journal,* May 27, 1987, p. 28.

Take Kitchen Privileges . . .: Caroline E. Mayer, "Cooking Up a Hot Idea," Washington *Post,* January 26, 1987, p. 1 (Business).

33   "Stand in the spotless . . .": John Merwin, "McOil Change," *Forbes,* August 11, 1986, p. 91.

C-1

61   ". . . the Japanese pulled . . .": Otis Port, "Making Brawn Work with Brains," *Business Week,* April 20, 1987, p. 57.

page   "The fastest growing companies": "The Riches in Market Niches," *Fortune*, April 27, 1987, article subhead.

"The car market has become": Bill Saporito, "The Smokestacks Won't Tumble," *Fortune*, February 2, 1987, p. 30.

62   "There has been an explosion": Rob Hof, "New Gourmet-Food Firms Hope to Dish Up Profits," *Peninsula Times Tribune*, May 11, 1987, p. B-1.

64–5 "Marketing should focus on": Regis McKenna, *The Regis Touch* (Reading, MA: Addison-Wesley Publishing, 1986), pp. 21–3.

67   Economist William Hall: Theodore Levitt, *The Marketing Imagination* (New York: The Free Press, 1983, 1986), pp. 136–7.

71   "One of the characteristics": Robert Christopher, *Second to None* (New York: Crown Publishers, 1986), p. 150.

75–6 "Franklin [Electric Company]": Pat Choate, *The High-Flex Society* (New York: Alfred A. Knopf, 1986), pp. 214–15.

C-2

79   "The best of ours": Jeremy Main, "Detroit's Cars Really Are Getting Better," *Fortune*, February 2, 1987, p. 95.

Percentage of West Germans: "Harper's Index," *Harper's*, March 1987, p. 15.

79–80 "Tennant Company was known": Roger L. Hale, Douglas R. Hoelscher, Ronald E. Kowal, *Quest for Quality* (Minneapolis, MN: Tennant Company, 1987), pp. 11–12.

80   "It has always been remarkable": J. Daniel Beckham, "The Power of Owning a High-Quality Market Position Can Be Overwhelming," *Healthcare Forum*, March/April 1987, pp. 13–14.

82   PIMS researchers now call: "Formulating a Quality Improvement Strategy," *PIMSLETTER*, no. 31, p. 5.

PIMS assesses both technical: "Product Quality," *PIMSLETTER*, no. 4, p. 4.

In 1985, Dr. John Groocock: John Groocock, *The Chain of Quality* (New York: John Wiley & Sons, 1986), p. 83.

The top third of TRW's: Ibid., p. 85.

"The PIMS results for": Ibid., p. 6.

82–3 "It would appear that": *Consumer Perceptions Concerning the Quality of American Products and Services* (A study by the Gallup Organization for the American Society for Quality Control, 1985), pp. 12–13.

84   The Rogers Survey, done only: Main, p. 93.

Another important Power survey: *The Power Report*, December 1986, p. 6.

Finally, *Consumer Reports* conducts: James K. Glassman, "The Wreck of General Motors," *New Republic*, December 29, 1986, p. 21.

86   "Let me tell you": Laurence Shames, *The Big Time* (New York: Harper & Row, 1986), p. 102.

"You can't become emotionally": Steven Prokesch, "Remaking the American CEO," *The New York Times*, January 25, 1987, p. 8 (Section 3).

page 87　"I don't think you": James Kouzes and Barry Posner, from the working papers for *The Leadership Challenge: How to Get Extraordinary Things Done in Organizations* (San Francisco: Jossey-Bass, 1987).

"Now step back": H. James Harrington, *The Improvement Process* (New York: McGraw-Hill Book Co., 1987), p. 58.

88　"pour money into computers": Joel Dreyfuss, "Toyota Takes Off the Gloves," *Fortune,* December 22, 1987, p. 78.

In 1960, Toyota's suggestion system: Michael A. Cusumano, *The Japanese Automobile Industry* (Cambridge: Harvard University Press: 1985), pp. 358–9.

89–90　Recall Roger Hale's comment: Hale, Hoelscher, Kowal, p. 31.

90　"Measurement is the heart": H. James Harrington, *Excellence: The IBM Way* (IBM Technical Report, 1986), p. 19.

91　"Data recording comes first": Richard Schonberger, *World Class Manufacturing: The Lessons of Simplicity Applied* (New York: The Free Press, 1986), pp. 18–19.

For instance, with one: Harrington, *Excellence: The IBM Way,* pp. 45–6.

"Western industry must put substantially": Schonberger, p. 215.

93–4　"The billing process consists of": Harrington, *The Improvement Process,* pp. 13–14.

94　"Many teams received credit": Pat Townsend, *Commit to Quality* (New York: John Wiley & Sons, 1986), p. 103.

95　"Champions can . . . come from": Hale, Hoelscher, Kowal, p. 68.

96–7　". . . I got the phone number": Ibid., pp. 35–6.

97　"As greater quality is built": Norman Augustine, *Augustine's Laws* (New York: Viking Penguin Inc., 1983, 1986), p. 104.

99–100　From Harrington, *Excellence: The IBM Way,* pp. 73, 75, 85.

102　"We have to grant quality": Edward Tenner, "The Meaning of Quality," *Quality: America's Guide to Excellence,* p. 37.

103　"Seamstresses [who] hold requiem services": Joseph Campbell, *The Masks of Gods: Oriental Mythology* (New York: Penguin, 1970), p. 478.

103–4　"Although Japanese lumbermen": Joel Kotkin, "The New Northwest Passage," Joel Kotkin, *Inc.,* February 1987, p. 94.

C-3

110　Employees even declare that Jim Nordstrom: "Nordstrom Chain Sets Itself Apart with an Old-Fashioned Service Policy," Los Angeles *Times,* September 30, 1984, p. 1 (Business).

111　The PIMS data base once more: *PIMSLETTER,* no. 33, p. 8.

112　The Total Product Concept: Theodore Levitt, "Marketing Success Through Differentiation—of Anything," *Harvard Business Review,* January/February 1980.

117–8　"[I]t is common . . .": McKenna, pp. 41, 43–4.

C-4

page 133   U.S. retailers such as: "How High-Tech Tailors Are Saving a Stitch in Time," *Business Week,* April 14, 1987, p. 92G.

134   "bottom up than top down": Jennifer Lawrence, "Frito Play," *Advertising Age,* March 30, 1987, p. 1.

"Basically there's no such": Ibid., p. 1.

"We are tailoring": Ibid., p. 1.

136   "(1) Reduced order lead times": Louis Stern and Patrick Kaufmann, "Electronic Data Interchange in Selected Consumer Goods Industries: An Interorganizational Perspective," *Marketing in an Electronic Age* (Boston: Harvard Business School Press, 1985), edited by Robert Buzzell, p. 56.

"has pioneered a retailing": James L. Heskett, *Managing in the Service Economy* (Boston: Harvard Business School Press, 1986), p. 67.

137   "transmits [by computer] its production": Davis, p. 20.

140   "All Japanese motorcycle companies": Robert Hall, *Attaining Manufacturing Excellence* (Homewood, IL: Dow Jones-Irwin, 1987), p. 107.

144–5   "A corrugated box company": Hall, p. 249.

145   "The development of [the] system": Robert Hall, *Zero Inventories* (Homewood, IL: Dow Jones-Irwin, 1983), p. 9.

C-5

151   "American management in the past": Gary Blonston, "The Translator," *Science '85,* July/August 1985, p. 80.

152   Natural gas owned by: Walter Wriston: *Risk and Other Four Letter Words* (New York: Harper & Row, 1986), p. 152.

153   Despite the hiatus: Nicholas D. Kristof, "Japan Winning Race in China," *The New York Times,* April 29, 1987, p. 41 (Business).

154–7   Material, except on Buckman Labs and IBM, derived from Christopher, pp. 8, 19, 143, 6, 7, 46, 55, 70, 9, 43, 45, 57, 37, 83, 4, 60; and from Lennie Copeland and Lewis Griggs, *Going International: How to Make Friends and Deal Effectively in the Global Marketplace* (New York: Random House, 1985).

158–9   "Several factors explain": Raymond Vernon, "Gone Are the Cash Cows of Yesteryear," *Harvard Business Review,* November/December 1980, pp. 153–4.

160   Coca-Cola took the lime taste: Christopher, pp. 122–3.

162–3   "The Americans still talk": Steven Schlossstein, *Trade War* (New York: Congdon & Weed Inc., 1984), pp. 63–4.

C-6

167–8   "The point about Dayton-Hudson's": Subrata N. Chakravarty, "Federated Chooses Not to Choose," *Forbes,* April 8, 1985, p. 87.

page 168   Sears lived by the slogan: Julien R. Phillips and Allan A. Kennedy, "Shaping and Managing Shared Values," in *The Leader-Manager*, ed. by John N. Williamson (New York: John Wiley and Sons, 1984), p. 198.

168   "The three generic strategies": Michael Porter, *Competitive Strategy* (New York: The Free Press, 1980), pp. 35, 41–3.

169   A 1985 study: Alex Miller and Bill Camp, "Exploring Determinants of Success in Corporate Ventures," *Journal of Business Venturing*, Winter 1985, pp. 87–105.

170   it turns out that: Groocock, p. 85.

171   The "straddle" strategy: Levitt, p. 137.

172   "Leadership is heading into": Warren Bennis and Burt Nanus, *Leaders* (New York: Harper & Row, 1985), p. 44.

C-7

178   "The U.S. does more": Michael A. Verespej, "The R&D Challenge," *Industry Week*, May 4, 1987, p. 33.

179   "Take ceramics, for example": Ibid., p. 33.

181   "When patients understand the": David Perlman, "Medicine That Emphasizes Role of Patient," San Francisco *Chronicle*, September 12, 1985.

184   "on the road *half the time*": McKenna, p. 108.

184–5   "Despite the increased ease": Perry Pascarella, "In Search of Universal Designs," *Industry Week*, July 22, 1985, p. 37.

187   "I've never been surprised": Roy Rowan, *The Intuitive Manager* (Boston: Little, Brown and Company, 1986), p. 97.

196   "Americans have made money": Draft version of *Tales of a New America*.

197   "The technical community": David Noble, *Forces of Production* (New York: Alfred A. Knopf, 1984), p. 191.

198   "[Harvard's Ramchandran Jaikumar] studies 35": Barnaby Feder: "American technology backfires as much as conquers," *Peninsula Times Tribune*, November 2, 1986, p. D-9.

199–200   "There's . . . the issue of": Roland Schmitt, "Wanted: Hands-on Engineers," *High Technology*, April 1987, p. 10.

200   "the most efficient engine": Schonberger, pp. 57–8.
"A recent study of production": Dreyfuss, p. 78.
"(1) New American plants often": Hall, pp. 18–19.

201   *World Class Manufacturing* ends with an Appendix: Schonberger, pp. 232, 230, 229.

203–4   "A [major] strength of Japanese": Masaaki Imai, *Kaizen* (New York: Random House, 1986), pp. 36–7.

205–7   "*Our largest challenge*": Alan M. Kantrow, "Wide-Open Management at Chaparral Steel," *Harvard Business Review*, May/June 1986, pp. 99–101.

C-9

pages 215–6 "Despite the rigidity": Tom Bonoma, *The Marketing Edge: Making Strategies Work* (New York: The Free Press, 1985), pp. 93–4.

216–7 "Consider Dan Siewert": Bonoma, pp. 106–10.

220–1 ". . . Management attempts to": Bonoma, p. 53.

221–2 "Two [real] donut chains": Ibid., pp. 7–8.

I-1

239 "U.S. firms have a": Verespej, p. 33.
"You can't get the": Ibid.
"Where is all this": Adams and Brock, p. 64.

240 "[Breakthrough] projects the entrepreneurs": George Gilder, *The Spirit of Enterprise* (New York: Simon and Schuster, 1984), p. 246.

241–4 Information from James Lardner, *Fast Forward* (New York: W. W. Norton & Co., 1987), pp. 92, 38, 311, 188, 324.

244 "For God's sake": Christopher Cerf and Victor Navasky, *The Experts Speak* (New York: Pantheon Books, 1984), p. 207.

245 "Because you are a": Paul Hawken, *The Next Economy* (New York: Holt, Rinehart and Winston, 1983), pp. 172–3.

247 Du Pont's loss of leadership: Richard Foster, *Innovation: The Attacker's Advantage* (New York: Summit Books, 1986), pp. 121–35.

247–8 "At Saclay, outside Paris": Gary Taubes, *Nobel Dreams* (New York: Random House, 1986), p. 48.

248 "Until Rubbia came along": Taubes, p. 28.

249 "[These firms] are neither": "Factory of the Future: A Survey," *The Economist*, May 30, 1987, p. 14.

250–1 "Kaisha respond and rarely": James Abegglen and George Stalk Jr., *Kaisha: The Japanese Corporation* (New York: Basic Books, 1985), pp. 9–10.

252 "We shouldn't be afraid": "How to Stop a Russian 'Surge,'" *U.S. News & World Report*, June 15, 1987, p. 43.

I-2

258–9 "[D]esigners designed a car": Walton, pp. 139–40.

259 "With Taurus . . . we brought": Ibid., pp. 140–1.
"We went to all": Ibid., p. 143.
"The common way of doing": Ibid., p. 141.

260 "One lighting firm": Ibid., p. 142.

260–1 "In another departure": Ibid., p. 143.

261 "The prototypes were also": Ibid., p. 143.

I-3

page 269   "[D]on't get too prepared": From working papers for Kouzes and Posner.

274–5   Young and Rubicam: Eileen Prescott, "An Agency's Turn to Madcap Ads," *The New York Times,* June 7, 1987, p. 8 (Business).

I-4

279   "When we want to": "Productivity and Japanese Management Style" (Meyer Michael Cahn, interviewer), "Maurie" Kaoru Kobayashi, *Japan: The Most Misunderstood Country* (Tokyo: The Japan Times Ltd., 1984), pp. 42–72.

280   The Presidio Theaters in Austin: Curtis Hartman, "A Night at the Movies," *Inc.,* October 1986, pp. 101–6.

282   Despite a high batting average: Faye Rice, "The Media Star of Wall Street," *Fortune,* October 13, 1987, p. 100.

I-5

291–2   "Word-of-mouth communication": McKenna, pp. 58–9, 61.

293   "Most individuals do not": Everett M. Rogers, *Diffusion of Innovations* (New York: The Free Press, 1962, 1971, 1983), p. 18.

I-6

297–8   "[T]he entrepreneurs sustain": Gilder, p. 19.
"The prevailing theory of": Ibid., p. 15.

298   "their [leaders'] unfettered and somewhat": Ibid., p. 16.
"Curt and Tom were considered": William J. Broad, *Star Warriors* (New York: Simon & Schuster, 1985), p. 32.

299   "Any account of Honda's": Richard Pascale, "Perspective on Strategy: The Real Story Behind Honda's Success," *Strategy and Organization* (Boston: Pitman Publishing Ltd., 1984), ed. by Glenn Carroll and David Vogel, p. 42.

299–300   "On December 10, 1984": Taubes, pp. xiii, 6, 8.

302–3   "A few months ago": William Allan, "Factory Workers' New Design Saved 2-Seater for Ford," San Jose *Mercury News,* June 29, 1986, p. 19D.

I-8

315   [Limited founder Les Wexner] actually likes: Steven B. Weiner, "The Unlimited?," *Forbes,* April 6, 1987, p. 77.

I-10

page 333   "a drug": Porter, p. 18.

P-1

340   A 1985 study: "Seeking and Destroying the Wealth Dissipators," A. T. Kearney (Chicago).

346   And yet, a poll of: Adam Clymer, "A Times Poll of M.B.A.'s," *The New York Times Magazine,* December 7, 1986, p. 28.

349   "It's really amazing": Kantrow, p. 99.

350–1   The *average* workers there: Robert Zager and Michael Rosow, *The Innovative Organization* (New York: Pergamon Press, 1982), pp. 127–30, 139–43.

351   "Traditionally, the welding department's": Hale, Hoelscher, Kowal, p. 76.

352   "In a departure from": Mary A. C. Fallon, "McDonnell looks to rank and file to help set management strategy," San Jose *Mercury News,* November 3, 1986, p. 15D.

353–4   "The QWL . . . process began": Zager and Rosow, p. 320.

P-2

358–60   From Tom Peters' foreword to *Transforming the Workplace* (Princeton, NJ: Princeton Research Press, 1985), by John Nora, O. Raymond Rogers, and Robert Stramy.

360–1   "a decision [was reached in 1981] by": Zager and Rosow, pp. 57–8.

362   One recent assessment: Ibid., p. 9.

P-4

381   "asked all kinds of": Thomas Melohn, "Screening for the Best Employees," *Inc.,* January 1987, p. 105.
      "has only three Ph.D.s": Imai, p. 34.

382   "I strongly believe in": Melohn, p. 105.

384   "To get your recruiting": Ibid., p. 106.

P-5

387   "We've documented the savings": Michael Brody, "Helping Workers to Work Smarter," *Fortune,* June 8, 1987, p. 87.

388   TRW policy analyst: Choate, p. 217.

page   *Training* magazine's 1986 survey reports that: Jack Gordon, "Where the Training Goes," *Training,* October 1986, p. 49.

390   In four short years: From working papers for Kouzes and Posner.

P-6

399   A Yankelovich poll: Christopher, p. 106.

400   "The chief problem of big": Oscar Schisgall, *Eyes on Tomorrow: The Evolution of Procter & Gamble* (Chicago: J. G. Ferguson Publ. Co., 1981), pp. 45–6; and Martin Weitzman, *The Share Economy* (Cambridge, MA: Harvard University Press, 1984), p. 80.

403   At Steelcase, tools for: Robert Levering, Milton Moskowitz, and Michael Katz, *The 100 Best Companies to Work for in America* (Reading, MA: Addison-Wesley Publishing Co., 1984, 1985), pp. 416–22.
       At Publix, a Florida grocer: Ibid., pp. 348–52.

403–4   Andersen Corporation of Bayport: Ingrid Sundstrom, "Profit Sharing Puts Glow in Andersen Corp. Windows," Minneapolis *Star and Tribune,* January 25, 1987, pp. 1A, 7A, 10A.

405   "If a store's employees could keep": Christopher Eklund, "How A&P Fattens Profits by Sharing Them," *Business Week,* December 22, 1986, p. 44.

406–7   Information derived from conversations with Lowe's spokesperson and Corey Rosen, and from *Employee Ownership in America,* Corey Rosen, Katherine J. Klein, Karen M. Young (Lexington, MA: Lexington Books, 1986), and *The 100 Best Companies to Work for in America.*

P-7

413   "If we have too many people": Bill Saporito, "Cutting Costs Without Cutting People," *Fortune,* May 25, 1987, p. 27.
       When a company: Levering, Moskowitz, and Katz, p. 97.
       "marks for the first time": *News from the UAW,* for release May 13, 1987, p. 1.

414   Case-IH won: *News from the UAW,* for release May 13, 1987, pp. 1–5.
       UAW's historic 1984 agreement: *UAW-GM Report,* September 1984, p. 1.
       union accepted American Airlines': Jocelyn Gutchess, *Employment Security in Action: Strategies That Work* (New York: Pergamon Press, 1985), p. 14.
       the idea of employment security: Jerome M. Rosow and Robert Zager, *Employment Security in a Free Economy* (New York: Pergamon Press, 1984), pp. 17–18.

415   introduced a minimum: Levering, Moskowitz, and Katz, p. 346.

415–6   1. Accept management proposed changes: Rosow and Zager, pp. 33–4.

416   1. Maintenance of productivity: Ibid., p. 35.

417   Different classes of employees: Ibid., pp. 21–2.

page 419   staffs for 80 to 85 percent: Ibid., p. 64.

which targets for: Ibid., p. 46.

(a) switches assignments: Levering, Moskowitz, and Katz, p. 167.

Shifting people to sales: Rosow and Zager, p. 92.

In 1981–1982: Ibid., p. 92.

Kimberly Clark used: Ibid., p. 92.

420   During the same slump: Gutchess, pp. 20–1.

Digital Equipment has: Saporito, p. 30.

Its Employee Development Center: Rosow and Zager, p. 70.

421   In the 1981–83 recession: Gutchess, pp. 64–5.

P-8

425   "We have the poorest": "Seven Wary Views from the Top," *Fortune,* February 2, 1987, p. 60.

426   James O'Toole, professor of: James O'Toole, *Work and the Quality of Life: Resource Papers for Work in America* (Boston, MA: MIT Press, 1974).

430   "Many writers on organization": Ginzberg and Vojta, pp. 29–30.

431-2   "The overall aim": Ginzberg and Vojta, pp. 221, 160–1.

432   A meticulous 1985 study: "Seeking and Destroying the Wealth Dissipators," A. T. Kearney (Chicago).

"better support with [fewer] people": Schonberger, pp. 39, 43.

433   "William Dowdell, a 45-year-old": Mark L. Goldstein, "What Future for Middle Managers," *Industry Week,* December 8, 1986, pp. 52–3.

P-9

441   "Management excellence cannot": Hall, p. 154.

"Perhaps the biggest change": Schonberger, p. 147.

443   "As a country, the UK": Malcolm Trevor, *The Japanese Management Development System* (Wolfeboro, NH: Frances Pinter Ltd., 1986), pp. 5–6.

446-7   "Consider the following": Jan Carlzon, *Moments of Truth* (Cambridge, MA: Ballinger Publishing Co., 1987), pp. 61–3.

447   "the need for manufacturing engineers": Hall, p. 157.

448   "Having salaried people": Schonberger, p. 40.

P-10

453   "I find it mind-boggling": "Overheard," *Newsweek,* May 18, 1987, p. 21.

The New York Times recently reported: Prokesch, p. 8 (Section 3).

454   "[Ross] Perot claims he operated": Rowan, p. 9.

page   "He drives a compact Oldsmobile": Brett Duval Fromson, "A Hero in the Rust Belt," *Fortune,* January 5, 1987, p. 103.

455 "How *much* of a head slap": "Getting the Winning Edge Sums Up the Essence of Sports," Kansas City *Star,* January 4, 1987, p. 2 (Sports).

459 Upon being questioned: "Now Hear This," *Fortune,* May 25, 1987, p. 14.

461-2 "The miners filed into the pit": " 'This Is About It, Lads,' " *Newsweek,* March 18, 1985, p. 41.

463 "Frank Smith is a good": Hale, Hoelscher, and Kowal, p. 65.

463-4 "The emphasis on quality and pride": Levering, Moskowitz, and Katz, p. 420.

L-2

483 "The very essence of": Ezra Bowen, "His Trumpet Was Never Uncertain," *Time,* May 18, 1987, p. 68.

484 "Leaders articulate and define": Bennis and Nanus, pp. 33, 21.
      "We had the chance": From working papers for Kouzes and Posner.

487 "When asked what he": Bennis and Nanus, pp. 29–30.

488-9 "The controls are not": Working papers for Kouzes and Posner.

489 "Trust is the lubrication": Bennis and Nanus, pp. 43–4.
      "The leader's job is to": Working papers for Kouzes and Posner.

492 "The leader may have been": Bennis and Nanus, p. 82.

497 "Example is leadership": Mark Green and Gail MacColl, *There He Goes Again: Ronald Reagan's Reign of Error* (New York: Pantheon Books, 1983), p. 8.
      "My moment of truth": Working papers for Kouzes and Posner.

506 Stanford researcher Joanne Martin: Ibid.

L-4

521-2 "Valley Medical Center developed": Julie Herrod, "Innovator Award Winners," *Healthcare Forum,* March/April 1987, p. 59.

L-6

535 "Everybody talks about ["Celtics Pride"]": Alan Webber, "Red Auerbach on Management," *Harvard Business Review,* March/April 1987, p. 85.
      "The 'visible' half of execution": Bhide, p. 65.

536 "I love 'em all": John Madden: *One Knee Equals Two Feet* (New York: Villard Books, 1986), p. 15.

539 "Isn't this beautiful work?": *20 Teachers,* Ken Macrorie (New York: Oxford University Press, 1984), p. 7.

L-7

page 546   "Dalgliesh had accepted": P. D. James, *A Taste for Death* (New York: Alfred A. Knopf, 1986).

L-8

559   "At Sequent Computer, company president": Working papers for Kouzes and Posner.

S-1

584   "Data recording comes first": Schonberger, pp. 221–2.
585–6   ". . . the manager good at monitoring": Bonoma, p. 150.
587–9   Information from H. Thomas Johnson and Robert S. Kaplan, *Relevance Lost: The Rise and Fall of Management Accounting* (Boston: Harvard Business School Press, 1987).
590   For instance, Schonberger reports on Uniroyal's: Schonberger, pp. 133–4.
590–1   "He was responsible for": Groocock, p. 50.
591   "The number of believers in zero": Schonberger, p. 13.
592   "[Chairman Jim Robinson] started preaching": Monci Jo Williams, "Synergy Works at American Express," *Fortune,* February 16, 1987, p. 80.

S-2

602–3   "He began 'by planning' ": Cdr. Greg Gullickson, USN, Lieut. Cdr. Richard D. Chenette, USN, "Ch. 12: As the Captain So Is the Ship," *Excellence in the Surface Navy* (Naval Postgraduate School, 1984), p. 51.

S-3

609   "An individual without information": Carlzon, p. 35.
"Promoting information exchange": Schonberger, p. 174.

Second Thoughts

636   In writing the foreword to: Ed Feigenbaum, Pamela McCorduck, Penny Nii, from a draft version of *The Rise of the Expert Company* (New York: Times Books, 1988).

page 641   Upon retiring from Westinghouse: Walter Kiechel III, "Corporate Strategy for the 1990s," *Fortune*, February 29, 1988, 34.

642   It's the product of: David Birch, *Job Creation in America: How Our Smallest Companies Put the Most People to Work* (New York: The Free Press, 1987), p. 3.

643   19 of the 48 firms: T. A. Heppenheimer, "1988's Hottest Superconductor Companies," *High Technology Business*, January 1988, p. 23.

645   An extensive study by the American Business Conference: *The Challenge of Global Competitiveness: Views of America's High Growth Companies*, American Business Conference, 1987.

646   In early 1988: "Smart Design: Quality Is the New Style," *Business Week*, April 11, 1988, pp. 102–117; and Jeffrey A. Trachtenberg, "How Do We Confuse Thee? Let Us Count the Ways," *Forbes*, March 21, 1988, pp. 156–160.

646   In *The Design Dimension*: Christopher Lorenz, *The Design Dimension: Product Innovation and Global Marketing Strategy* (London: Basil Blackwell, 1986).

648   Yet the January 4, 1988, *Industry Week*: Brian S. Moskal, "Doing It All Yourself . . . and Ensuring Worldclass 'Underperformance,' " *Industry Week*, January 4, 1988, p. 47.

648   "When manufacturers were in oligopolies": Moskal, p. 48.

648   the trend in manufacturing: Moskal, p. 47.

648   In "The Great American Revival," Kotkin observes: Joel Kotkin, "The Great American Revival," *Inc.*, February 1988, p. 53.

648   "People have developed": Kotkin, p. 54.

648   "In sharp contrast to": Kotkin, p. 52.

648   Drucker, too, now turns his back: Peter F. Drucker, "The Coming of the New Organization," *Harvard Business Review*, January/February 1988, pp. 45–53.

649   "It is internally so consistent": John Case, "Managing by the Book," *Inc.*, February 1988, p. 80.

649   "We've got to nuke the GM system": "The GM System Is Like a Blanket of Fog," *Fortune*, February 15, 1988, p. 48.

649   The reason, said *The Wall Street Journal*: Michael W. Miller and Paul B. Carroll, "IBM Unveils a Sweeping Restructuring in Bid to Decentralize Decision-Making," *The Wall Street Journal*, January 29, 1988, p. 3.

651   It capsulized an interview with Honda's president: Frederick Hiroshi Katayama, "Japan: Hands on at Honda," *Fortune*, November 9, 1987, p. 88.

Index

Abegglen, Jim, 250–1
accessibility
  see also visible management
  fear and, 575, 576
accountants, 431
accounting, 587–91
acquisitions, *see* mergers and acquisitions
Acura automobile, 280
Adams, Walter, 20, 23–4
Advanced Micro Devices (AMD), 421
agriculture, 6, 16, 65, 66
aircraft, small-start strategy in design of, 251–2
airline industry, 73–4, 119
Allan, William, 302–3
Allen-Bradley, 22, 249
Allied-Signal, 570
ALOFS, 204
AMAX, 348
AMC, 29
Amdahl, 390–2
American Airlines, 74, 136, 286
American Express, 592
  Travelers Cheques, 70
American Family Life Assurance, 154
American Hospital Supply, 136, 156
American Society for Quality Control, 82–3
American Standard, 70
Ampex, 241–3
Andersen Corporation, 403–4
appeals process, goal-setting and, 620–1
Apple Computer, 65, 157–8, 328, 536
application-oriented small starts, *see* small starts, application-oriented

appraisal, performance, *see* performance evaluation
assumptions, old, 14–5
AT&T, 74
Atari, 621–2
Atkinson, George, 243
attention, paying, *see* listening
augmented level, 113–5
Augustine, Norman, 97
automated teller machines, 71–2
automation, 39, 197–201, 344–5
automobile industry, 65
  see also specific companies
  Japanese *(see also individual firms)*, 84, 240
  new car model development cycle time, 265; quality, 87, 88
  niche strategy in, 29
  quality and, 83–5
autonomy, small-start strategy and, 247
awards
  see also recognition
  anti-bureaucracy, 557
  customer satisfaction and, 125
  for innovation, 310
  for listening to customers, 183–4

Bain, Joe, 21
Baird, John, 244
Baltimore, Md., 128–9, 224, 227
banks (banking industry), 32, 118
  failures, 5
Beckham, J. Daniel, 80
Benetton, Luciano, 203, 380
Benetton company, 136–7

Bennett, Don, 269
Bennis, Warren, 172, 484, 487, 489, 492, 493, 497, 498, 630–1
Bergen Brunswig, 136
Berra, Yogi, 177
Bhide, Amar, 132, 535, 569
bigness (big firms)
  American penchant for, 15–25
  decentralization of, *see* decentralization
  efficiency and, 20–3
  innovation and, 23–5, 240–1
  small-start strategy and, 245–9;
    acquisitions, 246; applications other than new product or service development, 249; breaking the "think big" mind-set, 245–6; customer orientation, 249; funding, 247–8; independence of new-product teams, 247; stopping or modifying small starts, 248; surrounding big projects by small-start and partial projects, 246
Biles, Dan, 181–2
Birch, David, 298
Blay, Andre, 243
Blue, Vida, 574–5
Boardroom Reports, 426
Boeing, 164, 251–3
Boise Cascade, 460
Bonoma, Tom, 215–7, 220–2, 585–6
bonuses, *see* incentive pay
Borman, Frank, 343
Bouleware, Lemuel, 343
Boyer, Dave, 318
Bressler, Phil, 116, 228, 233
Broad, William, 298
Brock, James, 20, 23–4
Brooks, Fred, 323
Brunswick Corporation, 432–3
Bryant, Bear, 551
Buckman Labs, 44, 154, 213, 346–7
budget deficit, 7–8
Buick, 420
  QWL (Quality of Work Life) program at, 353–4
bureaucracy
  see also regulations
  destruction of, 554–9
  reducing, 452–8, 464–5
Burr, Don, 73–4
Bush, Sam, 539
BusinessLand, 171, 214

"business-mindedness," 431
Business Week, 61, 136, 327, 405–6, 458
Buzzell, Robert, 63

Cadillac engine plant (Livonia, MI), 358–60
calendar
  changing your, 496–503, 509
  line personnel's importance as reflected by, 537–8
call-backs, 116
Calloway, Wayne, 216
Campbell, Joseph, 103
Campbell Soup, 31, 134–5, 246
capital-gains tax, 40, 41
CARE (Customers Are Really Everything), 115
Carlzon, Jan, 72, 442–4, 446–7, 449, 609, 612
Carrigan, Pat, 390, 393
Cartridge Television Inc., 241–2
Case-IH, 413–4
Casstevens, Bill, 413
Catholic Church, 430
Cavanagh, Dick, 63–4
Celanese, 247
celebrating, 366
  see also recognition
centralization, 434, 435, 437
  see also decentralization; recentralization
ceramics industry, 179
champions, 296–304
  average people as, 302–3
  characteristics of, 298–302
  executive, 302
  first steps in encouraging, 304
  need for, 297–9
  piloting and, 270–2
  in public sector, 304
change
  see also disruption; innovation
  corporate capacity for, 332, 334
  love of, 55–6, 468, 470, 560–6
Chaparral Steel, 21, 205–9, 253, 257, 349, 369, 430, 478
chemicals industry, 65
  specialist producers in, 29–30
Chick, Charlie, 280
China
  Coca-Cola in, 160–1
  United States and Japan in, 153

Choate, Pat, 75, 388
Christopher, Bob, 157
Chrysler Corporation, 8, 22, 29, 137, 249, 459
  convertible, 307
  quality of cars, 84
CIM (computer-integrated manufacturing), 264
Citicorp, 153
Citytrust, 124, 284
Clancy, Tom, 252
Clark & Rockefeller, 245
cleanliness, 461–4
Clifford, Don, 63–4
Coca-Cola, 156, 160–1, 282
Cohen, Ted, 455
Cole, Robert E., 79, 84
Coleman, "Old Man," 86, 230
Coleman, Debi, 87
Cole National Corporation's Optical Division (CNCOD), 216–17
co-location, 146, 147
  team product development and, 263
Comissionà, Sergiu, 487
commissions, sales, 122
communication(s)
  see also telecommunications linkages to customers
  team product development and, 263–4
compensation
  customer-as-appreciating-asset approach and, 122
  of line personnel, 536–7
  linking innovation goal to, 329
  measurement of customer satisfaction and, 125
  of middle managers, 449
  public disclosure of decisions on, 600
  quality as basis for, 92
competition (competitors), 40
  determining identity of, 280–1
  more cooperation required by more, 474
competitive analysis, 280–5
  as everyone's business, 283–4
  in public sector, 287–8
complaints, customer, 112, 126
  surveys of, 124
complexity, passion for, 197–9
computer industry, 65, 66
  see also semiconductor industry
  specialist producers in, 30

computer-integrated manufacturing (CIM), 264
confidence, fear and, 575–6
Conner, Dennis, 493
conservative financial targets, 618–22, 624
Consumer Reports, 84
consumers, see customers
control (control systems), 586–7
  increasing spending authority and, 614
  revising tools of, 596–607
Control Data, 419
Cooley, Richard, 219–20
Cooper, Philip C., 180, 182
cooperation
  see also partnership relations
  more competition requires more, 474
  rewards for, team product development and, 262–3
copying ("creative swiping"), 279–88
  competitive analysis and, 281–4
  customer perceptions and, 286–7
  first steps in, 288
  NIH (Not Invented Here) syndrome and, 284–5
  in public sector, 287–8
  uniqueness and, 285–6
corporate structures, see organizational structure
corruption, 606
Corvette, 246
Cosmos computer system, 122, 135
cost-accounting systems, 587–91
cost reduction
  quality improvement and, 97–9
  small yields and, 475
costs, labor, 26–8, 587–8
craft tradition, 25–6
Crandall, Bob, 74
Cray Research, 253
"creating dangerously," 485
"creative swiping," see copying
Credo Challenge (Johnson & Johnson), 488
Creech, Gen. Bill, 47
Crosby, Phil, 85n., 90–3, 100, 104–5
CSI (Customer Satisfaction Index), 84
cultures, foreign, 156–7
Customer Action Teams (CATs), Milliken's, 138–41
customer complaints, 112, 126
  surveys of, 124

customer information system (CIS),
   190–1
customer listening, 176–92
   case studies of, 179–80
   characteristics of good, 182–91;
      "educate" versus "listen," 188;
      foreigners, customers as, 188–9; fun,
      listening as, 189–90; "hanging out"
      in the marketplace, 184–5; intensity,
      183–4; involvement of everyone,
      186–7; persistence, 187; taking what
      you hear seriously, and acting fast,
      185–6; every listening post you can
      find, 186–7
   customer information system and,
      190–1
   first steps in, 192, 377
   "naïve," 182, 191
   in public sector, 191–2
customer obsession, 226–33
   see also customer responsiveness
   getting started in, 232–3
   revenue enhancement and, 228–30
   revolution as mandatory for, 230–2
customer perceptions
   "creative swiping" and, 286–7
   intangibles and, 115–8
   "under-promise, over-deliver" approach
      and, 118–20
   uniqueness and, 167–71
customer responsiveness, 45, 48, 58–233,
   570, 573
   see also listening; service; total
      customer responsiveness
   disruption and, 336–7
   intangibles and, 115–8, 229
   internationalism and, 10–11, 42,
      150–65, 231; China, U.S. versus
      Japan in, 153–4; decentralization
      and, 158–9; first steps in, 164–5;
      Japan, American firms in, 154–7,
      160–1; local tastes and requirements
      and, 159–60
   manufacturing and, 202–10; building,
      208–9; characteristics of, 202–5;
      market creation through
      manufacturing, at Chaparral, 205–8;
      new model of the role of
      manufacturing, 209–10
   market creation and, 63–67
   measurement of, 590–3

quality and, see quality; quality
      programs
   service and support people's role in,
      acknowledgment of, 217–8
   small-start strategy and, 243–4, 248–50
   uniqueness and, 166–74, 231, 488 (see
      also differentiation of products or
      services); consensus on strategy of,
      172–4; copying and, 285–6; first
      steps toward, 174; involvement of
      everyone in organization's, 172–3; in
      public sector, 174; "stuck in the
      middle" strategy versus, 167–71;
      value of, 173–4
customers
   see also customer responsiveness
   as appreciating asset, 120–3
   educating, listening to customers
      versus, 188
   linkages to, 132–7; electronic, 135–7;
      143, 146–7, 230–1; regional offices,
      134–5
   listening to, see listening
   in manufacturing plants, 204–5
   uncertainty and, 12–3
   word-of-mouth marketing and, 292
customer satisfaction, measurement of,
   123–7
Customer Satisfaction Index (CSI), 84
customer service, see service
Custom Vêtement Associates, 133

Dale Carnegie courses, 122, 391
Dana Corporation, 448
Darwin, Charles, 286
Data General, 263
David-Edward Ltd., 179–80
Davis, Martin, 28, 86–7
Dayan, Moshe, 550
Dayton-Hudson, 168
debt, international, 11
decentralization, 427–8, 435
   in information, 608–12
   innovation and, 245
   overseas operations and, 158–9
   tighter control through, 476
Defense, Department of, 457, 464, 590
defiance of rules and regulations, 321–2
DeFouw, Gene, 204
de Gaulle, Charles, 507
de-humiliating, 452, 458–61, 465

de-integration, 475
  vertical, 146, 208
Delco-Remy: Fitzgerald, Georgia plant,
  350–1, 358
delegation, 544–53
  to act "horizontally," 553
  empowering and, 545–50
  establishing context for, 550–2
  first steps in, 553
  as "really letting go," 544–50
Deluxe Check, 147–8, 586
Deming, W. Edwards, 14, 90, 141, 345,
  354, 597
design, 12
details, visions as lived in, 490
development of products, see product
  development
differentiation of products or services,
  67–77, 229, 230
  see also uniqueness
  first steps in, 77
  in Japan, 70–1
  misguided, 71–2
  in public sector, 75–7
  quantifying differentiators, 72
Digital Equipment, 3, 327, 420, 422
direct labor costs, 587–8
Disney, 156, 217
  training at, 389, 391–2
disruption
  capacity to accept, 336
  as opportunity, 336–7
distortion of information, 513–5
distribution, 12, 66
  electronic linkages and, 135–7
  in foreign countries, 157–8
distributors, enhancing role of, 220–3
domestic content legislation, 41
Domino's Pizza, 116, 124, 142n., 228,
  351–2
  Distribution Olympics, 372–4
Dowdell, William, 433
Drucker, Peter, 387, 430, 603–4
dumb questions, 529–30
Du Pont, 30, 247, 427, 433

Eastern Airlines, 62
Eastman Kodak, 160, 488
Eckstut, Michael, 179
Economist, The, 22–3, 30, 249
efficiencies of scale, 475

efficiency
  bigness and, 20–3
  smallness and, 21–2
Electronic Data Interchange (EDI), 136
Electronic Data Systems, 147
electronic linkages, 135–7, 143, 146–8,
  230–1
Elgin Corrugated Box Company, 68–9,
  202–5
emotional involvement
  see also involvement
  living the vision and, 493
  urgency and, 574
empiricists, leaders as, 477–9
Employee Stock Ownership Plan (ESOP),
  398, 400, 406–7
employment guarantee, 412–23
  advantages of, 415–7
  characteristics of, 417–8
  costs of reneging on an, 421
  first steps in developing an, 423
  larger context of, 422–3
  for managers, 422
  tactics that enable a firm to offer an,
    418–21
empowering, 525
  delegation as sine qua non of, 545–50
  sales and service people, 219, 230
engaged listening, 528–9
engineers
  flexible manufacturing systems and,
    198
  hands-on, 199, 201, 335
  process, 140, 202
entrepreneurs, 297–8
errors, see failures
evaluation, see performance evaluation
excellence, end of era of sustainable, 3–4
executive champions, 302
executives, incentive pay for, 407–8
experts, staff, 448

"failing forward," 318
failures, 314–24, 479
  accelerating the success rate and, 476
  "do it right the first time" philosophy
    and, 319
  encouragement of, 317–8
  "fast," 317–9
  first steps in supporting, 324
  innovation and, 242

failures *(cont.)*
    learning from, 318
    little, 319–20
    need for, 316–7
    in public sector, 324
    results of failing to support, 320
    sloppiness and, 318
    small-start strategy and, 248
fear, urgency and, 575–6
Feder, Barnaby, 198
Federal Express, 70, 113, 120, 121, 128,
    135, 219, 352, 368, 401
    training at, 389, 391–2
Federated Stores, 167
feedback, listening and, 182–5
"feel," manufacturing innovation and
    responsiveness and, 208
Ferrell, John, 274–5
financial community, word-of-mouth
    marketing and, 292
financial management and control, 54
financial objectives, conservative, 618–22,
    624
financial services, 66
    specialization in, 32
Financial World, 30
Finland, 240
first-line supervisors, 435
    eliminating, 360–1, 363
first mover advantage, 147
Fitzgerald, Edmund, 156
Fletcher Granite Company, 371
flexibility
    factors that induce, 569–72
    new systems in support of, 605
    strategic planning and, 616
flexible manufacturing systems, 198–201,
    249
focus groups, measurement of customer
    satisfaction and, 124, 125
food industry, specialist producers in, 31
Forbes, 9, 33, 167–8
Ford, Henry, 73
Ford Motor Company, 4, 16, 22, 23, 29,
    38, 73, 196, 280, 281, 287
    Employee Involvement (EI) programs
        at, 360–1
    Escort EXP, 302–3
    quality of cars, 84, 87, 92, 93, 102,
        104, 105
    Taurus/Sable program, 285

team development of Taurus at,
    258–61
foremen, eliminating, 360–2
forest products, 66
Fortune, 17, 61, 454, 592
Fortune 500 firms, 5, 17, 340, 427
Forward, Gordon, 22, 205, 254, 257, 315,
    349, 478
Foster, Richard, 241, 494
France, 203
franchisees, enhancing role of, 220–3
franchising, specialization in, 33
Fraser, Doug, 85
Frito-Lay, 134, 135, 231–2, 258, 328
    salespersons at, 215–6
front-line people, *see* line personnel
Fuji, 158
fun, 480
functional barriers, absence (or breaking
    down) of, 203–4, 262, 442–4
    listening and, 530–2
funding, small-start strategy and, 246–8

Gagnon, Christopher, 6–7
gain sharing, 41, 45
    see also profit-distribution plans
Gale, Bradley, 63*n*
Gardner, John, 502
Garvin, Clifton, Jr., 245
Garvin, David, 97
Gendron, George, 127
General Electric, 17, 34, 199, 218, 263
    acquisitions by, 4, 8
    plastics operation of, 141–4
    training at, 393
General Motors, 20–2, 38, 73, 120, 133,
    147, 197, 414, 427, 443, 458–9, 538
    competitive analysis of, 284
    involvement of people at, 350–1, 353
    NUMMI venture with Toyota, 341,
        349–51, 456, 460, 583
    quality of cars, 85
    self-managing teams at, 358–61
    small-start strategy at, 246
    training at, 390, 393
generic level, 113
Germany, 7, 201, 345
giantism, *see* bigness
Gilder, George, 240, 297–8
Gillette, 157
Ginzberg, Eli, 24, 430, 431

global marketing, 428
goals (goal-setting)
    conservative, 618–21, 624
    emphasizing the achievable in, 601–3
    innovation, 329
Golden Needles Knitting and Glove, 202
"Gold Seal" Laser Parts, 69–70
Gonzalez, Louie, 62
Goodyear, 299 n.
Gore, William L., 322, 323
Gore & Associates, W. L., 322, 334
Granite Rock Company, 115–6
Grayson, Bob, 531
Great Britain, 16, 443, 461–2
Groocock, John, 82, 105, 170, 229, 590–1
growth, infrastructure and, 621–4
guarantee of continuous employment, see
    employment guarantee

Haavind, Bob, 134
Hale, Roger, 80, 89
Hall, Edward T., 151
Hall, Robert, 140, 144–5, 200–1, 441, 447
Hall, William, 171
Hallmark, 419
Harrington, H. James (Jim), 87, 91,
    99–100
Hartman, Ron, 128, 224
Hawken, Paul, 245
Hawthorne Effects, 94
Hayes, Bob, 196, 200
health-care industry, 32–3, 66–7, 117, 119
Henri Bendel, 246
Herman-Miller, 443
Hertrich, Adolph, 103
Hesburgh, Fr. Theodore, 483
Heskett, James, 136–7
Hewlett-Packard, 91, 154, 202, 249, 253,
    258, 367, 393, 419, 584
    interviews with job applicants at,
    379–80
high-energy physics, 247–8
High Technology (magazine), 30, 137
high value-added goods (or services),
    26–7, 29 and n, 49, 60, 230
    see also differentiation of products or
    services; uniqueness
hiring, see recruiting
Hoelscher, Doug, 96
Honda, Soichiro, 299, 301, 315, 318
Honda corporation, 280, 299, 381

Hong Kong, 153
"horizontal" action-taking, 479
"horizontal" delegation, 553
"horizontal" management, 554, 558–9,
    612
Hormel, 421
Horton, Tom, 513
Hospital Corporation of America, 32–3
hospitals, 69
    see also health-care industry
Hotchkiss, W. R., 586
hotels, 71
housekeeping, 452, 461–3
humiliating conditions, eliminating, 452,
    458–61, 465
hustle, 131, 132, 146, 153–4, 570
    see also urgency, sense of
hypocrisy, as enemy of integrity, 631

Iacocca, Lee, 307, 459
IBM, 30, 70, 127, 219, 230, 253, 327,
    493, 561, 562, 590, 630
    employment guarantee at, 414, 417–20
    in Japan, 154–5, 157
    quality programs at, 90–4, 99–100,
    104–6
    surveys for evaluation of managers at,
    368, 370
    training at, 389
Ibuka, Masaru, 243
Imai, Masaaki, 70, 92, 93, 334, 381
imitation, 333
impatience, purposeful, 308–9
Implementing In Search of Excellence
    (seminar), 43–4
Inc. (magazine), 103, 127, 375
incentive pay, 398–410
    see also gain sharing; profit-distribution
    plans; rewards
    program for, 400–10; executive
    incentives, 407–8; first steps, 410;
    involvement and, 409;
    pay-for-knowledge programs, 401;
    productivity and profit-based
    incentive pay, examples of, 401–5;
    recommendations, 404–5; setting
    base pay above the norm, 400–1;
    share ownership by employees,
    406–7
    in public sector, 410

incrementalism (incremental
    improvements), 475
  bold change and, 565
  in manufacturing, 196–202, 208–9
  product development cycle time and,
    265
Individual Training Account, 41
industry-watchers, word-of-mouth
    marketing and, 292
Industry Week, 22, 179, 239, 433
inertia, 564–5
informants, protecting, 518
information
  distortion of, 513–15
  leaks of, 611
  sharing of, 608–12
  training in the use of, 613
infrastructure, growth and, 621–4
initiative-taking, encouragement of, 351–3
innovation (innovativeness), 45, 48, 53,
    236–338
  see also incrementalism; product
    development
  bigness and, 23–4
  champions and, 296–303
  clearing away hurdles that impede, 323
  corporate capacity for, 332–8; constant
    search for new ideas, 335; eliciting
    innovation from everyone, 334; first
    steps, 337–8; long-term commitment
    to building innovation skills, 333–5;
    owning up to magnitude of the task,
    335–7; turning adversaries into
    partners, 337, 338
  "creative swiping" and, 278–88;
    competitive analysis and, 281–4;
    customer perceptions and, 286–7;
    first steps in, 288; NIH (Not
    Invented Here) syndrome and,
    284–5; in public sector, 287–8;
    uniqueness and, 285–6
  definition of, 327–9
  failures and, 242; *see also* failures
  measurement of, 326–31, 591–3;
    compensation linked to innovation,
    329; definition of innovation, 327–30;
    first steps, 330–1; involvement of
    everyone, 330; uniform innovation
    targets, 329–30; widespread use of
    innovation target, 330

modeling (symbolizing), 306–11, 323;
    asking for innovation, 309; first
    steps, 311; mundane actions, 308;
    purposeful impatience, 308–9;
    rewards for innovation, 310; rewards
    for small innovations, 310; seeking
    out and celebrating innovators, 310;
    support people, 310–1
  piloting and, 268–77; bits and pieces
    of, 271; first steps in, 277; fostering a
    quick-test environment, 274–5; as
    "hard" approach, 273; as
    inexpensive, 273–4; mastering the
    piloting mentality, 272–3; process of
    innovation shortened by, 271; public
    sector in, 276; reduction in "time to
    first tangible test," 275
  small-start strategy for, 239–55; big
    firms and, 245–9; examples of
    small-start possibilities, 253; first
    steps, 255; no exceptions to
    small-start strategy, 250–1;
    preconditions of "small-starts"
    approach, 255; public sector, 254–5;
    small firms and, 250
  unpredictability of innovation, 240–4
  word-of-mouth marketing and, 290–5;
    first steps in, 295; small, progressive
    buyers and, 294; systematizing, 294
innovation goals (or targets), 329–30
In Search of Excellence, 43, 427
  word-of-mouth campaign for, 293–4
inspectors, higher quality with fewer,
    476
inspiring vision, *see* vision(s)
insurance companies, Taurus
    development and, 260
intangibles, 115–8, 229
integration, forward (distribution channel,
    customer) and backward (supplier),
    146
integrity, 626–32
  as consistency, 630–1
  first steps in commitment to, 632–3
  front line and, 628–9
  hypocrisy as enemy of, 630
  quality and, 629
  "squeaky clean" approach to, 630
  systems support for, 631–2
Intel, 25, 95

internationalism, 10–1, 41–2, 150–65, 231
  China, U.S. versus Japan in, 153–4
  decentralization and, 158–9
  first steps in, 164–5
  Japan, American firms in, 154–8,
    160–3
  local tastes and requirements and,
    159–61
interviews, job, 378, 379, 382
inventory, just-in-time (JIT), 144–5, 448
involvement
  in bureaucracy-bashing, 557
  by everyone in everything, 340,
    342–55; attitudes of management as
    obstacle to, 344–6; cases illustrating,
    346–8; first steps to start, 355;
    initiative-taking, encouragement of,
    351–3; listening and, 366–70; in
    public sector, 354–5
  incentive pay and, 409
  urgency and, 575
ITT Europe, 590–1
Iverson, F. Kenneth, 345, 407, 425, 426,
  454, 460

Jaikumar, Ramchandran, 198
James, P. D., 546
Japan, 7, 16–17, 103–4, 286, 383–5; see
  also Ministry of International Trade
  and Industry (MITI)
  American firms in, 154–8, 160–3
  automobile industry of (see also
    individual firms): in Finland, 240;
    new car model development cycle
    time, 265; quality, 84–5, 87–8
  ceramics industry in, 179
  in China, 153
  corporate capacity for innovation in,
    334, 335
  differentiation in, 70–1
  distribution system in, 157–8
  employment guarantee in, 417, 419
  in "global village," 151–2
  incentive pay in, 399
  managers in, 443
  manufacturing in, 196–203
  middle managers in, 448
  motorcycle companies in, 140–1
  partnership relations in, 157, 158
  semiconductor industry of, 6
  smallness, passion for, 17–20

small-start strategy in, 240–3, 250–1
tailoring products or services to
  customers' tastes in, 160
J. D. Power Survey, 84
job creation, 474
job descriptions
  "connection to the customer" in, 125
  doing away with, 604–7
  in public sector, 606
Jobs, Steve, 486
job-sharing, 421
Johnson, H. Thomas, 588
Johnson, Kelly, 43–4, 251
Johnson, S. C. (Johnson Wax), 371
Johnson & Johnson, 488
Johnsonville Sausage, 35, 345, 361, 393
joint ventures, 475
Jones, Conrad, 86
Jones, Paul, 141–2
Jordan, Mike, 134
Journal of Business Venturing, 169, 264
just-in-time inventory management (JIT),
  144–5, 448

kaizen, principle of, 200, 341
Kami, Mike, 167, 174
Kane, Edward, 93–4
Kansas City Times, 32
Kanter, Rosabeth Moss, 343
Kaplan, Robert S., 588
Karl, Stuart, 244
Kaufmann, Patrick, 136
Kawasaki, 448
Kearney, A. T., 340, 432
Keller, Maryann, 29, 282
Kennedy, Allan, 171–2
Kennedy, Donald, 489
Kennedy, Richard, 141
Kentucky Fried Chicken, 158
Kimberly Clark, 419–20
King, Martin Luther, 506
KITA (kick them in the ass) supervision,
  515–6
Kitchen Privileges, 31
Klein, Katherine, 406
Kobayashi, Kaoru, 279–80
Kodak (Eastman Kodak), 160, 488
Koichi, Kakimizu, 162–3
Korea, 17
Kotler, Phil, 102
Kouzes, Jim, 484, 489, 559

Kowal, Ron, 463
Krupp, 201
Kugelman, Stephanie, 275

labor
  involvement of, *see* involvement
  minimization of role of, 25–8, 344
  more productivity through more
    people, not fewer, 474
  skilled, 27, 345
  specialization of, 25–6, 344, 345
  see also recruiting; training
labor contracts, 456
labor costs, 26–8, 587–8
labor unions, 456
Land, Edwin H., 487
Landry, Tom, 574
Lardner, James, 241–3
large corporations, *see* bigness (giantism)
Latini, John, 303
laughter, urgency and, 574
Lawrence Livermore Labs, 298
layoffs, 412–6
  see also employment guarantee
leaders (leadership), 45, 49, 53
  calendar changes and, 496–503
  definition of, 484
  as empiricists, 477–9
  empowering and, 525
  by example, 496
  integrity and, 628–30
  line personnel and, 539–42
  listening and, 524–32; breaking down
    functional barriers, 530–2; engaged
    listening, 528–9; first steps, 532;
    note-taking, 526–8; visible
    management, 525–6
  paradoxes and, 472–7
  promotion of, 451–2
  promotions and, 496, 503–5
  storytelling and, 506–7
  as symbolic action, 505–9
  vision of, *see* vision(s)
leaks, 506–7
Lee, O-Young, 18–9
Lee, Philip, 181
legislation, 148
Leonard, Stew, 120–2, 128, 172, 284,
    380, 527, 600, 630
  company newsletter, 375–6
  training by, 391, 392

Lerner store chain, 531
Levi Strauss, 138–9
Levitt, Ted, 111–3
Likert, Rensis, 443
Limited, The, 81, 128, 137, 246, 531
Lincoln Electric
  employment guarantee at, 415, 417
  incentive pay at, 402, 408–9
line personnel, 534–42
  first steps in enhancing, 442
  indicators that reveal status and
    importance of, 536–8
  "measuring" managers' attention to,
    539–40
  pride in accomplishments of, 539–40
Linjeflyg, 72
linkages to customers, 132–7
  electronic, 135–7, 143, 146–8, 230–1
  regional offices, 134–5
listening, 231, 479, 524–32
  see also customer listening
  breaking down functional barriers and,
    530–2
  empowering and, 527
  engaged, 528–9
  environment for, 367–70
  formal, 368
  informal, 367–8
  involvement of work force and, 366–70
  naïve, 229, 286
  note-taking and, 526–7
  visible management and, 518, 519, 526
Litton Industries, 9–10
Livonia Engine Plant, 358–60
local tastes and requirements, tailoring
    product/service to, 159–61
Lombardi, Vince, 551
Lorenzo, Frank, 74
Louisville Redbirds, 113–4
Lowe's Companies, 406
LSI Logic, 31
LTV, 10
Lutheran parish, Bendersville,
    Pennsylvania, 181–2

MacArthur, Douglas, 506–7
McCartney, Paul, 297
McConnell, John, 409, 461
McDonald's, 220
McDonnell, 352
McGowan, Bill, 75

Machiavelli, 298–9
machines, old, modified, 200–5
McKenna, Regis, 64, 117, 184, 229, 272, 328
   on word-of-mouth marketing, 291–2
McKesson Corporation, 135–6, 147, 286, 591
McKinsey & Co., 9, 200, 426, 615
McMahon, Jim, 493
McNutt, Thomas R., 405
Macrorie, Ken, 539
Madden, John, 493, 536, 574
Maidique, Modesto, 185, 261
Malone, Tom, 87, 140, 527
Malthus, Thomas, 286
management
   see also leaders; managers
   "horizontal," 554, 558–9
   layers of, 424, 430 (*see also* organizational structure)
   by objectives (MBO), 603–4
   as symbolic action, 505–9, 573
   visible, 510–22, 584–5; listening and, 518, 519, 525–6
   by wandering around, 514
management information systems (MIS), 54, 283
management theory, prescriptions in this book as, 47–50
managers
   see also leaders; management
   employment guarantee for, 422
   middle, 435, 440–50, 571; as experts on call, 448; first steps in changing role of, 450; horizontal management and, 444–5; in Japan, 443, 448; passing on news as function of, 448–9; turning organization upside down and, 444–7
   plant, 204–5
manuals, 452, 455–8
manufacturers reps, enhancing role of, 220–3
manufacturing (or operations), 12, 195–210, 231
   customer-responsive, 202–10; building, 208–9; characteristics of, 202–4; market creation through manufacturing, at Chaparral, 205–9; new model of role of manufacturing, 209–10

first steps in improving, 210
flexible systems, 198–201, 249
incrementalism in, 196–202, 208–9
in Japan, 196–203
reorganization of, 140
market creation, 63–7, 229, 623
marketing, 41
   total customer responsiveness (TCR) as tool of, 146–7
   word-of-mouth, 290–5; first steps in, 295; small, progressive buyers and, 294; systematizing, 294
market research, 178, 229
market share, competitive analysis and, 281–2
market sharing, 64–5
Marriott, 217, 372, 380
Mars, Inc., 430–1, 456, 629
Martin, Joanne, 506
Martin, Pieter, 346
Martin-Marietta, 362
mass markets, 28
Materials Research Corporation, 154, 420
matrix concept, 428–9
Mayone, Lowell, 413
Mazda, 19–20
MCI, 74, 75
measurement
   of customer responsiveness, 590–3
   of customer satisfaction, 123–7
   of innovation, 326–31, 591–3; compensation linked to innovation, 329; definition of innovation, 327–30; first steps, 330–1; involvement of everyone, 330; uniform innovation targets, 329–30; widespread use of innovation target, 330
   of managers' attention to the line, 539–40
   more appropriate, with fewer measures, 477
   of prescriptions in this book, 591–5
   of quality, 90–1, 590
   simple (and visible) techniques of, 583–6
   as symbolic action, 586–7
   top managers and, 586
   "what gets measured gets done," 580
   of what's important to the business, 582–4, 587–93; first steps, 595; nontraditional measures, 589–93;

measurement *(cont.)*
   traditional measurement systems as
      misleading, 587–9
Melohn, Tom, 380, 392, 393
memos
   elimination of, 452, 455, 457
   notes in margins of, 507–8
mergers and acquisitions, 8–10
   small, 247
   as strategic alliances, 333
Merrill Lynch, 32
metals industry, 65
   see also steel industry
Metcalf, Adm. Joseph, 453
Michigan, 75
middle managers, 435, 440–50, 571
   as experts on call, 448
   first steps in changing role of, 450
   horizontal management and, 444–5
   in Japan, 443, 448
   passing on news as function of, 448–9
   turning organization upside down and,
      444–7
Miles, Ray, 9
Milliken, Roger, 39, 85–6, 92, 139, 335,
      526–8
Milliken & Co., 39, 87, 204, 253, 336,
      443, 630
   innovation at, 309
   just-in-time inventory management
      and, 144–5
   manufacturing organization at, 140
   quality programs at, 93–7, 100, 104–6,
      138–9
   shop towels, 67–8
   total customer responsiveness (TCR)
      program of, 137–41
   uniqueness of, 173–4
Ministry of International Trade and
      Industry (MITI), Japanese, 155,
      241–2
Ministry by Wandering Around, 181–2
Minit-Lube, 33
mistakes, *see* failures
Mitsubishi, 158
Model Installation Program, 464
Model T automobile, 73
Moe, Doug, 173
Monaghan, Tom, 372
Monsanto, 29–30
Montgomery, Fld. Mshl. Bernard, 602

moral dimension of quality, 102–4
Morgan Bank, The, 118
Moritani, Masanori, 70–1, 203–4
Morse, Skip, 118
motivation, competitive analysis as, 284
Motorola, 390, 419, 421, 423
Mountain Bell, 433–4
multi-function teams, 256–66
   first steps in adopting, 266
   reorganization for reducing product
      development cycle time and, 265
   success factors of, 262–4; co-location,
      263; communication, 263–4;
      multi-functional involvement, 262;
      outside involvement, 264; "shared
      resource" trap, 264; simultaneous
      full-time involvement, 262–3
   supplier involvement in, 260–4
   Taurus automobiles and, 258–61

names of firms, 10
Nanus, Burt, 172, 484, 487, 489, 492,
      493, 630–1
Napoleon Bonaparte, 550
NASA, 428
National Science Board, 23–4
Navy, U.S., 252, 410
naysayers to change, dealing with, 564
networks, word-of-mouth marketing and,
      292–4
Neumann, Gerhard, 263
new product development cycle time, *see*
      product development cycle time
new products and services
   see also innovation
   word-of-mouth marketing of, 290–5;
      first steps in, 295; small, progressive
      buyers and, 294; systematizing, 294
New York Times, The, 153
niche markets, creation of, 63–7
NIH (Not Invented Here) syndrome,
      278, 284–5
Nippon Telephone & Telegraph (NTT),
      156
Nissan
   training at, 390, 392
Noble, David, 197, 198
no-frills approaches, 74–5
Nordstrom, 230, 380, 382, 401, 444,
      454–6, 486
   salespersons at, 214–5, 217

service at, 109–15, 128
training at, 393
Nordstrom, Jim, 111
North American Tool & Die (NAT&D), 380–1, 382, 384
Norton Company, 141
"no substitutes" rule, 264
note-taking, 518, 526–8
Nucor Corporation, 21, 345, 419, 421, 430, 454
incentive pay at, 402
NUMMI, 341, 349–51, 456, 460
NUMMI venture, 341, 349–51

offices, 510, 516–7
Ohmae, Kenichi, 184–5
Ohsone, Kozo, 243
Oklahoma, 75–6
Olsen, Ken, 244, 413
Omark, 202
One Idea Club, 284
organizational pyramid, flattening of, 440, 444–7, 612
organizational structure, 424–38
see also decentralization
excessive, 424–9
recentralization of, 428–9
simplifying and reducing, 430–8; alternative control schemes, 435–6; duplication, problem of, 436; examples, 432–4; first-line supervisors, 435; first steps, 437–8; forces pushing toward centralization, 434, 435, 437; limit management layers to five, 430; middle managers, 435; put staff in the field, 430–2; senior managers, 434–5
Orr, Robin, 180–2
O'Toole, James, 426
"overstaffing," 113, 231
overtime, 418–9
Owen, Robert, 414–5

Pacific Bell, 246, 420
Pacific Presbyterian Medical Center, 180–3
packaged goods, 31–2, 66
Pagluica, Jess, 215–6
paradoxes, 468–9, 472–7
core, 478–9
empiricism and, 477–9

first steps in dealing with, 480
tips for the paradox-loving manager, 479–80
parallel structures, quality programs and, 95
Pareto, Vilfredo, 514
parking spaces, executive, 452, 458, 459
partnership relations, 45, 132–3, 118–9, 230
corporate capacity for constant innovation and, 337, 338
at Milliken & Co., 139–40
overseas operations and, 157–8
Pascale, Richard, 299
Passion for Excellence, A, 44, 170, 263, 284, 427
Patton, Gen. George, 602
Paul Revere Life Insurance Company quality programs at, 92–7, 105
pay, see compensation
pay-for-knowledge programs, 41, 392, 401
Pearl, Jayne, 191–2
People Express Airlines, 73–5, 122, 488
PepsiCo, 282
Pepsi-Cola, 134
per capita GNP, 4–5
perception, see customer perceptions
Perdue, Frank, 527
Perdue Farms, 92, 124
performance evaluation, 596–601
categories for, 598–9
constant, 598
contract for, 600, 605
"customer orientation" in, 125
first steps in changing, 606–7
goals of, 600
of middle managers, 449
in public sector, 606
simplifying procedures and forms for, 599–600
as small part of recognition, 600–1
team product development and, 262
as time-consuming, 598
Perot, H. Ross, 197, 257, 269, 388, 454, 458–9
persistence
internationalism and, 155–6
in listening, 187
small-start strategy and, 242–3
pet food industry, 71

philosophy, 482
  see also vision(s)
P-I-E Nationwide, 136
pilots, 269–77
  bits and pieces of, 271
  first steps in, 277
  fostering quick-test environment, 274–5
  as "hard" approach, 273
  as inexpensive, 273–4
  mastering the piloting mentality, 272–3
  process of innovation shortened by, 271
  public sector in, 276
  reduction in "time to first tangible test," 275
PIMS (Profit Impact of Market Strategy), 63 and n., 81–2, 111
Piore, Michael, 25
Pizza Hut, 160
Planetree Model Hospital Project, 180–3
planning, strategic, 477, 615–7
plant managers, 204–5
policy manuals, 452, 455–8
poor-quality cost, 91
porous organization, 48
Porta Copy, 240
Porter, Michael, 8, 168, 333
Posner, Barry, 484, 489, 559
potential level, 113, 114
Powell, Casey, 559
Power Survey, 84
PPG, 145
preaching, 519
predictability, 11–2, 119–20
prescriptions, 43–56
  see also specific topics
  how to use, 50–1, 55
  measurement of, 591–5
  as organization theory, 47–50
  public sector and, 47
Presidio Theaters, 280
press, the, word-of-mouth marketing and, 292
Preston, Sam, 371
pride in accomplishments of others, 539
Primerica, 426
problem-solving, sequential, 258
process engineers, 140, 202
Procter, Cooper, 400
Procter & Gamble, 31–2, 135, 399–400, 415

product definition, 12
product (or service) development, 203–4
  see also innovation
  multi-function teams in, 256–66;
    co-location, 263; communication, 263–4; first steps in, 266; multi-functional involvement, 262; outside involvement, 264; reorganization for reducing product development cycle time, 265; "shared resource" trap, 264; simultaneous full-time involvement, 262–3; success factors, 262–4; supplier involvement, 260–4; Taurus automobiles, 258–61
product development cycle time, 253
  reduction of, 44–5, 265
productivity, 4, 7
  incentive pay based on, 402–5
  through more people, not fewer, 474
profit
  incentive pay based on, 402–5
  quality and, 81–3
profitability, measurement of, 588–9
profit-distribution plans, 41, 399–400; see also gain sharing; incentive pay
promises, "under-promise, over-deliver" approach to, 118–20
promotions, 496, 503–5, 509
  of leaders, 451–2
  of those who deal best with paradox, 480
protectionism, 40
public sector
  champions in, 304
  "creative swiping" in, 287–8
  failures in, 324
  incentive pay in, 410
  involvement of people in, 354–5
  listening in, 191–2
  performance appraisals and job descriptions in, 606
  piloting in, 276
  prescriptions in this book and, 47
  quality programs in, 107
  recognition in, 376–7
  recruiting in, 384
  service and support people in, 223–4
  service in, 128–9
  small-start strategy in, 254–5
  uniqueness in, 174

value-adding, differentiation strategy in, 75–6
Publix, 403
Puckett, Allen, 529
purchasing department, 590
multi-function teams and, 262–3
purposeful impatience, 308–9

quality, 4, 28, 78–107, 229, 230
calendar changes and, 499
customers' perception of, 100–2
customers' willingness to pay for, 82–3
integrity on the front line and, 629
measurement of, 90–1, 590
moral dimension of, 102–4
obsession with, 85–9
paradoxes of, 476
permanent commitment to, 88
profit and, 81–3
quantitative assessments of quality in America, 83–5
return on investment as a function of price and, 169–71
rewards for, 92
small improvements in, 94
team approach, 92–4
training in assessment of, 92
quality circles, 92–3, 361, 362
see also quality programs
quality programs
attributes of, 85–100; constant stimulation for improvements, 94–5; cost reduction, 97–8; guiding system (ideology), 90; measurement of quality, 90–1; never-ending journey, quality improvement as, 98–9; obsession of management with quality, 85–90; parallel organization structure for quality improvement, 95; rewards for quality, 92; small improvements, 94; suppliers, 92, 95–7; team approach, 93–4; training, 92
first steps in, 107
at Milliken & Co., 93–7, 100, 104–6, 138–9
patterns and priorities in, 104–6
in public sector, 107
questions, dumb, 529–30
Quinn, James Brian, 6–7

raiders, corporate, 40
railroad industry, 16
Raychem Corporation, 484–5
RCA, 241, 242
Reagan, Ronald, 489–90, 506
recentralization, 427–8
recognition
see also awards
control systems and, 586–7
first steps in, 377
formal appraisal as small part of, 600–1
for line personnel, 538
public forums for, 370–6
in public sector, 376–7
recruiting, 379–85
credentials of prospective employees and, 381
first steps in, 384–5
in public sector, 384
values of company and, 379–81, 383–4
redeployment, employment guarantee and, 419–20
Reed, John, 535
Regent Air, 71
regional offices, 134–5
regulations
see also bureaucracy
supporting defiance of, 321–3
Reich, Robert, 26–7, 196, 344
Reichert, Jack, 566
Reid, James, 454
re-integration, 475
relationship-building, foreign markets and, 156–7
relationship management, 111
reliability, 118–20
reorganization
for reducing product development cycle time, 265
total customer responsiveness (TCR) and, 140
repeat customers, as appreciating asset, 120–3
report card, bureaucracy, 558–9
reputation. see word-of-mouth referrals
research and development (R&D)
bigness and, 24
tax breaks for, 42
responsiveness to customers, see customer responsiveness

restructuring, 9–10
retailing, 66
retraining, 386
    see also training
    employment guarantee and, 419–20
return on investment
    see also profit
    uniqueness and, 168–70
revenue enhancement, 228–30
Revere, Paul, see Paul Revere Life
    Insurance Company
reverse pyramid organization chart, 440,
    444–7
rewards
    see also compensation; recognition
    linking innovation goal to, 329
    for small innovations, 310
    team product development and, 262–3
Richardson, David M., 195
risk-taking, above the "waterline," 322–3
Rivers, Lee, 178, 239
Robinson, Jim, 592
Robinson, John, 493
robotics, 197
Rockwell Semiconductor, 368, 369
Rogers, Ev, 293
Rogers Survey, 84
Roodman, Richard, 521–2
Rosen, Corey, 406
Rosendahl, Paul, 464
Rowan, Roy, 187, 454
Rubbia, Carlo, 248, 299–302
rules, see bureaucracy; regulations
Runyon, Marvin, 195–6

Saba, Andrea, 14
Sabel, Charles, 25
Sabre system, 136
Sadoulet, Bernard, 300
sales commissions, 122
salespersons, 212–20, 231–2
    examples of giving priority to, 213–7
    first steps in making heroes of, 224
    increasing number of, 219
Sanders, Betsy, 111, 214, 217, 223–4,
    380, 455
Santo, Ted, 516–7
Sanwa Bank, 153
savings rate, 5
Scales, Anthony, 372

Scandinavian Air System (SAS), 442,
    445–7
Scanlon, Joe, 402
Scanlon Plan, 402
Schaefer, William Donald, 47, 227, 233,
    335, 464, 527, 552–3, 573
Scherer, Frederic, 9, 21
Schick, 157
Schlossstein, Steven, 162–3
Schmitt, Carl, 401
Schmitt, Roland, 199
Schonberger, Richard, 91, 92, 200–2, 432,
    441, 448, 584–5, 590, 591, 609
Schwartz, Laurie, 552
Schweitzer, Albert, 497
scintillator technology, 247–8
Sculley, John, 187, 536, 538
Sears, 168, 241
Seattle First National Bank, 219–20
Securities and Exchange Commission
    (SEC), 9
self-managing teams, 340, 356–65, 444
    elimination of first-line supervisors and,
        360–2
    examples of, 357–60
    first steps in using, 364–5
    market demand for, 364
    pitfalls on the road to, 361–2
semiconductor industry, 6, 66
    specialist producers in, 30–1
sequential problem-solving, 258
service, 108–29, 229
    see also customer responsiveness
    call-backs, 116
    customer-as-appreciating-asset
        approach to, 120–3
    first steps in improving, 129
    intangibles and, 115–8
    measurement of customer satisfaction
        and, 123–5
    at Nordstrom, 109–14, 128
    as profitable, 111–2
    in public sector, 128–9
    strategy for upgrading, 218–20
    technology's role in, 128
    Total Product Concept and, 112–5
    "under-promise, over-deliver" approach
        and, 118–20
service companies (service sector)
    decline of, 6–7
    specialist producers in, 32–3

service development, *see* product (or service) development
ServiceMaster, 33, 144, 154
    training at, 392
service people, 231–2
    acknowledging customer-responsiveness role of, 217–8
    first steps in making heroes of, 224
    inducing heroics among, 218–20
Sewell Village Cadillac, 214
"shared resource" trap, 264
Sharper Image, 240
Shaw, George Bernard, 297
shop towels, 67–8
Siewert, Dan, 216
"siloing," 257–8
simple systems, rejection of, 197–9
simplification, quality improvements via, 97–8
size, *see* bigness; smallness
skill enhancement, 40–1, 387–9
    see also training
Sloan, Alfred, 21
sloppiness, 318
Smaglick, Paul, 260
small firms
    see also smallness; start-up firms
    small-start strategy for, 250
    as uniquely successful at innovating, 298
small markets, small starts for, 240–1
smallness
    see also small firms; specialist producers
    efficiency and, 21–2
    Japanese passion for, 17–20
small starts, application-oriented, 239–55
    big firms and, 245–9
    examples of small-start possibilities, 253
    first steps in strategy of, 255
    in Japan, 240–3, 250–1
    no exceptions to strategy of, 250–1
    preconditions of a "small-starts" approach, 255
    in public sector, 254–5
    small firms and, 250
    unpredictability of innovation and, 240–4
Smith, A. O., 260

Smith, Fred, 109, 486
Smith, Ray, 113
Smith, Roger, 239, 459
Snyder, Irving G., Jr., 15, 101–2
software, electronic linkages and, 135–6, 146–7
Soki, Tessen, 19
Sony, 19
    VCR development and, 241–3
Sony Walkman, 243
span of control, 426, 430
specialist producers, 29–35, 63, 65–6. *See also* market creation
    in service sector, 32–3
specialization of labor, 25–6, 345
spending authority, 435, 454, 613–5
stability of purpose/employment, 474
Stabler, Ken, 541, 551
Stalk, George, Jr., 250–1
Standard Products, 454
start-up firms, 40, 41
    in semiconductor industry, 31
Staubach, Roger, 541
Stayer, Ralph, 345
"stealing" ideas, *see* copying
Steelcase, 220, 403
    truck fleet of, 463–4
steel industry, 65
    mini-mills and micro-mills in, 21, 29
Stegmayer, Joe, 404, 614
Stengers, Isabelle, 473 and *n.*
Stern, Louis, 136
Stew Leonard, *see* Leonard, Stew
Stone, Bob, 464
stories about "constructive defiance," 321–2
storytelling, 496
    control systems and, 587
    leadership and, 506–7
Stramy, Bob, 358
strategic planning, 477
    genuine "bottom up," 615–7
Strategic Planning Institute (SPI), 63
strategy for growth, 621–4
structure, *see* organizational structure
"stuck in the middle" strategy, 167–71
"stump speech," 492–3
subcontractors, 419
successful firms, 35
    characteristics of, 34

suggestions
  customers', 129
  Taurus development and, 259
suggestion system
  anti-bureaucracy, 557
  Toyota's, 88
supervisors
  first-level, eliminating, 360–1, 363
  first-line, 435
  ratio of nonsupervisors to, 426
  training, 394–5
suppliers
  more productivity through fewer, 475
  quality programs and, 92, 95–7, 100
  team product development and, 260–4
  uniqueness and, 173–4
support people, 231
  customer-responsiveness role of, 217–8
  for dealers and reps, 223
  first steps in making heroes of, 224
  inducing heroics among, 218–20
  rewards for, 310–1
support systems, 122, 128, 140, 582
  for integrity, 631–2
surveys
  of customer satisfaction, 123–7
  as feedback (listening) devices, 368
Sussman, Bernie, 390–1
Sutton, Doug, 448
symbols, 496
  leading and, 505–9
  management and, 87, 573–4
  management commitment to quality
    and, 87
  of support for (or rejection of)
    innovation, 306–11, 323; asking for
    innovation, 309; awards for
    innovation, 310; mundane actions,
    308; purposeful impatience, 308–9;
    rewards for small innovations, 310;
    seeking out and celebrating
    innovators, 310; support people,
    310–1
systems, 580

Tampa Bay Buccaneers, 382
Tandem Computer, 368, 403
Taubes, Gary, 248, 299–300
Taurus automobiles, team development
  of, 258–60, 285

tax incentives, for training and
  pay-for-knowledge programs, 40–2
TCR, see total customer responsiveness
  (TCR)
teams (team approach)
  multi-function, in new-product/service
    development, 256–66; co-location,
    263; communication, 263–4; first
    steps in, 266; multi-functional
    involvement, 262; outside
    involvement, 264; reorganization for
    reducing product development cycle
    time, 265; "shared resource" trap,
    264; simultaneous full-time
    involvement, 262–3; success factors,
    262–4; supplier involvement, 260–4;
    Taurus automobiles, 258–61
  quality and, 92–4
  self-managing, 340, 356–65, 444;
    elimination of first-line supervisors
    and, 360–2; examples of, 357–60;
    first steps in using, 364–5; market
    demand for, 364; pitfalls on the road
    to, 361–2
  small-start strategy and, 253; autonomy
    required, 247
Technical Assistance Research Programs,
  112
technology, 12. See also innovation
  research and development (R&D)
  intangibles and, 117
  service and role of, 128
telecommunications linkages to
  customers, 135–7, 143, 146–8, 230–1
telecommunications industry, 74
  in Japan, 156
Teleflex, 318
temporary employees, 419
temporary services, 33, 67
Tennant Company, 79, 346, 351, 463
  quality programs at, 88, 93, 96–7, 104,
    105
tension, 50–1
testing, see pilots
Texaco, 10
Texas Air, 8
Texas Instruments, 87
textile industry, 65
The Limited, 81, 128, 246, 531
Thompson, Allyn, 177
Thomson, Ian, 163

3M, 35, 201, 246, 329, 592, 623
  small-start strategy at, 253
  "time to first tangible test," reduction in,
    275–6
Topham, Jon, 284
Toshiba America, 185–6, 218
total customer responsiveness (TCR),
    130–48
  see also customer listening; customer
    responsiveness; listening; service
  factors necessary to achieving, 145–7
  first steps in strategy of, 148
  GE's plastics operation, 141–4
  just-in-time inventory management
    and, 144–5
  linkages to customers, 133–7; electronic
    linkages, 135–7, 143, 146–8, 230–1;
    regional offices, 134–5
  Milliken's program, 137–41
  training your customer's people and,
    144
Total Product Concept (Levitt), 112–5
Tower Board Report, 545
Townsend, Bob, 503, 599
Townsend, Pat, 92, 94
Toyota, 88, 200, 219, 230, 281
  NUMMI venture with General
    Motors, 341, 349–51, 456, 460, 583
trade deficit, 5
training, 219, 386–96
  beating the competition through, 387–9
  of customers' employees, 134–5
  elements of good programs, 391–4
  entry-level, 391–2
  examples of programs, 388–91
  first steps in, 396
  line-driven, 393–4
  listening environment and, 369
  of middle managers, 449
  national investment in, 388–9
  on-the-job, 393
  in quality assessment, 92
  revolution in, 395
  supervisors, 394–5
  tax credit for, 40–1
  vision and values of firms and, 393
Training (magazine), 62, 388
Trammell Crow, 407
Trevor, Malcolm, 442–3
Trus Joist, 183
TRW, 82, 105, 137, 170

Tupperware, 160
Turner, Phil, 486, 490

U.S. News & World Report, 22
uncertainty, 8–14
"under-promise, over-deliver" approach,
    118–20
understaffing, employment guarantee and,
    418–9
uniqueness, 166–74, 231, 488
  see also differentiation of products or
    services; innovation
  consensus on strategy of, 171–3
  copying and, 285–6
  first steps toward, 174
  involvement of everyone in
    organization's, 172–3
  in public sector, 174
  "stuck in the middle" strategy versus,
    167–71
  value of, 173–4
Uniroyal, 590
United Airlines, 8
United Auto Workers (UAW), 345–6,
    349, 350, 413–4
United Food & Commercial Workers
    (UFCW), 405
United Mine Workers (UMW), 348
United Technologies, 8
University National Bank & Trust (Palo
    Alto), 401
urgency, sense of, 568–77
  creating a, 570, 572–5
  fear and, 575–6
  first steps in instilling a, 576–7
USAir, 8
USX (formerly U.S. Steel), 20–1, 240–1,
    458

Vaill, Peter, 569
ValCom, 115
Valley Medical Center (Seattle), 521–2
value added, see high value-added goods
    (or services)
value-adding strategy, see differentiation
    of products or services
values
  see also vision(s)
  recruiting and, 379–81, 383–4
Vanport, 104
Venture Project, 287

Veraldi, Lew, 259, 261
Vermont, 223
Vermont National Bank, 62
Vernon, Raymond, 158–9
vertical de-integration, 146, 208
vertical integration, 475
vertical re-integration, via data exchange, 146
"very promotable item" (VPI), 189
Victoria's Secret, 246
video cassette recorders (VCRs), 241–4
Video Club of America, 243
visible management, 510–22, 584–5
  fear and accessibility, 575–6
  listening and, 518, 519, 526–8
vision(s), 482–94
  as clear and challenging, 487
  as compasses and controls, 488–9
  control systems and, 586–7
  definition of, 486
  delegation and, 544, 546
  in empowering work force and customers, 489
  as fad, 485–6
  first steps in developing a, 494
  getting a, 490–2
  as inspiring, 486–7
  as lived in details, not broad strokes, 490
  living the, 492–3
  as making sense in the marketplace, 487–8
  preaching, 492–3
  as preparing for the future, but honoring the past, 489–90
  as stable but constantly challenged, 488
  static, 493–4
Vlcek, Don, 372
Vojta, George, 24–5, 430, 431
VPI (very promotable item), 189

wages, 4, 27
  see also compensation; incentive pay

Wal-Mart Stores, 189
Walnut Creek, California, 287
Walton, Mary, 258–60
Walton, Sam, 189
warehouse stores, 32
Warner, Harry, 244
Waterman, Bob, 293
Watson, Thomas J., 155, 244
Weaver Popcorn, 161
Weick, Karl, 551
Weitzman, Martin, 41
Welch, Jack, 17, 141
West, Tom, 263
West Germany, see Germany
Wexner, Les, 315, 531
Wheelwright, Steve, 200
Wiggenhorn, Bill, 387
Wilson, Bob, 132
Woodside, William, 425
word-of-mouth marketing, 290–5
  first steps in, 295
  small, progressive buyers and, 294
  systematizing, 294
word-of-mouth referrals, 122
work force, see labor
Work in America Institute, 415–8
work-sharing, 420–1
work weeks, short, 420–1
Worthington Industries, 202–5, 393, 456
  incentive pay at, 403–5, 408, 409
Worthington Steel, 400, 614
Wriston, Walter, 151–2

Xerox, 158, 281

Yankee Group, 426
Young, Karen, 406
Young & Rubicam, 274–5

Zais, Lieut. Gen. Melvin, 573
Zenger, Jack, 361
Zirger, Billie Jo, 185, 261

Permissions Acknowledgments

Grateful acknowledgment is made to the following for permission to reprint previously published material:

Addison-Wesley Publishing Company, Inc.: Excerpts from *The 100 Best Companies to Work for in America* by Levering, Moskowitz, and Katz. Copyright © 1984 by Addison-Wesley Publishing Company, Inc., Reading, MA. Excerpts from *The Regis Touch* by Regis McKenna. Copyright © 1986 by Addison-Wesley Publishing Company, Inc., Reading, MA. Reprinted by permission.

Alfred A. Knopf, Inc.: Excerpt from *Forces of Production* by David F. Noble. Copyright © 1984 by David F. Noble. Excerpt from *The High-Flex Society* by Pat Choate. Copyright © 1986 by Pat Choate and J. K. Linger.

American Association for the Advancement of Science: Excerpt from "The Translator" by Gary Bloston reprinted from the July/August issue of *Science '85.* Copyright © 1985 by the American Association for the Advancement of Science. Reprinted by permission.

Ballinger Publishing Company: Excerpts from *Moments of Truth* by Jan Carlzon. Copyright © 1987 by Ballinger Publishing Company.

Basic Books, Inc.: Excerpts from *Beyond Human Scale: The Large Corporation at Risk,* by Eli Ginzberg and George Vojta. Copyright © 1985 by Basic Books, Inc. Reprinted by permission of the publisher. Excerpt from *Kaisha: The Japanese Corporation* by James C. Abegglen and George Stalk, Jr. Copyright © 1985 by Basic Books, Inc. Reprinted by permission of the publisher.

Business Week: Excerpt from "Making Brawn Work with Brains" by Otis Port. Reprinted from the April 20, 1987, issue of *Business Week* by special permission. © 1987 by McGraw-Hill, Inc. Excerpt from "How A&P Fattens Profits by Sharing Them" by Christopher Eklund. Reprinted from the December 22, 1986, issue of *Business Week* by special permission. © 1986 by McGraw-Hill, Inc.

Congdon & Weed, Inc.: Excerpt from *Trade War* by Steven Schlosstein. Copyright © 1984 by Steven Schlosstein. Reprinted by permission of Congdon & Weed, Inc.